West Coast Jazz

WEST COAST JAZZ

Modern Jazz in California

1945–1960

TED GIOIA

NEW YORK   OXFORD
OXFORD UNIVERSITY PRESS
1992

Oxford University Press

Oxford   New York   Toronto
Delhi   Bombay   Calcutta   Madras   Karachi
Kuala Lumpur   Singapore   Hong Kong   Tokyo
Nairobi   Dar es Salaam   Cape Town
Melbourne   Auckland

and associated companies in
Berlin   Ibadan

Published by Oxford University Press, Inc.,
200 Madison Avenue, New York, New York 10016

Oxford is a registered trademark of Oxford University Press

Library of Congress Cataloging-in-Publication Data
Gioia, Ted.
West Coast jazz : modern jazz
in California, 1945–1960 / Ted Gioia.
p. cm.   Includes index.   Discography: p.
ISBN 0-19-506310-4
1. Jazz—California—1941–1950—History and criticism.
2. Jazz—California—1951–1960—History and criticism.
I. Title.   ML3508.7.C28G5   1992
781.65'5'09794—dc20   91-23902

9 8 7 6 5 4 3 2 1

Printed in the United States of America
on acid-free paper

This book is dedicated to my parents,
Michael and Dorothy Gioia—the first West Coasters
I ever met, and still my favorite.

Preface

During the last half-century, New York's preeminence in the jazz world has faced a serious challenge only once. For a brief period following World War II, California captured the imagination of jazz fans around the world. "West Coast jazz" suddenly became a catchword, a fad, a new thing. Jazz writers even wrote about a *battle* of West Coast versus East Coast, as though an actual war were taking place.

Yet if this was a war, it was one the West Coast eventually lost. And the maxim that the winning side writes the history was never more true than in this instance. Jazz writing of the last two decades leaves little doubt as to the critical consensus: It treats the West Coast phenomenon as an aberration—at best a distortion of taste, at worst a marketing ploy contrived by Hollywood studios. And like any war, this one produced more than a few casualties. In the early 1950s, Art Pepper placed second in the *Downbeat* poll, losing to Charlie Parker by only a handful of votes. Yet by the early 1970s, Pepper's reputation in the jazz world had sunk so low that he thought about switching careers to bookkeeping. Jazz fans in the mid-1950s voted Chet Baker to the top spot in the *Downbeat* poll, easily placing him above Dizzy Gillespie, Louis Armstrong, and Miles Davis; in the early 1970s, Baker was pumping gas in a service station back on the West Coast. In the 1950s, Shorty Rogers and Jimmy Giuffre were at the top of the jazz world, but by the 1970s, Rogers had completely retired from playing, while Giuffre struggled to find a record label willing to issue his music. In 1955, Dexter Gordon released three of the finest records of his career, yet he would not enter a recording studio again during the decade, and by the early 1970s, he was an almost forgotten figure, plying his trade overseas.

All of these musicians fought their way back over the next decade, and their success in re-establishing themselves as important artists was perhaps the first signal, initially unrecognized as such, that a re-evaluation of the earlier West Coast scene was under way. Less fortunate than these few were West Coasters such as Sonny Criss, Harold Land, Curtis Counce, Carl Perkins, Lennie Niehaus, Roy Porter, Teddy Edwards, Gerald Wilson, and those others whose careers languished without achieving either a later revival or even an early brief taste of fame. Certainly some West Coast jazz players have been awarded a central place in jazz history, but invariably they have been those who, like Charles Mingus or Eric Dolphy, left California for Manhattan. Those who stayed behind were, for the most part, left behind.

The time has come for a critical re-evaluation of this body of work. With more than forty years of perspective—since modern jazz came to California—we can perhaps now begin to make sense of the rich array of music presented there during those glory years. But to do so, we need to start almost from scratch. We need to throw away the stereotypes of West Coast jazz, reject the simplifications, catchphrases, and pigeonholings that have only confused the issue. So many discussions of the music have begun by asking, "What was West Coast jazz?"—as if some simple definition would answer all our questions. And when no simple answer emerged—how could it when the same critics asking the question could hardly agree on a definition of jazz itself?—this failure was brandished as grounds for dismissing the whole subject.

My approach is different. I start with the music itself, the musicians themselves, the geography and social situation, the clubs and the culture. I tried to learn what they have to tell us, rather than regurgitate the dubious critical consensus of the last generation. Was West Coast jazz the last regional style or merely a marketing fad? Was there really ever any such thing as West Coast jazz? If so, was it better or worse than East Coast jazz? Such questions are not without merit, but they provide a poor start for a serious historical inquiry.

I ask readers hoping for quick and easy answers to approach this work with an open mind and a modicum of patience. Generalizations will emerge; broader considerations will become increasingly clear; but only as we approach the close of this complex story, after we have let the music emerge in all its richness and diversity. By starting with some theory of West Coast jazz, we run the risk of seeing only what fits into our theory. Too many accounts of the music have fallen into just this trap. Instead, we need to see things with fresh eyes, hear the music again with fresh ears.

Ten years from now this book would have been much more difficult to write. As it was, I was able to benefit from the input of those who, unlike myself, were active in the West Coast jazz scene during the years under discussion. In particular, I want to thank the following individuals who consented to be interviewed for this book. Their contribution has been enormous. They answered my questions, responded to my challenges, and taught me those things about West Coast jazz I could learn in no book or magazine. They are Vernon Alley, Benny Barth, Richard Bock, Dupree Bolton, Froebel Brigham, Dave and Iola Brubeck, Bob Cooper, Lucy Criss, Ron Crotty, Joe Dodge, Eddie Duran, Teddy Edwards, Russ Freeman, Harry "the Hipster" Gibson, Jimmy Giuffre, Chico Hamilton, Bill Holman, Barney Kessel, Harold Land, Mel Lewis, Nathaniel "Monk" McFay, Big Jay McNeely, Lawrence Marable, Dodo Marmarosa, Lennie Niehaus, Walter Norris, Marty Paich, Art Pepper, Roy Porter, Nadi Qamar (formerly Spaulding Givens), Shorty Rogers, Marshall Royal, Pete Rugolo, Howard Rumsey, Bud Shank, Jack Sheldon, Bill Smith, Sir Charles Thompson, Dave Van Kriedt, Leroy Vinnegar, Max Weiss, Forrest Westbrook, Dick Whittington, Claude Williamson, and Gerald Wilson.

In addition I have benefited from the oral history work of others. I extend particular thanks to Dan Morgenstern and his staff at the Institute for Jazz Studies at Rutgers in Newark, New Jersey. Other collections of documents, recordings, and newspapers were of enormous value in putting together this book: the Green Library at Stanford University, the Archive of Recorded Sound at Stanford University, the Doe Library at the University of California at Berkeley, and the Los Angeles Public Library.

I have also gained enormously from individuals whose expertise greatly added to the work presented here. I am especially grateful to Grover Sales, Dana Gioia, India Cooper, Terry Teachout, Tara Gioia, Devre Jackson, Charlea Massion, John Rogers, Joseph Mailander, Lori Dobbins, Mark Lewis, Phil Elwood, Leonard Feather, and Richard Figone for their generous help. Peter Bergmann provided invaluable research materials related to Paul Desmond. Peter Pabst shared his collection of tapes and documents relating to Chet Baker. I must extend particular thanks to John Miner, who gave greatly of his time in tapping his personal archieve of jazz materials in order to answer many of my questions. I am indebted as well to Wendy Lesser for allowing me to incorporate into this book part of a profile I wrote on Chet Baker for *Threepenny Review*. Other thanks are due to Schirmer Books for allowing me to reprint sections of Art and Laurie Pepper's *Straight Life*, and to Don Asher for permitting me to use extracts from his collaboration with Hampton Hawes, *Raise Up off Me*. I would also like to thank Louise Tanguay for transcribing many of the interviews conducted for this book as well as for valuable feedback on the project over a four-year period. Finally I want to thank my editor, Sheldon Meyer, whose support and encouragement were instrumental in making this project a reality.

Palo Alto   T.G.
September 1991

Contents

West Coast Jazz

CHAPTER ONE

Central Avenue Breakdown

the linear neighborhood

Los Angeles has no true neighborhoods—instead its distinctive cultures stretch out horizontally along specific streets. Hollywood Boulevard, Sunset Strip, Mulholland Drive, Olvera Street, Rodeo Drive, La Cienega—these are to Southern California what Greenwich Village and Soho are to New York. They are Los Angeles's linear neighborhoods, its criss-crossing geometry of local colors. Each of these Southern California streets boasts a unique sensibility, one that defies city limits and zoning laws—a Sepulveda, a La Cienega might cut through a half-dozen separate townships without losing its special aura, although a couple blocks on either side of these thoroughfares city life collapses back into the faceless anonymity of cookie-cutter car culture. Travelers from other parts of the globe, faced with this specifically West Coast phenomenon, can see only urban sprawl—looking for village geography, they miss the stories encrusted alongside the pavement, the flora and fauna of the LA city street.

Years ago electric-powered streetcars ran their linear routes down many of these same streets, a patchwork of rails that tied together the fifty-six communities that comprise the Los Angeles area. That was before General Motors, leading a consortium that also included Standard Oil and Firestone, bought up the smog-free streetcar system and dismantled it. Ripping out the tracks, or paving over them, they made the automobile a necessity where until then it had been a luxury. Today over two million GM cars traverse Southern California roadways, bringing heady profits to Detroit and leaving a permanent haze of air pollution in Los Angeles and its environs. LA now stands as the epitome of car culture, with all its attendant curses and blessings. The linear neighborhood has been locked into place, almost certainly for good—or at least as long as fossil fuels remain—but now even the locals speed by, mostly oblivious to the stories of the sidewalk.

Along Central Avenue from 42nd to Vernon, few such stories remain today. Almost no visitors come here any more. The general perception among LA natives is that this section of Central is not safe for casual strollers. ("You want to get out of the car?" asked my wary companion on a recent visit.) But in fact this part of Central is too run down to pose much of a danger—so little is happening here that even street criminals must have left long ago. Anyone seeking the former centers of Los Angeles jazz, such as the Club Alabam or the Downbeat, today finds only vacant lots or deserted buildings. The only leftover signs of the Alabam are a small strip of rose-colored sidewalk that once led to its door and a couple of holes that years ago supported an awning; where the club once stood there is now a dirt lot littered with garbage.

Where buildings still stand—at the former sites of the Memo, the Last Word, the Bird in the Basket—they are bombed out, graffiti-covered wrecks. "For Sale" signs can be seen everywhere. Those seeking to purchase a piece of Los Angeles cultural history can get it at a bargain price in this neighborhood. But even without owning a parcel of land, historians of LA culture can learn quite a bit from visiting the area—little building has gone on here for half a century, and the neighborhood's surviving architecture retains the flavor of prewar years. For current residents, however, Central Avenue is the urban equivalent of a ghost town, the hollow middle of an economy now flourishing only at its edges. It is a depressing sight.

Yet in its heyday this stretch of Central stood out as one of the most distinctive of Los Angeles's linear neighborhoods. Central Avenue was not, as some have asserted, the West Coast's answer to 52nd Street. It was much more: an elongated Harlem set down by the Pacific. By 1920, some 40 percent of the black population in LA lived within a few blocks on either side of Central Avenue between the stretch from 11th Street to 42nd Street, and a panoply of businesses, residences, social clubs, eateries, and nightclubs had sprung up as part of this blossoming culture. With the enormous growth in the California black population—since 1900 it had doubled every twenty-years—the Central Avenue scene of the 1940s represented a city within a city. Entertainment was just one small part of what Central Avenue was all about, and jazz was just one small piece of the entertainment picture, co-existing over the years with R&B, song-and-dance, comedy, blues, revues, shake dancing, vaudeville, and the like. The Club Alabam, the best known of the nightspots that dotted the landscape, is sometimes spoken of by jazz writers as a West Coast Birdland or Village Vanguard, but it was both more and less. The Alabam featured lavish revues that covered the gamut of the entertainment spectrum, and though the jazz might be spectacular—with Charles Mingus, Dexter Gordon, or Art Pepper playing in the house band, it no doubt was—jazz was still just a small part of the show.

Sometimes much of the show took place in the street: Mercedeses and Bentleys, Cadillacs and Lincolns, movie stars and athletes, singers and dancers. The avenue contained a round-the-clock cacophony of comings and goings. Celebrities from the black community, both local and national—Jackie Robinson, Joe Louis, Duke Ellington, Bill "Bojangles" Robinson—gravitated to Central Avenue whenever they were in town. The Dunbar Hotel, next to the Alabam, was one of the first high-class black hotels in Southern California and attracted the cream of black society. When heavyweight champion Jack Johnson, one of the greatest boxers of his or any day, decided to open a nightclub in the mid-1930s, he established it in the Dunbar. When the Ellington band came to Hollywood in 1930 to be in the movie *Check and Double Check,* Duke stayed at the Dunbar, then newly built, as later did many other visiting jazz luminaries such as Louis Armstrong, Jimmy Lunceford, Don Redman, and Sy Oliver. When drummer Cozy Cole lived at the Dunbar, Lee Young (Lester's brother), a fine drummer in his own right, showed up regularly each morning, practice pad in hand, to run through rhythm exercises with the master. Nellie Lutcher rose to national fame as an entertainer only after she switched from piano playing to singing: a change that took place while she was performing for two dollars a night at the Dunbar. The hotel's name appears in few jazz history books, yet its halls are laden with many musical memories.

On Central Avenue, black music history was compacted within a few city blocks. The Downbeat, two doors past the Alabam and three doors beyond the Dunbar, boasted an equally rich past. Howard McGhee's pioneering bebop band—the first modern jazz ensemble on the West Coast, predating the more heralded arrival of Parker and Gillespie by several months—was formed there in early 1945. Charles Mingus and Buddy Collette premiered their short-lived group the Stars of Swing—perhaps the most important unrecorded jazz band in West Coast history—at the Downbeat a few years later. Saxophonists Wardell Gray, Dexter Gordon, and Teddy Edwards frequently engaged in tenor battle on the spot throughout the late 1940s. Edwards recalls the long rectangular room as "about my favorite place to play jazz," a sentiment shared by more than a few others.[1] The layout of the room focused everyone's attention on the music: The bandstand was in the center of the room, with patrons bordering it on three sides, while the long facing bar was backed with a mirror, so even hard-drinking patrons sitting on the barstools could check out the action without turning in their seats.

Between the Downbeat and Club Alabam was a café, run under various names over the years, which hosted more than its fair share of musical luminaries. Its inelegant piano would occasionally attract a prominent patron to the keys, with even Art Tatum known to engage in impromptu music-making on the premises. Across the street from the café stood the Last Word, another important club of the late 1940s—Hampton Hawes on the night of his high school graduation came there to perform with Big Jay McNeely. Less than a block south stood the Memo (pronounced Mee-mow by the cognoscenti), another jazz club of note. A little farther down at Vernon and Central one found Ivie Anderson's Chicken Shack, run by the celebrated ex-Ellington singer—an eatery that occasionally featured live jazz—as well as Lovejoy's, a black-owned nightclub favored by prominent musicians such as Art Tatum and Charlie Parker. Around the corner on Vernon was the Ritz, an after-hours club in a converted house some ways off the street, as well as John Dolphin's celebrated music emporium. Along that stretch of Central, black music flourished at every corner.

Nor was it only black notables who found their way to Central Avenue: Mae West, Lana Turner, Ava Gardner ("I saw all those bitches down there," attests one avenue regular), John Barrymore, Orson Welles, John Steinbeck, William Randolph Hearst—literally anybody who *was* anybody might show up at any hour. The war had made Los Angeles a round-the-clock town. Defense industry plants were operating twenty-four hours a day, and "swing shift" dances sprang up for the late-night workers, with bands playing from 2 a.m. until dawn.

On Central Avenue even retail stores kept odd hours. Dolphin's of Hollywood, the neighborhood record store—which, despite its name, was located miles away from Hollywood—*never* closed. Proprietor Big John Dolphin—a colorful local character—was true to his name. He smoked large cigars, wore oversized hats, talked a blue streak, and invariably carried a wad of big bills (which he never missed an opportunity of displaying). Dolphin was so committed to round-the-clock retailing that he eventually threw away the key to the building—and invited the local media to watch the event. Of course Dolphin, like many Central Avenue proprietors, always sought to stand out from the crowd. Around this time he had prominent local disk jockeys broadcasting from the front window of the store, while in the back room he ran his own record label. Dolphin's biggest publicity coup proved to be his last. One day a disgruntled musician confronted Dolphin in his office and demanded money he had coming to him. Dolphin, who hated to pay royalties, pulled out a switchblade. The musician drew a .32 caliber gun. Two shots were fired, and John Dolphin was dead at the age of forty-six.

The kind of late-night marketing that John Dolphin pursued was, of course, mostly legal, but the flagrant sale of alcohol during the wee hours was another thing entirely. Some after-hours clubs served booze in coffee cups and kept the police at arm's length with regular payoffs. Others simply sold setups, letting the customer supply the hard stuff—not a difficult task, since one or more dealers would usually be in attendance near the door. Still, drinking after hours could be a costly proposition: Street price at these odd times ran twice the going day rate in the liquor stores, and often only expensive name brands were available. In a pinch, those looking for a taste after 2 a.m. could make their way to the market parking lot at 53rd, where a strolling vendor of firewater seemed to be ever-present.

The after-hours and breakfast clubs—Jack's Basket, Brother's, Backstage, the Ritz, Glenn's Backroom, the Casa Blanca—dotted the landscape, and they often featured the finest jazz in the funkiest locales. Charlie Parker was not the only hot alto saxophonist to grace the Casa Blanca—proprietor Stanley Morgan occasionally brought along son Frank, later to become one of the top altoists in jazz, and patrons were impressed by the fourteen-year-old's precocious bebop chops. Brother, the proprietor of another after-hours gathering spot, might not have been able to match the plush interior of the Alabam, but his musical offerings were not to be overlooked either. "At Brother's once there was a two-day, nonstop jam session in which they kept on playing 'Stompin' at the Savoy,' " recalls pianist Nadi Qamar, then known as Spaulding Givens.[2] "I would play some, then somebody would take my place." On nights when he wasn't playing, Qamar would often get up at three in the morning, get dressed, and head over to Lovejoy's, where Art Tatum, Qamar's fourth cousin on his mother's side, would be just starting up at the piano. After hours was a way of life during these postwar years.

The history of Central Avenue is often told as a tale of black musicianship, but it is just as much an account of black entrepreneurship. "Central Avenue Assumes Gigantic Proportion as Business Section for Colored Men" boasted the front-page headline of the *California Eagle* of February 12, 1916—and with good reason: Two hotels, a dry goods store, a motion picture theater, the Booker T. Washington Building, a drugstore, and numerous other smaller black-owned businesses were either already running or in the process of being established on the street. The Angelus, the movie theater that had opened only weeks earlier on 9th and Central, advertised itself as "the only Show House owned by Colored Men in the entire West." A constant hubbub of construction signaled more black-owned businesses to come.

From the first, black music was part of this economic expansion. An easily overlooked notice from the last page of the same edition of the *Eagle* announced a dance at 19th and Central featuring the Black and Tan Orchestra. "The Black and Tan Band in Los Angeles was the only band around there playing ragtime for a long time," bassist Pops Foster recounts in his autobiography.[3] "I think the Black and Tan made some records around LA before Ory did." If so, they've never been found, but if one ever comes to light, it would establish the B&T as the first black jazz band to record.* Any precedence in this regard would be, of course, somewhat academic. Although the West Coast took the lead in recording jazz, it looked to New Orleans for inspiration. In the 1920s there was no "West Coast jazz," if by that one means a distinctive regional style. The Black and Tan was no exception—Paul Howard, the most prominent member of the band, had heard Freddie Keppard as early as 1915 and was soon trying to capture the same New Orleans sounds with his pioneering quintet.

Conventional jazz history tells how jazz first traveled from New Orleans by riverboat up to Chicago. Yet just as early, jazz came by railroad from the Crescent City to California. Jelly Roll Morton, Kid Ory, and other jazz notables played in the area before 1920, along with a host of local musicians. The story of these West Coast pioneers of prewar jazz is beyond the scope of this book, but the contributions of Les Hite, Sonny Clay, Paul Howard, Reb Spikes, Curtis Mosby, and others are far from negligible. The modern jazz scene of the 1940s would flourish a number of blocks away around 42nd and Vernon, but the lower streets, around 12th and Central, were a musical hotbed by the start of the "Jazz Age" in the 1920s.

Curtis Mosby, the honorary mayor of Central Avenue, bridged the gap between these two generations of black music. As such, he played an important behind the scenes role on the street during the transition years of the 1940s. Despite his importance, Mosby remains something of a mystery man, around whom more than a small amount of controversy rages. A businessman who founded the Club Alabam (then known as the Apex) in the roaring twenties, Mosby appears at first glance to be a black Renaissance man of the day; in addition to his career as the most prominent club owner on the avenue he could boast of his skills as drummer, composer, bandleader, music store owner, and man about town.

---

* Albert McCarthy, in his *Big Band Jazz* (New York: Exeter Books, 1983) says that the first known reference in print to the Black and Tan is from March of 1920, but in fact the local black press from World War I years and after is full of references. The most interesting one, perhaps, comes from an October 12, 1919, ad for an appearance at the Dreamland Café—here for the first time the band calls itself the Black and Tan *Jazz* Orchestra. This is not the first reference to jazz in print (that is another West Coast first, dating from a San Francisco newspaper account of a few years before), but may well be the first time a local California group adopted that innuendo-laden name.

Or could he? Virtually all these talents have been challenged. Mosby, one is told, couldn't drum to save his life, completely lacked skills as a composer, called in Lionel Hampton to play drums on key gigs and recording sessions, etc. Although recordings can be found of Mosby's soundtrack to the film *Hallelujah*, Marshall Royal—one of the most knowledgeable of Los Angeles old-timers—insisted to me: "He couldn't write a note. He didn't write any soundtrack music."[4] When I mentioned Mosby's music store, Royal replied: "Bullshit. The only music store on Central Avenue was Spikes Bros. Music at 12th and Central." But ads from newspapers of the day, as well as other accounts, clearly place Mosby's music store at 23rd and Central. Hampton, furthermore, has denied ever recording with Mosby's band. The criticisms just don't seem to stick. Such acerbic comments, however ungrounded in the facts, nonetheless reveal the low esteem in which Curtis Mosby was held by his fellow musicians.

The drummer-turned-businessman was equally unpopular with the legal authorities. Mosby declared bankruptcy in the late 1940s, but it was later discovered that he hid his part ownership of the Club Alabam, as well as other assets, from creditors and the bankruptcy court. A well-publicized trial ensued, with Mosby initially pleading guilty, but a few weeks later he suddenly changed his plea to not guilty and produced M. E. Brandenberg, who claimed to be sole owner of the Alabam. Judge and jury remained unconvinced: After ninety minutes the latter convicted the mayor of Central Avenue, and shortly the former, denying a request for probation, sent Mosby to prison. Without skipping a beat, Curtis's brother Esvan took over the job as honorary mayor—a position that included, among other duties, the job of leading parades for visiting black celebrities while perched on a horse. When Curtis was released after a short sentence, a homecoming party was held—where else?—at the Alabam. When not involved in equestrian or penitentiary pursuits, the Mosby brothers seemed to have ambiguous relations with most of the nightspots in the area. The Alabam, the Downbeat, the Last Word, the Oasis, and other venues found one or both Mosbys often running the show. Whether they owned, merely managed, or just hung around greeting patrons remained a matter of conjecture.

a certain change was coming

Modern jazz made its way to Central Avenue in strange and wondrous ways. Even before the local nightclubs became part of this mid-1940s musical revolution, many of the more savvy Los Angelenos were devoted to the new sounds from back east. Local stores rarely stocked bebop records, and supporters of the music were forced into the subterranean economy to supply their habit. Dedicated fans often found these cherished recordings coming to them through the oddest intermediaries, and prices might reach three or four dollars a copy. A major dealer of the fugitive 78s, Emery Byrd (a.k.a. Moose the Mooche) was the underground economy on his stretch of Central Avenue. He dispensed Mexican green marijuana, heroin, and bebop records out of his shoeshine stand. Nor was such a combination at all strange. Both hard drugs and bop may have come to Central Avenue through the same unusual distribution channel, moving eastward across the country via accommodating Pullman porters willing to pick up some spare change through such sideline occupations. Another purveyor of the new music was an itinerant salesman known simply as Bebop. Bebop would set up his wares on a portable fiberboard stand at various places in the black community, dealing Bird and Diz to the hippest of the passers-by. It almost seemed that music so strange and different required an equally odd means of finding its buyers, and these quirky dealers of the new sounds from Manhattan only added to its allure.

But these records were just a taste of what was to come. Byrd and Bebop were merely the John the Baptists of bop, heralding the forthcoming arrival of Bird and Dizzy, the acknowledged masters of modern jazz, from their East Coast home base. The opening night performance of Charlie Parker and Dizzy Gillespie at Billy Berg's in December 1945 is often cited as the debut of live bop on the coast, but two important predecessors paved the way for this much-noted engagment. Coleman Hawkins's trip to Southern California earlier in 1945 had found him with a coterie of modernists in tow, including trumpeter Howard McGhee, bassist Oscar Pettiford, pianist Sir Charles Thompson, and drummer Denzil Best. Categorizing the style of this band is a tricky proposition. When I asked Sir Charles Thompson—the only surviving member of the group—about the band's sound, he chose to engage in a jesuitical debate over the meaning of the terms "bebop," "modern jazz," and "jazz," ultimately refusing to label any of his work with such blasphemies. But if this wasn't a bop band it was at least, to borrow the popular phrase (*pace* Thompson), close enough for jazz.

The question of Hawkins's music is confounded by the watered-down recordings the group made for Capitol while out west. Dave Dexter, who supervised the recordings, insisted that Hawkins play in a more accessible style than was the band's wont and initially even tried to replace McGhee—the group's strongest bop soloist—with Red Nichols, a traditional trumpeter whose playing was completely out of touch with the band's cutting-edge approach. "Hawk had a tune that Red Nichols couldn't play in no kind of way," McGhee recalled not long before his death.[5]

I was just waiting to see what was going to happen, and when Red started to play, Pettiford cracked up laughing. And that made Dave Dexter mad. . . . But he had no business putting Red in there in the first place, 'cause Red didn't know what our band was like. He didn't know what kind of music we were playing. It was just about the time of the game that a certain change was coming about in the music. Because when we'd gone into the studio, we didn't go into there playing none of that old-time shit.

Dave Dexter provided a much different account of the session:

McGhee, I believe, was not drunk [but] was on some kind of narcotics. He was belligerent and uncooperative from the start of the session. He fluffed every bar, and Bean [Hawkins] was embarrassed. In sheer desperation I phoned Red Nichols, a dear friend of mine, who lived not far away and he drove down to the studio with his cornet. But while McGhee sat on a chair giggling, poor Red couldn't cut that near boppish music, and after a couple of hopeless takes he went home.[6]

McGhee eventually took Nichols's place and, despite Dexter's assertions, played soberly enough. But Hawkins played it safe on these California sides. "I said to Hawk, 'Man, you don't need Dave Dexter, you're Coleman Hawkins.' " McGhee continued. "And he said, 'Maggie, you don't understand. This is business.' " As it turned out the session was a strange mishmash: McGhee plays in a pure bop style, while Hawkins pursues his own hybrid style, one that revealed a rich harmonic sense, which even the most ardent modernist couldn't fault, but retained a rhythmic feel looking back to the 1930s. On a song like "April in Paris" one can feel the whole rhythm section adapt to each soloist. Behind Hawkins they are almost pushing a two-beat feeling, but when McGhee enters for the trumpet solo the time becomes much more fluid and modern-sounding. Hawkins was never a full-fledged bopper, but his live appearances in Southern California no doubt found him pursuing a more contemporary line than these recordings suggest—indeed, Hawkins's 78s made in New York before his California trip are more in a modern vein than any of the West Coast sides.

After Hawkins left town, McGhee stayed on with a group of bop-oriented locals, which included drummer Roy Porter, guitarist Stanley Morgan, saxophonists Teddy Edwards and J. D. King, bassist Bob Kesterson, and a rotating group of pianists, including Vernon Biddle, Dodo Marmarosa, and Jimmy Bunn. There can be no confusion about the brand of music this group played: It was modern jazz of the Minton's variety. Fast tempos, intricate head charts, a pressure-cooker rhythm section—no ingredient was missing. "I've never worked with anyone who played faster tempos than Howard McGhee," recalls Roy Porter, now in retirement in Los Angeles.[7] And Porter should know, for he went on to gig and record with Charlie Parker, Sonny Criss, Wardell Gray, Hampton Hawes, and Eric Dolphy, none of them a slouch at speed. McGhee's group was playing this authentic brand of bebop six nights a week at the Streets of Paris when Parker and Gillespie came out for their famous Billy Berg's stint.

McGhee let his sidemen know in no uncertain terms the kind of music he wanted to hear. Off the bandstand he was a warm and convivial person, but at the gig McGhee was a demanding, often authoritarian leader. "Teddy was playing alto, and Howard made him switch to tenor," recalls the band's first drummer, Monk McFay, now in his early eighties and also retired in Los Angeles.[8] "And Howard got him a tenor. Howard wanted a sound with more bottom to it from the horns. And he wanted my drumming to be lighter. I had just been playing with a big band, but Howard wanted to hear less of the bass drum." About the band's place in the history of modern jazz on the coast, McFay is emphatic: "It was *the* first, not one of the first." Roy Porter soon replaced Monk and further enhanced the group's bop credentials, for while Monk was more in a Jo Jones/ Sid Catlett mould with bop leanings, Porter was an uncompromising, bomb-dropping modernist. Tenorist Edwards was one of the first modern stylists on the instrument, boasting a conception that eschewed both Prez' and Hawk in deference to Bird—commonplace a few years later but still a novel conception for tenor players circa 1945. Bassist Bob Kesterson knew how to walk a tightrope both at and on the way to gigs. He would arrive, bass and all, on a tiny Italian motor scooter. But a brief stint by the young bassist Charles Mingus with the band bespoke no drop-off in quality. The piano spot was filled by a number of talented players, but when Dodo Marmarosa was in attendance, McGhee could boast the services of one of the finest modern jazz pianists on either coast, one whose fluid right-hand lines and preternaturally clean touch stand out on the band's recordings. All in all, the McGhee band had, for at least those few months before Parker and Gillespie's arrival on the coast, a monopoly on the finest modern jazz talent in Southern California.

Michael Marmarosa, nicknamed "Dodo" in honor of his prominent beak-like nose, had come to California from his native Pittsburgh as a member of the Tommy Dorsey Orchestra. After an engagement at the Casino Gardens, Marmarosa decided to leave the security of the big-band world behind and join the ranks of the LA beboppers. A skilled pianist with outstanding technique honed by years of classical studies, Marmarosa stood out as one of the most prepossessing pianists of the bop era. He seemed destined to join the ranks of Bud Powell and Thelonious Monk as one of the leaders of the new generation of jazz pianists. But his early retirement from the jazz world—he left Los Angeles to return to Pittsburgh before the close of the decade—prevented him from building on the reputation made during these brief glory days. Marmarosa only rarely ventured into the recording studio in later years, and rumors depicted him as a relentless perfectionist who preferred not to record rather than do it below his own high standards. Other accounts mentioned Marmarosa's dissatisfaction with his small hands, the meager span of which prevented him from realizing his Tatumesque aspiration.

Most jazz fans assume that Marmarosa passed away long ago, but in fact he is living in quiet retirement in Glenview, Pennsylvania, where he is described by those few people who have dealings with him as an extreme recluse who jealously guards his privacy. In my conversation with him he denied the stories that his retirement was precipitated by his reported eccentricities. As Marmarosa tells it, the record companies rarely sought his services in later years: "I just didn't have the chance to do a lot of records."[9] His desire to return to his native Pittsburgh had effectively shut him out of the jazz mainstream well before he had reached his thirtieth birthday. His few recordings from the late 1940s, most notably the informally recorded "Tone Paintings" with their adventurous avant-garde constructions, stand out as major statements by an artist undeservedly neglected.

McGhee's recordings from this California stint are among the finest of his career. These were the kind of bop records in which the progressive quality of the music is brandished proudly. McGhee plays with something approaching total abandon—a rough-around-the-edges approach that made the modern music of 1945 seem light-years distant from the swing idiom of the prewar years. McGhee would later salvage the July 29, 1946, "Lover Man" session—at which Camarillo-bound Charlie Parker bailed out midway—with two quartet numbers that burn brightly. Record producer Ross Russell was suitably impressed—McGhee "had never played better. The trumpet crackled," he later wrote.[10] A few months later, Russell recalled these heated performances when he began stockpiling masters in face of the looming recording ban. With Bird in Camarillo, the California state-run mental institution, Russell resolved to bring McGhee in on a separate leader date. The addition of Teddy Edwards for this October 18, 1946, date brought another bop voice to the musical fray, with Edwards shining on "Up in Dodo's Room" and "Dialated Pupils." Edwards recalled: "I ran into Fats Navarro some time later, and he said to me, 'Do you realize you changed the course of history?' He told me that "Up in Dodo's Room" was the first tenor solo that didn't draw back on either Lester Young or Coleman Hawkins."[11] When I asked Edwards point blank whether Dexter Gordon had developed his celebrated style by stealing from him—a claim I had heard from another musician of the day—Edwards somewhat hesitantly replied: "Well, Dexter dipped into my bag just to check it out.

Course he didn't need to learn from me, he had a thing of his own going. But if you listen to the 'Webb City' he did with Fats you'll hear him doing my bag."

These recordings are given little attention these days, but Edwards's innovative playing, combined with McGhee's virtuosity and the rhythm section's savvy, makes them some of the finest performances of the early days of bop. In the early 1950s, McGhee got caught in the downward spiral of drug addiction, eventually nursing a $500-a-week habit that sent him to prison at Riker's Island. Although he was eventually rehabilitated, McGhee's trumpet work in later years rarely matched the unbridled passion of these early recordings. "I used to go all out to excite people," he said in the 1960s, "but I believe that pretty music is just as important. My future plans are to play prettier than ever. Anyhow, I think that music without beauty ain't saying too much."[12] This was a radical and unexpected change of heart from the virtuoso stylist who, years earlier, had forged a feverish trumpet style largely purged of any overt lyricism. The later renunciation was perhaps McGhee's way of following the path of least resistance: As a soloist the elder McGhee simply could not match the power and scope of his earlier self. The newfound lyricism was perhaps his way of making a virtue of necessity. The reunion album of McGhee and Edwards, made a decade after this first collaboration, never matches the same musicians' first recordings together.

These early Dial sides, even with their high energy level, had established the trumpeter—much to his chagrin—as a major West Coast player. For the Tulsa-born (February 6, 1918), Detroit-raised, New York–inspired player, this was sometimes too much to bear. "They just took it for granted that I was a California boy," he complained years later.[13] "Everywhere I went, 'Hey, man! There's the California cat! Hey, man! How's California?' And I only lived there in '45–'46. I came back to New York in '47. And everybody still, *today*, they still ask me, 'When did you get back from the coast?' "

The "West Coast" label would soon become a pet peeve among a whole generation of players, even those who sold records because of the tag. "They coin a phrase and that becomes your identity," Art Pepper complained to me a month before his death—and Art, unlike McGhee, was not only California-born and -bred, but almost never performed as a leader outside of the Golden State until late in his career.[14] Wherever their birthplace, modern jazz musicians in the postwar years grew wary of any regional label that cut them off from the New York–centered jazz scene. The stigma still holds today, perhaps more than ever before: In interviews for this book, any inquiry about "West Coast jazz" inevitably resulted in a perceptible rise in tension in the interviewee, followed by vehement denials of any connection with *that* music, almost to the point of pulling out birth certificates to show out-of-state origins. The responses became so predictable that I eventually stopped asking. After decades of lambasting from the critics, the term inspires a Pavlovian reaction of aversion even among those who initially benefited from it, or who even defined it with their playing. McGhee, perhaps the first hard-core bop musician on the Coast, was ahead of the game in this regard. Long before such renunciations came into fashion, he wanted nothing to do with the West Coast.

CHAPTER TWO

The Bird in the Basket

a groovy atmosphere

If the journey westward of the Gillespie/Parker band was not a first, it was the most visible, the most celebrated, and the most controversial event in the development of modern jazz in California. If one is seeking a milestone, a disjunction, a rupture with the past, Billy Berg's one-story stucco building on Vine Street, December 1945, is the time and place. Billy Berg's would be the launching point for a musical invasion, a D-day landing of bebop on the Pacific seaboard. Proprietor Berg had learned about the New York beboppers through Harry "the Hipster" Gibson, who had come from 52nd Street to work at the Vine Street club. Gibson had recently risen to fame on the strength of his argot-laden recordings of offbeat original tunes such as "Who Put the Benzedrine in Mrs. Murphy's Ovaltine?" and "Get Your Juices at the Deuces." Having heard Bird and Dizzy (at the Deuces, among other nightspots), he hipped Berg to the new New York music.

Gibson recalled to me, in his staccato Bronx/Harlem accent, his change of coasts and its after effects:

> My album took off. The next thing, the Hipster is famous. I had been making $56 a week in New York—that's scale—and Billy Berg calls me and offers a grand a week. The biggest West Coast club. Wants *me* as the feature attraction, not Tatum, not Eddie Heywood. [Pause] I'm out there. Billy Berg asked me "Who has the hottest band in New York?" On 52nd Street all the cats were blowing good, you know, but I tell him Dizzy's band is *the* hottest. So Berg went and booked them.[1]

Berg had already run a handful of jazz venues in California before opening his eponymous locale at 1356 North Vine Street, and he would open sev-

16

eral more before his death in 1962. By that time the Vine Street location would be occupied by a beer-and-pizza joint, and the other nightspots were equally a matter of history. The Capri Club on La Cienega, the Trouville on Beverly and Fairfax, and the Swing Club on Hollywood and Las Palmas had paved the way for the Vine Street locale, while in later years Berg would be behind the 5-4 Ballroom, Kid Ory's, and other ventures. Berg brought everyone from Parker and Gillespie to Billie Holiday, from Louis Armstrong to Lester Young, into his venues—a boon for Southland jazz fans.

Yet perhaps more striking, and certainly more pioneering at the time, was Berg's insistence on allowing integrated audiences. This was still a sticking point in the Southern California nightlife of the late 1940s. At the Cotton Club in Hollywood—across the street from Dial Records' former offices—proprietor Hal Stanley booted out an integrated group in the audience, reportedly exclaiming "I'm not running a Cricket Club. I'm not going to have these 'paddy hustlers' bringing these ofay chicks in my place."[2] The Cricket Club, a major jazz club of the day on Washington Boulevard with more tolerant notions about race, considered suing. Stanley would seem to have been an unlikely opponent of civil rights—he had, after all, formerly run the Downbeat on Central Avenue!—and he later recanted, but not soon enough to save the business. A few months later the Cotton Club was on the skids, and Stanley implored his wife, vocalist Kay Starr, to pawn her engagement ring to keep the club afloat. She refused, and soon the Cotton Club was history. The same day the nearby Hollywood Empire, one of the classiest jazz clubs in the city's history, also folded. It had survived only a few months, but had already booked Armstrong, Ellington, and Tatum and had even imported the diminutive emcee Pee Wee Marquette from Birdland—obviously not enough to please the local jazz fans.

Black jazz fans had learned to be wary of almost all Hollywood nightclubs in those years. The Cotton Club incident was no isolated event. Mixed couples or groups were routinely stopped in their cars once inside the city limits—so often that even those with wheels often chose to take the #4 Melrose bus between Central Avenue and Hollywood. The bus drivers were comparatively cool, and the cops didn't want to hassle the public transit system. Yet Hollywood was not the only redneck area in late 1940s Los Angeles. Around the same time, Nat "King" Cole ran into resistance from his white neighbors when he tried to move into Hancock Park. Howard McGhee was harassed by Los Angeles police after going with his wife, a white ex-model, to a movie theater. In Glendale, the situation was so bad that blacks needed a permit to be in town after 6 p.m. Musicians who performed in the city were provided with a police escort after the gig—whether they wanted it or not—from the club to the city limits. Even on

Central Avenue, blacks were not free from police problems: Billy Eckstine was hauled down to the station simply for having a new Cadillac with New York license plates. The Newton Street station regularly brought in mixed couples for a pat-down on the flimsiest of excuses. Los Angeles was not the Deep South, but neither was it a model of integration. The police in particular, with more than a few relocated Southerners in their ranks, were an especially intransigent group of segregationists.

In this setting, Billy Berg's was a much-welcomed oasis of racial tolerance. "It was a sophisticated, cultured audience," recalls Sir Charles Thompson of his work there with the Hawkins band.[3] "It was also an integrated audience, which may have had something to do with it. Generally when you found sophisticated audiences, you found integrated audiences." Sonny Criss adds: "Billy Berg's was a unique club. . . . It was the first really cosmopolitan club with a great deal of publicity behind it where Negro and white people mixed without any pressure. It was a groovy atmosphere, an atmosphere that embraced people from all walks of life."[4] For the Gillespie/Parker group the integration carried over to the bandstand. Pianist Al Haig and drummer Stan Levey worked alongside bassist Ray Brown, vibraphonist Milt Jackson, and the two horn players. Although Gillespie was contracted to bring a quintet, he added Jackson as a sixth man to prepare for Bird's likely truancies. Once on the coast he also enlisted tenor saxophonist Lucky Thompson for the same reason. The rationale was sound, as events proved: Bird was apt to miss any given performance.

Billy Berg was an unlikely protagonist for modern music and civil rights. His attention was devoted, much of the time, not to the music or club management but to the nonstop gambling sessions he and his friends would pursue in the back room. "He was a little guy like me," Gibson remembers. "All his friends were Jewish comics—old vaudeville guys. He took a liking to me, and I fit right in. We'd gamble all night long." The gambling mentality—strangely common to a number of jazz club proprietors—carried over to his booking policies. With Dizzy and Bird (as with Gibson), he was willing to take a chance on new names with no West Coast track record.

Booking Charlie Parker, however, may have been more of a gamble than even Berg realized. As it was, Parker almost didn't make it to Los Angeles. At a train stop somewhere in the Arizona or New Mexico desert, Bird was roused from the narcotics-induced sleep that had kept him groggy since Chicago. Picking up his baggage, Bird wandered from the train and began making his way solo across the desert landscape. For a moment the other band members hesitated, afraid to chase after Parker lest they get left behind, but perhaps equally afraid of losing their Esquire poll–winning saxophonist in the sandy expanse. Finally drummer Stan Levey took off in pursuit of the peripatetic altoist and convinced him to return to the train. Bird was going through withdrawal. After he returned to the compartment, his fellow bandmembers had to strap him into the seat for the remaining twenty-hour trip to Union Station.

Dean Benedetti, an amateur sax player and jazz enthusiast, greeted the band on arrival and quickly informed Bird about the heroin supply in Los Angeles—availability was limited, and prices were appreciably higher than in New York. Parker was able to cop some morphine from an obliging physician that day, thanks to a phony tale about kidney stones supplemented by a twenty-dollar tip. For the remainder of his stay Bird learned to make do with a host of substitutes for horse: morphine, pills, cheap wine—whatever he could muster. When only a small amount of heroin was available, Parker might combine it with a dose of morphine for what he termed an "H&M." Especially after his connection Emery Byrd—whom the other Bird found through an introduction from Benedetti—was busted, the H proved increasingly difficult to find. For perhaps the first time in his decade-long history of addiction, Parker now felt the strain constantly.

Bird buffs like to compare his opening night performance at the Vine Street club with the premiere of Stravinsky's *Rite of Spring*, a riotous event that found concert patrons literally resorting to fisticuffs. No violence erupted at the Gillespie/Parker debut—although a few days later Gillespie and Slim Gaillard, the other headliner during the engagement, exchanged some backstage blows—but in almost every other respect the performance was the stuff of legend. Parker was more than fashionably late for the band's start, with the first two sets elapsing before he made his grand entrance from backstage, coasting over the changes to "Cherokee"—an appropriate clarion call for his debut out west. Parker's delay this opening night had nothing to do with being strung out—the morphine had brought him around—instead he procrastinated while eating two of Billy Berg's specialty Mexican dinners in the back room. This was the kind of cavalier behavior that Dizzy—who, despite his nickname, was a fiend for professionalism and punctuality—would never indulge in. But for Parker it was a comparatively minor infraction. When Bird did appear, walking through the audience in mid–musical phrase, he played with all the fire and creative energy that had characterized his finest work on record.

Only a few days before leaving New York, Parker had recorded the path-breaking "KoKo" session for Savoy—the finest modern jazz sides to date—and his playing, at least in these early California performances, found him in equally top form. More than a few musicians in the audience— including Sonny Criss and Hampton Hawes—felt themselves irrevocably marked by the music they heard that night. Radio broadcasts of the Berg sessions reached countless others over the next several weeks, not only in the Los Angeles area but, through Armed Forces broadcasts that carried the music, far beyond Southern California.

The conventional story of this engagement stressed the unhipness of the Los Angeles audiences. "They didn't understand our music" was Parker's alleged characterization of the West Coast upon his return to New York. Yet the standard account is worth scrutinizing more closely. Sonny Criss, who attended many of the Billy Berg performances, tells a different story: "I don't recall it that way because the club was packed every night. Contrary to the reports Bird and Dizzy did not play to audiences of ten or twelve people."[5] Harry "the Hipster" Gibson, who, along with Slim Gaillard, shared the stage with Dizzy's band during the engagement, tells a similar story: "Slim Gaillard was packing them in. I was drawing them in. And don't forget, all the musicians were coming around to check out Bird and Diz. We were packing the joint. The joint *was* packed." Roy Porter, who was playing in an equally high-powered bop band with Howard McGhee at the nearby Streets of Paris, adds:

> You can't go by the movie *[Bird]*, which had the West Coast scene all wrong. The clubs were packed where we played. I'm not saying that the people understood the music, because it *was* new, but they showed up and were there to listen. While Bird and Dizzy were at Billy Berg's we were playing six nights a week to packed audiences at Streets of Paris. I couldn't go down to check them out because we were working ourselves, but if we were getting big crowds I can imagine that the same was true for them.

The Billy Berg's gig of 1945–46 may not have been a complete success—it no doubt failed to match the kind of record-breaking crowds Dizzy drew when he returned to Los Angeles in 1948—but neither was it the fiasco some have claimed. Porter and Gibson are quick to add that the club patrons, especially the nonmusicians present, may not have appreciated all the intricacies of the new music—Gibson argues, no doubt correctly, that the 52nd Street audience was more knowledgeable (there, he recalls, "even the *customers* knew")—but they came nonetheless.

If the Vine Street engagement was ill-fated, it was due less to poor attendance than to other factors. Media neglect or outright hostility—a chronic problem with West coast jazz then and later—was real, as was the disdain of many older musicians, especially among the Dixieland players who had settled in Southern California. Above all, if the trip west resulted in disastrous consequences, they took place not inside the four walls of Billy Berg's establishment but in the Civic Hotel, the LA County jail, Camarillo and the other less savory locales that Charlie Parker frequented during his extended stay in California. Bird's ensuing nervous breakdown, more than anything else, casts the ominous shadow on the Gillespie band's West Coast engagement. Yet the Los Angeles audience for bop, which existed even before Gillespie and Parker left for Union Station, takes the brunt of the blame meted out by chroniclers of the music. "I once read a write-up," Howard McGhee recalled in reference to his own bop work out west, "that said that people walked out after every group. That's bullshit! They just stayed there and listened, to see what was going on."[6]

The real tragedy of Parker's stay on the West Coast began after the engagement at Billy Berg's, and as with many tragedies, it began almost as farce. The day after the close of the Vine Street gig, Ross Russell, a former merchant marine who was now proprietor of Tempo Music Shop on Hollywood Boulevard, attempted to record Parker with Gillespie before the band returned to New York. Everything seemed to go wrong with this date: Lester Young, then in town, was scheduled to be part of the session—if he had shown, the combination of Bird, Dizzy, and Prez would have been historic—but he never appeared. The rehearsal at the Glendale studio turned into a fiasco when a crowd of hipsters and hangers-on disrupted the proceedings and eventually caused a scene at the adjoining Forest Lawn Cemetery, where their consumption of cannabis and wild behavior were much out of place. For the recording session, scheduled for the following day, Bird joined Young as a no-show. The only usable take with Parker and Gillespie—a fairly daring polytonal outing on "Diggin' for Diz"—comes from the aborted rehearsal. Nor did Parker appear in time to board the flight back to New York. Instead he apparently cashed in the return ticket Gillespie had given him. His bandmates made a last-ditch effort to find him before leaving Bird behind. Shortly afterwards, Parker started working as a sideman in Howard McGhee's band at the Club Finale in the Little Tokyo district.

After the internment of Japanese citizens during World War II, this part of town had become another center of black-owned businesses. Bird was living down the street from the Finale at the Civic Hotel on 1st and San Pedro where, within a few doors, there existed a host of jazz venues. They included Shepp's Playhouse, with two separate floors of music perched above the ground-level businesses, the Cobra Room, and the Rendezvous. The Finale, at 230½ 1st Street, had been opened by vaudeville dancer Foster Johnston in late 1945 or early 1946 and soon became a favorite of modern jazz fans, with a house band that might include, on a given night, Charlie Parker, Miles Davis, Howard McGhee, Sonny Criss, Teddy Edwards, Art Farmer, Gene Montgomery, or Serge Chaloff in the front line. The rhythm section might feature Joe Albany, Dodo Marmarosa, Russ Freeman, or Hampton Hawes on piano, Bob Kesterson, Addison Farmer, or Red Callender on Bass, Roy Porter or Chuck Thompson on drums. No place on Central could match these line-ups.

The vice squad closed the Finale down after a few months, and Johnston bailed out of the business. But McGhee and his wife decided to run the club themselves. On Saturday night, March 16, the Finale reopened with Parker and Erroll Garner performing and a live radio broadcast going out over station KXLA. Given the sporadic appearances of their star performer, as well as the McGhees' decision not to sell alcohol, the venture proved short-lived, but not before establishing a musical environment unmatched in the country. In the spring of 1947, the Club Finale boasted the most exciting modern jazz from coast to coast. If California could ever brag of its own Minton's or Monroe's, the Club Finale was it.

Although Ross Russell's planned all-star record date had been a disaster, his next session with Parker hit pay dirt. Russell jumped at the recording opportunity provided by Parker's extended stay on the coast, and another session was scheduled for March 28 at Radio Recorders on Santa Monica Boulevard. Miles Davis, in town after coming west with the Benny Carter band, joined Parker in the front line, as did tenor saxophonist Lucky Thompson. The remaining sidemen included perhaps the finest bop-oriented rhythm section Southern California could muster in those days, with pianist Dodo Marmarosa, drummer Roy Porter, bassist Vic McMillan, and guitarist Arvin Garrison providing a strong foundation for the horns. These are not well-known names, even in the jazz community—the scant discographies of Porter, Marmarosa, and Garrison are almost scandalous, while McMillan, a strong bassist in the modern mould, soon dropped into almost total oblivion—but they were solid journeyman players with a deep grasp of the new rhythmic vocabulary of modern jazz.

Even so, Parker threw them a curveball with his playing on the date. Bird's stunning four-bar break on "A Night in Tunisia" broached a devastating kind of syncopation that still sounds astonishing some forty years after it was recorded. The novice listener may be impressed by the speed of Parker's execution on this passage, but the dexterity is nowhere as extraordinary as the contorted placing of accents within the phrases. Has any jazz player since—Coltrane, Dolphy, Ornette included—ever matched this mastery of rhythmic phrasing? Little wonder that Miles Davis had to signal the beat to the rest of the group during this part of the performance. The group had rehearsed at the Finale the night before, but this kind of music was not to be assimilated in a single evening. Yet Bird must have had a Midas touch that day, as his daunting performance seemed to inspire outstanding work from the rest of the band. All the performances recorded during the seven-hour session—"Ornithology," "Yardbird Suite," "Moose the Mooche," "A Night in Tunisia"—rank among the landmarks of jazz music. On a level with Louis Armstrong's Hot Fives and Hot Sevens and Ellington's work from the early 1940s, the Parker Dial sessions stand out as monumental achievements.

From then on it was a downhill ride for Parker on the cost. On May 3, Parker signed over half of his Dial royalties in perpetuity to his connection Byrd—whose nickname had inspired the title of Parker's "Moose the Mooche"—no doubt in exchange for a fix. Byrd, a onetime honors student at Jefferson High, was shrewd enough to get a notarized document from Parker, thus establishing a legal transaction that would hold up in court. Within weeks, however, Byrd faced a court ruling of a less felicitous nature. "I wish to announce, due to misfortune," he wrote to Dial Records on June 30, "my change of address from 1135 East 45th Street, Los Angeles, to Box A-3892, San Quentin, California."[7] He requested that any royalties from the Dial sessions be forwarded to this new—and, he hoped, temporary—residence.

Although he was still on the outside, at least for the moment, Parker, cut off from his major supplier, was strung out and short of cash. Around this time he disappeared for a number of days and was finally discovered by McGhee living in an unheated garage on McKinley Avenue. Bird was imbibing port wine by the gallon and hadn't eaten in days. He slept on a metal cot, using his New York overcoat for bedding. To any observer, he would have seemed just another skid row derelict, not the leading musician of his generation. McGhee brought Parker back to his own house on West 41st.

"[Bird] seemed drained and I really thought it was over," Miles Davis recalls. "I mean I thought he was going to die."[8] Unable to score heroin, Parker started downing a quart of whiskey a day—in addition to port, bennies, whatever he could hustle. Parker developed, around this time, a nervous mannerism in which, in mid-solo, his arms would shoot up into the air. When he managed to show for a gig, Parker's playing, for the first time in his career, was often lackluster and mechanical. "Bird was strung out. His nerves were going haywire. He couldn't sit still," McGhee remembers.[9] So I told Ross Russell, 'Man, Bird seems like he's cracking up.' He said, 'Man, we better get him in the studio.' Right away, he's thinking, 'Let's make money.' "* Parker readily agreed to record—he needed the

---

*McGhee, Davis, Parker, and others have lambasted Russell as an opportunist, a money-grubbing record company executive intent on exploiting the musicians under his contract. But in point of fact Dial was something of a financial nightmare at the time, and Russell—whatever his other faults might be—was risking money on modern jazz record sessions at a time when virtually no one else on the coast was willing to take a chance on the music. After Dial moved back east, major LA players like Teddy Edwards and Dexter Gordon found no comparable supporter among West Coast record producers—indeed, there never was a replacement for Dial on the coast. The later dominance of the cool West Coast sound partly reflected this absence of aggressive independent record companies pushing the more bop-oriented sound. It is worth adding that Russell's writings about the Los Angeles jazz scene of the postwar years are among the most perceptive and vivid documents we have of the era. To those with an abiding interest in the music, Russell stands out as something of a godsend to West Coast jazz in the late 1940s.

cash—and Russell managed to convince his partner, Marvin Freeman, the financial support on which Dial was built, to ante up the money for the date. A session was scheduled for July 29.

That day encompassed the most disastrous twenty-four hours of Bird's California career. Parker somehow made it to C. P. MacGregor's studio on Western for the start of the date, but once present he seemed almost comatose. Dr. Richard Freeman, Marvin's brother and a psychiatrist, was in attendance at the session and assessed Parker as suffering from malnutrition and alcoholism. After a ragged take of "Max Is Making Wax," Dr. Freeman supplied Parker with six tablets of phenobarbitol—Bird asked for ten—and the session continued. During the following take of "Lover Man," Parker was supported by producer Russell, who grasped the altoist from behind, yet Bird still staggered off mike at times. He slurred his phrases, lingered over uncomfortably long rests, and in general played with a wrenching, agonized sound. Some have called this the most poetic record Parker ever made. Bird, for his part, was later furious when the 78 was released. To some degree, both sides of the argument are right. The performance is pathetic, but the pathos is gripping: It is a record that few can enjoy, but once put on the turntable it is mesmerizing. The ensuing two songs—"The Gypsy" and "Bebop"—were, in contrast, merely unpleasant musical disasters. On "Bebop," drummer Roy Porter shouts out encouragement to Parker in mid-solo, trying to rouse the saxophonist from his stupor. One gets no enjoyment from listening to these pieces and hears them only as documents of a personality on the point of collapse.

The collapse came that night. From his room at the Civic Hotel, Parker came down to the lobby twice wearing only his socks. After being escorted back to his room the second time, Parker set it on fire, probably by nodding off while smoking. When the authorities arrived, the still unclothed altoist grew irate. The police responded with a blackjack, hand cuffed Parker, wrapped him in a blanket, and brought him to the station. For ten days no one in the jazz community knew his whereabouts—rumors circulated, including one that Bird was dead. When Russell and McGhee finally tracked him down, Parker was in the psychopathic ward of the county jail in East LA. Confined in a small, dingy cell, wearing a matching gray straitjacket, Parker greeted his visitors with an outburst: "For God's sake, man, get me out of this joint!"

relaxin' at camarillo

Parker had hoped that Russell and McGhee could free him on the spot. It proved much more difficult to spring the caged Bird, and consid-

erable legal wrangling was required to limit Parker's incarceration to six
months in a medical facility. Charged with suspected arson, indecent exposure, and resisting arrest, Parker was on line to go to a maximum security institution for the criminally insane. With the intercession of Judge
Stanley Mosk—today a prominent member of California's supreme court—
Parker was instead placed, for a minimum of six months, in the comparatively comfortable environment of the Camarillo State Hospital, located a
two-hours drive north of Los Angeles in the sparsely populated community of the same name.

Parker positively flourished under the regimen at Camarillo. His wife,
Doris Sydnor, came out from New York, found a job as a waitress, and
served as lady-in-waiting for her spouse. Parker gained weight and soon
looked healthier than he had in years. He worked in the institution's adjoining vegetable garden, played C-melody saxophone in the hospital band,
and welcomed the visitors who made the trek from down south. Rumors
spread. Parker was now a devotee, word had it, of clean living. He even
had told Dean Benedetti, or so it was said, that he was considering giving
up music to become a bricklayer. These stories, as they circulated through
the jazz grapevine, raised almost as many eyebrows as had tales of Parker's
excesses in days past.

As the months went by, Parker grew increasingly anxious to get out
of Camarillo. He now told his friends that he would escape "over the wall"
if a legal way out didn't quickly materialize. A group of especially ardent
fans was said to be plotting to free the Bird. Since Parker was a New York
resident, the conditions for his release proved convoluted, but a provision
in the state code allowed for the release of an out-of-state inmate into the
custody of an approved California resident upon the recommendation of a
Sacramento board. Newcomer Doris Sydnor could not qualify, so Ross
Russell accepted responsibility for Parker—who later complained that Russell refused to get him out until Parker had agreed to extend the Dial
contract—and in late January 1947 the rehabilitated altoist was set loose.

Parker would never be so healthy again. In addition to the ferocious
brilliance of his playing—which was now at a peak—Bird's appetite for
more normal types of consumption resumed. He ate voraciously and even
won a pizza-eating contest in Los Angeles. Around the same time he pa-
raded around the beach with Doris, where he went bathing in a new suit
from Zeidler and Zeidler. But soon Parker was again drinking heavily and
missing the well-paying engagements that Howard McGhee lined up. Another gig in Chicago fell through when word began spreading about Parker's new dissipation.

Parker was anxious to return to New York, but he agreed to do a final
session for Dial Records. As it turned out, Parker completed two more
sessions for Russell before returning east. Only two instrumentals resulted

from a February 19 date due to Bird's insistence on using vocalist Earl Coleman, against Russell's wishes, for the other numbers. Coleman, a friend of Parker's since Kansas City, had visited Bird at Camarillo. At the time Parker had promised to help the singer out, and though Parker's reputation for keeping promises was shaky at best, in this instance he stuck by his word. He rehearsed with Coleman at Jack's Basket, a local after-hours spot where music ran from midnight until dawn, and he convinced Russell to include the vocalist on the session. Coleman's presence, along with a more conservative rhythm section of Erroll Garner, Red Callender, and Doc West, made this Parker's least adventurous record date in years. Perhaps Parker was interested in shedding the more avant-garde trappings of his music—much as he did a few years later in his recordings with string ensemble—in search of the mass audience he never found.

A week later, Parker returned to the studio for a much different session. This was a more bop-based band: Parker and Red Callender were the only carry-overs from the previous date, while the rest of the group included veteran Parker sidemen Marmarosa and McGhee as well as newcomers Barney Kessel and Wardell Gray. Parker had agreed to write four new originals for the date, but by the time of the rehearsal two days before the session, only one had been penned. This sinuous blues, "Relaxin' at Camarillo," is further testimony to the subtlety of Parker's rhythmic phrasing. The melody was only twelve bars, but the other musicians struggled, despite their all-star credentials, to master the line. By the time of the session, however, the players had the head down, and though Parker arrived over an hour late, the date proceeded without a hitch. The performance of "Relaxin'" ranks as one of the most memorable from Bird's California stay. The other three pieces recorded that day are almost at the same high level.

Russell has stated that Parker left Los Angeles to return to New York the day after this session, but a letter to Chan Richardson from a month later suggests that Parker stayed in California until the end of March.* In any event, the altoist had determined long in advance to leave Southern California, and a benefit from the previous December had raised enough money for plane fare. Parker was already in bad shape—ten days earlier he had, in Russell's description to Chan, "folded completely and had to go to bed"—and for his return to the east was only "half sober." Accompa-

---

*This, and below, from letter from Ross Russell to Chan Richardson, a photo of which can be found in Chan Parker and François Paudras, *To Bird with Love* (France: Editions Wizlov, 1981), 73. This letter from Hollywood, dated March 25, 1947, announces "Bird is leaving here today." Russell, in his several accounts of the period, has claimed that Parker left for New York the day following (or a few days following) the "Relaxin'" session, February 27 or shortly after. The postmark on the envelope, also legible in the photo, is March 26, 1947, 5:30 p.m. The March date is almost certainly correct.

nied by Doris Sydnor, his long-suffering and eventually abandoned companion, Parker boarded a plane to Chicago, with an ultimate destination of New York. The supposed eight-week stint on the dream coast had stretched into a fifteen-month-long nightmare.

After Bird flew the coop, the modern jazz scene in and around the avenue experienced a temporary lull, but by summer word was spreading of a series of heated sessions taking place at Jack's Basket on 32nd and South Central. Jack Jackson's establishment, also known as the Bird in the Basket—named not in honor of the departed altoist, as some have assumed, but after the house specialty of chicken and shoestring potatoes served in a rattan basket—kept no musicians on the payroll. But it didn't need to. The location was such an ideal spot for impromptu jams that Jack's became the center of the Central Avenue modern jazz scene during these months. The working-class patrons maintained a healthy interest in the modern music being played on the stand, and the layout of the room gave the proceedings a concert hall aura. In fact, the restaurant must have served at one time as a cabaret or meeting hall, because a large stage, on which sat an old but serviceable upright piano, dominated one end of the room.

Visitors today can still make out the faded lettering "Bird in a Basket" above the storefront entrance of the now apparently deserted building. "Chicken ain't nuten but a bird" announces a barely legible and enigmatic script above the far right-hand doorway. The still surviving signs are something of a surprise—apparently little has happened in this building since Jack moved out. But in this instance, looks are deceiving. Finding one of the doors ajar, I made my way into what seemed, at least from the exterior, to be just one more casualty of the shell-shocked Central Avenue economy. Inside I found, to my surprise, a burgeoning business in operation: a sweatshop with rows of Mexican seamstresses laboring over their work. The boarded-up and rundown exterior of the building was, of course, the perfect cover—few immigration officials, or anyone else for that matter, would think to look inside this decrepit building. A remnant of West Coast jazz history, the apparently empty Basket serves today, it seems, as a front for a different kind of underground commerce.

Some forty-two years before my visit, Bird had helped put the Basket on the map, frequently jamming there as well as holding rehearsals at Jack's for his Dial session with Earl Coleman. Right after his release from Camarillo, an all-star session in Parker's honor had taken place at the Basket with virtually every bop saxophonist in town—Dexter Gordon, Wardell Gray, Sonny Criss, Teddy Edwards, Frank Morgan, and others—lining up to pay tribute. Parker held off contributing to the music until near the end, then outclassed the assorted minions with superb playing that was light years beyond his pre-Camarillo playing and the "Lover Man" fiasco.

The sessions at the Basket continued in the weeks following Parker's return to New York, with Gordon, Gray, and Edwards standing out as the major participants. The atmosphere of an ongoing tenor sax battle permeated the setting, with especially heated confrontations taking place between Gordon and Gray. Regulars at these late-night battles began keeping score, remarking the occasions on which one tenorist would outshine the other. The strolling vendor of modern jazz records known simply as Bebop would usually be in attendance, cheering on the crowd, sometimes rooting for Teddy Edwards or Lucky Thompson, sometimes for Dexter or Wardell.

If the jam session is, as some have claimed, the jazz world's equivalent of war, then Jack's Basket was a Waterloo for the Central Avenue scene, a heated encounter that, in retrospect, also seemed to signal the end of an era. Before long the clubs along Central Avenue would close down, one by one, and the open jam session would be relegated to a minor role in the world of jazz, a mere way of filling off-nights at the few remaining clubs. The Los Angeles musicians' union helped to speed up the process by threatening to fine members playing for free at local jam sessions. The death of the Central Avenue scene and the precipitious decline in the demand for live jazz were only part of the nightmare waiting just around the corner. A whole booming economy, a way of life, a social fabric would be other, even more pointed, casualties of the changes to come. Less visible than the tearing down of the Club Alabam or the abandonment of the Dunbar, these more gradual transformations wrought even more destruction in the long run.

But in 1948 no one on the street could have envisioned the coming Central Avenue breakdown. Certainly at Jack's Basket one had little thought for such arcane reflections on urban evolution. This was a place where one got caught in the here and now, in the radiating energy of live jazz at its finest.

The proceedings would just get started around midnight and often continue until close to dawn. "There'd be a lot of cats on the stand," Dexter Gordon explains, recalling the Basket battles. "But by the end of the session it would wind up with Wardell and myself. 'The Chase' grew out of this."[10] "The Chase," like so many of the finest things on the coast, drew from the best of the rest of the nation. It was a musical duel built from the age-old New Orleans clarinet showpiece "High Society," mixed up with a dash of East Coast bebop, and brought to a boil in the pressure-cooker jam session atmosphere of Central Avenue. The saxophone battle is by now a modern jazz tradition, perhaps even a cliché. But on the raised stage of Jack's Basket, this was no practiced attempt at musical anachronism or even just another afternoon jam session. It was nothing less than combat, a throwing down of the musical gauntlet, a duel in which the weapon of choice was neither pistol nor dagger, foil nor sword—just a tenor saxophone.

CHAPTER THREE

The Chase

The basic idea of the "chase" chorus is elegant in its simplicity. Two musicians alternate solos, which gradually shorten in length. After the briefest of introductions, they're off . . .

the thin man

They called him the Thin Man. He was no detective, the name notwithstanding—even so, a great deal of mystery surrounds the figure of Wardell Gray. Dead before his thirty-fifth birthday, under circumstances that defy easy explanation, Gray revealed as many contradictions in his life as in his untimely end. On one hand, Gray read books written by Sartre, Shakespeare, and Colette and was an articulate, even eloquent speaker who talked with conviction on, among other things, politics, Henry Wallace, and the NAACP. On the other hand, he was a heroin addict, an unpredictable character, one who would borrow a friend's horn and hock it for drug money. There is much we don't know about Wardell Gray— the massive *New Grove Dictionary of Jazz* fails to provide his date of birth or even his full name (Carl Wardell Gray) and is sketchy on the most basic biographical details. But the few facts that have come down to us seem to reflect a man of extremes, often of polar opposites.

Even his appearance posed contradictions. "He ate like a horse and was skinny as a rail," recalled Hampton Hawes.[1] "First time I saw him in his drawers, ribs showing like a starving alley cat, I thought if I blew at him he'd fall over. Scared me. He couldn't have weighed a hundred pounds." With his understated voice, delicate build, and soft features set off by a moustache so pencil-thin that it seemed hardly to exist, Gray conveyed a degree of effeminacy very much at odds with his music. For as a saxophonist, Gray was one of the few disciples of Lester Young who didn't fit the "cool school" pigeonhole: While drawing on Young's light tone, Gray stayed in the hot with his marked talent for spinning out the most complex melody lines at even the briskest of tempos. When Dexter Gordon, Teddy Edwards, Sonny Criss, or even Charlie Parker blew at him on the stand, Gray did anything but fall over, instead blowing back with a conviction and style all his own.

Years after Gray's death, jazz writers, especially those in America, tend to label him a journeyman musician, a transitional figure. The descriptions suggest he is more important for what he led to than for what he actually accomplished. Perhaps picking up on his name, critics have depicted his music as representing some gray middle zone, neither swing nor bop, hot nor cool. Certainly there is some truth to this view. Yet if Gray succeeded in forging a dialogue between bop and swing, even so his style represented nothing transitional. His was a mature, distinctive sound, one that could be lyrical and driving at the same time. No one has ever sounded like Wardell Gray, and likely no one ever will.

Herbie Butterfield, in a perceptive piece published years ago in England's *Jazz Journal*, described Gray's music as a "celebration of being alive" and remarked on its fundamental "gaiety."[2] Usually such armchair ruminations add little insight into jazz, but Butterfield hit on something worth noting. In the midst of the modern jazz movement, a musical revolution that, for all its virtues, often tended to be self-conscious, serious, and more than occasionally somber, Gray brought back a *joie de vivre* to the music. He conveyed a lightness and joy reminiscent in spirit, if not style, of the earlier Kansas City and New Orleans sounds. In this respect Gray was a harbinger of some of the best West Coast jazz of the early and mid-1950s.

Perhaps the inflections of both these earlier jazz styles came to Gray through the mediation of his model Lester Young, a tenorist who grew up near New Orleans and reached musical maturity in Kansas City. Young's legacy to modern jazz was perhaps greater than that of any other swing era instrumentalist. He showed a way of articulating intricate melody lines that allowed them to swing without constantly accenting the underlying beat. By freeing himself from the ground rhythm, Young was able to improvise with an insistent linear inventiveness no saxophonist before him had approached. It was this rhythmic aspect of Young's playing that Charlie Parker developed into his own conception of modern jazz. The other equally distinctive side of Young's playing, his light, airy tone, had less impact on Parker (although it too might occasionally surface, especially on a Kansas City–style blues tune like "Parker's Mood"), but even this aspect of Prez eventually attracted a small cadre of followers among postwar musicians.

Here also Gray was an important forerunner of things to come. For reasons that are far from clear, the West Coast saxophonists of the 1950s felt Young's influence more powerfully than most of their East Coast counterparts. Back east, saxophonists who echoed Young's distinctive sound were never in the majority—in earlier years Coleman Hawkins had been the predominant model, while among the 1950s generation Bird's penetrating sound held sway. But out west, the devotion and, above all, the talent of the Prez contingent made them a force to be reckoned with. Both Gray and, to a lesser extent, his frequent musical companion Dexter Gordon were among the initiators of the West Coast trend. They were already assimilating Young into the modern idiom in the mid-1940s. By the time of the 1950s, under the redoubled influence of Young through the success of Woody Herman's "Four Brothers" sax section (and especially that of the most famous "brother," Stan Getz), the number of Prez aficionados in California would be legion.

Gray was not a native of the West Coast but, like many of his generation, part of the large population of expatriate Oklahomans who lived in Los Angeles during and after the Dust Bowl years. He was born in Oklahoma City on February 13, 1921, and his dual position as a black and an "Okie" would have placed him at the focal point of two separate currents of discrimination in Los Angeles during the war years. Racism was a matter of statute as well as class attitudes in those days when, for example, many Southern California communities established curfews for the black populace. The impoverished situation of the Okies during the Dust Bowl era was more ephemeral but no less real: Like so many other recent arrivals seeking work, they formed a new underclass that took its place on the bottom rung of the depressed labor market, frequently relegated to low-paying jobs as crop-pickers or menial workers. The economic recovery spurred by the start of World War II gave many an opportunity to raise their standard of living through comparatively better paying jobs in the Southern California defense industry. For a few select individuals such as Gray (and other transplanted black Oklahomans Dupree Bolton and Marshall Royal), a career in music offered a rare chance to escape the limitations placed on so many others with similar backgrounds.

Gray's path to the West Coast was, however, more circuitous than that of most. At an early age he moved from Oklahoma to Detroit, where he spent much of his childhood. While in Detroit, Gray studied at Cass Tech High and developed his skills first on the clarinet, and later on the alto saxophone. Soon he began working with a local band led by Jimmy Raschel, which also included Howard McGhee and George "Big Nick" Nicholas. When Gray left to join Benny Carew's band, he was replaced by another outstanding local saxophonist, Sonny Stitt. Wardell and Sonny engaged in some impromptu saxophone battles that must have served both well when, later in life, each became famous for his skills in such encounters—Wardell in "The Chase" and his other duels with Dexter Gordon; Stitt in his heated exchanges with Gene Ammons.

These musical affiliations in the Motor City gave Wardell a chance to play in heavy company, but the tenorist felt that he had to move beyond the Detroit scene to make his name. Soon he got his big break. In 1943, Gray was asked to join the Earl Hines orchestra—a fortuitous event that threw the tenorist into the midst of what, in retrospect, must be viewed as one of the most innovative ensembles of its day. Hines's band then featured, among other novelties, a string section and a female vocal quartet. But the band's reputation for innovation had little to do with these musical accessories; more path-breaking, if less marketable, were the first stirrings of modern jazz, heard in this ensemble, largely under the impetus of Charlie Parker, unknown then except to a small group of initiates. Hines, perhaps best remembered for his pioneering early work with Louis Armstrong, seems an unlikely mentor for this new generation of jazz innovators. Yet the pianist's sensitivity to musical talent in whatever form, as well as his restless musical curiosity (attested to by a large body of fresh and striking piano work that would continue until his death in 1983), made his orchestra a testing ground for many of the best young musicians of the day. In addition to Parker and Gray, many important members of the younger generation, such as Dizzy Gillespie, Billy Eckstine, and Sarah Vaughan, served apprenticeships with Hines around this time.

Our knowledge of this important group is unfortunately limited by the recording ban then in effect. Gray's work with Hines was not recorded until 1945, by which time most of the early modernists had left. Gray's other major musical affiliation of the mid-1940s, with the Eckstine orchestra, is also poorly documented on record. Even the length of Gray's tenure with these bands is uncertain. Most accounts state that the tenorist left Hines in 1945, but the existence of several recordings Gray made with the group in Hollywood during the spring and summer of 1946 suggests that either Gray stayed with Hines for a longer period or rejoined the group when it was in Southern California. Gray's choice of instruments at this time is also open to question: jazz critic Leonard Feather reports that Gray started as an altoist when he joined Hines, only later switching to tenor, yet those who heard Gray in Detroit with Carew's band claim that he was already playing tenor.

In any event, Gray's reputation began to take wing only after he left the routine of traveling bands and, drawn by the musical activity of Central Avenue, settled in Los Angeles. As if to confirm the wisdom of this career move, one of his first sessions in Southern California found Wardell as sideman on a recording destined to be a jazz classic. The February 26, 1947, Hollywood date for Dial brought Gray into a front line with two now famous former colleagues, Charlie Parker and Howard McGhee. Parker by this time had already begun to acquire the status of a jazz legend, his mystique only magnified by his recent enforced stay in the state hospital at Camarillo. To celebrate his release, Parker had written a new blues for the session entitled "Relaxin' at Camarillo." The title notwithstanding, the process of learning "Relaxin' at Camarillo" proved to be anything but relaxing. Ross Russell recalls the rag-tag rehearsal held two days before the session:

> The entire rehearsal was spent in everybody's trying to learn this sinuous twelve-bar line. Actually, they didn't get it down anywhere near cold by the end. I remember driving [pianist] Dodo Marmarosa home later that night. He kept talking about this line. It was still bugging him. It was only twelve bars, but he just couldn't get it. He kept talking, talking, talking about it. He said the next day he hadn't been able to sleep; this thing bugged him all night.[3]

If Gray was unsettled by the unusual melody, it does not show in the finished recordings, for each of the takes finds Wardell soloing with assurance. Perhaps even more notable is Gray's assertion of musical individuality on this date. At a time when so many other saxophonists were imitating Parker, the Thin Man didn't budge from the Lester Young–inflected sound that had long been the foundation for his playing. The modest bebop influence on his music is, if anything, less prominent here than on Gray's other recordings of the period. Perhaps foreshadowing his later saxophone collaborations with Dexter Gordon, Wardell instinctively provided a contrast and complement to Parker, rather than, as others did, mere Bird imitations or rococo extensions of the master's style.

Parker constantly defied the expectations of his fans by picking just such understated sidemen. In this regard Gray represents the same kind of foil for Bird that, for example, Miles Davis, Chet Baker, or John Lewis was in other bands. There were many hotter players around when Parker made these often surprising personnel decisions, and outsiders were quick to second-guess such selections—even today jazz fans and critics lament Bird's decision not to have pianist Bud Powell, the fiery virtuoso of bebop keyboard pyrotechnics, in his working band. But Parker knew what he wanted, namely, a more melodic contrast to the roman candle explosions of his alto. Gray fit this bill perfectly. One might have expected, on the strength of this early encounter, a long history of later collaborations between these two players. Instead geography intervened: Soon after this session Parker returned to New York.

The Parker date signaled the beginning of the most productive period in Gray's career. The following day he performed with McGhee and Vido Musso at one of Gene Norman's Just Jazz concerts in the spacious 6,700-seat Shrine Auditorium. A performance with Erroll Garner from April resulted in "Blue Lou," an attractive rendition featuring a comfortable sweet-toned Gray solo, destined to win the French Grand Prix du Disque the following year. Five weeks later, on June 12, 1947, Gray returned to the MacGregor studio on Western Avenue near Eighth Street in Hollywood, site of the Parker session, to set down what proved to be one of the milestones in an all too brief career.

Over the next two decades the idea of two tenor saxes battling it out in a small combo setting would become a jazz staple. Al Cohn and Zoot Sims, Sonny Stitt and Gene Ammons, Eddie "Lockjaw" Davis and Johnny Griffin, even Coltrane and Rollins would carry on this modern jazz tradition. All of these saxophonists are indebted, at least in part, to their immediate predecessor, the quintessential bebop tenor battle recorded that day by Gordon and Gray as "The Chase." In this musical duel the two tenorists first trade 32-bar choruses, followed by 16-bar half-choruses, then 8-bar exchanges, and finally 4-bar. Rooted in the timeless call-and-response forms of the earliest African and African-American music, the "chase" format proves irresistible in the hands of first-class musicians—listen, for another striking example, as Clifford Brown and Harold Land follow the same approach in their extraordinary "The Blues Walk" record of the mid-fifties. The "chase" format succeeded not just because of its musical compactness, its structural elegance, but also because of its unmistakable battlefield overtones. In Dexter Gordon's words:

It wasn't somebody would say "I can play better than you man," but actually . . . that's what it was. It was serious—shit, dead serious. You'd think, damn, what the fuck was he playing? You'd try to figure it out, what was going on. To a degree, that was one of the things, to be the fastest, the hippest. The tenor player with the biggest tone—that takes balls, that takes strength.[4]

The various Gordon and Gray collaborations rank among the most energized and gripping performances from either coast during the postwar years. The sales of the initial 78 reflected its musical excitement. "The Chase" proved to be the best-selling Dial recording to date, surpassing even the sales of the Charlie Parker sides. Jazz fans were apparently not dismayed by the great length of a performance—at just under seven minutes it was one of the longest jazz recordings of its day and took up both sides of a 10-inch shellac 78.

Recording technology of that era was fairly primitive. Music from the microphone was channeled through amplifying equipment into cutting lathes that etched the frequencies into the grooves of an acetate master. Sound quality was often poor, splicing together different takes was impossible, and stereo records were, of course, years away. Recording microphones of the period were quite good, but modern multimiking techniques were yet to be adopted. Strict limitations in the length of music suitable for a 78 side further restricted the musicians; solos rarely went beyond one or two choruses and often were limited to only eight or sixteen bars.

Live recordings of the late 1940s may have found the musicians in more comfortable surroundings, but they offer even less refinement in sound quality. Technical limitations notwithstanding, these grainy-sounding bootlegs are much cherished by jazz fans today, if only because they offer a rare glimpse into how the early bop players performed when freed from the time limitations inherent in three-minute-long 78s. A concert recording of Gordon and Gray made only three weeks after "The Chase" reveals all these combined vices and virtues. On July 6, the two tenorists were involved in a performance at the Elks Auditorium at 40th near Central Avenue, where Ralph Bass captured the music with the aid of two portable disk cutters, the alternation of which allowed him to record without a break in the performance. The sound quality is mediocre, and the different characteristics of the two pieces of equipment cause marked changes in sound that occur in mid-song. Even so, the energy level and interaction with the audience provide a dramatic sense of the excitement Gray and Gordon could generate with their battling tenors. On numbers such as "Cherokee" and "The Hunt" the soloists stretch out for up to twenty minutes per song. Here the two saxophonists capture a building intensity scarcely possible within the confines of a 1940s recording studio.

For the jazz record buyer, however, these brilliant performances exacted a price. Since a single song such as "The Hunt" needed to be spread across several 78 rpm disks, devoted bop fans had to listen to their music piecemeal. Yet this degree of excess may have only added to the music's allure. The hipsters of the day marveled that, even with a twenty-minute performance of "The Hunt," Gray and Gordon apparently had no time to play the melody but immediately jumped into their solos. (The more prosaic—and likely—explanation, of course, is that Bass missed the song's opening in his amateur recording effort.) It comes as little surprise that Jack Kerouac selected this particular recording as one of the favorites of Dean Moriarty, his protagonist in On the Road. Moriarty stands "bowed and jumping before the big phonograph listening to a wild bop record . . . 'The Hunt,' with Dexter Gordon and Wardell Gray blowing their tops before a screaming audience that gave the record fantastic frenzied volume." Another beat writer, John Clellon Holmes, went even further in a memoir of the 1940s: "The Hunt: listen there for the anthem in which we jettisoned the intellectual Dixieland of atheism, rationalism, liberalism—and found our group's rebel steak at last."

Even more surprising than these half-baked visions of jazz nirvana are the puzzling predictions made by the concert promoters for this celebrated performance. Both impresario Jack Williams and trumpeter Howard McGhee advertised the event as a dance! *Downbeat* announced, a few days before the concert, that Williams was "out to prove that the same kind of music that draws people to jazz concerts will pull customers who are chiefly dance-minded."[5] Williams certainly had a strange breed of dancer in mind—one who would fox-trot through twenty-minute-long blistering renditions of "Cherokee" or "The Hunt." As if that were not enough, the weather on that July afternoon turned out to be exceptionally hot, even by Los Angeles standards. "It was hot as hell—no air conditioning of course," recalls Roy Porter, "and the place was packed like sardines."[6] "The Hunt" may have failed to live up to such high expectations on either side; but if it captured neither a new dance beat nor an innovative beatnik anthem, it nonetheless confirmed the musical prowess of these two powerful West Coast tenorists.

Of the live recordings of the duo, however, the most compelling is the follow-up version of "The Chase" performed during Gene Norman's February 2, 1952, Just Jazz concert at the Pasadena Civic Auditorium. To my ears, this surpasses even the original version in excitement, while sound quality is far better than the muffled results of the Elks Auditorium recording. The audience responds with enthusiasm from the opening introduction—clearly many present knew the original recording—and Dexter takes advantage of this familiarity by starting his opening solo, as he did in 1947, with a variation on the melody. By the first bridge, however, he is moving into uncharted waters with a series of striking interval leaps leading into two pulsating phrases built on a single note. Dexter takes three choruses, and Gray follows him with three of his own, each one more intricate than the last. Gordon comes back in by building off Gray's closing motive and soon has moved into the tenor's lowest register, evoking the sound of a baritone sax. When Gray's turn comes, he responds by mimicking Gordon's device—he now builds off Dexter's closing phrase and soon is answering his adversary with a stream of cascading notes. Dexter, in turn, storms back and quotes, among other things, "Bye Bye Blackbird" as well as one of Gray's own distinctive broken melodic figures. This tenor battle continues at a feverish pitch, both players listening attentively to each other and taking every opportunity to turn the opponent's weapon to his own use. As the exchanges continue, they grow shorter and shorter, while the audience becomes louder and louder with its screams and cheers.

By this time, the recorded live jam session had become a stock in trade, largely under the influence of jazz promoter Norman Granz. During the next few years, jazz fans often saw the most unlikely musical pairings take place as part of these concert hall jams. However, few of these contrived sessions matched the special magic evoked by Gray and Gordon, these two tenorists, congenial combatants who were also friends and colleagues. "The Chase" was the recorded jam session *par excellence.*

"man, tune up, tune up, man"

Dexter Gordon, Gray's sparring partner on these memorable sessions, provided as telling a contrast to Wardell in physical appearance as in musical matters. A 1940s description from Art Pepper's autobiography presents the statuesque and magisterial Gordon as the exact opposite of the willowy Gray: "Dexter Gordon was an idol around Central Avenue," Pepper remembers. "He was tall. He wore a wide-brimmed hat that made him seem like he was about seven feet tall. He had a stoop to his walk and wore long zoot suits, and he carried his tenor in a sack under his arm."[7] Gordon's imposing presence could rivet an audience's attention even before he started playing. Ira Gitler recalls early instances of Dexter's charismatic persona:

> Often he would make a belated entrance and attract interest merely by putting his saxophone together in view of the crowd. Once he showed up at Lincoln Square with a finger encased in a cumbersome bandage; though unable to play, he was the center of attention. . . . [At the Royal Roost] Gordon, booked to appear, arrived late. At 2 a.m. he began to descend the long staircase leading to the club. At that moment, a throng was coming up the stairs; but on seeing Dexter, these jazz buffs reversed their course.[8]

Dexter's rare stage presence, both in the 1940s and in later years, may have fascinated the beats and hangers-on (Kerouac, again, built one of his mini-obsessions on the tenorist), but for the jazz initiates Dexter made his mark not by his looks but by his mastery of the horn. Gordon developed one of the first great modern tenor sax styles, and—perhaps even more remarkably—did so by borrowing only modestly from Parker and Gillespie. Instead, Dexter created a new approach to the tenor, a persuasive and immediately recognizable sound all his own.

Gordon, unlike Gray, was a native of Los Angeles, where he was born on February 27, 1923. The Gordons were an established and fairly well-to-do family. Dexter's father, Frank Alexander Gordon, was a doctor whose patients included Duke Ellington (Dr. Gordon ranks a brief mention in

Ellington's autobiography, *Music Is My Mistress*) and Lionel Hampton (who would become Dexter's first major employer). The elder Gordon initiated his son's musical education by taking him to the Los Angeles theaters to hear the big bands. Before he was ten years old, Dexter had already met Ellington, who occasionally came to the house for dinner. Under these influences, Gordon discovered his talent for music at an early age. He started on clarinet (an instrument at which his father had dabbled) at thirteen, switched to alto at fifteen, and finally settled on the tenor at seventeen.

The money he made mowing lawns in the neighborhood bought secondhand records at fifteen cents each. His later recollections suggest that by his teens Dexter had already developed fairly mature listening habits:

> I had a nice collection when I was 13 years old. . . . I was listening to people like Benny Carter, Roy Eldridge, and Scoops Carry who played alto with Roy's little band. Of course I had heard Chu Berry, and Dick Wilson who played tenor with Andy Kirk, and Ben Webster. I first heard Ben on a record he made with Duke called "Truckin'." He was shoutin' on that. But then I got my first Basie record and that was it. I fell in love with that band. Duke was fantastic, but the Basie band really hit me.[9]

In an interview with Gary Giddins, Gordon elaborated on his enthusiasm for Basie saxophonist Lester Young: "He had that special thing that floored me. I tried to play like him. He was the first to play color tones, like sixths and ninths. . . . He must have listened to Ravel and Debussy."[10] Gordon's comments notwithstanding, many jazz musicians had used the sixth and ninth intervals before Young, but Prez's contribution lay in the way he employed them. They no longer were primarily passing tones, used in phrases that gravitated toward chord tones, but instead were often the crucial notes in a musical phrase. Young might start or end a phrase on a ninth; this imparted a gentle tension to the music, one lacking in the more traditional practice of using thirds or fifths to center an improvisation. Because of this harmonic color in his melody lines, Prez could retain tension in his music without pushing the rhythm to excess. Years later, Charlie Parker would build on Young's legacy by adding a whole range of higher intervals—elevenths, sharp elevenths, thirteenths—to his arsenal of tones.

When Basie and Young came to Los Angeles in 1939, Dexter ditched school to hear the opening 11 a.m. show. More than thirty years later, Gordon recalled: "They opened with 'Clap Hands Here Comes Charlie,' and Lester came out soloing—and he was just fantastic. I really loved the man. He was melodic, rhythmic, had that bittersweet approach. . . . It felt so good to hear him play."[11] In justification of the day's truancy, Gordon explained: "Prez was like going to school for us."[12]

Gordon's musical education at this point consisted of much more than listening to records and attending performances. From almost the start he was assisted by two of the finest jazz educators of the day: Lloyd Reese and Sam Browne. Both teachers are unsung heroes of West Coast jazz. Charles Mingus, Buddy Collette, Dexter Gordon, and a host of other Southern California musicians benefited from Reese's strict discipline and unrelenting emphasis on music fundamentals. Marshall Royal, who had played with Reese in the Les Hite band, recalls that Reese decided early on a teaching career, even though his playing skills might have carried him far: "He was a great player, one of the best trumpet players you ever heard, and he was also an excellent saxophonist."[13] In addition to his mastery of various instruments, Reese had also acquired a prodigious skill in harmony and transposition. Buddy Collette recounts an anecdote that substantiates his teacher's latter talent. The occasion is an informal battle between Reese and pianist Phil Moore, Sr.:

> Lloyd and Phil had a trumpet and piano competition at the union, with maybe 15 or 20 people present. They chose "Stomping' at the Savoy," and agreed to play the first eight bars in the original key of D flat and go half steps all the way until somebody fell out. D flat, then D, and so on. . . . They went on for about a chorus-and-a-half before Phil Moore dropped out. Lloyd was still playing the changes.[14]

Reese taught harmony through a system in which chord progressions were represented by a series of roman numerals. This not only facilitated transposition but also inculcated an understanding of the general harmonic rules underlying any set of chords. Gordon's later reputation for harmonic subtlety—during his days on 52nd Street, other musicians would testify that "Dexter really knows changes"—may stem from this early grounding in his mentor's system.[15] But studying under Reese was more than merely learning harmonic theory; pupils were given a chance to put theory into practice in Reese's rehearsal band, which met weekly at the union hall.

Sam Browne, who taught at Jefferson High, was the other important musical educator who shaped Gordon's early development. "In the entire school system," Buddy Collette explains, "no one compared with Sam Browne at Jefferson. There was no other teacher who had that dedication, who would stay after school hours to get Dexter Gordon and the others to practice, play scales. Only Lloyd Reese on the outside compared with Sam Browne."[16] Browne could boast of a group of home-grown musicians that would be the envy of any school bandleader. In addition to Gordon, Browne's students included Frank Morgan, Vi Redd, Ernie Royal, and Melba Liston. "He had all these wild young dudes," Gordon later said. "We used to call him Count Browne."[17] The Count gave his students a grounding in much more than just jazz; according to Gordon: "We had a school marching band, an orchestra that used to play light classics, plus a swing band that played stock arrangements of Benny Goodman and Basie hits." Pioneers such as Browne and Reese had few models for their efforts—the term "jazz educator" had not yet been coined in the 1930s—but the success of their impressive roster of former students provides eloquent testimony to their wisdom and vision. Their influence on West Coast jazz may have been indirect, but their impact was enormous.

In their musical development, Gray and Gordon show striking similarities. Both started on clarinet, switched to alto, and finally moved to tenor saxophone. Both shared a rare preference for Basie's band over Ellington's ("Basie is the greatest bandleader ever" was Gray's hardly understated praise). Finally, both modeled their saxophone style on Basie tenorist Lester Young. Even so, the differences between these two stylists were marked—differences that made their tenor battles into fiery exchanges of opposing musical viewpoints. Their conflicts took on the aura of a fraternal fight, one heightened by the genealogy binding the two combatants together.

Borrowing pugilistic parlance, one sees their battles as a classic matchup of puncher against boxer. Gordon's solos build off a fierce energy channeled into sharp, powerful strokes, while Gray's more baroque sensibility took flight in a series of small, subtle jabs. Gordon delighted in developing powerful rhythmic figures, and his melodic development was often driven by this percussive undercurrent, while Gray conveyed the opposite sense; his solos seemed to dance, Ali-like, above the rhythm as the horn explored a variety of strange melodic nooks and crannies. Their contrasting tones further reflected these different approaches: Gordon offering a bigger, fuller tenor sound, Gray reveling in a lighter, more ethereal tone, one that stayed truer to the model set by Prez.

Like Gray, Gordon showed an early proclivity for the saxophone duel. His solo feature with the Lionel Hampton band, almost at the beginning of his career, was a tenor battle with Illinois Jacquet on "Po'k Chops." Gordon joined the band in December 1940, a few months after leaving school. Hampton had recently left Benny Goodman, and his "Flying Home" band immediately gave great visibility to Gordon. The young tenorist's initial reaction was, at least partly, disbelief: "I thought Marshall Royal was kidding when he called me up to offer me a job with Hamp's band. I went over to Hamp's pad, and we blew a while, and that was it. We went right on the road, without any rehearsal, cold. I was expecting to be sent home every night."[18] In addition to hiring Gordon, Royal also took charge of the youth's musical education from the day he joined the band. If Reese and Browne had provided Gordon's basic music education, Royal served as a stern finishing school. Royal was unimpressed with the grounding Gordon had received from these two deans of LA jazz education. Alluding to his first dealings with Gordon during our interview, Royal remarked: "I taught him anything that was necessary—and a lot was necessary." Over and above his skills as an altoist, Marshall Royal is also known as a strict taskmaster, one who instilled musical discipline in a number of ensembles, most notably the Basie band. Gordon's recollection suggests that Royal's reputation is not ill founded: "He used to stay on my ass all the time in that section. I'd say, 'Oh, man, won't this man ever get off my back?' But everything he told me was right—breathing, phrasing. 'Man, tune up, tune up, man.' "

The big bands were "traveling academies" for many young musicians of the 1940s. But beyond the pedagogical function of his stint with Hampton, Gordon also gained by going to New York with the band in 1941. Dexter heard Bird at this early stage, and he also laid the groundwork for his successful return to New York a few years later. Upon leaving Hampton in 1943, Gordon longed for his native coast and returned to Los Angeles, where he worked in the band of drummer Lee Young, Lester's brother, and participated in the flourishing Central Avenue scene.

One night when Gordon was playing at a Los Angeles club, Louis Armstrong came up to compliment him on his tone. The next day Gordon was invited to join Armstrong's band. A six-month engagement with the legendary trumpeter followed, but Gordon (much like Charles Mingus, another Los Angeleno who was unhappy during his tenure with the New Orleans legend) found this less satisfying than his work with Hampton: "I had more to play than with Hamp, but the band wasn't saying too much. Pops was using all those old, thirtyish arrangements. . . . You played a job and that was the whole thing. Of course Pops sounded very beautiful at that time—I loved the way he sounded."[19] Despite their musical and generational differences, Gordon and Armstrong hit it off on a personal basis. Gordon later recalled:

> When we left LA, going on the road, I had a dozen Prince Albert cans of Mexican pot. Every night at intermission, Pops and I would go out and smoke. After a week, he didn't bring his shit anymore. . . . I said, 'Damn, Pops, I notice you don't bring out that New Orleans Golden Leaf." He said, "Man, that's like bringing hamburger to a banquet."[20]

The excitement of playing with a jazz legend hardly compensated for the confining atmosphere of the band, especially for an aspiring modernist of Gordon's persuasion. From this perspective, Gordon's next career move, into the Billy Eckstine band, was an ideal step. In 1944 the Eckstine band had inherited many of the young lions of bebop who had infiltrated the Earl Hines band the previous year. "I had had a little taste of bebop before, in and out of Minton's and so forth, but this was really face-to-face," Gordon would later recount. "Dizzy was still in the band. Bird had just left."[21]

In the Eckstine band, Gordon once again found himself a protagonist in a tenor saxophone battle. On "Blowing the Blues Away" Gordon matched up with Gene Ammons, another Texas tenor who has garnered little praise from jazz critics but was a powerful competitor in such encounters. The predominance of Lester Young in Gordon's work was at its greatest at this point in his career, especially on his other Eckstine feature, "Lonesome Lover Blues." This influence lingered over the next few years, remaining evident during Gordon's days on 52nd Street, and only gradually giving way to his more robust bebop-oriented style of later years.

Several accounts mention that Gordon's tenure with Eckstine lasted eighteen months, but Thorbjørn Sjøgren (Gordon's discographer) argues that Dexter's appearances on several New York recordings from the fall of 1945 imply that the Eckstine association continued for less than a year. Gordon's interaction with the young modernists in the Eckstine orchestra no doubt encouraged his exploration of the blossoming Manhattan bebop scene. In 1945, he returned to New York and soon became a regular at the nightspots presenting the new music. Although Gordon's motive for making the trip east was largely musical curiosity, the decision also proved to be a shrewd career move. On 52nd Street, Gordon gained the type of reputation that no musician could develop on the West Coast. "Diz asked me one night on the street if I wanted to make a date," Gordon recalled, describing an impromptu recording session of the time. "This was about four o'clock, something like that in the morning. I don't even remember the studio, except it was in midtown, and I was never there again."[22] The session produced results well worth remembering, however. The released side "Blue 'n Boogie" was a major statement by the new beboppers.

For many listeners this was their introduction to a tenorist who, they assumed, must be at the forefront of the modern jazz revolution. Yet Gordon's recordings from this period show him to be, if anything, a reluctant modernist. Dexter's work with Gillespie is still very much in a Lester Young vein, and his leader sides for Savoy, from October 1945, reveal an undeniable streak of musical traditionalism. On the latter performances a different aspect of Gordon's playing emerges, but not necessarily a more modern one. On the Savoy sides one hears a more forceful Coleman Hawkins–oriented approach that overshadows any influence of Charlie Parker. Here Gordon largely avoids the virtuoso double-time passages and displaced accents to typical of Parker's disciples, instead concentrating on straight-ahead blowing with few frills. A strong rhythm-and-blues element is also apparent on these and the later Savoy recordings, reinforced by Gordon's choice of material, mostly blues and "I've Got Rhythm"–

based songs. This session's highlight is Gordon's workout on "Dexter's Minor Mad," an original based on "I've Found a New Baby," which served to display the tenorist's impressive harmonic awareness.

Despite their many virtues, these early sides only hint at what was soon to come. The next few months must have been an important interlude in Gordon's development, for the follow-up Savoy session reflects a major step forward. This second date, from January 29, 1946, finds Gordon in a more adventurous mood, spurred perhaps by strong support from a world-class rhythm section composed of Bud Powell, Max Roach, and Curly Russell. On "Dexter Rides Again" and "Dexter Digs In," Gordon experiments with new rhythmic and intervallic twists in his solos (the former also includes an intriguing, month-late quote from "Jingle Bells"—could the stated recording date be wrong?). Powell keeps up every step of the way in breathtaking sympathy with the tenorist, contributing some of his best work from this period. The session's ballad, "I Can't Escape from You," is less successful, with Gordon sounding uncharacteristically restrained in a Hawkins vein, while Powell chomps at the bit with Tatumesque runs in the background. Gordon more than makes amends with his trenchant solo on "Long Tall Dexter," a modified blues that finds the tenorist bursting with energy over the altered changes. Here all the disparate elements of Gordon's work begin to come together in a distinctive way: the repeated figures reminiscent of Illinois Jacquet; the harmonic daring of the beboppers; the lyricism learned from Lester Young; the forcefulness gleaned from Hawkins. From now on these separate currents would flow together into a style reflecting the individuality of Dexter Gordon. With these Savoy recordings from 1946 we first encounter the mature voice of a major soloist.

When Gordon returned to Los Angeles in the summer of 1946, the musical currents had already shifted in his hometown. Modern jazz, which was all but unknown in Southern California at the time he left to join Eckstine, had now developed a small but devoted cult-following after the inroads made by visiting musicians such as Gillespie, Parker, McGhee, and Hawkins. With the added glamor of his East Coast achievements, Gordon was marked as one of the few native sons at the forefront of the new musical movement. After a brief stint playing in Hawaii, Gordon reestablished himself on the Central Avenue scene. With Parker institutionalized in Camarillo, Dexter stood out as perhaps the preeminent modern saxophonist on the West Coast.

Such notoriety, however, was not without its costs, especially in the combative environment of postwar Central Avenue. Being acknowledged as the top saxophonist is not a little like being known as the fastest draw in a Wild West town: Soon every new challenger wants to match up with the top gun. Gordon's instinctive attraction to such musical duels, as well as the heated jam-session environment on Central Avenue, only reinforced this undercurrent of competition. Dexter's comments years later, to oral historian Bob Rusch, suggest both the tenor of the times and the times of this particular tenor:

> [RUSCH]: There is an implicit aggressiveness in the two-tenor battle or pairing. Is it something you consciously try to develop?
>
> DG: Isn't it with everything? All my life. . . .
>
> [RUSCH]: How about competition between sax players trying to be the best.
>
> DG: It's every night, all my life. There was always ten players, a battle royal.[23]

Although Gordon was only twenty-three years old when he returned to Los Angeles, he already needed to meet the formidable challenges of other up-and-coming saxophonists such as Teddy Edwards and Sonny Criss. Now, however, the most heated encounters invariably involved an unlikely aspirant to the throne: a fragile-looking Oklahoman of intellectual bearing and soft-spoken ways.

the duel

Gordon had met Wardell Gray earlier, during the latter's Detroit years, and saw him again when Gray was playing with the Hines band at El Gratto in Chicago. Now on the coast he learned at firsthand that Gray had continued to expand his saxophone skills. The transplanted Oklahoman was beginning to convince the avenue's more aware listeners that he was one of the two or three finest saxophonists—some said *the* finest—on the LA scene.

If this had been, in fact, a boxing match, there would have been no competition. Dexter's 6-foot 5-inch frame and 240 pounds made him seem twice as big as his rival—around this time Gordon's friends nicknamed him Joe Louis because of his perceived resemblance to the heavyweight champion. But the smaller man played with a strength that belied his stature. In musical combat he proved that he was every bit the equal of his larger opponent. The judges who kept score at Jack's Basket and other after-hours haunts on Central Avenue frequently had to call the matches a dead heat.

One convert to the modern jazz camp from this time was Ross Russell, an entrepreneur who felt that recording the new music was both an economic opportunity and an aesthetic necessity. While operating Tempo

Music Store in Hollywood, Russell had become pointedly aware of the scarcity of modern jazz records. Fans of the new music, he noted, were often willing to pay three or four dollars for a single 78 disk. The sudden appearance of a cadre of bebop musicians in Southern California presented Russell with a rare opportunity.. He determined to record the musicians himself, to fill the bop void with original recordings of the modern masters. Thus Dial Records was born.

The whims of record company executives affect the world of jazz in strange and often unnoticed ways. The West Coast jazz movement of the 1950s may have reflected, in some degree, the surrounding geographical and meteorological environment, but it also reflected the tastes of producers Les Koenig at Contemporary and Richard Bock at Pacific, the two most influential West Coast jazz arbiters of the period. The fledgling Dial label was no exception to the rule: It reflected the musical instincts of its in-house producer, Ross Russell. Indeed, one can speculate that West Coast jazz would have been a much different phenomenon in the 1950s had Russell and Dial stayed in Los Angeles. The careers of Gordon, Gray, Edwards, and others would have not experienced the downturn, or at least not as precipitously, that came upon them a few years later.

Dexter Gordon was an ideal musician for Dial. He was a young lion of the tenor saxophone steeped in the new musical culture, one who was also close at hand. (The latter attribute should not be minimized: Russell's various accounts of different Dial sessions strikingly reveal that the personnel of many classic record dates was a result of who was around town.) Gordon responded with some of the finest music he had yet set on vinyl. A week before the "Chase" session, Gordon recorded with trombonist Melba Liston for Russell, once again at the spacious MacGregor studio in Hollywood. On "Mischievous Lady" and "Lullabye in Rhythm," Gordon shows the progress he had made, especially in rhythmic phrasing, during the preceding eighteen months. Liston seems unsure of her bebop chops but contributes a simple and lyrical solo that contrasts nicely with Gordon's more ambitious work.

The follow-up session on June 12 is noteworthy not only for "The Chase," but also for Dexter's performances without Gray done later the same day. "Chromatic Aberration," as its name implies, is built on a fairly abstruse chord progression—something along the lines of a 1940s "Giant Steps." Gordon takes the opportunity to show off his much-praised harmonic sophistication. His work on the minor blues "Bikini" (named for the nuclear test site island, not the bathing suit—Gordon's morbid subtitle was "All Men Are Cremated Equal")—is also first-rate. The session's ballad, "It's the Talk of the Town," shows Gordon still trying to find his own voice on slower pieces. Coleman Hawkins had recorded the same piece during his California stay, and again his influence on Dexter's ballad conception is pronounced. Gordon would eventually evolve into one of the finest ballad players of his generation, but on the early Dials, as with the even earlier Savoy work, his approach is still rooted in a 1930s conception strikingly at odds with his personalized and modern way of handling medium or fast numbers. Dexter's last session for Dial, from December 4, 1947, is noteworthy for producer Russell's attempt to re-create the excitement of "The Chase" with a tenor battle between Gordon and Teddy Edwards. The result was "The Duel." Although these two tenors offer less of a contrast than the earlier pairing with Gray, their exchanges are heated. This performance ranks among the better Dial sides of the day and makes it clear how much great music was lost by Edwards's lengthy absences from the recording studio during the next decade.

Shortly after this last session Gordon returned to New York. From that time until he came back to California in 1949, Dexter worked in a wide range of settings. Like Gray, he performed frequently with Tadd Dameron and Fats Navarro, but he could also be found exploring Afro-Cuban music with Machito's path-breaking band. Further, his presence in New York allowed him to resume recording with Savoy. In December of 1947, soon after coming back east, he went into the studio for that label on three separate occasions with some of the finest New York beboppers of the day, including Dameron, Navarro, trombonist J. J. Johnson, drummer Art Blakey, and baritone saxophonist Leo Parker.

These sides show Gordon continuing the evolution presaged in the Savoy sessions. His work here has lost the vestiges of the premodern rhythmic phrasing of the earlier period, and the influence of Charlie Parker is more evident that ever. "Dexter's Riff" and "Dextivity" are musical gems that show the wide range of sounds now available in Gordon's musical arsenal, including the Bird-like double-time passages absent in his earlier work. Moreover, "Dexter's Mood," from the final December session, was Gordon's most forward-looking ballad work to that date. (It should be noted that the maddeningly eponymous song titles here reflect the choices of Savoy, rather than any narcissistic preoccupation on the tenorist's part.)

By the time Gordon returned to California in 1949, the Central Avenue scene was already in decline. Dexter was reunited with Wardell Gray on a number of occasions, but performance and recording opportunities became increasingly scarce at the turn of the decade. Although the 1950s would be the period in which West Coast jazz was recognized as an important movement, the era was also the low point in the careers of many Central Avenue regulars. The sad irony of the situation was that both Gordon and Gray were playing at peak form precisely when conditions turned for the worse. A live recording from the Hula Hut from August 1950 finds both tenorists cooking over the changes of Denzil Best's "Move." This is an exhilarating, well-recorded performance, one that clearly lives

up to the standards the two protagonists had set in their earlier encounters.

Gordon's lean years in the 1950s reflected personal troubles as much
as the broader economic decline in the jazz world. Unlike Gray, whose
drug habit emerged relatively late in life, Gordon's problems with heroin
addiction dated back at least several years before his legal troubles of the
1950s. Art Pepper's account suggests that Gordon began using heroin around
1943 or 1944, while Roy Porter's description of a disastrous road trip with
Gordon from 1948 makes it clear that by that time the problem was already acute.[24] Gitler recalls that many stories circulated from Gordon's
52nd Street days about the tenorist's drug-related escapades, "some true,
some exaggerated, some false." He conveys Dexter's own account of playing a solo for his connection at the intersection of 111th Street and 5th
Avenue: "He had just gotten me high, so when he asked me to play, I
unpacked my horn and blew right on the street corner."[25]

bop is swinging

"If Wardell Gray plays bop, it's great, because he's wonderful," Benny
Goodman told the jazz press during the summer of 1948. Goodman's odd
conditional phrase marked, among other things, the bandleader's ambivalence toward modern jazz. The King of Swing had not welcomed the end
of the swing era. Goodman had earlier asserted that modern jazz players
were "just faking." They were "not real musicians." A short time later
he did an about-face and formed his own bop band.

Goodman's ambiguous assessment of Gray, however, was also a sign
of the odd position of the latter's music. Gray's style straddled two radically different—and often hostile—musical camps. Perhaps this middle
ground made Gray an ideal candidate for Goodman's experiments with
bebop. Gray's more traditional roots had already made him a perfect sideman in other bands led by halfway modernists such as Al Killian and
Vernon Alley. Gray's work with the innovative Hines band, the quintessential transitional band of the early to mid-1940s, had further emphasized
his compatibility with both swing and bop. The tenorist's later stint with
Basie built on these same skills.

Goodman had heard Gray when both were playing as part of Gene
Norman's Just Jazz concerts in California. When Goodman formed his
new bop septet in spring 1948, he enlisted the tenor saxophonist along
with clarinetist Stan Hasselgard. Hasselgard, like Gray, had forged a fresh

and evocative sound by drawing on the best of the old and new jazz styles—
and, also like Gray, was largely forgotten in the years following his early
death. Hasselgard had come to New York from his native Sweden in 1947
to study art history at Columbia University. Forced to leave the university
because of lack of funds, Hasselgard made his way to Los Angeles, where
he gained notoriety for his striking clarinet work. His recording sides for
Capitol from the Hollywood period, which find him in the company of
Red Norvo and Barney Kessel, reveal the qualities that attracted Goodman
to this young stylist. Although self-taught and unable to read music, Hasselgard boasted a lithesome tone and engaging melodic sense.

Gray's collaboration with Goodman produced much fine music that is
too seldom heard nowadays. In contrast, Gray's studio work as a leader
from November 1949 has gained a degree of fame for fairly extraneous
reasons. Gray's memorable blues composition "Twisted," which comes from
this session, was to show amazing versatility and longevity—first as a vocal number for Annie Ross (who captured a modern sense of *Angst* in her
lyrics, exemplified in the couplet "My analyst told me that I was right out
of my head/ But I said 'Dear Doctor, I think it's you instead') and later as
a cover version by Joni Mitchell. Although the other performances from
the session have had fewer claims on posterity, they are nonetheless first-
class examples of Gray's work. Accompanied by a strong rhythm section
of Al Haig, Roy Haynes, and Tommy Potter, Gray contributes an excellent
ballad version of "Easy Living" and on the up-tempo "Southside" sounds
uncannily like Stan Getz, another Prez disciple of the day. A Prestige record made in Detroit a few months later finds Gray with a slightly less
accomplished rhythm section, but the tenor work here is also on a generally high level. His original "Treadin' " conveys his mastery of the rhythm-
and-blues idiom, while the ballad "A Sinner Kissed an Angel" is only a
notch below "Easy Living."

These opportunities to be a group leader were the exception rather
than the rule during this period in Gray's career. Between the two "Chase"
recordings, Gray's work as a sideman not only provided most of his income but also gave him the kind of exposure in the jazz world not possible
within the confines of Central Avenue. Gray frequently collaborated during this period not only with Goodman but also with Count Basie, Tadd
Dameron, and others. The Basie band served as an ideal setting for Gray's
tenor work. The Lester Young elements in his playing came to the fore
here, while the light swinging approach of the group was in sharp contrast
to the more self-conscious modernism of the Goodman efforts. Like many
of the bandleaders of his generation, Basie was struggling to keep a large
group together during a period in which small combos were coming to
dominate jazz. Indeed, many of the recordings with Gray feature a bare-
bones octet, while some find Basie conducting a six-piece group. The Count's

approach in the face of a declining market for big bands—an approach that was ultimately to prove highly successful and allow Basie to maintain a full-time big band—was to emphasize the unpretentious Kansas City swing that had always been the group's forte. Composer Neal Hefti created a number of successful vehicles for presenting this new version of old music (anticipatory penance perhaps for his later work composing TV music, such as the particularly annoying theme to "Batman"). On Hefti's "Little Pony," from an April 1951 session in New York, Gray shows his affinity for this same type of material.

The other significant collaboration of the period, with Tadd Dameron, features Gray in a still different setting. As a bandleader and pianist Dameron ranks as a full-fledged modernist, yet his approach to the bebop idiom showed a tempered restraint that was fairly unusual, especially in comparison with the widely imitated models of Parker, Gillespie, and Powell. Dameron's place in jazz history builds more on his contributions as a composer than as a player, and his low profile on even his own recordings—he is rarely a featured soloist—suggests that he probably viewed his role as pianist as secondary. In this regard, his work might be best viewed as an application of Ellington's philosophy to a modern jazz setting. Like Ellington, Dameron sought less to demonstrate his keyboard acumen than to develop a cadre of strong soloists and a repertory of distinctive compositions. He was distinctly successful in this endeavor: His compositions such as "Lady Bird" and "Good Bait" are played by jazz musicians today, and his sidemen were always among the finest available. At the time of Gray's recording with the group, Dameron featured the great trumpeter Fats Navarro, a fiery soloist and impressive technician who was second only to Gillespie among the first generation of bebop brass players. The presence of drummer Kenny Clarke and bassist Curly Russell alongside Dameron in the rhythm section bore further testimony to the modern jazz credentials of this unit. During this same period Dameron led his band for an unprecedented thirty-nine-week engagement at the Royal Roost, at which Clarke, Russell, Navarro, and Allen Eager were the regular sidemen. The third horn in the group varied during the Roost engagement: Gray was an occasional participant, as were trombonist Kai Winding and altoist Rudy Williams.

In the Dameron front line Gray's fellow tenorist Allen Eager was another Young-inflected modernist, and the two of them provided a fitting contrast to Navarro's more extroverted virtuosity. On the "Lady Bird" date referred to above, the trumpeter's lines crackle with concentrated energy, while Gray appears more inclined to understate the beat. On "Jahbero," a Latin-inflected variation on "All the Things You Are," Gray uses his lead-off solo to forge a relaxed and concise countermelody, while Navarro prefers to bring the house down with an attention-grabbing exploration of the high registers of the horn. Great jazz performances are built on just such musical give-and-take, and Gray showed throughout his career an ability to play his own game while simultaneously underscoring the contributions of his fellow musicians.

By this time Gray was clearly adept, by necessity if not by inclination, at quickly adjusting to new musical surroundings. For example, during a single week in September 1948 Gray did recordings or radio broadcasts with Goodman, Basie, and Dameron! Or perhaps it is more accurate to say that Gray succeeded best by not adapting, by playing in the same vein whether standing alongside Parker or Goodman, whether the rhythm section was led by Basie or Dameron. His style could succeed in any of these settings without having to change. Historians of the music may find it convenient to pigeonhole Gray's playing as a style in flux, but the tenorist's consistency in these very different ensembles suggests that even had he survived for several more decades his playing would have changed little. If anything, the jazz scene, not Gray, was in transition during these years. Modern jazz was becoming more in tune with Gray's hybrid style—the musical mountain was slowly coming around to Muhammed. After a decade of avant-garde experimentation, modern jazz circa 1950 was about to witness a coalescing of bop and swing in developments such as the cool and funk schools of the following decade. Gray would have been very much at home in either of these settings. Similarly, one can envision him fitting in nicely with even later styles, such as bossa nova or the Blue Note sound of the 1960s.

Gray prefigured these developments in both his playing and his occasional remarks on the jazz scene. "Swing is coming back," Gray told *Melody Maker's* Ted Hallock in an extremely rare interview from the last year of the tenorist's life. "The bop movement will be integrated into it. Bop is swinging, and swing is taking on the harmonic advances of bop. If you follow me."[26] In line with this belief, Gray told Hallock that "Basie is the greatest bandleader ever. . . . It is *the* band in modern music. I believe it will hold together and recapture the same vitality and popularity that Basie won with his Kansas City band."

Hallock also makes repeated reference in this all too brief interview to Gray's interest in books, chess, and other nonmusical topics. The article begins: "Interviewing Wardell Gray is more like attending a literary tea . . . than questioning a jazz veteran." Certainly Hallock's impressions substantiate Hawes's description of his friend as an articulate, soft-spoken man with intellectual leanings: "When white fans in the clubs came up to speak to us, Wardell would do the talking while the rest of us clammed up and looked funny."[27] The various accounts of Gray tend to agree on this portrait of an intelligent young man determined to give the lie to whatever stereotypes his interlocutors might have of a black jazz musician from

Oklahoma. Chico O'Farrill, recalling the Goodman bop group, states that "Wardell Gray sometimes felt the brunt of racial discrimination in a very strong way."[28] Rather than buckling under this overt or subtle hostility, Gray responded by cultivating a sense of pride and self-worth built upon his rare abilities, both musical and otherwise.

By the time Gray returned to California in late 1951, he had established himself as one of the most important tenor saxophonists in jazz. "Of the regular players along Central Avenue," Hampton Hawes continues, "Wardell Gray, Dexter Gordon and Teddy Edwards (and Bird when he was in town) were the keepers of the flame, the ones the younger players held in esteem for their ideas and experience and consistency."[29] According to Hawes, Gray was also free at this time of the drug problem that afflicted so many of his contemporaries and, only a few short years later, would contribute to his early death. Red Callender substantiates this view: "Wardell was straight life. That meant when a cat did nothing— didn't drink or anything."[30] Earl Hines, Gray's first major employer, recalls Wardell as a studious youth who spent his time reading books when he wasn't involved in music.

But Vernon Alley, who had played with Gray in San Francisco before the latter's work with Goodman, describes Gray in different terms:

> He could play, but he was kind of frivolous. . . . He took my clarinet down to LA and hocked it. And so when I saw him next I said, "Wardell, where is my clarinet?" He said, "Oh man, I hocked that mother." I said, "Well, give me the [pawn] ticket. I'll get the clarinet. You don't have to get it." He said, "Man, I don't know what I did with that ticket." So I lost my clarinet.[31]

Alley's anecdote may represent an isolated incident. Yet even if Gray's private life was beginning to come unglued at this early date, he was still tending to business on the bandstand, and much of his finest work dates from this period. A studio recording from January 1952 for Prestige finds Gray contributing an outstanding performance on "Sweet and Lovely." Gray is the only soloist on this and "Lover Man," but elsewhere he shares the spotlight with two exceptional sidemen: trumpeter Art Farmer and pianist Hampton Hawes.

Art Farmer and his brother, bassist Addison Farmer, were both part of the influx of Midwest natives to the West Coast during the 1940s. These fraternal twins (Art was the elder by an hour) were born in Council Bluffs, Iowa, on August 21, 1928, and after their parents' divorce, the youngsters moved with their mother and grandparents to Phoenix, Arizona. Both continued their path westward by moving to Los Angeles in 1945, where they became important members of the thriving Southern California jazz scene. Addison played with Charlie Parker and Miles Davis and recorded with Teddy Edwards and Jay McShann during the late 1940s, while Art paid sideman dues with Lionel Hampton, Benny Carter, Johnny Otis, and others. Both had only brief affiliations with West Coast jazz. Art moved to New York in 1953, with brother Addison doing the same the following year. From a career standpoint, the move was a wise one: Art Farmer is widely recognized today as one of the finest trumpeters in jazz and continues to perform regularly, although most often in Europe. Addison, who died from a cerebral aneurism on February 20, 1963, did not live long enough to receive the laurels his talent warranted.

Art Farmer's contribution on the Gray session is especially noteworthy. His clean articulation and assured tone foreshadow Clifford Brown's work of a short time later. Hawes and Farmer are also prominent on one of Gray's live performances from later that year, preserved on an informal recording made by Bob Andrews on his portable Pentron recorder. As on the second version of "The Chase," also from 1952, this date shows precisely what the tenorist could do in a conducive setting. The location was the Haig, a cramped converted bungalow on Wilshire that served as a spawning ground for much of the finest West Coast jazz of the day. More than in any previous performance, Gray displays here the full range of his stylistic mastery: On "Donna Lee" he plays in a more idiomatic bop vein than he had even when in the company of Parker or Navarro and shows a high level of comfort with a driving tempo that gives trumpeter Farmer some pause. Yet on "Taking a Chance on Love" and "Pennies from Heaven" Gray digs in with a more relaxed Prez-inflected orientation. Here, as elsewhere in 1952 and 1953, Gray is playing as well as at any time in his career. Bop was swinging.

the end of the line

Dexter Gordon's music from the 1950s is mostly lost to us. He made few records, received almost no write-ups. Even before he reached his thirtieth birthday, his career was apparently in decline. At the close of 1952, Gordon was arrested for heroin possession, and he spent most of the next two years at Chino, the so-called prison without bars. During the decade Gordon also served time in federal institutions in Fort Worth, Texas, and Lexington, Kentucky. Finally, in 1959, a parole violation led to several months in Folsom Prison, a maximum security institution in California. "That was the end of the line," Gordon says of the last prison. "You couldn't get any worse than that."[32]

Even this degree of personal tragedy brought some attendant benefits. "In some respects it was good. Actually it's the only reason I'm living.

Otherwise I would have been dead a long time ago. . . . Fortunately all
the times I was in I was always involved with a band . . . I always had
my horn, or a horn somebody laid on me, so it wasn't so bad. There were
some positive aspects about it." With a heroin habit that, at its worst,
approached $200 a day, Gordon was slowly self-destructing during his time
on the outside. Yet prison not only provided Dexter with a chance to re-
habilitate—during this time, Gordon also discovered his talent for acting,
an avocation and part-time vocation that would sporadically overshadow
his work in music, most notably in the late 1980s when his performance
in the film 'Round Midnight garnered not only rave reviews but also an
Oscar nomination for best actor.

Gordon's initial exposure to the dramatic arts was scarcely so glamorous; it came about fortuitously as the result of a Hollywood movie about
Chino. Called Unchained, the movie featured several inmates and gave
Gordon a few lines to speak as well as an onscreen saxophone performance. In typical Hollywood fashion, the music one hears is not Gordon's
but an overdub from a studio musician.

Once back on the outside Gordon turned again to music, but even
when he was playing and recording his impact on the jazz world was negligible. From entering Chino until the close of the decade he made only
three studio recordings, all within a matter of weeks during 1955. Although each of these finds Gordon playing at peak level, they did little to
resuscitate his then moribund career. Only a short while later, Gordon
would be back behind bars, but one doubts that, even under the best circumstances, the tenorist would have tasted much success during the late
1950s. Ten years had now passed since Gordon first made his name on
52nd Street, and the jazz critics paid little attention to these new releases.
Perhaps they saw Gordon as an outdated figure. Perhaps his stay in prison
had tarnished his reputation. In any event, the critic's pen and the junkie's
needle proved mightier than the horn.

But if favorable reviews were scarce in 1955, the music was nonetheless happening. His playing on these recordings was clearly stronger than
during his 52nd Street days, and his sense of style had matured to the
point where Gordon could now boast one of the most distinctive and individualized saxophone sounds on either coast. Gordon's comeback date for
Bethlehem, Daddy Plays the Horn, also shows the renewed enthusiasm
that Dexter brought to his music after the long layoff. On the opening
title track, Gordon dispenses with the melody, à la "The Hunt," immediately jumping into a no-frills B-flat blues, which he comfortably navigates
for no fewer than fourteen choruses, finally relinquishing the solo spot to
pianist Kenny Drew, but not before closing with a double-time cadenza
executed with breathless ease. His slow tempo style, evident on "Darn
That Dream" and "Autumn in New York," had by now fully matured—

the latter piece in particular stands out as Gordon's finest ballad performance to that time. The previously overshadowing Hawkins influence on Gordon's ballads is now tempered. Dexter's phrasing is relaxed and imaginative; his tone has become deeply personalized.

The ballad performances from Gordon's date for the Dootone label, *Dexter Blows Hot and Cool*, are less compelling, but the medium- and up-tempo numbers find the tenorist in fine form. Dootsie Williams had started Dootone (originally known as Blue Records) in 1949, and by the mid-1950s had established himself as one of the leading independent producers in the nascent rhythm-and-blues industry. As part of his interest in serving the expanding black urban record-buying market of the Eisenhower years, Williams made occasional forays into the world of mainstream jazz. Out of his porch-front office on Central Avenue near 95th, Williams had just hit the big time early in 1955 with the million-seller "Earth Angel," recorded for Dootone by the Penguins. Turning his attention a few months later to Dexter's less commercial music, Williams may not have had the same potential for huge sales; but even so he did have his hands on a genuine jazz master playing at the top of his game. Williams wisely avoided any attempt to squeeze Gordon's massive talent into the narrow R&B sound of most of the Dootone releases. If anything, he did better by Gordon than he had by many of his other artists: Many of the Dootone releases suffer from poor recording quality—perhaps the result of Williams's penchant for recording out of Ted Brinson's garage on West 30th Street—but the Gordon session boasts fairly good sound to go with the outstanding music. Too much of the album is devoted to ballads, of which only "Cry Me a River" stands out as a major statement, but the other blowing tunes serve as strong vehicles for the whole group, especially Dexter and Carl Perkins.

Only ten days after the first Bethlehem date, Gordon was back in the studio for the same label, as a sideman on drummer Stan Levey's project, released as *Stanley the Steamer*. In contrast to the informal approach to his own session, Gordon now found himself sharing the front line with trumpeter Conte Candoli and trombonist Frank Rosolino in a more tightly arranged combo setting. In different hands these arrangements—for example, the adaptation of "La Chaloupee" from Offenbach—might have come across as somewhat strained, but Gordon and Candoli both turn in gripping performances.

Soon after this brief flurry of recording activity, Gordon was again behind bars on drug charges. His musical career would be mostly on hold until the early 1960s, when his acting skills also moved forward with his role in a West Coast production of Jack Gelber's play *The Connection*. At the same time Cannonball Adderley would revive the tenorist's recording career by producing *The Resurgence of Dexter Gordon*. This comeback would prove to be more lasting than the ephemeral 1955 return: The Adderley production would be followed by a series of successful Blue Note albums. Although Gordon lacked the cabaret card he needed to perform in New York, a second career in Europe provided him with even more economic security than he could have found in Manhattan.

In 1977 Gordon returned to the United States after fifteen years abroad. In his mid-fifties, he began receiving the critical acclaim and audience support that had eluded him in earlier years. A record contract with CBS produced outstanding recordings such as *Homecoming* and *Sophisticated Giant* and gave him media visibility, which few mainstream jazz players could garner in an age of jazz-rock fusion.

In 1980 he was selected as musician of the year by the readers of *Downbeat* and was enshrined as a member of that magazine's Jazz Hall of Fame. In the 1980s, the awards and honors poured in: Gordon received a U.S. Congressional Commendation; he was awarded a grant for lifetime achievement from the National Endowment for the Arts; Washington, D.C., honored him with Dexter Gordon Day. After Gordon's Oscar nomination, his fee for a single concert could be as high as $20,000—or more. By the time of his death in April 1990, Gordon was universally acknowledged as a jazz legend, and though his playing in the late 1980s was often below the standard of his own earlier work, his audience had never been larger or more devoted.

With the benefit of hindsight, we can call Gordon's career a success, but in 1955 Gordon faced a future far from secure. Legal problems and an indifferent audience were not the only traumas the middle of this decade had to offer. When Gordon was released from Chino in 1955, he immediately searched out his old musical adversary and friend, only to find that Gray had just gone on the road. Wardell had traveled to Las Vegas with the Benny Carter band to participate in the opening of a major new hotel. Three days later, Gordon heard the news of Gray's death.

the steeplechase

Sometime during this period, Wardell Gray became caught in the same entangled web of drug addiction he had earlier warned Hampton Hawes and other young musicians against. Hawes recalls his surprise when, returning to Los Angeles after his stint in the service, he encountered his senior colleague at the California Club. "As soon as I saw him I knew he was strung. It shook me up."[33]

The effects on his playing are difficult to gauge. Gray's recording career also came to almost a standstill during late 1953 and throughout 1954. This period marked something of a dry spell for many of the Central

Avenue veterans: not just Gray and Dexter Gordon, but also—to name a few—Hampton Hawes, Teddy Edwards, and Sonny Criss. Gray's last studio recording found him in the company of the young alto saxophonist Frank Morgan, heralded at the time, with only slight exaggeration, as the "new Bird." Morgan, son of guitarist Stanley Morgan, possessed a lightning-fast saxophone technique and fertile melodic imagination. In the early 1950s, he caught the tail end of the Central Avenue renaissance, working the house band at the Club Alabam and making his name at the few remaining local jam sessions. Under different circumstances, Frank Morgan might have become one of the leaders of West Coast jazz in the 1950s, but he too struggled with a heroin addiction that kept him off the scene for many years. When the Morgan/Gray session was being prepared for reissue by GNP in 1977, both producer Gene Norman and Leonard Feather, who wrote the new liner notes, initially assumed that Morgan was long dead. In fact Morgan was then on the brink of putting his life and career back together after interim gigs at San Quentin, Chino, and Synanon. His success was such that his career blossomed in the 1980s as it never had in the 1950s. Today he is widely acknowledged as one of the four or five most talented altoists in jazz.

In 1955, Morgan was just twenty-two years old, one of the up-and-coming products of Sam Browne's pioneering jazz education program at Jefferson High School. Producer Gene Norman had used Morgan at the Tiffany Club for Sunday afternoon sessions, along with Wardell Gray and Teddy Edwards, and as a sideman on a recording by Lyle "Spud" Murphy. Now Norman decided to record Morgan as a leader in company with an all-star band that included Wardell Gray, Carl Perkins, and Conte Candoli. Around this same time, Norman also featured Morgan in a very different session with organist Wild Bill Davis and Machito's Afro-Cuban-based rhythm section. The young altoist is a delight to hear in both settings. On Gillespie's bop standard "The Champ," Morgan lets loose with a breath-taking solo, very much in a Bird vein, which few saxophonists of any age could match.

Gray, not to be outdone, responds with one of his stronger recorded choruses. On the strength of these recordings, one would have predicted a promising future for both saxophonists, but Morgan, a heroin addict since seventeen, was already caught up in the drug habit that would cause a two-decade absence from the jazz scene. Gray's situation was even worse. He would be dead before the Morgan recording was released.

Any attempt to recount the circumstances of Gray's death is likely to raise as many questions as it answers. Several interpretations have been offered with varying degrees of plausibility. The basic facts are as follows. Gray was in Las Vegas with Benny Carter's band to open the Moulin Rouge, a $3 million racially integrated hotel, theater, and restaurant complex. Wardell failed to appear for the band's Wednesday night late show on May 25. The next afternoon his body was found in a weed patch four miles outside of town. Gray's neck was broken and his head injured, presumably from a beating with a blunt instrument.

An immediate suspect in the case was dancer Teddy Hale. Hale, who had previously served time on drug-related charges, had also failed to appear for Wednesday's second show. Later in the day on Thursday he was interrogated by police; he told them Gray had suffered his fatal injuries when he had fallen out of bed during a "heroin party" in Gray's room. Frightened by what had happened, Hale decided to dump the body in the outlying desert. Bandleader Carter, in a statement to the press, underplayed the narcotics angle; he claimed that the question of drug use had never come up in his conversations with the police. He maintained, however, that Gray had been in poor health and was drinking heavily during the days prior to his death.

After making Hale take a lie detector test, the police released the dancer and accepted his explanation that Gray's death was the result of a fall. A host of rumors continued to circulate, however, each offering a different interpretation of the mysterious circumstances.

Singer Richard Boone recalled:

> Of course it was supposed to be an overdose, but the talk before was that he'd burned the people in power, who supply the heroin. He'd done something wrong, not enough to kill somebody, but from their point of view they figured they'd snuff him out.[34]

Vernon Alley, who had employed Wardell in his San Francisco band on many occasions, also suspected murder, but for different reasons: "He was probably fooling around with somebody's old lady. [Las Vegas] was a real bigoted place at the time. And so they wasted him."

Dexter Gordon dismissed the suspicions of murder but disagreed with the police allegations of a fall as the cause of death:

> I know he had an OD. I spoke to the dancer who was with him, and he told me what happened. He had taken an overdose. They had gotten high together and Teddy went to his room to get ready for work and when he came back Wardell was out of it. They couldn't revive him. So he and another guy walked him out of the hotel like he was drunk. And took him out in the desert, in Vegas, and dumped him. In the course of the ride, with the dead weight, his neck got broken, but he was already gone.[35]

Red Callender, whose account agrees with Gordon's on most points, nonetheless put the blame on Hale:

He had an overdose, what they call a hot shot. If the guys he was with had any brains they would have taken him to a hospital, they could have saved him. Instead, he died and they dumped him in the desert. . . . Had he lived he would have been one of the truly amazing players of our time. He was anyhow.[36]

CHAPTER FOUR

Dave Brubeck and Modern Jazz in San Francisco

the last bastion of the moldy figs

The Southern Pacific train tracks, which cut a swath from San Francisco to San Jose, are devoted to a single passenger route these days. Roughly two dozen times a day a commuter train leaves the downtown San Francisco depot for a ninety-minute trip to San Jose, while a corresponding train makes the same trip north, each following a set schedule. It is a closed system, two adjacent tracks running over fifty miles, serving an assortment of businesspeople, tourists, and those few residents eccentric enough to make their way in California without an automobile.

As the train passes the Menlo Park station midway on its trip, an especially alert passenger might catch a glimpse of an amusing sign perched on the depot roof. One end of the sign, pointing north, reads "San Francisco 29 Miles." The other end, pointing south to the San Jose end of the line, mysteriously reads "New Orleans 2473 Miles." Most assume that the CalTrain officials who supervise the lines have added an uncharacteristic touch of humor to an otherwise dreary commute. After all, the SP line, as if in answer to the 1960s song, knows *only* the way to San Jose. When questioned, the officials at CalTrain admit ignorance about the origin or purpose of the sign. Representatives of the city's Chamber of Commerce, whose office is located inside the depot, claim not to have noticed the message, perched literally above their heads, until a local recently pointed it out—nor, for that matter, had the city manager, a resident of Menlo Park for thirty years.

The sign, despite the amusement of the few who notice it, represents no attempt at humor. Photos of the Menlo Park depot taken in the early 1900s show a similar sign in the same location. Those willing to do their homework would discover that the Southern Pacific lines have not always been restricted to commuter traffic. In the early years of this century, San Francisco was a major hub for Southern Pacific, and New Orleans was the ultimate destination of the only southbound transcontinental route. In those days, the Sunset Limited train traversed the whole distance from San Francisco to New Orleans, passing the Menlo Park station over rails now reserved for the local commuter line and continuing far beyond the now truncated tracks at San Jose, down through Los Angeles, and heading all the way to Louisiana.

The route, now long defunct, was extremely popular in its day. And though the story of New Orleans jazz traveling up the river to Chicago may be more or less true, the less glamorous account of railroad commerce between California and the Crescent City also deserves its due. More than people obviously traveled the line—a fair amount of musical culture seems to have made the trip as well. The first known use of the word *jazz* in print comes, not from the South, but from the *San Francisco Bulletin* of March 6, 1913, in an ambiguous reference to "ragtime and jazz" in a sports article. Knowledgeable Chicagoans will point out that Bert Kelly formed his "Jass Band" (as he called it then) in Chicago in 1916, thus being the first bandleader outside New Orleans to use the *double entendre* name (*jazz* served also as a slang expression for copulation)—but what they forgot to add is that Kelly had been playing tea dances at San Francisco's St. Francis Hotel in 1914; it was there, by his own admission, that he first formed a jazz band. Reb Spikes, the pioneering Los Angeles bandleader, reports that San Francisco musicians were significantly ahead of their Southern California counterparts in assimilating the New Orleans music. "When I visited San Francisco," Spikes has commented of his 1907 trip, "I think they just called the music ragtime. They could have called their music jazz."[1] Long before the first black jazz musicians made records in New Orleans (or anywhere else, for that matter), their music had come in person to both Los Angeles and San Francisco. Jelly Roll Morton played at the Cadillac Café on Central Avenue around 1917 and a short while later worked at the Jupiter in San Francisco with a ten-piece band. Somewhat later King Oliver's Creole Band played a memorable engagement in an upstairs hall on Market Street in San Francisco. Buddy Petit, Frankie Dusen, and Kid Ory also played California in the years following World War I.

Even at that early date, however, the talent that journeyed back east garnered most of the recognition. San Francisco bandleader Paul Whiteman did well to ignore Horace Greeley's advice: He traveled east, where he was soon dubbed, however briefly, the "King of Swing." Oliver too only hit his stride after coming back from California. Jelly Roll Morton, in words that could be written today, remarked about a trombonist from Oakland from the pre-Prohibition years: "Poor Padio, he's dead now, never got east so none of the critics ever heard him."[2] If Jelly Roll can be believed—always a matter for dispute—the pattern of East Coast ignorance of, or indifference to, West Coast talent was set from the start.

Whatever pioneering spirit San Francisco captured in those early days of jazz disappeared in later years. Modern jazz musicians found San Francisco an inhospitable environment long after the music had made inroads in many other cities. In the late 1940s, when jazz had already undergone a revolution elsewhere, San Francisco was still holding on to the same New Orleans–inflected music—now played mostly by white Dixieland enthusiasts—it had embraced after the Great War. Even worse, San Francisco remained one of the last major cities to perpetuate segregated musicians' unions, not merging Local 6 and Local 669 until April 1960. Throughout most of the period under discussion, black musicians found a less than equal opportunity to make their names while staying in San Francisco, with strong players like Richard Wyands, Jerome Richardson, John Handy, and others earning their stripes back east. Those who stayed, like Allen Smith, Curtis Lowe, and Vernon Alley, became anything but household names, even among sophisticated San Francisco jazz fans. That modern jazz could survive in such a setting was for some time open to question. That it would eventually thrive there was something approaching a miracle.

Today, of course, things are much different. Since the 1970s, the San Francisco area has become one of the world centers of jazz recording activity. Many of the finest independent labels focusing on improvised music during all or part of the last twenty years—Fantasy, Concord, Landmark, Windham Hill, Blackhawk, Palo Alto Jazz, Theresa, Quartet—have used the Bay Area as a springboard for serving the international jazz record buyer. The jazz catalogue of Fantasy Records alone, built up over the years by the strategic acquisition of a number of other jazz-oriented labels—Prestige, Riverside, Contemporary, Pablo—now gives it control over more outstanding jazz, especially modern jazz, than any of the majors. But for an earlier generation of jazz fans, San Francisco represented not the mecca of modern jazz but rather the last bastion of white traditional jazz, a final haven for the "moldy figs" (as jazz jargon would denote the antimodernists) of Dixieland.

The cast of characters involved in establishing the San Francisco area as a center of modern jazz recording is every bit as unlikely as the story itself. Sol and Max Weiss, the founders of Fantasy, were true jazz anomalies: They got into jazz for the money! Even stranger, they succeeded! Their local predecessor in modern jazz, Jack Sheedy, was an equally unlikely participant. The owner of Coronet Records, a faltering label devoted to Dixieland jazz, Sheedy agreed to record Dave Brubeck—then an unknown local pianist playing an odd brand of modern jazz—largely due to the intercession of disk jockey Jimmy Lyons. Lyons promised Sheedy that the project would cost him little.

As it turned out, it helped him very little, too. Unable to pay his bills, Sheedy forfeited his masters to the Weiss brothers, who owned the local pressing plant where Coronet had its records manufactured. From a background in plastics, the Weisses were thus thrust into the entertainment industry as an inadvertent result of collecting their bills. Despite these inauspicious credentials, the Weisses would in time achieve extraordinary success with their label, soon rechristened Fantasy after a popular pulp science-fiction magazine. The growing orders for the Brubeck sides, first from the Pacific Northwest and soon from around the country, inspired them to produce more records with the popular pianist. Eventually they found the recording business so successful that to meet demand they were forced to hire other pressing plants. The later sage advice of the film *The Graduate* to the contrary, the Weisses made the unlikely transition *out* of plastics, into the far riskier business of being moguls of modern music. The only lasting reminder of the company's roots in applied chemistry was the distinctive multicolored vinyl used to press Fantasy records. Red, blue, and green phonograph records never caught on with other companies, but for jazz fans the colorful plastic disks were part and parcel of the Fantasy mystique.

"This was the place where every bit of business got done," Max Weiss remarked to me over lunch, gesturing to the surrounding restaurant. "I still eat here."[3] One of the conditions of our interview was that I would meet Weiss over lunch at the San Francisco Italian restaurant, Original Joe's, where he has lunched for several decades. Having religiously pursued business there in the past, he saw no need to change his plans for me. The tape of our conversation features an unabated accompaniment of tinkling glasses, shuffled plates, and background chit-chat, amid which Weiss continued his monologue: "This place became the hangout for all the jazz musicians of the day. There was a table back there where, every day, they would eat lunch. And we'd just hustle our business. All the record distributors would hang out here. And whoever was appearing at any of the nightclubs." The setting nowadays is far from inviting: The surrounding neighborhood boasts an assortment of shabby bars, sex parlors, and cheap hotels, while the restaurant's interior is only slightly less down-and-out. As for the other customers, if any were record industry celebrities, they had come carefully disguised on this occasion.

"We weren't die-hard jazz fans, never were, still aren't," Weiss explained in his account of Fantasy's earliest days. "Anything that sold, we would sell. [We did] mainly jazz because that was the only thing that we were aware of that wasn't a flash in the pan." Weiss is well known as the master of the put-on—one of his most famous works was a tongue-in-cheek letter to *Downbeat* lamenting the continual failure of Fantasy Records. Although the business made a handsome profit, he explained in the letter, it in no way compensated for its tragic failure in realizing the owners' "high and mighty" artistic aims. In his candor to me about the brothers' business-as-usual attitude, Weiss was this time ringing true. "We would do anything that would keep the pressing plant busy, because that was the main business we were in," Weiss elaborated. "All we had to do was pay for the shellac or vinyl." As to what to record, the Fantasy owners' lack of musical expertise was seen as no hindrance. Indeed the company's artistic criteria were clear from the start: "If it sells, great. If it doesn't sell, forget it. That's the philosophy I think you have to have. You can't fall in love with your product."

Weiss provided a rare glimpse into the business of recording jazz during the early 1950s:

> In those days, with a group like Mulligan, we would go into a recording session. Sidemen got $40 each, the leaders got double. In a three-hour session, according to the union, we had to get fifteen minutes of music. When Brubeck or Tjader or Mulligan went in a session, in three hours if we didn't get an hour and a half of music everyone thought something was wrong. . . . For every additional fifteen minutes we used we had to pay them another $40 and $80. So in order to break even on a jazz artist, if we sold 5,000 units we were very, very happy. Today, an average album costs anywhere from $40,000 to $50,000 in studio time. Today these guys aren't rehearsed, they listen to it while doing it. So I mean, the market was different.

When the Brubeck "product" started shipping in quantities of 40,000 to 50,000 a quarter, Fantasy began reaping windfall profits. The company's later hit with Vince Guaraldi's "Cast Your Fate to the Wind" sold 100,000 copies right off the bat, signaling even greater financial success. But Fantasy's biggest coup came shortly after the Weiss brothers sold out to an investor group led by Saul Zaentz, a former Weiss employee who would go on to produce films, such as *One Flew over the Cuckoo's Nest* and *Amadeus*, in addition to expanding Fantasy's presence in the music world. A rock group from Berkeley High known as the Blue Velvets, which the

Weisses had signed and renamed the Golliwogs, changed their name once again, this time to Creedence Clearwater Revival, and had a string of million-selling hits for the new owners. This unexpected success financed Fantasy's move to a new upscale building in Berkeley and provided capital for the company's acquisitions of a string of other jazz labels.

Long before this the Weisses had expanded beyond the world of record producing by buying a part interest in the Blackhawk, the leading San Francisco jazz club of its day. And to show that they were not constitutionally opposed to Dixieland, they also became involved in the Tin Angel ("an entirely different audience," Weiss explained). Notwithstanding the continued success of the Tin Angel and other traditional jazz venues, the modernist leanings of Fantasy and the Blackhawk in the 1950s were crucial in turning a Dixieland town into a hotbed of modern jazz. "All those places are gone now," Weiss commented toward the end of our lunch, striking for the moment an uncharacteristic note of nostalgia. "The Blackhawk closed. The lease ran out. It's now a parking lot. Bank of America owns the building. They're making more money out of a parking lot than a dumb little nightclub."

The Blackhawk, during its glory days, was much more than a "dumb little nightclub." Originally an obscure venue known as the Stork Club, the Blackhawk had become something of a West Coast equivalent of Birdland or the Village Vanguard by the middle 1950s. "When Charlie Parker was playing San Francisco he'd be at the Say When," Harry "the Hipster" Gibson recounted, in one of the taped monologues he provided for this book, "but he'd go over to the Blackhawk to play whenever he got the chance. He liked the musicians there better." Not just Parker but a large group of jazz fans were, it seems, enamored of the Blackhawk's bands. If the club fell short of matching "the jazz corner of the world" (as Birdland's Pee Wee Marquette proclaimed its East Coast location), the Blackhawk was no doubt the most illustrious jazz corner on the Barbary Coast. For jazz players on the Fantasy roster—in particular Dave Brubeck's quartet and octet and Cal Tjader's various groups—the Blackhawk was something of a home base from which they could launch their distinctive assault on the world of contemporary jazz. Other major venues dotted the landscape—Bop City, the Say When, Fack's, and the like—but if San Francisco could ever lay claim to a truly indigenous jazz style, it sprang from the *sui generis* modernism fostered by the Blackhawk and Fantasy Records. The all-star sessions at Jimbo's Bop City, which were stunning on a good night, or a visit by Charlie Parker to the Say When may well have bested the Blackhawk's acts on many occasions, but those clubs remained, in essence, extensions of an East Coast sensibility. The Blackhawk was, in contrast, a distinctively San Franciscan center of modern jazz. Of course, visiting jazz dignitaries from back east, Charlie Parkers or lesser talents, were welcomed on the premises—Miles Davis recorded one of his finest live albums at the club—but the unique sounds that set the club apart were largely native to the Bay Area.

The guiding force and unlikely revolutionary behind this indigenous San Francisco modernism, this still controversial music, was without question pianist/composer Dave Brubeck. For the historian of West Coast jazz, Dave Brubeck is the sticky problem that won't go away. No figure associated with West Coast jazz is better known than Brubeck—and if fame was the sole or chief criterion of our historical inquiry, our task would be a simple one of citing the cover stories and sold-out concert halls that have marked his career. Such notoriety notwithstanding, no West Coast musician has been more controversial than Dave Brubeck. Brubeck's music is loved or hated, and rarely viewed with indifference. The historian who hopes to reflect the consensus view of his or her subject had better find another subject. About Dave Brubeck there is no consensus.

Even individual comments on Brubeck are apt to seem paradoxical or inconsistent. How else can we take Cecil Taylor's strange judgment on the subject:

> When Brubeck opened in 1951 in New York I was very impressed with the depth and texture of his harmony, which had more notes in it than anyone else's that I had ever heard. It also had a rhythmical movement that I found exciting. . . . I don't think that that music is important now for what it made, but I think it was important then for the gaps it filled.[4]

Somehow the music lost its importance along the way. Taylor, however, is oddly silent about how this decline took place—and one hopes, for Cecil's sake, that a similarly inexplicable drop in importance, a kind of stock market crash of the aesthetic, doesn't one day afflict his own music.

Of course such convoluted judgments about Brubeck are not restricted to Cecil Taylor. One could spend many hours attempting to decipher the attitudes toward Brubeck of many otherwise intelligent and straightforward commentators. Ralph Gleason, the elder statesman of jazz criticism on the West Coast, wrote laudatory liner notes to a Brubeck album, and then later announced in *Downbeat* that not only did he dislike Brubeck's music, he had never liked it from the moment he first heard it. Critics who were at least consistent in their hostility created quite ingenious reasons for their disapproval. Frequently cited criticisms of Brubeck in the 1950s emphasized the facts—all of them difficult to dispute—that (1) his group earned more money than the Modern Jazz Quartet; (2) his picture was put on the cover of *Time* magazine; (3) Duke Ellington's picture was *not* put on the cover of *Time* magazine; (4) the Brubeck quartet did not sound like Gerry Mulligan's.

Even the much-publicized criticism that Brubeck's band didn't swing like earlier jazz bands—the *bête noire* of Brubeckology—seems a little odd in retrospect. Since the early Brubeck recordings of the 1950s present so much that, for better or worse, is new and unusual (especially in rhythmic and compositional structure), one expects the critics to focus on elucidating these positive attributes of the music instead of merely pointing out the ways in which Brubeck was *not* emulating, say, Basie or Mulligan or the MJQ. Indeed the criticisms of Brubeck's sense of swing, harmony, and tone sound quite similar to those directed at another apparently un-swinging iconoclast: Thelonious Monk. In both instances the critics seemed less than interested in the extraordinary individualistic qualities of the music and content to interpret it in terms of what it was not. This parochial attitude fails miserably, in the case of fresh stylists like Monk and Brubeck, to get at the heart of the matter. In both instances, the music has held up well over the passing years. It is the early criticism that seems worn and dated.

The names Brubeck and Monk are seldom uttered in the same sentence by jazz critics, but this is puzzling when one notices the powerful similarities between the two stylists. Both were offering comparable alternatives to the dominant Bud Powell conception of modern jazz piano: fast right-hand melodic lines that made the piano sound like a horn. Instead Brubeck and Monk brought out the intrinsically pianistic and orchestral qualities in the instrument. From different starting points, they arrived at convergent solutions to their shared musical problems. Both began adopting more complex harmonic structures than their peers (and both were chastised for this reliance on "funny chords"). Both emphasized (almost to an extreme) the percussive nature of the piano, relying on rhythmic placements that delighted in unexpected accents and syncopations—and both were accused of not swinging. Both stressed this percussiveness by adopting a heavy touch, which imparted to their improvisations a looming, hard-as-bricks sound. Both strenuously reacted against the "blowing date" atmosphere then prevalent in jazz and focused as much on composing as on playing. And when they did improvise, their solos were almost compositional in structure and intent. Finally, despite these experimental tendencies, both Brubeck and Monk showed their allegiances to the jazz tradition by remaining within the confines of a standard jazz quartet and continuing to program music from the standard jazz repertoire.

Monk's reputation has, of course, changed dramatically over the years. With each new decade since the 1940s his achievements are more recognized, and since his death in 1982 his status has become, if anything, further enhanced. Nothing of this sort has happened to Dave Brubeck. One senses that many jazz writers would like to discredit or explain away his tremendous and lasting success. And this might be easy to do if Brubeck had obliged them by putting out blatantly commercial albums. But the pianist has tenaciously refused this option and, in his cussed way, has developed a huge following while recording a series of very uncommercial-sounding albums. His most successful releases feature dense and often experimental piano music in an acoustic setting, without relying on lush string arrangements, catchy vocal numbers, funky dance beats, and the like. Added to the enigma is the lasting popularity of Brubeck's music: Decades have passed since he was on the cover of *Time*, and for years now he has recorded for a small independent label that puts little marketing money behind his releases. Still he sells well and packs concert halls wherever he performs.

Although Brubeck's influence on other players (especially through his experimentation with odd meters) is quite evident, it is rarely acknowledged, at least in jazz circles. "['Take Five'] was as important to me," rock star Billy Joel explains, "as *Sergeant Pepper's* was to rock 'n roll aficionados in the '60s."[5] Could one imagine any jazz player daring to make such an unfashionable claim? But as soon as one leaves the inner cliques of jazz, where his name is seldom mentioned, one sees Brubeck's impact everywhere. The background music between news flashes on TV, a few seconds of filler, bounces around in a Brubeckian 5/4 before disappearing. Jethro Tull, the long-lived rock group, hits the charts with "Living in the Past," a lilting tune with a "Take Five" breakdown of 5/4 into a waltzy three-step followed by the two hard hits on beats four and five. The TV show "Mission Impossible" grabs listeners with the same Brubeck-derived rhythm. Although the jazz world may be sparing in its praise, the music community at large accepted Brubeck as an innovator long ago, as did the listening public.

If the critics are more than a little befuddled by this state of affairs, some blame lies in Brubeck's corner. He has often quite deliberately defied the conventional wisdom, never easily fitting into the mould. One of Brubeck's contemporaries tells that the pianist years ago confided his secret for success in music: It lay in having "stuff that others couldn't understand." For Brubeck this technique has proven, perhaps unintentionally, to be more than a matter of harmony, melody, and rhythm—his whole career stands out as some strange stuff indeed.

Even the first facts of Brubeck's biography contradict the stereotyped images of the jazz life. Jazz, we are told, is urban music that flourishes only in the heart of the city (hence labels such as "New Orleans jazz," "Chicago jazz," "Kansas City jazz"), yet Brubeck's musical development was completely divorced from any urban environment. He grew up on a

45,000-acre ranch in Northern California, far removed from city life of any kind. He later flourished within the confines of an academic environment, thus violating another cardinal rule of jazz: that the music defies teaching in a classroom setting. In recent years this dubious truism has fallen under increasing attack, if only because more and more jazz players have graduated from (or are now teaching at) institutions such as the Berklee School, The University of Miami, or North Texas State.

Yet even given a more favorable view of jazz education, Brubeck's choice of Darius Milhaud as an academic mentor must seem highly unusual. At a time when merely playing bebop was still viewed in most jazz circles as suspiciously modern, Brubeck was cutting his teeth on Milhaud, Stravinsky, Schoenberg (another of his teachers, albeit briefly), and Hindemith. This attempt to out-modern the modern jazz players was all the more strange for taking place in a Northern California jazz setting where the traditional playing of Lu Watters and Turk Murphy was considered by many the extreme of hipness. In a locale where virtually no modern jazz players resided, Brubeck was practicing one-up-manship on a modern jazz movement that simply didn't exist. Even in his teens, Brubeck was a phenomenon unto himself.

Brubeck's rise to fame similarly defied all the rules. It happened without the benefit of a press agent or a public relations campaign, and on the strength of music that was neither designed for mass public consumption nor destined for critical acclaim. It was promoted first by a faltering Dixieland record label, then picked up by a tiny independent company with experience only in applied plastics and no track record in music. Even in his choice of sidemen, especially his hiring of alto saxophonist Paul Desmond, Brubeck seemed determined to go off the beaten track by selecting the most unhip, unmodern player on either coast. Why, one wondered, was he emulating Milhaud and Hindemith on the piano, while at the same time featuring a saxophonist who seemed completely out of touch with musical modernism, who was in fact—heaven forbid—as lyrical as Johnny Hodges or Benny Carter?

For someone depicted by the jazz press as so straightforward, so immune from eccentricity and quirkiness (perhaps his avuncular good nature, they sometimes suggest, accounts for his otherwise inexplicable success), Brubeck has certainly done a good job of investing his life and times with more than a fair share of mystery. Is it any wonder that Dave Brubeck should be placed in the strange situation of being both extraordinarily well known and, at the same time, quite badly understood? For the plain truth remains that, for all the hype and criticism, Brubeck remains an enigma. This unfortunate judgment must be the starting point for any attempt to assess this unique man and his music.

shouting with Schoenberg

Thirty miles inland from the San Francisco Bay, Concord, California, is a rapidly growing suburban town, populated largely by commuters seeking a working relationship with the nearby metropolitan areas. Initially attracted to the area by relatively inexpensive home prices—at least compared with the astronomic costs of residing closer to the Pacific—or by the less hectic pace of life, Concordians have more recently found, to their dismay, that many of the problems of big-city life have followed them into the suburbs. Traffic jams, pollution, overbuilding—unheard of in these parts only a few years ago—have all become prevalent. Meanwhile corporate America has followed the suburbanites' lead, relocating their offices, clerical staffs, and back rooms to Concord and its environs. Concord today is in danger of being overwhelmed by its endless rows of office parks, recently built residences, and faceless franchises. Perhaps no other city better exemplifies California as it flounders in the shopping-mall era.

When Dave Brubeck was born in Concord in 1921, the community bore no resemblance to its present denatured state. The population of the city then was 2,600. (Some decades later, when Brubeck first performed at the newly built Concord Pavilion, located on land his father formerly managed, there were more than 10,000 people in the audience.) Brubeck describes early-day Concord as a ranching and farming community having little contact with nearby San Francisco and Oakland. "The road to the Pavilion I learned how to drive a car on. In fact I didn't learn, I just drove. . . . I was probably maybe eight years old. When I go up that road I'm going right towards ranches where as a young man I had gone with my father, riding on the back of his horse."[6] Dave's maternal grandfather was the local stagecoach operator who ran the mail and passenger transport from Concord to Oakland, then an arduous journey by way of a mountain road.

Dave's mother, who had studied as a concert pianist in Europe, undertook the musical education of Dave and his brothers. Brubeck's father was probably of Native American descent (the family tree is ambiguous at this point, although musical colleagues Dave Van Kriedt and Paul Desmond took it as a certainty, the latter often referring to the pianist as "the Indian"), a cowboy and rodeo roper who had grown up near the California/Nevada border. As a young man he had won first prize at the prestigious Salinas rodeo. In later years he earned his living as a manager of cattle ranches and a buyer of herd beef—a profession that led the Brubecks to move to the even more remote community of Ione, California, when Dave was eleven years old.

Unlike Concord, Ione has changed little with the passing years. Located some forty miles above Sacramento, the Ione ranch on which Brubeck spent his adolescent years spanned three counties. It still spreads over 30,000 acres today. Here Dave furthered his piano studies under his mother's tutelage. Reading musical notation posed a problem—and would continue to do so—but the youngster showed a striking knack for creating his own spontaneous sounds.

Despite his early evidenced musical talent, Brubeck showed no intention of pursuing a career in music. Many of his contemporaries in jazz entered the ranks of professional music by joining the traveling bands that passed through town, usually in replacement of a recently drafted section player. But Brubeck had little exposure, if any, to traveling bands in either Ione or Concord. San Francisco might have been less than fifty miles distant, but in spirit it was a world away.

What Brubeck did encounter in those rustic settings was, put plainly, cattle and farm animals. When his mother insisted he pursue a college education (she had to insist—"I wanted to settle down right on the ranch and never go to college," Brubeck recalled[7]), his first leanings were toward a career in veterinary medicine. At the College (now University) of the Pacific he struggled through a year of premed studies and made passing grades, but his interest and attention slowly gravitated to the activities in the nearby music building. At the end of Brubeck's first year, he was encouraged by a perceptive zoology teacher, who noticed the lackluster interest of his student, to switch from medicine to music. Soon Brubeck was flourishing as a full-time music student.

There was a problem, however. Brubeck still had little ability in reading music, the result perhaps of a childhood vision disorder. Usually such a limitation would have prevented the pursuit of a college music major, but Brubeck, here as elsewhere, seemed destined to break the usual rules. J. Russell Bodley, Brubeck's mentor on the music faculty, intervened to keep the young pianist in the department. "If it weren't for him, I would have never gotten through school," Brubeck said some thirty-five years later.

He used to keep telling them, "Well, he can't read, but he's got a lot of talent." When they discovered I couldn't read, the Dean wanted to kick me out. Dr. Bodley came to my rescue. He said: "Look, I have him in ear training, and in harmony. He can write and everything, he just can't read." He slowly turned it all around. Another teacher, Horace Brown, said "If you kick him out, you're going to kick out one of the most talented kids in the Conservatory." I couldn't believe that they were calling *me* talented. I was inclined to agree with the Dean.[8]

The dean exacted one condition: Brubeck had to promise never to pursue a career in teaching music. Dr. Bodley's recollections substantiate the claims made for his young student: "We all recognized such a tremendous talent. I had him in a class in which one of the assignments was to harmonize a melody by Mozart. After eight or ten students had played their version, all stolid and hack, of course, Dave came up and rocked that Mozart right out the window, to great applause."

Dave Van Kriedt, who later made important contributions to the Brubeck Octet, says that the young pianist was then living a fairly untamed bohemian life out of the cellar—which they affectionately referred to as "the bomb shelter"—of a large rooming house near the campus. "He was a super player, and playing with him people related to him immediately," Van Kriedt recalls.[9] But at least part of the fascination Brubeck exerted on Van Kriedt came from the aura of eccentricity that hovered about the pianist, informing everything from his attire—"Brubeck had a Zoot Suit coat which went down to his knees which was like his tuxedo—kind of like Pachucos wore"—to his ethnicity: "He seemed to play upon his strangeness, being Indian and Jewish (Polish)," Van Kriedt writes. "[He] seemed like he still lived with the tribe."

Bodley lived across the street from the "bomb shelter," and Dave soon convinced Van Kriedt to join him as one of Bodley's students. The earliest roots of the partnership that would come to fruition as the Dave Brubeck Octet date from this time. For Brubeck, Van Kriedt was a kindred soul, a musician who was both an experienced jazz player and attracted to contemporary ideas about classical composition. Both would soon make the move from Bodley at Pacific to Milhaud at Mills College. There the Brubeck/Milhaud clique would expand to include William O. Smith, Jack Weeks, and Dick Collins. The studies at Mills, however, signaled not so much a turning point as an extension of Brubeck's already evident inclination to plunge into new and strange waters. Even in the early 1940s, if the various accounts are at all accurate, Brubeck's piano work was out of keeping with conventional styles in the jazz world.

The unusual decision to serve his apprenticeship in academic institutions, especially when viewed in light of Brubeck's distinctive approach to improvisation, suggests that he was less familiar with the jazz piano tradition than most improvisers of his generation. This hypothesis is supported by Brubeck's relative isolation in Concord and Ione, where traveling bands rarely ventured and where the Brubeck family long lacked even a radio. The family's musicality was an ingrown affair—the musicians in the family listened primarily to each other. Brubeck was inspired, one might assume, by the process of improvisation rather than by its history; the result was a style with unique and unconventional roots. The pianist's tastes, as these evolved, were characteristically eclectic and shed little light on his own music. In later years Brubeck would cite among his early idols

Duke Ellington, Art Tatum, and Stan Kenton, while also lavishing praise on Nat Cole, Erroll Garner, George Shearing, and Lennie Tristano. Whether due to his eclecticism or iconoclasm, Brubeck's own evolving music came to sound like none of these models; from the first he sounded only like Brubeck. Even the classical influences from Milhaud and others, played up by the media when Brubeck later achieved a mass audience, were only marginal influences. A comparison of Milhaud's supposedly jazz-inflected works with his student's actual jazz work reveals, underneath the superficial borrowings, a world of difference.

Brubeck had, of course, played jazz before arriving at the Stockton campus, but only as one of many kinds of music. During high school and early college he worked a wide range of casual gigs in isolated Northern California communities: Lions Club gatherings, socials, cowboy and hillbilly swing dances. These left a lasting impact. When I asked Brubeck about the influence, if any, of this early musical background, he started reeling off from memory the lyrics to an impressive number of little-known—at least to me—cowboy ditties. "When Sonny Rollins recorded his *Way Out West* album," he concluded, "I felt he was invading my territory." West Coast jazz, for all its hype about geography, was far afield from this music. Indeed Brubeck's training at these diverse gigs hardly suggests anything resembling a single-minded interest in jazz, especially when seen in the light of his home-bred musical studies and the early premed course load.

When he first arrived in Stockton to attend the College of the Pacific, Brubeck came across as something of a country bumpkin, even though Stockton circa 1940 must have been anything but a center of city slickers. When Dave tried to sit in with a local band shortly after arriving in town, one of the musicians asked him where he was from. Learning that the youngster came from Ione, the California equivalent of Ultima Thule, the musicians simply ignored him. "I had to walk away!" Brubeck later recounted. "Later when they found me playing at the ballroom, they couldn't believe it. 'Aren't you the guy from Ione?' they said."[10] By now he was quickly making up for his small-town origins, frequently going to San Francisco to hear music or sit in with some of the better local players. In 1941 he had his first opportunity to experience the dominant San Francisco traditional jazz scene when he heard Lu Watters's Yerba Buena Jazz Band. Such studied attempts at musical anachronism apparently made little impression on him. As late as 1956 he was telling interviewers that at some point he wanted to learn more about the music of Jelly Roll Morton and Fats Waller but hadn't yet had the chance. Until the 1950s, Brubeck's jazz work was probably more influenced by his classical composition studies than by his assimilation of the jazz tradition. Brubeck tried to make his jazz playing accommodate his academic training in modern classical music, not vice versa. "If someone had mentioned Darius Milhaud using two tonalities, on the job that night I'd be using two tonalities."[11]

Brubeck's studies with Milhaud were interrupted by his service commitment with the U.S. Army, and even his approach to military life was typically uncharacteristic. He somehow obtained permission to continue composition lessons while in uniform, this time under Arnold Schoenberg. "We didn't get along at all," Brubeck hastens to explain.[12]

> It's completely misquoted that I studied with him. The first lesson was an introductory affair, and the second lesson, I had written something, and he wanted a reason for every note. I said, "Because it sounds good," and he said, "That is not an adequate reason," and we got into a huge argument in which he was screaming at me. And I asked him why did he think he was the man who should determine the new music, and he screamed, "Because I know more than any man alive about music." Maybe this isn't an exact quote, but it's the essence of it.

A shouting match with Arnold Schoenberg may seem like excessive hubris coming from an unknown composition student from the California backwoods, but the incident is indicative of Brubeck's strong-willed personality. His extreme individualism, perhaps his most salient trait, has been variously described as "obstinacy," "self-confidence," "stubborness," "a domineering tendency" and the like. What in others might have been an unmitigated character flaw served Brubeck as an asset. Without his preternatural determination, Brubeck might never have made his way in a jazz world in which the prevalent tendencies were so far afield from his own musical interests. Even the unique sound of his music must be seen, at least in part, as drawn from the iconoclasm of the man. Ralph Gleason, hardly a Brubeck supporter, would later admit almost begrudgingly:

> He has played his own music the way he wanted to. It happens I don't like it. But I still have to respect the fact that he did it his own way. And there wasn't anyone I ever met who thought he could carry it to the place he did. . . . There was no press agentry, no showmanship. He succeeded in spite of himself, and everything was against it. I still don't understand why, but I recognize that it has occurred.[13]

In 1946, after serving in Patton's army during the Battle of the Bulge (even Brubeck trivia experts have probably not caught his appearance in Studs Terkel's World War II chronicle *The Good War*), Brubeck returned to California to resume studies with Milhaud at Mills College. Mills was a women's college, but, ostensibly for patriotic reasons, it agreed to accept the tuition dollars of GI Bill male students in certain fields of study. During this period a number of like-minded jazz musicians had gathered around Milhaud, who in turn encouraged them to bring these influences into their formal composition work. Van Kriedt writes:

> As we were "jazzbos" Milhaud encouraged us to continue on that premise rather than going further into sonata, string quartet, but we did a lot of that anyway and also a bit of orchestration. We had a smaller orchestra directed by Howard Brubeck backing Greek plays, dance groups, etc. We started a group to play our individual compositions. The students in our group were Dave, Bill Smith (clarinet), Jack Weeks (my old friend from many years before), and I got hold of Dick Collins (trumpet) who was a similar type to Paul Breitenfeld. Dick was a Bix Beiderbecke type, in fact that became his nickname later on. That made it piano, tenor, trumpet and Jack played trombone or bass (later). Which wasn't enough.

It was necessary to bring in outsiders to form a full ensemble. "I got hold of Paul on alto," Van Kriedt continues, referring to the future Paul Desmond (then still going by his given name of Breitenfeld). "Dick got his brother Bob Collins on trombone. Then we geared for an octet."

a tender Mozartian twist

Paul Breitenfeld, later Desmond, was the antithesis of Brubeck in almost every way. While Brubeck was a country boy raised on a ranch, Desmond was a city sophisticate, born on November 25, 1924, in San Francisco, and reared in California and New York. While Brubeck was obsessed with the trappings of musical modernism, Desmond had little interest in studying with Milhaud and instead focused his efforts on polishing a retrograde, almost antimodern saxophone style. While Brubeck had a domineering nature and needed to be group leader: he later insisted that the octet be called the Dave Brubeck Octet, ostensibly to make it easier for the band to get bookings, and he actually forced a plebiscite of the group members on this issue—a vote he won: Desmond, in contrast, was all too happy to avoid leadership responsibilities, content to make his mark as a sideman. While Brubeck was the master of stage presence (from the start he had, Van Kriedt recalls, "tremendous powers of creating attention while just being on stage"), Desmond was unostentatious to an extreme. While Brubeck, especially after his more untamed early years, mellowed into a strong family man, Desmond remained ostensibly the happy bachelor and proponent of the high life until the end. And while Brubeck's public demeanor was high seriousness, Desmond's was inevitably tongue-

in-cheek, veering from subtle irony to thinly cloaked sarcasm. That two
such antipodal musicians could create powerful music together may be but
another proof of the compatibility of opposites. Perhaps the true mystery
was not that this musical partnership worked so well but that it lasted so
long—for a quarter-century—despite such a marked divergence in lifestyles and temperaments.

Paul was secretive about his family background. Few early acquaintances were invited into the Breitenfeld residence, just as later in life most
of his friends were unaware that this apparent lifelong bachelor had once
been married, albeit briefly. As with Brubeck, even Desmond's ethnicity
has been the subject of speculation. Gene Lees explains that "Paul thought
his father was Jewish until, near the end of his life, a relative told him he
wasn't."[14] Frederick Breitenfeld, Jr., Paul's cousin, is more ambiguous in
his account:

> Much kidding has gone on over the generations and across the lines of cous-
> ins throughout the family, about who is Jewish and who isn't. This was a
> favorite topic of Paul's when he was working for laughs, and it appears that
> even he might ultimately have taken the whole thing seriously. There was
> no religious training of any consequence, or any specific denomination for
> that matter, at [Paul's grandfather] Dr. Sigmund Breitenfeld's household, so
> the question of "Jewishness" reduces to one of what *other people* thought
> rather than what the *family* thought.[15]

"Paul was devoted to his father," Frederick Breitenfeld continues. Paul's
father worked as a theater organist and arranger, and much of Desmond's
early musical inspiration probably came through him. Early in his musical
career Paul used his father's arrangements when backing shows and acts.
Although some of the other musicians moaned about the corny tunes, Paul
was markedly enthusiastic about the old songs. His later repeated use of
quotations from old popular songs in the context of his solos perhaps reflects this apprenticeship with the elder Breitenfeld's music.

In stark contrast to his devotion toward his father, Paul was always
guarded and secretive about his mother, Shirley. Van Kriedt helps cast
some light on the matter: "Another time [Paul] brought up that his mother
was not mentally well—as a matter of fact, I would be practically the only
person he ever invited to his house to meet his family." The Breitenfeld
residence sat high on a hill and commanded a breathtaking view of San
Francisco. Inside, however, the home was uncommonly stark. Van Kriedt
continues:

> I was struck by the fact that there were no rugs or curtains on the windows—
> just plain yellow hardwood floors, bare windows and no pictures on the walls.

I had the impression I was getting the royal treatment and that I was to be shocked by meeting his mother. [Paul] had told me she was scared by disease, dirt, death—one never mentioned death around her, and she wore rubber dishwashing gloves while cooking. Anyway—I assumed a very passive, kindly, understanding personality and it turned out that she was a very likeable person. We all chatted while we had lunch and I was relieved that it wasn't as traumatic as Paul had led me to believe. . . . I wanted to go again to Paul's house but I think that the whole area was a deep-seated torment to him and he was highly protective of this.

There was clearly much more to Paul's strained relations with his mother. Her illness was evidently severe enough that, at age five, Paul was sent back east to live with relatives in New Rochelle, New York. He did not return to San Francisco until 1936—almost seven years later. One can see the stamp of this uneasy maternal relation on much of Desmond's later life, not only in his committed bachelorhood and frequent womanizing, but perhaps as much in the little satisfaction such pursuits seemed to bring him. Brubeck could perhaps tell much more, as he hinted to Gene Lees: "If you knew the story, you could forgive him anything."[16]

"He was the loneliest man I ever knew," remarks Lees, who also notes that Desmond was attracted most to his friends' wives. Desmond somehow found solace by fixating on the women who were the most unobtainable, even at the cost of wreaking havoc with his closest friends. Nor perhaps is it going too far to see these same elements figuring in Desmond's bittersweet music. Van Kriedt reflects: "Seeing his home and playing a lot with Paul, [I felt that] his deeper song had to do with a 'babe crawling into his mother's arms,' a kind of tender Mozartian twist for a jazzman rather than the drugged-up stud proving his manliness."

After returning to San Francisco, Desmond began studying clarinet at San Francisco Polytechnic, apparently at the instigation of his father, who advised him to drop his French class to make time for music. In 1943, Desmond switched to the alto. Soon he was drafted into the army, and he spent three years in San Francisco as part of th 253rd AGF Band. Through Van Kriedt, also a member of the ensemble, Paul was introduced to another young army musician, pianist Dave Brubeck. Brubeck was about to be shipped overseas, and Van Kriedt planned "to show him off to the band, hoping to get him in. So I prepared a little concert in the rehearsal room." Only a few people showed up to hear the audition—"about five," Van Kriedt recalls—including Paul Desmond. "They all came to the Band Room, and Dave played for all his life It was to no avail. Afterwards I asked Paul, who commonly played with and highly regarded Larry Vannucci (local pianist), what he thought of Dave. He wasn't terribly impressed and thought that Vannucci was much better." Paul's account to pianist Marian Mc-

Partland of that same audition is both much different and clearly in the mock serious vein: "We had a session in the band room," he explained. "I remember the first tune we played was 'Rosetta.' I was really dazzled by [Dave's] harmonic approach." Then, continuing with added slyness: "I went up to him and said, 'Man, like Wigsville! You really grooved me with those nutty changes.' And Brubeck replied, 'White man speak with forked tongue.'"[17]

Whatever early reservations Desmond might have had about his later longtime musical companion were clearly forgotten by the time, a few years later, he actively lobbied to become a member of the Dave Brubeck Quartet. "He wanted to be in that band so badly," recalls bassist Ron Crotty, a founding member of the pre-Desmond Brubeck Trio. "He made no secret about it. He used to say, I'm going to be playing with Brubeck. He's my piano player. I'm going to be in that band."[18] Soon he was.

Despite pronouncements about his future music career made to Crotty and others, Desmond had been for many years as interested in becoming a writer as in plying his trade as a professional saxophonist. At San Francisco State, however, he was thrust into one of the most creative gatherings of student jazz players on the coast. The musicians associated with Milhaud at Mills have garnered most of the attention, but SF State in the postwar years was every bit the equal of its East Bay rival, with Paul Desmond, John Handy, Cal Tjader, Allen Smith, Ron Crotty, and others among its student body. Perhaps this fertile music environment, combined with Desmond's interactions with the Mills group, pushed him from the pen to the horn.

During his SF State years, Paul was briefly married; as with his enigmatic childhood, the details are rather sketchy. Gene Lees, despite his close friendship with Desmond, writes that he learned about the affair only because he had met the woman before he knew Paul: "Paul never mentioned her to me, and I mentioned her only once, when we had both had a few too many drinks. Paul got tears in his eyes, and I never spoke of her again."[19] The former Mrs. Breitenfeld later remarried, while Paul maintained a confirmed state of noncommitment in his later relations with women.

Desmond was almost as secretive about his early musical influences as about his family. When asked by Arnold Jay Smith about his early sources of musical inspiration, the altoist was characteristically noncommittal: "Before we got the Quartet together I listened to everybody who was playing then. Afterwards I decided that I wanted to do something myself, get my musical ideas together and stick with them."[20] For his *Encyclopedia of Jazz*, Leonard Feather asked musicians to list their favorites on their instrument, and Desmond responded with the triumvirate of Charlie Parker, Lee Konitz, and Pete Brown—eclectic if somewhat unrevealing choices. Joe Dodge, who played with Desmond in a dance band in the mid-1940s, recalls that the altoist's style was unique even then: "He was still just as lyrical. His ballads were just sensational and his 'up' things had a little more aggression in them. His lines weren't quite as involved and he was a little more simple. A swinging style, you know. . . . Of course, Paul was such a strong individual, he always pretty much had his thing."[21]

playland-at-the-beach

By the spring of 1946, the octet (or "the eight," as they were also known at the time) had formed, and the various members were contributing to the group's repertoire. Although the group's first charts are less impressive than the later works, they still showed the broad scope of the members' musical ambitions. From the start, arrangements of jazz standards coexisted with original compositions: Brubeck's "Rondo" and "Closing Theme" were among the octet's first pieces, as were Van Kriedt's arrangement of "I Hear a Rhapsody" and Jack Weeks's reworking of "The Prisoner's Song." The "Rondo" has all the marks of a student work: It lasts only ninety seconds, and though its dense harmonies would have been daring in a jazz context, the piece studiously avoids any reference to the jazz idiom, instead sounding like a classroom exercise written for Milhaud's benefit. "Closing Theme" offers more jazz feeling, but its thirty-second duration hardly allows it much scope. The extreme brevity of these pieces reflects the tentative character of the earliest octet work. Only with time would the group begin to master the ambitious territory it had staked out for itself—essentially what a decade later would be called, somewhat infelicitously, "Third Stream" music. In 1946 there were few precedents for this music—perhaps only the early octet music of Alec Wilder or the work of Raymond Scott. For the most part the Mills student musicians had to create their own precedents, establish their own voice. Weeks's approach in his 1946 chart was similar to Brubeck's in adopting a somewhat stilted classical approach, although the smattering of counterpoint looks forward to the octet's later more successful use of multiple melodic lines. Van Kriedt's contribution, in contrast, is definitely a jazz chart, relying on a much more expanded harmonic vocabulary than one would find in any big band. This incremental advance is more impressive, with the benefit of hindsight, than the other more "daring" works of the octet's earliest repertoire. Soon the whole body of writers for the ensemble would learn that moving relentlessly ahead would benefit them little if they left jazz behind in the process.

Yet remember that this was a student group with no track record, no star players, no audience to speak of, and little thought for the views of jazz critics some half-century later. In this context even the earliest pieces of the octet stand out as harbingers of something new and important that was taking place. Few in the Bay Area were privy to this process yet. Despite a repertoire calculated to shock and surprise, the octet had little opportunity to do either for almost two years. By mid-1946 the group was, in Brubeck's words, "an organized band ready to work or record," but until 1948 the octet's activities were limited more to practice and rehearsal. The band's 1948 performance in San Francisco, (by then it had been rechristened the Dave Brubeck Octet), and its subsequent increased visibility through the efforts of Jimmy Lyons, then a disk jockey and later the guiding force behind the Monterey Jazz Festival, were key events in the group's (and Brubeck's) eventual rise to wider recognition. Yet even the band's newfound notoriety stopped far short of ensuring financial success. Brubeck recalls that between 1947 and 1949 the group had only three paying gigs: the celebrated San Francisco concert at Marines Memorial Auditorium, a warm-up performance for the Woody Herman band, and a College of the Pacific concert.

But even the band's free performances helped spread the word about the new music. "We started playing concerts basically for music departments at University of California, College of Pacific, Marin Junior College, San Francisco State, Stanford, etc.," Van Kriedt recounts. "They were all successful. It ended up being another innovation in that we played, because of Brubeck's insistence, our compositions in the first half, then after the intermission we played our jazz stuff. It set off the students into confusion, as jazz was not considered eligible to be played around the pristine environment of a classically legitimate training institution." This attitude toward jazz in academic circles may seem strange today, when campus concerts by jazz artists are commonplace. Indeed the octet's classical works are likely to seem more shocking to many modern listeners than the group's early jazz-oriented repertoire. However, campus jazz events became standard fare largely thanks to Brubeck's pioneering efforts. In the late 1940s, any jazz performance given under the auspices of an academic music department was, to put it mildly, an unusual event.

As the writers in the band gained experience, the quality of the octet's material improved markedly. In arrangements such as Brubeck's "The Way You Look Tonight," Bill Smith's "What Is This Thing Called Love?" and Van Kriedt's "September in the Rain," the diverse classical, jazz, and popular song elements blend in a manner that combines the best quality of each discipline: The strong melodic material of popular song is wedded to the broad harmonic palette of classical music, the resulting hybrid drenched in that irrepressible rhythmic vocabulary that only comes from jazz. The next decade, of course, would witness a glut of Third Stream works purportedly trying to mix the self-same jazz and classical ingredients, but few of these later works succeed half so well as these "student" attempts made without the benefit of manifestoes of "Third Streamism," without financial incentives, record contracts and the like—above all without a clear received tradition on which to build. The main impetus behind the octet's experiments was simply the musicians' fascination with new sounds. Such an attitude may sound naive, but it is perhaps the purest motivation for composing music one can imagine. This straightforward basis for the octet's music contributes in no small part to the work's continued ability to surprise and fascinate some forty years later. When Brubeck weaves together the bridge and main melody of "The Way You Look Tonight" in an ingenious counterpoint, he reflects not just another manifestation of the avant-garde, but as much an openness to hearing the music in fresh ways.

For the 1948 audition for NBC, the octet added Brubeck's "Playland-at-the-Beach" to its repertoire, as well as a collectively written series of variations on "How High the Moon." The former reveals the enormous strides Brubeck had made since "Rondo" and "Closing Theme." The piece, according to Brubeck a "short musical description of a San Francisco scene," shows a more flamboyant sense of composition and a more fluent command of counterpoint than anything he had attempted to date, and though it is hampered, like its predecessors, by extreme brevity (only eighty-seven seconds long!) it succeeds in capturing several distinct moods. "How High the Moon" is, in contrast, the longest of the octet's recorded works. During its seven-and-a-half-minute musical documentary, Jimmy Lyons serves as narrator, while the octet features a series of theme and variations in different styles on the jazz standard. The rendition is, by necessity, something of a novelty number—but what an ingenious novelty, with its subtle mimickry of Benny Goodman, Dixieland, eight-to-the-bar boogie-woogie, hotel tenor bands, etc., followed by the octet's own modernist reading of the song. A few years later Leonard Bernstein would team up with Miles Davis to do a similar job on "Sweet Sue," but these more illustrious collaborators fail to match the sheer creativity and aplomb of the earlier, lesser-known, octet endeavor.

Among the octet's "classical" repertoire, Van Kriedt's "Prelude" and "Fugue on Bop Themes" and Bill Smith's "Ipca" rank with Brubeck's "Playland-at-the-Beach" as the group's most impressive works, combining an authentic jazz feeling with an overtly modernist classical approach. Van Kriedt's fugue is an especially provocative and successful work, with all five horns engaging in a dazzling counterpoint exchange over the propulsive swing of the rhythm section. In the 1950s, a number of jazz writers would attempt to adapt this difficult formal structure to the African-

American tradition, but this early attempt at extended jazz counterpoint ranks among the very best of the genre. Van Kriedt wrote other jazz fugues, and one regrets that only this one stunning performance survives among the octet's recordings.

The album sleeve to the 12-inch LP that comprises the octet's complete recorded legacy gives no recording date, and Brubeck's liner notes give the only hint of chronology when the pianist expresses his "gratitude that someone had the foresight to bring a portable recorder around in 1946."[22] One can well understand Brubeck's desire to place these performances as early as possible, if only to establish his precedence over the Miles Davis Nonet of 1948–49, a band that has been christened *the* progenitor of the West Coast jazz scene's fascination with octets, nonets, tentettes, and the like. Yet it appears that few of these recordings date from 1946, although some of the compositions were written during that year. Various sources suggest that much of the octet's music was recorded after the trio recordings, probably in July 1950, while other pieces come from the 1948 NBC audition for Jimmy Lyons or from tapes of performances from around the same time. On the initial 10-inch LP release of the octet's music, Brubeck provided some composition dates for the pieces—information omitted from later reissues—that suggest that only a handful of the works—"The Prisoner's Song," "Rondo," "I Hear a Rhapsody," and "Closing Theme"—was in the octet's 1946 repertoire. In later years Brubeck's accounts have pushed the bulk of the band's work back farther into the past: In an interview from the 1970s, Brubeck states that the octet's work spanned only 1946 to 1948—a fact that, if true, would clearly give him the jump on Miles—this in the face of the 1950 record date and the established fact that the octet gave regular Sunday performances at the Blackhawk well into the 1950s!

This said, the achievement of the Brubeck Octet is scarcely tarnished by this revision in dates. The group clearly reached its mature style by the time of the Miles Davis Nonet recordings, and any influence of the latter group on Brubeck's ensemble was negligible at best. It would take a huge leap of the imagination to try to show "Playland-at-the-Beach" or "Fugue on Bop Themes" as derivative from, or even vaguely evocative of, the Davis/Evans work. Brubeck and his colleagues were as unique in 1950 as they were in 1946. By the same token, the Brubeck Octet, despite its partial chronological priority, had far less eventual influence, on either coast, than the Davis band. Marty Paich's comments are perhaps representative of the views of most of the later West Coast composers/arrangers: "I heard the album [of the octet], and I had that album and listened to it a few times. But when I was getting ready to write or work with anybody I would always fall back to Gil Evans or Gerry Mulligan. . . . [But] if Dave

Brubeck had pursued a couple of more albums, I might have been totally influenced by it."[23]

This last point is worth stressing. The octet, despite the remarkable breadth and freshness of its few recordings, is remembered today primarily as a forerunner of the later Brubeck small combos. Given more recordings the situation might have been reversed; certainly Brubeck's reputation in jazz circles might have been enhanced by a return to this provocative format later in his career. As its stands, we have only these few taped performances to assess a group that, despite its meager output must rank among the most creative ensembles of its day.

Although the octet, as a unit, left behind only a single album's worth of material, the band's members went on to produce, as individuals, an impressive body of work. Brubeck and Desmond's later recordings are well known, as is, to a slightly lesser degree, the extensive discography of Cal Tjader. Dave Van Kriedt won the Graduate Composition Award at Mills College in 1952, continued his studies overseas with Milhaud, and later performed and wrote with Stan Kenton. In the mid-1950s he recorded an excellent reunion album with Brubeck and Desmond for the Fantasy label. James Weeks and Bill Smith (Bill is his jazz musician name; he is known as William O. Smith in academic composition circles) pursued later careers that strikingly overlap. Both furthered their composition studies under Roger Sessions; both were graduates of the University of California; and both were awarded the Prix de Paris: Smith in 1951–52, Weeks in 1954–55. In addition to his successes as an academic composer, Smith has retained an active, if somewhat sporadic, involvement in jazz. In the 1950s, he wrote an extended clarinet concerto, which he recorded under Shelly Manne's leadership. In the 1960s and again in the 1980s, he reunited with Brubeck, and he currently records and performs frequently with the pianist. Dick Collins furthered his reputation as a member of the Woody Herman band. All in all, this group of unknown students, bound together simply by a shared interest in mixing up jazz and classical music, had an impact on the contemporary music world that extends far beyond the few exemplary recordings of the octet. Even in the cases of the celebrated musicians such as Brubeck, Desmond, and Tjader, the achievement of this early ensemble must be considered one of the musical highlights of their illustrious careers.

Brubeck tells that there are no unreleased recordings of the octet, but even so the group's whole legacy is not available to the public. Van Kriedt remarks that he has a number of charts that were never recorded, including several of his fugues. Desmond, shortly before his death, wrote him a letter in which he expressed an interest in recording one of these fugues. Van Kriedt sent him the chart but a few days later learned of Paul's death.

where the proletariat make merry at

The Dave Brubeck Trio was formed largely in response to the economic difficulties faced by the larger ensemble. Not just the octet, but virtually every large jazz ensemble of its day, was caught up in a constant struggle for survival. The much-changed economic landscape of the late 1940s put a stranglehold on the dominance of the big band and established the small jazz combo as the most feasible format for presenting improvised music. The reasons for this change were many and complex: a government tax on dance venues; the transformation of jazz from America's popular music to a fringe music, with the accompanying shrinkage of its audience; an overall decline in the demand for live music, spurred by, among other things, the postwar recession; the competition posed by television and higher quality recordings; and an increase in the cost of putting a band on the road, as $2.50-a-night hotel rooms became a thing of the past. The whole story of this crucial change has yet to be told, and the above list can only hint at this largely unwritten history.

For Brubeck, as for Miles Davis and his nonet, the most salient result of this shift in economic reality was the lack of work for their larger bands. The only alternative was to try to capture a similar aesthetic with a smaller unit. Brubeck's career after the octet, like Miles's postnonet period, was anything but the rapid rise to fame that many have portrayed or assumed. The later *Time* magazine cover boy paid some heavy dues during these years, made even heavier by the unpredictable behavior of future quartet member Paul Desmond.

"If you knew the story, you could forgive him anything," the pianist has had occasion to remark, as noted above, with regard to Desmond's earliest days. Although he invariably speaks well of his long-standing colleague, Brubeck himself had much to forgive. While still a struggling up-and-coming player, Brubeck landed a gig at the Geary Cellar, circa 1947, in San Francisco as co-leader of a combo. Desmond would occasionally come and sit in, and he had no qualms about stealing the band away when he got a job of his own at the Bandbox in Palo Alto. His way of making it up to Brubeck was by hiring Dave as sideman at the Bandbox—at a cut in pay, of course, from the Geary Cellar rates, from about $100 a week to around $40. To add insult to injury, Brubeck and the band were required to sing a song about the Bandbox, which bandleader Desmond had written for the occasion: "It's the Bandbox/that's the joint for you. . . . The whiskey is old/but the music is new/at the Bandbox. . . . Where the proletariat/Make merry"—etc., etc. "It wasn't the greatest scene in the world," Brubeck remembers of the Bandbox gig, "but it was the only thing I had."

Soon he didn't even have that much. Desmond took the band to the Feather River Inn but decided to bring along a different piano player. Not only that, but Desmond prevented Brubeck from taking over the Bandbox gig with a new group featuring Bill Smith. From leader to sideman to unemployed was the primrose path down which the altoist had led his pianist friend. With a wife and two children, Brubeck was now scuffling for his life, finally dredging up a $42-a-week gig at a down-and-out watering hole in remote Clear Lake. He and his family were living in a windowless shack built of corrugated iron. "I'm in despair at this point," Brubeck recalls. "I get a call from Jimmy Lyons. Lyons had landed a gig for a trio at the Burma Lounge in Oakland; was Dave interested? "I almost screamed over the phone: 'Yes!' "

CHAPTER FIVE

The San Francisco Scene in the 1950s

sixty one-nighters in a row

By the start of the 1950s, word had begun to circulate of an exceptional young jazz pianist plying his trade in, of all places, Oakland, California—the much-maligned city where, in the *bon mot* of Gertrude Stein, there was no *there* there. First in the Pacific Northwest, and gradually elsewhere in the west, record sales for the Dave Brubeck Trio started to pick up. Soon even East Coast jazz fans were hearing about the intriguing young modernist from the Golden State, a protégé of Darius Milhaud, who was applying contemporary compositional techniques to jazz music. Even after the Parker/Gillespie musical revolution, this new kind of experimentation held promise of more uncharted waters ahead.

"Every good thing that happened to me in those days seemed to come from Jimmy Lyons," Brubeck recalls. With the intercession of Lyons, Brubeck had arranged to record with Coronet, a Dixieland label run by Jack Sheedy. The initial response to the records had been far from impressive, but sales continued to increase steadily, aided by Lyons's nightly radio broadcasts, which boasted a clear signal up and down the coast. The success of the 78s came too late to help Sheedy—the masters were eventually acquired by Fantasy Records when Coronet folded—and for Brubeck the rise to fame came none too soon. After years of struggling, and with a growing family to feed, he was now feeling financially secure for the first time in his career. The Burma Lounge in Oakland, which featured the trio during this rise to fame, soon lost the band as it moved across the bay to the more upscale Blackhawk in San Francisco.

The trio's popular success had little to do with any overt commercialism in the group's music. With the very first trio sides Brubeck showed that the smaller ensemble could be just as unconventional as his earlier octet. Although jazz musicians had long before developed a reputation for taking extreme liberties with the music they played, Brubeck's interpretations from this first trio session were perhaps as idiosyncratic as any version of these songs yet done. This was all the more evident, even to casual listeners, given his choice of well-known pop tunes for material. It was almost as if Brubeck deliberately selected familiar, at times even banal, melodies to make his bold restructurings of the compositions all the more discernible. Many of his devices would become standard Brubeck fare in later years, but in 1949 few jazz fans were conversant with compositional techniques such as polytonality, unexpected modulations from major to minor (listen to "Blue Moon," where bassist Ron Crotty holds on to the original changes while Brubeck's harmonies take off into the stratosphere); the jolting switch from twentieth-century to eighteenth-century harmony at the close of "Indiana"; the rumbling, dissonant block chords that transformed "Laura" and "Tea for Two" into biting Bartókian vignettes.

Those who scolded Brubeck the pianist for his incessant pounding were right in at least this regard: He was determined to pound these songs into submission, to make them bear the full weight of his experimental leanings. While some modernists might clothe their avant-garde tendencies in titles such as "Opus in Abstract" or "Conflict in Three Sharps" (the Kenton band being, of course, the past master of pretentious titles), Brubeck was somehow able to squeeze his iconoclasm into the pedestrian changes to "Blue Moon." This strange modern mixture—half Tin Pan Alley and half progressive classical music—would also become a Brubeck trademark.

Then again, almost everything about the Brubeck Trio's first session was unconventional. Coronet Records (or Koronet, as it was later known), trombonist Jack Sheedy's failing Dixieland label, was an unusual launching pad for this exercise in musical modernism. Further, the decision to experiment at the session with erasable tape (an innovation then being developed by Ampex Company in nearby Redwood City) was an equally novel departure. As well as a disastrous one: The session engineer proved incapable of mastering the new technology, and after two hours of failed attempts to record the band on the Ampex system, the decision was made to switch to the proven method of cutting the tracks on acetate. With only a half-hour left in the studio the trio quickly laid down four tracks, each done in a single take: "Blue Moon," "Indiana," "Tea for Two," and "Laura."

Later recordings of the trio took this arsenal of modernist devices and expanded upon them, with results that may have raised controversy as to their musicality, but never could be accused of being uninteresting. On "You Stepped out of a Dream," another early trio side, Brubeck starts by playing his radical reharmonization at a ballad tempo in which he shifts back and forth from a 4/4 to a 6/8 feel. This became a common approach to ballads among many jazz rhythm sections in later years, used with particular effectiveness by McCoy Tyner in the classic John Coltrane Quartet. At the time of the Brubeck Trio, however, it was a relatively unexplored technique. At the end of the first chorus an even stranger rhythmic device emerges: Cal Tjader enters on bongos playing at double tempo, but Brubeck shifts into a half-tempo rendering of the changes, so that the form of the song now sounds as though it is four times as long as before! This highly unusual device now gives Brubeck enormous space to work in a variety of passing chords and cross-rhythms. The song proceeds for only one chorus in this oddly structured form, but the performance is absolutely compelling.

The Brubeck Trio, unlike most small jazz combos, left little to chance. Rather than let the band's arrangements evolve informally and gradually over a series of performances, Brubeck was fastidious, at this point in his career, in working out novel interpretations in advance. Given the short duration of 78 sides, Brubeck placed particular emphasis on bringing as broad a compositional palette as possible to bear on each number he recorded. When the trio was asked to perform live on a regular radio show hosted by Jimmy Lyons, Brubeck's continuing patron-in-residence, band was required to come up with several new pieces for each broadcast. "That's when the band really started taking off," Crotty recalls," and we had to rehearse every week five or six tunes, four or five tunes, that we hadn't played . . . We started getting better gigs and starting playing the Blackhawk." Years later the band's music would become more spontaneous, especially after expanding to a quartet—and to good effect, given Brubeck's and Desmond's ability to anticipate each other's musical moves—but at this early stage Brubeck was characteristically shying away from a jam session ethos, pursuing instead structured methods of bringing modernist compositional devices into the group's playing.

The trio, now at the height of its fame, promised Brubeck the means he had long sought of combining musical expression with a degree of financial security. Only a short while before the pianist had been living in a one-room apartment in a housing project; now he was on the brink of a successful international career. The quartet, of course, would come to achieve more fame and fortune than either the octet or trio, and we tend to evaluate Brubeck's work in terms of that later, long-lived ensemble. But at the beginning of the 1950s, Brubeck had neither the desire nor need to change his newly successful format. Indeed he might never have formed the quartet if it had not been for a tragic, almost fatal, accident.

While in Hawaii in 1951, Brubeck seriously injured himself in a swimming mishap. With a running start, Brubeck took a dive into what appeared to be a large wave; instead he crashed into a hidden sand bar. He was first taken to Queen's Hospital, but they refused to admit him when they found he had no money to pay for treatment. Learning that he was a veteran, they sent him to the Veteran's Hospital. The doctor's parting words to the two friends who were transporting the injured pianist were: "Don't let go of his neck because he'll be paralyzed for life." In this condition Brubeck was helped downstairs into an ambulance that was to take him to the Veterans' Hospital. "I heard the guys talking up front," Brubeck recalls. "They phoned in that they were on their way in the ambulance. They said 'We've got a DOA.' I knew enough about army talk. So I figured, 'Oh, I guess that's it.' "

Rumors circulated for a while that Brubeck had died from the injury. As it was, doctors thought he might never walk again, let alone play the piano. For years the pianist said little in public about the lasting effects of this accident, although they were severe and long affected his musical work. "I've never talked about that," he said in 1977, then briefly elaborated:

> There was a period of a few years where I physically couldn't do much—I was almost paralyzed. . . . I lost a certain amount of dexterity at that time, so I had to rely on chords for a while. It took years; muscle spasms would come and and go. . . . I've never explained it, because you can't go copping out, but there was a period where I couldn't even get up from the piano. I would wait until the stage was blacked out, and then I had to pull myself up for support.[1]

The accident, despite Brubeck's eventual recovery, proved to be decisive in a number of ways. It demanded an adaptation in Brubeck's playing, forcing him to make greater use of his block chord style and less of the fast single-note lines so common among his peers. In this regard, Brubeck's physical limitations simply reinforced a tendency evident from his first recordings. Perhaps more telling was Brubeck's concern about the exertions involved in leading a trio. After the accident he had to disband the trio, and even after he was released from the hospital he was initially unable to perform. As he went through the process of rehabilitation, he knew that he needed another strong soloist to lift some of the musical burden off his shoulders.

A short while after the trio's rise to fame, Paul Desmond was listening to the radio in New York, where he was playing with Alvino Rey's band. When the disk jockey played the record of his former octet colleague, announcing that Brubeck was the rising jazz star from the west, Paul realized, with no small amount of insight, that his earlier cavalier treatment of the pianist might have gone too far. Returning to his native San Francisco, Desmond began a long process of working his way back into Brubeck's good graces. He showed up at the trio's gigs, lobbied to join the group, even offered to work with the band for free on its ill-fated trip to Hawaii. Desmond, according to most accounts, was typically unambitious and lackadaisical in advancing her career, yet the facts of his biography reveal that, when he had his mind set on a certain goal, his character could turn around completely, motivating him to go to great lengths in attainment of the desired end. In this instance, he was determined to put the hard press on Brubeck, and the swimming accident was the turning point that made the pianist open to his protestations. While still in traction in the hospital, Brubeck wrote to Desmond, offering him a position in a quartet as soon as Dave was well enough to start playing again.

By late summer 1951, Brubeck was ready to return to performing in the newly constituted group. Whether due to the new setting or perhaps to the limits of his rehabilitation, the pianist's playing now showed as less aggressive, less percussive than in the earlier trio sides. Especially when comping behind Desmond, the pianist revealed his skills as a sensitive accompanist, a talent that few might have suspected given the bravura of his work with Tjader and Crotty. The quartet's first released recordings, made during a thirteenth-month period between August 1951 and September 1952, do not reach the heights of the exemplary work made shortly after, but they show clear signs of the new group's promise and provocative sense of style. The choice of repertoire—"Me and My Shadow," "Somebody Loves Me," "Star Dust," and the like—are similar to the kind of pieces Brubeck had favored with his trio: well-known, hummable melodies that would make his transformations of them all the more striking to the listener. Even so, the arrangements are less daring than on the trio sides, with pieces being used more as springboards for improvisation. Desmond's playing is occasionally tentative on these first quartet recordings, but already his unique alto conception stands out. His bright, lucid tone and talent for melodic construction are quite evident, while Brubeck immediately shows a knack for counterpoint conversations with the altoist—for example, on the early "Mam'selle." These two players' ability to mesh seems, on the basis of these sides, anything but an acquired skill; apparently it was a given almost from the start.

When the band gets into a more heated groove, as on "Me and My Shadow" or "Frenesi," the rhythm section proves capable of swinging, but in a manner more reminiscent of the big band idiom than of the work of the beboppers. At several other points in this work I suggest that the earlier Kansas City style exerted a profound influence on the emerging West Coast sound of the 1950s. Despite Brubeck's overt modernism, the same seems to hold for his bands of the period: despite their flirtations with the avant-garde, the group's sense of ground rhythm owes more to Basie and McShann than it does to Bartók and Milhaud, or even Parker and Gillespie. The band's rhythmic experimentations, at their best, were often superimposed on this steady ground beat rather than replacements for it.

Not that Brubeck had no interest in experimenting with rhythm: The later innovations with odd meters are perhaps the most obvious example, but even his earliest recordings reveal, in their often surprising syncopations and cranky tempos, a willingness to take chances with time. Yet these devices always coexisted with a basic conception of the rhythm section that was conservative in the extreme. Bassist Ron Crotty tells of Brubeck's insistence that his bass line stick close to the harmonic roots—so much so that Brubeck would pound out his own bass line on the piano if he thought Crotty deviated too far from the standard chords. Similarly the drummers featured in the early groups were expected to support the soloists in a fairly subdued, traditional manner. The kind of open sound that, say, Bill Evans sought in his collaborations with Scott LaFaro and Paul Motian would never have appealed to Brubeck, despite other striking similarities (especially in harmonic conception) between the two pianists. Nor was this necessarily a flaw or limitation on Brubeck's part. It was perhaps the underlying rhythmic conservatism of his music that allowed Brubeck to incorporate elements of modernism into his work without alienating—indeed while attracting—a large audience. The most obvious example is the band's biggest hit, "Take Five," where Brubeck combines an odd meter with a simple, memorable vamp. This combination of the eccentric and the simple (another tie to Monk) was one of the pianist's most salient and effective stylistic devices.

Little of this early music prepares us for the new high level of the October 1952 recordings made at Storyville, the jazz club in Boston. Only four numbers have been released from this live taping, but they are enough to qualify the performance as one of the musical high points for Brubeck and Desmond. The former's solo piano rendition of "Over the Rainbow" is an absolute gem. Brubeck opens with only the barest hint of the Harold Arlen song: A gentle reharmonization supports a new melody, which only flirts with the original. Gradually he shifts into his block chord mode, adapting it now to a more relaxed, muted style—first eight to the bar, then in more complex rhythmic patterns. Suddenly a countermelody emerges in the low bass register—it sounds as though it is executed with crossed hands at the piano—underneath an undulating treble chording. It comes as something of a surprise to hear Desmond now enter into the music, playing the original melody, which surfaces for the first time; his participation at this juncture sounds totally spontaneous, as though he couldn't help intruding on Brubeck's solo piano feature, because the tune was just too enticing to resist. Brubeck responds by becoming even more daring with his reharmonization, soon shifting into a minor mode—a stock device of his, but rarely used to better effect—with Desmond following along, changing the melody of "Over the Rainbow" to match the new chords. This sensitive collaboration lasts only a moment, before the pianist and altoist reach the end of the form. There, instead of returning to the major, they close on a held tonic minor.

This whole Storyville performance captures one of those magical musical moments that improvising artists now and then experience (almost never, it seems, in the recording studio, and only on rare occasions even on the gig). How else to explain the ensuring duet on "You Go to My Head?" Here again Brubeck and Desmond achieve a masterfully high level of playing, with almost extrasensory interaction—a level they would only match a few times in their voluminous later recordings, and never really surpass. Even a quarter of a century later, Desmond would still speak with reverence about the Storyville recording of the Coots/Gillespie standard. And rightly so. The melodic logic of Desmond's solos is well known, but here the poignant melancholy is so overpowering that cool ratiocination is swept aside, becomes secondary to the heartfelt confession he is sounding on the horn. Following such a solo is no easy matter, but Brubeck rises to the occasion. He digs deep into his most introspective mood and building from the original melody, erects a musical house of cards that seems almost too delicate to stand. Gradually the energy level of his solo rises, and three-quarters of the way into it he locks into a repeated chordal figure that sounds positively majestic. "Yeah!" Desmond can be heard responding in the background, half in encouragement, half in admiration.

This extraordinary level of performance, needless to say, could not be counted on from night to night—indeed Brubeck suffered from a pronounced variability in his level of musical inspiration. Partly this was due to his increasing reliance on improvisation after the formation of the quartet. Even more than most jazz musicians, Brubeck and Desmond relied on the inspiration of the moment and worked assiduously to limit their reliance on clichéd phrases. Joe Dodge, the quartet's drummer from this period, recalls: "Dave had a lot more arranged things when I first joined him. And then it got to be that the solos were so successful in their improvisation that the arrangements really became secondary." Of course this openness to the spontaneous creativity of the moment, which allows for such successful interaction, also courts disaster when things don't click.

Desmond once amplified this point in discussing Brubeck with Marian McPartland:

> When he's at his best, it's really something to hear. A lot of people don't know this, because in addition to the fluctuating level of performance that most jazz musicians give, Dave has a real aversion to working out things, and a tendency to take the things he can do for granted and spend most of his time trying to do other things. This is okay for people who have heard him play at his best, but is sometimes mystifying for those who haven't. However, once in a while somebody who had no use for Dave previously comes in and catches a really good set and leaves looking kind of dazed.[2]

For the most part, the seventeen months following the initial Storyville engagement found the quartet playing at a strikingly high level. These Fantasy recordings outshine, in most instances, the group's later work on the Columbia label. For the next decade, the Brubeck Quartet would follow a maddening pace in which they released a new record every twelve to fifteen weeks, in addition to pursuing an extraordinarily demanding road schedule. It comes as little surprise that the later recordings should be more uneven in quality. In this regard, the marketing clout of Columbia/ CBS has perhaps done more to tarnish Brubeck's reputation than to enhance it. Most listeners are more familiar with the Columbia sides, while the generally superior Fantasy sides are far less known. In particular, the live tapings from the Fantasy period rank among Brubeck's strongest works—the college concerts proved to be more than a marketing angle, standing out as one of the most fertile settings for the quartet's music.

One of the most exciting (and unusual) of the later Fantasy recordings is the March 1953 live date at Oberlin. Desmond sounds like an altogether different soloist on this album: He spits out rapid-fire lines like a tried-and-true bebopper, to the astonishment of all (not least the audience, which responds with rapturous applause). Brubeck has remarked that Desmond never enjoyed playing at fast tempos, yet on "How High the Moon" the band breaks into double time at the start of Paul's solo—perhaps in playful revenge for a reported preconcert tiff. If the altoist is flustered by the tempo, he hardly shows it. Desmond kicks in with apparent relish, contributing some his most driving work on record, including a dizzying array of quotes and, another Desmond trademark, a call and response in different ranges of the alto that magically creates an illusion of counterpoint on the single horn. As if this departure from his usual style were not enough, Desmond dishes out more of the same on "Perdido" and "The Way You Look Tonight." These gripping performances hint that there were perhaps musical sides to the altoist that surfaced only rarely on record if at all.

The widely scattered Fantasy discography suggests that a fair amount of unreleased material may have been recorded. An early album might draw on four or five separate recording dates, usually taped live performances, leaving one to wonder about the status of other numbers recorded at the same time. What is one to make, for example, of the discographical note attached to Brubeck's moving solo rendition of "My Heart Stood Still"? The listener is told that the music was recorded at a rehearsal at Bill Bates's house in Los Angeles. No date is provided, and one is left to speculate what else was taped that day. Other cut-and-paste records draw snippets of music from a potpourri of venues, including the Surf Club in Los Angeles, the Blackhawk in San Francisco, and Storyville in Boston. Often only three or four tracks have been released from a live date, with the remainder apparently ending up on the cutting room floor—and probably lost for good. Often discographers have to make do with only the vaguest indications of when sessions took place. (For example, a typical Fantasy citation runs "recorded in San Francisco between August 1951 and September 1952," while with the octet, as we have seen, even the ambiguous dates provided appear to be patently wrong.)

But though jazz historians lament, listeners can rejoice. Overall this convoluted recording history produced a number of outstanding performances, although in some strange venues. A lecture at the University of California at Berkeley resulted in the lovely March 1954 version of "Star Dust" (the best of several quartet versions of the song), at which Brubeck played an upright piano, Joe Dodge was pushed against the wall with his drum kit, and students strolled in and out of the hall. Evidently the odd setting did little to unsettle the musicians: Phil Elwood recalls that this version "was a sensation when first released," and one can well understand why.[3] Desmond pays little heed to the written melody, instead launching into a delicate improvisation with a pronounced polytonal flavor. Here, as in many of the live Fantasy recordings of the day, the sound quality is surprisingly good, despite the apparently informal nature of the taping.

A more orderly state of affairs surrounds Brubeck's ensuing recording career with the Columbia label. These are invariably impeccably recorded, finely packaged, and well-marketed releases, yet one often misses in them the air of spontaneity and free invention that the more informal Fantasy recordings so often captured. Brubeck, however, had good reasons to change labels, not just for the greater clout of a major company but also in response to his unhappy business relations with Fantasy. At the creation of the label, Brubeck believed that he was half-owner of Fantasy Records. After the company grew and prospered, Brubeck learned that the contract he signed gave him a half-interest only in his own master recordings. Early on he had served as a musical director of sorts to the label, encouraging the Weisses to record Gerry Mulligan, Chet Baker, Red Norvo, and

others. Only after the company's rise to success did he learn that he had
no financial stake in the success of these releases. Even as to his own
recordings, Brubeck was often kept in the dark by the Weiss brothers. Not
only would they release projects without his approval, but they went so
far as to record performances without his permission. At the Blackhawk
they resorted to wiring microphones through the ventilation system into
a mobile recording unit parked outside, all without Brubeck's knowledge.
Such goings-on made his move to a major label all but inevitable.

Once a part of the Columbia roster, Brubeck decided, at least at first,
to stay close to the formulas that had brought him success in the past.
Little wonder that the initial projects for Columbia included another campus concert album (Jazz Goes to College) and a follow-up recording at
Storyville. The former, while below the standards set by the Fantasy dates
at Oberlin and the College of the Pacific, offered a few memorable moments, most notably a long outing on the blues, "Balcony Rock." Earlier
in its history, the quartet had rarely focused on the twelve-bar blues form,
but from this point on both Brubeck and Desmond would have a field day
with slow- to medium-tempo blues. "Balcony Rock" anticipates a series of
such pieces, continuing with "Bru's Blues" and culminating in the exceptional blues choruses in the middle section of "Blue Rondo à la Turk."
Both the pianist and the altoist approached the blues form in distinctive
ways that stood out from the cliché-ridden work of many of their contemporaries: Brubeck's harmonically layered percussion added an exotic flavor
to the standard form, while the sophisticated worldliness of Desmond's
blues lines gave new meaning to the term "urban blues," conjuring up
images not of the gritty inner city but of glitzy views from a penthouse
apartment. These were some of the freshest blues performances of the
1950s and 1960s.

How does one interpret Brubeck's ambivalence, in the light of his
achievements, about continuing his work in jazz? As late as 1954, the
pianist told Downbeat that if he "ever got financially set" he would spend
six months of the year working solely on classical composition. Then almost as an afterthought, and in contradiction to this surprising prediction,
he added:

> This past year especially has shown me that there is as much possibility for
> me to say what I want to say through jazz as there is through composition.
> Before that I thought that I had to compose to fully express myself. . . .
> The point is that I'm getting more and more from jazz of what I had hoped
> to get out of formal composition. One of our tapes that hasn't been released
> yet has an "On the Alamo" that says as much for me in ten minutes of my
> best improvisation so far on record as any symphony I ever hoped to write
> when I didn't have as much command of the jazz idiom as I have now.[4]

The subsequently released recording of "On the Alamo" showed that Brubeck's stylistic "breakthrough," which pleased him so much at the time, was an extension of his earlier use of harsh, percussively placed chords. Only here the thick two-handed voicings are denser, their placement more aggressively rhythmic, and the solo setting more extended. In essence Brubeck was taking the existing elements in his piano approach and pushing them to an extreme. Such blitzkrieg attacks on the keyboard revealed Brubeck to be increasingly distancing himself from the pronounced lyricism exemplified by Desmond, as well as from public expectations formed by the "West Coast jazz" stereotype. Perhaps more significantly—and much at odds with the critics' contentions—Brubeck came across in such performances as completely disinterested in furthering his public acceptance. At this end of this massive post-Wagnerian solo, there is only the smallest smattering of applause from the audience—hardly a good sign for a solo that was, according to the pianist himself, his greatest musical achievement to date. Yet this very fact, in light of the comments made to *Downbeat*, suggests that Brubeck felt he had reached a point in his public acceptance at which he could risk alienating his audience and plunging into deeper musical waters. Brubeck's sense that he was now expressing himself more in jazz perhaps had as much to do with this newly felt freedom as with any purely musical breakthrough on his part.

To my ears, Brubeck's best work from this period came when he stepped back from the more radical implications of his style. Even at his most conservative, the extreme vertical conception of his solos was a refreshing departure from the pronounced Bud Powell–inflected linearity of most of his peers. His version of "Don't Worry 'bout Me," from the same session as "On the Alamo," is an impressive and moving study in voice leading and chordal phrasing, with the sensitivity to space lacking in "Alamo." This was the side of Brubeck's playing that, if it had emerged more often, would have put to rest critics' charges that his piano attack was merely "heavy-handed." It also shows that Brubeck's more dense playing was, like Monk's, not adopted out of necessity or an overstated conception of the instrument. Brubeck, like Kenton, *wanted* big sounds, the bigger the better. But when he so desired, Brubeck could move closer to the mainstream—as he has, in fact, done increasingly in recent years. His keyboard approach today is often surprisingly linear and straight ahead; his once pronounced eccentricities of style have mellowed into a modest quirkiness.

In the early days of the quartet, turnover in the bass and drum chairs had been frequent, but with the addition of drummer Joe Dodge in December 1953, Brubeck found a solid and supportive pulse-keeper, one with a good feel for swing and an acute sense of dynamics. At the time, Dodge was hesitant about quitting his day job for the uncertainties of gigging with a traveling jazz band. "When I joined," he recalls, "even then, I said,

'Gee, you're sure you work steady?' [Brubeck] said, 'Oh, we have to fight for a night off.' " Within a few weeks, Dodge learned that this was no exaggeration.

> I think at about February we started those college concert things. We did sixty of them in a row, sixty one-nighters in a row! Then I kind of believed them . . . I got in on the gravy because they had really struggled before that.

At the start of 1956 Brubeck made a personal decision that proved to be the most important change in his group since Desmond had joined five years earlier. After three years with the quartet, Dodge began to grow weary of life on the road, deciding to leave the group to spend more time at home. With his departure, Brubeck took a chance by hiring the first non–West Coaster to play in the quartet. Actually, little risk accrued to this decision: Joe Morello, a native of Springfield, Massachusetts, was a masterful choice. Morello's polished virtuosity and marked creativity immediately made a major contribution to the quartet.

Some critics had depicted the Brubeck band, with its studied sense of time, as a sort of purgatory for jazz drummers. But Morello absolutely flourished in the confines of this apparently "unswinging" ensemble. The group's high degree of visibility, its later experimentation with odd time signatures, its emphasis on daring improvisation—all these factors helped launch Morello to a position of preeminence in the world of jazz drumming. And with good cause. This leap into the limelight was no concoction of media hype but well-deserved fame for an exceptional musician. Marian McPartland, one of Morello's first employers, recalls the powerful first impression made on her by the young drummer. A fellow musician had told her repeatedly about "this 'fabulous' drummer from Springfield. But being so accustomed to hearing the word 'fabulous' used to describe talent ranging from mediocre to just plain bad, I was slightly skeptical."[5] Even so, given the big build-up, she was willing to hear Morello play. When he showed up at one of her gigs at the Hickory House, McPartland invited him to sit in even though, she noted, he "looked less like a drummer than a student of nuclear physics." Once he started playing, however, any doubt about Morello's jazz credentials was immediately put to rest. McPartland continues:

> I really don't remember what the tune was, and it isn't too important. Because in a matter of seconds, everyone in the room realized that the guy with the diffident air was a phenomenal drummer. *Everyone* listened. His precise blending of touch, taste, and an almost unbelievable technique were a joy to listen to . . . I will never forget it. Everyone knew that here was a discovery.

With the Brubeck Quartet, Morello continued to have the same effect on audiences, but now in large concert halls rather than in small clubs. Soon he was no longer a discovery, but a known commodity, emulated by a generation of younger jazz percussionists.

Despite the arrival of this powerful young workhorse on the drums, the first few Brubeck recordings with the reconfigured quartet were somewhat uninspired. By now the relentless schedule of a new album every three to four months, combined with the quartet's hectic touring schedule, was beginning to take its toll on the quality of the group's recordings. Certainly the group was as tight as ever, especially since the addition of Morello, but its repertoire began to wear thin as Columbia pushed the band into a steady stream of "theme" albums. By the time of *Jazz Goes to Junior College* in 1957, the band's umpteenth live campus date, it seemed as if the move to junior colleges came about because Brubeck had gone through all the four-year institutions around. Before continuing the move down the ladder to high school and junior highs, Columbia looked for other thematic projects, the results of which can be heard in fairly ho-hum albums such as *Dave Digs Disney* as well as a series of formulaic releases devoted to individual composers.

Given the tired format of these projects, the burst of creativity with the 1959 release of *Time Out* is nothing short of staggering. This was not only the most financially successful album of Brubeck's career, but also an immense artistic success. This latter fact may well have been hidden under the critics' continued gripes about Brubeck's dazzling rise to even higher heights of stardom, yet the snide comments and put-downs did no lasting damage. This album is still a delight to listen to a generation later, and not just because of the odd meters—others have come to master them with greater ease since 1959—but because of their winning incorporation into a series of exceptional and fresh sounding compositions. Perhaps no other jazz album of the decade exuded so much enthusiasm and such a sense of unbridled fun.

But even this move into uncharted musical territory came to be something of a formula for the band as it entered the 1960s. "Time"-oriented projects became a recurring staple for the *Time* magazine cover boy: *Time Further Out, Time in Outer Space, Time Changes, Time In* take their place as lesser or greater items in the Brubeck quartet's 1960s discography. Although the later recordings only occasionally matched the splendor of the first "Time" effort, Brubeck's lasting contribution in this regard stems perhaps less from what he himself achieved as from what it brought out of other, later musicians. As countless jazz bands across the country tackled "Take Five" and other of the group's compositions, odd meters came to be nowhere near as odd as they had once seemed.

The quartet's work in the 1960s is beyond the scope of the current study. The 1960 break-off point is a natural one for most of the artists dealt with in these pages. Most West Coast jazz players who stayed out of both the Big House and the Big Apple—Sonny Criss, Harold Land, Teddy Edwards, and others—learned to scuffle as never before. Others still, such as Carl Perkins, Curtis Counce, Wardell Gray, had already died, leaving behind only a small legacy of recordings. Needless to say, the immense success of "Take Five" and the *Time Out* works helped make Brubeck one of the few exceptions. He not only weathered the inhospitable jazz environment of the 1960s but actually flourished in the face of rock-and-roll. Yet though Brubeck continued to record and perform regularly, these later recordings, with few exceptions, fall short of the greater achievements of the 1950s. Moreover, they added fuel to the fires of criticism that have surrounded Brubeck from the start. By producing a steady stream of uneven albums, Brubeck only obscured the very real achievements from earlier in his career.

Desmond found a second wind late in his life. His recordings from the 1970s are among the strongest in his discography. The live albums on A&M and Artists House are exceptional works from start to finish, while his sideman work with Chet Baker, some of it only recently coming to light after the trumpeter's death, stands out as well. The new recordings with Brubeck, on the elegant 1975 album of duets and the following year's brief reunion with the quartet, showed that the old match-ups still could produce more than a few magical moments. Far from becoming stale, the classic quartet had aged well. The layoff from regular performances had, if anything, made the music sound fresher than it had in years.

For Desmond, the reunion with Brubeck was also something of a last hurrah. On May 30, 1977, he died, a victim of lung cancer. Brubeck continues to perform and record, often in company with his sons, and more recently alongside longtime colleague Bill Smith. Smith, a founding member of the octet, can trace his collaborations with Brubeck back over forty years. His work on clarinet is hard not to like; it is typically fresh, creative, and well executed. It is no fault of Smith's that the inevitable comparisons with Desmond continue; Brubeck's partnership with the late altoist, one of the most lasting legacies of West Coast jazz, proves irreplaceable.

a rara avis

Sometime in the late 1950s a Swedish student wrote to vibraphonist Cal Tjader to inform him that in northern Sweden a *tjader* is a rare wild turkey that is sometimes found running loose in the open fields. Tjader's response to the letter is not recorded, but the general drift of the etymology must have rung true for him. Long before this, Cal Tjader had proved that he too was something of a *rara avis*. In his music, his geography, even his ethnicity, Tjader seemed to have broken all the rules, only to find himself more successful for having done so.

Nowhere was this more striking than in his unlikely position as the father of Latin jazz on the West Coast. Tjader lacked all the obvious credentials for this pioneering role. To begin with, the West Coast in the 1950s was an unlikely setting for Tjader, or anyone else, to develop an authentic Latin jazz sound. Not that adaptation to new settings went against the grain of the music. If anything, contemporary salsa boasts the most unusual ethnic fusion of any music played in the twentieth century: It is, in essence, a school of Cuban music with African roots largely centered in New York and played, often, by Puerto Rican or other Latin American musicians. Needless to say, the West Coast is noticeably absent in this complex musical lineage, which spans three continents.

But if the West Coast was not the obvious place for developing a Latin jazz sound, Tjader must have seemed even less the obvious candidate to change this state of affairs. A Swedish-American from Missouri residing in Northern California, Tjader represented a different ethnic mix, one that included everything Latin jazz wasn't. One cannot minimize the problems presented by this striking incongruity. Poncho Sanchez, a Tjader protégé who now leads one of the finest Latin jazz bands around, recalls that during his own apprenticeship in the music, he was considered insufficiently "Latin" for the Latin music community, even though he was a Chicano. "They wouldn't even let me sit in," Sanchez says of the Cuban musicians in Los Angeles. "Are you Chicano?' they'd ask. 'Yeah, I'm Chicano and I play congas.' 'Get outta here. Chicanos don't know how to play.' "[6] Little wonder that Tjader, whose own ethnicity made him all the more suspect as an exponent of the music, was the first to give Sanchez a major break, hiring the talented conga drummer in 1975 and keeping him in the group for the next seven years, until Tjader's sudden death in 1982. And by comparison with Cal, Sanchez's background was positively *tipica*.

If his lineage and geography were two strikes against him, Tjader's odd musical background was a third. Born in St. Louis on July 16, 1925, Callen Radcliffe Tjader, Jr., was the son of two vaudeville entertainers. His father was a dancer who later became an army lieutenant-colonel, and his mother had been an aspiring concert pianist. Both left their mark on his earliest involvements in music: At the age of two Cal was already receiving piano instruction from his mother, and soon he was following in his father's terpsichorean footsteps. His initiation to show business had started by age ten when, as a precocious tap dancer in a Mickey Rooney vein, he began entertaining in public and even garnered a dance scene in a motion picture called *Too Many Parents*. In 1927, the family settled in

San Mateo, California, where Cal Sr. opened a dance studio. After high school, Cal Jr. served in the navy and then went to San Francisco State on the GI Bill.

During the postwar years, San Francisco State was an oasis of modern jazz activity in a Dixieland town. The student body boasted a host of outstanding talents, including Tjader, Paul Desmond, John Handy, Allen Smith, and Ron Crotty. Desmond, then still known as Paul Breitenfeld, was the crucial link between the SF State group and the other contingent of modern jazz musicians at Mills College across the bay. Eventually Tjader became part of the Mills avant-garde unit. His earliest jazz recordings with the Brubeck Octet and Trio not only find him in a musical idiom distinctly opposed to Latin music, but also working on an instrument, the drums, that he would not even include in his first mambo records. Tjader would have to re-educate himself musically from the groundup before he would be able to make his big step into Latin jazz.

Tjader's inspiration to change directions came while on the road with the George Shearing band in the early 1950s. "One of the chief compensations of being with Shearing," Tjader told John Tynan in 1957, "was that back east I got to hear a lot of Machito, Tito Puente and Noro Morales. Those bands had a tremendous effect on me. Immediately I wanted to reorganize a small combo along the same lines, only with more jazz feeling incorporated in the Latin format."[7] In 1954, shortly after leaving Shearing, Tjader made this aspiration a reality with his new San Francisco–based "mambo" quintet. A six-month debut stint at the Macumba Club proved to be a great local success, while the first of a long series of records for the Fantasy label brought Tjader's new music to the attention of jazz fans across the country.

Viewed in the light of his later recordings, the early Tjader Latin sides with the Macumba band are mostly a mixed bag. Some fairly tame cha-cha adaptations, such as "I'll Remember April" or "Midnight Sun," are only a step above Xavier Cugat. But the more aggressive "mambo" numbers, such as "Mamblues" or "Mambo Macumba," go a long way toward capturing the immense rhythmic potential of the idiom. Also among Tjader's recordings with this group was his first version of the Dizzy Gillespie standard "Guarachi Guaro." This piece, actually the creation of Chano Pozo during his brief tenure with the Gillespie band, would become Tjader's biggest hit some ten years later when the vibraphonist recorded it again under the title "Soul Sauce" for the Verve label.

These first recordings from the mid-1950s produced no "hit" numbers on the scale of "Soul Sauce," yet they sold well and helped spread the vibist's reputation beyond the clique who had followed him with Brubeck and Shearing. More successful were the March 1954 sessions that found Tjader recording in the Latin idiom with a different group of musi-

cians than he had used for the Macumba engagement. Bassist Al Mc-
Kibbon was perhaps, at the time, the most capable jazz musician on his
instrument in a Latin vein: having served as a member of Gillespie's rhythm
section during the Afro-Cuban years, McKibbon had played with and studied under Chano Pozo. McKibbon, who had been in the Shearing band
with Tjader, had also been a major influence in exposing the latter to Latin
music in the first place. Jerome Richardson and Richard Wyands, playing
flute and piano respectively, were two of the outstanding home-grown San
Francisco jazz players of their day; both eventually enhanced their reputations by moving east. Richardson, five years Tjader's senior, had also
been a student at SF State and went on to play with a series of stellar big
bands, including those of Lunceford, Hampton, and Hines. He moved to
New York in the early 1950s and later worked with Mingus and Oscar
Pettiford and served as a founding member of the Thad Jones/Mel Lewis
big band. Wyands, three years younger than Tjader, also gained greater
recognition for his talents after moving to New York in the late 1950s,
and went on to play with Mingus and Roy Haynes and serve an extended
stint in Kenny Burrell's band. The final member of this Tjader ensemble
was conga player Armando Pereza. Tjader doubled on timbales. On one of
the sessions pianist Eddie Cano replaced Wyands, and though he comes
across as a far less capable jazz player, his salsa work, especially on the
invigorating "Ritmo Caliente," stands out as some of the finest keyboard
work on any Tjader album of the decade. In general this sparsely recorded
band, whose work can be heard on the Fantasy *Ritmo Caliente* release,
represented a giant step above the working Macumba band of the period.
Tjader's finest Latin jazz albums were still to be recorded, but these early
sides show he had captured a powerful sound that could be much more
than a passing fad.

   At least initially, however, that was what Tjader and Fantasy must
have felt they had on their hands. The dizzying pace of recording Cal
would pursue over the next several years shows all the signs of a frenzied
attempt to capture the market for the Latin sounds before the next new
thing came along. As it turned out, Cal proved able to tap an audience
that did not disappear but stayed, for the most part, solidly in his corner
for the rest of his career. In just a few years Fantasy had issued over
twenty Cal Tjader LPs—an excess of exposure that might have diluted the
drawing power of many a lesser talent. But Tjader continued to find an
audience for new recordings: with the Verve label in the 1960s, again with
Fantasy in the 1970s, and on the newer Concord label in the 1980s. And
he did so, moreover, without the constant stretching for variety that has
contributed to the patchwork recording careers of so many other artists.

   For the most part, Tjader's records were of just two kinds: Latin albums and straight-ahead jazz albums. And of these the former provided most of the vibraphonist's bread and butter, outselling the jazz releases four to one early in his career and remaining a major drawing card until the very end. The jazz albums, despite their relatively lower profile, in many ways reflected Tjader's basic musical instincts. At heart he was a musical romantic, a highly melodic soloist who refused to adorn his playing with the tawdry frills that are often endemic to jazz in general and the vibes in particular.

The vibraphone invites overplaying almost by its very nature. The trumpet, by comparison, is at the opposite extreme: The visceral feeling of producing the tone is part and parcel of playing it. Each note counts. Moreover, horn playing inculcates a natural instinct for restrained phrasing, if only because of the player's physical need to catch a breath of air. Little wonder that some of jazz's most concise melodists, from Bix to Miles, have been trumpeters. The trumpet has an almost built-in barrier against merely facile playing; instead it, more than the percussion or even string instruments, invites a centered, Zen-like concentration on the melody line. The vibraphone has a much different personality. Unlike a horn player, the vibraphonist is unable to sustain notes for very long, even with help of vibrato and pedal. The vibes invite overplaying to compensate for such limitations. Added to these difficulties is the fact that finger technique is not required to play the vibes—instead a hitting motion is powered by the wrists. With the mastery of a steady drum roll, the aspiring vibraphonist is already capable of flinging out a flurry of notes and, given the repetitive motions used to build up drum technique, the vibes player is often tempted to lock into a "steady stream" approach in which one could say of the notes, following Lewis Carroll, "thick and fast they came at last/and more and more and *more.*"

Tjader's playing, however, was nothing like this. Although he was a drummer and percussionist by background, he seemed to draw on the instincts of a horn player in shaping his improvised lines. They *did* breathe. One might expect, given this distinctive quality, that Milt Jackson, whose horn-line approach revolutionized vibes playing in the 1950s, had been Tjader's prime influence. Indeed, in 1962 he said: "I'm so influenced by what Milt Jackson has done. He has been the Lester Young of the vibes. I find myself always thinking, 'How does this compare with something Milt did?' . . . Milt just revolutionized the instrument."[8] Tjader, however, also took care to cite the more musically verbose Lionel Hampton as his first inspiration, stating that Jackson became a model only later. These disparate strains in his playing came out most clearly in his jazz work, where Tjader melded them into a melodic, often introspective style that was very much his own. Even when playing more high-energy Latin numbers Tjader kept a low-key demeanor, building off the intensity of the rhythm section rather than trying to supplant it. For the most part, he came across as an introvert on an instrument meant for extroverts.

I remember seeing Tjader, the year before he died, sitting in with the Brubeck band at a San Francisco jazz festival. The event was heralded as the first reunion of the original Brubeck Trio in some thirty years—with bassist Ron Crotty making up the third member of the reconstituted band. The newly built Davies Symphony Hall was packed with an enthusiastic crowd of jazz fans, many of whom had been following the careers of Brubeck and Tjader, the proverbial town boys who made good, for years if not decades. After playing the drums, Tjader joined Brubeck on the vibes and contributed two delightfully sly and clever solos, both of them musical gems, short on technique but long on creativity and care. Tjader all the while looked nervously around, as though he felt he had little business being on stage at such high-powered proceedings. A number of other premier jazz acts were on the bill that night, and Brubeck's performance rose to the occasion, but the most striking thing about the event for me has remained the two choice Tjader vibraphone solos. Not just their beauty stood out, but also their contrast with the image of self-effacement Tjader gave on the stand. This same self-deprecating attitude came out in one of his comments from the early 1950s: "I am not an innovator, I am not a pathfinder—I am a participator."[9] Still in his twenties, at the start of his early successes as a bandleader, Tjader was even then anxious to dismiss outright any undue acclaim.

Tjader's recordings suggest that the vibraphonist had little grounds for such modesty. The disarming charm of his playing, especially on lyrical later albums like *Breathe Easy* and *The Shining Sea,* had a reassuring, distilled quality about it, as though Tjader dispatched each note with definite intent, with no wasted flourishes. This side of Tjader's music was most prominent in his jazz recordings, surfacing only occasionally in his more unrestrained Latin work. Tjader was anything but unaware of this unusual contradiction in his music: One of the established stars of Latin jazz, Tjader was also among its most vocal critics. "Latin has its definite limitations," he remarked in 1957, "especially from the standpoint of improvisation. It's like a hypnotic groove. First you set the rhythmic pattern, then the melodic formulae follow—until pretty soon you realize there's not much real music invention happening."[10]

The chief virtue of Latin music—this intricate, layered rhythmic structure—is also its vice in jazz setting. Although these rhythms boast a complexity that can almost rival the polymetric structures of jazz—as well as throw for a loop the uninitiated jazz musician who thinks one can just "sit in" without studying the idiom—Tjader also saw in them something of an improvisational straitjacket. "See," Tjader continued, "the Latin percussionist's conception of time is very straight, rigid. It's not really loose like it has to be for jazz. That's why there's nothing more of a drag than having a Latin percussionist sit in with a jazz group."

Such sentiments were the obvious motivation behind Tjader's June 1956 decision to reorganize his mambo quintet into a jazz band. The month before Tjader made the change, John Tynan had written a distinctly unflattering review in *Downbeat* of the Latin band's appearance at Zardi's.

> This attempted blending of Afro-Cuban and jazz suggests rather an uneasy shotgun marriage . . . an overall monotonous sound. . . . One is left with a decided impression of untenability. . . . For jazz listeners, the most perceptible excitement was generated when for the greater portion of one set, the conga drummer left the stand, permitting Cal to wail through several straight jazz numbers.[11]

These comments must have reflected Tjader's own view of the proceedings, for within a matter of weeks he had made the change to a jazz format, retaining a conga player for the Latin numbers but stocking the rest of the band with solid jazz players. Even before returning to San Francisco from the Zardi's gig, Tjader went into a Hollywood studio to record a straight-ahead quartet album with Gene Wright, Gerald Wiggins, and Bill Douglass. Despite his greater draw and record sales as a "mambo" artist, Tjader was determined to earn his spurs as a jazz player—a move that was marked by success. By the close of the decade, Tjader's jazz-oriented albums were selling virtually as well as his purely Latin outings.

When Tynan next reviewed the band—a Hollywood stint at the Interlude in late February of 1957—the transformation had already taken place. The new band boasted pianist Vince Guaraldi, bassist Eugene Wright, drummer Al Torres, and conga player Louis Kant. This would be one of Tjader's finest jazz ensembles of the decade. (For Latin numbers the band could still be fairly effective. Torres would switch to timbales and cymbal, and Guaraldi proved to be quite capable in the Latin idiom.)

Like Tjader, Guaraldi effected a successful hybrid between poignant lyricism and rhythmic drive. As musicians, Tjader and Guaraldi were ideally compatible. "I will never forget one night at the Macumba in San Francisco," later recalled critic Ralph Gleason of their collaboration, "when that group got a blues groove going that was something else again. It was so good that the band was giggling, the waitress stopped serving to turn and look, and the audience held its breath. It was one of the best moments of music in my entire life, believe me."[12] Another member of the San Francisco State scene during the postwar years, Guaraldi was a native of San Francisco, where he was born on July 17, 1928. In addition to his work with Tjader during the 1950s, Guaraldi also toured with Woody Herman, worked in smaller combos featuring Sonny Criss and Bill Harris, and recorded as a sideman with Frank Rosolino and Conte Candoli.

Despite these sideman credits, Guaraldi was far more comfortable as a bandleader. Max Weiss recalls the difficulties between Guaraldi and the talented guitarist Bola Sete, who worked and recorded with the pianist in the early 1960s.

> Guaraldi and Bola Sete were really a great group. We got bookings like crazy for them and also in colleges and concerts. But Vince could not handle the problem that Bola was getting more applause than he was. That's why they split up. And Vince thought it was because Bola was playing the guitar, but that wasn't it. You see, Bola was a showman. . . . Bola and Vince had other frames of reference and different values, and he couldn't handle it.

Weiss went on to contrast the two players with Brubeck and Desmond, who, as he saw it, had an ideal working relationship despite being two "star" players. "Vince was very determined to succeed in this business," comments another musician on the scene during those years, "and once he had a taste of success with 'Cast Your Fate' he got all the more feisty. He became all the more demanding with club owners and the like."

In early 1959, Guaraldi left the Tjader ensemble, perhaps due to similar tensions, and after a return stint with Herman and a brief engagement as a Lighthouse All-Star, decided to go out on his own: a decision that proved to be wise, given the immense success he experienced on the crest of his hit single "Cast Your Fate to the Wind." Guaraldi was one of the few West Coast players who found his career entering an upswing during the 1960s. In addition to "Cast Your Fate to the Wind," he released a series of albums that successfully broached commercialism without compromising on jazz content, including his soundtracks for the Charlie Brown TV specials, his Grace Cathedral Concert, and his collaborations with Bola Sete. Perhaps the only sour note struck was an unfortunate venture into singing. Guaraldi died on February 6, 1976, of a heart attack while resting between shows at Butterfield's Bar. He was forty-seven years old.

Another Tjader-sideman-turned-leader from the mid-1950s, Brew Moore, never achieved Guaraldi's wider public but had all the tools necessary to do so. "Everything he plays lays just right," a fellow musician once commented on Moore.[13] And indeed it seemed true. Ralph Gleason put across the same point when he remarked that "Brew has two absolutely golden gifts. He swings like mad and has soul." Gleason might have added Moore's knack for melody as a third virtue. Moore combined these striking attributes in a style unabashedly drawn from Lester Young. Moore's often-repeated comment on Prez—"Anybody who doesn't play like Lester is wrong"—seemed almost battle cry for West Coast saxophonists in the

1950s. Young's influence was heard across the whole expanse of Southern California geography, from urban Central Avenue (Gordon, Gray) to the suburban shoreline of the Lighthouse (Giuffre, Cooper, Shank). In Northern California, Moore was perhaps the most striking proponent of the Four Brothers sound, and one could scarcely imagine a more convincing exemplar of that approach to the tenor.

For a later devotee to Prez, Moore made an unlikely start on the saxophone by memorizing Coleman Hawkins's solo on "Body and Soul." "I made an awful mess of it," he said in 1949.[14] "My trouble was that I was reading Downbeat too much. Downbeat said then that Hawk was the man." If it took Moore some time to find his true inspiration on the horn, it had taken him just as long to find his true instrument. Born in Indianola, Mississippi, on March 26, 1924, Moore wanted to play trumpet in the high school band but was instead assigned a trombone. He switched to clarinet two years later; when he discovered that the clarinet was rarely featured on solos, he changed again to saxophone.

After high school Moore began a peripatetic career that brought him little fame but gave him a heady taste of life on the move. After a brief spell with a band in Texas, Moore studied at the University of Mississippi for a short while before moving to New Orleans, where he joined the Will Stomp band. Then to Memphis and on to New York, where, while waiting out his union card, he changed his mind, returned home to Mississippi, then back to New Orleans, and finally reconsidered and went back to New York—all this while scarcely out of his teens! The second time around, New York seemed hardly more inviting. After hearing Dizzy and Bird at Minton's and gigging for a while in Newark, New Jersey, Moore once again returned to Mississippi. He felt uncomfortable with the modern jazz idiom until he realized that, as he put it, "Lester was the foundation of bop. Then I knew I could keep playing Lester's style and play with a bop band."[15] When he next ventured to New York in 1948, he persevered and soon was working with Claude Thornhill, Machito, Howard McGhee, and others. In April 1949, he recorded for Prestige in a line-up including Stan Getz, Zoot Sims, Al Cohn, and Allen Eager for a session that featured Four Brothers–type arrangements. One of the tunes was appropriately called "Five Brothers."

Given the wanderlust-laden account of Moore's early travels, one can almost believe the story he commonly gave about his mid-1950s move to San Francisco: "Billy Faier had a 1949 Buick somebody wanted him to drive out to California, and he rode through Washington Square shouting, 'Anybody for the Coast?' And I was just sitting there on a bench and there wasn't shit shaking in New York so I said, hell yes."[16] By the time he moved to San Francisco, Moore had achieved a reputation for excellence among jazz insiders, something his West Coast years did little to either dispel or enhance. Jack Kerouac depicts a Moore performance in *Desolation Angels*, where Brew (or Brue, as Kerouac spells it) starts his solo with, the beat prosodist tells us, "a perfect beautiful new idea that announces the glory of the future world."

This future glory eluded Moore to the end. His quartet and quintet albums on Fantasy, made during his California years, were his last commercial recordings in the United States. These along with his sideman recordings with Tjader, find the tenorist at absolutely top form, stretching out over standards with an impressive melodic and rhythmic inventiveness. In 1961, he moved to Europe, where, except for intermittent appearances in the United States, he lived until his death in 1973 as the result of a fall.

Despite the loss of Moore, Tjader's growing reputation and draw was making it easier for him to attract world-class sidemen to his band. In 1956, Tjader broadened his exposure with an eastern tour that included a lengthy stint alternating with Dizzy Gillespie's band at Birdland, as well as opportunities to play Latin music in Spanish Harlem dancehalls. By 1957, Tjader was the largest-selling artist in the Fantasy catalogue and seemed to be releasing a new album for the label almost every ten to fourteen weeks. From 1957 through the turn of the decade, Mongo Santamaria and Willie Bobo, two of the most important Latin musicians of their generation, were frequent fixtures in the Tjader band. Both already had strong reputations in the Latin music community, but through Tjader they also reached a much wider jazz-oriented audience. "Since our success," Tjader explained, "the availability of good players has improved because I've been able to offer better guarantees. Money. That often makes the difference."[17]

Given this flexibility, Tjader put together in 1958 what was his finest working band of the decade and probably of his whole career. With Santamaria, Bobo, and Guaraldi, he had three sidemen who were leaders in their own rights. For a short while Pony Poindexter, one of the strongest (albeit rarely recorded) West Coast altoists of the day, was also a member of this band, but unfortunately he never recorded with it. With this high level of musicianship, Tjader's band could switch from Latin to jazz without sacrificing in either idiom. Whereas Tjader had earlier felt that the choice between Latin and jazz was an either/or situation, he increasingly tried to put together bands that could do both equally well. With Guaraldi's departure, Tjader found a strong substitute in Lonnie Hewitt, another player with the flexibility Tjader required. During his tenure with Tjader, the Oakland-born Hewitt built on his strengths in a blues and funk vein and grew into a well-rounded player with dual jazz and Latin skills.

At the first Monterey Jazz Festival in 1958, the Tjader band had been given the unenviable task of following Billie Holiday, Dizzy Gillespie, Sonny Rollins, and Gerry Mulligan, among other luminaries, to conclude the

Sunday night program with a 1 a.m. set. Defying these untoward circumstances, the band rallied the remaining several thousand members of the audience with a stunning performance that left the crowd clamoring for more. Encouraged by the group's showing at this graveyard shift performance, promoter Jimmy Lyons brought Tjader back several months before the next festival for what was billed as a "Jazz Festival Preview." On April 20, 1959, Tjader's group, joined by guest artist Paul Horn on flute and alto, made the journey down to the Monterey peninsula, several hours' drive from Tjader's Northern California home base, for their performance at Carmel's Sunset School auditorium. Lyons hoped that the concert would not only spur interest in the forthcoming second annual Monterey Jazz Festival (the first one had been, despite its artistic success, something of a financial failure), but also give the festival crew a chance to work out various concert production problems beforehand. But if the reason for the gig was forward-looking, the band was very much caught up in the here and now that evening. Eventually the full extent of the band's work that night was initially released on two records—*Cal Tjader's Concert by the Sea*, volumes one and two—which provide an excellent insight into the Tjader band at its full flowering as the decade came near its close.

The whole range of the band's repertoire—blues, bop, ballads, Latin, and the like—are showcased during the evening's proceedings. On "Doxy," Hewitt gets going on a riveting gospel-inspired groove and, with Tjader urging him on in the background, stretches out for several choruses. Santamaria's "Afro Blue," later picked up and disseminated by John Coltrane, is given an attractive streamlined treatment with strong solos by the composer and Horn's flute. Horn switches to alto to lead the band into an exceptional blues outing on "Walkin' with Wally," while on a Latin cooker such as "Timbao" the combination of Bobo and Santamaria kicks in with a fury. Despite the strong skills of his sidemen, Tjader was invariably the finest ballad player in his various groups, and here he shines on "Bess You Is My Woman" and "Laura," with " 'Round Midnight" given over to Hewitt for a Monkish interpretation. With this band, Tjader had achieved his stated goal of being able to cover all the bases with a single line-up. To a greater or lesser extent, Tjader's later bands all aspired to achieve the same controlled eclecticism.

Tjader suffered to some extent from the general lack of imagination that characterized much of Fantasy's jazz product in the late 1950s. While other jazz producers of the day, such as Norman Granz or Orrin Keepnews, constantly strived for different formats, personnel, and concepts for their artists, Fantasy tended to churn out a steady stream of similar-sounding albums, usually featuring Tjader's working band. One of the few exceptions to this rule, Tjader's collaboration with Stan Getz showed the benefits of mixing Cal with new blood from beyond the occasionally anemic

Fantasy roster. In addition to Getz, the session featured Scott LaFaro, Billy Higgins, Vince Guaraldi, and Eddie Duran. The band drew on some of the permanent fixtures in the Tjader repertoire—Cal's waltz "Lizanne," the blues "Crow's Nest," and Guaraldi's "Ginza"—with Getz leading the way with a charged tenor performance.

Eddie Duran, the guitarist on the session, was another Tjader colleague who was a group leader in his own right. Duran's brothers Carlos and Manuel had recorded with Tjader in one of his earliest Latin ensembles, but Eddie proved to be the family talent with the most staying power in the world of jazz. His strong chordal sense and fiery single-note lines elevated him to prominence as perhaps the finest of the postwar modern jazz guitarists in the Bay Area. A San Francisco native—he was born on September 6, 1925—Duran's reluctance to leave his California home base through much of his early career hindered him from making the national reputation his talent warranted. Early in his career, Duran turned down the opportunity to join Benny Goodman's touring band and instead chose to develop his reputation from San Francisco, recording with Tjader, Guaraldi, and Ron Crotty before being given a leader date by Fantasy.

Duran's formative years were spent almost entirely in Northern California. The guitarist's reluctance to leave the Golden State may have limited his fame, but it hardly affected his opportunities to play with outstanding jazz artists. He gigged with Charlie Parker during the latter's tenure at San Francisco's Say When club, and in the following years Duran recorded with Stan Getz and Earl Hines, among others. His 1957 debut as a leader, *Eddie Duran—Jazz Guitarist*, showcased, for the most part, a more reflective side of the guitarist, with a pronounced emphasis on slow and medium tempos. His earlier sideman date with the Ron Crotty Trio, released as part of Fantasy's 1955 *Modern Music from San Francisco*, shows a more free-wheeling side of Duran, especially on the Guaraldi original "Ginza."

Duran's career decisions began to move apace with his musical abilities in later decades. He finally accepted Goodman's renewed offer to join the band in the mid-1970s, and in 1976 Duran made his New York debut with the clarinetist at Carnegie Hall. In the late 1980s he served a brief residency in New York but soon returned to Northern California. In his mid-sixties, he stands as an imposing fixture on the San Francisco jazz scene, and though he now shares the spotlight with younger talented homegrown guitarists such as Bruce Forman and Tuck Andress, Duran remains a compelling and often brilliant soloist.

Fantasy's apparent reluctance to record black jazz artists is one of its less fortunate legacies from the 1950s. Pony Poindexter, an exceptionally talented and tragically underrecorded black altoist of the period, made no albums until Los Angeles–based Richard Bock brought him in as a sideman on two 1959 sessions. The Mastersounds, another outstanding San Francisco–based ensemble, buoyed by Buddy and Monk Montgomery, also recorded with Bock's Los Angeles–based label (although it later had a brief association with Fantasy long after the group had established itself as a major attraction). In his autobiography, *Pony Express*, a seldom-seen volume published in English by a small West German publisher, Poindexter lambastes what he perceives as a white/Jewish conspiracy to prevent black musicians from breaking into the Bay Area recording scene and pinpoints the Weiss brothers and Jimmy Lyons as the instigators of it. The problem, however, centered perhaps less on racism, overt or covert, than on the Fantasy owners' extreme conservatism and their formulaic approach to record producing during these years. This nickel-and-dime philosophy limited their openness to almost any kind of new sound. Once they found marketable artists, like Tjader and Brubeck, the Weisses preferred to record them every few months rather than take chances with new talent. And even these artists were anything but Weiss discoveries. The new artists they signed were almost invariably sidemen with groups Fantasy had already recorded—thus reducing the uncertainty of breaking in unknown talent. Even Brubeck was no find of the Fantasy owners, but rather a part of the Coronet catalogue they acquired by default. Unlike Les Koenig and Richard Bock, the Weisses had little confidence in their own musical judgment; so while a Koenig would tempt fate by recording Ornette Coleman and Don Cherry, the Weisses would play it safe by churning out another Tjader release. "Cal was bringing in some very, very good musicians," Max Weiss explained to me. "You know, at the time we didn't realize that they were the ones that would get even bigger than Cal. Vince Guaraldi, Mongo Santamaria, Willie Bobo."

Even today the attitude of Bay Area record companies to native talent is quite similar. It is all too telling that, even with the preponderance of jazz record companies in Northern California, the two biggest black jazz talents to emerge from the area in recent years—Bobby McFerrin and Stanley Jordan—were ignored by the local record labels and had to go back east to be "discovered." Julian Priester's complaint that he got more work in San Francisco after he moved away from the area is another symptomatic story of the strange distrust of home-grown musicians that has often characterized the local scene. If the need for New York legitimation is and has been a common complaint among West Coast players, much of the problem lies not with the New York critics—who, after all, have only the most limited opportunity to evaluate the California players—but with the strange failure of West Coast jazz institutions to recognize the talents of musicians right under their noses. This subject will be discussed in greater detail in the final chapter of this book.

The Mastersounds, an integrated band that came to San Francisco from the Midwest in the late 1950s, proved that the local black artists could, under the right circumstances, sell lots of records and attract large audiences. With the considerable talents of the Indianapolis-born and -bred Montgomery brothers, Monk and Buddy (with occasional help from middle brother Wes), drummer Benny Barth, and pianist Richard Crabtree, the Mastersounds stand out as one of the finest and most successful West Coast bands of the late 1950s. Barth recalls the circumstances surrounding the birth of the group:

> Back in Indianapolis Buddy Montgomery was a piano player—and he still is one of the best piano players I know of—but around 1955 or 1956 he got a set of vibes, and we started rehearsing at his house. It would have been Buddy on vibes, I would play drums, Al Plank played piano, and Wes [Montgomery] played electric bass. Monk wasn't around then. It was interesting to hear Wes playing the bass, because when he took his solos he would make it sound like a guitar. We did a few gigs and called ourselves the Indianapolis Jazz Quartet. But it wasn't a big thing. We never played a steady gig.
>
> Then around December of 1956 or January of 1957, Monk called to say that he had a gig for a quartet in Seattle. Al couldn't go, but Richard Crabtree, who was in Sidney, Montana, at the time, was available. So we headed out to Seattle, where we met up with Richard. There we had a steady gig at Dave's Fifth Avenue in Seattle, and also played at the Congo Club in Tacoma. We didn't want to call ourselves the Indianapolis Jazz Quartet any more, and Buddy's wife came up with the name the Mastersounds. I would have been content to call it the Buddy Montgomery Quartet or the Monk Montgomery Quartet, but it really was a cooperative group.[18]

A tape made of the group in Seattle was sold to producer Richard Bock, who released it as the *Jazz Showcase* featuring the Mastersounds. Around this same time, the band was invited to pursue a lengthy engagement at San Francisco's Jazz Showcase, a prominent club on lower Market Street not far from the Ferry Building. This venue had been a major jazz club as early as the 1940s, when it was known as the Downbeat. Now under new ownership, and with a no-alcohol policy, it was attracting a younger clientele. Anxious to try their luck in San Francisco, the band agreed to the offer and traveled down in two cars to set up shop in California.

Despite the success of their first release, the band's follow-up album was what put the Mastersounds on the map. Buddy Montgomery proposed doing an album based on music from *The King and I*, the successful Rodgers and Hammerstein musical that had already been made into a hit movie. Up until this time the Mastersounds sounded like a funkier version of the Modern Jazz Quartet; but with *The King and I* the band captured a more subdued, melodic sensibility, which obviously struck a resonant chord with record buyers. As Shelly Manne and André Previn were discovering in Los Angeles, many listeners otherwise reluctant to pick up a jazz combo album would do just that if it featured unthreatening renditions of familiar show tunes. Such projects often required the musicians to pull off the musical equivalent of alchemy, transmuting the leaden textures of songs torn out of their dramatic context into the pure gold of modern jazz. "The music didn't strike me at all," writes jazz critic Ralph Gleason of his first exposure to the material. "But I must confess it was not until I heard the young musicians who call themselves The Mastersounds do their medley from *The King and I* that I finally appreciated what marvelously melodic, visual and deeply rewarding music the composers had written."[19] The Mastersounds followed up with similar projects—*Kismet* and *Flower Drum Song*—as well as more loosely arranged releases such as *Ballads and Blues* and *In Concert*. The last two albums may have been more popular with the serious jazz audience, but the show tune compilations brought the band a wide public acceptance that few serious jazz groups have garnered in the modern era. On the strength of their growing popularity, the band moved from the Jazz Showcase to the Jazz Workshop on Broadway, where they began drawing overflow crowds. "We played there off and on for some time—it was our home base the way, say, the Blackhawk would be Cal Tjader's place," Barth explains. "We caused a big stir there—I'd go out on our break and see lines going around the corner. Up until that time the Workshop was really just for local talent, but after us they started bringing in name bands."

The group seemed poised to enjoy a long, successful career when it disbanded. At the close of the 1950s, only a short while after the Mastersounds had won the New Star Award for combos in the *Downbeat* International Critics Poll, the Montgomerys, Monk and Buddy, left to form a band with brother Wes. In the mid-1960s the Mastersounds reunited but, despite renewed offers to record and tour Europe, disbanded only a few months later.

Under other circumstances, the Mastersounds might have been one more San Francisco success story to buck the jazz jinx of the 1960s. Brubeck, Guaraldi, and Tjader each managed to have a hit record at the turn of the decade. And though none of them ever had a later success to match, respectively, "Take Five," "Cast Your Fate," or "Soul Sauce," the momentum of these chartbusters served to keep their careers alive during the heyday of rock and roll. In Los Angeles, matters were far worse at the close of the Eisenhower years.

CHAPTER SIX

Central Avenue Survivors

the most loyal subject in the land

The lights are out in the spacious gymnasium of the Los Angeles Police Academy. It is very late on a warm summer night. If there were a clock around it might be striking 2 A.M. about now. But there is no clock, and no one to ask the time. Visitors to this spot—isolated Chavez Ravine, several miles from downtown—are rare at any time and especially so at this odd hour. Burglars know better than to try their luck on their adversaries' home turf. But a by-stander tonight would encounter the strangest thing. From the inside of the dark gymnasium, the sound of music suddenly pierces the air. Our imaginary visitor, seeking the source of this unexpected commotion, wanders inside. A Steinway grand piano is set up in a dimly lit section of the gym. Seated at the piano is a wiry young black man, who attacks the keys with remarkable force, almost as if to defy the heavy stillness surrounding him.

The pianist is not alone. A bass player and drummer surround him in the semidarkness and join in the performance. They play as though urged on by an encouraging audience, but though the large gym occasionally doubles as an auditorium, it is now empty—or at least seems so at first glance. Closer inspection reveals an unusual exception: A single table has been set up behind the piano and outside the pianist's line of vision; there three women and two men sit quietly drinking beer. These visitors are easy to overlook; it is the man at the keyboard who immediately catches one's attention—not just for his impassioned performance to an invisible audience but also his striking appearance. Although he is only in his mid-twenties, he looks much older. His eyes are set deep, and the sharpness of

114

his features is only slightly softened by a pencil-thin moustache. His body and face are unnaturally thin, almost gaunt, but his hands are out of keeping with the rest of his physique. They are small and powerful, the hands of a carpenter or workman, someone who has learned to combine finesse with a degree of brute force. In the juxtaposition of these different qualities, he seems both old and young at the same time.

A short while before, Arthur Rubenstein had played this same Steinway piano. Tonight the pianist is Hampton Hawes. Unlike Rubenstein, Hawes is known to only a few people in the music world—almost all of them in Southern California—but within a year, largely on the strength of this strange late-night performance in Chavez Ravine, he will have become a well-known musician with opportunities to play at many of the best clubs across the country. Hidden in the recesses of the building this night, an engineer is recording the proceedings on portable Ampex equipment. By the time the musicians have finished, just before dawn on June 28, 1955, they will have recorded an entire album.

For many jazz fans this album, simply entitled *Hampton Hawes Trio*, marked their first exposure to this exciting young pianist from Los Angeles. Soon they would know him well. Just a few weeks earlier, Hawes had recorded an album with Bud Shank for the Pacific label, and over the next three years an impressive stream of records under his leadership would come out on the Contemporary label. The musicians in Southern California, however, had been aware of this young man's talents for quite some time. In early 1953, Shorty Rogers prominently featured him on Rogers's first RCA recording. Hawes was chief soloist on Rogers's appropriately titled "Diablo's Dance," and the pianist's driving improvisation and memorable four-bar break presaged great things to come. Only a month later Hawes recorded a version of "All the Things You Are" with the Lighthouse All-Stars, and his solo work here also raised eyebrows among jazz cognoscenti. This last recording found the pianist tackling an out-of-tune Lighthouse piano with impressive results. His powerful, fluid right-hand lines and forceful comping dominate the performance and stand in sharp contrast to the workman-like contributions of Frank Patchen, the other Lighthouse pianist on the session.

One of those struck by this memorable rendition of the Jerome Kern standard was Les Koenig, president of Contemporary Records. "In that moment I was determined to record him for Contemporary," Koenig would later recall. Almost two years would elapse before Koenig got his chance.

Like Anne Boleyn, Henry VIII's unfortunate second wife, Hawes had been born with six fingers on each hand. Although such accessories might be of more benefit to a pianist than to a queen, Hawes's extra digits were clipped off with a nylon string on November 16, 1928, three days after his birth. ("I wondered if it could have been some kind of omen," he would later remark.) The remaining ten managed to serve Hawes quite well over the next half-century.

The youngest of seven children, Hampton was raised in the Los Angeles neighborhood of Watts. His father was a Presbyterian minister, prominent in the community, who frowned upon his young son's interest in jazz—long after Hampton had become well known, his father still refused to attend his performances. His mother, who had been a professional pianist and organist before raising her family, provided more encouragement. From both sides Hampton was exposed to music, in the church and in the home. His formal training was practically nil—he could barely read music even as an adult—but his ability to mimic what he heard was phenomenal from the start. His first model was his elder sister, who performed classical music on the family upright. By age twelve Hawes was also imitating the recordings of Earl Hines and Fats Waller. In his early teens, Hawes caught the spark of the nascent modern jazz movement when his school friend Eric Dolphy (destined to become one of the founders of the jazz avant-garde) introduced him to the work of Dizzy Gillespie. Hawes quickly became a convert to the new sounds from the East Coast.

While still in Los Angeles Polytechnic High School, Hawes began playing professionally. When he was sixteen, he convinced his father to approve his application to the musicians' union. Over the next few years he would be a regular on the Central Avenue music scene, performing with Wardell Gray, Dexter Gordon, Charles Mingus, Teddy Edwards, and Sonny Criss. The night he graduated from high school he played at the Last Word on Central Avenue with Jay McNeely. McNeely recalls that Hawes then played in a style similar to Nat King Cole's, but soon he had evolved into a more aggressive bop stylist in the manner of Bud Powell.[1] Only a few weeks after graduation Hawes was playing with Bird, who had recently been released from the Camarillo State Hospital.

Parker was working in a quintet led by trumpeter Howard McGhee at the Hi De Ho. Hawes, eighteen years old at the time, was enlisted for the gig. Hampton grew close to the master by offering to drive him to and from work. Hawes later remarked, on more than one occasion, that Parker influenced him more than any other musician, more even than piano players. Parker's impact unfortunately went beyond musical matters: His troubled lifestyle also fascinated his young disciple. The elder altoist introduced Hawes to his first marijuana cigarette ("some light green from Chicago Bird pulled out as we were driving down Avalon Boulevard"). Later Hawes learned to emulate Parker's heroin habit—with disastrous consequences.

Over the next decade, Hawes's musical career and dependence on drugs would grow hand in hand. Inspired by Parker and word of the East Coast scene, Hawes flew to New York but quickly decided that he wasn't yet ready to take on Manhattan. ("Sometimes it's better to pass, wait for a better hand," he remarks in *Raise Up off Me*.) Hawes joined Wild Bill Moore's traveling band and worked the eastern seaboard. Then he played with Red Norvo for a San Francisco engagement before returning to Los Angeles to pursue opportunities on Central Avenue and elsewhere.

The Club Alabam, Downbeat, the Haig, Surf Club, Jungle Room—these now defunct clubs were the training grounds for the developing West Coast scene, and Hawes was one of the most notable young musicians in attendance. A half-dozen trio sides recorded at the Haig on September 22, 1951, are the first recordings of Hawes leading his own band—and they serve as a dazzling debut by almost any standard. The speed of his piano attack is the most obvious virtue of these performances, but Hawes's rhythmic daring is also noteworthy: Although the pianist prefers to phrase on the beat, at several points he engages in some ambitious cross-rhythms with drummer Lawrence Marable. Few West Coast pianists of the early 1950s could have pulled off this type of syncopated phrasing at such tempos, but Hawes does it with apparent ease. Hawes's polytonal statement of the melody of "What Is This Thing Called Love?" is equally striking—this intriguing, albeit uncharacteristic, bit of experimentation bears more resemblance to Brubeck circa 1951 than it does to Hawes early or late.

Much of our knowledge of Hawes's earliest work comes from amateur recordings. Several live performances by Hawes's trio from 1952 were recorded by Bob Andrews, a jazz devotee who brought his portable Pentron recorder to various Southern California jazz spots to capture the emerging sounds of West Coast jazz. These diverse performances do not match the early 1951 session; still they show that Hawes, by his early twenties, had already assimilated much of the jazz piano tradition. On fast and medium numbers he shows a penchant for the rapid-fire right-hand lines of Bud Powell—Hawes's December 23, 1952, performance of "Just One of Those Things" is especially impressive in this regard—while on slow ad lib introductions he tends toward baroque embellishments reminiscent of Art Tatum's.

Yet much of his playing, even at this early date, is pure Hampton Hawes. The distinctive timbre of his notes and the whip-cracking snap of his comping chords were the calling cards of Hawes's keyboard style. This inspired work in the local clubs led to his increasing presence on studio sessions, including the aforementioned recording with Shorty Rogers and the memorable 1953 live date with the Lighthouse All-Stars—the session that determined producer Les Koenig to feature Hawes on his Contemporary label.

In the interim, Hawes was drafted. By this time he was already suffering from heroin addiction. At the induction physical, the presiding doctor noticed the prominent needle marks on Hawes arm. The pianist was referred to a psychiatrist, who told him that he could be exempted from service but, if he thought he could handle it, could choose to be conscripted. Hawes agreed to serve. The decision proved to be a disastrous mistake.

Hawes never saw combat in the Korean War—the war ended one day after his ship left for the combat arena—but his luck stopped there. His chronic unsuitability for the rigid strictures of military life precipitated a string of disciplinary actions, ultimately leading to court-martial and incarceration. In February 1955, after serving time in both Japan and the United States, Hawes was released and returned to Los Angeles to resume his music career. Koenig, now given his opportunity to record Hawes, decided to avoid the sterility of the studio environment as well as experiment with the live acoustics of the Police Academy auditorium. Koenig afterwards reflected—in a classic understatement—that "it had been an unusual record date."

It was also an extraordinarily successful date. Critic Nat Hentoff, writing in *Downbeat*, greeted the release with the highest words of praise: "This is the most exciting album I've heard from the coast in the over two years that I've been reviewing records for the 'Beat." Red Mitchell, the bassist on the nocturnal session, later recollected "a whole stack of good reviews" resulting from the project. Opening with a heated rendition of "I've Got Rhythm," Hawes demonstrated the various qualities that would become trademarks of his playing. A whole generation of keyboard players imitated pioneering bebop pianist Bud Powell's linear style, but Hawes was one of the few who also captured the scorching intensity of Powell's pianism. The styles of Tommy Flanagan, Duke Jordan, Hank Jones, John Lewis, Barry Harris, Lennie Tristano, Ahmad Jamal, Jimmy Rowles, Thelonious Monk, Bill Evans, Dave Brubeck—to name just a few jazz pianists working in the 1950s—all revealed Powell's influence to some degree, especially in their conception of melodic development, but none could match the master's inner flame, the burning energy that made each note sizzle.

Hawes was drawn to precisely this aspect of Powell's playing. He developed a keyboard attack that, while remaining distinctively his own, achieved an inner power similar to Powell's. With Hawes, it is the quality of *sound* in his playing that can be almost mesmerizing, the music somehow transcending the individual notes played. This is the meaning behind Hawes's later boast: "I'm doing something with the piano that nobody else is doing."[2]; On fast tempos his playing was absolutely exhilarating, and his knack for blues progressions was such that one can hardly quibble with John Mehagen's early judgment: "Undoubtedly, Hamp plays the best blues in jazz piano today."[3] Hawes's sound was truly like no one else's.

He was the John Henry of the jazz keyboard, with the power of a steam drill, but still remaining all too human.

Hawes's ballad playing was still undeveloped at this point. His ad lib choruses relied too heavily on stock cocktail piano devices. Problems with creating a fresh, comfortable ballad style were fairly widespread among West Coast jazz pianists during the mid-1950s. Despite a stereotyped view of West Coast pianists as restrained melodicists, the truth was quite the opposite: Hawes, Pete Jolly, Claude Williamson, Lou Levy, Carl Perkins, and others were at their best on medium to fast tempos and showed, if anything, a reluctance to play ballads at very slow tempos. (The surprising exception here is Brubeck, whose cranky and deeply personal ballad statements from the 1950s rank among the finest achievements of his career). Part of their problem stemmed from the model set by Bud Powell. Powell's ballad approach, far less individualized and modern than his other work, relied heavily on devices assimilated from Art Tatum. Even at the peak of his career, Powell's ballads—for example, "I'll Keep Loving You" from 1949 or "A Nightingale Sang in Berkeley Square" from 1951—had little of the innovative spark of his other work. He approached these numbers in one of several ways: He imitated Tatum's older style; or he doubled the tempo (as he does briefly to good effect on "Nightingale") and played the piece as a medium up-tempo number; or he fell into a rhapsodic cocktail style. Hawes adopted these same basic mannerisms for his 1955 recordings of "So In Love" and "Stella by Starlight." By the late 1950s, however, a more modern ballad style had emerged in the playing of Bill Evans, Ahmad Jamal, Wynton Kelly, and others, with an indigenous approach to harmony and rhythm that followed the model of neither Powell nor Tatum. Today's mainstream ballad style builds off these later developments, just as Powell's basic innovations still are at the heart of the up-tempo work of virtually every modern straight-ahead pianist. Hawes also benefited from these later developments, for by the 1970s his ballad style was exceptional. One could hear the influence of younger players, such as Evans, Herbie Hancock, and Keith Jarrett, assimilated into his work.

On the strength of the initial trio recording, Hawes was chosen Arrival of the Year by *Metronome* magazine and finished sixth in voting in the 1955 *Downbeat* poll. Koenig, anxious to capitalize on the success of his new recording artist, scheduled a follow-up project for the pianist. Five months after the first date, Hawes returned to the studio to record a second trio album for Contemporary. This time Koening opted to record at what he euphemistically called the "Contemporary studio"—actually the back-room warehouse at the company's office. It was perhaps the dual function of this back room that served as the original inspiration for Koenig's repeated scheduling of sessions in the wee hours, the easiest time to clear the warehouse without disrupting business. Otherwise, Koenig was a perfectionist when it came to sound quality. He supervised disk mastering in-house—a rare step for an independent label—and developed such a reputation for quality that major labels began sending him mastering work. At the studio sessions, Koenig had a reputation for giving musicians free rein on most artistic issues, but he remained dictatorial when it came to getting the initial sound balance right. His acute care shows in the finished product; the Contemporary releases are among the best-recorded jazz albums of the 1950s.

Moving into a supposedly "cold" studio environment, Hawes maintained all the spontaneous energy that had characterized the earlier trio date. His ballad conception is still overly florid, but on numbers such as "Yesterdays" and "Steeplechase" he again displays the sweep and power of his keyboard attack. Koenig quickly followed up with a third trio release, and the band was soon being booked by Billy Shaw at top clubs around the country. Hawes was earning $1,500 per week at Basin Street, Storyville, the Embers, and other important jazz nightspots.

At Basin Street, Hawes was awarded the dubious honor of having three different critics assigned by *Downbeat* to scrutinize his performance. Nat Hentoff, Leonard Feather, and Michael Levin reported back to the magazine's readers on September 5, 1956, with three detailed assessments of this upstart trio from west of the Rockies. Levin was by far the most critical. Hawes was, he admitted, "a very soft-spoken, honest and pleasant gent," but his playing left much to be desired. His music was "played with a crisp but unvarying and unshaded tone; a rhythmic uneasiness at up-tempos, especially with regards to shifting fingering in the second and third fingers, right hand; a tendency to get florid at slow tempos, still with the same brittleness of tone."[4] Levin concluded that "either Basin Street ain't Hamp's dish, or he really has basic playing problems."

Today these criticisms seem terribly narrow-minded. One wonders at the mentality that could unhesitatingly classify the remarkable crispness of Hawes's piano tone—perhaps the most impressive aspect of his playing—as a technical flaw! Feather's comments were far more positive: Hawes was "a superb, swinging modern jazzman. . . . His touch is admirable, his technique exceptional, his taste almost perfect." Hentoff, who had favorably reviewed Hawes's album some months earlier, devoted most of his space to encomiums about the rest of the trip. "Red Mitchell," he wrote, "has become not just one of the better young bassists, but one of the most creative bassists in all of jazz. . . . Chuck Thompson, who sounded good enough on records, is even more memorable 'live.' He is an unusually spare, functional drummer who does not lean on his top cymbal all night, whose accessories are just that, and who possesses an unfailing sense of time."

Levin's reservations notwithstanding, the East Coast tour was an important success for Hawes, bringing his music to the attention of a large audience beyond the confines of Southern California. Hawes's increasing notoriety as a musician was, however, coming hand in hand with the disintegration of his private life. His growing income was as much a curse as a blessing, as more and more money went toward feeding his drug addiction. "I was no longer enjoying the recognition or the crowds, just waiting for my pay so I could try to cop and keep myself feeling human."[5] During his 1956 tour Hawes had trouble finding reliable sources of heroin on the road; he often resorted to flying his New York connection to wherever he was performing. In St. Louis, Hawes finally cancelled the last part of the tour, and he returned to Los Angeles.

Hawes's problems continued on the West Coast. Opportunity was knocking, but Hawes was in no mood to open the door. By the fall of 1956, he was regularly showing up late for performances—or missing them altogether. A Hollywood studio representative approached him about doing a soundtrack. A *Downbeat* editor wanted to talk to him about publishing his solos. The great jazz virtuoso Art Tatum invited Hawes to his house to exchange musical ideas. Hawes never found the time to follow up on these opportunities. It was during a gig with Stan Getz at the Tiffany Club that Hawes was greeted by his boyhood hero Tatum. "Son, you hot," he told the awed Hawes. "That's like the King telling you you're one of the most loyal and courageous subjects in the land," Hawes would later write in *Raise Up off Me.*[6] Only a few weeks later Tatum was dead.

As the Tatum anecdote suggests, Hawes's playing at this time showed little sign of the strains on his personal life. He *was* hot. But he was also burning out of control. Only a few days after Tatum's death, Hawes would undertake the most successful and impressive session of his career. But the growing acclaim awarded to Hawes's music was by now only accentuating the incongruity between the success of his public life and the dissolution of his personal affairs. Hawes was soaring high but would soon go into a tailspin that threatened to be fatal. He was, in his own words, the man with the 105° fever.

make it in my home town

When Parker and Gillespie played at Billy Berg's in December 1945, two local teenagers sat together in rapt admiration on opening night. For eighteen-year-old Sonny Criss and seventeen-year-old Hampton Hawes, this evening out proved to be a turning point in their lives. Billy Berg's provided both their Pauline experience—it was their road to Damascus by way of Vine Street. "I was molded on the spot," Hawes later described the evening, "like a piece of clay stamped out." Criss was even more moved—so moved that he decided to track down Parker at all costs. Learning of the group's accommodations, the young altoist made his way to the First Street Hotel, where Parker was staying. "I went to the desk. They told me what room. Then I knocked on the door. No answer. Then I knocked. I was really determined. I was still at school. No answer. So I wouldn't give up. I just kept knocking because they had told me he was there. And finally he peeked out of the peep-hole. I told him who I was, and he let me in."[7]

Both Criss and Hawes became intimates of their older role model, tending to his various needs and eventually earning the opportunity to perform with him. Because of his access to a Model T Ford with a rumble seat, Sonny was awarded the privilege of sharing Hampton's responsibilities as Bird's chauffeur. Parker in turn introduced his followers to an intense nonstop lifestyle unlike anything hitherto known at Jefferson High. Criss later recalled: "Bird and the fellows used to get into that car—seven or eight fellows in there, I don't know how we managed it—and we would go down to First Street in the Oriental section, up to Central Avenue in the Negro section and from there to Hollywood—we just went every place to play. We even played at Inglewood. Sometimes we used to go on like this for three or four days at a time without sleeping."[8] Criss became part of the expanded Howard McGhee band in which Parker was a sideman.

For the next thirty years, until Criss's suicide in 1977, this gifted musician kept faithful to the blistering bebop idiom he had learned firsthand from the master. Other West Coast alto saxophonists had different responses to the challenge of Parker's genius: Some switched to tenor or baritone, despairing of developing their own sound in the shadow of Bird; others, such as Paul Desmond and Lennie Niehaus, perfected a "cool" alternative to the bebop style, which allowed them a fair degree of individuality outside Bird's expansive shadow; still others, such as Dean Benedetti, simply gave up the saxophone altogether after hearing Parker, switching from being a musician to just being a fan of the new music. Bird's dominant influence was enough to drive many musicians (and not just altoists) to extremes.

Criss was one of the few to confront the challenge head on. More than any other West Coaster, Criss strived from the start to make Parker's music his own. As an unabashed bebopper during the years in which West Coast jazz was supposedly restricted to cool melodicism, Criss risked being the odd man out in a real-life version of musical chairs. Yet even though Criss never reached a large audience, he could boast of a cult following, one that is still going strong over a decade after his death. Jazz historian Bob Porter expressed the views of this devoted contingent of admirers when he wrote, shortly after Criss's suicide: "Sonny's was a talent too big to be

denied. For me, he comes immediately after Bird as an alto saxophonist.
. . . I don't know anyone who was exposed to his playing who didn't
enjoy him."

Perhaps the problem was, as Porter hints, that so few people were
exposed to Criss's music. Sonny's career took place in Los Angeles (except
for a short time, in Europe). He never made the East Coast move, which
benefited other West Coast talents such as Charles Mingus, Eric Dolphy,
and Dexter Gordon. And Los Angeles never appreciated the loyalty of this
adopted native son—Criss, like so many others schooled in the clubs and
after-hours spots of Central Avenue, struggled to find performance opportunities in Southern California. After the end of the Central Avenue era,
work dried up—especially for black bop-oriented players. Still Criss never
seriously considered making the move east. When interviewer Harvey Siders
later asked Criss why he returned to Los Angeles from overseas at the low
point for jazz in the mid-1960s, the altoist replied: "Why man, this is my
home. Sure, I had a ball [in Europe], but I've got to give myself the chance
to make it in my hometown."

Sonny Criss's musical development took place when the Central Avenue scene was at its peak. Born in Memphis, Tennessee, on October 23,
1927, Sonny began his musical studies on the saxophone at age eleven.
Lucy Criss, who still resides in Los Angeles, described to me the begin-
nings of her son's musical interests:

> He came home and said, "Momma, I'd like to play the saxophone." I told
> him he would have to work to earn the money for it. And he did. He worked
> at a local drugstore—he was a delivery boy. He earned enough money for a
> down payment. After that my husband and I helped with the payments.[9]

Four years later the Criss family moved to California. Sonny was
fifteen years old and, by all accounts, a natural musician who was advancing quickly on his instrument. In Los Angeles he practiced assiduously,
and while still attending high school he began working regularly on Central Avenue. "The first band I joined was an outfit with Hampton Hawes,
Buddy Woodson, Leon Moore, and we worked the Last Word. I was still
in school. In fact on graduation night I played a duet with Big Jay Mc-
Neely—I think it was Chopin's 'Minute Waltz'—in high school, and right
after we had to make it to the gig."

Criss had heard Parker on record long before he crossed paths with
the older altoist in Los Angeles. Ross Russell, in his biography of Parker,
Bird Lives, quotes Criss to the effect that he started "in a completely new
direction" after hearing the Jay McShann band's version of "Hootie Blues."[10]
Russell mistakenly explains that Criss heard Bird with McShann after buying
the latter's record on Central Avenue, but Criss claimed he was still in

Memphis when he heard the McShann recordings. And the degree of influence of the McShann work is open to question. To Bob Porter and Mark Gardner, Criss explained that on the McShann records Parker "sounded like he was moving with Prez. He hadn't really gotten into his own thing yet." At that time Criss was more impressed by his teacher Hank O'Day, one of the top saxophonists in Memphis during the war years. "Very strange looking man. With a head about so big," Criss described him. "But he had a kind of sound that I had never heard before. Very beautiful and very powerful. Even today, I haven't heard that kind of sound he had."[11]

But Criss had switched his allegiance to Parker by the time the latter came to California at the close of 1945. Bebop records were hard to come by on the West Coast during those days. Criss relates: "My mother had gone to Chicago. I had heard about the new records but I couldn't get them. So I told her to look for them, and she found them."[12] Among the records she brought back was "Congo Blues," recorded in New York on June 6, 1945, with Parker and Dizzy Gillespie in a group under the leadership of Red Norvo. Parker's work here was anything but a rehash of Lester Young: the technical virtuosity and dazzling melodic ingenuity he (as well as Gillespie) demonstrated on this piece must have been frightening to hear in 1945, especially for a young musician who hoped to imitate this high example. The disdain expressed by many older musicians for bebop made Criss's task all the more difficult: "We were the minority and we had a hard row to hoe. People just wouldn't accept it. The majority of musicians wouldn't accept it, the older ones wouldn't let us play. They used to say 'these be-boppers don't know what they are doing.' We had to form a kind of little clique among ourselves, just as Bird and Diz did in the East. We played at each other's homes."

Criss's home environment offered him the support that was lacking in the outside music community. Lucy Criss mentions that the family's move from Memphis to California was largely motivated by the desire to raise Sonny in a more tolerant environment. Once settled in Southern California, Sonny commuted every day to a racially mixed high school on the west side. Finally he balked when he learned that the best school band was "in the ghetto." Soon he was allowed to transfer to nearby Jefferson High School, where Sam Browne had created a strong jazz education program.

One side of Criss rarely appreciated by the jazz public was his strong work ethic. His powerful virtuosity on the alto was not, he took pains to point out, an untutored, inborn gift but was acquired by subjecting his native talent to hard work and discipline. Lucy Criss recalls: "I never had to tell him to practice. When the other boys would come to see him they would have to wait until he was done practicing." Criss's later comments on Charlie Parker are also revealing in this regard; while other onlookers praised Parker as the inspired genius of bop, Criss saw him in a much different light. He admired Parker's music as the product of extraordinary self-discipline: "There is a misconception about Bird. A lot of people say he was a born genius, but that's wrong. He wasn't born with anything except the ability to breathe. Unless you really apply yourself to music, nothing is going to happen." Criss clearly saw himself in the same light: as a self-made musician, one whose mature ability was the result of years of dedicated effort.

The celebrated Elks Club concert of July 6, 1947—best remembered for the tenor battle recorded that day between Dexter Gordon and Wardell Gray—served notice of another saxophone master on the rise. On "The Hunt," Criss takes four heated choruses that leave little doubt as to either the youngster's talent or his loyalty to the Parker model. His technique at this point—he was still several months shy of his twentieth birthday—is not as fluid as it would soon be, but even here the passion that always characterized his playing is evident throughout. For someone so soft-spoken and private offstage, Criss was a different person entirely in front of an audience.

Around this time Criss joined a small combo under the leadership of high-note trumpeter Al Killian. This band, which also included Wardell Gray, was initially formed to back up Billy Eckstine at Billy Berg's Hollywood club, but soon the group was on the road as a stand-alone unit. They played in Los Angeles, San Francisco, and Seattle and stayed for several months in Portland. A recording made in Portland on October 17, 1947, shows that Criss's advocacy of modern jazz continued even in this more swing-era oriented group setting. The rest of the group, despite Killian's stated goal of playing bebop, remained fairly rooted in the earlier style.

Trumpeter Killian, nominal leader of the Portland ensemble, would bring his high-note expertise to the Duke Ellington band later that same year. At the time of the Portland recording he was flirting with the modern jazz idiom, but he—like so many players of his generation—never managed to play the newer style with any conviction. His work alongside Criss shows that his conception is definitely premodern. (Like his two colleagues in the front line, Killian met a tragic and senseless end. Three years after these recordings Killian, only thirty-three years old, was murdered in his East 35th Street apartment by a deranged janitor.) Tenorist Gray solos with his usual aplomb, but very much in a prebop Lester Young vein. Teenager Criss, in contrast, is here undeterred by his older bandmates—he remains firmly entrenched in the bebop idiom. As with the Elks

Club concert, Criss's technical command of the instrument was not yet fully formed, but even at this young age he demonstrates a firm sense of musical direction. Criss manages to garner some musical support from drummer Tim Kennedy, who also sounds like a full-fledged modernist. He and the altoist take flight over the chord changes of "Blue Lou" and "Out of Nowhere." These recordings remained unissued for many years; their eventual release was made possible only because Criss kept the originals in his possession.

By the close of the decade Criss had developed into a virtuoso altoist in the Parker mold. A September 22, 1949, quartet session for Norman Granz finds Criss alongside his longtime friend Hampton Hawes and shows the strides Criss had made in the months since the Killian recording. On "Tornado" (actually a renamed version of the bop standard "Wee"), he provides some accompanying lightning with his relentless sixteenth-note barrage at high speed. His playing on "The First One" is only a notch less impressive. Hawes gets little of the solo space on the four-sides—an especially unfortunate circumstance given his ensuing two-year absence from recording studios—but his few contributions show that he, like Criss, was by now playing bop with a sure sense for the idiom. From spectators at Billy Berg's, the two players had advanced by the time of their early twenties into leaders of the new music on the coast.

Although Criss's sound and conception stayed true to the model set by Bird, several differences are striking. Criss tends more toward even streams of notes, only occasionally matching Parker's masterful start-and-stop rhythmic phrasing. And even more than Parker, Criss maintained a strong gospel-ish blues bent in his playing. A previously unknown recording from this period, which was released after Criss's death on the Pablo label, showcases this latter aspect of his style. The album, *Intermission Riff*, captures a live performance at the Shrine Auditorium in Los Angeles from October 12, 1951. Criss then only a few days shy of his twenty-fourth birthday, fronts a seven-piece band that included some of the finest modern jazz musicians of the time. Bassist Tommy Potter and drummer Kenny Clarke had performed and recorded frequently with Parker, while pianist Bobby Tucker was a 52nd Street veteran who could fit easily into either a swing or bebop setting. Joining Criss in the front line were tenorist Eddie Davis, trumpeter Joe Newman, and trombonist Bennie Green.

Electricity is in the air every time Criss solos. Although his colleagues on the bandstand make major contributions (especially Davis), it is the altoist who rivets the listener's attention. On "How High the Moon," Criss, Davis, and company play with fierce energy. At one point the audience interrupts Criss's solo with roaring applause for a particularly gripping chorus; Criss, oblivious of the crowd, plays on as if in the heat of a private jam session. On "High Jump" he digs in even deeper with cascading streams of Parker-like sixteenth notes that slowly build into a repeated blues riff. Time and time again Criss combines his rapid-fire technique, now fully polished, with a powerful emotional urgency and an unfailing instinct for the blues.

It is hard to understand why the tapes of this extraordinary session gathered dust for over thirty-five years before being rediscovered by archivist Eric Miller. Recorded by Norman Granz as part of his prolific Jazz at the Philharmonic sessions of the 1950s, the Criss date somehow got lost in the shuffle. It was only after the sale of Granz's Pablo label to Berkeley's Fantasy Records that the tapes were found on a shelf in a crowded Bekins storage room. The box was simply marked JATP/Shrine/'51. The neglect of the tapes may have been due to a few moments of sound problems still evident on the released recording. More likely, Granz became preoccupied with the better-known artists in his jazz entourage, such as Ella Fitzgerald, Oscar Peterson, and Lester Young.

The following year Criss had the opportunity to match musical wits with his early mentor when Parker returned to the coast for a series of performances with local players. Bass player Harry Babasin, who ran a regular jam session at the Trade Winds in Inglewood, a fairly undistinguished suburban nightspot with a pseudo-Polynesian decor, found himself in dazzling company on one particular Monday night in mid-June. Charlie Parker, Chet Baker, and Sonny Criss all showed up to front a rhythm section consisting of Babasin, Lawrence Marable on drums, and Al Haig and Russ Freeman sharing honors on the out-of-tune piano.

"Sonny made his reputation by cutting Parker on those few nights when Bird was strung out," recalls one musician from the period. "But then Bird would come back all the stronger the next night and give Sonny a lesson." Bird was more in a lesson-giving mood on this particular evening. He burns brightly on the alto, drawing on the seemingly bottomless fund of ideas that always made his playing a thing apart from his imitators'. Criss is not intimidated, or at least doesn't show it if he is. He comes across as, if anything, less Bird-inflected than usual, instead building on the same hard-driving blues vocabulary that had served him well with the JATP group. On "The Squirrel," Criss takes two solos, separated by contributions by Haig and Baker, before Parker finally enters; Sonny's first effort stands almost as an homage to Bird, while the second is Criss unadulterated. Although Baker, only weeks away from his leap to stardom with the Mulligan group, was gigging with Parker at the time, he appears less able to play his own game than Criss. The latter rose to the challenge on this evening, even if he stopped well short of "cutting" his idol. Then again, no one was going to approach Parker when he played at this high level.

Criss's style would change little in later years. As with many of his contemporaries, Criss felt little desire to go beyond the bebop idiom of the postwar period. He believed that this approach to improvisation, drenched in chromaticism and rhythmic pyrotechnics, still represented the greatest degree of melodic complexity possible within a tonal sytem. No wonder that any "advance" beyond bebop was likely to seem to Criss, and others of his temperament, as regress rather than progress. If Criss tempered his bop chops, it was not with a step ahead into the avant-garde but rather with a backward glance to the blues. By his early twenties Criss knew precisely what he wanted to achieve in his music. Over the next thirty years he pursued this vision with great tenacity and artistic, if not commercial, success.

By the time of the Inglewood jam, Central Avenue was a jazz ghost town. Most of the clubs had closed or would soon do so. A few downtown venues continued to flourish on Western Avenue or Hollywood Boulevard, but more often jazz was spreading beyond the city limits. Mimicking Southern California's growing urban sprawl, the jazz nightspots also moved to the suburbs. The next generation of clubs, such as the Lighthouse in Hermosa Beach, would reflect these changing demographics.

While many of the jazz musicians of his generation were entering the studios, if only for financial security, Criss continued to cling to the shrinking LA market for live jazz. "Sonny could have done the studio scene," recalls pianist Dick Whittington, who gigged extensively with Criss in the latter part of the decade.[13] "He could read the spots off the page. He certainly was capable of doing studio work. I don't know if he didn't care to, or maybe he didn't have the opportunities."

For whatever reasons, Criss supported himself during part of the 1950s by, among other things, playing at burlesque clubs. "The bottom dropped out so far as jazz work was concerned," he later said. Whittington recalls that "there were probably ten strip joints in LA, and they would hire a three-piece band. They'd have saxophone, piano, and drums. No bass— they didn't feel they needed that. They just wanted a melody and the rhythm, especially that drum beat. Everybody worked strip gigs. Hampton Hawes, Carl Perkins, Walter Norris, Herb and Lorraine Geller."

Occasional club performances and road trips helped Criss keep one foot in the jazz world, but his morale suffered throughout this period. Despite the sub-par conditions in which he often worked, Criss still maintained an attitude of total professionalism in his work. "He was business-like—I learned a lot about being a leader of a band from him," Whittington continues. "And he always dressed to kill, no matter how funky the place was we were playing. Sonny's shirt would be starched; he'd be wearing a diamond stickpin; and he might be wearing a Paris suit. Of course he was a handsome guy, and suave, and the chicks used to be falling all over him."

Like many jazz players of his generation, Criss encountered a degree of artistic acceptance and economic security overseas not possible in the United States. But though his work in Europe in the early 1960s was well received, Criss longed to be back in California. By 1965 he was home and again out of work. At this time Criss paid out of pocket to record a demo tape with a quartet and managed to land a contract with the Prestige label. This led to a second period of fruitful activity in the studio, one that lasted until the Prestige association ended in 1969. The Prestige recordings show that Criss had lost none of his spark. His musical instincts remained intact and were still imbued with the bop and blues idioms he had mastered two decades earlier.

In the early 1970s, Criss worked as an alcohol rehabilitation counselor and gave concerts for children in the Los Angeles school system. In 1972 he spoke to some 25,000 children about "the beauty, the importance, and the origin of jazz." For extended periods he would make two school visits per day, in addition to his counseling work and other commitments. Musical opportunities were picking up for the saxophonist, with renewed recording and performing activities, at the time of his suicide in 1977. Immediately before his death he had been planning a tour of Japan. Criss had spoken with enthusiasm of the coming trip; he was delighted when he heard that the mayor of Tokyo was planning to greet him upon his arrival. Everything suggested that Japan would be as receptive as Europe had been years before.

The trip never happened. On November 19, 1977, Criss took his own life. For more than a decade after his death, the reasons for Criss's suicide remained unclear. His playing toward the end was in peak form, and audiences were gradually reacquainting themselves with the pleasures of serious jazz such as Criss had to offer. The mystery of his motive was finally cleared up in 1988 when Lucy Criss revealed that her son was suffering from stomach cancer at the time of his death: "He kept still about it and worked for as long as he could."[14] One can easily imagine Criss remaining silent; he was an introspective man, one who carried both his disappointments and his joys quietly within himself. Criss's colleague Teddy Edwards once described him as "a closet full of coats with the shoes underneath," while Dick Whittington spoke of the altoist as "a dormant volcano." Criss rarely complained about whatever troubles he faced, medical or otherwise. Just as rarely did he dwell on his achievements or his hopes for the future. He let his music speak for him. Over a decade after his death, it still does.

blues in Teddy's flat

In the middle and late 1940s, Teddy Edwards was poised to emerge as one of the outstanding tenorists in the modern jazz world. Along with Dexter Gordon and Wardell Gray, Edwards was one of the few California tenors with a growing national reputation. His recordings for the Dial label not only were among the best tenor sides in modern jazz, they were among the first. No lesser an authority than trumpeter Fats Navarro, citing Edwards's early recording of "Up in Dodo's Room," credited the saxophonist with being the first bebop tenor player, the first to create an authentic modern sound freed from the models of either Coleman Hawkins or Lester Young. Whether this Edwards recording is, in fact, the birth of bop tenor on record may be open to question, but about the quality of these early sides there can be little doubt. One of the strongest players among the Central Avenue regulars, Edwards appeared to have laid the groundwork during the late 1940s for jazz stardom in the 1950s.

Yet if recording opportunies for Sonny Criss were rare in the early 1950s, for Teddy Edwards they became virtually nonexistent. During the short tenure of Dial Records in Los Angeles, Edwards emerged as one of the label's up-and-coming stars, but after Ross Russell moved to the East Coast, Edwards's recording career went into hibernation. With the exception of a brief recording stint with the Rex label, Edwards was entering a period not of stardom but of semiretirement. Not until the late 1950s would he begin appearing in the recording studio with any regularity, and by then the whole West Coast scene—white or black, hot or cool—was on the wane.

Although many West Coast musicians of Edwards's generation were beset by personal tragedy, few suffered more from pure bad luck. A series of recurring medical afflictions—gall bladder trouble as well as several oral surgeries necessitated by problems with his teeth—haunted Edwards throughout the 1950s, often sidelining him for months on end. When he was able to play, Edwards distinguished himself by being in the right place at *almost* the right time. At the start of the 1950s Edwards stood out as the most prominent member of the Lighthouse All-Stars, and his composition "Sunset Eyes" was the band's most requested number. Yet right before the All-Stars' rise to fame through a series of widely heard recordings, Edwards was dismissed by leader Howard Rumsey when a group of ex-Kenton players suddenly became available for active duty. Rumsey's decision was marked with eventual success, but Edwards was the unfortunate casualty of the affair. Nor was this all. In 1954, Edwards turned down an opportunity to go on the road with the Max Roach/Clifford Brown band because he had recently married and felt that the time was not right for an extended road engagement. The Roach/Brown band went on to become the most celebrated bop quintet of its day. Edwards never got another chance at such a high-profile gig. The tenorist's life during the heyday of West Coast jazz is an extended account of just such missed opportunities and misfortunes.

Born on April 26, 1924, in Jackson, Mississippi, Edwards began playing alto saxophone at age eleven and soon added clarinet to his repertoire. His early development must have been prodigious: Only six months after beginning musical studies he was performing with Doc Parmley and his Royal Mississippians. Precedents for Edwards's musical talent were not hard to find in the family. His grandfather, Henry C. Reed, had been a bassist, and his father, Bruce Edwards, had played trombone, violin, and reeds. "I was still in school then," Edwards recalls of his professional debut at age twelve, "but on summer vacations I would go on the road. I was good in school, so there was no problem." [15] Edwards's formal training on the saxophone was restricted to a few early lessons with Arthur Horne, who had played with the Don Dunbar band. "I was mostly self-taught," Edwards explains. "After those six months of lessons my teacher told me I had learned everything he could teach me."

True to form, Edwards became a West Coast jazz musician more or less by mischance. As a young man he had joined the Ernie Fields Orchestra because the leader promised him that the band was going to New York. Fields told him: "You can go to New York and have some money in your pocket." [16] Edwards recalls: "The next job was in Pensacola, Florida. The next job was somewhere in Louisiana. The next job"—at this point Edwards starts to laugh— "was in Tulsa, Oklahoma. He was taking me further and further away." Edwards eventually found himself with Fields at the opposite end of the continent: By way of Lincoln, Nebraska, they had arrived at the Club Alabam on Central Avenue. Although he left the city soon after with Field's band, before long he was back, this time playing rhythm and blues with Roy Milton. In Los Angeles, Edwards continued to work as an altoist until, after joining Howard McGhee's bop band, he switched to tenor at Maggie's suggestion.

A sideman date with the band on October 18, 1946, gave Edwards a chance to show off his talent for the new instrument. On an earlier session with the trumpeter, Edwards had been asked by McGhee to try to imitate Coleman Hawkins's sound on the tenor, but this time around Edwards decided to break away from the tenor tradition and, instead, aim at capturing his alto conception on the lower horn. His work on "Up in Dodo's Room" and "Dialated Pupils" showed the wisdom of this decision. Whereas McGhee's bop style depended on nonstop streams of notes, Edwards broached a more subdued style in which lyrical passages were countered with brief flurries of music, much in a Parkeresque vein. If one is looking for comparisons here, the obvious one is with the Parker recordings on tenor made with Miles Davis, yet this similar-sounding session was still some six and a half months in the future.

Edwards's growing reputation justified follow-up work for Dial. On the eve of the American Federation of Musicians recording ban, producer Ross Russell wanted to bring Dexter Gordon into the studio for a last session. In the light of the great success Dial had achieved with the Gordon–Gray tenor battle on "The Chase," Russell proposed to re-create the format with an Edwards–Gordon match-up. The same session also found Edwards recording "Blues in Teddy's Flat" as a leader. This piece features the tenorist from start to finish and is perhaps his most impressive work from the period. Opening with an a cappella introduction, Edwards leads into an earthy twelve-bar blues that becomes more adventurous as it develops. The second and third choruses contain an impressive recital of angular phrases, half Bird and half Monk, with constant surprises in the intervallic leaps. At the top of the fourth chorus, however, Edwards suddenly breaks into a shower of double-time phrases over a convoluted stoptime pattern. The rhythm section falters here for a moment, entering out of synch, but Edwards never hesitates. He continues his aggressive attack for several choruses, moving into a masterful exercise in syncopated accents at double time before settling back into a gospel-ish groove to conclude the number. This was Edwards at his best. Such performances promised extraordinary things to come.

As it turned out, this memorable date also proved to be Dial's last session in California, as well as one of Edwards's last recording opportunities for almost a decade. Edwards recorded a few sides during 1948, despite the recording ban, for the Rex label. Run out of a small record store on Hollywood Boulevard, Rex was a tiny independent with a reputation of not paying its artists. The illegal nature of the proceedings required using a nonprofessional home studio in the Valley. Edwards's playing is at a consistently high level on the eight 78 sides made for Rex, but these were poorly recorded and even more poorly distributed. At the time they did little to further Edwards's career. As it stood he would only record once more—and then as a sideman—during the next nine years. His career appeared destined to end just as it was ready to take off.

Edwards's one sideman date on the period was, however, glamorous by any standards. When Gene Norman first recorded the Clifford Brown/Max Roach Quintet during their Los Angeles stay, Edwards was holding down the tenor chair, having replaced Sonny Stitt. Edwards continued with the Roach/Brown Quintet through most of the band's lengthy 1954 engagement in Southern California. But when the group left to go on the road, Edwards decided to stay in Los Angeles with his recent bride, and he was replaced by Harold Land. In retrospect, it is clear that Edwards declined what turned out to be the most prominent tenor chair in the modern jazz scene of the day: Harold Land's reputation in the jazz world was enhanced enormously through this early association, while Land's successor, Sonny Rollins, used the visibility as a springboard into jazz superstardom.

Like other musicians outside the more publicized "West Coast jazz" movement, Edwards scuffled from gig to gig. In a 1962 interview for *Downbeat,* he recalled "taking anything that came along—rock and roll, burlesque and so on."[17] At this time his situation was aggravated by the aforementioned series of health problems that further restricted his playing. Finally, in 1957, an album as sideman with bassist Leroy Vinnegar brought him back into the recording studio. In 1960 his recording career took off in earnest with leader dates for Pacific *(Sunset Eyes)* and Contemporary *(Teddy's Ready),* two major Los Angeles labels, which had expressed little interest in Edwards in years past. Some belated recognition was starting to come his way, furthered by follow-up recordings for Contemporary throughout the early 1960s. By the time of his 1961 reunion album with Howard McGhee, released as *Together Again!* Edwards had reversed roles with his former bandleader. This session finds Edwards in superior form, combining his bop chops with a sensitivity to the more modern contributions of Coltrane and Rollins, while McGhee plays capably but a notch below his work of the earlier period. McGhee, in town as part of James Moody's group, had also gone through some lean years, at least partly due to his agonizing struggle with drugs. By this time Maggie's career was also on a modest upswing, but the trumpeter would never match the recorded legacy of his early career.

Edwards, in contrast, was still growing and maturing as a player, and these early 1960s works garnered strong reviews, for the most part, from the critics. However, it was a case of too little, too late. By the early 1960s, West Coast jazz was already in decline, with a shrinking audience for both recorded and live jazz. The breakdown of the Central Avenue scene a decade earlier now proved to be a harbinger of the collapse of the whole Southern California jazz community. Even the recently anointed stars of white West Coast jazz were being forced underground into studio work and other nonjazz gigs. Edwards's career suffered on both occasions. A few years earlier, these strong albums might have served to boost the tenor saxophonist into a position of preeminence in the jazz world. As it was the 1960s were years of retrenchment in which major stars struggled and new names (which Edwards's was to many fans) found it all the harder to make a reputation. The early 1960s comeback proved ultimately to be much like the earlier 1945–48 interlude in Edwards's career: a brief oasis in the midst of a much longer period beyond the pale.

the man with the 105° fever

A week after Art Tatum's death, Hampton Hawes returned to the studio to record what would be his greatest work. Trying to re-create the late-night ambience of Hawes's first session on Contemporary, producer Koenig planned another midnight recording date. This time the results were even more memorable—and more unusual. Starting in the evening of November 12, 1956, and working well into the night, Hawes and his group recorded no less than three complete albums' worth of material. To emphasize the spontaneity of the music, Koenig decided to issue the performances in the exact order in which they were recorded.

The three albums, released as *All Night Session!* volumes 1–3, reveal the wisdom of his decision. The two hours of music captured on these album sides highlight the virtues of Hawes's playing. His noted keyboard attack was a rare hybrid: He combined the clarity and swing of Oscar Peterson with the scorching intensity of bebop master Bud Powell. (It comes as little suprise that Hawes, in a 1955 interview in *Downbeat*, cited Powell and Peterson as his two favorite pianists.)[18] Hawes's crisp, percussive sound, his sure sense of time, his finely etched solos—all of these qualities are demonstrated time and time again on the *All Night Session!* releases.

Hawes's driving improvisation on "Blue 'n Boogie" is a case in point. He starts his solo with a string of isolated notes dropped like drum hits on the off beat. The melodic phrases gradually become more and more complex, and the rhythmic intensity rises perceptibly over several riveting choruses. Hawes finally kicks into an extended outburst of blues-inflected block chords that build to a climax. His improvisation is over—or so it appears. Guitarist Jim Hall tries to enter to take his solo, but Hawes now decides that he is not yet finished. He plays off Hall's melody line with a rhythmic flurry of notes, and the guitarist retreats into the background. Hawes, now driving at full speed, builds his solo up to an even higher pitch than before. Then he slowly brings the energy level down. A final gentle chorus of block chords eventually gives way to the guitar. Hall, chastised the first time around, hesitates for a moment and then embarks on his solo.

One day after the all-night session Hawes celebrated his twenty-eighth birthday. He had much to celebrate. Few live albums have ever captured the immediacy and presence Hawes had achieved during this lengthy studio outing. It stands out as Hawes's most expressive musical legacy of the decade. The response from jazz fans was appropriately enthusiastic. The releases garnered favorable write-ups in the national media. That same year Hawes received the *Downbeat* New Star Award. For exactly two more years Hawes would be at the pinnacle of his career.

Hawes's most frequent accompanist during these years was bassist

Red Mitchell. Years later both Hawes and Mitchell would vividly recall the circumstances under which they met. Hawes wrote in his autobiography:

> John Bennett, owner of the Haig on Wilshire Boulevard, phoned and said if I'm available he wanted me to come in with a trio, and there was a bass player standing right next to him who would be perfect for me . . . I drove down there, and the bass player said, "I'm Red Mitchell, and I think we might have fun playing together." I said, "Well, let's go in and see." Four bars into "All the Things You Are" I turned to him and said, "I think we're going to have fun playing together."[19]

This felicitous collaboration would continue for the rest of Hawes's life. Mitchell participated in almost all of Hawes's projects on Contemporary: He held down the bass chair on the early trio albums, figured prominently on the *All Night Session!* quartet releases, and showed up again on the quartet project *Four*. After Hawes's release from prison, Mitchell would rejoin him on *The Seance* from 1966, one of the pianist's best later works. With Mitchell's move to Europe in 1968, the collaborations with Hawes grew less frequent. At the time of Hawes's death in 1977, however, the duo was scheduled to make a tour of Japan. In 1984, Mitchell told Mike Davis: "I miss him a great deal. He was so much a part of my life, and the world is an infinitely poorer place through his absence."[20]

This memorable musical partnership might never have taken place had it not been for a few cartons of cigarettes. Mitchell, who was born on September 20, 1927, in New York, did not become a bass player until relatively late in life. He studied the piano from the age of five until fourteen, and it remained his chosen instrument when he attended Cornell University on scholarship to study engineering. After being drafted, he played piano and alto sax in an army band, but while serving in Germany he traded fifteen cartons of cigarettes for a bass. The barter proved to be a wise one. Shortly after his release from the army, Mitchell was playing opposite Charlie Parker at the Onyx on 52nd Street. Although this gig only paid $15 a week, Mitchell remembers that "it was just like going to school." With his 52nd Street education under his belt, the bassist went on to work with Jackie Paris, Mundell Lowe, Charlie Ventura, and Woody Herman, among others.

The Herman association was cut short in 1951 by Mitchell's hospitalization for tuberculosis. For over a year he kept away from the music world while he recovered. In 1952 he began performing again, first with Red Norvo and then with Gerry Mulligan. Mitchell decided to remain behind when Mulligan left for New York. Settled in Southern California, he became an important presence on the West Coast jazz scene. In March

1957, Mitchell debuted as a leader on the Contemporary label. This project, released as *Presenting Red Mitchell* (and later reissued under the name
Red Mitchell Quartet), is in keeping with the Hawes recordings of the
same period: The music is hard-swinging jazz in the bebop tradition. The
group, which consisted of Mitchell, drummer Billy Higgins, pianist Lorraine Geller, and saxophonist James Clay, made few concessions to the
stereotyped "West Coast sound"—only the occasional use of counterpoint
lines and Clay's flute work fit in with the more typical California currents.
Shortly after the album's release, when James Clay left for an induction
physical in Dallas and Lorraine Geller departed to devote time to mother-
hood, Mitchell's group disbanded.

One other bassist during this period matched Mitchell's ability to bring
out the best in Hawes. Charles Mingus joined Hampton and drummer
Dannie Richmond in a trio recording made in New York on July 9, 1957.
The quality of the music—in particular Hawes's memorable rendition of
"I Can't Get Started"—was in stark contrast to the turmoil of his personal
life at the time. Hawes later said of his extended stay in New York: "Trying
to remember that trip is like asking someone who has had a 105° fever for
a couple of months how he felt, what went down. . . . Sometimes the
music happened, sometimes it didn't."[21]

Hawes's recordings of this period reveal that it mostly happened. The
Mingus collaboration, a quartet date with Harold Land, Scott LaFaro, and
Frank Butler, work with guitarist Barney Kessel—these showed that Hamp's
keyboard prowess could adapt successfully to many different settings. The
quartet recording *Four* is outstanding—although somewhat strange. Hawes's
piano attack here is even more biting than usual. His playing increasingly
relies on short, choppy phrases that come out of the piano soundboard as
if they were being shot out of a cannon. Land, perhaps to contrast with
this keyboard grapeshot, concentrates on long, elaborate lines on the tenor.
Bass player Scott LaFaro seems at first blush an unlikely choice for a session with Hawes—La Faro's oblique bass style, most prominent in his work
with Bill Evans, no doubt made him one of the most important innovators
on the instrument, but Hawes's strongly percussive approach seemed to
require a more straight-ahead player. LaFaro, however, works surprisingly
well on the date, concentrating on setting a full-sounding, four-to-the-bar
foundation as uncharacteristic of him as it is successful. This is a gripping
record, but the fierce, acerbic quality in Hawes's playing on this date is
somehow disturbing. He is fighting the instrument as much as playing it,
as though he were presciently rebelling against the vicissitudes in store for
him.

Hawes' thirtieth birthday, which took place a short while after the
Four recording, brought an end to the musical accolades. On November
13, 1958, Hawes was arrested for selling narcotics to a federal agent. He

was sentenced to ten years in prison. Incarcerated in a Fort Worth penitentiary, Hawes finally broke himself of his addiction. In 1971, Hawes recalled the agony of quitting cold turkey: "I was so sick that I used to stick lit cigarettes against my arm to change the pain."[22]

After more than two years in prison, Hawes inquired about applying for a pardon from newly elected President John F. Kennedy. Prison officials told him that any hopes for executive clemency were unrealistic, and over a year passed before he could even learn the name of the government's pardon attorney. By March 1963, Hawes had collected eighteen letters of recommendation and completed the government's complex paperwork. On August 16, 1963, Hawes learned that President Kennedy had granted him clemency.

Back on the outside, Hawes began putting together his interrupted career. The 1960s were bad years for the postwar generation of West Coast jazz musicians, and Hawes, like many of his colleagues, had to face an audience that was increasingly indifferent to the bop-inflected music he had to offer. Moreover, Hawes's poor reading ability prevented him from pursuing the studio work that supported so many others during those years. Producer Les Koenig, who had championed the pianist throughout his career, brought Hawes back into the Contemporary fold and over the next several years recorded projects such as *The Green Leaves of Summer, Here and Now, I'm All Smiles,* and *The Seance.*

These albums did not advance very far beyond Hawes's earlier work. Nonetheless they were far better than the projects he made after signing with Fantasy/Prestige in the early 1970s, which found him on electric keyboards in a series of undistinguished efforts neither artistically gratifying nor, as he might have hoped, commercially successful. Like so many other jazz musicians, he now turned to audiences in Europe and Japan, which were keeping the spirit of the music alive while it languished in America. On a trip to Tokyo, Hawes was recorded by both RCA and Columbia in a single week—something virtually inconceivable in Los Angeles.

Perhaps the most important project of his later years was one he did away from the keyboard. Together with writer/pianist Don Asher, Hawes put together his gripping autobiography *Raise Up off Me.* This book, first published in 1974, is an important document in the history of the music. Still more it is a readable and moving work, tragic and comic by turns. It stands out as one of the finest autobiographies in the jazz literature.

The last few years of his life found Hawes performing on the acoustic piano—"the wood," as he liked to call it—with increasing regularity. He finally returned to Contemporary, the label for which almost all of his best work was recorded, for several first-rate projects. On *Living Legend,* Hawes was paired with Art Pepper, another troubled survivor of the West Coast scene—who, like Hawes, had battled with the horrors of addiction and prison only to pull his career together again. These two phoenixes of West Coast jazz proved to be both kindred spirits and sensitive musical collaborators.

As he aged, Hawes's body lost its sharp angularity; he came to look something like a black Elvis, a big, almost bloated presence. But if his looks had lost their lean and hungry quality, Hawes had not lost his appetite for new sounds and new perspectives. Another late project, a duet album with bassist Charlie Haden on the Artists House label, revealed that Hawes had assimilated the music of younger pianists such as Herbie Hancock and Keith Jarrett. Hawes was still very much growing as a musician as he approached the end of his fifth decade.

He never quite made it. In the spring of 1977, Hawes was felled by a cerebral hemorrhage. After lingering in a coma for two weeks, he died on May 22. He was buried in Los Angeles, his hometown, inside Lincoln Memorial Park. His grave lies next to that of Hampton Hawes, Sr., who had died only a few months before his son.

CHAPTER SEVEN

Big Bands out West

the great orchestras of the future

In October 1948, disk jockey Hunter Hancock, who a few weeks earlier had become a columnist for the *Los Angeles Sentinel*, enthusiastically
told his readers about a new big band in town. The group, a seventeen-
piece modern jazz ensemble led by drummer Roy Porter, was just in its
infancy. Its first engagement, according to Hancock, had taken place the
previous Saturday. Even so, the columnist had already heard enough to
predict great things from the group: "I was privileged to attend a couple
of the band's rehearsals last week, and heard what may be one of the great
orchestras of the future. The fellows are relatively young as far as years
go, but wise in the ways of music way beyond their years." Hancock
continued: "Perhaps one or two of the men will eventually become great
sidemen."[1]

For once, the standard hype of such puff pieces proved to be right on
target—or even understated. Hancock concluded by listing the band's line-
up, which included at that time Eric Dolphy (in his first major jazz gig)
and Art Farmer—two musicians who became much more than strong
sidemen. The article also cited the arrangements of Leroy "Sweetpea"
Robinson, Joe Howard, and Robert Ross, and praised the band's tight ensemble work and driving rhythm section, suggesting in passing that the
group might be somewhat weak in terms of soloists.

The year 1948 was a bad time to start a big band in California—or
almost anywhere else. Unlike the jazz orchestras of earlier days, the en-
larged combos and big bands of the postwar years existed only in defiance
of the economic climate. From the time of the Brubeck Octet and the Roy
Porter Big Band in the late 1940s, the larger West Coast ensembles that
presented modern jazz struggled for existence. It was becoming increas-

ingly clear to jazz fans that the big band was dead or dying. The only disagreement was over what dealt the fatal blow: Some said bebop, others criticized a tax on dance venues, still others pointed to brunt economics or a secret media conspiracy. The one thing virtually all parties agreed on was that the big band had lost its central place in popular culture, pushed to the periphery if not quite yet to extinction. Even Roy Porter, whose dazzling bebop big band had more work than many others of its day, felt the pinch. "That band was built on love," Porter explained to me, "because it damn sure wasn't built on money."[2]

Porter had developed his bop chops by recording and performing with the earliest modern jazz bands on the coast—first with Howard McGhee and later with Charlie Parker—and had taken part in some of Bird's seminal sessions for Dial. He was arguably the finest bop drummer in the west during the period, and his presence added a spark to many of these classic recordings. In the late 1940s, however, Porter turned away from combo work to devote his attention to this short-lived but outstanding big band. Only a few recordings were made (some of which apparently remain either unreleased or lost by the Savoy label), but they reveal a powerful, hard-swinging ensemble propelled by Porter's crisp drumming and a crop of strong soloists.

Porter describes the circumstances leading to the formation of his big band:

> I was back in Cleveland working the Tijuana Club with Tiny Grimes. I wanted to come back to Los Angeles, not so much to form a big band but to get together a band of my own. I thought maybe a small combo. When I got back I got some guys together . . . and we started rehearsing a small group at the Chicken Shack on Vernon and Avalon. One day a guy came by and heard me rehearse. He said that if I got together a 7- or 8- piece band I could do some USO shows. Well, I added a couple more horns, but the USO gigs fell through. But I started getting a little following at the Chicken Shack. Joe Howard, an arranger, told me that he had some charts for a 17-piece band— 5 saxes, 4 trumpets, 3 trombones, and rhythm section. Within the next few days I had a 17-piece big band.

Without planning it, Porter found himself at the helm of a scorching modern jazz orchestra. This was an unlikely role for a young bop drummer who, although he had a glowing reputation for small combo work, lacked a formal music education and could not read music. Years later Porter would devote himself to serious formal study of music and not only teach himself to read notation but also master the fundamentals of composition and arranging. At the time of the formation of his big band, however,

Porter had to delegate many of the technical aspects of leading and re-hearsing to section leaders. Fortunately he could rely on the considerable expertise of the individuals he chose: Art Farmer took charge of the brass players, while the reed section was entrusted to Eric Dolphy.

Known for the most part as Roy Porter and his 17 Beboppers, this band lived up to its name. Of all the postwar big bands on the coast, Porter's ensemble had the deepest bebop roots. Joe Howard's charts are outstanding statements in the bebop idiom, and the section work and solos run deep with passion. Leroy "Sweetpea" Robinson's alto work is espe-cially impressive—little wonder Dolphy's biographers have wanted to at-tribute it to the then twenty-year-old LA City College student. Robinson showed here every sign of being a first-class player in a Parkeresque style. This promising career was cut short when Robinson was killed with a shot-gun by his wife.

While on a tour of the Southwest, one of the band's cars overturned a short distance outside of Deming, New Mexico. In the car with Porter were Art Farmer, Clyde Dunn, the band's valet Cisco, and the driver—all of whom needed to be taken to a local hospital. The musicians were unable to play for some time, and though Porter eventually recovered and reor-ganized, the accident signaled the beginning of the end for his big band. A number of the Porter big band recordings have never been available in LP, not to mention compact disk—in addition to the missing sides recorded for Savoy, masters recorded for Knockout Records, a small local label, were destroyed in a fire. Porter has copies of the 78s of these last works, one of which showcases Eric Dolphy on his only recorded feature with the band. Other reported participants include Bob Gordon (in his first session), Russ Freeman, and Joe Maini, with Jimmy Knepper and Hadley Caliman re-turning from the Savoy session—certainly a tantalizing line-up by almost any measure. It is unfortunate that these important documents of a vital band and extraordinary soloists remain unavailable to the wider audience of jazz fans.

The story of West Coast big bands from the 1950s, especially those featuring black leaders, was largely one of neglect. Like Porter, Gerald Wilson was one of the more talented and stylized West Coast bandleaders of the postwar years. Despite the excellence of his early ensembles, Wil-son's recording career was, except for a few brief interludes, deferred until the 1960s. His first brief stint as a bandleader ran from 1944 to 1946, when he fronted a bebop-inflected orchestra that featured, among others, pianist Teddy Buckner, Melba Liston, and, for a time, vocalist Joe Wil-liams. Despite accounts suggesting that this band broke up for lack of work, Wilson decided to call it quits for other reasons. With two successful East Coast tours under his belt, as well as dozens of 78s under his name, Wilson disbanded because of dissatisfaction with his own writing and a desire to devote more time to refining his craft. "I had hit the top," Wilson describes it, "but I decided that if that was it, I wanted to do more."³

Wilson dropped out of music briefly to run a corner grocery store, continuing musical studies on the side. An urgent request from Duke Ellington for an arrangement that was due overnight began an ongoing partnership with the famed bandleader in 1947. The following year Wilson began working with Count Basie, and in 1950, Wilson briefly gigged with Billie Holiday in a road band that also included drummer Philly Joe Jones. With these impressive credentials, Wilson decided to return to bandleading. He organized a new ensemble in San Francisco in the mid-1950s. This band, which included saxophonist Jerome Richardson, recorded one LP for the Federal label.

By the time Wilson joined forces with the Pacific Jazz label—the association for which he is best known—he had been a prominent bandleader for some fifteen years, fronting large groups on and around Central Avenue, in San Francisco, and on the road. Even so, his 1961 debut release for Pacific, *You Better Believe*, brought Wilson much wider exposure than he had before. Wilson describes this group's formation: "That band had gone into the Flamingo in Los Vegas with Earl Grant for six weeks. We were hot." On returning to Los Angeles, Wilson signed with Dick Bock to produce the new band's debut album. Buoyed by outstanding soloists such as Harold Land, Teddy Edwards, and Carmell Jones, as well as by Wilson's outstanding writing, the group went on to record a series of excellent albums for Pacific throughout the glory years of rock-and-roll.

Wilson's writing leans toward thick, textured sounds in which the arrangements are as prominent as the soloists. Some have traced a Kenton influence in Wilson's work, and though such a lineage is not out of the question, it could well be that the influence worked the other way around. Wilson's early "Yard Dog Mazurka," written for the Lunceford band, became the Kenton orchestra's "Intermission Riff" (where it was credited to Ray Wetzel). Much commerce went both ways in the two bandleaders' later careers, with Wilson eventually contributing to Kenton's Neophonic Orchestra. Even more than Kenton, however, Wilson maintained a quintessentially West Coast band during the 1960s—in terms of both its structured compositional approach and geography. The Wilson band kept close to Los Angeles during these later years—indeed, its ability to attract top-notch talent depended, to some extent, on its "no road trip" policy. The group finally disbanded in 1971.

"Your first ten years are thrown away," Wilson has commented. "If you did pretty good for ten years, you're just starting."⁴ Here Wilson is perhaps making a virtue of necessity—as well as outlining his autobiography. The lack of recording opportunities determined that his work as a bandleader during the 1950s would be ten years largely lost to posterity. Comebacks are, however, part of the Wilson arsenal: Both his 1960s Pacific recordings as well as the later 1980s releases for the Discovery label (with his "Orchestra of the '80s," as he called it), indicated that Wilson's skills did not suffer from long layoffs.

At age seventy, Wilson embarked on a rare, high-profile East Coast tour—including a month of conducting stints in New York, Boston, and Philadelphia—in the fall of 1988. "Writing is easy for me now," he told Jon Garelick of the *Boston Phoenix.* "Writing is just a memory anyway— you just remember everything you've learned and put it down."[5] When I interviewed Wilson in late 1989, the seventy-one-year-old bandleader announced enthusiastically: "This week I've got a new album coming out on Albert Marx's label. It's my Orchestra of the 1990s."

For Porter and Wilson, as for the leaders of many 1950s aspiring West Coast big bands, recording opportunities were few and far between. Their discographies are marked by long gaps, and their records stand as mere hints of what might have been. Defying the economics of the day, which almost proclaimed "Thou shalt not form a big band," they managed to put together a handful of documents testifying to their vision of music. The impact they made on the wider music public was negligible—certainly far from the notoriety their bands might have experienced in an earlier day.

The big band most jazz listeners associate with the West Coast in the postwar years is neither Roy Porter and his 17 Beboppers nor the Gerald Wilson Orchestra, but rather the much different (if equally modern) ensemble led by Stan Kenton. For many listeners, the Kenton sound with all its vices and virtues, *was* the starting point for West Coast jazz. And not just because of Kenton's frequent recordings and performances (the massive Kenton discography includes well over 150 entries just for 1945–55). The specter of Kenton's music haunted a whole host of West Coast jazz bands, either through personnel, stylistic approaches, or simply the underlying, almost unconscious, assumptions of what modern jazz was all about.

Kenton's fascination with what he called the "neophonic"—from Greek roots meaning "new sounds"—was either the tragic flaw or the saving grace (depending to whom you talked) of much West Coast jazz during the 1950s. It was this neophonic sensibility that so many of his alumni— many of whom criticized Kenton on the one hand, yet emulated this aspect of his work—brought with them to their own bands. The constant and sometimes strained striving for new effects, the openness to different sounds, the ceaseless variety and churning musical activity—these underlying themes of the period found their fullest expression in Stanley Newcomb Kenton.

the Kenton writers

The jazz big band is the sound of motion as much as emotion. It is a music of movement, an aural poetics of activity. A tried-and-true big band device from the early days was to make the group sound like a train—and no one could achieve this mysterious orchestral effect better than Duke Ellington. Although this might seem to be a strange and pointless endeavor in program music, the transformation of a jazz orchestra into a steam locomotive was so often employed that it had to represent something more than a novelty effect.

In fact this mechanical masquerade is quite apt. The rhythmic intensity in jazz is not a stop-and-start affair, chugging along like a bus following its downtown route. Instead, with the constant undercurrent of a driving rhythm section, momentum and propulsion are ever-present factors in swing jazz. Just as the early New Orleans/Chicago jazz musicians conveyed the sound and feel of the riverboats traveling the Mississippi, the big bands captured the sound of the steam locomotive. And, in the late 1950s, jazz bands strained to present musical images of rockets and outer space; on the West Coast, Shorty Rogers, Curtis Counce, and Bill Holman were some of the chief culprits. This "innovation" was never fully realized: Otherwise the age of Ellington might have been succeeded by the era of Sun Ra. It wasn't.

Nor was it succeeded by the age of Kenton, despite what some of that bandleader's more fervent fans might have you believe. Just ask the Kenton critics. If the Ellington band was a train and Sun Ra a spaceship, the Kenton band was, some might suggest, more like one of those overbuilt Detroit cruisers of the 1950s. "Too many chrome gadgets," said bandleader Ward Kimball in his description of the Kenton group, "and not enough fundamental design." [6] The opponents of the Kenton band—of which there were (and are) many—focused on its penchant for excess, for "more is better" as a way of life. These were seen as serious flaws that negated the contributions of even the admittedly outstanding soloists the band attracted. An Art Pepper, a Shorty Rogers, a Bob Cooper, Kenton's critics would suggest, could succeed only in spite of the band. Perhaps only a Maynard Ferguson—with his inbred taste for the bombastic and overstated—could flourish in such a setting. Yet for other jazz fans of the postwar years, the Kenton band epitomized the excitement and energy, the freedom and broad scope, of modern jazz. For these devotees, the Kenton band was the only big band still moving ahead, still exploring new ground.

The emerging consensus—and one that, to my mind, strikes the right note—is that the Kenton output was, as a whole, neither as terrible as its critics insisted nor as celestial as its devotees pretended. At times, of course, it could be either of the extremes, but the plain truth about the Kenton orchestra was that it was so much else as well. One should speak of the "Kenton sound" only with trepidation; it is better to refer to the "Kenton sounds." For this band boasted as many different styles as it had writers. Bill Holman, Bob Graettinger, Pete Rugolo, Gerry Mulligan, Lennie Niehaus, Bill Russo—each brought the Kenton ensemble into different territory; each drew on different resources of the great individual talents Kenton featured in his ensembles. The band even showed, on occasion, some steam locomotion of its own—especially with the help of a Bill Holman or Gerry Mulligan chart. But the group could also be as ponderous as a Sherman tank. The band's range of expression was, in fact, nothing short of awe-inspiring. There may have been better big bands, certainly there were more consistently excellent big bands, but for sheer expansiveness, none could match the Kenton ensemble of the postwar years. Kenton once recorded an album featuring all the major national anthems of the world—a typically Kentonian exercise—but even when he stayed close to home, he seemed intent on swallowing the whole world of sound with his musical ambitions.

Born in Witchita, Kansas, on December 15, 1911, Stan Kenton was the son of the idealistic, job-hopping Floyd Kenton—who had worked as, among other things, a tombstone salesman, grocer, mechanic, roofer, and carpenter—and the more practical-minded Stella Newcomb Kenton, a college-educated native of Colorado. At age five, Stanley moved with his family to Southern California, where, at age ten, he started piano lessons under the tutelage of his mother. His musical restlessness was apparent almost from the start. He changed instruments as often as his job-hopping dad switched careers; after trying his hand at banjo, saxophone, clarinet, and trumpet, Stanley finally focused his energies on arranging. In 1928, while still in his mid-teens, he sold his first arrangement—for seven dollars—to a local octet.

Kenton did better than most musicians during the Depression, landing a series of gigs that brought little notoriety but gave him both experience and a steady paycheck. After lengthy stints on the road, he settled down in 1939 with a secure, high-paying gig as leader of a pit orchestra at Earl Carroll's in Hollywood. Soon he was chafing under the limited opportunity for musical experimentation on the job. Kenton had increasingly been devoting his spare energies to writing and arranging, and now he wanted a forum to have his own music heard. With this in mind he started a rehearsal band in 1940 that met two or three times a week for several months and played Kenton original compositions and arrangements almost exclusively. On November 1, Kenton brought the band to Music City in Hollywood to record some audition pressings to help attract steady work for the band. Up until this time the band members had been paid no money for their services—their only remuneration from Kenton had been some bottles of Jim Beam bourbon whiskey. The test pressings paid off. They resulted first in a number of one-night stands, and eventually in Kenton's booking at the Rendezvous Ballroom in Balboa.

The group's success at the Rendezvous, a popular hangout for local college and high school students, was out of proportion to even Kenton's expectations. The enthusiasm spread not only to local fans but also to a national audience who heard radio broadcasts hosted by Jimmy Lyons— making his debut as a coast-to-coast announcer. Before the close of the year, the band was recording for the Decca label, appearing at the Hollywood Palladium, and preparing for its first trip back east.

While Kenton was trying to win over audiences on the East Coast, a business partnership was being formed in Southern California that would have a profound impact on the band's career. Johnny Mercer, G. B. "Buddy" DeSylva, and Glenn Wallichs pooled $17,000 to start the record company eventually known as Capitol Records, which would help push Kenton— and a host of other talented musicians—into the limelight. As one of the few record companies with talented musicians in high-level executive jobs, Capitol proved capable, over the next decade, of combining quality music with a profitable bottom line. When a controlling share of the company was sold to EMI in 1955, the price paid was $8.5 million—an attractive return, to say the least, for the initial investors' $17,000 commitment.

The next several years would mark a slow but steady rise by the Kenton band to a preeminent position in the world of jazz, despite a number of setbacks along the way. The draft board would decimate Kenton's line up, leaving the 1943 band with only three of the original sidemen. By the close of the year, however, Kenton had replaced Skinnay Ennis as Bob Hope's bandleader, and the exposure to forty million Americans through Hope's radio show more than compensated for the musical strictures, resented by Kenton, that the show's format imposed. That same month Art Pepper joined the band, and a few weeks later Kenton made his first recordings for Capitol. Then, while playing an engagement at the Golden Gate Theater in San Francisco, Kenton made the acquaintance of the aspiring composer/arranger Pete Rugolo. Things were on the upswing on several fronts.

One of the band's more influential supporters at the time, prominent jazz writer Dave Dexter, served almost as a one-man promotional unit for the Kenton ensemble. The story of Dexter's initiation as a Kenton apostle long ago passed from history into legend and remains one of the tales Kentonians most like to recount. One day in the summer of 1942 Kenton's manager, Carlos Gastel, reportedly walked into Dexter's New York office and demanded that he give a hearing to the sensational new band on the West Coast. Instead of giving Dexter a record to listen to, Gastel insisted, so the story goes, on driving Dexter to the band's gig—in Balboa, California! Several days later, Valdez's dusty Cadillac pulled up in front of the stucco and Spanish-tiled Rendezvous Ballroom, with Dexter in the passenger seat. The newcomer was almost immediately, converted to the Kentonian faith, and he began doing whatever he could to further the group's fortunes.

Over the next few years Dexter proved he could do quite a bit. He wrote up the band in *Downbeat* and other periodicals; at Capitol Records, where Dexter later worked, he lobbied for Kenton; he lauded the group in his book *The Jazz Story;* and on one occasion he even lent Kenton most of his life's savings—some $800—to help meet the band's payroll. This devotion was in sharp contrast to the more ambivalent, if not outright hostile, reactions of other jazz critics to Kenton's experiments. Barry Ulanov compared the band's sound to "a moving-man grunting under the weight of a concert grand," while George Fraizer determined that the Kenton orchestra was "neither fish nor flesh, but pretty foul."[7]

Dexter was not, however, the only person off the bandstand to have an impact on the band's fortunes. Perhaps the most important figure, after Kenton himself, in establishing the band's reputation for big sounds and dramatic flourishes was Pete Rugolo, Kenton's chief arranger from 1945 to 1949. Rugolo shared Kenton's Wagnerian aspirations and ambitions for creating a new big band vocabulary. Rugolo recalled his first encounter with the maestro:

> Jimmy Lyons, who was then a disk jockey, had heard my service band, and he told Stan about me. He told him that there was a guy who wrote just like him, and that he was going to send me to see him. So when Stan was playing at the Golden Gate Theater I went up to him and handed him five or six arrangements I had brought. I was so green that I actually asked him to send them back to me if he didn't like them because I had spent a lot of time hand-copying them. Well, for a long time nothing happened. Then one day in the barracks I got a call, and it was from Stan Kenton. He had been on the road and had forgotten about my arrangements, then one day at a rehearsal the band had run out of new things to rehearse, so Vido Musso reminded Stan about the charts I had given him. So Stan went searching in his trunk and dug up the music and passed it out to the band. After they played it, Stan was excited about the music and called me up. He said I wrote more like Kenton than he did. He offered me a job for when I got out of the service.[8]

Born in San Piero Patti, Sicily—a small village near Messina—on Christmas Day 1925, Rugolo had come to America at age six, making the ocean journey with his mother by way of the Statue of Liberty and Ellis Island. The family settled in Santa Rosa, California, where Rugolo studied music in the local schools. He went on to San Francisco State, then Mills College, where he was among Darius Milhaud's first jazz-oriented students. "I was the first boy they allowed in Mills," Rugolo recalls. "I had good grades from SF State, and I wrote to Mills saying that I wanted to study with Milhaud. And they accepted me. I think it was the year after that Dave Brubeck and his brother came to Mills. When I got to Mills it was so different. At SF State, Ravel and Wagner were about as modern as they got, but at Mills everything revolved around modern classical music, the twelve-tone row, and the avant-garde. I felt behind." As pianist at Sweet's Ballroom in Oakland, Rugolo had patterned his music after the swing styles of Teddy Wilson and Art Tatum. Now he took to assimilating the much different musical idiom of twentieth-century classical composition. As with the other West Coasters who underwent this ordeal by fire at the hands of Milhaud, Rugolo's jazz music would never be the same again.

After Rugolo's discharge from the service, he joined the Kenton squad full-time, with a $150 a week salary and—even rarer for a staff writer—constant public acknowledgment by Kenton for his contributions to the band. The Kenton position was demanding. "For the four or five years I was with the band full-time, I wrote probably about ninety percent of the band's material," Rugolo recalls. "Stan wasn't writing much then, and occasionally someone else would contribute a chart. But most of it I did." Time pressures aggravated the situation:

> I never had time to write during those years. Sometimes I'd have to come up with three or four arrangements in a couple of days. Or with seven arrangements in four days, like when we did a June Christy project. I listen back to those pieces and sometimes I wish I had had more time, but sometimes I'm surprised at what I came up with. You see, it was hard to find time to write when the band was on the road. I don't know why, but Stan wanted me to show up every night at the concerts—sometimes I would sit in on the piano for the last hour of the concert, while Stan would go mix with some of the people.

The 1950 Kenton band, which presented "Innovations in Modern Music," allowed Rugolo more time to work on his arrangements, and the resulting compositions and arrangements of "Mirage," "Conflict," and "Lonesome Road" rank among his most successful classically oriented charts for the band. In later years Rugolo's work found him exerting more and more experimental zeal with less to show for it. Work for the Columbia and Mercury labels found him pigeonholed as a "commercial" arranger, and even his more jazz-oriented projects began to show a facile slickness that had rarely seeped into his music in earlier decades.

During the postwar years, however, Rugolo proved to be an ideal collaborator for Kenton. He played Billy Strayhorn to Kenton's Duke Ellington, and as with the Ellington/Strayhorn collaborations, Kenton and Rugolo could each create individual music that flowed seamlessly into the work of the other. Rugolo recalls their working sessions:

> Stan might have an idea. He'd maybe say, "Let's do something for Safranski," or he'd want something for Shelly [Manne] or Vido [Musso]. Sometimes we'd sit for a few minutes at the piano and work on some ideas. A lot of times we would write what we'd call a menu. Stan would say, "Let's start with a piano introduction, then a piano solo of sixteen bars, then Vido"— things like that. Then I'd go and do all of the actual writing. Stan wasn't writing much at all at that time. He never really changed anything I wrote. Even though I would do some daring things with time signatures or dissonances, or classical things.

Rugolo once described this association with Kenton as "an arranger's idea of Paradise. . . . I felt like I was walking through the pearly gates when, fresh from the army, I went to work with Stan Kenton."[9]

Kenton apparently shared these celestial aspirations. Maybe his band lacked a host of harp-playing angels, but virtually every other instrumental sound eventually made its way into the group over the next several years—a process that reached its culmination in the Innovations group of 1950. Jazz listeners, for the most part, were willing participants, at least initially, in this attempt to take the big band into the world of high art. In 1946 the Kenton band won the *Metronome* poll as the outstanding big band in jazz; June Christy was chosen outstanding vocalist; Eddie Safranski finished first among bassists; Kenton placed seventh among pianists; arranger Rugolo and saxophonists Vido Musso and Boots Mussulli also finished among the top ten in their respective categories. The Kenton band was widely viewed—at least by the fans—as the preeminent big band in jazz.

On this high note Kenton decided to break up the group. In the spring of 1947 he wired his booking agency and asked them to cancel all engagements. At the same time, he gave notice to all his band members, providing them with a month's severance pay and a ticket home. An exhausting tour of the South and Southwest had been the final straw, with several band members falling ill and Kenton reportedly suffering from both clinical exhaustion and a failing marriage. At a personal low point, Kenton climbed aboard his Buick and drove to Arkansas, where he tried to get a job as an unskilled laborer at a lumberyard. Only a few months before, drummer Shelly Manne had told the jazz press, in a moment of indiscretion, that playing in the Kenton band was like chopping wood—the bandleader was now literally ready to start wielding the axe. The yard boss told Kenton there was no work available. A few days later Kenton, whose whereabouts were unknown even to family and friends, phoned home from Mineral Wells, Texas, saying he was ready to come back to California. When he returned, he started a diligent program of psychoanalysis—an experience he viewed so positively that he later spoke of quitting music to become an analyst himself.

This hiatus, however, was a short one. By late summer Kenton was rehearsing a new band for a September engagement back at the Rendezvous in Balboa. Kenton announced that the new band would focus on "Progressive Jazz," a label that soon stuck for better or worse, just as the other various Kenton dynasties had their futuristic-sounding titles: the Innovations band, the Neophonic Orchestra, etc. (Even when Kenton needed to scale down his ambitions, he gave an impressive title to the endeavor. His slimmed-down 1952 band toured as—pause to take a breath—"New Concepts in Artistry in Rhythm.") To launch the "Progressive" sound, Kenton booked the band into a series of impressive nonjazz venues, including Carnegie Hall, Boston's Symphony Hall, and the Chicago Civic Opera House.

The band's repertoire drew strongly on originals by Rugolo and Kenton. A whole string of "Artistry" numbers (following the successful "Artistry in Rhythm")—"Artistry in Bolero," "Artistry in Percussion," "Artistry in Boogie," "Artistry Jumps"—featured different orchestral textures and soloists. Kenton originals such as "Fantasy" and "Opus in Pastels" captured a similar classical flavor. Perhaps the most ambitious piece was the oxymoronically titled "Prologue Suite," a four-piece work for concerthall performances. A few dance numbers remained in the Kenton book, but the symphonic pretensions of the band now held greater sway than ever before.

Although many critics expressed doubts about the band's direction, most of the fans remained in Kenton's corner. In 1947, the band won the *Downbeat* poll, with many individual members of the group again copping high honors, and *Metronome* named the group its top big band for the second consecutive year. This time the critics were closer to the truth. Despite the acclaim of a boisterous fan base, the band's work from this period is beset by a troubling unevenness—perhaps inevitable, given Kenton's desire not only to do new things in jazz but to do several at once. A piece like Rugolo's "Fugue for Rhythm Section" impresses with its daring—indeed, Rugolo was always a musical risk-taker—but too often Rugolo's conception of modern music in the mid-1940s boiled down to making jazz sound like a movie score, an ambitious score to be sure but one that seems to be supporting a series of visual images to which we are never privy. His "Elegy for Alto" could well be the background to a hard-boiled mystery movie set in the 1940s. As such, it would be quite successful, but as a jazz piece it falls flat. Rugolo's "Impressionism," recorded a month later on October 22, 1947, is similarly ponderous. However, "Monotony," recorded two days earlier, defies its name, standing out as one of the more successful Rugolo works of the period, with its expressive cross-rhythms more than compensating for the screaming brass.

Rugolo's ventures into Latin music are perhaps the most striking of his works from this period. The strong performances of "world music" are usually the last thing recalled in accounts of the band's achievements. Nonetheless, this is an area in which the Kenton band consistently excelled over the years. "Cuban Carnival" and "Introduction to a Latin Rhythm" have none of the rarefied flavor of the academy to hamper their exuberance. While not up to the caliber of the Kenton classic *Cuban Fire* release of some years later, these charts showed that progressive music could boast a heady rhythmic flair and an earthy flavor.

Soon Kenton would push the limits once more. If Rugolo's and Kenton's writings for the band made the critics chafe, the music of Bob Graettinger was more than even many Kenton loyalists could stand. Graettinger was, in the eyes of some, more fit for the looney bin than for a staff arranger job with a big band. His gaunt, unsightly figure, his ill-fitting clothes, his tormented demeanor, his bizarre lifestyle all contributed to the effect. But even without these personal quirks, Graettinger's music was strange enough to make him stand out as a forbidding figure.

Graettinger's music could not be described as typical of the Kenton orchestra's music—indeed, it could hardly be said to typify anything—but the bandleader's commitment to this musical and social outcast in many ways exemplified Kenton's aspirations for jazz. If the new and different were Kenton's guiding lights, then Graettinger represented a perfect fit. Graettinger's most ambitious work—a four-part suite of massive proportions—was recorded and released by Capitol over the fierce objections of the company's executives and finally was marketed more as a favor to Kenton than as any sign of commitment to the music. Kenton, for his part, seemed willing to pursue this unremitting quest for the "neophonic," wherever it might lead. In this instance, it led to the *City of Glass*.

CHAPTER EIGHT

City of Glass

dance before the mirror

In a ramshackle room above a garage, a pale, vampirish figure pounds out a succession of dissonant chords on a tiny upright piano that seems both too big for the smallish room and too small for the reverberating harmonies that come out of the instrument's sounding board. The room is sparsely furnished: a single card table, a few apple crates, a mattress lying on the floor, a frying pan, a few odd kitchen utensils, assorted bottles of vitamins. Ten dollars a month does not buy much in the rental market, even in 1948 dollars. But this tenant seems scarcely bothered by the meager surroundings. Lifting himself from his reverie in the music, he picks up a pad of paper and begins to draw small figures in bright colors on the page. It seems he has gone from the realm of music to that of visual art in an instant, but closer examination shows that the paper contains some strange hybrid work. It appears part sketch pad, part musical manuscript, part poetic notebook, all done up in striking, multiple colors. After a moment, he puts down the paper and starts again on the piano.

It could well be a scene from a Hollywood movie: tormented genius at work. But though the neighborhood is, in fact, Hollywood, California, the scene is real life, not cinema. Sequestered in a series of spartan garrets, Bob Graettinger struggled day after day for over a year on what he felt would be his magnum opus: a four-part work he called *City of Glass*. Graettinger worked at the piano as many as twelve to fourteen hours each day, seven days a week, stopping reluctantly only to sleep and eat. An aesthetic ascetic, Graettinger viewed food and rest as evils to be partaken of only as necessary; one would get plenty of sleep, he often remarked, in the grave. As for food, Graettinger lived primarily on fried eggs and milk (the key, he felt, was to maintain a high level of protein) supplemented by vitamins. Whenever Kenton tried to raise his salary, he protested that he could not take any more than $25 a week. Graettinger occasionally allowed the bandleader to buy him a new suit—but only after Kenton insisted that the current one was not presentable attire for meeting the public; band members recall Graettinger's long attachment to a single blue suit. When he didn't have a belt, a piece of rope sufficed.

His musical script was as nonconformist as everything else about him. Instead of using musical manuscript paper, he wrote on graph paper—the kind with the smallest grids. Instead of using pencil or pen, he worked with multiple colors—blue, orange, red, violet, green. The instrumental parts were written with the highest range at the top of the page, with descending registers following accordingly. Graettinger's meticulously crafted drawings were integral to the manuscript; they formed diverse figures and hieroglyphs—a private argot whose Rosetta stone we still lack. More decipherable comments dotted the margins: "RIPPLES THEN WAVES . . . DESERT SOUNDS . . . THOSE FOOL BIRDS AGAIN" are typical examples.[1] Stumpy Brown recalls the musicians' "look of disbelief" when they saw the *City of Glass* score. "This music was way ahead of our time."[2]

Born on Halloween in 1923, Graettinger had started on saxophone at age nine. He began working professionally, as a writer and player, with Bobby Sherwood at sixteen. He later worked with Benny Carter, Johnny Richards, Alvino Rey, and Jon Savitt before retiring from performance to focus on composition. This decision to abandon his career as a saxophonist took place shortly after he was given a medical discharge from the armed forces for alcoholism—a recurring problem for Graettinger—toward the close of World War II. Graettinger's education as a composer took place at the Westlake School of Music, an institution more suited to churning out studio musicians than disciples of Stravinsky or Hindemith.

By all accounts, his skills as an arranger developed slowly, his pre-Kenton work showing little of the dramatic flair of his mature pieces. When he had first approached Kenton at the Hollywood Palladium in 1941, the charts Graettinger offered the bandleader were clumsy efforts that gave only a hint of the composer's messianic vision. Kenton encouraged the young writer to persevere but soon put the encounter out of mind. Six years later, when Kenton was back in Hollywood for a rehearsal of the Progressive Jazz orchestra, Graettinger reappeared with another arrangement for the bandleader's inspection. This time the music, a Graettinger piece called "Thermopylae," made a powerful impact on Kenton. Privately he admitted to friends that he didn't know if the piece was "genius or a bunch of crap," but he decided it was provocative enough to demand a hearing.[3] Within months Kenton had recorded the work, and Graettinger was added to the band's payroll.

The reaction of others in the band to the newcomer was, for the most part, apprehensive reservation. Various comments, culled by Kenton historian Carol Easton, capture the general sense of discomfort at Graettinger's arrival.[4] "Bob Graettinger was frightening," Gene Howard said. "He was a very *weird* person" was Jan Rugolo's verdict. "He had this terrible coloring—sick. He looked like he was just out of the picture all of the time. Just very *weird*." To Shelly Manne he was simply an enigma: "Graettinger was the kind of guy you don't know what to say about him! Even though we were on the road with him, spent time with him, we never really knew him." Bill Holman was equally mystified: "We were kind of in awe of him. None of us understood his music."

The most sympathetic appreciation of Graettinger given to Easton came from, of all people, Art Pepper. Pepper, a street-wise, hard-blowing altoist with movie-star looks, would seem to be an unlikely companion for this consumptive Kentonian composer of atonal jazz. But Pepper, despite the accolades, always saw himself as something of a loner, misunderstood and rejected by the insiders. Given this self-image, strikingly at odds with the way others viewed him, it is little wonder that the altoist felt a deep affinity for the outcast Graettinger. "I was one of the few people who would spend time with him," Pepper recalled. "We'd smoke pot together and just talk. When he died I was very unhappy, because I always had the feeling that if he had lived he would've been someone I could've went to and talked to and possibly gotten some direction or understanding or sympathy or whatever it is that you need." There is clearly some heavy psychology hidden in this depiction of Graettinger, the "weird, frightening loner" who turned off everyone else in the band, as the one person whose advice Pepper would seek in a time of need. About Graettinger's music Pepper had no reservations. "He *was* a genius."

It was to Pepper that Graettinger explained in the greatest detail the story represented in *City of Glass*. The opening section depicts the approach to the city, with the colors and activity slowly building as the city gates draw near. Images of trees or signs on the graph paper would be converted into musical notation, with the range of instruments reflecting the intensity of the image. A bright tree would be translated into music in the higher register with bright-sounding instruments, while a gloomy tree would fall into the lower register with trombones or bass.

Graettinger strived to capture not just the character of each instrument but the personality of each Kenton player. Pepper recalls that Graettinger saw the altoist as having a tragic and lonely sound—this before Pepper's fall from grace, and when, for example, writers like Shorty Rogers would invariably feature Pepper as a player of pretty and dreamy ballads. But Graettinger's much-different characterization was, as Pepper saw it, an uncanny prophecy—"The way he described my sound is exactly the way my life went," Pepper said. Graettinger's ability to combine individual sounds into a musical whole was crucial to his compositions—much as was the case with the very different work of Duke Ellington. Also like Ellington, Graettinger was never held back by the conventional section-writing techniques in which brass, reeds, and rhythm serve as the basic building blocks, rather than the individual sounds of specific horns. The opening of *City of Glass* is atomistic, analytic; it breaks down the sections into individual parts, isolated sounds.

The second section takes the place within the city and consists of a walking tour of the precincts. Different families of instruments—brass, strings, reeds—are used to represent the various buildings encountered during this stroll. The third part, the most dramatic section of the work, is entitled "Dance Before the Mirror." Graettinger described it as a view of the surrounding structures as "though one were viewing them while whirling around in a spirited dance before a huge mirror. There is a frenzied climax and then abrupt silence."[5] Here Graettinger combines his flair for flamboyant orchestral colors and spine-tingling dissonances with a powerful jazz rhythmic drive. This section of the work is wholly successful as a fusion of avant-garde classical techniques with a jazz band idiom; as such it compares favorably with the much more celebrated *Ebony Concerto*, which Stravinsky crafted for the Herman band during the same period. The final movement, "Reflections," creates a musical vantage point from which the city can again be viewed as a whole. It is comparatively soothing, at least by comparison with what comes before. The work ends with a flaming sunset over the city of glass and a final plunge into the darkness of night.

The *City of Glass* premiere was as unusual as the work itself. Kenton took the opportunity of a concert at the Chicago Civic Opera in 1948 to launch the piece and assigned Graettinger the rare opportunity of conducting the band. A capacity crowd showed up for the Progressive Jazz Concert, as it was billed, with little idea of quite how progressive the proceedings would be. After the band completed the grueling four-movement work, Graettinger and the band members nervously awaited some response for several moments while a stunned silence continued—the audience could well have been turned into glass for all their reaction. Then Kenton seized the initiative by literally leaping in front of the band and, with a dramatic gesture, signaling the group to take a bow. The audience responded with an enormous ovation. Then they stood and began cheering. Perhaps befuddled, they knew nonetheless that they had witnessed, on that night, something quite out of the ordinary.

Graettinger's output for Kenton was always slow in coming, and he only produced one or two pieces a year during his tenure with the group. In the mid-1950s, Graettinger grew even more reclusive, and his writing activities became ever more sporadic. He died in the spring of 1957, shortly after undergoing surgery for lung cancer. At his death, he was working on an unfinished septet for classical instrumentation. Forrest Westbrook, a friend and student of Graettinger's, undertook completion of the work. Westbrook recalls:

> The first two movements were completed, and the third movement was almost finished. I made an attempt at completing it. I needed to exercise my judgment about the duration of some notes and the instrumentation of certain parts. Also there were virtually no dynamic markings for the last movement. I had the manuscript in my possession until around 1967 or 1968 when I had a friend return it to Kenton. Later someone at Eastman was trying to track it down, and they contacted Kenton, but he didn't have any knowledge of it . . . The piece is almost certainly lost which is a great tragedy. Bob was working on it for at least three years that I know of and maybe longer.[6]

Despite the popular success of his Progressive Jazz, Kenton continued to experience doubts about his career. In December 1948 he announced that he was again disbanding the group. A few months later, word broke that Kenton planned to give up music to become a psychiatrist—quite an ambitious goal for someone who not only had never attended medical school, but had not even gone to college. With some thirteen years of higher education facing the thirty-seven-year-old pianist, Kenton could look forward to opening his psychiatry practice sometime in his early fifties. (Strangely enough Stan Getz, a former Kenton sideman and another player who never attended college, would later announce to the jazz press similar aspirations to become a doctor. Is life as a celebrated jazz musician so bad as to spur such dramatic plans for career change?) These far-fetched dreams lasted, as it turned out, thirteen weeks rather than thirteen years. In June, Kenton announced his plan of forming a new band, one even more progressive than the Progressive Jazz orchestra. It would tour under the name "Innovations in Modern Music."

"About that Stan Kenton band," comedian Mort Sahl was telling audiences around this time, "a waiter dropped a tray and three couples got up to dance."[7] Sahl was, in fact, one of Kenton's greatest boosters, but his quip was a revealing expression of the bandleader's general reputation, by now well earned, for the unusual and excessive. Actually Kenton never went quite so far afield again as he had done with Graettinger's works—much to the relief of many jazz fans. Even so, he managed to capture a wide range of sounds in his early 1950s bands. The Innovations band of 1950 aimed at integrating a large string section permanently into the group. This presented numerous problems, both musical (the strings were easily drowned out by the screaming brass) and practical (the band put Kenton some $125,000 in the red after just four months). The Innovations band's repertoire was built around a series of eponymous pieces designed to feature individual group members—Shorty Rogers's "Art Pepper" and "Maynard Ferguson," Kenton's "Shelly Manne" and "June Christy"—as well as workout pieces for individual sections of the band, such as Bill Russo's "The Halls of Brass" or Graettinger's "House of Strings." The compositions occasionally buckle under the weighty self-consciousness of the writing as well as a tendency toward pomposity, but for the most part they capture the listener's interest. The string writing in particular is surprisingly good, given how little experience writers such as Kenton and Rogers must have had in this area. Rogers's string underpinning to "Art Pepper," Kenton's string accompaniment to "Shelly Manne," Graettinger's string feature—all of these are quite successful. If there is a down side to this music, it is less the presence of violas and violins than it is the overly demonstrative brass work. On the whole, the recordings of the Innovations band hold up well today, and one suspects that this music must have had a powerful effect when heard live in a concert hall. The band and its composers formed the strongest unit Kenton would ever field: Pepper, Rogers, Bud Shank, Manne, Ferguson, Christy, Bob Cooper, Russo, Graettinger, Laurindo Almeida. After two tours, however, the physical and financial strain of maintaining such a large working band proved to be too much. Briefly considering an Innovations III tour, Kenton decided to drop the fiddlers and go with a "small" band consisting of five reeds, ten brass, and four rhythm instruments.

in a jazz orbit

Kenton's two chief arrangers in the early 1950s, Bill Holman and Bill Russo, displayed strikingly opposed approaches to writing for the band. "Russo objects to the soulful, romantic approach to composition," announced the liner notes to his 1954 project for Kenton, *The Music of Bill Russo*. "He feels that music, like all art, should be consciously designed to express basic truths." In contrast, Bill Holman's counterpart record, *The Music of Bill Holman*, quoted the composer as saying: "What I like to capture is a real jazz spirit—so that no matter how much is written down, the music should have all the *feeling* of improvisation." One writer sought an ideal music, far removed from the commonplace, while the other looked precisely to capture the heat of the moment, the epiphany of the everyday.

From 1950 to 1954, Bill Russo had a major impact in shaping the experimental tendencies of the Kenton band. Russo's high-art seriousness exemplified everything the critics disliked about Kenton. And Russo did little to mollify his detractors. His massive 825-page study *Jazz Composition and Orchestration*, published by the University of Chicago in 1968, was a representative gesture. This detailed and impressive tome goes sharply, and self-consciously, against the grain of those who would like to depict jazz as an intuitive art recalcitrant to articulation in systematic and quasi-scientific method books. And as if Russo's positivistic view of jazz were not enough, he peppers the book with allusions to high culture, starting with an epigraph from Aristotle and continuing with quotations from Shakespeare, Napoleon, Mao and others. His self-satisfaction is all the more grating when one notes that virtually all of the hundreds of examples of exemplary composition and arranging included in the book are from Russo's own writings.

Though it is easy to chafe under Russo's demeanor, his skills as a writer and arranger must be evaluated on their own merits. Judging these works on "purely" musical considerations is, however, far from a straightforward task. The Third Stream, that infelicitously named combination of the two pre-existing streams of classical music and jazz, was long ago discredited in the world of jazz criticism for its rarefied academic tendencies. Although a thorough re-evaluation of Third Stream works is beyond the scope of this book, some comment is necessary to assess the Kenton band, not to mention several other West Coast musicians of the period under discussion. Part of the problem one faces here is the lack of a critical tradition and vocabulary required to "place" such works. To judge a Third Stream work by Gunther Schuller or Ran Blake with the same standards one uses to assess an Art Blakey or Sonny Rollins performance is clearly to stack the deck against it from the start. Yet precisely some such approach seems implicit in so many dismissals of Third Stream writings, pieces that, we are told, fail because of their "cold intellectualism," their "cerebral character," their lack of "solid swing," etc. Yet even Mozart and Bach would rate poorly if their work were to be evaluated by the standards of hard bop. Like all hybrid musics—fusion, bossa nova, Afro-Cuban, even jazz itself—Third Stream is both more and less than its constituent parts and must be so treated. Early jazz, a hybrid of African and European elements, might well have been seen as a failure if it had ben evaluated by the standards of either of these "streams"—an African griot and a nineteenth-century classical composer might have been equally unimpressed with the music of King Oliver or Jelly Roll Morton, whose works succeed unabashedly when evaluted as what they are, namely, jazz. Third Stream music, comparably, is a hybrid music lacking a corresponding critical tradition. Without such a perspective, any critical assessment of these works must approach them gingerly, careful not to apply blindly the various jazz pieties that have little bearing on such compositions.

In Russo's case, perhaps the wisest course is to evaluate his writings on the standards to which they seem to aspire. The virtues of Russo's writing stem from his impressive command of the jazz orchestra. The works are marked by their variety of textures, voicings, and contrapuntal devices, as well as a strong sense of formal structures and an instinctive feeling for musical tension and release. The jazz idiom, however, soon became too constricting for Russo's tastes. In the late 1950s, a grant from the Koussevitzky Foundation enabled him to establish the Russo Orchestra, a large ensemble with strings, while teaching stints in classical music conservatories further enhanced his highbrow credentials. Never closely associated with the West Coast sound, Russo chose in later years to shift his focus increasingly more and more toward these nonjazz settings for his music.

Bill Holman stands as the antithesis of Russo. The most traditional arranger that Kenton ever hired, Holman was also among the very best. His charts, more than any other 1950s additions to the band's repertoire, proved to the skeptics that the Kenton band could swing as hard as any of its peers. Holman was something of a departure from the norm for Kenton. "I spent some time trying to figure out what kind of material I could write for the band," Holman explains.[8] "I knew I wanted to do something different from what it had been doing previously, but I knew that Stan was not interested in Basie types of charts. But the things Gerry Mulligan had done with the band gave me a glimmer of light of what could be done with the band." The precedent set by Mulligan allowed a more streamlined approach—one that sounded modern without completely abandoning the swing era idiom. "I could describe my ideals in jazz writing as: continuity and flow, combined with swing and vitality, with a fairly traditional base," Holman said in 1987.[9] "It's got more involved as time's gone by, but basically those are my guiding principles."

Although most accounts claim that Holman was born in Orange, California, on May 21, 1927, the event actually took place in a tiny nearby farming community named Olive—"I don't even know if it still exists," Holman says. Holman's father ran the local general store and post office. In junior high school, a musical aptitude test administered to the students revealed Holman's promise as an instrumentalist, and he was assigned a clarinet to play in the school band. Soon he decided to switch to saxophone. "When I started listening to the radio, I heard most of the top forty and the hit bands, and I realized that saxophones were what was needed for that music. I had tried to play some stock arrangements on clarinet, and it just didn't cut it, so I decided to get a saxophone." Despite his strong native ability, Holman only gradually decided to pursue a career in music—after first studying engineering at the University of Colorado and UCLA. Like Graettinger, Holman decided to study music at Westlake, the prototype jazz conservatory then being run out of an old house on 6th and Alvarado. Here Holman learned the fundamentals of big band writing and immediately been creating his own charts. One of these, an ambitious twelve-bar blues, caught the interest of Gene Roland, who referred Holman to Kenton. Holman at this time had already left Westlake and apprenticed with the Charlie Barnet band, but this group, despite its increasing orientation toward modern jazz, gave Holman little chance to expand his writing skills. "Barnet was winding down his band and wasn't buying many charts. I think he might have bought one." Kenton, in contrast, was constantly on the lookout for new material for his group and provided Holman with a regular forum.

However, Kenton's decision to feature Holman's writings exclusively on the Capitol 10-inch record *The Music of Bill Holman* came, strangely enough, shortly after Holman had left the group on bad terms. "When I had left the band I had had a few words with Stan—nothing serious, but still I figured that that was it with me and him. Then I turned around, and he was doing an album of my charts." Although most listeners assumed that Holman was involved in this project, he participated neither in picking soloists and personnel, conducting nor selecting which charts would be featured. He does not recall whether he came to the sessions, but Holman is certain that he was not consulted about the particulars of the project.

Holman's records as a leader from the late 1950s offered him much greater artistic control than the Kenton association. His live work as a leader during these years was restricted to small combo settings, but on his three 1957–60 record dates he returned to a big band setting. The first of these projects, 1957's *The Fabulous Bill Holman*, finds him drawing on a strong cast of West Coast players—Conte Candoli, Richie Kamuca, Herb Geller, Stu Williamson, Lou Levy, Al Porcino, Charles Mariano, Mel Lewis—many of whom would go on to grace the Holmanesque big band led by Terry Gibbs two years later. The music reveals the essential qualities of Holman's sound. He works from no-nonsense charts immersed in the syncopated big band idiom of the swing era, built to support the soloists with solid frameworks for improvisation. Just as striking, however, are what Holman leaves out: the overly textured writing, the strained efforts at modernism for the sake of modernism, the attempts to built compositions at the expense of improvisation—in short, all of the most controversial elements of the Kenton band. As Holman describes it: "I had all these more traditional big band sounds in my head that I never could have done with Kenton. *The Fabulous Bill Holman* gave me a chance to get those out of my system.

"But the next project," he continues, describing the follow-up *In a Jazz Orbit*, "was more modern." As with its predecessor, *In a Jazz Orbit* almost got canceled even before it was recorded. Red Clyde had commissioned the earlier album for Bethlehem, but by the time the arrangements were finished, the label had lost interest. The project was saved when Shelly Manne persuaded the Coral label to back it. After the Bethlehem fiasco, Clyde found a new home at Mode Records and commissioned Holman to write material for a new album. Once again Holman completed the charts, only to find that his opportunity to record had lapsed. Again he improvised a new outlet, in this instance the owners of Andex, a tiny label that briefly hit the big time with Sam Cooke before he went with RCA. "They didn't know much about jazz; in fact they didn't know much about music—the company mostly made aircraft instruments," Holman explains. "But after what happened with Sam Cooke, they decided that the record business was a snap. It wasn't much work to convince them to do my project. But they really didn't know what to do with it, so it didn't make much of an impact at the time."

In a Jazz Orbit has, however, worn well with the years despite the dated neo-Sputnik theme promoted by its tacky cover. The entire second side of the album is devoted to Holman originals, and on "Theme and Variations #2" he presents a wholly written chart with no sections for soloists. Even on a standard, such as his version of "You Go to My Head," the arrangement stands out as a provocative restatement of the piece that goes well beyond the "bare-bones" aesthetic of Holman's earlier works. At the same time, Holman stays true to the hard-swinging ethos that had characterized his writing to date.

At the start of the 1960s Holman pursued a final big band date as a leader for Capitol, *Bill Holman's Great Big Band,* the most commercial of his leader dates from the period and one below the standards of his previous projects. Like so many others associated with the West Coast scene of the 1950s, Holman found the age of the New Frontier to be lean times for jazz. He was increasingly writing for pop groups like the Fifth Dimension and the Association, as he broadened his credentials to encompass almost the whole scope of commercial music. His jazz writing never fell completely by the wayside—he wrote sporadically for Gerry Mulligan, Woody Herman, and others—but not until the 1980s would he get the chance to record again with a big band under his own name. Like Roy Porter, Gerald Wilson, and most of the other big band leaders out west during the 1950s, Holman's work in this idiom remains a tantalizing hint of what he might have achieved had conditions been more favorable for larger ensembles.

The addition of Holman was one sign among many of Kenton's growing tendency, after the break-up of the Innovations band, to return to a more mainstream jazz style. His willingness to hire players like Zoot Sims, Lee Konitz, Billy Root, and Curtis Counce reflected, despite their brief tenure with the group, an attempt to reach out to a more straight-ahead style. The hiring of Mel Lewis for the band's drum chair was also a major plus. With the further addition of bassist Curtis Counce, the band had perhaps the strongest rhythmic foundation since Shelly Manne had left the group. Writers like Bill Russo, Joe Coccia, or Johnny Richards could still provide the band with ambitious and path-breaking arrangements—Richards's *Cuban Fire*, recorded shortly after the band's return from Europe in May 1956, is an especially impressive example of Kenton's willingness to tackle new things—but the mid-1950s band veered more and more toward a traditional big band vocabulary.

Another major addition to the band at this time was alto saxophonist Lennie Niehaus. Niehaus is perhaps best known today for his scores for movies and his widely used method books for saxophone. But in the 1950s Niehaus stood out as one of the strongest altoists on the West Coast, as well as an impressive writer/arranger. Born in St. Louis on June 1, 1929, Niehaus came west with his family in 1936. His father, a professional musician who trained his son to play the violin, sought a studio music career in Hollywood. Starting on the violin at age seven, Niehaus progressed to oboe and bassoon before focusing on the more jazz-oriented alto saxophone and clarinet. After graduating from Los Angeles State College (now known as Cal State Los Angeles), Niehaus began a several months' stint with the Kenton band around February of 1952; an induction notice from the draft board cut short his tenure with the group. Niehaus was sent to Fort Ord, but not before recording several numbers with the band and leaving behind an arrangement of "Pennies from Heaven."

At Fort Ord, Niehaus played in a variety of ensembles, including an octet, a pianoless quartet, and a big band. "Many of the ideas for the recordings I later did with Contemporary came from the work I did during this time," Niehaus recalls.[10] "I made these into productive years. I practiced; I worked with different groups." (The years were also beneficial in ways Niehaus wasn't aware of at the time: another Fort Ord regular, future actor/director Clint Eastwood, would remember Niehaus's playing years later and enlist the altoist to score a series of movies, including the Charlie Parker bio-film *Bird*.) Niehaus's Kenton ties continued even after his induction: "I remember one night when I was in the service a number came on the jukebox, and it was Kenton's recording of my arrangement of 'Pennies from Heaven.' Stan had recorded it after I left." Niehaus played the number over and over on the jukebox that night.

He left the service in 1954, and an opening came up almost at the same time in the Kenton sax section. Soon Niehaus was reunited with his former bandleader, an association that lasted until the close of the decade. Niehaus stood out as one of the group's strongest soloists during these years and also contributed a number of charts to the band's repertoire: "When I joined the band, Kenton couldn't really play a dance. There weren't that many dance things in the book, maybe things like 'September Song' or 'Street of Dreams.' Stan had liked the 'Pennies from Heaven' chart and wanted to know if I could do other things like that, so I did a number of charts based on more basic show tunes." During his tenure with the group several of Kenton's albums were devoted solely to Niehaus's writings, with a strong emphasis on Broadway material and ballads.

Niehaus also was making a reputation outside the Kenton organization during this period. After leaving the service, Niehaus had caused a stir when he sat in at the Haig and the Lighthouse, and soon several record companies were clamoring for him to work as a leader. He also fronted a successful working quintet, alongside Bill Perkins, during his breaks from the Kenton band. His powerful technical command of the saxophone, his inventive linear approach to improvisation, and his sweet tone made Niehaus a likely candidate as the next alto star on the coast. His series of albums made for the Contemporary label, rarely heard nowadays, make compelling listening. Despite the striking virtues of his playing, Niehaus never achieved more than passing notice from the critics. One notable exception, however, was Max Harrison, whose insightful essay on Niehaus, reprinted in *A Jazz Retrospect*, captures the essential virtues of the altoist's work:

> Niehaus had little to learn about playing the alto saxophone. His ease and fluency conveyed a feeling of relaxation and security that is always rare, and his attack and swing were almost equally striking. But the most notable single feature . . . is the consistency of his inventive power in improvisation. He never seems at a loss for a good melodic idea, and, though his phrasing is concise and preeminently logical, an element of the unexpected is never absent.[11]

This is high praise, and mostly on the mark. Niehaus is one of the more unfortunate casualties of the general neglect of West Coast players. For this he himself is partly to blame. In the 1960s he began a long retirement from jazz playing to concentrate on scoring motion pictures and television shows. While many West Coast players returned to jazz in the 1970s, Niehaus were not among their ranks. In the middle 1980s, however, he did begin playing the saxophone in earnest once again, with occasional performances. His first album as a jazz soloist in some thirty years was recorded shortly before my interview with him.

This comeback album finds Niehaus in the company of tenorist Bill Perkins, whose strong saxophone voice was also a fixture of the Kenton band in the mid- and late 1950s. Perhaps best known for his work on the tenor, Perkins has also distinguished himself on flute, clarinet, and baritone saxophone. Perkins's early work showed him to be one of the most polished disciples of Lester Young on the West Coast during the decade, although in more recent years he has favored a more aggressive, rougher-edged sound. Born in San Francisco on July 22, 1924, Perkins spent part of his youth in Chile before returning to California. Like Bill Holman, Perkins studied both engineering and music in school—he holds an electrical engineering degree from Cal Tech—before choosing the life of the road musician. In the 1950s, Perkins became a big band journeyman, working in the orchestras of Jerry Wald and Woody Herman before settling in with Kenton for the last half of the decade.

Although the Kenton affiliation had many musical high points, Perkins's most memorable work of the decade is his outstanding collaboration with John Lewis on the 1956 album *Two Degrees East, Three Degrees West*. Recorded in a single afternoon in a vacant Los Angeles theater, the album relied on head arrangements put together on the spot by pianist Lewis. Far from resulting in a haphazard jam session, this informal approach produced a subtle, winning album that has held up well. As in his collaborations with Jimmy Giuffre, Lewis revealed that he was perhaps the East Coast musician with the greatest sensitivity for developments on the West Coast. In his later championing of Ornette Coleman, Lewis would do even better. He showed that he understood musical happenings in California even better than most of the natives.

a dream band

"I don't think there was ever a better band than this one," remarked drummer Mel Lewis of the Terry Gibbs Dream Band, "including my own."[12] At first glance, such high-flown praise must seem puzzling. Little in the Gibbs band's history or personnel suggests that it was destined for greatness. Most of the band's charts were hand-me-downs from other ensembles. Many of the arrangements from *The Fabulous Bill Holman* on the Coral label ("Airegin," "Bright Eyes") and the same leader's *Big Band in a Jazz Orbit* ("Kissin' Bug," "You Go to My Head") show up intact on the Dream Band's recordings. The personnel, for all their strengths, were also by no means unique. Most of the players had recorded on the Holman dates, and many were regular participants on a host of other sessions of the day. Nor can we attribute the band's reputation to shrewd marketing and wide exposure. The Dream Band was virtually unknown, especially outside Southern California, during its brief existence. It never went on the road, and its most important recordings were not released commercially until almost thirty years after the band broke up. And the band proved to be something of a financial disaster. Gibbs later estimated that he lost some $1,000 a month during the group's existence.

Gibbs paid his sidemen $14 each as he tried to support a big band on a quartet budget. Gibbs had been booked into the Seville, a struggling nightspot on Santa Monica Boulevard later converted into an adult movie theater. Though Gibbs was contracted to bring in a combo, owner Harry Schiller agreed to let him front a big band for a one-night trial, as long as it cost no more than the smaller group. Anxious to make the most of this onetime opportunity, Gibbs and his sidemen pulled all the strings they could to publicize the event and even garnered a plug on Steve Allen's Sunday night television show two days before the opening. On the Tuesday night the normally deserted Seville was packed to the rafters with celebrities, musicians, and fans, including Ella Fitzgerald, Dinah Shore, Louis Prima, Johnny Mercer, Steve Allen, and Fred MacMurray. "From the first bar of the first number," recalls John Tynan, who represented *Downbeat* that night, "the impact of this band was as breathtaking as swallowing a double shot of tequila straight."[13] What started as an off-night rehearsal band became, for its brief moment in the sun, an all-star sensation. Soon the band settled into the Sundown on Sunset Strip, where it spent most of its two-year life.

All these circumstances would seem to warrant only a marginal place for this band in the history of West Coast jazz. Yet the Dream Band was an outstanding, spirited ensemble, one whose few recordings are full of gripping performances. The factors that set this unit apart from the common garden variety big band defy precise definition. It could boast of what one calls, for want of a better term, "chemistry," combined with that equally ineffable element, "swing," in this instance a wonderfully loose yet powerful swing that seemed to uplift each member of the ensemble. A simple comparison of the Holman band's version of some of the charts with the Gibbs renditions brings this out quite clearly. The material and even the musicians overlap almost completely at times, but the Gibbs band is like a turbocharged roadster compared with the Holman group's economy model. Some of the difference can be explained by the tangible crowd enthusiasm that permeates the Dream Band records, combined with the greater familiarity of the musicians with the charts. But the band's pizzazz also stems from Gibbs's penchant for dramatic flourishes and high-energy music. "Terry always knew exactly what he wanted," Holman recalls. "There's a joke between the two of us that Terry always wants a big chord on the end of every chart." Gibbs, who has compared leading a big band to being a psychologist, also apparently had a flair for bringing the best out of his musicians.

Born in New York on October 13, 1924, as Julius Gubenko, Gibbs established himself as a major jazz player in the 1940s on the strength of his work with the Dorsey, Goodman, Herman, and Rich bands, as well as his prolific output as a leader. By the time of his move to California in

1957, he stood out as one of the leading vibraphonists in jazz, one who brandished an aggressive, note-filled, two-mallet style perfectly suited for the bebop idiom. He came west with the intention of pursuing a studio career in Southern California. He was soon offered a staff position at NBC, but when he learned that this required him to forgo outside jazz gigs, he backed out. The Dream Band stands as his most successful jazz endeavor of these early California years.

Mel Lewis played drums for the band and later claimed that he rarely played better. Lewis possessed the rare skill of being able to propel a big band without overplaying—a talent of vital importance during his tenure with the Kenton band, whose heavy textures had been known to over-power more than one drummer. (Anita O'Day recalls that the Kenton band had some ten different drummers during her ten months with the band: "I never heard of any of 'em again. I think it must've scared them out of the business.")[14] The rest of the usual suspects—Conte Candoli, Frank Rosolino, Stu Williamson, Bill Holman, Bill Perkins, Al Porcino, Lou Levy—with their Lighthouse, Kenton, or Herman credentials, also played prominent roles, as did altoist Joe Maini, an often overlooked Parker-school player.

The Dream Band was a potent musical force while it lasted, but its reputation was long hindered by Gibbs's refusal to release the tapes of the band's finest performances. For years they were heard only by occasional visitors to Gibbs's house, while the vibraphonist turned down all offers to make them commercially available. In the late 1980s, Gibbs in conjunction with Fantasy Records, finally put out several releases that showed what all the hoopla was about. Running any big band in the postwar years was more of a nightmare than anything else, but for a short while this dyna-mite band was a dream come true.

CHAPTER NINE

Chet Baker and
the Pianoless Quartet

Oklahoma is a cultural wasteland

A picture of trumpeter Chet Baker, circa 1953, figures prominently on the cover of a recent book on hipsters and the beat generation. One could scarcely imagine a better photograph to represent *The Hip* (which is, in fact, the book's name): Baker lies casually sprawled across two folding chairs, apparently backstage at a concert. His slicked-back hair is a hipster's dream: Every strand conveys an image of casual semidisarray. His right hand gently cradles his trumpet, while his left embraces one of the chairs; his eyes stare out intensely into empty space. His face looks like a Greek marble sculpture. He bears an uncanny resemblance to a young James Dean.

Photographs of Chet Baker taken in later decades could well be of another person altogether. The back cover of his 1978 album *You Can't Go Home Again* shows the grim image of a man who has gone through a wringer. If you didn't know about Baker's problems with narcotics—and they have been extremely well publicized—you could probably guess them from this photo. Even here, however, Baker holds himself with dignity. He stares straight into the camera, almost with defiance, and his visage—although having suffered a sea change—is every bit as compelling as in the earlier photo.

Despite the travails of his offstage life, Baker stands as one of the finest soloists jazz has produced. In later years his performances might be erratic, but even then most of his work remained fresh and captivating. A few days before Baker's last San Francisco performance, his former producer Richard Bock asked me to report on the caliber of the trumpeter's playing. Bock wanted to feature Baker on a recording but had heard conflicting stories about the level of his music. That weekend any concerns Bock or I might have had were put to rest as Chet gave an inspired and riveting performance to a packed house of admirers. His ballad work was as compelling as ever, but even more impressive was his easy mastery of faster tempos. True, his range was limited, but even in the first flush of youth he had never made his mark as a high-note player. In the middle register, however, Baker always remained nonpareil.

Despite the virtues of his playing, not everything seemed right that evening with Chet Baker. The accomplished trumpet work belied his worn, emaciated looks—although Baker was in his late fifties, his features showed not so much advanced years as advanced dissipation. He was the antithesis of Dorian Gray: All his assorted voices were written in the lines of his face. The audience's warm applause reflected the quality of the music, but it was heightened by their realization that Baker might not be around much longer. After the performance Baker readily agreed to give me an interview for this book and set a time for it on the following day. He never showed up for the interview—another in a career of missed appointments. He phoned a few days later, but I wasn't home to receive his call. His next scheduled San Francisco performance was canceled because of poor health. A few months later he died under circumstances that defy clear explanation. Accident, homicide, suicide have all been offered as possibilities.

Though the facts surrounding Baker's death may continue to raise questions, his passing came as little surprise to the jazz community. If anything, Baker's relative longevity was nothing short of miraculous—and not just for medical reasons. From the start of his career, Baker had embodied the stereotypical figure of the young trumpeter who makes a powerful impact on the jazz world but then disappears from the scene. In the history of jazz, this image is not romanticized legend but tragic reality—attested to by the abbreviated careers of Buddy Bolden, Bix Beiderbecke, King Oliver, Bunny Berigan, Fats Navarro, Sonny Berman, Clifford Brown, Lee Morgan, and Woody Shaw. Baker, with his fast-paced and careless lifestyle, fit the pattern with uncanny perfection, better than even these other illustrious figures. He was, to quote the old saw, an accident waiting to happen. "People said I'd never make 35," Baker told an interviewer in 1978, "then I'd never make 40, 45; now I'm almost 50, so I'm beginning to think maybe they might be wrong."[1] At the time of his death, Baker was fifty-eight years old, not the average life span for a white American male, but remarkable for someone with Baker's history.

Posterity will likely look kindly on this musician—although he took little heed of it. Often pressed by necessity, Baker recorded frequently, and the body of work he left behind is immense. I have suggested that

Baker's work was uneven, yet from another perspective his work is the epitome of consistency: More than almost any of his contemporaries, he revealed a unity of vision and clarity of intent that remained unchanged during his forty-year career. Unlike Miles Davis, with whom he has often been compared, Baker did not vary his style with the passing decades and passing fads. His trademark virtues remained the same: His phrasing and use of space were always distinctive, as was his airy tone, which was especially pure for a jazz musician. He rarely distorted his notes with the variety of bends, moans, and growls that often characterize jazz trumpet; his notes were so clean and their positioning so straightforward that one could almost imagine them being read from some private mental score. He played very softly and was one of the few trumpeters who required amplification even in an intimate setting. His singing was softer still, often lingering just above a whisper. His technique and range were modest, especially in later years, but he did so much with his limited musical tools that one scarcely kept track of what he couldn't or didn't do. In an age of incessant virtuosity, Baker's work was a telling and much-needed reminder that technical mastery was not the only path to musical expression, and indeed could often be a beguiling dead-end street.

Chet Baker was born in Yale, Oklahoma, on December 23, 1929. Despite its Ivy League name, Yale was a modest farming community. A few scattered oil rigs marked the otherwise rural landscape. Until the Dust Bowl forced the local population into a nomadic existence, things changed slowly in Yale. Chesney Henry, as he was named, was born on the same farm as his mother. He moved to Oklahoma City the following year, where he stayed with his aunt until he was ten.

The larger town offered little in the way of modern musical culture. Chet's father played guitar in a western band that broadcast regularly on station WKY. Baker would later take every opportunity to lambaste the music of his native region. "Oklahoma is a cultural wasteland. . . . I mean those people listen to the most terrible kind of music in the world—hillbilly, rock-a-billy, and all that crap."[2] Baker goes too far. Much of the country music of his childhood bore a close resemblance to swing jazz. Certainly Baker's father had strong jazz roots: He encouraged his young son to listen to the music of Jack Teagarden (whose compatible brass work and vocal style somewhat foreshadow Baker's later work). Moreover, Oklahoma's home-grown jazz talent was far from unimpressive. The state could later boast of numerous native sons who became significant jazz players (often after moving to the West Coast): Charlie Christian, Don Byas, Wardell Gray, Marshall Royal, Barney Kessel, Dupree Bolton, Don Cherry, and many others.

Chet's father came to California to take a job with Lockheed around 1940—shortly after Steinbeck's *Grapes of Wrath* had publicized the plight of Oklahomans transplanted to the Pacific Coast. Soon he sent for Chet to join him. They settled first in the quiet city of Glendale, and later in the coastal community of Hermosa Beach. In these new surroundings, Chet's mother took the youngster, not even in his teens, to sing at various amateur talent contests in the Los Angeles area. ("I had to compete with girls playing accordion and tap dancing. I never won, but I was second once.")[3] His father, in contrast, tried to build upon his son's enthusiasm for Teagarden by bringing home a trombone. "It was too big, and I could hardly reach the bottom position," Baker later recalled.[4] Not long after, at age thirteen, he switched to the trumpet and began playing with school bands. By this time he was listening to Bix Beiderbecke and Harry James.

At age sixteen Baker enlisted in the service. Originally assigned a position as a clerk, Baker later became part of the 298th Army Band in Berlin. Listening to V-disks, Baker first discovered modern jazz. Stan Kenton and Dizzy Gillespie forced the young trumpeter to re-evaluate his allegiance to Harry James. After his 1948 discharge, Baker continued studying the bebop idiom, now listening to Miles, Fats Navarro, and Red Rodney as well as to West Coast locals such as the Candoli brothers. Playing opportunities as a civilian were few, and Baker re-enlisted in 1950, this time joining the Presidio band. This San Francisco–based ensemble provided Baker with the opportunity to experience the growing modern jazz scene in Northern California. "I played in the band all day, went to sleep in the evening, got up about 1 a.m. I'd go [into town] and play until 6, then I'd race back for reveille, play in the band, and go back to sleep."[5] After being transferred to Fort Watchuka in the Arizona desert, Baker lost his enthusiasm for military service. He went AWOL and returned to San Francisco, where he surrendered. After three weeks of treatment in a psychiatric clinic, Baker was found to be "unadaptable to army life" and was discharged.

Back in Los Angeles, Baker again found few opportunities to play modern jazz. In 1952 he settled in Lynwood with his wife, who worked in a dress shop, and played in a Dixieland band led by Freddie Fisher. Baker's jazz career was at a standstill. This would now change with a vengeance. Over the next twelve months, Baker would make dozens of now classic recordings, be written up in *Time* magazine, and serve an apprenticeship with the greatest jazz legend of his day.

a little white cat in California

Beyond the swinging doors of the Tiffany Club on 8th Street, it is quite dark. The sound of a large crowd of people comes as a surprise in a setting that is usually well populated only at night. Outside the daylight of late afternoon still lingers—it is about 3 p.m.—but inside the dimly lit club it might as well be midnight. In addition to the sounds of an audience, musicians can be heard performing on the stand. As one's eyes adjust to the surroundings, aided by the reflected light from the mirror over the piano and stage, the interior slowly becomes visible: the low bandstand, the tacky wall pattern (depicting clumsy drawings of phonograph records, violins, keyboards, almost anything connected with music), and some thirty to forty people sitting or standing around. Many are familiar jazz figures: Jack Sheldon, Pete Candoli, Conte Candoli. It looks as though someone has called a convention of Los Angeles jazz trumpeters.

The musicians suddenly stop playing. The one alto saxophonist in this sea of brass players walks to the microphone. Even in the semidarkness there is no mistaking who *he* is. The year is 1952. Charlie Parker, the altoist on stage, is a figure larger than life in the jazz world. Bird has grown physically since his extended LA stay of the mid-1940s—almost as though his body has expanded to match his increase in reputation. He stands much larger, heavier, fuller faced, than before. Jack Kerouac's comparison is apt: Bird does look like the Buddha now—a black Buddha in a suit and tie.

At the microphone Bird asks: "Is Chet Baker here?" A moment later, the response: "Yeah, Bird, I'm here." A lanky, baby-faced, twenty-two-year-old trumpeter steps to the bandstand. Parker announces a song and counts in a tempo, and the group is off at a precipitous rate. After finishing the first number, Parker counts in a second. Then he returns to the microphone. He thanks the other musicians for having come. The audition is over. Chet Baker will be Parker's trumpeter during a three-week Southern California engagement.

Baker would later credit much of his success in jazz to being in the right place at the right time. On this occasion he came dangerously close to missing his big opportunity. Baker had learned about the audition only a few hours earlier. Arriving at his Lynwood home that afternoon, he found a telegram from Dick Bock telling him about Parker's scheduled audition. Bock, who would later produce many of Baker's best recordings, also came to the Tiffany to make sure Bird was aware of the young trumpeter. Baker lived up to his advance man's praise. "[I was] twenty-two and scared to death! But fortunately I knew the tunes that he called."

The work with Parker soon extended to other venues and other cities. He performed with Bird at the Say When in San Francisco, in Oregon, and in Canada. Bird's relationship with his sidemen could be highly strained and often tempestuous—as Miles Davis has revealed with telling detail in his autobiography. But Baker's interactions with the celebrated altoist took on an entirely different character: "He was gentle and protective of me.

He wouldn't let anyone give me anything. And at the end of every job when he got paid, he would always try to get more money than the contract called for to split up with the musicians, to get the guys something extra." More than money, Baker's affiliation with the leader of the bebop movement brought him notoriety in the jazz world. When Parker returned to the East Coast, he reportedly told Dizzy and Miles: "There's a little white cat out in California who's going to eat you up." On the West Coast, Baker had established himself as an up-and-coming star. His drug problem had not started yet. In short, Baker was poised for success.

This was only the beginning. The fame Baker gained by playing with Parker was modest in comparison with the recognition he soon received from his collaboration with Gerry Mulligan. In the spring of 1952, baritonist Mulligan secured a regular Monday night job at the Haig, a small Los Angeles jazz club on Wilshire Boulevard. From the outside the Haig appeared an unlikely place to launch a major jazz career. This free-standing converted bungalow looked more like a modest residence than a major nightclub. The building was surrounded by a picket fence, shrubbery, and an assortment of palm trees. The only indication that this idyllic hideaway housed a commercial establishment came from the towering sign: "THE HAIG DINNERS COCKTAILS." The club's location, of course, overcame any limitations in its façade: Down the street was the celebrated Brown Derby, a much-touted restaurant where movie stars obligingly came to watch the tourists dine; across the street stood the luxurious Ambassador Hotel, which, sixteen years later, would become infamous as the site of Robert Kennedy's assassination. In 1952, the Ambassador was better known for housing the Cocoanut Grove, one of Los Angeles's priciest nightclubs. All these landmark establishments are now gone, but in their day they ranked among the most glamorous locations in Southern California. The Haig could boast neither the spaciousness nor ritzy clientele of the Cocoanut Grove or the Derby—its capacity was less than a hundred—but owner John Bennett had developed the club's reputation by featuring some of the finest jazz bands of the day. Even before the Baker–Mulligan success, popular artists such as Red Norvo and Erroll Garner had played the club, and soon, inspired by the new band's rapid rise to fame, the Haig would rank with the Lighthouse as the major springboard for West Coast jazz talent. A list of the groups that would debut at the Haig reads almost like a Who's Who of West Coast jazz in the mid-1950s; it includes, in addition to the Mulligan–Baker ensemble, Shorty Rogers and his Giants, the Laurindo Almeida/Bud Shank Quartet, the Hampton Hawes Trio with Red Mitchell, and the Bud Shank Quartet with Claude Williamson.

Baker had been sitting in with Mulligan's group at the club's regular jam sessions. The much-praised rapport between the two musicians was not immediately apparent, but with each performance their mutual chemistry grew. In the weeks preceding his meeting with the trumpeter, Mulligan had been preparing to record with a new small combo. A first session, recorded on the afternoon of June 10, 1952, featured Mulligan with bassist Red Mitchell and drummer Chico Hamilton. The three sides cut that day were unimpressive: Mulligan obviously felt that the instrumentation was too sparse (according to Bock, pianist Jimmy Rowles was hired for the date but never appeared), and he spent much of the session doubling on piano. Over the next few weeks Mulligan met Baker and played with him at the Haig; on the strength of these performances, Mulligan tried another line-up for his July 9 recording session. This time the instrumentation was baritone sax, trumpet, piano, and bass. The musical results were an improvement over the previous date, and a few passages of counterpoint horn lines hint at developments to come. But the presence of a piano, despite Rowles's strengths as an accompanist, prevented the music from taking flight.

The third session, on August 16, represented an important breakthrough for Mulligan. The three selections recorded that day are powerful musical statements that go far beyond the previous efforts. By now Mulligan had decided on the instrumentation that would launch his quarter to fame. Pianist Rowles was now gone, and drummer Chico Hamilton had returned, to constitute a quartet of trumpet, baritone sax, bass, and drums. Mulligan's ability to extract a wide range of sounds from three monophonic instruments and percussion would prove to be nothing short of amazing, as even these first pieces show. On "Bernie's Tune" the initial rendering of the melody is tightly orchestrated for trumpet, baritone, and bass, with a carefully arranged drum part underscoring the proceedings. This ensemble statement leads into brief solos by baritone and trumpet; behind Baker's solo, Gerry adds his understated complementing line in the lower octave, then joins Chet for an extraordinary chorus of counterpoint punctuated by a tight eight-bar drum solo. Every nuance, every note contributes perfectly to the performance. The Mulligan Quartet had discovered its sound—one in which composition and arrangement would become every bit as important as improvisation.

These early recordings were completed under primitive conditions, even by the standards of the day. The group had assembled each time at the Laurel Canyon bungalow of engineer Phil Turetsky, where an Ampex tape recorder was run off a single RCA 44-B microphone. In October the quartet was booked for two sessions at the more upscale Gold Star Studios in Los Angeles. These two dates, as well as the September sessions for Fantasy, show that the musical rapport of the August date was no fluke. The Fantasy sides in particular include some of the finest work by the Mulligan Quartet: Baker's performance of "My Funny Valentine" has been much praised and imitated (perhaps most often by Baker himself), but even more striking are the performances of "Line for Lyons" and "Lullabye of the Leaves." The tight polyphony, subtle dynamics, and cohesive group inter-play—all Mulligan trademarks—would never be better.

Much of the publicity surrounding the Mulligan Quartet stemmed from the absence of a pianist. The jazz journals frequently referred to it as the "pianoless quartet," as if the group were more noteworthy for what it lacked than for what it did. Today the omission of a harmony instru-ment does not sound unusual, and other virtues of this group are more salient: its effective use of counterpoint, its understated rhythm section, its melodic clarity, and its willingness to take chances. Not since the days of New Orleans ensemble playing had the individual members of a small combo been so willing to merge their personal sounds into a cohesive whole. These characteristics, rightly or wrongly, became viewed by the jazz public as trademarks of West Coast jazz.

Different reasons have been offered for Mulligan's decision to drop the piano from his group. Richard Bock recalls that it was a product of necessity:

The Haig had booked the Red Norvo Trio [which consisted of bass, guitar, and vibraphone], and Norvo didn't want a piano onstage. So John Bennett moved it away. This seemed to make it difficult to run sessions, but Gerry said it was all right. They started working without a piano—at first there would be long stretches when just the bass and drums would be plodding along, and John Bennett was worried. But each week it got better, and by the third week it was exceptional.[6]

Other accounts, notably Mulligan's own, stress the bandleader's conscious desire to free his music from the explicit harmonic presence of a chordal instrument. Probably the truth lies somewhere in the middle: The absence of a piano at the Haig simply pushed Mulligan in a direction that matched his inclinations.

With regard to Baker, Mulligan again showed his ability to take best advantage of the circumstances at hand. Although the original repertoire of the pianoless quartet was almost entirely penned by Mulligan, these compositions indicate that Mulligan was focusing on new material per-fectly suited to Baker's strengths. "Chet had a fantastic ear," Mulligan would later remark. "Although he couldn't sight-read music at all, he would pick up on things I improvised as if we had them all written out in ad-vance."[7] In other musical settings, Baker's ambivalence about sight-reading/and his constant reliance on playing by ear might have been limitations, but Mulligan realized the tremendous asset he had in Baker's native talent and extraordinary sense for melodic invention.

The band's chamber music approach also helped further the Mulligan

Quartet's appeal to the public. In the early 1950s, jazz was undergoing a major upheaval; it was ceasing to be the popular music of the land and evolving into a serious music for dedicated aficionados. The attitude of the jazz audience was increasingly resembling that of the audience for classical music. And any attempts by jazz musicians to emulate the patterns of classical music consumption were likely to meet with success. Mulligan, whether consciously or not, played to the new stereotype of jazz as a serious endeavor. Pictures of the group's performances from that period show the bandsmen dressed in well-tailored suits (in contrast, photos of an early recording session find Baker wearing an undershirt and Mulligan a plain plaid shirt), but the highbrow demeanor of the band was much more than a matter of sartorial splendor. The article in *Time* clearly played off a wide range of stereotypes associated with classical music: Mulligan, the readers were told, opens his eyes "only occasionally to glower at customers who are boorish enough to talk. . . . Mulligan is extremely serious about his music. . . . [He looks] for ideas in his favorite composers—Stravinsky, Ravel, Prokofiev and Bach."[8] Much like Brubeck to the north, Mulligan was forging a whole new image of what the jazzman was all about.

the end of the dance band

Mulligan, like many of his contemporaries, was never happy about being associated with the West Coast movement. "My bands would have been successful anywhere," he said in 1977. "I didn't live in California. I went to California, scuffled around for a while, wrote some charts for Stan Kenton to survive, and started my group—I had very little contact with anything that was going on out there—and then left."[9] Like many others, Mulligan was rewarded for moving back east. There he gained the reputation and opportunities that often seemed inaccessible to musicians who stayed in California.

Mulligan was a New Yorker by birth, as well as by inclination. Born in Queens Village, Long Island, on April 6, 1927, the future baritonist was the son of a management engineer who moved his family around the East Coast and Midwest. "My first instrument was piano, my second was clarinet, my third was alto sax. Each one of these I had to save up my money and buy."[10] He later added the tenor sax to his musical arsenal, finally turning to the baritone. Under the influence of Harry Carney and Skip Martin, Mulligan decided to focus on the baritone. In 1944, at age seventeen, he left home as an arranger with Tommy Tucker's big band. Two years later he returned to New York, where he survived by arranging and playing. During this time he began a fortuitous association with Claude

Thornhill's big band. Through the band's chief arranger, Gil Evans, he met
a group of like-minded young musicians who would ultimately influence
not only Mulligan's career but also the later development of jazz.

This clique of musicians has come to be known, in retrospect, as the
"birth of the cool" group. Their ranks included many pioneers of cool
jazz: Miles Davis, then best known for his association with Charlie Parker,
but soon to emerge as the most important bandleader of his generation;
John Lewis, who would rise to fame with the Modern Jazz Quartet; Lee
Konitz, a young altoist who was developing a different branch of cool jazz
under the influence of pianist Lennie Tristano; and Mulligan, who would
be a major exponent of the cool movement on the West Coast. These were
just some of the musicians who had gathered around Evans. Their brief
period of musical collaboration resulted in a handful of important recordings and a few live performances.

Despite this band's powerful influence and its later critical acclaim,
commercial prospects at the time were bleak. The band's three-week stint
at the Royal Roost failed to lead to steady work. The impact of the group's
recordings, which featured a nine-piece unit under the nominal leadership
of Davis, was far out of proportion to the band's limited output. Virtually
all of the members of the nonet would be permanently marked by this
early association. Countless other bands, across the country and around
the world, would also bear the stamp of the new cool jazz sound. The
name attached to the group was not misleading: If there were such a thing
as a birth of the cool, this was it.

And Gil Evans was its midwife. The group's meeting place was Evans's
apartment, a modest one-room basement lodging behind a Chinese laun-
dry on West 55th. The setting was less than elegant, but to the musicians
it was a haven for their new ideas. George Russell's description captures
the atmosphere of the locale:

> A very big bed took up a lot of the place; there was one big lamp, and a cat
> named Becky. The linoleum was battered, and there was a little court out-
> side. Inside, it was always very dark. The feeling of the room was timeless-
> ness. Whenever you went there, you wouldn't care about conditions outside.
> You couldn't tell whether it was day or night, summer or winter, and it
> didn't matter. At all hours, the place was loaded with people who came in
> and out.[11]

Russell quickly adds: "Mulligan, though, was there all the time."

One can well believe it. Davis and Evans have been given much of
the credit for the musical success of the enterprise, but Mulligan's influence is heard throughout the group's few recordings. John Carisi recalls:
"Between Gil and Mulligan, I think they conceived the instrumenta-

tion."[12] This novel choice of nontraditional jazz instruments was one of the group's most distinctive features: The nonet emulated the Thornhill band's use of the French horn, a neglected jazz voice even today. The tuba, a throwback to New Orleans days, was also brought into play. ("The problem," Carisi noted, "was to get a tuba player that could play delicately enough, that wasn't a German-band-sounding tuba.") The other horns were trumpet, trombone, and alto and baritone sax. Gerry served as the group's most prolific writer, penning almost half of the pieces it recorded.

After the Capitol recordings were made, Mulligan hitchhiked to California, where he sold arrangements to Stan Kenton and played odd jobs. The change in Mulligan's musical setting was as pronounced as the difference in geography. Kenton represented, in the baritonist's view, the antithesis of the nonet. With Davis and Evans, Mulligan had created a scaled-down big band, one that featured a lighter sound and relaxed swing. Kenton's band represented the opposite approach: It kept expanding and constantly created bigger and bigger sounds. "I hated what that band stood for because it was like the final evolution of wrongly taken points. The way the band kept growing. . . . It was symbolic to me of the end of the dance band. It was so pretentious. It was the last straw."[13]

Mulligan's own philosophy of large-group writing is better demonstrated by the recordings he made for Capitol with his ten-piece band. The Mulligan Tentette built on the foundation of the earlier Davis/Evans Nonet and featured an array of the finest West Coast musicians of the day. Baker and Chico Hamilton were carryovers from the quartet; joining them were, among others, Bud Shank, John Graas, Pete Candoli, and Bob Enevoldsen. In this setting, Mulligan was preaching to the converted. The spirit of the "birth of the cool" sessions had already taken root on the West Coast. Shorty Rogers had recorded with an octet for Capitol over a year earlier, and only two weeks before Mulligan's date, Rogers brought a nonet (also featuring Graas on French horn) into the studio for RCA. Graas, an Iowa native born in Dubuque on October 14, 1924, had been advocating the French horn as a jazz instrument long before Davis's nonet. In 1942, he had worked with Claude Thornhill, and after his army service, Graas graced the bands of Tex Beneke and Stan Kenton and served in the Cleveland Orchestra. In the early 1950s, he settled in Hollywood, where he figured prominently on the jazz and studio music scene until his death in 1962. When the "birth of the cool" sound spread west, Graas—one of the few jazz-oriented French horn players on the scene—was a major beneficiary of the new instrumentation.

Over the next decade many similar bands—octets, nonets, tentettes—would record and perform on the West Coast, but these early Mulligan sides rank among the finest. From the quiet moodiness of "A Ballad" to the swing era echoes of "Simbah," Mulligan showed that he was a skilled and flexible arranger with a mastery of many different idioms. As with the quartet, the larger ensemble's work served as an impressive compendium of the range of sounds Mulligan could extract from his instrumentation.

Only three weeks after the *Time* article, the quartet returned to the studio. The four compositions recorded on February 24, 1953, at Gold Star Studios in Los Angeles reveal two different sides of the ensemble. On "Makin' Whoopee" and "Cherry," Mulligan shows the deep premodern roots of his work; the pronounced two-beat feel, combined with the fairly simple counterpoint, give these recordings a Dixieland flavor. It would be hard to justify the group's growing importance in the modern jazz world on the basis of such works alone. "Motel" and "Carson City Stage," with their use of rhythmic displacements and intricate melody lines (the former piece is reminiscent of Monk's "I Mean You") show, in contrast, Mulligan's bop roots. Drummer Hamilton pushes the band along with greater intensity than usual, and the solos and counterpoint are full of surprising twists and turns. Follow-up sessions from March and April found Mulligan increasingly relying on popular songs instead of original compositions. The performances, while capable, rarely matched the earlier quartet recordings. Mulligan had apparently mined most of the possibilities of this instrumentation, and there are few surprises on these new sides.

The real neglected gems recorded by this band came from outside the studio; they are the quartet's several collaborations with alto saxophonist Lee Konitz. Long thought to be recorded in June of 1953, these dozen pieces now appear to have been taped before the *Time* article. Konitz, who had worked with Mulligan on the "birth of the cool" sessions, forces the group into an aggressive blowing style, and the results are memorable. The altoist dominates the proceedings. On "All the Things You Are" and "I'll Remember April" he plays with fire and ice, supplying both the hot and cool in equal doses. One of the finest soloists of his era, Konitz has rarely played better than on these spontaneous sessions of a generation ago.

No later work by Baker would achieve the degree of renown earned by his early collaboration with Mulligan. This is unfortunate. Baker's best work as a soloist was still in the future at the time of the pianoless quartet. The Mulligan Quartet achieved its success through a group effort in which collective rapport was more important than the work of any individual soloist. As such, this band's work did more to reveal Baker's abilities as an ensemble player than as a soloist proper. Baker sounds as if he is holding back on many of the quartet's performances: He appears to concentrate on providing ingenious counterpoint lines and short, compelling improvisations, rather than on presenting the full range of his capabilities. Even years later, in Baker's several reunion recordings with the baritone saxophonist, his solos rarely matched the level that he frequently achieved with his own ensembles.

The body of recordings Baker made with his own quartet provide a far better sense of the trumpeter's skills as a soloist. They show that Baker continued to grow after his apprenticeship with Mulligan. Although non-musical reasons precipitated Baker's decision to go out on his own, he was ready to lead his own group. The circumstances leading to the break-up began with Mulligan's arrest on narcotics charges in 1953 and his subsequent six-month stay at the Sheriff's Honor Farm. After Mulligan's release, he and Baker had a falling out over money matters. Baker had been working for $125 per week during the quartet's eleven-month stint at the Haig. On the strength of the band's success and Baker's strong showing in the *Downbeat* and *Metronome* polls, the trumpeter felt he deserved more. When he ran into Gerry on Hollywood Boulevard shortly after Mulligan's release, Baker demanded $300 per week: "He and this chick he was with, Arlene . . . for a minute they laughed in my face and said that's ridiculous, $300 a week; and that was the way the Gerry Mulligan Quartet ended."[14]

Baker now found in pianist Russ Freeman a musical collaborator as stimulating, if less well known, than the baritone saxophonist. Like Mulligan, Freeman was both an instrumentalist and a composer. Less restrained than the emotionally cool writing by Mulligan, Freeman's compositions, as well as his supportive comping style, gave Baker free rein to stretch out. In fact, Freeman's pieces stand out as among the finest musical settings Baker ever found. Freeman, in return, saw Baker as the ideal interpreter of his music. "He's the only one who could play my songs the way I hear them," Freeman would say in 1963. "He had such an innate feeling for them."[15]

But Freeman was much more than composer-in-residence for the new Baker quartet. He also served, in a rare combination, as musical director, road manager, and personal advisor all rolled into one. In Richard Bock's words:

> He was the perfect pianist for Chet at that time. He gave him an enormous amount of room. He was really the musical director, you know, and he was largely responsible for the success that the quartet had as far as being able to be a unit to work. Not only did he pick the tunes, he wrote the tunes, he taught Chet what he needed to know to play them, [and] took care of business on the road.[16]

Freeman, born in Chicago on May 28, 1926, was three years older than Baker. Like many others of his generation, he had been profoundly influenced by Parker and Gillespie's performances in Los Angeles in 1945 and 1946. Even before the celebrated engagement at Billy Berg's, Freeman had become one of the few West Coast initiates into the new music, largely through the influence of alto saxophonist Dean Benedetti. A prototypical hipster, Benedetti became famous not for his music but for his obsessive preoccupation with Charlie Parker. "He had his saxophone lacquered black," Freeman recalls.[17] "I suppose it was because Bird was black—although I don't know if he felt it would make him play any better. It was strange. I've never heard of anyone else, then or now, doing that." Through Benedetti, Freeman discovered the early Parker and Gillespie sides, which were then surfacing out west. "We heard the Parker and Gillespie albums, and our mouths just dropped in awe. When they came out here, we heard Parker at Billy Berg's every night."

Benedetti's fame in the jazz world stems almost entirely from his private recordings of Parker, released in 1990, several decades after they were made. Long thought to be lost, these tapes contain hours of previously unknown Bird solos, much of it of extraordinary musical—if not sonic—quality. Benedetti came equipped with a portable recorder with which he preserved countless musical utterances of the master. He combined his Bird fixation with his continued efforts—at least for a time—as a professional saxophonist, and Freeman served as the band's pianist. The Benedetti band was not lacking in talent—in addition to Freeman, the group also included trombonist Jimmy Knepper and trumpeter Dale Snow. Charles Mingus also worked with some of these musicians and may have been an occasional member of the Benedetti band.* Despite its array of talent, the band seemed destined for financial failure from the outset. "We would get together and play," Freeman remembers. "Sometimes we'd even rent a hall ourselves for a few dollars to have a place to play. And then we got a real gig. We got together and practiced, got arrangements, even got uniforms. That was the only gig we had. It lasted maybe a week." Tragedy also seemed to follow many of the individual members of the band. Snow was soon committed to a mental institution; Ray Rosser, another pianist who played with the band, was killed in a hotel fire in Chicago; Benedetti followed Parker's descent into drug addiction and died at an early age.

Freeman, however, flourished in the years following this early initiation into bebop. Around the time of Parker's release from Camarillo, Freeman was working with Howard McGhee, whose band often featured Bird during the post-Camarillo period. After McGhee, Freeman further honed his skills by working with three of the finest Los Angeles saxophonists of

*Surprisingly, this group of white hipsters is credited by Mingus's biographer with exposing the young bassist to the virtues of Charlie Parker's music. Brian Priestley quotes Jimmy Knepper as follows: "Years later Mingus told me that it was the first white band he'd worked with . . . and that he hadn't paid much attention to Parker. But these guys were so enthusiastic. All they could listen to was Charlie Parker." Brian Priestley, *Mingus: A Critical Biography* (London: Quartet, 1983), 28.

the day: Dexter Gordon, Wardell Gray, and Art Pepper. By the time he met Baker, around 1952, Freeman had already established himself as one of the leading West Coast pianists. When Baker's musical partnership with Mulligan soured, Freeman was an obvious choice as a new musical collaborator.

The music Baker and Freeman recorded for Pacific Records forms the trumpeter's most important legacy from the 1950s. Baker's playing would never again be at such a consistently high level, and seldom would he find a group of sidemen as stable and sympathetic as those on these sessions. Further, Baker's most outstanding work as a singer also dates from this period. These initial vocal performances are free of the questionable intonation and pitch problems that mar much of his later singing work. Instead they reveal a crystal-clear choirboy voice that could attain an almost haunting beauty. On his versions of standards such as "Time After Time," "I Fall in Love Too Easily," or his remake of "My Funny Valentine," Baker created a classic "cool" vocal approach, one that would have a refracted influence in many strange and surprising ways: João Gilberto's moving bossa nova singing style of the next decade would borrow heavily from Baker in its use of understatement and its relaxed delivery, while Gilberto indirectly delivered Baker's influence to later pop singers such as Kenny Rankin and Michael Franks.

It should come as little surprise that much of Baker's influence as a singer took place beyond the confines of mainstream jazz. His style was almost too low-key for jazz. It captured a melancholy world-weariness, a lovelorn ennui foreign to the currents of hard bop and vocalese that dominated jazz singing in the late 1950s. But if Baker failed to reflect the broader currents of jazz, he succeeded in understanding and building on the basic appeal of his narrow yet singular talent. In these early experiments in singing, Baker developed the most relaxed jazz vocal sound ever heard. If the work of an Ella Fitzgerald or a Sarah Vaughan grips an audience with a breathtaking vocal virtuosity, then Baker proved that the exact opposite approach could also be effective. His was an antivirtuoso style. It relied on the meagerest of tools, ones that underscored the starkness of the emotions conveyed. Baker seemed to suggest to his listeners that his was a feeling too deeply felt to be betrayed by superficial frills or mere technique. Baker's singing, it is worth noting, also seemed to bring out some of his finest trumpet playing. When I asked Richard Bock which record he thought represented Baker's best work on trumpet, he unexpectedly cited Chet's first vocal album; Baker's brief solos on those vocal numbers are uncommonly lyrical, even by Baker's standards.

In assessing the Baker quartet of this period, one's attention is invariably drawn to Freeman's contributions as a composer. His collaboration with Baker brought out the best in him as a writer, just as his compositions in turn evoked some of the finest improvisatory work from the trumpeter. It is difficult to generalize about this large body of work, and this reflects the music's strengths: There is an invigorating range and breadth in these recordings, a wideness of musical inquiry that belies the stereo-typed view of Baker as a limited specialist in moody ballads. Much of Baker's reputation at this time was, of course, based on the success of his recording of "My Funny Valentine," but these first Pacific dates avoided the obvious temptation to focus on only one side of Baker's talent. The quartet's first sessions, in late July 1953, show his comfortable mastery of Freeman's Latin-tinged "Maid in Mexico" and his fast bop chart "Batter Up." A follow-up session from October 3 produced especially memorable up-tempo work from Baker and Freeman on the latter's "No Ties," "Bea's Flat," and "Happy Little Sunbeam."

Richard Bock takes credit for Baker's venture into vocal music: "I encouraged him to sing, and it turned out that he had an exceptional talent for it." Only two vocal numbers were recorded that first day, but they justified Bock's high hopes. The jaded sentiments of "The Thrill Is Gone" and "I Fall in Love Too Easily" provided an ideal vehicle for Baker's emo-tionally restrained style. Early in the following year, Baker and Bock scheduled a more ambitious vocal session. This one resulted in other gems, including "But Not for Me," "Time After Time" and "There Will Never Be Another You." Perhaps the most moving moment is the new, slower take of "I Fall in Love Too Easily," which features an all too short, bitter-sweet trumpet solo.

Less than a week later, Baker returned to the studio to complete a project pairing him with string orchestra. Seven weeks earlier he had added Zoot Sims to his quartet for a string orchestra session, and now he re-turned with Bud Shank in Sims's place. Despite an illustrious group of arrangers—Marty Paich, Jack Montrose, and John Mandel—and generally strong contributions from the soloists, the music rarely ventures beyond superficial prettiness. Of course Baker was not the only jazz musician of the day who pursued ill-advised flirtations with strange musical contexts—even Charlie Parker was drawn into some tawdry settings during these years. But for Baker such musical detours and dead ends became a recur-ring theme. And the overt lyricism of his playing made it all the more desirable for him to avoid such saccharine settings.

Freeman's work is essentially obscured on the string sessions (al-though his composition "The Wind" is set in a rather graceful Mandel arrangement), and it is hardly more noticeable on the vocal sessions. The pianist was thrust into the forefront, however, in the touring band Baker put together the following month. Along with Carson Smith and Bob Neel, Baker and Freeman spent several months on the road at some of the most illustrious venues of the day: Birdland and Basin Street in New York,

Storyville in Boston, the Blue Note in Philadelphia, and the Streamliner in Chicago. In Ann Arbor, Michigan, a recording of the quartet's Mother's Day performance was later released by Pacific. Here Baker plays with an intimacy and delicacy one would think scarcely possible in a large concert setting. Opening with an understated "Line for Lyons," Baker works the middle register of the horn with a sure touch, repeating and refining a series of melodic motives with a lazy relaxation that belies the tight compositional structure of his phrases. On "Lover Man," Baker merely suggests a few bars of melody before moving into a whirlwind improvisation that Freeman follows with a daring interlude soaked in substitute scales and dense harmonies. Most jazz performers play few ballads on a gig, fearing they might lose their audience without constantly mixing in brighter tempos. But Baker at Ann Arbor kept drawing from the till with ballad after ballad—"Lover Man," "My Old Flame," "My Funny Valentine"—and held the audience enrapt. On the uppish "Maid in Mexico" Baker outdoes the group's studio recording of the piece with a definitive performance of the Freeman tune. This was Baker's trumpet playing at its best.

Beyond his work with Baker, Freeman's recordings in the 1950s were impressive in their scope. In addition to his trio album on Pacific, Freeman experimented with more unconventional settings, such as his piano/drum duets with Shelly Manne and his even more iconoclastic trio work with André Previn—a trio that featured *two* pianos and drums! In many ways Freeman exemplified the modest experimental current at the heart of West Coast jazz during this period. Like many of his contemporaries', Freeman's experimentation was probing, rather than path-breaking, building on a firm tradition instead of merely renouncing past techniques; yet despite its appreciation of the jazz heritage, it was always open to new sounds, new instrumentations, new song structures. This pervasive openness paved the way for a more revolutionary form of experimentation on the West Coast in the later work of Ornette Coleman and Don Cherry.

Freeman's duets with Manne are a case in point. This recording grew from the empathetic work between the pianist and the drummer in their live performances. "Playing on the job," Freeman explained, "Shelly and I used to do things together in the rhythm section, not just counterpoint to the horns, but between us. Instead of playing a drum solo or a piano solo, in some spots, we'd play a solo at the same time, trying to feel each other out, with an awareness of each other being there. Incidentally, both of us like playing with a good bass player."[18] Freeman's afterthought is well taken; even so, the bass is not missed on these sides. Both players seem positively inspired by their newfound freedom. Freeman in particular, not held down by any predetermined bass line, plays with an impressive harmonic daring that assimilates Monk and prefigures Bill Evans. Two years later, aided by Baker, he would create an even finer example of this harmonic style with his moving composition "Summer Sketch." On the strength of these few recordings, Freeman must be considered one of the most sophisticated harmonic minds on the West Coast during the decade.

On September 6, 1955, Baker left for a four-month European tour. Like so many other things in Baker's life and times, the scheduled itinerary soon gave way to more spontaneous demands, and eight months elapsed before the Baker group returned to the United States. Even the initial incentive for the tour—Baker's affair with a Frenchwoman—testified to the trumpeter's impulsiveness. Around this time Baker was first experiencing the drug problems that would follow him for the remainder of his career.

"Chet wanted me to go to Europe with him," Freeman explains, "but I could see where he was heading with the drugs. I was also having trouble with migraine headaches at the time, so I didn't go with him. Instead he went with Dick Twardzik." Both Freeman and Baker had heard Twardzik during their engagement at Boston's Storyville club in late 1954 and had been amazed at the striking keyboard conception of the pianist, then only twenty-three or twenty-four years old. "When I heard him play he sounded so unique and so different that I called up Dick Bock. I told him about this fantastic piano player I had heard. And Dick said, 'Why don't you do a recording?' So we went up to New Jersey to Rudy Van Gelder's studio and did the album. I'm glad we did it, because it's one of the few things Dick ever recorded." This seldom-heard recording, which features Twardzik with bassist Carson Smith and drummer Peter Littman, is one of the most exciting piano trio albums of the mid-1950s. Perhaps the oldest cliché in criticism cites an artist as being "ahead of his time," but Twardzik's rhythmic and harmonic daring on this, his only recording as a leader, warrants this description.

When Freeman declined the opportunity to tour overseas, Twardzik became the natural choice for the spot. Although Freeman has often been credited with referring Baker to Twardzik, he explains that "Chet already knew about him. We were hanging out together. Chet might even have driven up with us to Rudy Van Gelder's studio for the [Twardzik trio] session."

This long tour found Baker performing for the first time in a wide range of European locales, many of which would become familiar haunts in later years, including Amsterdam, Geneva, Copenhagen, Paris, London, Stuttgart, Cologne, Berlin, Baden-Baden, Milan, San Remo, and Rome. For much of the rest of Baker's life, Europe would serve as a home away from home, more of a home than he ever had on the West Coast and certainly more than his native Oklahoma could offer. Had he stayed in Southern California, Baker eventually would have scuffled for work, like Sonny Criss, Teddy Edwards, Harold Land and the other LA talents who were taken for granted by the natives. And given his predilection for the drug underworld, Baker, like Art Pepper, would probably have spent half his career in institutions of one sort or another. Even in Europe Baker's run-ins with the law were frequent, but in the more tolerant atmosphere of the northern countries he eventually forged a lifestyle that gave him the freedom he craved, one supported by admirers who would tolerate his excesses and an audience that apparently never tired of his music. This extended stay overseas was simply the first stage of a lifelong love affair—perhaps "working relationship" is the more apt term—with continental ways.

For all its devil-may-care spontaneity, this first road trip was marked almost from the start by tragedy. On October 21, while the group was staying in Paris, Dick Twardzik died from a heroin overdose. "We really don't know whether it was an intended thing or not," later commented Baker—in words that could apply to the equal ambiguity surrounding the trumpeter's own death years later. "He was alone and the door was locked."[19] Freeman suspects that Twardzik had been a novice with drugs: "You know, you don't find people who are really strung out dying from overdoses—which leads me to believe that he probably hadn't been deeply into it. He probably hadn't built up a tolerance to it." Twardzik was only twenty-four years old when he died; his complete discography consists of a scant half-dozen recorded performances—three made during this tour with Baker. Despite this meager output and his short career, Twardzik had already shown promise as one of the finest pianists of the new generation. Baker's praise leaves no doubt as to the trumpeter's verdict: "His playing reached an unbelievable level. He was a true genius."[20]

Twardzik's presence also had a noticeable effect on Baker. He brought out an even greater introspection in the trumpeter's music, akin to the way Baker played in the Mulligan Quartet. Like that earlier ensemble, Baker's group with Twardzik created a subdued chamber music atmosphere in which every note resonated a depth of meaning. One wanting to prove that less is truly more would look to just such sessions as these for evidence.

In a much different vein is Baker's work with pianist Bobby Timmons in the trumpeter's 1956 quintet. Timmons's funk-oriented style is best known through his still widely-played compositions "Moanin'," "Dis Here," and "Dat Dere" and his later associations with Cannonball Adderley and Art Blakey. His work was the antithesis of the cool melodicism associated with Baker, yet his presence in the 1956 group was anything but an anomaly. Baker was clearly interested at this point in pursuing a more hard-bop approach, and to this end he also brought along tenorist Phil Urso in a front line supported by the East Coast rhythm section of Timmons, Philadelphia-born bassist Jimmy Bond, and Bostonian drummer Peter Littman. During the last week of July 1956, Baker went into the studio several times with this band in the midst of one of the busiest periods of this career; that same week also found him recording in vocal sessions with the accompaniment of Russ Freeman, as well as involving himself in a somewhat disappointing session with Art Pepper (discussed in chapter 14).

The fluency of the recordings with Urso and Timmons suggest a band that is quite comfortable and well-meshed. "To Mickey's Memory," a spirited romp over the changes to "I'll Remember April," reveals the much greater energy in Baker's playing in this new setting. His new musical personality reflected a tendency that would surface again from time to time in Baker's career, perhaps most notably in his series of Prestige recordings from the 1960s. This much-different Chet Baker hoped to shuffle off his reputation as a dreamy balladeer by surrounding himself with a group of hard-driving musicians who could light a fire under his own playing. These forays into the hot often surprised those listeners expecting one more version of "My Funny Valentine." For the most part they were successful attempts to broaden Baker's musical horizons.

a sensuous, feminine instrument

In early 1954 Gerry Mulligan was released from the Sheriff's Honor Farm. Returning to his native New York, he learned—no doubt to his dismay—that he was now inextricably linked in the public's mind with "West Coast Jazz." Labels aside, the music he now played stayed true to the model he had set in California. Over the next year the baritone saxophonist performed in various settings, often relying on trumpeter Jon Eardley or valve trombonist Bob Brookmeyer to fill the role initiated by Baker. For many fans and concert promoters, the break-up of the original pianoless quartet was much lamented. When Mulligan traveled to Paris to perform at Salle Pleyel in June, Charles Delaunay and others expressed apprehension at Baker's absence and the substitution of the lesser-known Brookmeyer. The recording of the concert shows, however, that the valve trombonist filled the brass chair admirably. Brookmeyer, like his musical colleagues Gerry Mulligan and Stan Getz, resided briefly in California during the 1950s. Despite his compatibility with a cool aesthetic, he (again like Getz and Mulligan) remained ambivalent about being associated with West Coast jazz.

At the close of 1954, Mulligan returned to California for a recorded concert at Hoover High School in San Diego, this time relying on Jon Eardley on trumpet. Both Eardley and Brookmeyer made strong contributions to Mulligan's band; even so, their work represented little, if any, advance over the pianoless quartet, either in quality or conception. The old magic was difficult to recapture. Even when Mulligan was rejoined by Baker—as on their 1957 reunion sessions—the music remained a notch below their earlier collaborations. The addition of tenor saxophonist Zoot Sims to Mulligan's mid-1950s group had a more positive impact on the music. Sims, one of the finest soloists of his generation, gave the band a new sound to draw on—and one distanced from the now overworked Baker–Mulligan model.

In later years, Mulligan was disinclined to build on his reputation as a West Coast player, even though many of his finest later albums found him paired with California natives such as Paul Desmond, Dave Brubeck, and Zoot Sims. At the close of 1957, Mulligan even returned to the Pacific Jazz fold to do the first of several reunion albums with Baker. Although the results were below the level of the first pianoless quartet, they renewed Mulligan's perceived ties to the West Coast jazz community. Despite his aversion to such recognition, Mulligan continued to exert a strong influence on the California scene until the end of the decade. The use of counterpoint, the emphasis on relaxed tempos, the restrained drum sound, the experimentation with different combinations of instruments, the heavy reliance on compositional structures, the openness to new sounds—all of these remained trademarks of West Coast jazz in the 1950s. Not only that, but Mulligan's own work—on whatever coast—continued to reflect many of these same attributes.

Drummer Chico Hamilton was one of those who learned the most from Mulligan's model. Hamilton had performed on many of the early quartet and tentette sides before leaving the group to tour with Lena Horne. Along with Shelly Manne, Hamilton contributed greatly to the establishment of a West Coast style of drumming. "It is a very melodic instrument," Hamilton has said of the drums, "very soft, graceful in motion as well as sound: a sensuous feminine instrument."[21] Hamilton reached back to prebebop drummers such as Jo Jones and Sonny Greer in developing his sound. Despite these roots in the big band era, his drum attack was far from old-fashioned; his sensitivity, taste, and dynamic range were fresh and invigorating in the wake of the modern jazz revolution. "When Chico Hamilton took a drum solo," critic Ralph Gleason once wrote, "it was probably the first time in history that a jazz drummer's solo was so soft you had to whisper or be conspicuous."

Unlike many at the forefront of West Coast jazz, Hamilton was a native of Los Angeles, where he was born as Foreststorn Hamilton on September 21, 1921. He began playing at age sixteen while a student at Thomas Jefferson High School. "I didn't study with Sam [Browne]," Hamilton recalls, "but I was part of an outside-of-school band with many of the musicians who were playing for him."[22]

The "unofficial band" rehearsed at Ross Snyder Playground Recreation Hall, located between Jefferson High and the White Sox Ballpark. This inconspicuous site proved to be a minor league training ground for major league jazz talent. In addition to Hamilton, other participants included Dexter Gordon, Charles Mingus, Ernie Royal, Buddy Collette, and Jackie Kelso. On occasion Wardell Gray, Illinois Jacquet, or Britt Woodman might join in on the music-making. It is hard to think of this group—any leader's dream come true—as a "student band."

Between 1942 and 1946 Hamilton served in the army; during this time he abandoned his given name for "Chico." ("They had trouble pronouncing Foreststorn.") Upon discharge, Hamilton learned that the four short years of his military service had witnessed a jazz revolution: "When I came out I discovered that there had been a complete switch in drumming. Oh, the basic foundation of keeping time remained, but otherwise the whole conception of drumming changed. It threw me." With, in his words, "considerable shock" Hamilton heard and learned from the beboppers, but unlike many musicians placed in a similar situation, he carefully avoided slavish imitation and instead continued to develop his more stylized approach to the drums. His postwar work with Lester Young, Count Basie, Ella Fitzgerald, and Lionel Hampton helped him maintain and refine this tempered alternative to the modern drum methods.

Hamilton returned to Lena Horne for a year before deciding to branch out on his own. He followed the example of his former bandmates Mulligan and Baker by recording as a leader for Pacific Jazz. His first project, a 10-inch LP that featured Hamilton with guitarist Howard Roberts and bassist George Duvivier, received generally good reviews. Strengthened in his conviction that his future lay in leading his own ensemble, Hamilton decided to experiment with more diverse instrumentation than this trio allowed. The subsequent addition of Buddy Collette, a Los Angeles native born on August 6, 1921, was a major coup. Collette—who was fluent on flute, clarinet, tenor, and alto—gave Hamilton access to a rich variety of tonal colors. Hamilton also asked French horn player John Graas to join the group, but Graas was committed to his steady if mundane gig with the pianist Liberace. Hamilton's other choice for an "exotic" instrumentalist was Johnny Mandel, whose work on bass trumpet briefly graced the band, but Mandel was also unavailable for a full-time commitment. The unusual voice Hamilton was seeking emerged fortuitously when he learned that Fred Katz, primarily known in jazz circles as a pianist, was interested in exploring the jazz potential of the cello. Katz, guitarist Jim Hall, and bassist Carson Smith constituted the "string section" in the new Hamilton unit.

Katz was not the first to use the cello in jazz, but he was perhaps the first significant jazz player to play it without doubling on the contrabass.

Oscar Pettiford, for example had experimented with the cello after pur-
chasing one at a pawnshop in 1949 and recorded with it the following year.
Even earlier, Harry Babasin had recorded pizzicato cello solos with pianist
Dodo Marmarosa in 1947. At the time of the Katz/Hamilton collaborations, the cello was still viewed as a jazz anomaly—it was usually perceived, if considered at all, as a second instrument for ambitious bass players. Katz also doubled on piano (and had played that instrument with Lena
Horne and Tony Bennett, among others), but his adoption of the cello was
not, as in the case of Pettiford, the late addition of someone already in
mid-career. Katz had studied with Pablo Casals and was devoted to establishing the cello as a legitimate jazz voice, anticipating the later work of
other dedicated cellists such as David Darling and Abdul Wadud.

The Hamilton's quintet was one of the most stylized groups to emerge on
the West Coast scene. All the elements associated with Mulligan and West
Coast jazz—unusual instruments, intricate arrangements, a refined sense
of swing—figured prominently in the group's sound. For many listeners,
the Chico Hamilton Quintet was a quintessential West Coast jazz band.
More to the point, the group reflected the excesses of the West Coast
sound. The Hamilton ensemble was not a good barometer of the California
music scene at its best, or even of the group's members in particular. The
band's work on early recordings such as *Chico Hamilton Quintet* and *Chico
Hamilton Quintet in Hi Fi* has not worn well with the passing years. Its
heavy string orientation evokes a pronounced "elevator music" quality.

The problems with Hamilton's music had nothing to do with the in-
dividual talents of the band members. During this period and in later years
Hamilton's various groups consistently featured some of the most outstanding soloists in jazz, including Eric Dolphy, Ron Carter, Paul Horn,
Jim Hall, Larry Coryell, Buddy Collette, Gabor Szabo, Dennis Budimir,
Arnie Lawrence, Charles Lloyd, and Roy Ayers. With the early Hamilton
Quintet sides, however, the overly arranged settings prevented these fine
musicians, Hamilton included, from playing at their best. Especially on
ballads like "My Funny Valentine" and "The Wind," Collette's lyricism
is undercut by the string section, while on faster tempos the cello often
only adds an unneeded layer of sound. Like the flute and oboe work pursued by the Lighthouse All-Stars, this particular "innovation" helped feed
the fires of criticism repeatedly launched at West Coast musicians ever
since Kenton began toying with new instruments. The critics were often
correct. The new instruments were often treated as ends in their own right.
The challenge of fitting them into the group was addressed only after the
fact.

Collette and Hall provided the strongest jazz solo voices in the original quintet, but their contributions were not enough to compensate for the
meandering arrangements and generally dainty sound of the band. Col-

lette, who recorded prolifically as a sideman in the 1950s—with, among others, Frank Sinatra, Benny Goodman, Carmen McCrae, Red Norvo, Buddy Rich, Jimmy Giuffre, and the Hi-Los—was better served by his less frequent sessions as a leader. His first LP recorded under his own name, *Man of Many Parts*, as well as his subsequent project *Tanganyika* (ostensibly credited to disk jockey Sleepy Stein, but clearly under Collette's direction), gave him the room to blow he rarely found in the Hamilton ensemble. True to its name, *Man of Many Parts* successfully showcased a number of different sides to Collette's playing and composing. His sensitive lyricism comes through on his wistful ballad "Cheryl Ann," written for his daughter; "Jazz City Blues" includes several tasty tenor choruses in a Lester Young vein; "Zan," another twelve-bar blues, captures a more bop-like feeling with Collette's up-tempo alto work. "Makin' Whoopee," in contrast, is a straightforward standard that sticks to a medium groove throughout, but Collette is equally persuasive here with an offhand sense of swing that floats nicely over the rhythm section. Elsewhere on the album, Collette plays flute and clarinet, features an original composition written in Lyle Murphy's twelve-tone system, works with Latin rhythms, and in general lives up to the eclecticism implied in the album's title.

Like other similarly accomplished multi-instrumentalists (Roland Kirk comes to mind), Collette was hindered in gaining wider public recognition by the very breadth of his talent. In a jazz world where winning polls and being master of a specific "category" are important contributors to success, too wide a musical grasp is a curse rather than a blessing. Collette's longstanding work in the studios also contributed to his continued low profile in the jazz world. As one of the first black musicians to play a major role in the film studios, Collette was a pioneer who paid a price through his reduced visibility in jazz.

In early 1958 Hamilton went back to a standard trio format on his *Chico Hamilton Trio* album, this time using the common configuration of piano, bass, and drums. The string section was not missed—except, perhaps, by the captive dentist-chair audience—but in this new setting Hamilton's sidemen fell below the standard of previous groups. Pianist Freddy Gambrell was simply not a strong enough soloist to sustain the new band. Later in the year, Hamilton tried to convince Collette to rejoin the group, but Buddy, by now firmly established in the studios, was understandably reluctant to leave town. Instead he recommended a young reed player who, like Collette, showed a prodigious talent on both saxophone and flute: Eric Dolphy, who would, of course, soon prove much more than an accomplished sideman. Dolphy, whose career on the West Coast will be discussed later in this book, set off a revolution in the jazz world.

one long nightmare

As the 1950s progressed, Chet Baker's problems with drugs came to overshadow his musical achievements. "My whole life became one long nightmare," he would later reflect.[23] For years Baker had had his share of run-ins with the law, but now everything around him began to crumble. Around the time he signed with the Riverside label, he was arrested and sent to the federal hospital in Lexington. Shortly after his release, he was arrested once more, again on drug charges, and spent four months on Riker's Island.

"I couldn't get a job after that, so I headed for Europe," Baker later explained. In July 1959 the trumpeter arrived in Italy, but his encounters with the law became even more pronounced in the Old World. In August 1960, he was arrested while trying to fix in a gas station in Lucca, Italy. After eight months of legal wrangling he was convicted of forging prescriptions, importing narcotics, and drug abuse.

According to Baker, his heroin use began in 1957, when he was twenty-seven years old. In interviews with the jazz media, Baker's various accounts of his addiction were often extended exercises in bad faith, but in this instance Baker's claim is substantiated by Russ Freeman. "He started after everybody else stopped," Freeman attests.[24] Richard Bock also describes Baker, from the early days, as athletic, clear-headed, spending his recreation time on weekend ski trips—hardly the profile of a heroin addict. Yet long before Baker's narcotics problems deepened, his character showed striking signs of a constant reliance on quick fixes; going AWOL from the service is an obvious example. But Russ Freeman provides an even more telling anecdote from the quartet days: Baker took $3,500, which had been set aside for the quartet's IRS payment, and used it—no, not for drugs— to fly to Detroit and buy a new car! Immediate gratification was Baker's way almost from the start.

And kept its hold throughout his life. The trumpeter's fascination with expensive cars never diminished. Toward the end, when his appearance suggested a junkie on his last legs, Baker's breakneck driving in his Alfa Romeo astonished and terrified many fellow passengers. In light of these early warning signals, Baker's heroin addiction and constant legal problems should come as no surprise. "If my habit hadn't been illegal and expensive," he once offered in justification, "I might have been alright."[25] But then he added, with obvious pride: "At one time, I was spending $800 to $1,000 a week on heroin. How did I get the bread to pay for that? I worked, and every cent I made went for drugs. Using heroin is a full-time, 24-hour-a-day thing." Like a true native Oklahoman, Baker could boast of his Bible Belt work ethic even when it was applied to supporting drug use.

During his Italian internment, Baker spent his time playing the trumpet and solving chess problems. At his release, he seemed poised to put all his energies into his career. He had composed twenty-two songs while in prison and was anxious to return to the recording studio. But only six months later, Baker was again arrested, this time in Munich, and charged with narcotics law violations, theft, and forgery. In preliminary questioning, he admitted to taking about seventy pills a day. After three weeks in a Munich clinic, he was released and ordered to stay out of Germany for the next three years. He tried to return to Italy but was denied entrance. In desperation, he settled in Paris, where he began a lengthy engagement at the Blue Note.

The story of Chet Baker's life from the late 1950s until his death repeats like a broken record. Arrest, imprisonment, release, change of residence, comeback attempt, and then another arrest to start the cycle all over. In the early 1960s, Baker's comeback attempts and rehabilitations still held some promise. We wanted to believe that the bad boy of jazz would come clean. After all, didn't he have everything to gain by rehabilitating—movie stardom, a crossover pop music audience, fame and fortune—and everything to lose from addiction and incarceration? And for brief moments, Baker appeared to be back on track. In late 1962 he was working on a film in England, *Summer Holiday* starring Susan Hayward. A film based on his life was planned by an Italian film company, and Baker had been given an advance of 2.5 million lire to play himself.

These promises of film stardom never panned out, although Baker was an ideal candidate for movie success. Years later film critic Pauline Kael would lament this lost career: "As a young man in the nineteen-fifties, the cool jazz trumpeter and singer Chet Baker had the casual deviltry and the 'Blame It On My Youth' handsomeness to become a screen idol."[26] At the end of his life Baker finally played himself in Bruce Weber's film *Let's Get Lost*, but by then he was no material for a romantic lead, just a burnt-out addict who interested his audience through his decadence as much as through his music.

Then again, Baker's cinematic life outdid anything the Hollywood studios could have invented. In January 1964, Baker was again arrested in Germany after playing the Blue Note in West Berlin. This time he spent forty days in a German psychiatric hospital and was deported on March 3, 1964. Two days later he returned to the United States, penniless but apparently unchastened by his disastrous European experiences. At JFK Airport he was interrogated, searched by customs agents, and detained for more than an hour.

Pressed by financial necessity, Baker recorded frequently, first in New York and later in California. By the middle of the decade he had hit a new artistic low. Faced with a shrinking audience for jazz in an age of rock-

and-roll, he began recording with the Mariachi Brass, a feeble imitation of Herb Alpert's then successful, but musically impotent, Tijuana Brass. While under contract to Liberty Records, the owners of World Pacific, Baker made six pathetic albums: four with the Mariachi Brass and two with strings.

This was the worst music of his career. But his personal life had yet to hit bottom. That came in 1968, while he was in Northern California for an engagement at Sausalito's Trident Club. Five men jumped Baker and beat him severely. Baker lost his teeth—and almost his music career—as a result of the assault. In Weber's *Let's Get Lost*, the trumpeter gives his version of the circumstances: On a previous visit to the site—a heroin connection in San Francisco's Fillmore district—Baker encountered a suspicious character who, so Baker thought, was planning to rob him. In response Baker held his hand in his pocket, as though he were holding a gun. Nothing happened at that time. On Baker's next visit, according to this puzzling version, the same man had five assailants attack Baker. An ambiguous gesture made with a hand hidden inside a pocket seems an insufficient motive for such a violent outburst. Weber himself implies as much in *Let's Get Lost*. Moreover, the nature of the attack suggests that Baker's enemies knew who he was. They wanted to impair the trumpeter's ability to earn a living. After the attack, the remnants of Baker's teeth were pulled ("one at a time," Baker would later stress to his interviewers), and his career was apparently at an end. Twenty years later, Baker's death in the heart of Amsterdam's drug culture suggested that he had perhaps again made an enemy who bore a deep grudge. After the 1968 attack Baker found himself unable to play the trumpet and was forced to work, at least for a time, as a service station attendant, pumping gas and wiping windshields from 7 a.m. to 11 p.m. During this hiatus from jazz—a five-year enforced retirement—Baker supplemented his paychecks through occasional government assistance programs. His drastically reduced income had, however, the one positive effect of limiting his narcotics intake. From 1970 to 1973, he took part in a methadone program—participation that ended, perhaps not coincidentally, around the same time that he returned to performing and the big-time money of the overseas jazz circuit.

Some critics have suggested, not without reason, that Baker's reputation in jazz circles would be far greater had he died young. The romantic myth of the jazz trumpeter who meets an early end has become a stereotype—with disturbing corollaries in the history of the music, from Bix Beiderbecke and Buddy Bolden to Lee Morgan and Woody Shaw. Baker was hardly so obliging. If anything, he sabotaged the stereotype at every point. Instead of conveying the clichéd image of the boy trumpeter dying before age could tarnish his youth, Baker took on the appearance of advanced years and dissipation while still in his thirties. Instead of leaving behind a small body of classic recorded work, Baker made more records—

good, bad, and ugly—than almost any other jazz musician of his generation. Instead of dying suddenly from tragic circumstances beyond his control, he lasted longer than anyone thought possible. And the circumstances
surrounding his eventual demise could evoke little sympathy—they suggested that Baker was perhaps culpable, at least in part, for his own death.

Once again, the comparison with Art Pepper comes to mind. In the
1950s Baker had recorded with Pepper as "the Playboys of Jazz." And like
Pepper, Baker soon lost even the tawdry glamor of the neighborhood bad
boy. But with both the music remained fresh and good until the end. For
the last half of his career, Baker constantly faced hostile critics who wanted
to treat him as a has-been—someone who had either never deserved praise,
or else had long ago passed his peak. Max Harrison's early critique of the
trumpeter's "monotonous, emasculated style" is the typical party line of
those who could not or would not hear the powerful emotional directness
of Baker's cool aesthetic.[27] But the music tells a different story. Baker's
early recordings on the Pacific label are among the lasting masterpieces of
postwar jazz. There were always bad Baker albums—economic quick fixes
to support his habit—especially in the 1960s. But there were many more
outstanding ones. His recordings from the 1980s—even the very last ones—
were much stronger than most admitted at the time. Some subconscious
sense of fair play made us want to believe that Baker's music was on the
decline. How could a life of such dissipation not take its toll on the artist's
work?

But Baker had no patience for the expectations others put on him:
neither for the early romanticized image imposed on him nor for the mor-
alistic posturing taken toward his later life. At the end he refused the
Dorian Gray stereotype, just as decades before he had sabotaged the pinup-
boy image others had of him. At every step, in both his music and his
life, Chet Baker went his own way. The initial press reports of his death—
some of which stated that the police had found a *thirty-year-old* trumpeter
dead from a fall—seemed like Baker's last laugh. He refused to be a has-
been even at the end.

CHAPTER TEN

From the Lighthouse

shoot the pier

The combat between East Coast jazz and West Coast jazz was waged by means of album covers. Covers from New York's Blue Note label lived off the mystique of East Coast intensity, with monochromatic images that evoked an essentially macho view of the jazz experience: drummer Art Blakey drenched in sweat caught mid-solo; saxophonist Sonny Rollins taking a smoke between smoking takes; trumpeter Lee Morgan threatening to pop a vein with the next high note. Such stolen moments of jazz in flight captured a musical intensity that was the antithesis of West Coast cool. The Blue Note musicians were invariably shown indoors, blanched in the double darkness of the studio inner sanctum and East Coast gloom. This music achieved its diamond-edged sharpness, such covers suggested, through hard work, unbounded energy, and occasionally plain brute force. The music's underlying sophistication seemed continually tempered by a blue-collar, New England work ethic mentality. Recall the anecdote about an importunate audience member asking drummer Blakey why he wore overalls to the gig. The response came back quickly enough: "Because I'm going to *work!*"

Covers from California's Contemporary label fought back with their own distinctive arsenal. West Coast record companies didn't even need to show musicians on their covers. Being savvy marketers, they knew how to sell their product—with image advertising, sometimes with humor, often with unabashed pandering to the baser instincts. A honey in a skimpy bathing suit, a nurse with her blouse half open, an attractive model climbing out of the bell of an enormous saxophone. What did these images have to do with West Coast jazz? Very little perhaps, but they did sell records. The Contemporary cover for Russ Freeman and André Previn's *Double*

Play, for example, could even evoke a sexual *double entendre* from the title, by depicting an attractive young woman, apparently naked except for an incongruous baseball cap (which mysteriously bears the initial *H*), who holds both her thumbs up in the air. The nurse featured on the cover of a Curtis Counce release is shown applying a stethoscope to her partially covered left breast (apparently measuring the palpitations inspired by the enclosed music).

All these images were, moreover, displayed in full-color, splashy lay-outs—another sharp contrast with the no-frills, spartan look Alfred Lion instituted at Blue Note. And if the leader of a Contemporary date did get his mug on the album jacket, he certainly wasn't shown perspiring in Rudy Van Gelder's recording studio. On the basis of the record covers, one might wonder whether these musicians ever saw the inside of a studio. Contemporary covers seemed to find the bandsmen playing in the most low-key locations: Harold Land blowing tenor at the Watts Towers, Red Norvo playing vibes in a meadow, Art Pepper fingering his horn in a tree-lined garden. Even East Coast players were susceptible, it seems, to this baneful influence: When Sonny Rollins recorded *Way Out West* for the Contemporary label, he posed for the album cover on the desert plains of the Southland, dressed in a mock cowboy outfit, brandishing his saxophone like a gunslinger's weapon.

The Lighthouse All-Stars went the furthest to imprint this ultra-cool West Coast ethos on their album covers. Each Lighthouse release seemed to outdo the previous one in presenting West Coast jazz as an offshoot of Southern California beach culture. The inevitable end-point was reached with the cover of the All-Stars' sixth Contemporary album: The band is actually shown set up to play on the Hermosa Beach strand. The waves roll gently onto the shore a few dozen yards in the background. Dressed in suits and ties (in sharp contrast to the one, possibly naked, bather discernible in the distance) and apparently captured in the middle of a serious impromptu performance (only saxophonist Bob Cooper wears a giveaway grin), the All-Stars act as though this beach setting is the most natural place in the world for a California band's jam session.

Perhaps this simply underlines the timeworn injunction not to judge a book (or record) by its cover. Even so, if the New York critics wanted to prove that West Coast jazz was all image and no substance, certainly these flighty jackets played right into their hands. Yet with the Lighthouse albums, more than perhaps any others, reality seemed to approach the stereotyped image. The Lighthouse brought West Coast jazz about as far west as it could go, at least in terms of geography. Only a few feet past the door to the Lighthouse Café, which even today stands near the end of Hermosa Beach's Pier Avenue, the sidewalk disappears, its place taken by the sandy beach shown on the aforementioned cover. A pretentious statue of a surfer now stands here on a huge pedestal at the brink of the pier—locals call it the Tomb of the Unknown Surfer. Another hundred feet or so past the sundry sunbathers and volleyball enthusiasts, the waves of the Pacific Ocean lap on to the shore. At the end of the avenue, the Hermosa Beach pier juts out over the ocean. Surfers who frequent these waters will try, in moments of daring or foolhardiness (take your choice), to "shoot the pier," cascading on their boards between the large supports underpinning the structure. This is how the continent ends, not with a bang, but on a surfboard. Or, if the waves roll wrong, with a bang on a surfboard.

A picture-perfect setting for the celebrated Lighthouse Café. Yet even a legend occasionally needs some help. The towering lighthouse shown on the cover of *Music for Lighthousekeeping* (another Contemporary release) was not *the* Lighthouse, but an attractive surrogate. The actual club, for all its proximity to the shore, boasted no beacon for fog-bound sailors, no towering turret, no crusty keeper (unless one wished to award Howard Rumsey that dubious distinction). With its unassuming façade and dark, cramped interior, the club proper was unsuitable for glossy cover photos. First-time visitors to John Levine's inelegant dive soon learned that it was a lighthouse in name only.

And even the proximity to the Pacific could be misleading. True, the Lighthouse was situated as far west as you could go without getting your feet wet. True, it was intimately associated with the West Coast scene—in fact was almost synonymous with it in the minds of many listeners. Yet the music played within its four walls was often strikingly at odds with the critics' stereotypes of jazz on the Pacific Coast. In contrast to the emphasis on composing and arranging characteristic, say, of Mulligan, Rogers, Giuffre, Holman, and many other West Coast bandleaders, the Lighthouse All-Stars frequently worked within the context of fairly free-form jam sessions. Even when many of these same musicians played with the Lighthouse group, their work on the Pier Avenue bandstand differed markedly from what they did in the studio. The various live recordings suggest that the Lighthouse was no center for California cool but was as boisterous and lively a setting for jazz music as any dive found east or west. A constant undercurrent of talk, tinkling glasses, cash registers ringing, and other assorted crowd noises provided a nonmusical counterpoint to the often frenetic activities onstage. Whatever introspective tendencies West Coast jazz may have had, they rarely took wing in this high-energy environment.

The site was an unlikely locale to make jazz history. Built in late 1934 and opened as a restaurant named Verpilate's (after the building's contractor), it served patrons of a nearby dime-a-dance ballroom. After only six years, the room underwent its first major face-lift, changing owners, format, and name all at once.[1] the new proprietor's previous experience in club management came from two San Pedro bars. There he had attracted a clientele of merchant seamen to his beach community watering holes. Now he decided to apply this same tried-and-true formula to the new locale. The changed name, the Lighthouse, and the newly added bamboo and Polynesian decor were likely chosen to arouse the seafaring nostalgia of a grounded merchant marine. Apparently they did the job: The room did boomtown business during the Second World War, serving drinks until 2 a.m. and selling food around the clock. But by the late 1940s, the novelty had worn thin—Polynesian pastiche had perhaps lost its luster for vets returning from island-hopping escapades in the Pacific. Business declined sharply. The club was sold in 1948. John Levine became its new owner.

Levine, one of the forgotten businessmen who spurred the West Coast renaissance, is an interesting character in his own right. A rabbi's son from Canada, he was already a former millionaire by the time he took control of the Lighthouse. Gambling had been his downfall, but with the bettor's eternal optimism—he *knows* the next million is right around the corner—Levine embarked on his new venture full of confidence and élan. With, alas, little success—at least at first. Enter stage left: Howard Rumsey, a bassist caught up in the musician's eternal search for the next gig. One spring day in 1949, Rumsey's search brought him to Hermosa Beach, where he had once played in the dime-a-dance ballroom near Verpilate's. Although the Lighthouse did not feature live music at that time, Rumsey noticed that the room had a serviceable bandstand. He approached the new owner about adopting a jazz format:

> I asked him, "How about putting on a Sunday jam session?"
> "Kid, are you gonna try to tell me what to do with this place? Everybody else has."
> I talked some more; finally he said, "Okay, let's try it out." The next Sunday I put together a fine combo, opened the front door—there was no p.a. system, but we kept the music loud enough to roar out into the street—and within an hour Levine had more people in the room than he'd seen in a month. That was Sunday afternoon, May 29, 1949.
> It was a classic case of all the elements converging: the right place at the right time for the right people.[2]

In seeking a steady short-term gig, Rumsey stumbled upon what became a lifelong career. Of course Rumsey, born in Brawley, California (a few miles from the Mexican border), on November 7, 1917, had already shown a knack for spotting the right place at the right time. Even as a player he was something of an opportunist: Starting as a pianist, then switching to drums, Rumsey focused on the bass after a musician friend told him there was a shortage of solid players on that instrument. The advice was well taken; after completing a year at Los Angeles City College, Rumsey landed a choice job with Vido Musso's band, soon following it with a lengthy stint with Johnny "Scat" Davis.

The next opportunity Rumsey spotted was, however, far bigger. When former Musso sideman Stan Kenton decided to form his own band, Rumsey immediately signed on as bassist. Almost from the start of its engagement at the Rendezvous Ballroom in Balboa, the Kenton ensemble proved to be a huge success, quickly parlaying its local following of college and high school students into a dedicated radio audience from coast to coast.

Musicians who played for Kenton frequently reached for religious metaphors when describing the maestro. Art Pepper incurred Kenton's displeasure when he told *Downbeat* that the bandleader could have been as big as Billy Graham if he had gone into the religion business. Pepper had intended the remark as a compliment—and many of the group's fans shared the charismatic fervor. "We were wired that first summer at Balboa," Rumsey adds.[3] "We were glued in. We all had houses or apartments down there; my wife and I lived within sixty yards of the ballroom for thirty-six dollars a month. I was so wrapped up in the music, I didn't even know I was married! We used to follow Stan around. He was like a god to us!"

Rumsey soon lost the faith. He incurred a rapid departure from the ensemble when he was literally heaved off the bandstand by Kenton after an onstage disagreement. Upon leaving Kenton, Rumsey worked for several first-class bandleaders, including Charlie Barnet and Barney Bigard, but finally decided that road life was not his ideal. Settled in Southern California, working as, among other things, a tile layer, Rumsey again began searching for the right opportunity in music. The one he found came in the unlikely guise of a 180-seat room, thirty-five by ninety feet, with outdated Polynesian decor.

the dropping-off station

The success of the initial Sunday trial strengthened Levine's commitment to the new format. As the jazz policy expanded, the last straggling merchant seaman soon abandoned their beloved watering hole to the new crowd of modern jazz fans and casual listeners. At first the group performed only on the weekends, with Rumsey spinning records as an in-house deejay from Tuesdays through Thursdays. Eventually live music became a nightly affair, with Sunday featuring a grueling day-long musical marathon.

The Lighthouse, for all its eventual fame, was a challenging—and often exasperating—jazz venue. The long hours were legendary, the quarters cramped and incommodious, the audience frequently loud and disrespectful. The musicians responded, however, with a positive energy that was often surprising, given the inclement surroundings. Jimmy Giuffre, Shorty Rogers, Shelly Manne, and other Lighthouse regulars later gained renown for bringing chamber music restraint to jazz combo playing, but the early work documented in their live Lighthouse recordings shows no such cool and controlled neoclassicism. These were spirited blowing dates with no holds barred, as rambunctious and unpredictable as the turbulent surf waves outside the door. Even Giuffre, arguably the king of cool understatement (he later mastered the technique of constructing a whole solo from an extended, pitchless, breathy sound), often worked up an uncharacteristic sweat when playing on Pier Avenue.

The initial Lighthouse album on Contemporary captured precisely this informal spontaneity. From the riff-like swing of the opening number, Jimmy Giuffre's "Four Others," to the crowd-rousing finale, an extended jam on the same composer's "La Soncailli," the All-Stars take off on the musical material at hand with considerable abandon. This band was loaded with arrangers, but its charts were mostly bare bones and at times even nonexistent. Hampton Hawes's noteworthy work on "All the Things You Are" is a case in point: There is no apparent arrangement or elaborate game plan here, just a quartet blowing its way through one of the oldest standards in the book. Yet Les Koenig found the results memorable enough to give Hawes a contract with Contemporary.

An earlier private recording of a Lighthouse session featuring Shorty Rogers and Art Pepper (later released on the Xanadu label) reveals an even more free-wheeling ensemble. In fact, the music recorded here might seem to be completely at odds with the personnel. Supported by a rhythm section consisting of Rumsey, Patchen, and Manne, Pepper and Rogers led a veritable West Coast all-star band. But the music taken down by Bob Andrews's portable Pentron recorder is New York bebop plain and simple. Tearing through "Scrapple from the Apple," "Cherokee," "Tin Tin Deo," and other East Coast standards, the front line was driving hard—and clearly driving under the influence of Bird and Dizzy. Here again the Lighthouse setting roused the musicians to a higher level of intensity than was their wont. The change was not always for the better—sometimes the Lighthouse performances took on a ragged quality—but the music more often captured an infectious spark that many of these musicians rarely matched elsewhere.

The earliest regular Lighthouse band—a little-known ensemble that unfortunately never recorded—was a throwback to the Central Avenue scene. Rumsey drew around him some of the finest avenue regulars—

including Teddy Edwards, Sonny Criss, and Hampton Hawes—to form the first group advertised as the Lighthouse All-Stars. "Teddy Edwards's composition 'Sunset Eyes' was the first tune we played in the club that people started asking for," Rumsey remembers. Edwards also recalls pianist Frank Patchen, drummer Bobby White, and trumpeter Keith Williams as regular members of the All-Stars during this period.[4] Although he was a star attraction for almost two years, Edwards received two weeks' notice when a new group of musicians became available for the gig. Shorty Rogers had been invited by Rumsey to play at a New Year's Eve performance during his Christmas break from Kenton, and then was asked to join the band full-time. Along with other new additions Jimmy Giuffre and Shelly Manne, Rogers and Rumsey formed the nucleus of a new Lighthouse All-Stars—one much different from its Central Avenue–infused predecessor. This group would soon become established as a bellwether of the new jazz movement on the coast.

This largely unnoticed shift in personnel marked a symbolic turning point distinguishing the new "movement" of the 1950s from the Central Avenue–dominated scene of the 1940s. The black bebop-drenched sound, inspired by Parker during his lengthy California sojourn, now took a back seat to the white heavily-arranged music that would become known simply as "West Coast jazz." The new name implied a homogeneity of musical styles that in fact never existed on the coast. But the mythical world of images has a reality of its own. Fostered by record companies in search of a marketing angle, a new sound was christened: one that, according to the hype, was tanned by the seaside sun and tempered by the cool Pacific breeze. For better or worse, jazz fans began talking about a new style, a new music, a new aesthetic.

"The West Coast jazz style soon began to evolve," Rumsey explained in a 1966 interview.[5] "Music with a definite character took shape, with a special library of its own written by the sidemen. The next few years were very exciting; musicians would bring in new charts and we'd rehearse them right on the job." The last point was amplified in a *Downbeat* photo caption from March 11, 1953, which mentions that Giuffre and Rogers both wrote one new composition each week for the band. The attractions of the gig for the members were many: regular employment, a chance to try out new material on an ongoing basis, and a respite from the road. "I'd been on the road for five years," Shorty Rogers points out, "and it felt like it was time to come out here and stay home a lot, so that's what brought me there and at a later time brought Shelly Manne. It was kind of a dropping-off station for guys that had been on the road too long."[6]

The 78s recorded on the short-lived Lighthouse label in July 1952 show that these new All-Stars were anything but big band burn-outs.

Rogers's "Swing Shift" is a well-arranged up-tempo piece that gives solo space to everyone but Rumsey. Although Patchen, Rogers, Giuffre, and Bob Cooper each make praiseworthy contributions, drummer Manne steals "Swing Shift" with a shifting swing that builds energy without obscuring the subtlest details. The same composer's "Viva Zapata" is surprisingly successful, with none of the awkwardness one finds in many other early recordings of jazz players attempting Latin music. As the name implies, the piece is more Mexican than Afro-Cuban, and Rogers sounds as though he had just served a long apprenticeship in a mariachi band. Giuffre's "Out of Somewhere" is a more subdued contribution, in line with the prevailing image of West Coast understatement. But his "Big Girl" provides a radical contrast. Here the composer honks and shouts in a rhythm-and-blues vein that seems like parody . . . but one is never quite sure. Manne obliges with a hearty backbeat, and some enthused if unknown bandmember occasionally lets loose with an orgiastic holler.

In late 1953, Rogers left the All-Stars to form his Giants and began an extended engagement at the Haig. He brought Giuffre and Manne with him, essentially "borrowing" the nucleus of the Lighthouse All-Stars. Under circumstances that might have been a death knell for Rumsey's ensemble, the bassist responded by forming a new group of regulars, who matched the quality level of the former band in most regards. Bud Shank and Bob Cooper, two of the finest saxophone soloists on the scene, formed the core of the new front line, with Rolf Ericson (and later Conte Candoli) filling the brass chair initiated by Rogers.

Rumsey's real coup, however, was in bringing bebop legend Max Roach to the club as Manne's replacement. For the next several months Roach served as the unlikely drum-keeper of the Lighthouse flame—a period that proved exciting not only for inimitable percussion work, but also for Roach's many friends who sat in with the band. "When Max Roach came in from New York to take over Shelly Manne's drum chair," Rumsey relates, "he drove up with Charles Mingus and Miles Davis in the car with him."[7] Roach's arrival signaled a reversal of compass points from west to east. During the drummer's brief tenure, the Lighthouse hosted some of the brightest jazz stars from the East Coast scene. Rumsey continues:

Miles was just starting to play again after a long sabbatical back home in St. Louis. He hung around for a while, stayed at my home for a week, and did a couple of guest shots at the club. . . . Mingus never played bass for me, but he sat in several times as intermission pianist. As for Max, he set the whole town on fire. Out of his stint I developed long-lasting friendships: Dizzy, Sarah Vaughan, Charlie Parker. The night Bird came in to see and sit in with Max, he was playing a saxophone that was in terrible condition. After an hour of frustration he went outside down the alley and heard someone playing a tenor sax in another club. It was a brand new horn. He asked if he could play it. When the cat said yes, Charlie jumped on the stand and we all left the Lighthouse and listened to him while he blew for two fantastic hours.

Clora Bryant, who was playing at the High Seas—the other jazz club on Pier Avenue at the time—was also present the night Parker came by.

> Right before Charlie Parker was going back to New York, he came down to see Max. They tried all afternoon to get him to sit in, but he left and came over and spent the afternoon playing with *us*. The guy I was working with, Sid Calloway, his horn was so bad, but Charlie played it—he played the you-know-*what* out of it! It was a tenor, and Charlie blew it. Everybody emptied out of the Lighthouse to hear that.[8]

Not all the excitement, however, happened outside the club. Roach's very first Sunday on the job—September 13, 1953—marked one of the most exciting nights in the Lighthouse's history. Miles Davis, Chet Baker, Russ Freeman, and Lorraine Geller all sat in alongside regulars Shank, Cooper, Ericson, and Rumsey, and recent Lighthouse alumni Giuffre and Manne returned to take part in the festivities. Cecil Charles Spiller, a jazz fan/photographer, was on hand with both his monaural tape machine and camera, and he captured the musical proceedings. For many years rumors circulated about these unreleased recordings, especially because of the speculated encounter between Davis and Baker. In his expansive 1983 biography of Davis, *Milestones*, Jack Chambers repeats the hearsay but mistakenly suggests (on what source is unclear) that Baker was not present that day.[9]

All rumors were set to rest in 1985—thirty-two years after the event— with the release of two albums' worth of material from that night: Both Davis and Baker did play at the Lighthouse on that occasion but, at least on the released material, never shared the stage together. What an exciting match-up that might have been: an encounter of the two greatest trumpeters in the cool school! The recorded performances are interesting and intriguing documents nonetheless, and they boast other unusual musical combinations. Davis plays with the boppish flair that characterizes much of his early work, even tackling the four-bar break on "A Night in Tunisia" with a double-time cadenza that sounds more like Gillespie than Miles. On the up-tempo numbers Shank proves to be a surprisingly compatible foil for the trumpeter, contributing some of his most driving recorded work of the decade. Davis dips into the cool with a delicate version of " 'Round Midnight," a song that would help revitalize his career two years later when he played it to acclaim at the Newport Jazz Festival. Baker plays, for the most part, with uncharacteristic aggression—again revealing how the Lighthouse setting brought out the hardball side of West Coast jazz.

These recordings suggest that the new rhythm section struggled to find common ground. Roach preaches fire and brimstone on the drums, definitely showing he was the right man to assume Manne's rights, but his pointillistic rhythms elude pianist Lorraine Geller, who pounds out the beat unmercifully. (One might think to attribute this overbearing piano sound to the microphone placement on what is, after all, an amateur recording. But when Russ Freeman and Claude Williamson play the piano on other numbers, the problem disappears.) Rumsey stays true to the West Coast tradition of a solid, if somewhat flatfooted, bass line. Leroy Vinnegar was the strongest exponent of this powerful, no-nonsense manner of bass playing then prevalent on the coast—a role Ray Brown would later assume and refine. But Rumsey could match neither Brown's strong sound nor Vinnegar's propulsive fills. Studio recordings with Roach made five weeks later show much greater rhythm section coherence, but this live date is touch and go, especially until Freeman and Williamson take over the keyboard duties.

These later studio sessions, made for Les Koenig's Contemporary label, feature an augmented Lighthouse group of from seven to nine members. Like its predecessor, this edition of the All-Stars shows a remarkable affinity for Latin rhythms. Bob Cooper's "Witch Doctor," also played by the band on the live session with Baker, is heard again in a spirited nonet version. This song would soon become one of the All-Stars' most requested numbers.

With Roach's eventual departure, Rumsey again scored a coup in attracting Stan Levey as a replacement. (Finding musicians was one of Rumsey's major skills: I conducted an informal count of some seventy-five musicians who performed at one time or another as part of a Lighthouse All-Star ensemble—and mine is surely only a partial list. An alumni gathering of the group could easily fill the whole club!)[10] Levey, who had come west with the Gillespie/Parker ensemble almost a decade before, was one of the finest modern jazz drummers on either coast. *Drummin' the Blues*, a recording made for Liberty, features both Roach and Levey with the Lighthouse band. The program consists simply of blues tunes, four by each drummer. But any risk of monotony from this limited repertoire is dispelled not only by the strong trap work by both parties but also by noteworthy solo contributions from tenorists Bill Perkins (with Roach) and Bob Cooper (with Levey).

Despite band turnover and noisy club patrons, the Lighthouse All-Stars seemed poised at a creative peak. Rumsey more than made up for his limitations as a player through his unflagging efforts as a promoter and talent scout. Until the gimmicks set in, his band showed promise of becoming the dominant modern jazz ensemble on the coast.

flute 'n oboe

West Coast jazz is littered with the obscured careers of long-neglected figures, but Bob Cooper's case is more unfortunate than most. Unlike so many others who went into the studios in the 1960s, Coop's later reappearances in the jazz world have been largely unheralded. Part of the problem stems from his association with Albert Marx's Discovery label—a company that does so little promotion of its releases that they are truly "discoveries" to the jazz fans who stumble upon them. But Cooper's diffidence and subdued lifestyle also contribute to his low profile.

While browsing through old musicians' union documents from thirty-five years ago, I noticed that Cooper resided then at the same address in Sherman Oaks where he still lives. The fact is a small one, but it is typical of Bob Cooper. Musicians are a nomadic lot, but Cooper is a homebody even by the standards of middle-class suburbia. There is little headline material in his life. He comes across as a paragon of personal stability, a person not prone to taking drastic steps and seemingly indifferent to publicity as well as criticism. In my conversations with him for this book, he appeared ambivalent—indeed, almost completely uninterested—in talking about the history of his musical career. Yet this indifference shows up nowhere in Cooper's music. Onstage he is a powerful, often fiery player.

Born in Pittsburgh on December 6, 1925, Cooper was the son of a professional hockey player who moved from Canada to play for the local team. The elder Cooper eventually married and settled in the area. Influenced by his brother, who was learning the banjo, Bob began playing the tenor guitar at age twelve. He was soon working in a small ensemble with two neighborhood children who were cousins of the great altoist Benny Carter. Cooper's first horn, like so many tenor players' later attracted to Lester Young, was the clarinet, which he began playing in 1940. The following year, while still in high school, he switched to the tenor saxophone.

Cooper first began working in territory bands, his big break coming when a last-minute call to fill in with the Kenton band led to a six-year association. The Kenton connection had several even longer-lasting consequences: Through this band, Cooper not only established himself as a premier soloist but also met his wife, June Christy, and traveled to California, which became his adopted home. Like his father, Cooper pursued a glamorous profession only to eschew the glitz and settle down. Even at this early date, Cooper presented a striking contrast to the typical road musician: Neither a smoker nor a drinker, he was, in the words of Kenton biographer Carol Easton, "quiet, boyish and virginal, with an absolutely even disposition." This was in marked contrast to Christy, of whom Easton writes: "Although she was young and appeared naive, a reputation for drinking and carousing had preceded her."[11]

Kenton, despite his personal magnetism, was a difficult bandleader, not just because of his demanding road trips but also due to his intense personality. Cooper and Christy's marriage had to accommodate itself to the bandleader's strict discipline. Even their wedding ceremony, in Washington, D.C., on January 14, 1947, had to wait until after the band had finished its last show that day. Both were wearing their band uniforms when they married. And the honeymoon was brief: The newlyweds were on the bandstand promptly at 10 a.m. for the next morning's show.

The couple's stormiest encounter with Kenton was precipitated by the singer's illness. "She got high fever and laryngitis so bad she could hardly talk, let alone sing," recalls Cooper.[12] Kenton was reluctant to let his star singer take a leave of absence, and when he finally relented he was aghast to learn that Cooper wanted to accompany his wife. Although the tenorist had found a substitute for his place with the band, Kenton balked. Finally both Cooper and Christy left, but not without temporarily straining their relations with the boss.

After he settled on the West Coast, Cooper's new musical pursuits followed in the progressive direction of his former employer. "The thing that [Kenton] left me was the feeling of wanting to learn to grow in music," Cooper explains. "So many people just stay in their same place, and Stan with that progressive jazz attitude wanted to do something different all the time. . . . It left me with that kind of an attitude to learn and to study a little. So when I came out here I started studying oboe and orchestration."

Cooper became a dedicated student of Mario Castelnuovo-Tedesco. Castelnuovo-Tedesco, born in Italy before the turn of the century, was one of the European highbrow composers who fled to Hollywood to escape the rise of fascism, as well as to collect a paycheck from the movie studios. His film scores were apparently quite few—he joked to Cooper that the studios kept him around to meet prestigious guests rather than to write music—although some have said that he composed scores under an assumed name. Certainly as a teacher his impact on film music was significant. His students included such later important cinematic composers as Henry Mancini, Jerry Goldsmith, and André Previn. During the postwar period, Castelnuovo-Tedesco maintained an active involvement in classical composition, and Cooper recalls his teacher sending him postcards from Venice (the Italian city, not the California beach community of the same name), where one of his operas was being premiered. His pedagogical method focused strictly on classical composition. Cooper's assignments included, for example, the orchestration of Ravel piano pieces.

These academic pursuits coexisted with Cooper's growing involvement with the Los Angeles jazz scene. His affiliation with the Lighthouse All-Stars began as part of the lengthy Sunday afternoon-to-evening sessions, in which guests were encouraged to sit in, if only to take the strain off the other bandsmen during these twelve-hour marathon gigs. "Bud [Shank] and I would just go down Sundays, and then they got to hiring us to come down for Sundays. We didn't really start working there steadily until Shorty, Shelly, and Jimmy left." The new additions radically changed the sound of the group. Although Cooper's tenor playing shared Giuffre's cool school affinities, both he and Shank boasted deeper bebop roots and greater technical fluency than their Texas tenor predecessor. Giuffre's and Rogers's departures also meant the loss of their writing skills, but under the tutelage of Castelnuovo-Tedesco, Cooper was ready to fill the void.

Cooper's work as a leader during the mid-1950s also shows a gradual switch in emphasis from playing to writing/arranging, but not always to the best effect. Only gradually did the quality of his writing begin to match his impressive skills as a soloist. His sextet work as a leader from 1954, released on a 10-inch LP for the Kenton Presents label, is most noteworthy for his rapid-fire work on two Jerome Kern standards, "The Way You Look Tonight" and the lesser-known "She Didn't Say Yes." A second Kenton Presents project, recorded in spring 1955, features more ambitious arrangements for an octet under Cooper's leadership. For better or worse, this music captured the stereotyped West Coast sound of the day. Cooper is found working tenor sax, oboe, and English horn; John Graas joins in on French horn; other participants offer smatterings of flute, valve trombone, and bass clarinet. The quaint version of " 'Round Midnight" would be appropriate at a Renaissance fair.

Cooper's writing skills began to blossom during the second half of the decade. The debut 1957 recording on Rumsey and Levine's Lighthouse Records, *Jazz Rolls Royce*, proclaims on the cover that it features "Howard Rumsey's Lighthouse All-Star Big Band." The album, in fact, relies exclusively on Cooper's arrangements from start to close and includes some of the finest writing of the tenorist's career. The music was commissioned for one of the All-Stars' infrequent performances outside their home base— a concert at UCLA's Josiah Royce Hall. Only the year before, Igor Stravinsky had conducted his seventy-fifth birthday concert at Royce, and the deflected glow of respectability was a central theme in the proceedings. Write-ups from the time emphasize that the occasion presented "the first jazz commissioned by a major American university (UCLA) for performance at an official event."

This music, eventually released as re-recorded in the studio, was also taped at the concert. The performance at Royce Hall was, according to Rumsey, "much better." Technical difficulties, however, necessitated a studio re-creation. Even so, it is difficult to find much fault with the music as it stands. The "official event" proudly and ambiguously proclaimed above was homecoming, and the group started the concert with Cooper's new arrangement of "Strike Up the Band," a piece familiar as a fight song to the student audience. The following "Prelude to the Queen," probably a musical backdrop to the selection of the homecoming queen, showcases the more classical style of composition Cooper was pursuing with Castel-nuovo-Tedesco. It's easy to dismiss such works as pretentious attempts to disguise jazz as something other than it is, but "Prelude" is such an attractive composition that it is difficult not to like it. The piece is also noteworthy for featuring some of Cooper's finest oboe work on record, several steps above the earlier, lackluster *Flute 'n Oboe* release on Contemporary. The other titles belie their corny names (the UCLA motif recurs in inane titles such as "Coop Salutes the Co-Op," "Bruinville, My Bruinville" and "Mambo del Quad-O") with powerful straight-ahead blowing by the Lighthouse band, augmented with ten additional players (including Larry Bunker on tympani and Red Callender on tuba).

Exactly two months before the UCLA concert Cooper had recorded the *Coop* album for Les Koenig's Contemporary label. His twenty-four-minute "Jazz Theme and Four Variations," which comprised all of side one of the album, is an ambitious and innovative work. Cooper departs from traditional practice by taking enormous liberties with the variations, often building them from a single motif of the original theme. The structural unity of the work is elusive, but the piece succeeds nonetheless—largely because Cooper is able to integrate his strengths as an improviser into the elaborate formal structure of the work. This album contains perhaps the finest solo work of Cooper's career, not just on the extended composition, but even more so on the standards that grace the second side of *Coop*. On "Frankie and Johnny" the tenorist burns with intensity against the shifting meters (alternating 3/4 and 4/4) of the arrangement. Here one first begins to hear the more driving, aggressive strain in Cooper's playing that would become increasingly evident in his music over the next three decades.

Cooper's career reveals an uneasy tension between the cool and the hot elements in his music. This later evolution in Cooper's playing marks, in many ways, a return to his earliest roots—his first major influences on tenor were Coleman Hawkins and Chu Berry. But most critics still associate Cooper with his Lester Young–inflected work of the 1950s. The tenorist explains: "Lester Young came later for me. I always liked him, but I never had quite the feeling from him that I got from the robust sound of Hawk. But then I realized what fantastic time Lester had, what beautiful ideas and total originality. That really came more after I was with the Kenton Band, and Stan Getz and Zoot Sims were making big names for themselves with Woody [Herman]." Jumping on the Prez bandwagon, Cooper switched mouthpieces in an attempt to develop a lighter sound.

Like most of the musicians from the early West Coast period, Cooper claims to have thought little about the difference between the two seaboards: "I really didn't relate to it as east and west." But later in the same interview, he suggests that on the Pacific Coast there might have been "a pressure for the young guys to all play the same with the Lester Young thing." Certainly the later, harder styles of Cooper, Bud Shank, Art Pepper, and others indicate that the full flowering of their individual styles happened slowly, while earlier in their careers something along the lines of this stylistic convergence was taking place. In a pointed polemic, Brew Moore, another West Coast saxophonist of the period, once asserted, "Anybody who doesn't play like Lester is wrong."[13] Perhaps the essence of geographical styles in the age of the global village boils down to just this: a diffused pressure among younger artists to follow certain models and neglect others.

Bud Shank, who joined the Lighthouse group at the same time as Cooper, has also shown marked ambivalence about the "cool jazz" connotations of West Coast jazz. Certainly Shank has demonstrated throughout his career that he can play in an understated, melodic style—most notably on his recurring collaborations with Laurindo Almeida, first in the 1950s and then again two decades later in the LA Four. Yet Shank's basic instincts, like Cooper's, led him toward hard-blowing work on the saxophone. Also like Cooper, Shank was drawn toward "exotic" instruments—he was among the first jazz saxophonists to double on the flute. In recent years, however, he has abandoned it to concentrate on the alto. As a composer, he avoided the classically inspired forms that fascinated many of his peers, developing instead into a tunesmith whose best pieces were often simple springboards for improvisation.

He was born Clifford Everett Shank, Jr., on May 27, 1926, and was raised on a country farm ten miles outside Dayton, Ohio. The future altoist's musical education began through an experimental program initiated at his small rural school. He was ten years old when he started on a fifteen-dollar clarinet purchased on the installment plan. Only four weeks later he made his public debut as a soloist with piano accompaniment in downtown Dayton. ("A very simple piece," he recalls. "I still have the music.")[14] At age twelve he began studies on the saxophone, traveling into downtown Dayton for weekly lessons. After his family moved to North Carolina, where his father was stationed in the armed forces, Shank began as a music major at the University of North Carolina. "I was spending most of my time playing with a jazz band. And about when I was in my third year, which was in 1946, the whole band quit school together to go on the road—to take the world by storm." The high hopes of the band members turned into something of a nightmare. The group lasted only six weeks before breaking up.

Shank, intent on making it in the music world, balked at the idea of returning to school ("The best you could come out was a high school music teacher or store owner") and instead decided to try his luck in a major city. He had already visited New York, on occasional day trips to take music lessons from Walter "Foots" Thomas, but now he decided to try the other coast. Borrowing money from his father, Shank purchased a flute, and he hitched a ride with a friend to Los Angeles. There he shared a house in Hollywood with three other musicians, and soon learned that life in the Southern California entertainment industry was not all glamor and movie stars. Scraping by with occasional gigs, and supplementing his income by parking cars and taking other odd jobs, Shank could not afford flute lessons. Instead he picked up tips secondhand from a roommate: "One of the guys had enough money to take some flute lessons from this flute teacher at a school in Hollywood. He would tell me what his teacher told him."

Much of Shank's earlier saxophone work was on the tenor, but after joining Charlie Barnet in 1947 he changed to alto. Shank returned to Los Angeles in 1949, where he freelanced and worked with a small band under the leadership of Alvino Rey. Shank's piecemeal education on the flute paid off when he auditioned for Kenton's new Innovations in Modern Music orchestra. Kenton's increasing fascination with different instrumental colors made Shank an ideal choice for the group. For two years Bud served an apprenticeship in this hothouse of West Coast jazz talent, an ensemble that also included Art Pepper, Shorty Rogers, Shelly Manne, Bob Cooper, Maynard Ferguson, Laurindo Almeida, Bill Russo, Milt Bernhart, and John Graas.

For many listeners and critics, this band was an anomaly: It boasted an impressive group of individual players, but as an ensemble it often sagged under the weight of Kenton's Wagnerian ambitions. Shank shares their ambivalence:

> That band was too clumsy to swing—because of the instrumentation and voicings. On the other hand the sounds that came out of it were really big noises, really impressive. That's what that band was all about, making these really big noises. As far as swinging, it never did swing. Maybe it wasn't supposed to, I don't know. There sure were some players in it who swung.[15]

As a tenor player Shank had preferred, like many of his contemporaries on the West Coast, Lester Young to Coleman Hawkins: "Coleman Hawkins even at that time was old-fashioned to me, which was really not fair because he wasn't, but I appreciated more where Lester was going." But in 1947, when Shank switched to alto, Charlie Parker was launching a musical revolution on that instrument, and Shank naturally gravitated to the more modern idiom: "The sound Bird got with Jay McShann, the sound he got on those strings records, was just something that fascinated me. More than anything about him. The freedom in his playing I think soaked through later on, but the initial thing was that sound."

It is difficult to gauge the immediate impact of Parker on Shank's work. His solo opportunities were limited in the Kenton band. As first saxophone he led the section, while Pepper served as chief soloist. The Parker influence, much in evidence on the Lighthouse recordings, is hardly apparent on the 1953 collaboration with Laurindo Almeida, released on a 10-inch Pacific LP as *Laurindo Almeida Quartet Featuring Bud Shank*. this group, which also included bassist Harry Babasin and drummer Roy Harte, grew out of a duet engagement for Babasin and Almeida at a Sunset Strip club. Soon the band expanded to a quartet, which practiced in the back room of Harte's Hollywood drum shop. The quartet began playing Monday nights at the Haig during the celebrated Mulligan/Baker engagement at the same club. Richard Bock, whose early success at Pacific Records seemed to be built on recording performers from the Haig, set up a session for the band in September 1953.

This excellent music is not, as some have suggested, the first example of bossa nova jazz. Although the later bossa nova musicians were aware of the Almeida/Shank recordings, their combination of samba and cool jazz was built from a lighter, more relaxed guitar feeling than the classically restrained Almeida chose to employ. Almeida is quite an anomaly in the world of jazz: Although he is neither an experienced jazz soloist nor a traditional Brazilian samba player, his formal technique and understanding of Brazilian classical music created a distinctive sound in the 1950s jazz world. Born in São Paolo on September 2, 1917, Almeida had been a staff radio musician and performer in Rio de Janeiro before coming to the United States to join the Kenton band in 1947. His style had none of the lick-oriented Charlie Christian roots of virtually every other American jazz guitarist's of the day—indeed, it was so far from the norm that even his Kenton bandmates were initially skeptical about whether Almeida could swing in a jazz setting. The early recordings show that Almeida could swing hard, albeit in his own South American manner. Shank's playing in this ensemble includes some of the most reflective and unabashedly pretty alto work of his career.

The gentle Brazilian musings of these collaborations bear little resemblance to Shank's hard-nosed work with the Lighthouse All-Stars. The live sessions with Miles Davis and Chet Baker are particularly revealing of the altoist's bebop roots, as is another long-lost tape of Shank's work as a leader from the Haig, unreleased until 1985—thirty years after it was recorded. These late discoveries force one to reassess the conventional view of Shank's work from the 1950s; they show a more impassioned and heated soloist than, for example, do the Almeida collaborations or the flute and oboe performances with Cooper. If Shank was pigeonholed as a quintessential West Coaster, it was the lyrical restraint of the latter works that the critics had in mind. The stereotyped view, in the words of critic Gene Lees, was that "[Shank's] playing was pretty and lyrical but, according to the eastern orthodoxy, it lacked balls."[16] Such criticisms find little support in these recently unearthed live performances at the Haig and the Lighthouse. They reveal a different side of Shank and suggest his work took on a gutsier intensity in the heat of a club performance—especially when he was unaware that the tape was running.

In sharp contrast to these heated alto performances were Shank's ongoing flute and oboe collaborations with Bob Cooper. During their early period at the Lighthouse, the two saxophonists had tried combining the former's flute work with the latter's developing oboe style in informal practice sessions. Encouraged by other members of the group, they tried out the unusual instrumentation in front of the Lighthouse patrons one Wednesday night toward the end of 1953. The audience reaction was positive, and the new sound became a regular part of the two players' repertoire, both on albums and in performance. On February 25 and 26 of the following year, the All-Stars undertook the first of several recording sessions designed to exploit the new sound. Most of the recordings of this unusual instrumental combination now seem dated. On slow mood pieces the distinctive timbres can be intriguing, at least in small doses, but on faster-blowing numbers the music sounds unidiomatic and gimmicky. The continued rarity of the oboe in straight-ahead jazz situations contributes to this impression; perhaps if more later musicians had pursued this lead, these early experiments would not sound so odd to modern ears. The flute and oboe work had the further unintended effect of distracting critical attention from the continued vitality of the pair's saxophone performances.

One of the finest examples of the pair's saxophone work comes from their January 19, 1956, concert at Cal Tech. Shank's quartet was booked to play a campus performance at the unlikely time of 11 a.m.—the usual slot for student assemblies, but a painfully early hour for jazz players. Cooper, despite his warm tone and gift for melody, has always sounded more comfortable on faster tempos, but at Cal Tech his ballad performance of "How Long Has This Been Going On?" shows him at top form. But even here Coop chomps at the bit; soon he has abandoned the song in mid-flight, shifting gears into a double-time version of "Tea for Two." Less heated than Cooper, and far more restrained here than on his Haig recording, Shank is content to show off a more lyrical side of his playing. His tone tends toward Desmond/Konitz warmness, and the Bird calls are more muted. These performances capture, on the whole, an attractive midpoint between the bebop intensity of Shank's other live work and the extreme cool of the Almeida collaborations. The flute and oboe make an obligatory appearance on "Lullabye of Birdland," where they add variety without dominating the proceedings.

The waters were muddied, however, by the next Shank/Cooper collaboration on Pacific: *Flute 'n Oboe*. As the title suggests, this project exploited the new instrumentation to painful excess. On all but three selections, the group is augmented by a string quartet. Records like this gave West Coast jazz a bad rap—and deservedly so.

Although Cooper was Shank's most persistent front-line companion during the decade, the mid-1950s found the altoist co-leading recording sessions with a number of other horn players. A date with Shorty Rogers, recorded in March 1954, features Rogers's writing from start to finish. With the characteristic polyphony, counterpoint, and tight compositional sense of the trumpeter's music, these pieces work like a charm, but they push Shank's contribution into the background. He seems like a sideman on his own date. The May 2, 1955, session with Bill Perkins is a looser affair, and the two saxophonists are backed by a fine rhythm section consisting of Hampton Hawes, Red Mitchell, and Mel Lewis. Hawes, recently returned to Southern California after his unsuccessful attempt at military service, would record the first of his celebrated albums for Contemporary the next month. Here he shows all the crisp swing that would contribute to the success of the coming trio date. Shank rises to the occasion, contributing especially fine solos on Clifford Brown's "Paradise" and the ballad "A Sinner Kissed an Angel."

Given Shank's increasing prominence as a leader, his tenure as a sideman at the Lighthouse inevitably ended. On New Year's Eve 1955, both Shank and pianist Claude Williamson gave their notice at the Hermosa Beach club. On the first Monday of 1956, they began an engagement at the Haig in a quartet under Shank's leadership. Dick Bock, who was recording Shank as a leader for his Pacific label, was anxious for the altoist to get more exposure as a group leader. After lengthy engagements in and around Los Angeles, the new band, which also included bassist Don Prell and drummer Chuck Flores, went on a lengthy cross-country tour with stops in Chicago, St. Louis, Philadelphia, New York, and Boston. Williamson and Shank already boasted a long history of working together—both had served their apprenticeship in the same Charlie Barnet band, and both had refined their craft with the Lighthouse All-Stars. This collaboration was destined to continue for years to come. With few changes (most notably the substitution of Jimmy Pratt for the 1958 world tour), the Bud Shank Quartet would stay together until early 1959. For twelve years Shank and Williamson would remain frequent musical partners in some of the finest West Coast bands of the day.

Williamson's background was much different from the altoist's. Born in Brattleboro, Vermont, on November 18, 1926, Williamson was exposed early to jazz through his father, a drummer who led a territory band in the New England states. Despite his father's background in jazz and dance bands, Claude's studies focused on classical music from the start. He began piano lessons at age seven. These continued for ten years, then Claude began full-time musical studies at the New England Conservatory of Music. In contrast to these highbrow surroundings, Williamson knew from the start that he wanted to make his career as a jazz musician: "I wanted to study theory and composition and further my work on the piano. Fortunately I had a teacher who included both jazz and classical music in my studies."[17] Sam Saxe, Williamson's teacher, was a somewhat unorthodox conservatory teacher for the 1940s. In addition to emphasizing the mastery of keyboard fundamentals, Saxe gave Claude transcriptions of Art Tatum piano figures to be practiced in all twelve keys. In late 1946, Saxe moved to Southern California, and in February 1947, Williamson followed, not only to continue his studies but also to take advantage of the growing musical opportunities Saxe promised on the West Coast.

Saxe, along with Lloyd Reese and Sam Browne, stands out as one of the forgotten jazz educators who played an important role in shaping the postwar generation of West Coast players. In addition to Williamson, Saxe's other piano students included Lorraine Geller, Don Friedman, Arnold Ross, Dick Whittington, Joanne Brackeen (then known as Joanne Grogan), and even, for a short time, Hampton Hawes. "I don't know what he could do with Hampton," Whittington remarks. "Hamp seemed to be born with his gift. But I talked to Hampton once about it, and he seemed to feel that it had been a help to him."[18]

Whittington describes the Saxe regimen:

> Sam's goal was to get you to playing gigs as soon as possible, and he used to run a referral service and would send you on gigs when he thought you were ready. He emphasized theory—almost to the point of a fault. He would make you play a Parker ii-V lick in different keys, things like that. Any jazz pianist you wanted to study, he had copies of their music he had transcribed. In his studio he had these two grand pianos and these ottomans all around, and in them, neatly filed, would be this music he had copied on onion skin paper. Whatever you wanted, he'd have it—Latin music, Oscar Peterson, Bud Powell. He would train you for jazz or studio music, and he would have these things he would give you on, say, ten rules for being a studio musician. They would include things like: learn to be able to read everything; cultivate connections; live close by to the studios—a lot of these things would have nothing to do with music. But he could teach you anything, and he had a lot of successful students.

Williamson continued studying with Saxe while waiting the then obligatory six months to get a Los Angeles union card. Immediately after joining the union, Williamson became pianist for the Charlie Barnet band. Barnet's ensemble was evolving into a more bop-oriented band, much like the Woody Herman Herd of the same era. Like other young musicians then joining the band—such as Bud Shank and Doc Severinsen—Williamson was increasingly drawn to the modern jazz idiom. During the two years he remained with Barnet, his piano style evolved from its swing era roots in Teddy Wilson and Jess Stacy to a more contemporary approach rooted in the innovations of Bud Powell. His best-known work with Barnet was his piano feature on "Claude Reigns" (a punning reference to both Williamson's keyboard prowess and Hollywood actor Claude Raines).

After leaving Barnet in December 1949, Williamson served as musical director for June Christy before being drafted in September 1951. He narrowly escaped serving in Korea by discovering his calling as a percussionist—a talent he was unaware of until he learned that it would get him off a boat to Korea and into an army band on Okinawa. "I ended up playing the bells in a marching band," Williamson notes.

Within two weeks of his release in late summer 1953, Williamson got a phone call from Russ Freeman, who was leaving the Lighthouse All-Stars and looking for a replacement. This was musical *dejà vu* for Williamson—here he was reunited with Barnet bandsmate Shank and with Christy's husband, Bob Cooper. The Lighthouse move also provided Williamson with an opportunity to work with many of the finest jazz musicians of the day; including Max Roach, Conte Candoli, Frank Rosolino, and Stan Levey, as well as the various artists who would sit in at the Pier Avenue nightspot.

The careers of both Shank and Williamson during the 1950s show an evolution away from the cool style associated with the West Coast. The most revealing music from this period comes from the surreptitiously recorded session from the Haig. This is the only amateur jazz recording that I know of from the period that boasts top-notch *stereo* sound (from 1956!). But even more remarkable are the performances by the quartet. Shank plays with a degree of uninhibited energy that apparently only came in live performances during the mid-1950s. The hints of Desmond and Konitz are still apparent, especially on a tasty ballad version of "Lover Man," but on faster numbers such as "How About You" Shank gives a virtuoso display that had yet to surface in his studio recordings. Williamson is even less restrained, frequently stretching out in a fiery bebop idiom.

The West Coast label has been particularly unfortunate for both Shank and Williamson. At best it served as a substitute for evaluating the individual merits of their work; at worst—especially for Williamson, who by the mid-1950s was a full-fledged bebopper in the spirit of Bud Powell—it was completely misleading. "I hate the term 'West Coast jazz,' " Williamson told me, "and to this day I can't get away from it. I went to Barcelona

to perform a few years ago, and what does the poster say? 'West Coast
Jazz.' This is the 1980s." Williamson has made a pointed, if unsuccessful,
effort to dissociate himself from the label, going so far as to damn with
faint praise his early recordings that fit the stereotype—"they were *cleanly*
done," he remarks, giving the adverb a strange pejorative twist. His several recordings as a leader after the middle of the decade never looked back
to the earlier style.

Williamson's 1955 recording for Stan Kenton's jazz label for Capitol
is called, true enough, *Keys West,* but the trio music shows clearly the
new East Coast inspiration in Williamson's playing. On "Get Happy" the
pianist sounds on the brink of going out of control, like a drag racer running curves at a dangerous speed. Few keyboardists have truly perfected
this style. Bud Powell was its most noteworthy exponent (indeed, he practically invented it), but though Powell had many followers, few of them
captured this aspect of his playing. They tried to play Bud's licks as precisely as possible, whereas the manic intensity of Powell's work made the
apparent sloppiness in his playing part of the effect. This was feverish
music that was *supposed* to sound ragged. Williamson more and more
captured this neglected aspect of the bebop master in his later work. He,
too, thrived when working in overdrive.

Shank's musical evolution followed a similar pattern—and over an
almost identical period of time. One wonders whether the mutual influence of these longtime collaborators did not play a vital role in the transformation. The decade of the 1950s found Shank undergoing a gradual
shift from a cool player to a hot one, a change that reached its culmination
only in the 1980s. Anyone who has experienced a Bud Shank performance
during the past several years can hear the huge gulf between his current
work and his playing from the early 1950s. Unlike the stylistic continuity
that marked the work of Chet Baker, Shorty Rogers, or Paul Desmond,
Shank's playing has continued to evolve, especially since his departure from
his 1970s band, the LA Four.

The seeds of these later changes might well have been predicted early
in Shank's career. An interview Shank gave in 1956 is strikingly prescient.
"There is a tremendous leaning towards a sort of pseudo-intellectual, too-
cool approach," Shank explained, in a manner many jazz fans must have
found surprising at the time, as Shank was one of the players most associated with just this kind of "too-cool" sound. Shank continued: "Groups
that base their entire thing with this in mind, I think are losing the basic
part of jazz, which to me is: it's got to swing!"[19] Other comments in this
interview are equally forward-looking. Several decades later Shank would
abandon the flute (in our 1988 interview he announced in no uncertain
terms: "I think the flute is a stupid instrument to be playing jazz music
on"), but he hinted at his disaffection with it in this 1956 interview. Asked

about recently being named an outstanding flutist in a magazine poll, Shank responded with apparent reservations: "I feel that jazz is the reason for the saxophone's existence, and that's what I am. A jazz alto player, not a jazz flute player, primarily."

The Shank Quartet's 1957 release on Pacific, simply entitled *The Bud Shank Quartet*, gives little hint of these sentiments. In general, the group successfully pursues a more introspective vein than revealed on the (then unreleased) Haig session or hinted at in the 1956 interview. The band's rendition of Cole Porter's "All of You" includes some of Shank's tastiest alto work of the decade and features an especially appealing stop-time section after the piano solo. Here, as on the Basie number "Jive at Five" or Williamson's "Theme," the altoist presents an attractive balance between lyricism and unadulterated bebop. His flute work from this period typically reflected a more innocent prettiness, especially moving here on his ballad version of "Polka Dots and Moonbeams" and in his introduction to "The Lamp Is Low." But on Gillespie's "A Night in Tunisia," Shank attempted a more bop-oriented attack on the instrument. And with good results—perhaps he was making amends for the uninspired earlier flute and oboe recording of this piece (although he still fails to match his alto solo on this same number from the then unreleased Lighthouse date with Miles Davis). Also worth noting is Williamson's contribution of an extended suite, "Tertia," which, unlike most of his work from the period, reflects the then current West Coast preoccupation with intricate compositional structures. This album is mostly an exercise in cool jazz; despite Shank's stated desire to move in a different direction, it is an extremely successful recording.

In March of 1958, the Shank Quartet, joined by Bob Cooper and June Christy, undertook their most ambitious tour yet. "There were some promoters in Europe who were very anxious to get June Christy over there," Williamson recalls. "While they were dickering with her, they found they could get a whole group of West Coasters." The tour began as a series of European bookings that brought the band to Amsterdam, Rotterdam, Brussels, Copenhagen, Hamburg, West Berlin, Milan, Rome, and other locations. Bootleg recordings from the tour find the group in fine form.

At the last minute the tour was expanded to include South Africa, where the group gave separate concerts for black and white audiences. The visit to South Africa was marked by Shank's intriguing attempt to assimilate the indigenous musical culture. "While we were there Bud discovered a little instrument called the pennywhistle," Williamson describes, "and we recorded a single 45 called "The Pennywhistle Blues," and it was number one on Johannesburg radio for three weeks." Soon after returning to the States in June of 1958, Shank abandoned his promising career as the leading pennywhistle exponent in jazz.

The Bud Shank Quartet broke up in 1959. Williamson continued to take occasional trio gigs, but soon he, too, was putting more and more of his energies into projects as an arranger and performer in the lucrative Southern California entertainment industry. "I realized around 1961 or 1962," Williamson explains, "that people weren't listening."

For a while Shank continued to work with a quintet at the Drift Inn in Malibu. This three-night-a-week gig was a last hurrah for the saxophonist—soon he would be dedicating most of his time to studio work—as well as a creative turning point. Just when the bottom was dropping from the LA jazz market, Shank was finding the fullest expression of his new, more aggressive style. His turn-of-the-decade release *New Groove* reveals a bluesiness and bite not matched in any of his earlier studio releases. Joined by twenty-five-year-old trumpeter Carmell Jones, who had recently moved west from Kansas City, Shank spits out biting alto and baritone lines far removed from the gentle musings with Almeida or the flute work with Cooper. Shank's disappearance into the studio netherworld was all the more unfortunate coming at this promising juncture in his evolution as an artist.

Like many other West Coast musicians who moved from the nightclubs to the studios in the 1960s, Shank and Williamson bore the stigma of having "sold out" to the system. In a 1987 interview, for example, a European critic suggested to Shank that his choice of studio employment was a betrayal or a copout. The altoist's heated response was to the point:

> You have to eat. You have to survive. When I became a full-time studio musician, I had been unemployed for a long time since jazz music left us in 1962–63 or whenever. At that time, I don't think any of us realized what was going on, but some American jazz musicians ended up here in Europe, some gave up playing altogether, some went off into never-never land by whatever chemical they could find, and there were some others who went into another business. That's what I did. I went into another business using the tools I had, which was playing the flute and the saxophone. Consider that a copout? No, I don't.[20]

musical chairs

In the latter half of the decade, the Lighthouse All-Stars made fewer commercial recordings on location. "The studio became the recital and the Lighthouse the rehearsal hall," Rumsey explains. For a while it seemed as though the opposite would take place. The installation of $5,000 worth of recording equipment, including an Ampex 350 stereo recorder and a two-channel, eight-line mixer, in the club facilitated informal live recordings. "The recording equipment was set up with remote starting and stopping, which I could activate from the bandstand," Rumsey continues. "We utilized the house microphones for recording as well so the audience was unaware of the set-up." A number of performances were recorded, but not with the intention of commercial release. Although these were made primarily so the musicians could review their work, they may someday be made available to the public. Rumsey recently negotiated the sale of a number of tapes to a Japanese buyer.

These tapes might add considerably to our understanding of West Coast jazz in the late 1950s, and not just with regard to the All-Stars. One would give much to hear a recording of the Sunday intermission band from late in the decade, which featured, from time to time, Don Cherry, Scott LaFaro, Billy Higgins, Charles Lloyd, Dick Whittington, and others. Meanwhile, the studio recordings by the regular Lighthouse group still maintained a fairly high level of quality through the mid-1950s. True, the band's approach had become somewhat formulaic—its recipe called for a handful of original compositions, a dose of standards, a hint of flute and/ or oboe, all leavened by some straight-ahead blowing—but formulas pose no problem as long as they continue to work. As with Art Blakely's more successful but similarly oriented group, the Lighthouse All-Stars continued to succeed as long as it maintained top-notch soloists.

The All-Stars' December 1954 date for Contemporary was one of the better features for the mid-1950s unit. It showcased the group's expanded line-up, which included Shank, Cooper, Conte Candoli, Rosolino, Williamson, and Levey. Shank, who had been studying composition with Shorty Rogers, was beginning to focus more on writing original material, and his "Sad Sack" shows the progress he had made. The piece spurs what Rumsey rightly described as "one of our best recorded efforts. It just moves and moves." Despite the name, this is a buoyant performance, taken at the kind of medium up-tempo Cooper devours. Shank, Candoli, Rosolino, and Williamson each follow the lead-off tenor solo with strong contributions of their own. Two other Cooper compositions stand out from this session. The first is "Mad at the World," a lyrical work in the same vein as the composer's "Prelude to the Queen" from the UCLA concert. These pretty, meditative works may have incurred the critics' scorn during the controversy over east versus west. They were the "oh, so palatable West Coast stuff" (to repeat the "oh, so" complacent put-down by critic Brian Priestley[21]). Yet these works still sound good today precisely because they are unpretentious, because they are quite content to work on the level of melodic and compositional elegance. Many of the more ambitious West Coast compositions from this period have aged far less gracefully. The All-Stars, with Stu Williamson's valve trombone replacing Rosolino's slide work, recorded again on February 22, 1955, and once more a week later, this time with no trombone. These sessions maintain the high standards of the December date, with Cooper's Getz-inspired work on "Prelude to a Kiss" and Shank's start-to-finish feature on "East of the Sun" standing out in particular.

From the time of Rogers's departure with Manne and Giuffre, the history of the All-Stars was marked by the growing size and steady turn-over of the group. The year after Shank and Cooper were added to the band, Jack Sheldon joined on trumpet, but he was soon replaced by Stu Williamson, who also played valve trombone. Late in 1954 trumpeter Conte Candoli was added. In May 1955, Candoli left, and trombonist Frank Rosolino joined the ensemble. Between 1956 and 1957, piano responsibility moved from Claude Williamson to Sonny Clark to Lou Levy. Levy, a Chicago native (born on March 5, 1928) was an especially important addition who brought to the Lighthouse skills honed through his work with Woody Herman, Shorty Rogers, and others. Sonny Clark also provided a strong rhythmic and harmonic underpinning to the band. But though the caliber of musicianship was high, none of these bands had much time to develop a distinctive musical voice.

Appraisals of Frank Rosolino's outstanding work have been overshadowed by the tragic and senseless circumstances surrounding his suicide in 1978. Indeed the most detailed essay about Rosolino by a jazz critic, Gene Lees's thoughtful piece reprinted in his collection *Meet Me at Jim and Andy's*, includes only a passing account of the trombonist's career, instead trying to come to grips with the facts of his death. After first shooting his two children, killing one and blinding the other, Rosolino turned the gun on himself. The terrible event struck virtually all who knew the trombonist as jarringly out of character: Although the jazz world has more than its share of oddballs, Rosolino had always come across as the epitome of light-hearted joviality. Among musicians he was almost as famous—and certainly as welcome—for his nonstop wisecracks and jokes as for his undisputed mastery of the horn. Yet in retrospect, even this irrepressible gaiety became suspect. "When somebody cracks four jokes a minute," pianist Roger Kellaway reflected, "we all should have known there was something wrong."[22]

Rosolino was the son of immigrant parents from Sicily who settled in Detroit, where Frank was born on August 20, 1926. His father, a talented musician who played mandolin, clarinet, and guitar, started instructing him on guitar at age nine and encouraged him to study the accordion at thirteen. This old-country instrument did not appeal to the youngster. Instead he convinced his father that he was big enough to learn the trombone. Beginning on a $25 model purchased at a pawnshop, Rosolino spent much of his practice time mimicking the exercises his brother Reso played on the violin. "Maybe that's why I started thinking of playing with speed," Rosolino later mused.[23]

Rosolino's *Free For All*, issued posthumously on Specialty Records, stands out as one of the trombonist's strongest leader dates. The eighteen-year delay between recording and releasing this project is somewhat mystifying. "Frank and I were excited about this album," producer Dave Axelrod recalls, "because it was going to be the first hard bop album recorded and released on the West Coast. . . . We worked for weeks on planning the personnel and the songs; the results were terrific. It was a great disappointment to us both that the record, for reasons we never understood, wasn't released."[24] Although Axelrod's claim for being the first hard bop album from the Coast is ill founded (earlier projects by Clifford Brown, Curtis Counce, and Harold Land are just a few of its predecessors), his views on the music's quality are well substantiated. With a strong supporting band composed of Harold Land, Stan Levey, Leroy Vinnegar, and Victor Feldman, Rosolino created some of his finest work of the decade. The arrangements are well crafted; familiar standards such as "Star Dust" and "What is this Thing Called Love?" take on new luster through provocative tempo and rhythm changes. The Cole Porter song starts with a funky horn arrangement—akin to Lee Morgan's successful work on the Blue Note label—doubling the tempo into a brisk walk in the bridge before settling into a medium groove that inspires one of Rosolino's better recorded solos. One can well understand the trombonist's frustration when these performances remained in the can. Nine months after the session, he wrote to the record company: "I feel it's the best album I have ever recorded; everyone who was on the date feels the same. I've played the dub for numerous musicians and they all think it's just great."

Conte Candoli, Rosolino's companion in the Lighthouse All-Stars front line, shared his sympathy for a more aggressive, hard bop approach. An exuberant trumpeter, with none of the pensive moodiness of a Chet Baker or Jack Sheldon, Candoli was best at uninhibited blowing in a jam session setting. In fact Candoli, when he was paired up with East Coasters Kenny Dorham and Al Cohn for a mid-1950s tour and recording, came across as much more of a bombastic bebopper than his more subdued East Coast counterparts. An unaware listener would likely pick out Dorham and Cohn, on that date, as the ones with the West Coast sound.

Like Carl Perkins, Leroy Vinnegar, and Buddy Montgomery, Candoli was a West Coast musician by way of Indiana. He was born Secondo Candoli in Mishawaka on July 12, 1927. As his true name suggests, Conte was the second son in this highly musical family. During much of his career, Conte has collaborated with his older brother, trumpeter Pete Candoli, born June 28, 1923. At age twelve Conte began his musical studies, in emulation of his brother's playing. By his mid-teens he had developed enough proficiency to join the Woody Herman band—an engagement that was interrupted when the younger trumpeter was forced by his mother to return home to finish high school. In January 1945, diploma in hand, Conte embarked on a full-time career as a professional musician. After leaving Herman, he worked with Chubby Jackson, Stan Kenton, and Charlie Ventura before finally leading his own group in Chicago in 1954. Later that year he settled in California, where he soon signed on as a regular member of the Lighthouse band.

Brother Pete had a more flamboyant stage presence. During his tenure with Herman he was dubbed "Superman with a horn" for a crowd-pleasing routine in which, dressed like the Man of Steel, he would display his high-note expertise. Conte's extroversion, in contrast, comes out more in his playing than in his personal demeanor. His trumpet stylings, though less rooted in the upper register than his brother's, possess a devil-may-care verve that is quite appealing.

Shortly after his arrival on the coast, Conte undertook a date as leader for Bethlehem Records, released as *Groovin' Higher*, in which he was joined by Bill Holman on tenor sax and a rhythm section comprised of Leroy Vinnegar, Lawrence Marable, and Lou Levy. Here the basic elements of Candoli's style are evident. He first and foremost shows a knack for constructing long phrases with a variety of rhythmic twists and turns; unlike most players, who strive to play complex phrases with an appearance of ease, Candoli seems to aim for the opposite effect—his playing, particularly on fast numbers, sounds as though it is running at full steam and perhaps in danger of overheating. Also contributing to this effect is Conte's strong sense of dynamics. While Pete might build up to a musical climax by working his way into the highest register of the horn, Conte achieves the same effect through shifting dynamics, not only between phrases but often within a specific phrase. Conte's music is like a caldron on the boil, with individual notes and groups of notes bubbling above the surface. On the *Groovin' Higher* album, his work on "Full Count" is a striking example of these various qualities. For a comparison of the two Candolis' styles, their exchanges on "Caravan" (from the *Jazzin' Around* album) provide a good starting point. Like so many of their contemporaries, these two brothers have in recent years established themselves as first-call Hollywood players somewhat at the cost of their reputations in the jazz world. Yet their occasional forays into straight-ahead jazz still find them playing at peak form.

As suggested above, the All-Stars had always been somewhat unaffected by the cool jazz ethos prevalent on the coast. Even when Giuffre, Rogers, and Manne had been in the band, they played with more abandon than in their work as leaders. With the exception of the flute/oboe work, the later editions of the All-Stars only furthered this tendency. By the time of the 1956 All-Stars recording *Music for Lighthousekeeping*—with

Rosolino, Candoli, Cooper, Levey, and pianist Sonny Clark—the band had lost the last vestiges of the low-key, cool approach that many listeners still associated with the Lighthouse name. This was a hard bop band plain and simple, even if the jazz public still thought of it as a refuge for cerebral jazz *artistes.*

Clark, a strongly rhythmic pianist with roots in the Bud Powell tradition, made a strong contribution to this hard-nosed ensemble. Although he is not typically associated with the West Coast scene, during his several years' residence in California Clark's work contributed not only to the Lighthouse All-Stars but also to sessions under the leadership of Frank Rosolino and Sonny Criss. Later in the decade, Clark moved to New York, where he died in 1963 at the age of thirty-one, a figure who had yet to gain his due as a musician. Recently his work, long neglected, has experienced a much deserved revival.

One of the most surprising attributes of this new edition of the All-Stars, as well as its predecessors, is its surprising affinity for Latin jazz. There is nothing in the individual or collective background of the various musicians, other than talent and musical curiosity, to explain this recurring predilection, all the more remarkable given the many forced attempts to blend jazz and Latin music in the postwar years. Two of the biggest hits of the Lighthouse All-Stars during the 1950s—Cooper's "Witch Doctor" and Rogers's "Viva Zapata"—reflected sizeable borrowings from Latin music, as had a host of other successful Lighthouse charts: "Mambo Los Feliz," "Mexican Passport," "Mambo del Quad-O." The new band featured on *Music for Lighthousekeeping* continued this tradition with two outstanding Bill Holman compositions, "Mambo Las Vegas" and "Latin for Lovers." The rhythm section is especially effective on the former number, in which Clark starts his fiery solo with a hint of montuno before breaking into crisp single-note lines and finishing with a percussive flurry of block chords. Of course this group could also shine on more traditional fare, as Holman's composition "Love Me or Levey" and Cooper's "Jubilation" prove. On the basis of such a recording, one would classify this edition of the All-Stars as a strong hard-bop band. Yet just the week before this album was recorded, the All-Stars undertook a far different session with the revived bland flute and oboe formula. Buddy Collette was called in to fill the flute chair of the departed Shank, while Rosolino and Candoli lay low. If the All-Stars never gained the reputation they deserved for bop prowess, the reason lies here. Far better had they spent the time doing a whole album of mambos.

Although the Lighthouse All-Stars would continue as an ensemble well into the 1960s, the middle 1950s represents its last hurrah as a major jazz ensemble. The turnover then did little to dilute the quality of the band. But by the turn of the decade, the Lighthouse All-Stars increasingly relied on lesser-known regulars and guest artists such as Don Sleet, Daniel Jackson, Nick Martinis, Tony Ortega, Carrington Visor, Dick Shreve and Terry Trotter. A group from the summer of 1960 included, for example, trumpeter Johnny Anderson, altoist Gabe Baltazar, pianist Dick Johnston, drummer Roy Roten, and Rumsey. The decline in quality, however, had perhaps less to do with the Lighthouse than it did with the general state of West Coast jazz in the 1960s. A complex set of circumstances, some of them social, others personal, had sapped the Los Angeles scene of many of its finest players, while the shrinking audience for nightclub music in general, and jazz in particular, made work sporadic for those who remained. As the 1960s progressed, the Lighthouse was forced to shift gears: Only by booking well-known out-of-town acts could the club hope to draw significant crowds.

The Lighthouse would continue for some years under this policy as a viable entertainment venue, but its intimate connection with the local music scene was lost. By the 1970s, the club had to compete with Howard Rumsey's more upscale Concerts by the Sea club, located down the beach at the Redondo pier. Even then the Lighthouse continued for some time as a major jazz venue, with its odd church-pew seating giving the intimate space a ceremonial, almost religious, atmosphere that the glitzier new club could not match. Today the building still stands at 30 Pier Avenue and is still known as the Lighthouse Café. But the club no longer operates as a major jazz venue, instead serving as an eatery and watering hole for the crowds who flock to the nearby beach. The club looks much the same as it did in years gone by, and old-timers who remember the Lighthouse's livelier days still hope for an eventual return to a regular jazz policy.

Perhaps all it would take is another enterprising young bassist anxious to run a free-wheeling jam session well into the wee hours. Meanwhile, art continues to imitate art. Almost forty years after the group's founding, a Lighthouse All-Stars alumni group, under the guidance of veteran jazz photographer William Claxton, reassembled on the same Hermosa Beach shoreline where they had posed for the celebrated cover of their 1950s' Contemporary release. Now they were back to shoot the cover for a 1988 reunion album. The nearby Lighthouse club might have halted its jazz policy; group founder Howard Rumsey might have retired; other Lighthouse alums might have passed on; but some things had not changed. Standing on the shore, the All-Stars, now a group of near–senior citizens, still played to their frivolous beach boy image of the 1950s.

CHAPTER ELEVEN

A Ring-tail Monkey

he's into nature, understands tree worship

> "He has had great influence on my life." Pause.
> "His scope of music is limitless." Second pause.
> "It has given me the staff of life." A moment of silence.
> "It would be impossible to say too much about him."
> By now the conclusion is almost anti-climactic: "It was a rare stroke of good fortune that brought me to him." '

The speaker is saxophonist Jimmy Giuffre. The subject of this high-flung laudation is Wesley La Violette.

La Violette's name appears in few accounts of the history of West Coast jazz. Yet if one is looking for the hidden influences on the LA scene, his contribution can hardly be ignored. A classical composer whose students included not only Giuffre but also John Graas, Red Norvo, and Shorty Rogers, La Violette raised eyebrows by teaching much more than musical technique. Put simply, he was a prototypical guru.

A decade later, as part of the mind-altering ethos of the 1960s, the combination of Eastern mysticism and contemporary music would become almost a cliché. Even the Beatles would make their pilgrimage East—to sit at the feet of the Maharishi Mahesh Yogi—as part of their bid to capture the musical markets of the West. But in the Truman and Eisenhower years, even a garden variety mystic was something of an anomaly. In their beachside enclave, however, the Lighthouse sect was ahead of the wave: La Violette was the West Coast jazz players' own 1950s' Maharishi. One, moreover, who was also a celebrated classical composer. Could they ask for more?

A world traveler and student of Eastern philosophy, La Violette impressed his students not only by his striking and fresh orchestral pieces (which, according to Giuffre, were remarkable for their "untraceable roots")[2] but also by the "holy aura" that emanated from his tall, striking frame. Giuffre studied with him off and on for fourteen years. The master apparently responded with affection to his disciple's dedication, once announcing that Giuffre had a protective aura surrounding him for a radius of twenty-five feet that would prevent any harm from coming to him. No, a student could ask for no more.

La Violette's aspirations as a guru may ultimately have overshadowed his contributions in music and perhaps even gave him, in the eyes of skeptics, the aura not of a holy man but of a charlatan. Yet few of them were aware that La Violette's book on religious mysticism, *The Crown of Wisdom* (1949), had been nominated for the Nobel Prize in literature, or that he devoted considerable energies to translating works of Indian philosophy into English. His contributions in music were also far from inconsequential—as educator, author of *Music and Its Makers* (1938), and composer. La Violette's compositions were often strongly contrapuntal with marked rhythms and a tendency toward atonality—features that began to appear in Giuffre's work during his apprenticeship years with his mentor.

Perhaps La Violette's impact explains the radical transformation in Giuffre's work in the 1950s. From his earliest roots as a big band tenor player, Giuffre eventually evolved into an iconoclastic composer and multi-instrumentalist. His later works are truly *sui generis*. Perhaps La Violette deserves the lavish praise quoted above. Maybe he fell short of being the staff of life, *pace* Giuffre, but his influence certainly was a stroke of good fortune.

And if this mentor's mysticism was an anomaly at the time, his musical influence was quite in fitting with the direction of West Coast jazz in the 1950s. Giuffre's deep-seated musical curiosity and almost childlike fascination with new sounds and formats, with counterpoint and compositional structures, seem superficially in keeping with what we find in Mulligan, Rogers, Manne, Hamilton, and others of this generation. Yet there the similarity almost certainly ends. Giuffre's work from the 1950s, with its increasingly eclectic mix of West and East (in Giuffre's case, the Far East rather than New York), tonal and atonal, jazz and classical, is extremely difficult to pigeonhole. Perhaps Giuffre, too, had achieved the "untraceable roots" he so admired in his teacher.

Perhaps, too, this deeply personal element of Giuffre's music explains the surprising neglect of his work by later critics and commentators—explains but hardly justifies. If Giuffre's contributions cannot be squeezed into the conventional linear accounts of jazz history, perhaps the problem is with the historians and not Giuffre. Given the Hegelian zeal with which the story of jazz has been portrayed as a succession of progressively higher developments, each growing dialectically from pre-existing schools . . . well, such accounts miss quite a bit. For one, they leave no room for stylists who fail to transform the art form in their own image. Such histories lack the terminology for addressing those musicians who create artistic statements that reflect themselves and not the fashions of the day.

"Censorship by definition—You can't do that, it isn't Jazz—has been the bane of innovative musicians from James P. Johnson to Anthony Braxton," writes Graham Lock in a perceptive essay. He adds: "But few can have suffered from its effects quite so comprehensively as Jimmy Giuffre."[3] By blissfully ignoring virtually all of Giuffre's important recordings as a leader, Robert Gordon's book *Jazz West Coast* avoids the problem of categorization altogether. Yet for those less inclined to run away from the subject, Lock's point is well taken: The only way to deal with Giuffre's music is on its own terms.

When one listens to Giuffre's music for what it is—and not for what one thinks it should be—the beauties of this rich and strange musical landscape begin to emerge. Or rather, landscapes. For Giuffre never found a single musical Garden of Eden, a definitive style or format he could stay in for long. Like his more celebrated contemporary Miles Davis, Giuffre remains a musical chameleon, a distinctive stylist who constantly feels compelled to change his sonic setting.

A single album, such as *The Jimmy Giuffre Clarinet* from 1956, might boast a vertiginious array of compositional approaches. The record starts with a relaxed passage of solo clarinet—the first solo horn recording in jazz since Hawkins's daring "Picasso" of the previous decade—accompanied only by Giuffre's tapping foot. ("I wanted to get the effect of a musician playing in his back room all alone," he explains.) This is followed by a duet with Jimmy Rowles playing celesta (!) on the standard "Deep Purple." Next comes an atonal piece, starting in 5/4, for flute, alto flute, bass flute, clarinet, and drums (on which Shelly Manne plays with only his fingers). The first side closes with "My Funny Valentine," but anyone expecting a straightforward rendition of this old chestnut is immediately set straight by Giuffre's arrangement for clarinet, oboe, bassoon, English horn, and bass. The remainder of the album includes a clarinet trio, a nonet playing a funky blues, clarinet performing with piano and drums, and clarinet playing with bass and drums. Finally the album ends, as it began, with the leader playing alone against the insistent tapping of his foot—a strange finale to an album that seems to delight in not repeating itself. Something old, something new, something borrowed, something blue. One would be hard-pressed to think of another jazz album that explored so many different facets of a single musician in such rapid succession.

This degree of iconoclasm must come as some surprise after the more conventional approach of most of Giuffre's early work. His debut session with Red Norvo from 1947 finds him exchanging saxophone licks with Dexter Gordon. The result is something less than "The Chase," and Giuffre's playing here shows him to be a solid if unadventurous player who, like so many other young saxophonists on the coast, had listened carefully to Lester Young. (Interestingly, the predilection for Prez would remain in his later, more experimental efforts, but by then it would be Young's lesser-known—though not less brilliant—clarinet playing that would hold sway.)

At the time of this first session Giuffre, born in Dallas on April 26, 1921, was twenty-six years old, a fairly advanced age to begin recording jazz. Even so, he already had a significant amount of musical experience under his belt. After starting on the E-flat clarinet in a YMCA Beginners' Band at age nine, he soon switched to tenor sax, and during his high school years he performed in ROTC and dance bands and began formal studies in harmony. Inclined to pursue music as a career, he attended North Texas State Teachers College, where he earned a bachelor's degree in music in 1942, meanwhile working in many informal dance bands ("We played sorority and fraternity dances for $2.50 a night") as well as playing clarinet in a symphonic group. North Texas State, in an unlikely ascendancy, would eventually become a premier center of jazz education in America, but even during Giuffre's tenure the college boasted an excellent music department under Dr. Wilfred C. Bain. Giuffre remembers: "I roomed with Herb Ellis when we were at North Texas State. We rented an eight-room house where we would jam for hours and hours. Gene Roland came by one of our gigs, and a short time later he had moved in, too. That class at North Texas State really started the reputation for jazz at that institution."[4] Bain would soon leave for Indiana University, where he would be a vital force in developing another exceptional music program.

Any postcollege plans Giuffre had were interrupted by four years in the armed forces, during which he played in a seventy-piece air force orchestra ("like Kostalanetz," he recalls). Brought to Los Angeles through the air force, he decided to enter the master's program at USC in 1946. After a short period there, he left to pursue private lessons with La Violette. Only gradually did Giuffre's career in jazz develop; in his early work with the Boyd Raeburn and Jimmy Dorsey bands, his skills as an arranger tended to overshadow his work as an instrumentalist. Although the Raeburn stint is often cited in his biography, Giuffre clarifies that his performing career with Raeburn lasted only one week when he substituted for a regular. Hardly a promising apprenticeship!

This slow start may well have left a positive mark on Giuffre's later work. Like the styles of others whose recording careers started late (Lester Young and Bill Evans come immediately to mind), Giuffre's would eventually show the marks of a mature restraint—perhaps a result of focusing on his instrumental voice at an age when peer pressure and fad-following have lost much of their allure. The classic late bloomer in jazz was Duke Ellington, a master whose eventual stylistic sophistication more than made up in maturity and scope for what it lacked in precociousness. Perhaps late developers in jazz actually have, in some strange way, a head start.

If Giuffre's earliest work as an instrumentalist bordered on the conventional, his arranging skills were already noteworthy. During the summer of 1947, Giuffre had worked with saxophonists Stan Getz, Herbie Steward, and Zoot Sims as part of an eight-piece group led by trumpeter Tommy DeCarlo at Pontrelli's Ballroom in Los Angeles. The striking nature of the band's sax section would soon become well known in the jazz world as the "Four Brothers" sound, its name taken from a soon-to-be-famous Giuffre composition. Yet even here it would be wrong to credit Giuffre as anything more than a partial contributor to this novel scoring technique. Arranger Gene Roland had experimented with a similar saxophone lineup in New York the previous year and now was developing it in the DeCarlo band. This emphasis on orchestrating a light, Young-inflected saxophone sound was, however, compatible with Giuffre's musical background and interests, and soon he would put it to good use in the famous Woody Herman chart.

Herman took on the new sound as part of an ambitious package deal. With characteristic prescience, he hired three of the saxophonists with the DeCarlo band and commissioned Giuffre to write arrangements for his new Herd. The immensely successful "Four Brothers" brought together a number of disparate elements: a bop-inflected melody line built on the chord changes to one of the hoariest swing standards, "Jeepers Creepers," played by a sax section steeped in early Lester Young. The seamless interplay of these varied sources in Giuffre's arrangement proved to be nothing short of marvelous. In addition, Giuffre incorporated subtle changes in the lead line to add variety to the melody. Giuffre recalls:

[At Pontrelli's] we would alternate who played lead. I might do it for a set, and then maybe Stan Getz would do it. I incorporated this change in lead into "Four Brothers." If you listen closely, you can hear the lead change from phrase to phrase. I wrote a song for Woody called "Frantisi" that did the same thing for the other sections as well. But he never recorded it. It is extremely difficult to get an original composition into a big band's repertoire. Leaders don't want to call numbers unless they know beforehand that they are going to work really well. With "Four Brothers," the musicians wanted to do the song, so they would try it out during the last set. That's how it got rehearsed. It might not have been recorded if it hadn't been for the recording ban that was coming up. Woody recorded everything in the band book because the recording ban was coming up. Otherwise who knows? "Four Others" [another Giuffre chart from that period] sat in the bottom of the book for five years.

Over the next two years the Herman band would be one of the most exciting ensembles around, eventually winning the *Downbeat* readers' poll as the outstanding big band in jazz. Its financial failure, however, only confirmed the sad reality: The days of the big bands were all but over. Herman later estimated that over the two-year life of the band he lost $180,000.

Giuffre's financial situation was equally precarious at this point. He found it necessary to take a day job at J. C. Penney's in Los Angeles. For six months he worked his way up from the yardage department to men's clothing. Meanwhile his musical life languished. Giuffre's advancing career in retailing ended when a referral from Hal McKusick gained him a spot in Buddy Rich's band as arranger and tenorist. Soon he was responsible for writing the band's book, supervising rehearsals, and conducting. Yet work for Rich's band was irregular and Giuffre's situation far from secure.

In 1949, Giuffre joined Woody Herman's Second Herd, which meanwhile had done well with his "Four Brothers" arrangement—an arrangement he was now performing as a replacement for Zoot Sims. (Sims, in the mirror image of Giuffre's move, left to join Buddy Rich.) In addition to reuniting Giuffre with his most famous composition, enlisting with Herman also brought him into close contact with two frequent future collaborators, Shorty Rogers and Shelly Manne. Again Giuffre's saxophone work from the period suggests that he was a solid player, but by no means an innovator or even a distinctive stylist. In general Giuffre seemed content to be a conventional swing era tenor saxophonist—a noble occupation to be sure, but far less than what proved to be his ultimate potential.

When Herman disbanded during the 1949 Christmas season, Giuffre returned to Los Angeles, where, along with Rogers and Manne, he became part of the Lighthouse All-Stars. Giuffre's regular stint at this popular Hermosa Beach club put him into the midst of a heated jam session environment in which any tendency toward his later, more cerebral style would have been out of place. A largely forgotten recording from this period finds him playing heated rhythm-and-blues with some Lighthouse cohorts in a song that seems half-parody and half-serious. For a short while Giuffre attracted a following among rambunctious teenagers—and then lost it when the fickle youngsters discovered that this journey into heavy R&B was only a onetime pit stop for the stylistically peripatetic saxophonist. In contrast, Giuffre's composition "Four Others," prominently featured on the first live Lighthouse album on Contemporary, prefigures the relaxed downhome blues approach of many of his later works. But in the midst of a noisy nightclub the piece never achieves the effortlessness that is essential to Giuffre's performances in this vein.

In general, Giuffre's work on tenor for the Lighthouse band is solid if somewhat flat-footed. His solos show little of the feel for the bebop idiom that, strange to say, is reflected in some of his arrangements. As an improviser Giuffre, even more than other "brothers," such as Getz or Sims, stays true to the premodern roots of his music. The recently released live recording of Chet Baker with the Lighthouse All-Stars from September 13, 1953, shows that even at this relatively late date (Giuffre was thirty-two) the tenorist's Lighthouse work gives little hint of the direction his music would take over the next few years. On "Loaded" Bud Shank comes out smoking in a Charlie Parker vein, obviously inspired by Max Roach's driving drum support in the background, and trumpeter Rolf Ericson continues with no letdown in energy. Giuffre's solo, which follows, is a somewhat uncomfortable attempt to play a swing era solo in the company of a driving bebop band. Few would imagine, on the strength of this performance, that a decade later a major jazz authority would announce that Giuffre "has long been a leader of the jazz *avante garde.*"[5] Here he seems more like the last defender of the *ancien régime.*

Yet there may be more connection to Giuffre's early conservatism and later revolutionary zeal than appears on the surface. Precisely this uneasiness with the clichés and unremitting aggression of modern jazz spurred Giuffre to reconsider his musical allegiances. Unlike those who came to free jazz through either a born-again conversion or a gradual extension of mainstream techniques, Giuffre's later penchant for experimental work was rooted in his long-standing ambivalence about the bebop idiom. In this regard he is very much the musical equivalent of those intriguing political figures who move from reactionary to revolutionary movements without ever professing moderate views. This drastic shift in his musical bearings made it all the more difficult to pigeonhole Giuffre's work according to the common labels of 1950s jazz criticism.

Whether under the influence of La Violette or through a process of self-examination, Giuffre's changed musical priorities had already become apparent in much of his non-Lighthouse work. His tenure with the Rumsey band, for all its financial security, did not provide a suitable environment for the directions he was now pursuing. Seven weeks before the Lighthouse session with Baker, Giuffre had recorded his "Fugue" for Contemporary Records. This atonal piece of counterpoint would hardly have gone well with the Lighthouse crowd—indeed, the piece must have struck most 1953 listeners as an incongruous, if not downright spiteful, contribution from the composer of "Four Brothers."

But "Fugue" was anything but an exception. The chameleon was intent on changing still further. Exactly one month later Giuffre's collaboration with Teddy Charles and Shorty Rogers, released as *Collaboration: West,* further accentuated this new side of his playing. Charles's ballad "Margo" barely avoids atonality with its constantly shifting tonal center.

The sound here is not entirely dissimilar to the much-heralded work Miles Davis would undertake a few years later on "Blue in Green;" if anything, Charles's moody piece is more daring than Davis's. "Bobalob," from the same session, also looks ahead to *Kind of Blue* with its pronounced modal emphasis. Although Charles was the composer of these pieces, Giuffre proved to be an almost ideal sideman. The tenorist sounds more comfortable on these sophisticated experimental works than on many of his own compositions from that period.

In a well-known critique of West Coast jazz, André Hodeir complained that there was too great a gap between the "normal" and "experimental" works it produced.[6] Giuffre's recordings from this period are especially open to this criticism. A work like "Fugue," for all its supposed daring, seems somewhat like a student's class project in composition. Yet Hodeir fails to realize that some of Giuffre's finest work (as well as that of many West Coast players of the postwar years) bridged this gap with music that had both the freshness of experimentation and the fire of modern jazz. The excitement West Coast jazz generated as a so-called movement during the 1950s was due, at least partly, to the promise of merging these two extremes. Charles's compositions from *Collaboration: West* are a definite step in this direction, and Giuffre's best pieces from the mid-1950s succeed precisely on these same grounds, for their radicalism is no longer steeped in the rarefied atmosphere of the academy.

In 1954, Giuffre became an exclusive recording artist for Capitol Records, and the opportunities he now had to record as a leader furthered the evolution of his music into a more personal sound. The diverse results of his session from April 15, 1954, show how far he had come, although at the risk of revealing his growing musical split personality. Perhaps the obligatory rendition of "Four Brothers" was the idea of some Capitol Records executive; certainly its swinging ensemble passages bear little resemblance to the contrapuntal emphasis of Giuffre's newer pieces. "Sultana," recorded the same day, begins with unaccompanied horns, a device that would become increasingly central in his compositions; even when bass and drums enter, they are used not in the traditional manner of supplying support and momentum for a soloist, but as separate melodic voices.

The key element in Giuffre's compositional approach at this important turning point was his now almost obsessive interest in counterpoint. Countermelodies had been an integral part of early New Orleans jazz, but later generations of jazz writers showed less and less interest in counterpoint. Charlie Parker had experimented, for example in "Chasin' the Bird," with bringing this approach into the bebop idiom, but his model was not widely imitated. Most modern jazz writing emphasized either monophonic doubling of parts or else tight polyphonic ensembles. In one of the strange twists of musical fate, counterpoint became almost *de rigeur* in the new

West Coast sound. The best-known exponents were perhaps Mulligan/ Baker and Brubeck/Desmond, but the music of other West Coasters—Rogers, Manne, Hamilton, Shank, Cooper—also reflected the general tendency. Giuffre's interest in contrapuntal writing was probably the most extreme of any of his colleagues': "Once I discovered counterpoint," he could comfortably assert, "this was my direction, and I'm sure it will continue to be."[7]

In keeping with his mentor's blending of musical and philosophical instruction, Giuffre characteristically sees his use of counterpoint as fulfilling the demands of both composition and a humanist philosophy: "In studying counterpoint I began to see that each guy wants to express his own individuality. . . . I began to think, well, if this man is playing, give him a part to play that's good. Give the guitar, give the bass or whatever I use, a line that sounds like he is playing his own melody." Pursuing a quite unusual analogy, Giuffre elaborates:

> Like in industry, the Ford Company is one big sound, and it takes a lot of individuals to make that, but a lot of those individuals don't need, from Ford's standpoint, to have any individuality. They've been given a job and they do that job, and they don't use their imagination. Well, that's fine if that's the way it has to be done. But in making music you don't have to be so cold about it.

Clearly this is a unique rationale for contrapuntal writing! Giuffre implies that how much the artist enjoys producing the work of art is important to our evaluation of it. And Giuffre's actions lived up to these odd ideals: for example, his later decision to form a pianoless *and* drumless trio. This instrumentation, he claimed, had little to do with what sounds he wanted to hear. The band was so constituted, he explained, because this particular threesome—Giuffre, Ralph Peña, and Jim Hall—got along so well together.

In September 1954, Giuffre had his greatest opportunity yet to put such theories into practice in his collaboration with Manne and Rogers on *The Three*. Without any chordal instrument and lacking even a bass line, the three musicians needed to make extensive use of contrapuntal devices, if only to avoid the potential monotony of such a limited instrumentation. At times the spartan character of this music is a bit much; one craves the kind of harmonic grounding that it positively delights in avoiding. *The Three* was a frankly experimental work, perhaps the most daring West Coast recording to date, and the musicians were clearly anxious to explore the limits of their new musical ideas, with all the risks that entailed. Rogers tackled the twelve-tone row technique on his "Three on a Row," while the group's collective composition "Abstract #1" was a totally spontaneous work with no preconceived chord pattern, melody, or rhythmic structure. As such, it is perhaps more impressive for what it attempted than for what it actually achieved. But on the two standards recorded that day—"Autumn in New York" and "Steeplechase" the harmonies are more implicit, and the soloists' melodic twists and turns are more compelling. Manne's exquisite drum solo on the former piece ranks as one of the finest musical statements of his career.

Giuffre's follow-up session for Capitol from January 1955 finds the tenorist backing off from the more extreme tendencies of *The Three*. Accompanied by trumpeter Jack Sheldon, bassist Ralph Peña, and drummer Artie Anton, Giuffre showed that he could work with conviction in a more traditional vein. The interest in counterpoint is still quite evident, if not as obsessive, but the song structures and improvisations are more rooted in a common jazz idiom. This new middle ground, between the radical experiments of the "Fugue" and the casual jam sessions at the Lighthouse, would produce Giuffre's best work as both composer and soloist. This session's "A Ring-tail Monkey," an attractive light swinger with an intriguing melody, reflects precisely this successful new hybrid. (The piece was apparently named for Sam, Giuffre's pet monkey who shared his Manhattan Beach residence around this time.)

Giuffre's choice of accompanying instruments may have seemed strange enough, but the selection of his own horns now equally reflected his iconoclasm. Giuffre had the neck of his tenor rebent to help create a distinctive sound; when playing the clarinet, itself something of a rarity in modern jazz, Giuffre used an A-natural clarinet, rather than the standard B-flat horn, and his preference for the woody resonance of the instrument's deep register (what Ed Michel called the "isn't-this-a-nice-day-for-a-picnic sort of tone") further pushed Giuffre beyond the musical mainstream. Little wonder jazz fans had difficulty categorizing the unusual output of this former Woody Herman bandsman.

Giuffre's ensuing project for Capitol did little to reassure those who thought his penchant for experiment had already gone too far. The appropriately named *Tangents in Jazz*, recorded in June 1955, would be the furthest musical extreme Giuffre had yet tackled, and it remains the most controversial project of his career. In an unprecedented move, Capitol went so far as to include a lengthy interview with Giuffre on the back cover to defend the composer's approach. "What is this music?" the unknown questioner asked Giuffre. The composer replied:

> Jazz, with a non-pulsating beat. The beat is implicit but not explicit; in other words, acknowledged but unsounded. The two horns are the dominant but not domineering voices. The bass usually functions somewhat like a baritone sax. The drums play an important but non-conflicting role.[8]

The follow-up questions ("Why abandon the sounded beat? . . . But isn't the sounded beat an integral part of jazz? . . . Don't the soloists have a good deal less freedom than before?") suggest that either Giuffre or Capitol—most likely both—well understood the hornet's nest of criticism they were courting. Perhaps they felt it best to acknowledge the controversy in advance. But the result was still rather strange: Certainly few jazz artists have undergone such a hostile interrogation as part of the liner notes to an album.

By the mid-1950s the modernist belief in the necessity of constant musical radicalism had, of course, become accepted by all but the most retrograde jazz critics. After the furor surrounding bebop and the subsequent deification of its inventors, few critics wanted to risk being caught on the wrong side of jazz history. (This fear no doubt contributed to the striking bandwagon effect of critical support experienced by Ornette Coleman's avante-garde work a few years later. When the "free jazz" train came through town, no one dared to be left behind.) But even if innovation was welcomed in principle, the particular nature of Giuffre's experiments was such to raise eyebrows. By questioning the driving rhythm of modern jazz, Giuffre had challenged the most sacrosanct area of the music—the propulsive beat was viewed by many, both musicians and critics, as the essence of jazz. "It don't mean a thing, if it ain't got that swing," Ellington had announced long ago, and if the jazz critical establishment ever took the time to outline their ten commandments, Duke's admonition would likely be the first. Any attempt by Giuffre, or anyone else, to eliminate the propulsive beat was seen by these guardians of the jazz tradition as not progress but the most heinous reaction. To these true believers, Giuffre was essentially advocating musical heresy when he insisted:

> I've come to feel increasingly inhibited and frustrated by the insistent pounding of the rhythm section. With it, it's impossible for the listener or the soloist to hear the horn's true sound, I've come to believe, or fully concentrate on the solo line. An imbalance of advances has moved the rhythm from a supporting to a competitive role.

Despite Giuffre's rhetoric, the pieces on *Tangents in Jazz* do swing. In many ways the listener is even more drawn to the rhythmic element of the music, by the way it moves from instrument to instrument, instead of resting solely with the "rhythm" section. On *Tangents* Giuffre was again joined by Peña, Sheldon, and Anton, and though none of them stretches out at length during the course of the album, each is very much put in the spotlight as Giuffre employs a wide range of compositional devices: call-and-response figures, two- and three-part counterpoint, unison and harmony lines, canonic devices. These take the place of solos in Giuffre's new conception. As a filmmaker conveys a sense of momentum through a sequence of rapidly shifting camera angles, Giuffre's constant movement from one musical device to another achieves a similar effect. Part of the achievement of *Tangents in Jazz* is that, despite the leader's stated disregard for a "propulsive" beat, these pieces are constantly propelled, if not by a metronomic beat, certainly by Giuffre's constant changes in compositional focus. If anything, Giuffre overcompensates on *Tangents*, avoiding lengthy solos and shifting musical gears with abandon. The result is a highly concentrated music—which may be pleasing to the listener, but also makes severe demands on the attention.

By this time Giuffre clearly saw himself at the forefront of the "new thing" in jazz. Only "an imbalance of advances" had kept these innovations from taking root sooner. Yet with the perspective of the ensuing three decades, Giuffre's music can be seen to have had little influence on later jazz players. A few years later Bill Evans would use the term "internalized beat" to describe his trio's similar sense of rhythm, but at no point does he cite Giuffre as an influence. Other later rhythmic developments— for example, those of the John Coltrane and Miles Davis bands of the 1960s—also showed no signs of having assimilated the *Tangents* approach. For the most part, jazz of the next two decades continued to evolve while maintaining the propulsive rhythmic foundation Giuffre so much disliked.

But the sensibility Giuffre evoked would have a musical lineage, albeit outside of jazz. New Age music would not only create an independent style of improvisation in which rhythmic drive would be eliminated, but it would do this in the context of precisely that kind of blending of music and lifestyles Giuffre prefigured in the 1950s. The Eastern philosophical bent of Giuffre's work, borrowed from his guru La Violette; the exotic instrumentation of his music, as well as its meditative overtones; and all this practiced on the Pacific Coast—these are strong evidence for Giuffre's position as a forefather of New Age. California during the Cold War, however, had yet to develop an audience for this music-cum-lifestyle; being ahead of his time meant, for Giuffre, being shut out of his own time.

Giuffre's compositional mannerisms, to be sure, also included several elements far afield from the later New Age bag. First, his rhythmic approach, for all its dislike of steady swing, was anything but emasculated. Instead, like a fighter varying his attack, he tossed out a series of short, choppy rhythmic punches and counterpunches, never letting them fall into a predictable groove. Despite the stereotyped view of these performances as effete attempts to cut off jazz from its vital African roots, one returns to them with a constantly fresh sense of their enormous rhythmic variety. Giuffre's approach to harmonic construction is also far removed from the diatonic conservatism of New Age music, and despite his allegiance to Far Eastern philosophy, his compositional techniques from the 1950s rarely employed the static modal structures of meditation/New Age music. Finally, Giuffre's fascination with a wide range of compositional techniques, including counterpoint and atonality, brought him onto rocky terrain where few New Agers have yet dared to tread. These considerations notwithstanding, the starkness and restraint, the slow tempos and melodic integrity, his penchant for folk-style themes, and the philosophical trappings surrounding the music are harbingers of that later West Coast style of music.

Despite the assured pronouncements surrounding the release of *Tangents in Jazz*, Giuffre's musical temperament was still in ferment. Timed with the coming of the vernal equinox in 1956, Giuffre's debut session for Atlantic was another new beginning. The resulting clarinet album, discussed above, moves in a half-dozen different directions at once. Whereas *Tangents* had stood out by exploring the various possibilities of a narrow instrumentation—bass, drums, reeds, trumpet—the new recording offered a different combination of instruments on every track. In total, Giuffre drew on no fewer than fourteen musicians playing fifteen different instruments during the two days in the studio. Giuffre's new compositions called for clarinet, bass clarinet, celesta, flute, alto flute, bass flute, oboe, English horn, bassoon, trumpet, tenor sax, baritone sax, piano, bass, and drums, as well as his own percussive foot tapping.

In spite of this intimidating musical arsenal, the clarinet album reflects a clear step back from the experimentation of *Tangents in Jazz*. Indeed Giuffre seems to be looking as much backward as forward here, as he draws on a variety of blues and folk styles that warmly counter his more abstract leanings. On "Down Home," "The Sheepherder," and the opening unaccompanied "So Low," Giuffre captures a plaintive, pastoral quality only hinted at in his earlier work. Even the album's most obviously experimental piece, the atonal "The Side Pipers," does little to dispel this melancholy, open feeling. *The Jimmy Giuffre Clarinet* is very much that blessed rarity: a quite accessible experimental recording. It remains Giuffre's finest recording from his most productive decade.

Giuffre was one of the few resident West Coasters to keep a high profile on the East Coast during the second half of the decade and well into the early 1960s. Through teaching stints at the Lenox School of Jazz in Massachusetts, performances at the Newport Jazz Festival and elsewhere, and his growing involvement with the East Coast exponents of the new Third Stream movement, Giuffre had a coast-to-coast visibility no other saxophonist on the Pacific shore—Art Pepper, Sonny Criss, Bud Shank, Harold Land, Dexter Gordon—could then match. (Two decades later these roles would be reversed, with Giuffre finding fewer recording opportunities in the 1970s than any of the others.) A residency with the members of the Modern Jazz Quartet at the Music Inn near Lenox in the summer of 1956 led to his collaboration with the MJQ for a recording on the Atlantic label. Giuffre and John Lewis would continue to cross paths for some time to come, but their shared musical sympathies are apparent at even this early date, with both contributing restrained pieces of contrapuntal writing for the record date. Giuffre's clarinet sound here is strangely reminiscent of Paul Desmond's alto, and his solos take on an uncharacteristic daintiness, which is nonetheless beguiling, especially on the album-closing "Serenade."

Giuffre's deep sense of sound becomes increasingly apparent during these years on both his leader dates and his sideman work, eventually becoming more integral to his music than even his contrapuntal techniques. The saxophone tradition in jazz, more than any other instrumental lineage, is as much a matter of sound as of the actual notes played. Adolphe Saxe's invention, a bastard instrument removed from the classical tradition, can boast no one "correct" sound. Instead, it invites each player to invent a distinctive voice. The great players do just that, forging musical identities so vivid that they almost surround the listener with a strange new atmosphere, one sensuous and almost tactile in its presence: If Coleman Hawkins was a sultry, penetrating wind, then Ben Webster simply floated by in an evening mist, and Lester Young enveloped the listener like a drifting fog. Their styles *were* sounds. Giuffre's growth during these years focused on just this truth, and both his writing and playing evolved accordingly. Perhaps as a composer he was obsessed by the one quality that could not be captured in musical notation; perhaps he wanted to compensate for his limitations of technique by an excess of individuality in his tone. Whatever the underlying cause, by 1955 Giuffre's playing is as much a matter of texture as of melodic lines. By 1957, he goes so far as to take a solo on Shorty Rogers's LP that is nothing but the sound of his breath. "He has us work on horn phrasing like a Tibetan would have you bring up an *om*," explains Mark Rossi, a collaborator with Giuffre from the 1980s.[9] Rossi then adds, somewhat enigmatically, "He's into nature, understands tree worship, and has kept branching and growing."

Such "branching" continued to be evident in the new trio, comprised of Giuffre, bassist Peña (whose garage served as the group's practice room), and guitarist Jim Hall, who had recently left Chico Hamilton. The tree metaphor is quite appropriate to Giuffre's development at this stage, because the newness now is very much rooted in his past work, as demonstrated on *The Jimmy Giuffre 3*, his follow-up leader project for Atlantic. Certainly Giuffre's use of a fairly stark instrumentation after the varied tonal colors of the clarinet project is reminiscent of *Tangents in Jazz*, but the traditional element in this music is more a matter of composition than of instrumentation: The opening "Gotta Dance" harks back to the swing idiom of "Four Brothers," while the melodic, folk, and blues elements of his playing are still present, tempering the abstract, formalistic tendencies in his music. The academic coldness that is so stifling in Giuffre's least successful work is held at bay on these attractive trio performances. "The Train and the River," perhaps Giuffre's most popular composition after "Four Brothers," is anything but cerebral with its joyous down-home feeling and easy swing. On this song, indeed on the whole album, Giuffre feels free to violate the dogmas he had zealously articulated in the past. The beat is more propulsive, and the bass line frequently falls into a comfortable walk, which would have been anathema to the composer of *Tangents in Jazz*. Giuffre even stretches out at a fast tempo on "The Song Is You," apparently having made his peace with bebop. A bootleg recording of the same group, taken from a TV broadcast of January 1957, confirms this return to the tradition: The trio goes so far as to play a scaled-down arrangement of "Four Brothers," with Giuffre again conjuring up Prez on the tenor. The maligned propulsive beat is, once again, very much evident. Giuffre had apparently come full circle.

These return visits to the jazz heritage never lasted for long with Giuffre, and even the saxophonist's most conventional works seemed to have a subversive undercurrent. Giuffre later argued that he had committed the ultimate blasphemy, at least from the perspective of the jazz world, in forming this new trio: Not only had he abandoned the drums in his group, but he had also been guilty of following a model from classical music. "It came out of Debussy, actually, that Jim Hall group," he later admitted. "Debussy's sonata for flute, viola and harp. So Jim was the harp, Ralph the viola and I was the flute. I'd been looking for someone who could play great drums and also wanted to play more of a chamber-type music—and it was hard. I couldn't find a drummer interested in playing softly, in listening and resting. So I heard this Debussy piece, I liked it, and I thought, well, why not the three of us."[10] Giuffre's trio would undergo many transformations over the next few years—with Peña, Ray Brown, Red Mitchell, and Steve Swallow taking the bass chair, guitarist Hall playing in bands both with and without bass, and the third member of the trio including valve trombonist Bob Brookmeyer and pianist Paul Bley—but the absence of drums was to become a staple of these small groups.

Moving from town to town in a Volkswagen van, the Giuffre Three brought its new sound to the jazz community with an almost missionary-like zeal. With Hall and Brookmeyer in the band, Giuffre had assembled an ideal working unit. Each of the three was as skilled in listening as in playing, and with such an unconventional instrumentation the musicians needed to have big ears. Despite their extended West Coast residencies, Buffalo-born Jim Hall (December 4, 1930) and Kansas City native Bob Brookmeyer (December 19, 1929) are seldom associated with the West Coast sound. Yet in terms of style and associations, both had more than a passing acquaintance with the music. Brookmeyer had already replaced Chet Baker in the Mulligan Quartet and performed in a Los Angeles–based group alongside Stan Getz. For Hall's part, his sensitive, often pensive guitar stylings are quite in concordance with much of the creative focus of West Coast jazz during those years—as evidenced by Hall's collaborations then and later with Giuffre, Paul Desmond, and Chet Baker, as well as by the guitarist's early trio album on the Pacific label. The Giuffre/Brookmeyer/Hall threesome was a persuasive argument in defense of the new music on the Coast. Their work, for example on the Atlantic album *Trav'lin' Light*, successfully captured the folksy, pastoral elements and blues inflections that marked Giuffre's strongest work. These same qualities emerged, perhaps with even greater success, on the trio's later *Western Suite* recording, also on Atlantic. By this time, Giuffre's group had melded into an almost telepathic unit whose exceptional rapport made it easy for the listener to forget the strangeness of the instrumentation. This was powerful music, pure and simple. Bass and drums would have only intruded on the proceedings.

Consistency, the so-called virtue of small minds, was not the most salient attribute of Giuffre's work during the later 1950s. His interviews and public statements may have seemed like the polemics of a monomaniac, but his recordings revealed an increasing scattering of energies on a wide range of fronts. An album of Giuffre playing four overdubbed saxophones (à la the Four Brothers), a record of songs from Meredith Willson's *The Music Man*, a blowing date with a quartet, a Third Stream composition recorded with the Sudwestfunk Orchestra of Baden-Baden, a continued series of performances with his eccentric trios—these many efforts led one to ask: Which is the real Jimmy Giuffre? In a sideman such versatility is forgiven or even praised, but in a leader these split personalities were somewhat disturbing. Perhaps Giuffre's lack of recording opportunities a decade later reflected his audience's difficulty in digesting these exotic tidbits from the 1950s.

A few years earlier André Hodeir had written:

> The medium-size group sessions with Giuffre, Holman, Rogers . . . show us what mistakes can be made by estimable jazzmen working without any doctrine except, perhaps, the most detestable—eclecticism. . . . The only results obtained are negative. Jimmy Giuffre gives new proof that the fugal style is inappropriate for jazz.[11]

The dismissal of the fugue as "inappropriate for jazz" smacks of that unsettling control of jazz by definition Graham Lock has rightly criticized. But Hodeir's attack on eclecticism cuts deeper (and is perhaps even more relevant today when eclecticism has become the "style without style" of so many—perhaps most—younger jazz players), and in the case of Giuffre was more prescient. In the closing years of the decade, when the others cited by Hodeir were narrowing their focus and refining their stylistic integrity, Giuffre was more in flux than ever before.

Not that the various projects were without merit. Giuffre's blowing date with Jimmy Rowles, Red Mitchell, and Lawrence Marable from 1957, released on Verve as *Ad Lib*, is every bit as enjoyable as it is unexpected. In the liner notes Giuffre explains that he "finally got up the nerve to throw the rock off the cliff and just play anything I wanted to play when I wanted to play it. It was a revelation."[12] Giuffre's playing must also have been a revelation to those critics who had chastised him for his poor technical command of the saxophone. On *Ad Lib*, he sounds more comfortable than ever before on tenor, and even the up-tempo closer "Problems," despite its name, poses no difficulties. A further surprise is the new influence of Sonny Rollins on Giuffre's playing, now especially noticeable at faster tempos.

The Music Man is an equally incongruous effort. The instrumentation was once again highly unusual: The rhythm section included no chordal instrument, relying solely on bass and drums, while Giuffre's work on three horns (clarinet, tenor, and baritone) was supported by three trumpets and three saxophones. Giuffre had tried a similar instrumentation on his clarinet album and was now adapting it to a very different context. Other elements of Giuffre's earlier works are also featured in heady doses: the nonpulsating beat, the reliance on counterpoint, the constantly shifting instrumental groupings. This was no off-the-cuff jam session based on lead sheets from the show, but a full-scale effort to fit Willson's music into the confines of Giuffre's stylistic and theoretical tendencies.

Giuffre here proves the validity of Stan Getz's assertion that irreverence is one of the four greatest virtues a jazz musician can possess (the others being taste, courage, and individuality). Certainly Giuffre pays no undue respect to the Meredith Willson songs in this setting; changes in tempos, meter, phrasing, harmony, and instrumentation are applied liberally. This was Giuffre's first album as a leader that involved no original compositions, and the saxophonist/arranger perhaps compensated by attempting what was, in effect, a re-composition of the music involved. Giuffre succeeded in making this music his own—perhaps his small-town Texas roots found a resonance in the Midwestern sensibility of the material—and the transformation of the pieces resulted in more than a few magical moments: Giuffre's duet with drummer Ed Shaughnessy on "Shipoopi"; his moving coda on "Till There Was You" after the affecting stop-and-start ballad rendition; the interaction of brass, reeds, and soloists on "76

Trombones." In its freedom and flexibility, above all in its constant surprises, *The Music Man* earns a place among the best Broadway adaptations
of its day.

Once again, Giuffre refused to linger in a musical genre. No more
Broadway albums were forthcoming from him. The turn of the decade
found him increasingly involved in his trio work, but even here the instrumentation constantly shifted. A Giuffre trio might include almost any
combination of instruments: clarinet, bass, and guitar; clarinet, valve
trombone, and guitar; clarinet, piano, and drums; clarinet, bass, and drums;
clarinet, piano, and bass. At the close of the period under discussion, Giuffre
began working frequently in the last format with the able assistance of
pianist Paul Bley and bassist Steve Swallow, two of the finest musicians of
their generation. The trio's work on *Fusion* and *Thesis* (both released on
the Verve label) shows Giuffre increasingly immersing himself in the lan-
guage of the then-emerging jazz avant-garde. His 1959 recordings of "Piece
for Clarinet and String Orchestra" and "Mobiles," also released on Verve,
are orchestral works very much in the same adventurous vein. With the
tonality often attenuated, and the musical structures based more on disjunction than on the uninterrupted flow of, say, "Four Brothers" or "A
Ring-tail Monkey," Giuffre was entering the 1960s at the end of a process
of personal development that, to a casual listener, must have seemed a
complete renunciation of his early roots in swing. These are difficult works
with little of the charm that radiates from Giuffre's most memorable efforts. Especially when he abandons a tonal center in his works, Giuffre
seems to lose more of his individuality than he gains by the supposed
freedom. At their most derivative, his evocations of Ornette Coleman—
apparently heightened by the presence of Bley—are nowhere as convincing
as the real thing. With Coleman (as well as with Bley), the freedom from
conventional structures comes across as being truly liberating, whereas with
Giuffre the plunge into atonality is never completely satisfying or convincing. To be fair, this apparently final stage in Giuffre's development was
clearly no haphazard result, but truly the logical end-point of a decade of
personal growth. To this listener, one who considers himself one of Giuffre's
defenders, this evolution ranks as one of those journeys, much like that of
Huck Finn or Phileas Fogg, in which the stopping points along the way
are much more interesting than the final destination.

Soon after this point, Giuffre disappeared from the musical scene.
More progressive critics had hailed these final recordings as Giuffre's greatest
achievement, but the response among the majority of jazz fans was anything but enthusiastic. After the second trio album with Bley and Swallow,
Verve dropped Giuffre from the label. The third album of the group appeared on CBS, but the new label also quickly became disenchanted with
the response to the music. Many of Giuffre's admirers had found in his

earlier music, such as the popular "The Train and the River," "Gotta Dance," or "Trav'lin' Light," a fresh, distinctive sound unlike anything else in jazz. Now they were disappointed to hear Giuffre plunging into an idiom in which the most personal aspects of his sound were all but lost. But Giuffre, ever anxious to move ahead into new areas, again refused to rest on past achievements.

In a strange contrast to this increasingly experimental work of the late 1950s, Giuffre closed the decade with one of the most winning traditional efforts of his career. His late 1959 collaboration with singer Anita O'Day, released by Verve as *Cool Heat*, is now seldom heard, and certainly not as widely heralded as the Bley/Swallow work, yet it must be considered one of the most striking collaborations of singer and arranger during the decade. These are not typical singers' charts by any means: Giuffre's use of space borders on the extreme; his control of dynamics is almost obsessive; his metronome markings and instrumentation are far from conventional. On "It Had to Be You" the arrangement shifts back and forth between full orchestra and guitar trio; after the first languid chorus, the tempo doubles—a common arranger's device—but after the second chorus, the tempo doubles again. Suddenly O'Day has shifted gears from ballad mode to medium groove and now into blistering up-tempo bop. The experience is exhilarating. In O'Day, Giuffre found the perfect singer for his efforts: Her strong sense of time and phrasing allowed her to deal with his various "nonpropulsive beat" devices as well as these radical tempo changes. Further, Giuffre's probing arrangements had a positive influence on the singer, leading her to eschew the florid excesses of her most facile work and dig deeply into the songs. This album, too, saw no follow-up efforts in a similar vein.

Indeed, in the eyes of the jazz world Giuffre seemed to do little of anything after 1963. Ostensibly much of his efforts since that time have been devoted to teaching. His few forays into the recording studio have been, as one would expect, quite eclectic. The hints of a combined New Age philosophy and music, always implied in his work and lifestyle from the 1950s, are increasingly pronounced on such later releases as his 1975 *River Chant*. On this, he even remakes his earlier "The Train and the River," only this time one hears how this distinctive mixture of folk, jazz, and blues had anticipated the work of so many later musicians, especially those associated with the ECM label. But Giuffre is not the type to carry such retrospections to an extreme, and his work in the 1980s has diverged between these backward glances and ongoing attempts at still different things, now in the world of synthesizers, electronics, and rock-inflected music. (Some things, however, have not changed: In a 1989 interview he still referred to La Violette, over a decade after the latter's death, as "my teacher.")

Yet if Giuffre is largely unacknowledged as a pioneer, he perhaps has only himself to blame. The extraordinary diversity of his musical output has made the exact nature of his contributions to jazz difficult to pinpoint for all but his most devoted fans. Yet with a little effort one can trace many lineages through Giuffre's oeuvre, and more than one contemporary school of jazz could look to him as a forebear. Homage from the younger generation (whether of musicians or critics) has not, however, been at all apparent. Nor is it likely to be forthcoming.

CHAPTER TWELVE

Martians Go Home

sprezzatura

Shorty Rogers's music exemplifies what the Italian courtier Castiglione called *sprezzatura*—the ability to do difficult things with apparent ease. For Castiglione, this attitude of studied nonchalance was the trademark of the Renaissance man. Half a millenium later, members of the beat generation described this same world view as being "cool"—and thought they had invented something new. The only difference was that the beats held up their "cool" demeanor as an attitude of rebellion against the system. Castiglione's ideal courtier was an organization man. He may have had a bit of Bogart, a good measure of Chet Baker (circa 1952), and even a dash of James Dean, but his Renaissance cool never pushed things too far. Sprezzatura was beat without the bite.

Shorty Rogers is much the same. During the West Coast musical renaissance of the 1950s, Rogers offered his listeners sprezzatura in 4/4 time. His arrangements could swing without ostentation; his solos were executed with untroubled fluency; his compositions seemed to navigate the most difficult waters with a relaxed, comfortable flow that belied the often complex structures involved. Rogers's lifestyle, in its refusal to call attention to itself, followed a similar philosophy. While many of his colleagues on the West Coast found it easier to make headlines through their counterculture ways than through their music, Rogers had little to do with such excesses. He paid his dues and his monthly bills with equal equanimity. This was perhaps *too* cool. Rogers was easy to take for granted.

Rogers's visibility in jazz has been further hindered by his virtual retirement from performing situations since the early 1960s. Like his longtime colleague and collaborator Jimmy Giuffre, Rogers recorded prolifically between 1951 and 1963, only to fade from the scene afterwards. It is almost as if the amazing early fecundity had crammed a whole career of music-making into a dozen years. Nothing was left for an encore. Of course, neither Rogers nor Giuffre actually left the music world; they simply applied their skills elsewhere, in studio work or academic pursuits. But to the jazz community this was tantamount to retirement.

In reaction to Rogers's retreat into studio work, some jazz fans have been even less generous. They have viewed this change in careers as nothing short of treason, a betrayal of the serious music Rogers had once strived to create. But no matter how one interprets Rogers the musician, his lengthy absence from the jazz world has meant that his work, once widely known, is now largely unfamiliar to many jazz fans and critics. As for Rogers the man, the criticisms voiced by those unhappy with his studio work have had little effect on him. Unlike others similarly lambasted, Rogers shows no desire to answer his accusers. Today Shorty Rogers impresses those who deal with him as a spiritual man, a gentle man, soft-spoken and quietly dedicated to his music. Recently he returned to performing and recording, and whatever responses Rogers may have to the jazz establishment are to be found in his music rather than in outspoken public comment. No polemics, à la Giuffre, accompany his recordings. In his attitude toward his music as well as in the ease and grace of the music itself, Rogers practically invites us to overlook his achievements.

This even-tempered approach to music goes against the grain of most modern jazz. Jazz, whether by its nature or circumstance, has evolved into a music that constantly calls attention to itself. To work up a sweat during the performance is almost *de rigeur*, while to transform the act of playing into an athletic event, in the manner of a John Coltrane or Cecil Taylor, is much prized and praised. When Charlie Parker's life was recently made into a movie, actor Forest Whitaker portrayed Bird swinging back and forth with energy while he played the alto. In point of fact, Parker remained stock still when he improvised, but the mythifiers of jazz have difficulty dealing with that degree of restraint. To play this kind of music, the conventional wisdom goes, you have to be swinging your limbs.

Not so Rogers. Even in the most heated passages, the listener never loses the beauty of the details, the subtleties in his music. And it swings too, but always swings comfortably. Just as Count Basie had done years earlier, Rogers pursued an ideal of swing in which dynamics and space played a role, in which rhythmic inspiration was not equated with mere perspiration. Those who delight over the ragged edges in music must be dismayed over such performances. Here the rough spots never show. The shirttails are always neatly tucked in.

The mention of Basie's name is not haphazard. Nor is it by chance that one of Rogers's finest albums from the 1950s was entirely devoted to Basie's music. The Count's work exerted a strong influence on Shorty

Rogers's music and was also an important (and often unacknowledged) inspiration for the West Coast sound. The Kansas City style, with its easy swing, seemingly moved west to take on a second life in California. Commentators have often noted that Basie's saxophonist, Lester Young, served as the most prominent model for a whole generation of West Coast players (Wardell Gray, Dexter Gordon, Art Pepper, Jimmy Giuffre, Bill Perkins, and Brew Moore, to name just a few), but less understood has been the influence of the Basie band as a unit on the West Coast music. At a time when the Ellington ensemble ruled supreme among many connoisseurs of big bands, a large number of West Coast players went on record as preferring the Basie orchestra.

Some representative comments:

DEXTER GORDON: "I got my first Basie album and that was it. I fell in love with that band. Duke was fantastic, but the Basie band really hit me."

WARDELL GRAY: "Basie is the greatest bandleader ever."

BUD SHANK [asked by *Metronome*'s Fran Kelley, "What's your favorite band?"]: "It's got to be Count Basie. . . . That's since adolescence up until now and probably will be for the next twenty years."

SHELLY MANNE [complimenting a rival band]: "I haven't had such a thrill from a big band since the last time I heard Basie's band."

ART PEPPER: "The first time I heard Prez was Basie's band. . . . That's my whole inspiration of black music. . . . That was music to me for years. It still is. Just that thing."

SHORTY ROGERS: "Where did West Coast jazz come from? Maybe Count Basie. . . . In my case, one of the strong influences was the Count Basie Kansas City Seven."[1]

As he tells it, Rogers's first strong impression of jazz came from a Count Basie 78 that belonged to one of his siblings:

I can't remember if it was my sister or brother, but one of them had some jazz records in the house, and one of them was a Count Basie record. . . . I played it and fell madly in love with Sweets Edison's solo on there, so one of the first things I can remember learning was just playing that over and over, learning his solo and playing along with the record.

Rogers, born near Lee, Massachusetts, on April 14, 1924—as Milton Michael Rajonsky—began playing the bugle at age five. Walter Raith, who assisted the elder Mr. Rajonsky at his tailor shop, had introduced the youngster to the instrument. Before long Rogers was part of a drum and bugle corps run by the local American Legion. His father, Abraham Rajonsky, an immigrant from Romania, and his mother, Anna Sevitsky Rajonsky, originally from Pinsk in Russia, had met years earlier in New York, and when Rogers was nine years old, his parents decided to return there. Rogers soon found himself living on Claremont Parkway in the Bronx, where he joined another drum and bugle corps. This musical apprenticeship continued until he was thirteen.

For his bar mitzvah, Rogers's father offered to give the youngster a present of his choice. The resulting gift, a $15 trumpet, was acquired at a local pawnshop. Without instruction of any sort, Rogers began experimenting on the new horn, and soon he was emulating the music he heard on records, not just Sweets Edison, but also Bunny Berigan, Roy Eldridge, Bobby Hackett, and others. Four months after acquiring the instrument, Rogers entered the High School of Music and Art. Although he had initially failed the entrance test because of his poor music-reading skills, a subsequent ear-training test revealed his strong native ability. This proved sufficient to gain him admission to the school.

During his school years, Rogers played in local bands around the Bronx at weddings and bar mitzvahs, supplemented by summer gigs in the Borscht Belt. At one of these engagements he was offered a job by bandleader Will Bradley. Bradley told him a job would be waiting for him when he finished school. Three months later, diploma in hand, Rogers joined the Bradley band. The drummer in that ensemble, Shelly Manne, would remain a lifelong companion. Ten years later and three thousand miles away, these two East Coasters would collaborate in forging what would be called the "West Coast sound."

After several months with Bradley, Rogers joined the band of Red Norvo (who would marry Rogers's sister Eve several years later). Through Norvo, Rogers played briefly on the 52nd Street scene, until his musical career was interrupted by a stint in the service. This intermission lasted, Rogers recalls with precision, two years, four months, and seven days. Afterwards, Rogers found another job waiting, this time with Woody Herman.

The Herman band, one of the most important institutions in the history of jazz, was also one of the strangest. Beset by a turnover rate that made the Ellington and Basie ensembles appear paragons of stability; frequently losing money and initially forced to organize, against union objections, as a cooperative in which group members held shares of the band; commissioning band scores from an unprecedented range of sources, from Igor Stravinsky to Dizzy Gillespie—Herman seemed intent on proving that one could break all the rules and still make an indelible mark on the jazz world. Perhaps just this ambiguity motivated Phil Wilson's memorable *bon mot:* "Nobody does what Woody does as well as he does. [Pause] If we could only figure out what it is he does."

What Herman did, of course, was little short of incredible. Forming his group out of the remnants of Isham Jones's sweet band, Herman transformed it first into an outstanding hot band and eventually into the preeminent bop big band of its day. Each of these jumps—from sweet to hot, and from swing to bop—was an immense leap beyond the ken of most other bandleaders of the day. But Herman took them in stride, moving ahead with the support of a growing legion of enthusiastic fans. And despite the turnover and personal problems of his bands, Herman thrived—largely through his almost unfailing knack for bringing in high-powered replacements. The alumni rolls of his Herds contain an impressive listing of jazz masters past and present: Stan Getz, Zoot Sims, Herbie Steward, Al Cohn, Serge Chaloff, Pete and Conte Candoli, Shorty Rogers, Bill Harris, Sonny Berman, Jimmy Giuffre, Jimmy Raney, Terry Gibbs, Ernie Royal, Jimmy Rowles, Phil Urso, Dave McKenna, Richie Kamuca, Bill Perkins, Bill Chase, and Phil Wilson, to name just a few.

On the strength of a recommendation from Red Norvo, Rogers replaced Conte Candoli in the band's trumpet section. "[Pete] sat next to me," Rogers recalls, "and treated me like I was his brother Conte. Conte got the raw end of the deal—he got drafted. I got his chair, and he went to Camp Lee, Virginia, where I got out from." It was soon after Rogers's arrival in the band that Herman's work with Stravinsky on the *Ebony Concerto* began. The trumpeter's presence apparently had a soothing effect on the elder statesman of classical modernism. Later Stravinsky reportedly remarked: "I can listen to Shorty Rogers's good style, with its dotted tradition, for stretches of fifteen minutes and more and not feel the time at all, whereas the weight of every 'serious' virtuoso I know depresses me beyond the counteraction of Equanil in about five."[2] This admiration extended to influence. According to Robert Craft's *Conversations with Stravinsky*, the composer used the flugelhorn on his "Threni" at least partly as a result of hearing Rogers play the instrument. Rogers returned the favor, in his own manner, by composing "Igor" for the Herman band.

Rogers's contribution to the Herman ensemble were significant; some of his numbers such as "Steps" or "Nero's Conception" became important parts of the band's repertoire. But just as things seemed to be taking off, Herman—again breaking all the rules—disbanded the group. To jazz fans at the time this was both a tragedy and a mystery, and a number of conflicting explanations were given as to Herman's motives. Herman's eventual explanation of an illness in the family was a euphemistic reference to the alcohol and pill addiction of his stay-at-home spouse, Charlotte.

When he re-formed in 1947, after taking care of problems at home, many of the earlier members were unavailable. But Rogers returned. During the interim, Shorty and his wife had settled in Southern California and legally changed their name from Rajonsky to Rogers. Here the trumpeter tried to find work—with mixed results. "Nothing was happening," Rogers later explained. "I literally couldn't even pick up the phone and call anyone. I didn't know anyone to call. . . . As soon as they let me know that Woody was re-forming, I was back!"[3] Rogers exaggerates his level of inactivity—during the interlude he performed with Charlie Barnet, Stan Getz, and Herbie Steward, among others. But the decision to rejoin was the right one. This Herman unit became the celebrated Four Brothers band, and Rogers gained increased notoriety as well as arranging and playing experience in a series of charts, including "Lemon Drop," "I've Got News for You," "Keeper of the Flame," "More Moon," and, with Ralph Burns, "Keen and Peachy."

This band, despite its extraordinary run of musical successes, was plagued with difficulties: The drug problems were extreme even by the lax standards then prevalent in the world of modern jazz (although, it should be added, most of those involved in drugs in the band later stopped using them). In addition, the new group was losing money at a prodigious rate. Herman was again forced to disband in late 1949, and Rogers soon joined the Stan Kenton orchestra.

Kenton was reportedly apprehensive about hiring Rogers because of the latter's strong association in the jazz public's mind with the Herman Herd. Rogers, for his part, may have been equally reluctant to join a band that, unlike Herman's, had developed a reputation as much for bombast as for swing. If Rogers held any reservations about the move, however, he kept quiet about them. When I asked him about his reactions to the "Kenton sound," he replied with characteristic diplomacy: "There was such a variety there, I think to really analyze it or really take a good look at it you'd have to go one piece of music at a time." Rogers sees his own contributions to the band as a case in point: "I got out some paper and a pencil and I just wrote, you know, as if I was still with Woody's band"; he adds, almost as an afterthought, "with maybe a few little things that would be in the Kenton flavor." But almost as quickly, he counters: "But if I did it was unintentional."

Rogers's comments notwithstanding, the trumpeter's arrangements showed his adaptation to the new musical surroundings. The screaming brass and thick voicings of "Jolly Rogers," for example, definitely fit in with the supposed tenets of Kentonian jazz. On a chart like "Art Pepper," Rogers showed that he could make excellent use of the added strings and French horn, as well as the overall freedom, which Kenton wisely instilled in his writers, to experiment with new sounds and approaches. This openness was perhaps Kenton's greatest virtue; it gives the lie to critics who saw "neophonic music" or "progressive music" (those ever-cryptic Kenton neologisms) merely as the bandleader's narrow-minded adherence to his own dogmas. Rogers's arranging and writing skills benefited from this institutionalized openness to new musical ideas.

According to some sources, including Robert Gordon's seminal *Jazz West Coast*,[4] Rogers's membership in the Kenton Innovations band ended with the close of its first tour in June 1950. When the band re-formed later in the year, Rogers was supposedly not a part of the new unit. Rogers's comments have tended to substantiate this: For whatever reasons, he depicts his tenure with Kenton as a matter of a few months. Yet the Rogers discography tells a different story. It shows the trumpeter involved with the Kenton band for recordings and broadcasts on no fewer than twenty-three separate occasions between his supposed June 1950 departure date and the fall of 1951.

Most of these recorded documents come from the band's stint at the Hollywood Palladium, and thus might be explained as Rogers's work as a local freelancer who was not a permanent member of the band. But this period also finds Rogers apparently participating in recorded Kenton performances in New York and New Jersey. Rogers's comments in my initial interview with him were ambiguous: "That lasted, I think, less than a year. I really don't remember. . . . I'm just guessing, because after I left the band, I left to join the group at the Lighthouse." Rogers recalls his first Lighthouse gig as being New Year's Eve, probably in 1950, but the first recorded evidence of his playing at the Lighthouse comes from the December 27, 1951, bootleg recorded by Bob Andrews. Given these circumstances, it seems likely that the traditional accounts of Rogers's career from the mid-1950s are one year out of synch: Most probably, his involvement with Kenton ended in the summer of 1951, not the summer of 1950, while his Lighthouse engagement began at the close of the same year. Andrews, who now lives in Mission Viejo, substantiates this view; his recollection is that Rogers began playing regularly with the All-Stars around the time Andrews recorded the Pepper/Rogers ensemble.

This tape incurred Howard Rumsey's displeasure when it was released without his permission on the Xanadu label. (Although he was paid for the date, Rumsey claims he never cashed the check.) But from the standpoint of jazz history, the availability of this session is quite a blessing. It reveals a heated, bebop side of Rogers's playing, unlike anything else in the trumpeter's recorded legacy. The Lighthouse, as I have mentioned, brought out the more driving side of the various musicians who played there. This factor combined with the presence of Hampton Hawes and Art Pepper, and the break from the restrained Kenton setting, to push Rogers into a different musical vein than was his wont. The versions of "Scrapple from the Apple" and "Cherokee" from this taped performance suggest

that Rogers's later "cool school" persona was built on a careful appreciation and assimilation of Parker and Gillespie.

The much more celebrated Rogers session from October 1951 showed
a much different side of the trumpeter. With the production help of local
deejay-cum-jazz-impresario Gene Norman, Rogers undertook what would
later be recognized as a historic record date. These seminal performances
were released the following year after Norman sold the tapes to Capitol.
They are justifiably considered not only one of the classics of Rogers's
career, but also one of the pioneering statements of the "West Coast sound."
And rightly so: If the later nonet, octets, and dectettes of Dave Pell, Marty
Paich, Lennie Niehaus, and others have a West Coast progenitor, the sources
must be looked for in Rogers and Mulligan. Brubeck's octet may demand
equal respect for its music, but its influence, for better or worse, was min-
imal in comparison with Rogers's or Mulligan's.

Not that Rogers's music was without precedent. Much has been made
of the influence of the Miles Davis nonet, which had earlier set the model
for Rogers's use of French horn and tuba. Rogers adopted those instruments but diverged from the "birth of the cool" instrumentation by sub-
stituting tenor saxophone for baritone and omitting the trombone. These
subtle changes, along with the personnel and charts, served to make the
Rogers octet sound less bottom-heavy than the Davis nonet. Again the
influence of the Basie band should not be overlooked, especially in the
easy, relaxed swing of these performances.

"Popo," the opening number, is a telling indicator of one of the distinctive sounds Rogers was forging. It was nothing short of a new way of
playing the blues. The standard twelve-bar form was left intact, but the
flavor of the composition and arrangement mimicked neither the gut-bucket
blues of an earlier day, nor the more abstract structures (such as Parker's
"Blues for Alice") the beboppers had built on this foundation. Even the
East Coast cool school, in its diverse Miles- and Tristano-inflected streams,
never achieved such a light and airy approach to this time-honored form.
Part of the credit here accrues to the rhythm section. Shelly Manne's
pointillistic drumming avoids the heavy rhythmic ground most percussionists would have added to this setting. Even in a large ensemble, Manne
rarely tried to emulate a big band sound. In much of his best work he
pursued the exact opposite philosophy; his apparent goal was to make a
large group swing with the intimacy of a small combo. Hampton Hawes,
in contrast, followed a more aggressive rhythmic approach. In the context
of the Rogers ensemble his comping chords gave a percussive push to the
soloists with a staccato crispness that never clouded the bass register. These
elements merged with Rogers's "Popo" chart to create an effortless swing,
an atmosphere in which melody could float above the beat and the blues

(perhaps the most flexible form in the history of jazz: its sonata, concerto, and symphony all rolled into one) could take on a new face.

The success of "Popo" eventually led to its use as a theme song for Rogers's group, but it was far from the only highlight of this session. A number of memorable musical moments were immortalized at the early autumn date: Rogers's building off a call-and-response interlude in "Didi" to start his solo; Art Pepper's bittersweet feature on "Over the Rainbow," which became, at the time, his best-known recorded work; Hampton Hawes's unexpected solo break after the introduction of "Apropos." This early leader date showed all the ingredients that would characterize Rogers's work throughout the decade: a continual emphasis on musical surprise coupled with a modest willingness to experiment with new approaches; a predilection for a relaxed, nonbombastic sense of swing; a reliance on strong, melodic soloing by the finest improvisers available on the coast; an emphasis on carefully and creatively arranged settings, designed with these specific soloists in mind; and, in general, a unique musical style that remained modern without being abrasive or cold. Unlike Giuffre, Rogers's willingness to experiment rarely found him straying too far afield from these foundations. He discovered the recipe that worked for him, and his goal from then on was to apply it in a way that kept it fresh, so that his winning formula never became merely formulaic.

Over the next year, Rogers's energies were largely occupied by his association with the Lighthouse All-Stars, as well as by sideman projects with Maynard Ferguson, Shelly Manne, June Christy, and others. When he returned to the studio as a bandleader in January 1953, this time for RCA, he took up where he had left off fifteen months previously with the Gene Norman sessions. For the two January dates Rogers convened a nonet almost identical to the earlier group, the only difference being the addition of Milt Bernhart on trombone and the substitution of Joe Mondragon for bassist Don Bagley. This reluctance to change musicians, even after a lengthy interval, was not surprising. Rogers's writing here sounds as though composed for precisely this group of players: Pepper's feature on "Bunny" recaptures the innocent prettiness of his early work, so much so that one cannot imagine any other soloist in his place; "Diablo's Dance" was a much different composition, but once again Hampton Hawes's playing on it is part and parcel of its success. These pieces, as well as such Rogers staples from this same project as "Powder Puff," "Pirouette," and "Morpo," rank among the strongest works of the trumpeter's career.

They also reveal the strongly traditional approach of his writing. The free-flowing melodic writing that characterized most modern jazz composition—exemplified in Parker tunes such as "Confirmation" or "Donna Lee"—made even composed lines sound as though they were improvised.

Such melodic writing was complex and ingenious, and usually drenched in chromaticism. Rogers's melodies, in contrast, reverted to more basic motivic writing. The phrases followed one another with an easy logic, often being mere restatements, slight alterations, or inversions of the previous phrase. Listening to the opening of, say, "Powder Puff," one is struck by the childlike simplicity of the melody, one that bears little or no resemblance to the kinds of melodies typically found in Parker, Gillespie, Powell, or Tristano. But instead of lapsing into the monotony such devices risk, Rogers used this technique to set up the listener for the eventual surprising shift that breaks out of the expected pattern. In the case of "Powder Puff," the attractive transformation of melody, rhythm, and mood in the bridge is captivating for just this reason. What sounded like a simple nursery song with a predictable development is suddenly transmuted into an evanescent Latin-tinged dance, which briefly works its magic before retreating into the wings. Rogers's compositions typically work in just such a manner: The "hooks" are built out of surprisingly simple devices. Afterwards we marvel at the amazing contrast between the ambitious ends achieved and the modest means used. It is as though an old-school craftsman has shown us how to build a house using only a basic toolbox and a stack of bricks.

In late March and early April, Rogers returned to the studio, this time in the company of a seventeen-piece big band, complete with tuba and French horn as well as full brass and reed sections. The eight tracks resulting from the two dates with the band, released by RCA as *Cool and Crazy*, reveal the Kenton influence, which had been just barely detectable on the preceding octet and nonet projects. If anything, listeners might have heard the earlier records as a reaction against the bombast of Kenton. But now Rogers revealed that his stint with the Cecil B. deMille of jazz had left its mark. The light effervesence of the earlier octet and nonet sessions appears only sporadically on this date; instead Rogers seems intent on presenting a broader array of sounds, ranging from the softest musical whisper to the most boisterous screaming and shouting.

"Infinity Promenade," from the March 26 session, is representative of this change in Rogers's music. The introduction is low-key in the extreme, with Shelly Manne softly playing a single cymbal, as though he were alone in the studio after everyone else had gone home. A moment later the whole band enters, over a throbbing dominant pedal point, bellowing out a quintessentially Rogerian melody built off a simple five-note motif moving in an easy stepwise pattern. The volume builds through an interlude leading in to an Art Pepper solo, in which the tension is suddenly released by the removal of the pedal point and a drop in dynamics. During this Pepper improvisation, as well as in Rogers's following solo, the group sounds like the earlier Rogers octet with its relaxed underpinnings. But then the ensemble returns with Maynard Ferguson's trumpet screaming in the stratosphere. The band now milks this melody for all it is worth in a fortissimo shout before again giving way, this time to a tinkling Marty Paich piano solo, which lasts only a few bars before the band returns stating the melody, even louder than before. One might think that the performance is now ending, but Rogers throws in one of those musical surprises so typical of his work. Just as the piece seems to be moving into a coda, the band again abruptly fades away, this time leaving Shelly Manne alone on his drums. Manne begins with a flurry of energy, then suddenly shifts gears as he works his way back to the simple solo cymbal pattern that began the performance. After a moment of this gentle cymbal work, Rogers brings back the band for one last rendition of the piece's simple melody, this time playing it at a moderate dynamic level and closing on a held unresolved chord. *Cool and Crazy* was the right name for this record, for both extremes were juxtaposed at close quarters in the music.

When I asked Rogers which of his records, if any, were personal favorites, he cited this first big band date for RCA. (He referred to it as *Shorty Rogers Express*—the name of a later 12-inch LP reissue of the project, which also included some additional tracks from July 1956.) One can understand his pride, for this project, more than any one before it, reflected the full range of his musical skills, capturing not just the intimacy and gentle moodiness of *Modern Sounds*, but a panoply of other sounds and approaches. Perhaps the project also served, in his eyes, as an answer to those criticisms, now being voiced for the first time, of the newly celebrated "West Coast sound." Those hostile to the California movement lambasted its lack of variety and, above all, its insufficient intensity. With *Cool and Crazy* Rogers created a music immune to such criticisms: This was music that prided itself on both its variety and intensity.

His follow-up big band recording for RCA was a strange affair, anticipating in some degree the later mania among West Coast jazz musicians for theme albums based on Hollywood or Broadway music. Here Rogers presented his arrangement of four compositions written by Leith Stevens for the Marlon Brando movie *The Wild One*. These pieces, for all their elán, were rather poor vehicles for Rogers's talents, certainly not up to the par of the movie material André Previn would later borrow for his successful theme albums. The high point of this project is perhaps the strong solo contributions of saxophonist Bill Perkins. The featured soloist on "Blues for Brando," Perkins comes across as anything but a musical counterpart of the cinematic "wild one," instead offering a gentle, musing improvisation representative of the tenorist's best playing of the 1950s.

During this period, Rogers was increasingly returning to the music of his first model: Count Basie. "We like to play a lot of Basie things on the gig," he told Ralph Gleason in a 1954 interview. "It's our tribute to Basie.

. . . It expresses the way myself and all the guys feel about him."[5] Over the course of three sessions in early 1954, Rogers regrouped his big band in the studio to record a tribute album dedicated to this music. For the project Rogers arranged nine pieces associated with the Count and added three original pieces written in a Basie style. As in *The Wild One*, Rogers was content here to submerge his own style in someone else's—something many jazz musicians are loathe to do under any circumstances. But here the music involved proved the wisdom of Rogers's decision. Rogers glistens in the company of his early hero Harry "Sweets" Edison. The whole band—which also included Jimmy Giuffre, Bud Shank, Shelly Manne, Marty Paich, and Zoot Sims—seems to be having a great deal of fun emulating the group that had inspired so many of them as youngsters. The album radiates a heady enthusiasm.

There were many sides to Shorty Rogers's musical activities during this period. The unabashed traditionalism of the Basie project, the film-inspired music from *The Wild One*, the big bands, nonets, and octets—these projects were quite eclectic, yet they reflected only part of Rogers's wide-ranging interests. Much of his most striking and experimental music from this time comes from his work as a sideman. Projects with Shelly Manne, Jimmy Giuffre, and Teddy Charles revealed an iconoclastic side of Rogers that only rarely surfaced on his dates as a leader. In this regard the contrast between Rogers and his colleague Jimmy Giuffre could not be greater: Giuffre preferred to experiment on his projects as a leader, while his dates as a sideman show off the traditional side of his playing. With Rogers, the opposite was true during most of the mid-1950s. As the decade proceeded these two, once like-minded partners, diverged even more sharply: While Giuffre advanced further and further into the avant-garde, Rogers slowly abandoned the more extreme aspects of his experimentation and increasingly focused on straight-ahead playing and arranging.

In at least one regard—his adoption of the flugelhorn—Rogers's work from the mid-1950s must be viewed as distinctly innovative. Between sets at Zardi's one night early in 1954, Rogers encountered a fellow brass player who lent him his flugelhorn. "The guy said he had been playing it himself and asked me if I wanted to blow it for a set," Shorty later recollected.[6] "I loved its mellow sound immediately and kept that horn for two years until I arranged for another friend, who was going to Paris, to bring me back by own Besson." Within a few weeks Rogers used the borrowed instrument on a session with Bud Shank; he employed it again a month later on a date for Jimmy Giuffre, and again the next month with Shelly Manne. His continued reliance on the horn in ensuing years confirmed that this new sound was no mere novelty but an important expansion in his music, while the gradual adoption of the instrument by many other trumpeters suggests that his enthusiasm was not an isolated case.

Rogers's use of the new instrument was not the first instance of flu-gelhorn jazz playing: Joe Bishop had played the instrument with Woody Herman's band in 1936; and only a short while before Rogers's adoption of it, Chet Baker had been seen playing an old rotary-valve flugelhorn at gigs. But with Baker, one was never sure whether the move was a con-scious decision to experiment or simply the trumpeter's making a virtue of necessity. Baker's flugelhorn, it turned out, had been acquired for ten dollars in a pawnshop as a replacement for his missing trumpet. But Rog-ers proved to be much more influential than these sporadic predecessors. In addition to the abovementioned influence on Stravinsky, Rogers also anticipated Miles Davis's much-lauded use of the horn on his *Miles Ahead* record. The Rogers/Davis/Baker connection in this manner is quite telling. As such names might suggest, the flugelhorn proved to be an ideal instru-ment for trumpeters working in a cool idiom. The horn's relatively mel-lower sound and exceptional warmth made it suitable for melodically ex-pressive work. As in the related case of the flute, the flugelhorn slowly lost its reputation as an "exotic" instrument. By the 1970s the horn had become accepted in the jazz world as a standard addition to the brass rep-ertoire. Both these now overlooked innovations were spurred largely by the work of musicians on the West Coast.

relations with the constellations

As the decade progressed, Rogers's recordings and performances in-creasingly focused on his smaller combo work. Often joined only by Giuffre in the front line, Rogers worked out sparse arrangements with greater room for soloing. The most typical rhythm section from this period is a stellar match-up of Shelly Manne, Curtis Counce, and Pete Jolly. This group's recording session for RCA on September 10, 1954, produced four strong, swinging tracks with the kind of powerful no-nonsense tenor work from Giuffre rarely found on the latter's leader dates. The use of counter-point was crucial to Rogers's conception in this Quintet, but not the sparse moody counterpoint of, for example, the Mulligan/Baker collaborations; Rogers opted for a tighter, more energized interaction between the two lead voices. But like Mulligan (and Giuffre, for that matter), Rogers came across as determined to extract as much variety as possible from his lim-ited instrumentation. It is almost as if these musicians' experiences ar-ranging for big bands made them more dissatisfied than their peers with the limited conventions of small combo work. While most small groups from the 1950s were content with a predictable formula—melody, then solos, then fours, then melody again—the big band emigrés on the coast were constantly struggling against these selfsame conventions.

Rogers kept the same line-up and general approach when he switched his allegiance to Atlantic in 1955. Atlantic's Nesuhi Ertegun had become close friends with Rogers and frequently attended the group's performances at Zardi's, the Haig, and elsewhere. Rogers described him as "a fixture and our closest friend; we'd go to eat after every work night."[7] Ertegun's familiarity with the repertoire of Rogers's working group proved to be an asset when the band was brought into the studio. "So when we'd run into the studio," Rogers continued, "he knew everything we played, and he'd say, 'Do this tune,' or: 'Last night you did something you hadn't done before—let's record it.' It was a special time, and it was just like coming into the club and doing it live."

Pianist Jolly, whose hard-swinging piano work made a significant contribution to this quintet, became part of the group only after Rogers's first two keyboardists departed for apparently greener pastures. Russ Freeman, who had served in Rogers's band when it first formed at the Haig, left to go on the road with Chet Baker. Freeman's replacement, Marty Paich, also departed after a brief stint because of his increasing outside commitments as a player and arranger. Like Paich, Jolly had followed the unusual path of learning the piano after studying the accordion, but unlike Paich, Jolly continued to play the accordion in jazz settings even after his piano career took off. On the piano Jolly boasted a crisp, hard-bodied sound and a predilection for intricate Bud Powell–inflected lines. Born in New Haven, Connecticut, on June 5, 1932, Jolly spent his early music career in Phoenix, Arizona, where he played with guitarist Howard Roberts. In the early 1950s, first Roberts and then Jolly made the move to Southern California. Rogers first heard Jolly, then still known by his birth name, Pete Ceragioli, when the young pianist sat in at the Lighthouse. When the piano spot in the Giants became open, Rogers brought the up-and-coming twenty-two-year-old keyboardist into the fold.

This band was by now a group of strong individual players, each a leader in his own right. In fact, Atlantic needed to get permission from Capitol Records to use Giuffre, permission from Contemporary to use Manne, and permission from RCA to use Jolly—Counce was the only band member free to record without a release, and only a short time later he got a contract from Contemporary. Despite the increasing fame of these sidemen, there was no individual grandstanding on this project. The band blended together effortlessly. The two sessions held on March 1 and 3 produced no fewer than thirteen usable tracks, as well as additional numbers that have apparently never been released.

This debut project for the new label ranks among Rogers's finest albums of the decade. The most celebrated track on the album, "Martians Go Home," served as a minor hit for Rogers. Here the trumpeter adopts a variety of experimental techniques seemingly more characteristic of

Giuffre's work than of Rogers's: the solo horn passages; the frequent absence of a stated beat; long stretches of silence. The unusual "hook"—
which no doubt helped generate airplay and sales—is a repeated two-bar
break in which *nothing happens.* One expects to hear a soloist come in,
and on a few occasions we are rewarded with a single piano chord coming
at the end of the break. But for the most part, the break leads only to this
unexpected rest. This is precisely the kind of perversely simple device that
would appeal to Giuffre in one of his more esoteric moods, although the
mock seriousness with which it is presented reveals more than a small
share of Rogers's light-heartedness. Rogers's mark is also felt in the infectious riff-like melody that allows "Martians Go Home" to sound experimental and traditional at the same time.

Rogers was never so serious as to neglect a possible marketing angle.
The "Martians" theme was one he accordingly milked for all it was worth.
His follow-up recording was appropriately titled *Martians Come Back*, and
over the next few years he recorded a steady string of related titles: "Planetarium," "Martian's Lullabye," "Saturnian Sleigh Ride," "March of the
Martians," and "Astral Alley," to cite a few examples. Somehow the modernistic notions surrounding the concept of outer space implied, at least in
the 1950s, that any music related to it would be equally modernistic, equally
at the cutting edge. Around the same time, pianist and arranger Herman
Blount rose to fame in the jazz world by changing his name to Sun Ra
and founding a "Solar Arkestra," which propagated various types of forward-
looking cosmic music. But where Sun Ra usually tried to be taken as dead
serious, Rogers never got much beyond the tongue-in-cheek. Sputnik fever gave new life to his cosmic pretensions. In 1958, Rogers was quoted
by a major jazz magazine as advocating the development of "interplane-
tary jazz": "We have several pre-Sputnik compositions in our repertoire,
and there are many more to come. Man, you gotta mind your relations
with the constellations."[8]

Despite the success of the "Martians" theme, other less cosmically
oriented pieces from this period are also deserving of comment. Rogers's
sensitive work on "Michelle's Meditation" may be his strongest ballad
performance of the decade. The melancholy side of Rogers's playing, so
striking here, surfaced rarely in his recorded work. Typically his compositions tend toward the major mode (except on the blues), while their tempos gravitate toward a medium range. But here, as on the earlier recording
of "Lotus Bud," Rogers saves some of his finest playing for an unmarac-
teristic minor key ballad. Two Richard Rodgers compositions—"Isn't It
Romantic?" and "My Heart Stood Still"—also stand out in a much different manner, as powerful vehicles for improvisations from both Rogers and
Giuffre. Two years after this first Atlantic release, Rogers would record a
whole album of Richard Rodgers compositions, but as early as this project

the trumpeter showed that his affinity with the great show-tune writer depended on much more than a homonymic similarity in names. On both tunes, one hears elements of Clifford Brown's influence on Rogers's playing, particularly in tone and phrasing and to a slightly lesser degree in melodic ideas. Brown's ability to forge powerful horn lines without ever losing the warmth and clean articulation in his notes was an inspiration to many other players, both younger and older, although few were able to live up to the impressive examples set by Brownie's playing. The previous year Brown's work with Max Roach had made a mark in Los Angeles jazz circles, and Rogers shows that he was not immune to such bebop-inflected influences. One can well understand why: Brown's apparently effortless virtuosity, his ability to execute the most difficult passages without losing melodic clarity and crispness, were very much in keeping with Rogers's own musical ideals of sprezzatura.

Nesuhi Ertegun provided an interesting, lengthy set of liner notes to the Atlantic release, ostensibly to defend West Coast jazz against its critics. "Who said West Coast jazz doesn't swing?" he demands at the opening. But his heated attack on a straw man version of East Coast criticisms perhaps only added fuel to the fire. It is probably far from a coincidence that the most prominent writers of west-versus-east copy were record company executives like Ertegun or Richard Bock. But if "West Coast jazz" were a movement formulated on the basis of public relations considerations, it would not be the first nor last artistic school to be so tainted. In the case of West Coast jazz, most musicians were content to let record company executives say whatever they wanted about the music, especially if it increased sales and performance opportunities. The record company people, in return—and this is important—never tried to force the musicians to play in a certain style. Bud Shank, who recorded for virtually all the major jazz record producers on the coast, put it bluntly: "I never had anybody telling me how to play from a record company." Whatever hype may have surrounded the music, it remained limited to the marketing effort.

Soon after this recording, Rogers found it impossible to retain his all-star group of sidemen. Ralph Peña replaced Curtis Counce; Lou Levy replaced Pete Jolly. Perhaps the changes in the group were the cause of the difficulties Rogers faced in preparing his follow-up album for Atlantic. Whereas the previous quintet had been extraordinarily prolific in the studio, the new group had trouble recording Rogers's material. Three sessions from late October produced a meager total of four releasable tracks. Additional sessions on November 3 and December 6, 9, and 16 were only slightly more productive. Two albums—*Martians Come Back* and *Way up There*—were culled from these seven sessions (with some tracks only showing up on the English release *Martians Stay Home*.) These sessions are among the oddest of Rogers's career. The Clifford Brown inflections in Rogers's conception are more pronounced in some of this music, with "Barbaro," "Planetarium" and "Baklava Bridge" sounding like they were culled from a hard bop Blue Note release. Giuffre is also surprising here, contributing some ballsy playing that looks forward to his *Ad Lib* album on Verve two years later.

Rogers was trying his hand at an impressive range of projects during this period. The recording a few weeks later of Kansas City staples such as "Dickie's Dream" and "Moten Swing," with the added presence of Harry "Sweets" Edison, are another thing altogether, strongly rooted as they are in the swing era idiom. In a still different vein, "Martians Come Back" and "Martians Stay Home" return to the minor blues but with far fewer of the spacey quirks that distinguished their celebrated Martian predecessor. Sprinkled among these divergent styles are occasional ventures, such as "Chant of the Cosmos," that, in their all too cool medium tempo groove, hark back to the established Shorty Rogers sound of the early 1950s.

Rogers was involved in a variety of other projects around this time. He has a bit role in *The Man with the Golden Arm*, a strange Hollywood affair in which an addict becomes a jazz musician to get away from drugs! Rogers participated in the soundtrack recording of the Elmer Bernstein score. In a few years Rogers would be concentrating most of his energies into studio work, but already in 1955 his leanings in that direction could be clearly detected.

For years it was assumed that Rogers's recording relationship with Atlantic ended at the close of 1955. Rogers had signed a one-year contract, and with its expiration he returned to RCA. But in 1976, critic and discographer Todd Selbert, while searching through Atlantic's master log book, discovered that two sessions from March 1956 had produced eight tracks that had never been released. No notes survived from the sessions, but aural identification, supplemented by photographic documentation of the session by William Claxton, reveals an all-star front line consisting of Rogers, Giuffre, Bud Shank, Herb Geller, and Bill Holman supported by the rhythm section of Peña, Levy, and Manne. This octet is somewhat underarranged in comparison to earlier Rogers extended groups, but the strong contributions from the individual soloists more than compensate. Indeed, it is puzzling why this date, featuring Rogers plus sax section, was never released when originally recorded. But then again, the ways of major record companies are mysterious and strange: So much so that, when the tapes were discovered, Atlantic told Selbert that they had no interest in releasing them, and the same response came from the company's affiliates in Japan and Europe. Finally Atlantic UK reconsidered, and—surprise of surprises—the project became the best-selling jazz release in England during the winter of 1978–79. And in the nick of time: A vault fire took place at Atlantic a short time later, and these tapes would have been irretrievably lost if it hadn't been for Selbert's invaluable intercession.

Rogers's return to RCA found him recording frequently but breaking little new ground. His initial work after returning to RCA showed a promising return to the *Cool and Crazy* format, as Rogers added a few numbers to that project to make it available for release on 12-inch LP, but future RCA efforts in general fell far short of his earlier success on the label. Unlike Giuffre, whose albums during this period constantly ventured into new waters—perhaps too much so—Rogers seemed more content to work on sporadic theme albums (revolving around diverse themes such as *Gigi, The Wizard of Oz, Tarzan, The Nutcracker*, etc.) supplemented by an increasing schedule of studio work. Perhaps Rogers's growing involvement in various Hollywood projects is the underlying cause of these uninspired projects; in any event, his output from the latter part of the decade comes across as workmanlike and far less daring than before. Even the surprises, so characteristic of his music, fall into increasingly expected patterns.

The quality of Roger's nonjazz commitments also shows a decline over time. In the late 1950s, we find Rogers on Eartha Kitt and Bobby Troup sessions—hardly the most promising settings for his work. Yet these were virtual gold mines of musical merit compared to some of his work from the following decade. The 1960s witnessed the demise of Shorty's Giants—the band's hectic recording schedule sputtered to a halt in 1963— after which we encounter Rogers working with Bobbie Gentry, or arranging Lovin' Spoonful songs for Bud Shank or music from *Hair* for Bobby Bryant. Rogers was also in demand in the movie studios, sometimes composing scores but more often serving as an arranger. Earlier Rogers's studio efforts could be justified as providing economic support that allowed him also to do serious jazz, much as today jazz fans forgive Herbie Hancock his funk albums because he continues to release occasional jazz records of significant merit. But with Rogers, once the serious jazz disappeared and the quality of the studio work dropped, it appeared as though he had become a nomadic musical talent, now available to the highest bidder, no matter what type of music was involved.

To Rogers's credit, it should be noted that his departure from the jazz scene coincided with a general drop-off in demand for jazz among the record-buying public. Even given the most extreme commitment to the music, Rogers's jazz activities would have diminished in the 1960s. The obsessive growth of the rock-and-roll industry dictated as much. The exodus to the studios was more a matter of economic necessity than of crass opportunism. Yet unlike Shank, Collette, and many of the others who made the move to the studios, Rogers went a step further by completely retiring from jazz performance.

Finally, in 1982, Rogers agreed to play for some performances in England, and the following March he began working sporadically with longtime colleague Bud Shank. Three months later Rogers and Shank recorded *Yesterday, Today and Forever* for Concord. "Every time I saw Shorty when we were working together on a film scoring job," Shank told Leonard Feather at the time of their 1985 follow-up album *California Concert*, "I would bug him about starting to play again. I'm so glad I finally convinced him."[9] This album, even more than its predecessor, showed that Rogers had not lost his touch, either as player or writer. Once again his knack for constructing musical surprises came to the fore—in the breathtaking triplet passage in his composition "Aurex"; in the unexpected double-time section in "Makin' Whoopee"; in the meter changes in "Echoes of Harlem." In such moments Rogers revealed a renewed desire to push beyond the expected and tried-and-true.

Since his comeback, Rogers has shown no desire to return to his pressure-cooker pace of the 1950s, which demanded a new studio project every few months. That high level of output was the bane of too many West Coast masters of the 1950s—Rogers, Giuffre, Brubeck, Tjader—and led to a situation in which, despite their commitment to the music, the quantity of their output began to affect its quality. Shorty Rogers, in the midst of the fifth decade of his career, is now more content to take matters at his own speed. That, too, is part of his sprezzatura.

But this relaxed pace, like the whole low-key ethos of Rogers's life and music, seems to hide a deeper streak of obsessiveness and persistence. The tremendous output of the 1950s and the studio successes of the 1960s and 1970s, suggest that Rogers's cool demeanor is no mere attitude of nonchalance. When I interviewed him at his Southern California home, Rogers's trumpet was sitting nearby, and the room was full of signs of ongoing musical activity. "You can see the horn there," Rogers mentioned at one point. "I have to practice every day. . . . I'm working daily, very tenaciously to get stronger chops. They're getting stronger, they're getting better. But it's a never-ending scene."

CHAPTER THIRTEEN

The Anti-drummer

choppin' wood

In the 1950s the role of a West Coast drummer was beset by many contradictions. The experimentation of the Los Angeles musicians focused on the innovative use of horn lines, harmony, and composition and only occasionally approached new ways of treating the rhythm section. Little wonder that the stereotypical West Coast approach to percussion, exemplified by Shelly Manne and Chico Hamilton, attempted to make the drums into a horn-like instrument, one in which rhythmic drive was often subservient to melodic continuity. Nor was it surprising, given the strong interest in writing and arranging on the coast, that the drums should become viewed increasingly, by drummers and arrangers alike, as a compositional tool, integrated into the music as an instrumental voice that needed to provide more (or perhaps less) than just a driving beat.

Given these bearings, West Coast percussionists came to be viewed as antidrummers. Their distinctive approach to time keeping was seen by many as a subversion of the modern jazz tradition of high-energy jazz drumming. In the eyes of their critics, such drummers meant their instruments to be seen and not—or only barely—heard. Whether rightly or wrongly, this new approach to percussion, so central to the West Coast sound, became one of the most controversial aspects of the music.

Shelly Manne was the drummer most associated in the jazz public's mind with this new approach to drumming. Yet Manne's recorded legacy from the 1950s reveals that his highly stylized approach to jazz drumming was anything but narrow and parochial. From 1953 until the close of the decade, Manne's work as a leader for the Contemporary label covered an impressive variety of bases—ranging from hit records featuring show tunes (*My Fair Lady*) to highly experimental combo work (*The Three* and *The*

Two), ambitious extended compositions *(The Gambit* and *Concerto for Clarinet and Combo)*, and high-gear straight-ahead work *(At the Blackhawk)*. All in all, it constitutes one of the strongest bodies of work made on the coast during the 1950s.

It is also one of the least listened to today. Manne's work represents what Robert Frost called "the road not taken." With the benefit of hindsight, we can see that the great revolutions that were to come in the development of the jazz rhythm section—spurred by the Bill Evans Trio, the John Coltrane Quartet, and the Miles Davis Quintet during the 1960s—made little conscious reference to the precedents set on the West Coast during the 1950s. If we judge a jazz artist by his influence, Manne—like many West Coasters of his day—is at best a minor figure.

Yet the value of a body of work is more than a retrospective assessment of its influences. Perhaps the greatest flaw of existing studies of jazz lies in their substitution of genealogies of influence for appreciations of merit. Manne's body of work becomes well worth consideration and praise when we evaluate it less as a stage in the history of drums, and more as a body of *music*. Manne himself would have wanted it that way. Perhaps the key to understanding his achievement is to realize that, despite the virtues of his instrumental skills, he viewed himself, perhaps more than any of his contemporaries, as a musician first and a drummer only second.

This is part of the contradiction involved in typecasting Manne as the leader of "West Coast drumming." Despite Manne's strengths as a drummer—and they were considerable—he carefully avoided the pitfalls of many drummer-led groups. Given his relentless interest in seeking out the finest composers, arrangers, and sidemen available, his drum work was often pushed into the background on his own dates. This, too, was part of Manne's role as the antidrummer. Even as a leader he was something of a sideman.

Manne's appearance played into the role as well. He did not look the way a modern jazz drummer should. If jazz writers compared the young Chet Baker's looks to James Dean's, the most apt comparison for Manne was the cover boy for *Mad* magazine, the toothy-mouthed perpetual adolescent Alfred E. Neumann. And while Baker soon had aged into the picture of Dorian Gray, Manne—even decades after he had emerged on the scene—still looked like the boy wonder of the drums, caught in some time warp with his boyish features and offhand demeanor. His was an engaging, well-groomed kind of youthfulness with overtones of what today would be labeled East Coast "preppie" mixed with what even then was known as California cool. One could almost hear him query: "What, me worry?"

Such a characterization is more than an exercise in armchair physiognomy. Manne *had* been something of a prodigy on the drums. Born in New York City on June 11, 1920, Manne was raised in a musical household. His father was a drummer/tympanist, and Shelly expressed early in life an interest in following in the elder Manne's footpedals. But—in a strange reversal of the typical father/son relation—Mr. Manne told his son to forget about the drums. Learn a wind instrument, he admonished. Shelly's father brought home a saxophone, hoping it might capture the youngster's imagination. When it failed to elicit a response, he eventually relented and let Shelly study the drums.

Manne did not begin on drums until age eighteen, an exceptionally late start for a professional musician. But even more exceptional was the speed with which he learned his chosen instrument. Within a few months, Manne was playing professionally, first with minor bands but soon with major jazz groups. "I was very fortunate. I came into the profession at a time when one of the main things musicians wanted to do was get to play in a big name band," Manne would later say. "Goodman and Basie and the Dorseys and Ellington represented the ultimate, and every kid knew the names of every third and fourth trumpet player."[1]

One of the few West Coast musicians to develop his skills on 52nd Street in New York, Manne used that opportunity to hear and play with some of the best players in jazz. In 1939, he caught the attention of Ray McKinley, who heard him sit in with Kenny Watts and his Kilowatts—an unconventional band whose renditions of Basie charts on kazoos (supported by rhythm section) were an innovation whose time had not yet come (and, with luck, may never). McKinley told bandleader Bobby Byrne about the talented young drummer. Hired by Byrne, Manne stayed with the band for eight months before undertaking the more stressful job of replacing Dave Tough (who had left to join Goodman) in Joe Marsala's band. Before Tough took the new job, Manne also held down the Goodman drum chair for two or three days—quite an undertaking for a youngster who had been playing drums for less than two years! Manne also gigged over the next several years with Raymond Scott, Will Bradley, and Les Brown before leaving the scene in 1942 for a three-year stint with the coast guard.

By 1946, Manne had already recorded with Dizzy Gillespie, Coleman Hawkins, and other leading luminaries of the East Coast jazz establishment. He was poised on the brink of establishing himself as one of the elite New York drummers. In a fateful decision, however, Manne joined the Kenton band in 1946, beginning an intermittent association that would last until 1952. The day before he joined Kenton, Manne had recorded the *52nd Street* album for RCA. By the time he parted ways with Kenton six years later, these 52nd Street ties would be almost forgotten by the jazz public. By then, Manne had entered the musical maelstrom that would become known as "West Coast jazz."

The relation with Kenton was not a peaceful one. When the drummer left the band for a period in 1948, he told *Downbeat:* "A night with that band made me feel like I'd been choppin' wood." Yet a short while later Manne was back in the group—an event *Downbeat* commemorated with a cover photo. It showed Kenton supervising Manne while the latter literally chopped wood with an axe. From then on, Manne was more circumspect in his public assessments of the Kenton sound.

In addition to his Kenton work from this period, Manne developed his craft in a variety of settings, including engagements with Charlie Ventura, Jazz at the Philharmonic, and Woody Herman. In 1950, Manne settled in Northridge, California, and after two more years of road work with Kenton began concentrating his energies on combo playing in Southern California. His work with the Lighthouse band and later with Shorty Rogers and his Giants soon established him as the quintessential drummer in the new West Coast movement.

The opportunity for regular employment, ready acclaim, and financial security without the hassles of leading a group has led many of the finest drummers in jazz to work mostly as sidemen. But for Manne the attractions of leading his own ensemble more than compensated for the troubles involved. Like other successful drummer/leaders—Art Blakey and Max Roach come to mind—Manne was motivated not so much by a desire to have his own group as by a clear vision of the music he wanted to make. As early as 1953, Manne had paid enough sideman dues to be signed by Les Koenig at Contemporary as a bandleader. Shelly Manne and His Men was primarily a studio band at first, but even then it was one of the most talked-about ensembles on the Coast. Before long Manne had established himself as one of the most important artists on the Contemporary roster, recording over a dozen projects as leader or co-leader for the label before the close of the decade. He was simultaneously involved in almost nonstop sideman work for Koenig, backing up everyone from Lennie Neihaus to Ornette Coleman.

At the first session under his own name for Contemporary, from April 1953, Manne followed the formula that would characterize most of his best projects over the next half-decade. He commissioned original compositions or arrangements from some of the finest writers on the West Coast and recorded them with the best jazz soloists he could find. For most of the 1950s, this simple recipe continued to work. His ability to get new wine out of old bottles stemmed perhaps from his insistence, especially in his early albums, on taking chances with the music. He encouraged his writers to think ambitiously, and they usually rose to the occasion. The charts Bill Holman, Charles Mariano, Marty Paich, and others wrote for Manne's group during the 1950s stand out as some of the most adventurous and outstanding works these writers would ever produce.

This first session featured an all-star band consisting of Art Pepper, Jimmy Giuffre, Bob Cooper, Bob Enevoldsen, Marty Paich, and Curtis

Counce and drew on arrangements by Bill Russo and Shorty Rogers. Of the four numbers recorded that day, Rogers's "La Mucura," a pseudo-Latin chart reminiscent of the Lighthouse fare of that period, is perhaps the least interesting. The other three numbers, however, are engaging works with the subtle experimental flair that characterized much of the best music coming from the nascent California scene of that time. (Little wonder that, when these recordings were released on LP, Contemporary entitled the project *The West Coast Sound*.) Rogers's "Mallets" is a more ambitious dialogue between the horns and Manne's mallet work on the drums. On this number, as well as on his "Afrodesia" from Manne's next session in July, Rogers tried his hand at some daring and, at the time, highly unusual minimalist devices, which look forward to the 1980s work of composers Steve Reich and Philip Glass. On "Mallets" Rogers built off static harmonies—principally a repetitive two-chord horn motif—to underline Manne's drumming. On "Afrodesia" the introduction is an extraordinary, if all too brief, piece of program music in which the horns emulate the buzzing of insects and various birdcalls. The two Bill Russo charts from the April session, "Gazelle" and "You and the Night and the Music," are also strong works. The former is a bit of ingenious and intricate part writing that leads into an outstanding Art Pepper solo. The latter is a strange mixture of sweet and hot that starts as an imitation of a Guy Lombardo band, with Manne and the rhythm section keeping discreetly in the background. A surprising twist comes when some burning bop horn lines rupture the mood. By the end of the piece the band is working off a modern jazz vocabulary that has left Lombardo far behind.

This music was fairly daring by the standards of 1953, but it seems positively conventional by comparison with Manne's follow-up session, held only fourteen weeks later. Jimmy Giuffre's "Fugue" stands out as one of the most strikingly avant-garde pieces any jazz group, on either coast, recorded during the early 1950s. The use of fugal form, in its own right, would have been cause for some raised eyebrows in the jazz world, but Giuffre's particular piece, with its atonality and its obvious destruction of the typical roles played by the rhythm instruments, made this work especially iconoclastic. Even today, some thirty-five years after it was recorded, it is a disturbing, unnerving piece to listen to. Marty Paich's arrangement of "You're My Thrill" seems, perhaps, conservative in comparison, but by almost any other standard it stands out as an ambitious chart with its effective reharmonization and use of counterpoint. "Afrodesia," discussed above with regard to the minimalist echoes in its opening, eventually settles into a prototypical Rogers ballad featuring Bud Shank's alto. In its middle section the piece bears striking similarities to the series of ballad charts Rogers wrote for Art Pepper ("Over the Rainbow,"

"Bunny," and the Kenton showpiece "Art Pepper")—so much so, one suspects that this piece, too, was written for Pepper, who had played on the first Manne session. Shank, however, takes a commanding solo, which leaves little doubt about his ballad-playing credentials. Bill Russo's "Sweets," the final number recorded at this session, stands in striking contrast to the other charts. Named for the celebrated Basie trumpeter Harry "Sweets" Edison, the piece is a relaxed swinger, as informal as Giuffre's "Fugue" was cerebral.

Given the extraordinary variety and depth of these performances, Manne's fans soon learned to expect the unexpected from the drummer's recordings, and Manne did little to refute this reputation for musical eccentricity over the next several years. The two projects recorded in mid-September 1954, initially released on separate 10-inch albums as *The Three* and *The Two*, are cases in point. *The Three* found Manne as the sole rhythm instrument supporting Jimmy Giuffre and Shorty Rogers. This was an almost perverse exercise in "less is more"—brought to the extreme of "least of all is the most." Although the music wears its experimental bias on its sleeve, the record exerts a certain odd fascination. Like tightrope walkers working without a net, the three musicians court disaster as they try to hold together an ensemble without bass, piano, or guitar to provide a harmonic underpinning. *The Two*, with pianist Russ Freeman, was a far more accessible project. Although stark in its neglect of a bass, the music was positively lush in comparison with the Giuffre/Manne/Rogers session of four days earlier.

Freeman stands out as the most compatible of all the pianists who worked with Manne during the decade. In contrast to Freeman's performances with Chet Baker, where the pianist's harmonic knack was brought to the fore, the Manne collaborations evoked some of the strongest rhythmic playing of Freeman's career. One might expect pianist and drummer to be tentative without a bassist, but Manne and Freeman take more rhythmic chances in this setting than they typically did in the context of a full ensemble. When Freeman later joined Manne's working band—where he served for some eleven years from the mid-1950s to the mid-1960s— the two musicians continued to build off this striking rapport. On gigs they often had the rest of the group fall out for a chorus or a bridge while they worked their striking interplay on piano and drums.

"When he was at his best," Freeman describes Manne, "he was the most fun of any of the drummers I've ever played with. He was a very sensitive player. And when he set a tempo he would hold it like a clock— which is not true of even some of the famous-name drummers. But with Shelly the time was solid as a rock."[2] "With a Song in My Heart" and "Billie's Bounce" from *The Two* stand out as especially persuasive examples of the musicians' mutual chemistry, especially the call-and-response section on the former in which Manne tries to imitate Freeman's piano lines in a series of two-bar exchanges.

In his discussion of these early Manne projects, Robert Gordon has aptly characterized the strangely contradictory response they engendered: "At first they were lavishly praised as fresh and original; then a reaction set in and they were damned (often by the same critics!) as straying too far from the jazz heritage."[3] For the most part, these records still sound fresh and original today. Their influence on later jazz, however, has been negligible—and perhaps this accounts for the critics' about-face. One expects to see such ambitious music—proclaiming itself at the forefront of progressive trends—validated by later developments. Manne's work, for all its virtues, is that most cursed of all artistic artifacts: the self-proclaimed masterpiece without a lineage.

the polemical manne

In 1955 Manne took the unusual step of writing an article on his conception of drums for *Downbeat*. Although most musicians, then and now, are content (perhaps unwisely) to leave jazz writing to professional journalists, Manne's decision was yet in keeping with the ethos of West Coast jazz. Jazz, for many among this new generation of musicians on the coast, was no longer to be viewed as a mysterious art form born of ineffable moments of inspiration. It was seen rather as a body of practices, techniques, and formal knowledge that could be explained clearly and taught to those willing to listen, learn, and practice. Never before had a group of jazz players boasted such a commitment to music education. Many of the masters of the LA scene had music degrees, and a surprising number of them continued to take music lessons long after they had become major jazz stars. The cold intellectualism that some critics asserted was at the heart of the West Coast music may, in fact, have stemmed less from the performances themselves (which were often bathed, almost to excess, in a sensuous emotionalism) than from this novel approach to talking and writing about the music. Like conjurers who have given away the tricks of the trade, the West Coast players who talked openly of the theoretical underpinnings of their work were less respected than their more taciturn contemporaries. Put simply, they made fans and critics uneasy with their positivist attitude toward music.

"I have always felt that the drums have great melodic potential," Manne began his essay.[4]

I have tried to play melodically for about ten years now. In the last few years, through the study of composition and devices used by the composers, I feel I have found a definite path I need to follow. . . . If a drummer must play an extended solo, he should think more about melodic lines than rudiment lines. If I play a solo of this sort, I will try to use devices such as imitations, diminution, extension. Never prepared, always improvised. By using these composition devices, a drummer can make his solo a composition in itself instead of a display of practice pad technique. Technique is a means to an end and not an end in itself. . . . On some of my records, the writers have written definite 'melodic' lines for the drums to play, and if these lines were left out, it would be like one of the horns dropping out.

At the close of the article Manne adds, almost in apology, "I hope all this makes some sense. I dislike becoming so analytical about jazz."

For all his theorizing, Manne never neglected the necessity of swinging. "All these things I've said would mean nothing if swinging were ignored," he adds in the *Downbeat* piece. Or, as he said on another occasion, "[For drummers] the most predominant thing is that they have to swing. I feel if a drummer could swing, he can play with anybody. It doesn't matter whether he's playing with Art Hodes or Ornette Coleman."[5] Here Manne's indirect praise of the ideal drummer is, quite clearly, directed at himself—he *did* play with everyone from Art Hodes to Ornette Coleman. One of the telling virtues of his apparent eclecticism was his ability to propel these different ensembles without radically altering his basic style of drumming.

Around the time he wrote this article, Manne entered a brief musical partnership with Stan Getz, who was trying to ride the West Coast wave then at its peak in the jazz world. In the early 1950s, Getz had lived in Southern California, and his celebrated band with Bob Brookmeyer had its home base in Los Angeles. But a more frequent presence on the road, combined with his affiliation with record producer/impresario Norman Granz (who, despite his California ties, maintained an arm's-length relation with the new sounds on the Coast), made Getz at best a peripheral participant in the West Coast scene. But soon enough, both Getz and Granz made the plunge. On July 27, 1955, Getz became a late entrant in the West Coast sound when he opened at Zardi's with a California quintet consisting of Getz, Shelly Manne, Leroy Vinnegar, Conte Candoli, and Lou Levy. The same band went into the studio to record an album under Granz's supervision, released as *West Coast Jazz*. Outside of his choice of sidemen and a title for the project, Getz made little attempt to adapt his style or repertoire for the occasion. The compositions played—Gillespie's "A Night in Tunisia," Miles Davis's "Four," Gershwin's "Summertime," etc.—were, without exception, East Coast standards. In fact, one wonders whether Getz's decision to open the record with "East of the Sun" (which, over and above

the giveaway title, was written by Princeton graduate Brooks Bowman)
was not a fairly unsubtle jab at the title and unabashed marketing bent of
the album.

In terms of playing style, Getz meshed well with Manne and the
other musicians on the date. Getz's light-swinging tenor shared the same
Lester Young roots that characterized the work of so many other outstanding California saxophonists of the decade, and his playing throughout the
album exemplifies the tasteful, inventive creativity that has long been a
trademark of Getz's recordings. Had he been signed with Pacific or Contemporary during the 1950s, Getz might have made a number of excellent
collaborations with other musicians from the Coast. As it was, his expe-
dition into West Coast jazz was of short duration.

In early 1956, shortly after the Getz date, Manne brought his own
group into the studio for a new recording project. In the course of three
sessions at Radio Recorders in Hollywood, the new band laid down eight
tracks eventually released under the title *Swinging Sounds*. The group at
this point was a strong, well-meshed unit featuring Charlie Mariano on
alto, Stu Williamson on trumpet and trombone, Leroy Vinnegar on bass,
and Russ Freeman on piano. Mariano, a Massachusetts native born in Boston on November 12, 1923, was the one newcomer to the West Coast in
the group. After a two-year stint with the Kenton band in the mid-1950s,
Mariano made his residence in Southern California from 1956 to 1958,
spending most of this period in Manne's ensemble. Mariano's vigorous,
impassioned saxophone work established him as one of the most talented
"hot" altoists, along with Art Pepper and Sonny Criss, in the midst of a
musical culture that tended toward the cool. Williamson—another alumnus of the Lighthouse All-Stars—had come a long way since moving to
Los Angeles in 1949. By this period he had matured into a top-notch brass
player, fluent on both trumpet and valve trombone. Vinnegar and Freeman had long before established themselves among the finest rhythm players
on the coast.

As was his practice until the later 1950s, Manne built his project around
a strong body of original compositions, including his own "Parthenia," a
melancholy ballad that ranks as one of his most memorable pieces. Mariano contributed two interesting compositions: "The Dart Game," which
opens the album, a dazzling bit of counterpoint in which trumpet and alto
carry on a high-speed conversation, and "Slan," a medium-tempo piece
that alternates between major and minor mode. Russ Freeman added "Bea's
Flat," a polytonal blues line originally written for Chet Baker but recast
for Williamson and Mariano. Bill Holman's variant on rhythm changes
"A Gem from Tiffany"—named for the 8th Street jazz club of the day—
closed the album, as well as most of Manne's sets during the period.
Swinging Sounds stands out as one of Manne's most informal albums from

the mid-1950s. In contrast to his next three Contemporary leader dates—which would emphasize extended, highly arranged works—this project showcased a more carefree, soloist-oriented music. Manne seemed intent, at least for the time being, on re-creating the spontaneous approach of his earlier days at the Lighthouse.

Shortly after recording *Swinging Sounds*, Manne's group began a nine-week road trip, which covered much of the Midwest and East Coast and finished with a highly successful engagement at Storyville in Boston. In an interview with *Downbeat*, Manne expressed his pleasure with the band's performance on the road and announced his intention of immediately recording the group: "I'm happy with our sound, and I really like the guys. . . . The first thing we're going to do is Bill Holman's 'Quartet.' I think that's the best thing Bill has ever written. He's a great writer, developing all the time. He's done some great things, but this is his greatest."[6] The band had previewed the work to audiences on its tour and was heartened by the enthusiastic response.

During the course of three recording dates held in midsummer, Manne's band taped the four-movement Holman piece as well as four other tracks for the group's next Contemporary release. While Mariano's "Pint of Blues" and Freeman's "The Wind" are represented in strong versions, the centerpiece of the album is the extended Holman work. The hope of bringing successful longer forms into the standard jazz repertoire has been an unrealized dream for most jazz composers. Holman's approach in this instance was, as he explained in the program notes, to model his piece on "the four movements of the classical sonata form." This decision, he hastened to add, was made "not because it is a classical form . . . but because it has proved itself, thru centuries of use, capable of supporting (as framework) a composition of this length."[7] The inclusion of "program notes" on the album jacket was, like Manne's earlier *Downbeat* manifesto, an unconventional step toward intellectualizing the music. As if that were not enough, Contemporary commissioned a Jesuit philosopher, Father G. V. Kennard, to provide additional liner notes. His speculative ruminations ("Jazz responds to a void in modern man"), concluding with the assertion that "to swing is to affirm," almost seem deliberately designed to irritate the jazz "primitivists" who resented any highbrow approach to the music.

The music, however, is the main drawing card here. Nat Hentoff assessed Holman's piece as follows: "The work had considerable impact on me when I heard it at Basin Street in New York, and it becomes even more valuable and integrated for me after several hearings. I think it's a significant success in the widening of jazz form."[8] The first and last movements are strong statements, mainly built on a blues form, with contrast coming from a slow second movement and a third-movement drum solo intermittently interrupted by a stark minor melody. The fourth movement is perhaps the most striking. Its intriguing opening alto statement surprisingly prefigures Ornette Coleman's "Lonely Woman" melody. Even when bass and drums enter playing a blues progression, the initial absence of the piano combines with Mariano's expressive playing to sustain the avant-garde feel. Holman was one of the first supporters of Coleman's music on the West Coast, and this unexpected later affinity makes sense in the context of this piece.

Manne's work as a leader during this period was slowly evolving from the highly experimental work of the early Contemporary albums to more informal, hard-swinging projects. This process would culminate in the exceptional four albums recorded at the Blackhawk toward the close of the decade, one of the high points in the drummer's illustrious career. By then Manne would have come full circle to a more mature realization of the kind of soloist-oriented approach he had worked with at the Lighthouse at the start of the 1950s, informed by the period of experimentation and re-evaluation he had gone through in the interim. The recordings from the middle 1950s are, however, much more than documents of a transition period. These projects find Manne trying to bring together the best of both worlds, to create a musical hybrid that combined the innovative writing of his first leader dates with the greater freedom for blowing of his Lighthouse and Blackhawk recordings.

the gambit

In January 1957, Manne's quintet returned to Contemporary's studio in Los Angeles to record another extended composition, this one written by group member Charles Mariano. The new piece, "The Gambit," was another four-movement work in the same vein as the earlier "Quartet." The band was the same—except for the substitution of Monty Budwig for Leroy Vinnegar—as the one that had tackled the first Holman extended work. The similarity between the two works, however, stops there. While Holman had used blues structures as the essential foundations of his work, Mariano's work is more harmonically and rhythmically complex—which perhaps explains why the group needed three recording sessions to tape the nineteen-minute composition—with more obvious ties to the European classical heritage. The first movement, "Queen's Pawn," starts with a mock processional that moves through a series of shifting meters, finally settling into a relaxed 6/4 for the solos. The second movement, "En Passant," builds off a series of static harmonies, first basing Mariano's somewhat "outside" solo on a repeated vamp. The piece then shifts into a minor drone behind Williamson's trumpet solo. The third movement, "Castling," opens with an unaccompanied counterpoint duet between Mariano and Williamson, which evolves into another shifting meter pattern in which 4/4 alternates with a subdivided 8/8. The movement closes with a restatement of the coronation march that opened the work. The final section, "Checkmate," starts with Manne soloing on mallets in a slow 3/4 meter; Freeman, Mariano, Williamson, and Budwig gradually enter, setting up rhythmic variations in the still restrained tempo, until a sudden leap into a fast 4/4 underlines extended solos for each of the band members. This section ends as suddenly as it began with an unexpected and brief restatement of the opening processional.

The third extended jazz work presented by Manne during this period was Bill Smith's ambitious "Concerto for Clarinet and Combo," a twenty-minute, three-movement work recorded by a ten-piece band under Manne's leadership in mid-1957. Smith had earned his stripes as a member of Dave Brubeck's octet and had continued to combine work in jazz with his career as an academic composer. His studies with Milhaud were succeeded by work with Roger Sessions and stints overseas for winning the Prix de Paris and the Prix de Rome. Despite this immersion in academia, Smith's jazz work remained completely indigenous. Although one is tempted to apply the term "Third Stream" to his concerto, his work actually is much jazzier than that term, or the choice of concerto form, might suggest. Smith's experimentations, especially his use of nonsymmetric phrases, co-exist with his mastery of the traditional jazz vocabulary, while his clarinet playing shows him to be an outstanding modern soloist on that neglected instrument.

Despite the virtues of these three extended works—each of which is first-rate—it is precisely ambitious compositions such as these that have been the forgotten legacy of West Coast jazz. The reasons for such neglect are difficult to pinpoint. "Quartet," "Concerto for Clarinet and Combo," and "The Gambit" are well-written works full of musical surprises, which increase their appeal with repeated listenings. But this apparent bias against extended works in the world of jazz is a phenomenon by no means restricted to the West Coast in the 1950s. Even Ellington, the greatest composer jazz music has produced, often found a less than sympathetic response to his longer works. The criticism often launched against such pieces—namely, that they are merely a group of shorter works arbitrarily grouped together—certainly does not hold for the three works under discussion. These pieces make a special point of tying together separate movements through the repetition and development of specific musical motives, as well as through the programmatic themes used in outlining the compositions.

"The Gambit" in particular stands out, despite the marginal attention lavished on it, as perhaps Manne's most ambitious and successful work of the decade. The labyrinthine structure of the piece presented particular challenges in live performance—usually the group attempted only the first and third movements in their nightclub appearances—and the limitations on solo space were even greater than in the Holman work. Little wonder that Manne, in the liner notes to the album, felt obliged to explain: "Although we do play works—and sections of works—like Charles Mariano's four-part 'The Gambit,' we do plenty of blowing things, too. We don't want to break away from that. I enjoy getting into a blowing groove too."[9]

These words served as a prophetic announcement of the direction Manne would take in the ensuing years, both as a bandleader and a sideman. While their former Lighthouse colleague Jimmy Giuffre moved more and more into the avant-garde, Manne and Shorty Rogers both backed off from their highly experimental work in the mid-1950s, as part of a retrenching that eventually found them firmly established as conservative members of the jazz mainstream. By the early 1960s, Manne's and Rogers's credentials as daring jazz radicals had become completely tarnished by their involvement in tepid theme albums and anonymous studio fare.

This move in Manne's recordings first became evident in two trios featured prominently on numerous Contemporary recordings from the mid-1950s: the Poll Winners, a collaborative trio that also included Barney Kessel and Ray Brown, and Shelly Manne and His Friends (alternately known as André Previn and His Pals), a standard piano trio that also featured bassist Leroy Vinnegar. The Poll Winners' first recording was made in March 1957, between the several sessions required to complete *The Gambit*. Although the group seems to have been put together primarily for marketing reasons—because, as the liner notes to their debut project explain, "all three won all three of the major American jazz popularity polls for 1956"—the musicians displayed a stylistic compatibility and shared sensibility that made the collaboration a natural fit. Bassist Ray Brown, who would settle permanently on the West Coast in 1966, stood out even by the mid-1950s as the most prominent heir of the Jimmy Blanton–Oscar Pettiford tradition of full-toned, no-nonsense swing. Much like Manne himself, Brown made his reputation by his willingness to work in the trenches. He could carry a whole band by himself, if need be, with his powerful, in-the-pocket groove—a Brown trademark—yet do so without grandstanding or ostentation, one whirling cog locked into an integrated rhythm section.

This band, however, didn't need to be carried. Like Manne and Brown, guitarist Barney Kessel boasted a seamless, effortless sense of swing tied to an overriding understanding of group interaction. A true "Okie from Mukogee," where he was born on October 17, 1923, Kessel had learned jazz guitar firsthand from Charlie Christian, the legendary Oklahoma-born player who revolutionized the role of the six-string instrument in jazz before his untimely death in 1942. Kessel was sixteen years old at the time he met the budding guitar legend, while the "veteran" Christian was only four years his senior. Christian's expressive playing contrasted strikingly with his laconic approach to discussing music ("He spoke in grunts. . . . you'd almost have to piece it together as to what it meant," Kessel later said.)[10] In sum, his advice to the young guitarist had been, in Kessel's paraphrase: "The main thing is to concentrate on swing first. Then if you can make some interesting harmony after you know how to swing, that's fine. But to begin with, swing alone is enough to get you by."[11]

Kessel learned this lesson well from Christian and soon was doing much more than getting by in his work with road bands in North Dakota and Minnesota. Kessel came to California in 1942, the same year that Christian died of tuberculosis, with less than a dollar in his pocket and lots of musical aspirations. He soon began an apprenticeship (along with vocalist Mel Tormé) in the band of Chico Marx of Marx Brothers fame. Later he played with heavier jazz company on Central Avenue. Despite his allegiance to Christian—one of the earliest jazz modernists—the bebop revolution of the mid-1940s, especially the new music of Charlie Parker, initially came as an unwelcome surprise:

> I remember being in California, and [Parker] was there with Dizzy Gillespie playing there, and he made some records for Ross Russell on Dial, and I remember buying those records, even though I did not like them, and one day it's just like a mist lifted and I could see what it was. . . . From the minute I began to like it and began to understand what he was doing, I did not like *my* playing because I wanted to articulate that way and didn't know how.[12]

Already an established jazz player with a growing reputation, Kessel was forced to re-evaluate his own playing and rebuild it from the ground up.

By the time Parker was released from his enforced stay in Camarillo, Kessel had mastered enough of the bebop idiom to join in on jam sessions with the altoist. Shortly before Bird's return to New York, Kessel participated on the celebrated "Relaxin' at Camarillo" session for Dial. Although much of his work during the next decade—with Oscar Peterson, Jazz at the Philharmonic, and others—would keep him on the road, Kessel maintained his Southern California home base for a number of years and recorded frequently for the Contemporary label.

The Poll Winners were, in many ways, the antithesis of the groups Manne had been leading for Contemporary. While composition, arranging, and experimentation had been the catchwords of his earlier efforts, the Poll Winners looked toward Manne's later recordings with their spirited versions of loosely arranged jazz standards. The Poll Winners succeeded almost solely through pure musicianship. Their debut release featured such timeworn numbers as "Satin Doll," "Green Dolphin Street," and "Mean to Me"—in short, the standard repertoire of cocktail lounge acts from coast to coast—the only original being an inauspicious riff-based minor blues penned by Kessel. The polish and taste, as well as the sheer exuberance, of the group members, individually and collectively, were what raised the tepid material into something worth hearing.

The other band Manne led for Contemporary—Shelly Manne and His Friends—had begun the previous year as a piano trio featuring André Previn and Leroy Vinnegar. The trio's August 1957 recording of songs from *My Fair Lady* became a huge hit for Contemporary and inspired Previn to churn out a series of follow-up theme albums, some with Manne and Vinnegar. These projects varied greatly in terms of quality and jazz content, but at his best Previn could be a persuasive, moving jazz musician.

Born in Berlin on April 6, 1929, Previn was a child prodigy with wide-ranging talents in both jazz and classical music. In addition to his enviable credits as a performing pianist, Previn today boasts a glittering résumé as a conductor, writer, and arranger, although his ties to the jazz world have gradually lessened over the last thirty years. Despite his deep roots in symphonic music, Previn largely steered clear of Third Stream classicism in his jazz work, aiming more at an earthy, hard-swinging piano style at times reminiscent of Horace Silver. Long before his eventual retreat from most jazz activities, Previn had become something of a popularizer of jazz rather than a serious practitioner of the music. At his best, however, his music reflected a strong indigenous feel for the jazz idiom.

Although the drummer's collaborations with Previn sold well, Shelly Manne and His Men remained the major venue for Manne's music during the last half of the decade. By the close of the 1950s, the Men, originally one of the most daring of the West Coast groups, had created a new image in the jazz world. Largely on the strength of four live albums recorded at San Francisco's Blackhawk in September 1959, Manne's Men had emerged as a high-powered blowing band with deep hard-bop roots. Two personnel changes earlier in the year had paved the way for this transformation.

Joe Gordon, a Boston-born trumpeter, had started his working life selling sandwiches on the Boston-Albany train line in the 1940s. A later job selling newspapers near the local jazz clubs was a decisive step, exposing him to the developing modern jazz scene. After studying at the New England Conservatory, Gordon worked as a leader in the Boston area, gigged with the fathers of modern jazz—Parker, Gillespie—and recorded with the young lions of hard bop, Art Blakey and Horace Silver. These were rare credentials for a 1950s West Coast trumpeter.

Moving to Los Angeles in 1958, Gordon began an association with

Manne that would last until 1960. This focal activity was supplemented by work with Benny Carter, Harold Land, and Barney Kessel. After leaving Manne, Gordon waxed a July 1961 leader date for Contemporary, *Lookin' Good*, which promised big things from the trumpeter in the years to come. As it was, Gordon was near the close of his all too brief career; a tragic injury in a fire ended his life on November 4, 1963, at age thirty-five.

The other new addition to the Manne ensemble, tenor saxophonist Richie Kamuca, boasted a more conventional West Coast lineage. Kamuca, too, had East Coast roots—he was born in Philadelphia on July 23, 1938—but in the early 1950s he followed the typical apprenticeship pattern for a California saxophonist by joining the Kenton band. After Kenton, Kamuca worked with Woody Herman, finally settling in Southern California in 1957. If Kenton and Herman represented indoctrination in the ways of the West, Kamuca's next major gig, with the Lighthouse All-Stars, served as the finishing school for LA jazz talent. Despite this résumé and Kamuca's roots in Lester Young, his tenor playing avoided the extremes of West Coast cool, tempering its native lyricism with a pronounced rhythmic bite. A leader date recorded for the Mode label in June 1957 found Kamuca demonstrating these attributes in a strong line-up featuring Carl Perkins, Leroy Vinnegar, and Stan Levey. Joining Joe Gordon in Manne's front line in 1959, Kamuca provided an ideal tenor voice for the more loosely configured sound the drummer was then pursuing.

The final newcomer to the Manne group for the Blackhawk session was an unexpected last-minute substitute. Manne regular Russ Freeman had left on a road trip with Benny Goodman around the time of the San Francisco engagment. Looking for a replacement on short notice, Manne settled on Victor Feldman, a London-born multi-instrumentalist who had moved to the United States in 1957. More familiar to some listeners as a vibes player, Feldman made clear his piano credentials during the Blackhawk gig—his ensuing engagement with Cannonball Adderley is reported to be the result of the latter's favorable response to the Manne recordings. In the early 1960s, Feldman would also find favor with Miles Davis, with whose band Feldman briefly recorded shortly before Herbie Hancock joined the group. Miles recalls in his autobiography:

> We played a date in LA at John T's It Club and there I decided I wanted to record some music. I replaced [Harold] Mabern on piano with a great piano player from England named Victor Feldman, who could play his ass off. He also played vibraphone and drums. On the recording date we used two of his tunes: the title track "Seven Steps to Heaven" and "Joshua." I wanted him to join the band, but he was making a fortune playing studio work in LA, so he'd be losing money if he came with me. I came to New York looking for a piano player. I found him in Herbie Hancock.[13]

Despite its brevity, this association with Miles produced some excellent music. The pianist's solo on "Summer Nights" on Davis's *Corcovado* album is a textbook example of outstanding ballad playing. Feldman, who died in 1987, never gained the jazz reputation he deserved, although he eventually established himself as one of the premier studio musicians in Southern California. In this capacity, he brought his jazz sensibility to the music of Steely Dan and Joni Mitchell, while maintaining occasional jazz ties in his work with Stan Getz and others. His piano playing was anything but the limited "two-fingered" approach of many doubling vibraphonists and instead revealed a rich harmonic texture, a strong percussive element, and a good sense of space and melodic development.

Along with Monty Budwig, the one holdover from Manne's earlier group, this ensemble ventured north to San Francisco in mid-September 1959 for an extended engagement at Guido Cacianti's Blackhawk, then the crown jewel of Bay Area jazz clubs. After the first week, Manne excitedly phoned Les Koenig. "I've never asked this before," Koenig recalled Manne saying, "but we all feel you should come up and record the group in the club."[14] The following day Koenig and crew were on hand, setting up their equipment at the Blackhawk. For the next three evenings they taped everything that took place on the bandstand.

Koenig and Manne had originally intended to produce a single album from the Blackhawk tapes, but after listening to the music recorded they decided that virtually all the material was worthy of release. Few other record companies would have dared to issue four albums of live material from a single club engagement, but Koenig had already developed a reputation for doing the unconventional. A few years earlier he had culled three albums from Hampton Hawes's single November 1956 all-night session, thus producing one of the masterpieces of the decade. Koenig would do the same thing two decades later with the extraordinary series of recordings made by Art Pepper at the Village Vanguard. By 1959, in addition, Koenig had already produced Ornette Coleman, another highly controversial decision that later proved to be a brilliant call. By this time, Koenig was more than ever willing to trust his gut instinct.

Nor was the choice of issuing four full albums of live material the sole unusual feature of this Manne release. Despite the great amount of vinyl allocated to the project, fewer than a dozen full selections were featured on the four albums, most of the numbers running over ten minutes each. This, too, marked a daring move on the part of Contemporary, for few of these lengthy numbers would fit easily into a jazz radio format accustomed to rapid rotation of a large number of selections. Another contrast with Manne's previous habit lay in the band's heavy reliance on commonly done standards such as "Summertime" and "What's New?" in place of the originals and extended compositions of earlier projects. It was almost as if Manne were intent on doing with a vengeance all the things he had so long purposely neglected in his recordings. On "Vamp's Blues," from the second Blackhawk album, the band stretches out for twenty minutes on a twelve-bar blues. "It's hard for a guy to play jazz if you're going to tell him, 'Only two choruses,'" Manne announced in the liner notes, apparently unaware of the irony of this statement in the light of the meticulously arranged pieces he had fostered in years past.

Joe Gordon's strong showing on these albums makes his scant discography especially unfortunate. Dick Whittington, pianist on Gordon's Contemporary leader date, recalls the powerful impact the trumpeter could have on a group: "I've never heard a horn player better at pulling a group into a groove. He was almost like a drummer in his ability to put it in the pocket. And that's a hard thing for a horn player to do. Yet Joe could do it, and his playing was still relaxed and loose."[15]

As part of the final flowering of jazz on the coast at the decade's close, Manne's Blackhawk sessions remain among the most vital releases in the whole Contemporary catalogue. Although Manne was one of the few to weather the jazz drought of the 1960s with a certain amount of success, his ability to do so built as much on his strengths as a businessman as on his talents as a musician. Whether through some preternatural knowledge of the coming collapse in jazz venues or mere chance, Manne opened the new decade of the 1960s by securing his own jazz establishment, Shelly's Manne Hole, an underground bomb shelter where he could wait out the rock-and-roll fallout taking place in the open musical environment. In this self-contained atmosphere, Manne continued to play, as well as book outside acts, well into the revival years of the 1970s. Meanwhile he continued to enjoy the reputation he had developed in the Southern California studios, and the 1960s found little abatement in his recording activities as leader or sideman.

By the time the Manne Hole finally closed its doors in 1973, the prospects for many of the West Coast old-timers were beginning to look up again. For Art Pepper, Hampton Hawes, Chet Baker, and many of the West Coast stars of the postwar generation, the 1970s represented an opportunity for renewed careers. New venues to play—in Europe, Japan, even California—were supplemented by new recordings and reissues. Manne, like many of his contemporaries, began witnessing a resurgence of interest in his jazz work. His participation in the LA Four, which began concurrently with the closing of the Manne Hole, as well as continued projects as a leader, showed that he was prepared to make the most of this reviving interest in jazz.

His sudden death in September 1984 cut short the diminutive drummer's music for good. In the spring of 1986, the city of Los Angeles held a commemorative event honoring him on the site of the original Manne

Hole. Many of Manne's closest musical associates were in attendance: Conte Candoli, Bob Cooper, Bill Holman, Dave Pell, Jack Sheldon, and Leroy Vinnegar, among others. Afterwards a jam session, held at the city's expense, took place in the street. The mayor dedicated a bronze manhole cover to mark the occasion.

CHAPTER FOURTEEN

Straight Life

serve the master

Any account of Art Pepper's tumultuous career risks being a pale shadow of the story Pepper tells in his autobiography, *Straight Life*. Even the most candid outsider's description of the altoist's life and times would have a hard time matching Pepper's unflinching honesty, while even the most diligent investigative reporter would never dig up the kind of nasty details on Pepper's life that the altoist calmly presents himself. Pepper's worst enemies could hardly outdo his self-incriminations, but then again few panegyrists could match his self-praise. At one point in his book he interrupts the detailed account of his travails to announce:

> I believe I'm above anybody I meet. Anybody. Everybody. I think that I'm more intelligent—innate intelligence; I feel that I'm more emotional, more sensitive, the greatest lover, the greatest musician; I feel that if I had been a ball player I'd have been in the Hall of Fame.[1]

The reader of *Straight Life* is left to reconcile such statements with the harrowing account of personal dissipation presented elsewhere in the book. While most jazz autobiographies are a predictable recital of honorary degrees received and polls won, Pepper eschews the surface gloss and digs deep into a gritty account of his passage from Stan Kenton to San Quentin and his ensuing attempts, none of them entirely successful, to put his life together again—all told with a clinical detachment almost as fascinating as the story itself. He neither relishes the seamier details, in the manner of so many kiss-and-tell books, nor whitewashes the tale of his life. Nor finally does he assume the smug attitude of the born again, justifying his transgressions through the self-righteousness of his final conversion to the

straight life. Like all real redemptions, Pepper knew, his had to be earned
again every day. At the end of the book he comes across as no self-confident
victor over his problems, but a man every bit as anxiety-ridden and haunted
as the convict incarcerated in San Quentin. Art Pepper almost certainly
never read St. Augustine or Rousseau, but this latter-day confession is
rooted in those predecessors, just as his blistering alto sound grew out of
Charlie Parker, Benny Carter, and Willie Smith.

Pepper the musician is portrayed vividly in the pages of his book, but
so are Pepper the addict, the thief, the pervert, the narcissist, the voyeur,
the convict. As if this self-revelation were not enough, Pepper quotes his
"friends" at length as they add to the charges. In a lengthy passage included in *Straight Life*, Freddy Rivera says this about Pepper's self-
proclaimed sensitivity and intelligence:

> Art was very sensitive and I would say cunning in many ways. . . . The
> sensitivity is largely an expression of selfishness. He is sensitive to such a
> degree about himself. . . . At times his concern for other people would be
> expressed as sentimentality: "I really *love* you, man." Even histrionics. But
> I question whether at any time the concern with the self was ever put aside.
> . . . The cunning was a result of great natural intelligence, but it was really
> a form of childishness. Instead of taking the form of advancing his career and
> getting work, which he had every right to have, it was diverted into the
> manipulation of flunkies. . . . The child must be taken care of. He must be
> given things. Infantile gratification. For an infant it's perfectly appropriate;
> he's weaned in three years. One time we were at a place and I bought him a
> pizza and then I wanted to take a bite. He wouldn't let me have any! Haha-
> haha! What would you call that? That was selfishness. And then, of course,
> he would have a student, a guy named Joe Martin, and the student would
> drive him everywhere and do things for him. The *Master!* We must serve
> the *master!* That type of thing. Art used it to the hilt.[2]

Certainly there are far worse things in *Straight Life* than hoarding
pizza. Even so, one can only marvel at Pepper's willingness to include such
passages in his book. Has any entertainer's autobiography ever gone to
such lengths to tell the whole story, to present a rounded and unflinching
portrait of the artist as a young scumbag?

"Art's lifestyle is complaining and bitching," states Ann Christos in
her contribution to *Straight Life*. "I guess the only thing that I know of
that has *really* been important to Art in his life is dope." "Art is a patho-
logical physical coward," adds Jerry Maher elsewhere in the book.[3] And
one could go on and on. Certainly other jazz autobiographies have included passages written by friends of the subject, but most outside contributions have all the authenticity of speeches made at a testimonal dinner—
for the ultimate example see Dizzy Gillespie's comprehensive *To Be or*

Not to Bop, where the platitudes never stop. Pepper's friends and acquaintances come across, by comparison, as participants at a celebrity "roast," albeit one in which the implicit good humor typical of such events is noticeably absent.

Pepper the addict may incur our criticism; Pepper the writer may draw our amazement; but it is Pepper the musician who earned his place in the history of jazz. Yet an individual does not exist piecemeal; links between life and art have been the critics obsession at least since the time of Vasari. And rightly so. Who can deny that, in Pepper's case, this extraordinary candor, which overwhelms the reader of *Straight Life*, also played its part in the man's music? Emotional honesty of an extreme degree gave Art Pepper's music its raw edge. If Pepper told all in his 1979 autobiography, he was also letting it all hang out night after night on the bandstand. Especially at the end of his life. It was almost as if writing the book had a cathartic effect on his playing; there too his attitude was increasingly "Here I am, warts and all." The missed notes, the painfully bent tones, the honks, the distorted sounds—all mixed with the sweetest lyrical passages.

His late ballad "Everything Happens to Me"—which was being prepared for release on the *Roadgame* album at the time of his death on June 15, 1982—brings all these things together, and though you would swear that so many disparate elements could never cohere in the context of a thirty-two-bar solo, somehow Pepper pulls it off. Pepper never agreed with Lester Young's statement that you need to know the lyrics to play a ballad. "I don't know the words to any song. Maybe 'America the Beautiful,' " he said in 1981—then added: "No, I don't even know that."[4] But the poignant world-weariness and self-pitying lament of these lyrics seemed echoed in every note of this gripping performance. If Pepper was an egomaniac (And could anyone who spent more than five minutes in conversation with him deny it? When I interviewed him, he dwelled at length on the injustice *Downbeat* had done him by never putting him on the cover.), it was only another side of the intense self-assertion that brought his music so tellingly to life. The whole man, with all his contradictions and flaws and pains, entered into his music.

The music of Art Pepper from the 1950s had more of the sweetness and less of the *Angst* that one finds in his later playing, and this, too, was reflective of the man. Thirty years before *Roadgame*, Pepper recorded "Everything Happens to Me" as part of one of his first dates as a leader for the Discovery label. The easy, relaxed mastery of the song was as fitting then as his later anguished rendition was in his changed circumstances. In 1952, everything bad had yet to happen to Art Pepper. For two years running, he had finished second in the *Downbeat* poll, placing behind only the legendary Charlie Parker. If not universally accepted as the

greatest alto saxophonist in the world—that being his often stated goal—
Pepper was recognized as one of the masters of his instrument. At only
27, Pepper must have felt his best was yet to come.

By then Pepper had already come a long way. His troubles began
MacDuff-like, according to his autobiography, while still in the womb. His
teenage mother tried various methods of inducing miscarriage. Although
she failed, her child was born—on September 1, 1925, in Gardena, California—sickly and frail. Pepper attributed his early poor health, including
rickets and jaundice, to her attempts at self-induced abortion. At age five
he left home to live with his grandmother on a ranch farm near Perris,
California; and soon they moved to Los Angeles before finally settling in
the nearby beach community of San Pedro. At nine Pepper began studying
clarinet—he wanted to learn trumpet, but a local music teacher advised
him that his teeth were not strong enough for the instrument—and at
twelve he started playing the alto saxophone. By the age of fifteen, he had
lost his interest in school bands, and he began looking for opportunities to
sit in with working jazz groups.

Soon Pepper was gigging on Central Avenue, where he learned about
an opening in Gus Arnheim's band in San Diego. It took little prodding
for him to leave school—his attendance at Fremont High was sporadic at
best—and take the job. After three months in San Diego, he returned to
Central Avenue, where, from Dexter Gordon, he heard of an opening in
Lee Young's band at the Club Alabam. Pepper auditioned for the spot at
the black musicians' union—the unions would remain segregated in Los
Angeles for years to come—and won the job.

Lee Young's band provided heady company for a seventeen-year-old
white alto saxophonist from San Pedro. Lee's brother Lester was Pepper's
earliest idol. (Pepper described Lester as "one of the greatest saxophone
players that ever lived in this world. The most fantastic—equalled only
fairly recently by John Coltrane. Better than Charlie Parker. In my hum-
ble opinion, better than Charlie Parker, just marvelous, such beauty.")[5]
While gigging on Central Avenue, Pepper also played with some of his
most promising LA contemporaries, such as Dexter Gordon and Charles
Mingus. After work he could go to the nearby after-hours clubs to hear
the legendary players of the older generation: Louis Armstrong, Lester
Young, Art Tatum, Ben Webster, Coleman Hawkins, Johnny Hodges, and
others. Little wonder Pepper would claim, years later, "I attribute whatever ability I have to play jazz to those times on The Avenue. I didn't
know what chord it was, but I was in an atmosphere of great jazz feeling,
and I think it stayed with me."[6] Pepper's musical education at the Alabam
took place both onstage and in the back room. The precocious altoist was
getting by on his strong ear at this time; not only did he lack any knowledge of harmony, but he was also a poor reader. Between shows, fellow

saxophonist Jack McVea gave Pepper impromptu music lessons on reading stock arrangements. "I'd go into the dressing room with Art and I'd go over his parts with him," McVea relates. "He learned real fast, you know."[7]

Central Avenue was home turf for the leading black jazz musicians in Southern California, and though integrated bands were something of a rarity, they posed no problem in the black district (in striking contrast to some other Los Angeles neighborhoods). Harry James, Artie Shaw, Buddy Rich, and Vido Musso, among others, were known to sit in on Central Avenue when they were in town. Lee Young had already featured Jimmy Rowles in his band before Pepper joined on. Barney Kessel, Russ Freeman, and other white musicians of the period invariably describe their experiences on the avenue as positive ones in which racial tension rarely came to the fore.

The Central Avenue days perhaps also contributed to the essentially black aesthetic that remained at the heart of Pepper's music for the rest of his life. The experiences of the black underclass have long served, in the words of critic Gary Giddins, as "the best possible source for self-examination" for the most probing white jazz musicians. The oppression of a minority—whether political, religious, or ethnic—has long borne an uncanny relation to the production of art of lasting value. (I recall a literary critic once pointing out to me that the history of poetic masterpieces in English literature characteristically showed that poets produced their finest works when their own political party was out of power. The argument, however tendentious when set out in such an extreme form, contains more than a grain of truth.) The undaunted vitality of black music during much of this century is no accidental circumstance: It is the bitter fruit harvested by a race that has been forced, by its very existence, into constant self-awareness and uneasy self-assertion. This was an element of the jazz experience white musicians could appreciate, at best, only second-hand. The tension and intensity characteristic of the jazz experience had, for the black creators of the music, all too many corollaries in their non-musical lives.

The best white jazz artists have often felt, whether consciously or subconsciously, that they belonged to an underclass. And even if the black/white dichotomy was not the cause of this inner sense of isolation, the situation of their black colleagues must have served as an apt symbol for the alienation they experienced in their own lives. Pepper's autobiography is full of telling anecdotes in this regard, and one imagines that the psychology of a Chet Baker, a Bill Evans, a Stan Getz, or even a Bix Beiderbecke, were it probed as deeply as Pepper has done in his book, would reflect similar feelings of isolation from the norms and expectations of society. Perhaps such musicians were initially attracted to jazz because it was (and is) the art of an oppressed, underclass sensibility. Jazz is the art form of the outsider, whether racially, musically, or psychologically. In 1979, Pepper recalled the roots of his early identification with jazz musicians: "At the beginning, when I was very young, playing on Central Avenue, I asked someone about [alto saxophonist] Willie Smith and that he looked so white, and they told me that he was a seventh-grain negro, and I remember wishing that I was. I wanted to be black because I felt such an affinity to the music."[8] Years later when Pepper recorded as a sideman under the pseudonym "Art Salt," he was delighted to learn that some listeners thought Salt was a black alto player. Freddy Rivera, amplifying on this undercurrent in Pepper's self-image, suggests that the altoist was very much at home during his later prison terms, because he was then in "an environment where he could *identify*, believing unconsciously that he was a black sheep, ostracized from the 'respectable' world. Feeling that way all of his life, he could readily identify with all these other outcasts."[9] Jack Sheldon recalls that Pepper retained the isolated convict mentality even when on the outside: "He would stay in his room all the time. His life was like he was still in prison."[10] Drugs, legal problems, alcohol, eccentricity, isolation—perhaps these are not haphazard elements in the biographies of Pepper, Baker, Getz, Evans, Beiderbecke, but are as representative of their true selves as their affinity with jazz. They craved the position of the outsider, the loner, the oppressed.

For the young Art Pepper, his music, even more than his lifestyle, was well suited to the Central Avenue setting of his first efforts at public performance. Only a few years later, West Coast jazz would gain notoriety for its supposed emphasis on complex compositional structures, unique instrumentation, and a laid-back improvisational style, but Central Avenue in the 1940s gave little hint of this emerging sound. The music in the air at Lovejoy's, the Downbeat, or the Last Word was typically hard-swinging, loosely arranged, often informal, with an emphasis on improvisational brilliance rather than compositional ingenuity. Throughout his career Pepper's music would bear the stamp of these same mercurial qualities: With few exceptions (the most noteworthy being his collaborations with Marty Paich), the best work of his career came from informal small-group sessions, often done with little preparation.

It is telling that Pepper, in his autobiography and various interviews, tried to understate the amount of preparation he actually did—for example, he explains that he had not touched his horn for months when he recorded *Art Pepper Meets the Rhythm Section*, yet his discography shows that he participated in several sessions in the weeks preceding the date. Similarly, he always claimed to practice the horn very little, implying that his technical fluency simply emerged through native talent. "I don't practice much, but I think about music all the time," Pepper told me during our interview. Obviously there is a fair degree of truth mixed with the hyperbole in Pepper's assertions, but it is equally clear that his ideal of what a jazz musician should be involved a rejection of conventional notions of diligence, practice, and decorum. His ethos was of inspiration, not preparation.

In the same vein, Pepper prided himself on his compositions, but he never followed the model of Mulligan, Giuffre, Rogers, and other West Coast players in pursuing writing as a serious form of self-expression. His compositions were invariably vehicles for his own soloing, and they succeeded or failed on that basis. Indeed many of his pieces follow the bebopper's practice of adding a new melody to a standard chord progression—Pepper's composition "Straight Life," for example, is based on the chords to "After You've Gone"—the result being new compositions that remained familiar and comfortable settings for straight-ahead blowing. Above all, Pepper followed the Central Avenue model in his unrelenting emphasis on swing. More than any other white jazz musician's of his day, Pepper's sense of swing was at the very heart of his music. Stoking the rhythmic fire was second nature to him, akin to breathing or walking. In each of these respects Pepper stayed true to the culture of this early setting for his musical exploits.

Through Lee Young's intervention, Pepper got an audition for the open saxophone chair in the Benny Carter band. Pepper made the band, and though he played second alto behind Carter, occasionally the latter would let the youngster take the lead and play his solo spots. It is easy to hear echoes of Carter in the later Pepper, especially in his appealing manner of combining sweet-toned lyricism with a strong sense of swing. The older altoist was a past master at this rare hybrid: There were plenty of "hot" players around at the time, but few could match Carter at driving the band without losing this underlying sweetness. Pepper flourished in this conducive setting for his musical development.

At this point Pepper was still playing by ear, unaware of chord structure and harmonic progressions, but his strong musical talent let him go further within these limitations than most could go even with the deepest grasp of theory. His colleagues with the Carter band were as impressive as his musical companions at the Alabam. In addition to Carter, the group brought him into contact with such present and future jazz luminaries as Freddie Webster, J. J. Johnson, and Gerald Wilson. The band played in and around Los Angeles, and Pepper also accompanied the group to Salt Lake City. But when Carter was preparing to embark on a tour of the South, he was forced to drop Pepper from the band. It was far too risky to bring an integrated group to that part of the country.

Carter talked to his manager, Carlos Gastel, who also represented the Stan Kenton band. Soon Pepper was part of the Kenton orchestra, just in time for its new recording association with Capitol Records. His experience playing with Carter held him in good stead in the new ensemble; at the same time, the more complex arrangements of the Kenton orchestra forced him to learn to read chord changes instead of relying on his ear alone. Pepper was with the group for only about three months before receiving his draft notice, but before leaving he made his recording debut with a solo on two takes of "Harlem Folk Dance," recorded on November 19, 1943. He was barely eighteen years old.

A few months earlier Pepper had married his first wife, Patti Moore, sixteen years old at the time, whom he had met while still in school. Although his father objected to the marriage, Pepper borrowed his cousin's car and drove with Patti across the Mexican border to Tijuana, where they were married. The marriage seemed, at least initially, to be a reasonably happy one. Pepper's musical career was taking off, and he was making good money with the Kenton band. As yet unafflicted by his heroin addiction, Pepper was at the beginning of what promised to be a productive and successful period in his life. Little wonder that the altoist resolved to avoid the draft if at all possible. Pepper tried various ploys with this end in mind: He paid a chiropractor to write a letter saying he had a heart murmur; in preparation for his physical he walked around in the evening, soaking wet from a shower—he hoped to come down with tuberculosis; he even fainted during his induction physical. Despite these strategems, he was inducted at Fort MacArthur on February 11, 1944, and soon sent to Fort Sill, Oklahoma, for basic training. Right before he was scheduled to be shipped out to combat, he was transferred into a military band. Most of his remaining time in the service was spent playing in bands and serving as an MP in England.

At the close of 1946 Pepper left the army and returned to California, where he soon discovered, much to his dismay, that a musical revolution had taken place during his absence. While overseas he had not even heard the word *bebop*, let alone encountered the music being played by Parker, Gillespie, and the new generation of modernists. "When I came out, I didn't know anything about what was happening over here," Pepper later explained.[11]

> I got home, a friend of mine came by and said, "I want you to hear these records." He had two records, and one he had was with Sonny Stitt and Dizzy—"Oop Bop Sh'Bam" and "That's Earl, Brother." That record was the first one I heard, and I said, "Oh, my God," and I just got sick. I just couldn't believe it. And then the next record I heard was, I think it was "Salt Peanuts," and that other real fast one—it was "Shaw Nuff." That thing was so fast. . . . When I heard Bird I just got deathly sick. I couldn't stand any more, and he was going to play something else, and I said, "No, no, I can't stand it. I can't listen to any more."

This initial sense of musical vertigo soon gave way to the altoist's kindled desire to master the new music. Already an accomplished professional, having gained notoriety with Benny Carter, Stan Kenton and others, Pepper was forced to return to the woodshed to keep pace with the rapidly changing musical environment of the postwar years. Eventually he would forge a partnership between swing and bop, hot and cool, that would stand out as one of the most authentic alto sounds of the 1950s. Indeed, much of the beauty of his later style stems from the lyrical prebop underpinnings that meld with the modern and postmodern jazz inflections in his playing: "I really dug Bird, but I didn't want Bird to destroy me. I didn't want that to happen to me that I heard so many other guys do. . . . I really worked at that very hard. I more or less gave myself a pep talk that I've got to go out and play, and I couldn't ignore the new thing because I had to be modern but I had to keep me, I couldn't lose myself." [12] Two decades later Pepper would weather another crisis of confidence in the face of the new music of John Coltrane—so much so that he even temporarily switched to tenor saxophone—but here, too, he eventually succeeded (and reached a higher level in his own playing) by incorporating the more modern approach into his own distinctive alto voice. Much of Pepper's genius lay in this serpentine ability to swallow whole the styles of his most illustrious contemporaries while remaining true to himself.

Resettled in Los Angeles, Pepper worked on assimilating the new bop sounds, meanwhile doing casual gigs. This same time period found the altoist becoming increasingly dependent on alcohol, marijuana, and pills. For a brief time Pepper took a day job in a meat-packing plant, until an unexpected phone call from Stan Kenton led to Pepper's rejoining the band. Soon he was again living the nomadic life of a road musician. During the second Kenton stint, Pepper's music continued to develop, and his solo work with the band began to show the mature presence of a strongly personalized saxophonist. At the same time his private life started its painful downward spiral, which would soon lead to the first of many periods of incarceration. A brief attempt to have his wife and their young daughter, Patricia, travel with him proved unfeasible. Following with painful fidelity the model set by his parents, Pepper had originally been upset at his wife's pregnancy and resentful of his newborn daughter. Now he responded by making Patti feel she had to choose between husband and child. When she returned to Southern California with Patricia, the decision signaled the beginning of the end of their marriage.

Even more destructive was Pepper's newfound heroin addiction. While in Chicago with the Kenton Band, Pepper was introduced to his ultimate high by some fellow musicians. In *Straight Life* the experience is explained with epiphanic vividness:

I said "This is it. This is the only answer for me. If this is what it takes, then this is what I'm going to do, whatever dues I have to pay. . . ." And I knew that I was going to get busted and I knew that I would go to prison. . . . All I can say is that at that moment I saw that I'd found peace of mind. . . . I realized from that moment on I would be, if you want to use the word, a junkie. That's the word they used. That's the word they still use. That is what I became at that moment.[13]

Pepper's music from the period reflects what seems a different man from the anguished addict portrayed in *Straight Life*. In due course, his playing would communicate more than a small dose of these painful emotions, but his solos with the Kenton band are another thing entirely. On his feature number, the Shorty Rogers composition "Art Pepper," the altoist begins with a long, slow interlude that is simply and unaffectedly pretty. Like Getz, who did something similar in his "Early Autumn" feature with the Herman band, Pepper somehow was able to pull this off without sounding saccharine or sentimental. It came across not as a shallow or contrived prettiness, the calling card of so much popular music, but more like the innocent beauty of a child. Even when the tempo doubles on this piece, Pepper's complex melodic lines do not destroy the earlier impression. There is something carefree about this whole performance, almost in defiance of the pretentious instrumentation.

Rogers obviously found this particular aspect of Pepper's playing especially moving, because his several later attempts at writing and composing for the altoist typically tried to recapture this same kind of simple sweetness. Rogers's arrangement of "Over the Rainbow" is noteworthy here, but perhaps the most striking example is "Bunny"—the piece named for Art and Patti's French poodle—from the January 12, 1953, session for Rogers and his Giants. (Rogers's predilection for naming compositions after pets borders on the extreme: "Popo," "Didi," and "Sam and the Lady," for example, all are dedications to various cats owned by producer Gene Norman.) Like its predecessor "Art Pepper," "Bunny" begins with a meditative calmness that is broken by a lilting up-tempo section.

At the close of 1951, Pepper left the Kenton band. Although he was one of the highest-paid members of the orchestra and developing a national reputation for his alto work, Pepper was tired of the hassles of life on the road—aggravated by the difficulties of scoring heroin in constantly changing locations—and anxious for more musical freedom than the modest degree allowed him in a big band setting. His departure was part of a larger exodus from the Kenton band at this time, which also saw Shorty Rogers and Shelly Manne leaving the fold. Pepper's decision to go on his own put him, at least temporarily, in an uncertain financial state. With the expenses of married life and his increasing drug dependency, Pepper found himself with a number of outstanding bills and no regular source of income. The almost immediate opportunity to record with Shorty Rogers and his newly formed Giants was a godsend. Pepper's feature on "Over the Rainbow' became one of the most popular recordings of his career (he kept the number in his repertoire until the end of his life, recording a much more harrowing version of it in the late 1970s) and was an important success at a time when he was about to form his own group.

Largely on the strength of the notoriety earned with Rogers and Kenton, Pepper formed a group under his own leadership early in 1952. He brought the band into the Surf Club, a tiny jazz nightspot located at the corner of 6th and Manhattan in Hollywood. Despite the name, the Surf was no hangout for jazz-loving beachcombers, but rather a ramshackle saloon, located miles from the nearest surfing spot, which could hardly seat more than fifty or sixty fans. In contrast to the low-key surroundings, the caliber of the entertainment was world-class: Pepper's sidemen included pianist Hampton Hawes, Shelly Manne, or Larry Bunker on drums, and bassist Joe Mondragon. Richard Bock, then an unemployed student taking classes at Los Angeles City College on the GI Bill, was one of the enthusiastic listeners who first heard Pepper in person during this engagement.* Bock had recently completed a two-year apprenticeship as Albert Marx's assistant at Discovery Records. Although Marx had ceased operations, his former understudy tried to interest the new owner of the Discovery masters, New York distributor Jack Bergman, in letting him produce the Pepper quartet for the label. With Bergman's go-ahead, the musicians assembled on March 4, 1952, at MacGregor Studios in Hollywood to cut Pepper's first date as a leader. The four tracks recorded that day, in particular the fast-paced "Surf Ride," showcased Pepper's exuberant and effortless alto stylings, with Hawes providing a perfect piano counterpart. It is easy to view Hawes, like Pepper, as a tragic figure, an anguished victim of addiction, but the music here seems more a statement of pure exultation. Perhaps this is the other side of the junkie's live-for-the-day mentality: This is uplifting music of the here-and-now.

Three days after this session, a glowing article on Pepper, written by Bock, appeared in Downbeat. (Such disregard of obvious conflicts of interest were—and are—not uncommon among a few of the "old school" critics.) "This year may well prove to be the most important one yet in the career of Art Pepper. . . . He has earned an enviable reputation and large following as one of the most consistent of the modern jazzmen."[14] Bock's

*Bock's way with the dates and other facts, one should be warned, was quite cavalier: In the liner notes to the 1978 reissue of this session on United Artists, he mentions that this first chance to hear Pepper took place in 1950. In his liner notes to the Mosaic reissue of a few years later Bock mentions again his first encounter with Pepper at the Surf Club, this time placing it during the spring of 1951. In fact, both dates are almost certainly wrong. Pepper's stint at the Surf Club was in early 1952.

questionable impartiality aside, Pepper clearly had come into his own by the time of the Discovery date. He had always been a distinctive soloist, but now for the first time he began to focus his attention on composing original material. Two of his finest compositions—his ballad "Patricia" and the barn-burner "Straight Life"—were penned during this period. The former piece was named for his daughter, whom he finally grew to know and love during this relatively happy time in his life. Pepper's career was on the upswing. With his earnings from the Surf Club and other venues, he was able to buy a tract house on the GI Bill. In a manner typical of his topsy-turvy ethics, Pepper refused to use his music earnings to support his drug habit, instead relying on the money he made from dealing to subsidize his own use.

Finally, on the urging of his father, Pepper entered a sanitarium in Garden Grove, where during a several-week stay, he was slowly broken of his addiction through a process of gradually decreasing injections of morphine. His father had taken out a mortgage on his home to pay for the treatment, and Pepper had entered the program in good faith, but after only a short period on the outside he was using again. Finally, in 1953, he was forced to quit cold turkey under less comfortable circumstances. He was arrested on heroin possession charges and incarcerated in the Los Angeles County Jail. Later he claimed that during this anguishing period of breaking the habit, he went seventeen days and nights without sleeping, plagued by chills and pains, constantly vomiting and unable to eat. The only "treatment" available at the jail was an occasional aspirin. At his trial, Pepper pled *nolo contendere* and was sentenced to two years in the federal hospital at Fort Worth.

the route

In 1954, Pepper was paroled from Forth Worth and returned to Los Angeles. Some casual gigs with tenor saxophonist Jack Montrose led to a recording session for the two horn players on the Discovery label. On August 25, they entered the studio, where they were ably supported by a rhythm section comprised of Claude Williamson, Larry Bunker, and Monty Budwig. Montrose proved to be an ideal collaborator with Pepper—years later Pepper would mention that only with Montrose and Warne Marsh was he able to share the front line and still play freely. The group's performance of "Deep Purple" bears witness to this claim with its spontaneous opening counterpoint, which segues nicely into Pepper's lead-off solo. A more tightly arranged opening graces the equally compelling "Nutmeg." (Spices seemed to be on the altoist's mind during this session.

In addition to "Nutmeg," the other originals include "Cinnamon," "Art's Oregano," and "Thyme Time." Drug culture cognoscenti of the time might have appreciated the titles—ingestion of large amounts of spices was one of the few legal highs available to an addict cut off from contraband.) More noteworthy than the kitchen cabinet song titles was Pepper's playing on the date. Here we begin to hear a more probing, impassioned soloist than the one who graced the Kenton or Rogers bands, or even the Surf Club quartet. Despite, or perhaps because of, the tribulations of his private life— in addition to the ignominy of imprisonment, Pepper had just suffered an unwanted divorce from Patti, who had immediately married drummer Remo Belli—Pepper's music comes across here as stronger and deeper than ever.

Born December 30, 1928, in Detroit, Montrose had attended high school in Tennessee before journeying west to study music at Los Angeles State. In addition to being a leading saxophonist on the Southern California scene, Montrose also distinguished himself as a composer and arranger with a flair for the indigenous contrapuntal sound so popular in California jazz in the 1950s. His writing credits grace record dates for, among others, Clifford Brown, Chet Baker, and Bob Gordon. For a brief period Montrose seemed on the verge of establishing himself as a major force in West Coast jazz, but instead his career went into a tailspin after the mid-1950s. Relegated to playing the LA strip club circuit and odd studio gigs, Montrose decided to resettle in Nevada. There he has kept himself busy in the financially secure surroundings of the casino entertainment world.

The Montrose date would be Pepper's only studio recording before another period of imprisonment. By the end of 1954, Pepper was using forty caps of heroin a day, and his weight was down to 128 pounds. On December 7, 1954, he was arrested while trying to score heroin, but the only charge that could stick was possession of codeine tablets—for which he was sentenced to six months in the county jail. The arrest was perhaps a hidden blessing. Later he would say, "I could have been using maybe a hundred caps a day in another month if I had access to that much, because the demand just builds and builds."[15] Given his past record, Pepper was forced to serve nineteen months, most of it at the federal penitentiary on Terminal Island, near his boyhood home in San Pedro.

In the late spring of 1956, Pepper was released from Terminal Island. Despite his newfound freedom, his situation at this time was far from enviable. His marriage had failed; he had lost his house and car; and he had not worked a steady jazz gig since November 1954. Moreover, his reputation was tainted by the now widely publicized details of his addiction. To make matters even worse, he was soon using again. Pepper was befriended by a big-time drug dealer, Mario Cuevas, who became enamored of the altoist's talent and provided him with a regular (and steadily increasing) supply of heroin. Pepper later wrote and recorded a song for

Cuevas: the poignant 5/4 blues "Las Cuevas de Mario" from the altoist's 1960 *Smack Up* album. In his autobiography Pepper calls Cuevas, in another example of the altoist's odd value system, "one of the greatest people I've ever met in my life."

By the beginning of 1957, Pepper's increasing dependency on heroin was taking its toll on his career. He missed gigs. He stopped looking for work. He did not return phone calls or would not take them even when he was in. With the exception of an occasional record date, he stayed at home behind locked doors and windows and, in his words, would "fix all day and night." Whatever money he had went to Cuevas in return for drugs: "Whenever I came to I'd just cook again. Sometimes the spike would be lying on the floor or still stuck in my arm so when I woke up I'd have to clean it out, get it unplugged. I'd start cutting the light fixtures. I'd be cutting the cords and the plugs to get wires to stick into the spike to clean it. I would have ripped up anything in the house to unplug that needle."[16]

One Saturday morning near the close of January, Pepper was awakened by his girlfriend Diane (soon to become his second wife) and told that he had a record date scheduled for that day. Les Koenig and Diane had arranged the session behind his back, fearing that he would back out unless it were set up as a *fait accompli*. Miles Davis was performing in Hollywood that week, and Koenig had arranged to bring Davis's world-class rhythm section into the studio for a session with Pepper. Davis's band featured drummer Philly Joe Jones, bassist Paul Chambers, and pianist Red Garland—perhaps the finest working rhythm section in jazz during that period. Koenig, one of the altoist's staunchest supporters, felt this was the perfect opportunity to feature Pepper in a setting that would challenge him to the utmost.

In Pepper's circumstances, the challenge must have seemed almost too great. He had played the alto only infrequently during the six months since his release from prison. Trying to prepare his horn for this unexpected session, Pepper discovered that he had not taken it apart since the last time he played. Now, when he tried to remove the mouthpiece, the cork on the neck of his saxophone came off with it. With no time to repair the damage, he put the mouthpiece back on—the cork still in it—and taped it into place. Before leaving the house, Pepper fixed one more time, so he would be steady for the recording. Arriving at the studio, he met the other players. The title of the eventual album, *Art Pepper Meets the Rhythm Section*, was no exercise in poetic license; he truly met them for the first time at the session. Needless to say, he had never played with them before, and there was obviously no time for a rehearsal. Even the basic task of choosing songs had not yet been done.

Despite these unpropitious circumstances, Pepper recorded one of the finest albums of his career. His playing here begins to show the mature qualities that would characterize his work to the end. In the past, it seemed, two different musical personae had made up Art Pepper: a lyrical, sweet side, epitomized in the several feature pieces Shorty Rogers had written for him, and the saxophone virtuoso, whose biting improvisations on the earlier recordings of "Straight Life" and "Cherokee" were full of spark and flash. By the time of his early thirties—he was thirty-one when he recorded *Meets the Rhythm Section*—these two selves had begun to coalesce. From now on, even Pepper's ballads probed deeper and took on the biting intensity formerly reserved for up-tempo work; at the same time, his fast work no longer relied so heavily on technical displays. Now each phrase came across as deeply felt, a personal statement that refused to be reduced to a manifestation of virtuosity. In time, Pepper would develop almost an antivirtuosity, one in which his missed notes, jagged phrases, distorted tones, honks, and cries would stand side by side with the passages of effortless fluency. Hints of this transformation can be heard on *Meets the Rhythm Section*. In the 1970s, this aspect of Pepper's playing would reach full flower in a series of brilliant recordings for the Galaxy and Contemporary labels.

What comes across on this 1956 recording is the focused vitality of a player for whom every note counts. Describing music in words is always a challenging task, but pinpointing the change in Art Pepper's music during this period is especially elusive. Above all one gets a sense here of musical conviction, difficult to define but easy enough to feel, which goes beyond Pepper's previous efforts. Even when he lets his fingers fly, as on the group's re-recording of "Straight Life," one hears a deeper level of commitment than on the earlier version of the tune. That this should happen at a point in Pepper's life when his involvement in music seemed most detached is difficult to comprehend. Perhaps the musical side of him, which for so long had been undernourished, asserted itself in reaction to the dissipation of his personal life. One can only speculate, and perhaps such speculations should be left to the psychologists. In any event, Pepper's performances during these darkest days recall the truism of the spirit being willing while the flesh is weak. This playing exemplifies willing and willfulness *par excellence*.

Not that all of Pepper's performance from this period are at a uniformly high level. Almost immediately after his release from Terminal Island, he was slotted by Richard Bock to record with Chet Baker for Pacific Records. The combination of Art Pepper and Chet Baker, the two bad boys of jazz, must have seemed to many West Coast jazz fans like a musical match made in heaven. Beyond the compatibility of their boyish good looks and fast-paced lifestyles (the pairing was marketed as the "Playboys of Jazz"), their playing indicated a powerful affinity. As much as any two musicians of the 1950s, Baker and Pepper represented the most telling mixture of the sweet and the hot: Their playing was pretty without being saccharine or shallow, and their soles could burn without ever losing their melodic integrity. Their music could be appreciated on the surface, where it glistened with all the mellow beauty that *was* "West Coast jazz" according to the pundits, but those who wanted to probe deeper could hear a raw honesty that was anything but superficial. Truly one had high hopes for such a pairing.

The Baker–Pepper collaboration, to be sure, produced some noteworthy performances, but one leaves them vaguely disappointed. The first session, from July 26, 1956, finds the duo joined by Richie Kamuca in the front line and supported by a rhythm section consisting of Leroy Vinnegar, Pete Jolly, and Stan Levey. On "Minor Yours" and "Little Girl" both Baker and Pepper contribute individually strong solos, but there is no sense of chemistry between the two—as one finds, for example, in Baker's collaborations with Desmond or Mulligan or, to perhaps a slightly lesser degree, in Pepper's work with Jack Sheldon. Johnny Mandel's sophisticated arrangements, which would have been well suited for the Lighthouse All-Stars or Shorty Rogers's Giants, are too constricting for Baker and Pepper. On "Tynan Time," written for *Downbeat's* West Coast correspondent John Tynan, Pepper sounds like a parody of himself. His playing always had a swashbuckling quality in which the jagged rhythms of his phrases were set off by pregnant pauses, but here the phrases are uncommonly stark and the rests uncomfortably protacted. Put simply, Pepper sounds angry: "This is my session and I'll sulk if I want to." "The Route" is much better and noticeably unarranged, with Pepper's blues solo starting sweet as honey and slowly building to a heated conclusion. Baker follows, and he makes it clear that he wants to follow a different road map on this route. He begins gently, as though he were playing a lullaby to a tòddler, and only barely raises the energy level during the solo. He sounds as though he is back in the Mulligan Quartet and trying to be as low-key as possible.

This playing at cross-purposes is representative of the whole session. Baker and Pepper (and for that matter Kamuca) do not seem to be listening to each other. It is perhaps no coincidence that the altoist's best work from this session took place when Baker and Kamuca sat out, leaving Pepper to stretch out on the "Cherokee"-based "Ol' Croix." This gradual attrition, whether planned or spontaneous, continued with Jolly departing and Pepper attempting two numbers with just bass and drums. The whole event, especially given Bock's piecemeal way of releasing the music, has the look of a desperate attempt to find some combination of these talented musicians that might click.

Follow-up work from a Halloween date follows a similar formula. Again Baker and Pepper are joined by a third horn player, this time tenor saxophonist Phil Urso. Again a guest arranger is brought in, this time Jimmy Heath, who relies heavily on his own compositions. The addition of pianist Carl Perkins is quite welcome, especially in light of the exceptional later collaborations between Perkins and Pepper, and the supporting presence of Curtis Counce and Lawrence Marable promised a first-rate recording date. While a step above the first session, this second Baker–Pepper pairing still gets bogged down by the overly elaborate arrangements and the unnecessary third horn. One craves hearing just Pepper and Baker, backed by the rhythm section, work their way through some standards.

Perhaps part of the problem was simply that, for all their shared peculiarities of lifestyle, Pepper and Baker never really warmed up to each other as individuals. Baker, in an unprecedented display of prudery, has gone on record as being aghast at Pepper's lifestyle. Pepper, in contrast, stops short of this pot-calling-the-kettle-black mentality. He remained oddly silent on the subject of Baker. It comes as some surprise that Pepper had absolutely nothing to say about Baker during the course of some five hundred pages of *Straight Life*. In many articles published on Pepper, the journalist or interviewer reached for the obvious comparison with Baker, but Art never did so. This uncharacteristic reticence combined with the duo's surprisingly few collaborations suggests that some hidden feud or bad blood separated the two. Perhaps the answer is simpler still: Each may have seen too much of himself in the other.

Despite the mixed results of the Baker collaboration, these works have been reissued in many formats and are widely known. The same cannot be said unfortunately, for the masterful work Pepper recorded a short time later for Omegatape. These January 1958 performances are far less known than the celebrated work with Miles's rhythm section, but they are no less compelling. If one is looking for a neglected Pepper masterpiece from the 1950s, this is where to go. The reason for the neglect no doubt stems from the strange fact that these performances were originally issued solely on reel-to-reel tape format, and thus were unavailable to the vast majority of jazz record buyers. These electrifying performances, long overlooked, should now take their rightful place as key jazz recordings from the late 1950s.

The original session was instigated by Manny Koppelman, a sometime record producer with no track record in jazz. In early 1958, he brought Pepper's working quartet into a small Hollywood studio to record a project for what he hoped would be a growing home market for reel-to-reel tapes. Even then Pepper and his bandmates must have realized that this was a fairly arcane project, not likely to be widely heard, and this perhaps contributed to the relaxed informality of the session. Over a dozen successful takes were made, possibly in a single session, of a uniformly high quality.

The supporting cast of Carl Perkins, Chuck Flores, and Ben Tucker may be less well known than the Garland/Chambers/Philly Joe unit, but on the strength of these works they must be considered one of the strongest rhythm sections on the West Coast during the decade. Perkins's tremendous talents were, of course, no secret in Los Angeles. Although his reputation never made much headway on the East Coast (despite the deep admiration Miles Davis had for his ability), he retains a cult following among California jazz aficionados some quarter-century after his death. January 1958—some six weeks before Perkins's death—was a fruitful period for the pianist, with the Pepper date as well as sessions with Curtis Counce and Harold Land producing outstanding work. Pepper told *Downbeat* in October of that year that Perkins's work on the Omegatape recordings was the finest of the pianist's career. Pepper's praise, at least on this occasion, represented neither empty hype nor sentimental eulogizing.

As for the other members of the band, Flores and Tucker were not viewed as major innovators in West Coast jazz during the 1950s, but you might think otherwise on the strength of these recordings. Bassist Tucker, a Tennessee native born in Nashville on December 13, 1930, graced the bands of Pepper, Bill Perkins, Warne Marsh, and Chico Hamilton before moving to New York in1959. Chuck Flores, a Californian born in Orange on January 5, 1935, had recorded with Shorty Rogers, Woody Herman, and Al Cohn, among others, by the time of the Omegatape date. Both were strong journeyman players on the LA scene, and both were at peak form for the Pepper/Perkins date. The band is tight and swings like crazy.

Some might attribute the cohesion of this group to their long experience as a working band. Yet though these four did in fact work together, their engagements were anything but steady. Flores recalls the band working on no more than a half-dozen occasions between 1956 and 1958. Pepper's prison record may, in fact, have resulted in a blacklisting in many Southern California nightspots. In any event, work for the altoist was sporadic at best. Moreover, when the band did work, Perkins was never a permanent member, often being replaced by Russ Freeman or Pete Jolly. Yet this was as close as Pepper ever got to a working unit during the decade, and the chemistry between the band members is quite apparent. All three musicians had also recorded with Pepper in the past, Flores and Tucker in particular having shared several sessions with him.

The previous May, *Downbeat*'s John Tynan had reviewed the group during their two-week stay at the Tiffany Club. "Pepper never has sounded better," Tynan wrote. "The sidemen provide superior support and solo well. Eastern exposure is strongly recommended—fast."[17] Despite Tynan's admonition, Pepper received virtually no East Coast exposure with this group—or any other of his bands from the 1950s. However, the recorded evidence suggests that this band might have taken Manhattan by storm with its easy mastery of a variety of musical moods. On "Without a Song" Pepper's opening break sets a powerful bluesy mood, and from then on it sounds as though he and Perkins are trying to outdo each other in down-home funkiness—a duel that culminates in a memorable series of exchanges between the two soloists. "Fascinating Rhythm" serves as an ideal up-tempo feature for Pepper—Gershwin wrote the melody, but its quirky syncopation sounds like something Pepper would compose himself—and he stretches out comfortably on its changes. The rap against Perkins was that he couldn't play ballads, but on "Body and Soul" he takes a majestic two-handed solo that proves otherwise, while Pepper merely states the melody, but with a kind of conviction that looks forward to his anguish-laden later work. The all too short Latin vamp leading into "Begin the Beguine" was also anticipatory: His later extended use of such vamps would bring out the very best in Pepper, so much so that they would come to dwarf the song they introduced or completed. Here the vamp lingers briefly before settling into a comfortable medium-groove rendition of this convoluted (a 108-measure-long form!) Cole Porter composition.

Pepper's large-group collaborations with Marty Paich struck a different vein entirely. Both Pepper and Paich had been impressed with Gerry Mulligan's ten-piece group, and they decided to emulate that instrumentation, but the similarity with the Mulligan band ended there. Their conception was to create a hotter, more bop-oriented sound than typically found in the nonets and tentettes that were a staple of West Coast jazz during the 1950s. Paich recalls that the original model for the *Art Pepper plus Eleven* album was not, as most have assumed, the Miles Davis Nonet or the similar ensembles headed by Rogers and Mulligan but the small combo music of Charlie Parker.

> Lester Koenig, who owned Contemporary records, put us together and said, "Why don't we do an album of Charlie Parker songs?" That's exactly the way it came about. So I got together with Art and we had about 25 songs, then it got down to 20, then down to 15, and it got down to the normal 10 or 11 songs that were on the album. . . . The Charlie Parker stuff up until that time was just done with two front line, alto and trumpet. . . . Our idea was to do the same thing with a band.[18]

Certainly the influence of the Miles Davis Nonet is not totally absent in these recordings, but to focus on that element alone is to miss most of the story. The enduring appeal of these performances resides in their willingness to break out of the Miles/Evans/Mulligan mold, to combine the birth of the cool with the coming of age of the hot. In this regard, Pepper was the ideal soloist. He had deep roots in the cool, melodic approach followed by Miles and Mulligan, but he also instinctively knew how to push up the energy level of a performance, how to kick a band into overdrive. His unique blending of gentle lyricism and raw passion brought the Paich arrangements to life.

tears inside

Marty Paich is one of the unsung heroes of West Coast jazz. His personal lifestyle had none of the flamboyance and eccentricity of his long-time friend and collaborator Art Pepper's, and his years of extended labors in the studio make it all too easy to overlook his contributions to jazz. Difficult to pigeonhole, Marty Paich followed an idiosyncratic musical development almost from the start. Paich was born January 23, 1925, in Oakland, California, and his early musical background was equally distanced from the New Orleans revivalism and the contrasting blues sounds, both of which contributed to Oakland's musical orientation during his adolescence. In 1940, while Lu Watters was forming his Yerba Buena Jazz Band in that city, Paich was still playing his first instrument—the accordion! Even in the ancient years before World War II, this was a rare starting point for a jazz musician: "I came from a very nonmusical family, and it was just the fact that they liked me to bring the accordion along, so that when we went to picnics and stuff like that, I would play."

While in high school Paich added the trumpet to his repertoire. These two instruments remained his chief musical outlets until he was assigned to an air force band during his service career. "There was no pianist in the band that I was attached to, an air force band. And being that I was the accordion player, closest to the keyboard, they said, 'Paich, sit at the piano.' My right hand was all right, but I had no left hand at all." Under the necessity of learning a new instrument, Paich eventually developed into a first-class jazz pianist—a talent that has been overshadowed by his greater recognition as an arranger. His trio album on Mode from the 1950s, for example, shows a side of this musician which rarely surfaced in later years.

Paich's interest in orchestrating, however, was no late addition to his musical arsenal, for his precosity in this regard was nothing short of amazing: "I started arranging when I was about twelve years old. . . . By the time I was sixteen years old I was actually selling my arrangements, I think for about $20 or $25." This description of early-blooming musical talent is no idle boast. "Martin Paich's terrific crew is a leader's dream come true," wrote *Downbeat* correspondent Dixon Gray in 1942 of the then seventeen-year-old prodigy.[19] "The boys have worked like demons and have outclassed anything of like size or style in the area." The band's "solid jive" featured Paich's arrangements for "four saxes, four rhythm and seven brass including Mart's trumpet." The notice concludes by announcing the group's intention to tour—high hopes that came to nought when the band folded within a few months. Paich's "street smart" arranging skills were refined by periods of study at San Francisco State and, after the war, by continued work at the Los Angeles Conservatory, from which he received a master's degree in composition with high honors in 1951. The GI Bill allowed him to study with composers outside the conservatory faculty, and Paich took advantage of this leeway to begin working under Mario Castelnuovo-Tedesco: "I spent four years with him being my composition and orchestration teacher. And that's how I got ninety percent of my formal knowledge." His work with Castelnuovo-Tedesco involved no explicit study of jazz, and Paich's assignments included the writing of two string quartets, a woodwind trio, classical overtures, and a symphony.

Over the next decade Paich divided his time between his work as a pianist, with a diverse group of bandleaders ranging from Shorty Rogers to Peggy Lee, and his increasing activities as an arranger/composer. In addition to his work with Pepper, Paich's arranging for Mel Tormé, Anita O'Day, and Dave Pell stand out from the period. Also noteworthy was a sporadically recorded big band under Paich's leadership. The Marty Paich Big Band, in its various configurations, featured some of the finest West Coast players of the day, including Pepper, Jack Sheldon, Bob Cooper, Conte Candoli, Bill Perkins, and Herb Geller. For the band's June 1957 sessions for Cadence (later reissued on the Discovery label), Paich still held the piano chair in his ensemble, but by the time of his 1959 Warner Brothers project he had relinquished that spot to Russ Freeman. By the close of the 1950s, Paich had almost completely abandoned his performing career.

The Paich big band sessions for Warner Brothers, coming only a few weeks after the recording of *Art Pepper plus Eleven*, serve in many ways as a counterpart to that work. Once again Pepper is featured prominently, and Paich, relying heavily on Ellington compositions, shows that he has also learned Duke's technique of fitting the arrangement to the players involved. On "It Don't Mean a Thing (If It Ain't Got That Swing)" and "Violets for Your Furs," the charts are perfectly built around Pepper's sound. The collaborations between these two artists remain among the most satisfying meetings of musical minds West Coast jazz produced. Paich recognized this compatibility and went out of his way to include Pepper as often as possible in the various projects he pursued—for Tormé, Jesse Belvin, the Hi-Los, and others—at a time when Pepper's drug-related notoriety made him *persona non grata* in most studio sessions. Between 1958 and 1960, Paich was directly or indirectly responsible for almost half of the recordings in the Pepper discography. Although many of these sessions find the altoist making only an occasional contribution as a soloist, still Paich's advocacy was vital in documenting much of Pepper's recorded legacy from this period. Paich recalls:

> Art would not conform like the other musicians in town. . . . He was such a devoted saxophone player, he didn't want to try to double on flute or do any of the stuff that the usual musicians had to do in order to make a living. So a lot of guys didn't hire him for that reason. I hired him because he was such a great alto saxophone player that I had to have that sound on my records. . . . When I first heard Art Pepper I just couldn't believe what a beautiful sound he had. . . . He and Chet Baker were, I think, the two most important people in West Coast jazz.

Paich's sensitivity to Pepper's distinctive talent is evident throughout *Art Pepper plus Eleven.* Other arrangers had been able to capture specific sides of Pepper's musical personality;—Shorty Rogers, for example, had created several successful settings to feature the lyrical quality in Pepper's ballad work—but Paich was able to develop settings that wrapped perfectly around the full range of Pepper's sound, not only utilizing his alto voice in different contexts, but also effectively exploiting his seldom-heard playing on clarinet and tenor sax. The former finds perhaps its ultimate bebop expression on "Anthropology," while the tenor solo on "Move" ranks among the finest of Pepper's career. He comes out of the opening ensemble with a simple repetition of a single note, but the quality of swing he is able to put into that one note is remarkable. Pepper was a master of precisely this kind of device; the repetition was almost like a melodic stutter, an opening incantation, a moment of hesitation that throws the listener temporarily off balance. From this musical mantra, Pepper moves into a free-flowing, rapid-fire phrase that cuts through the initial tension. At their best, as on this solo, Pepper's improvisations seemed to suggest that he was discovering his craft anew each time he played. Listening was like watching a child just learning to ride a bicycle, fearful that at any moment he would topple, when suddenly he balances himself, picks up speed, and races off with the wind. Earlier in his career, Pepper's solos seemed to demonstrate his alto virtuosity at every opportunity, but by the middle of the 1950s, he had learned to keep such displays in reserve for the most telling moment. By the time of *Meets the Rhythm Section* or *Art Pepper plus Eleven,* he had become a master at merely suggesting a phrase; a few hurried notes convey the impression that one is hearing just the extracts of a more elaborate musical demonstration, which has been compressed and concentrated for our benefit.

Pepper's nonmusical life continued to show all the terrible symptoms, if anything aggravated, of the addict's lifestyle. To support his drug habit,

Pepper's day-to-day activities began to include burglaries, shoplifting, forgeries, armed robbery (in a reference to the last in *Straight Life*, the only regret Pepper espouses is that he wished his partners had let him hold the gun). This was the lowest point Pepper would reach in his whole career, and it was a period that also, in many ways, would seem to be his last hurrah. After 1960, fifteen years would go by before Pepper would again record as a group leader. For all intents and purposes his career appeared to be over, but this last year of recording found Pepper at absolute top form. It was almost as if he sensed that he needed to make these musical statements while still in a position to do so.

The year 1960 is chock full of recording projects in which Pepper's music literally explodes out of the starting gate, including three leader dates of the highest caliber. On Leap Day, Pepper reunited with the Miles Davis rhythm section, this time comprised of Wynton Kelly, Paul Chambers, and Jimmy Cobb, with trumpeter Conte Candoli joining the front line. As with the earlier *Meets the Rhythm Section* date, this project was squeezed into one day, with half of the project devoted to basic blues and rhythm changes. On "Rhythm-a-Ning," Pepper plays with the fate-tempting abandon that would come to characterize his later style. "Diane," named for Pepper's second wife, is aptly described by Martin Williams, in the liner notes to the album, as "an *emotionally* sustained piece of improvised impressionism" and forms a kind of Sadie Hawkins Day tribute to a relationship on the rocks. ("The tune was way too beautiful for her," was Pepper's later comment.)[20] The other ballad, "Why Are We Afraid?"—an André Previn piece Pepper had played on the soundtrack of the film *The Subterraneans*—is only a notch lower in quality. *Intensity* and *Smack Up*, two other albums from this time, are equally powerful. The former finds Pepper teaming up with pianist Dolo Coker in a hard-hitting series of performances, while the latter shows Pepper digging into daring material, including Ornette Coleman's "Tears Inside."

These projects, despite their marked excellence, could do little to boost Pepper's career. By the time of their release Pepper was back behind bars, this time at San Quentin.

time on my hands

The name notwithstanding, no patron saint—Quentin or otherwise—looks over this stark federal penitentiary, incongruously situated in prosperous Marin County, California. The city and its eponymous institution are named for an Indian leader Quintin, slain on the site sometime in the last century, who was mysteriously canonized when the township was founded. Other oddities persist in the most desolate of West Coast prisons; perhaps the most striking is the perennial crop of outstanding jazz musicians brought within its walls. In 1942, a San Quentin–based dance band gained enough renown to broadcast regularly on the Mutual radio network. The group was, needless to say, unable to follow up this success by going on the road—although the band members would no doubt have been willing. The group's theme song was—what else could it be?—"Time on My Hands."

Each of the California prisons of the 1950s had a character of its own: Chino provided a minimum security environment for relatively nonviolent offenders; Soledad was known for its vocational programs; Vacaville was a medical institution/prison; Folsom was for older offenders who were seen as beyond rehabilitation. San Quentin was reserved for the most violent younger prisoners, repeat offenders with serious records. Dupree Bolton, another jazz musician turned professional inmate, declared to me without hesitation that "San Quentin was the worst"—and Bolton's twenty-plus years of experience in the Big House give his judgment some weight. Prison is never a picnic, but this Marin County institution was perhaps the worst the West Coast had to offer.

After his October 1960 arrest for heroin possession and subsequent conviction, Pepper was incarcerated at San Quentin. He was sentenced to two to twenty years—an ambiguous although comparatively light punishment given his previous convictions. Pepper was a three-time loser, with a record that could have resulted in a sentence that would last the rest of his life. But Pepper viewed this as harsh treatment. It was, he believed, a response not to his criminal record, but to his unwillingness to give evidence against his connections. With his topsy-turvy sense of values, Pepper prided himself more on this fidelity to his dealers than on almost any other moral decision related in his life story. Not being a "rat," a "snitch," was his recurring boast, but one that must have provided little consolation in the degrading surroundings in which he now found himself. To survive, Pepper amplified on the technique he had developed while at Terminal Island. He pretended to be crazy, adopting a repertoire of eccentric behaviors in an attempt to keep other inmates at bay: stumbling, mumbling, slobbering, throwing things—a whole series of oddball actions designed to give him breathing space. During his working hours, he labored in the paymaster's office in the South Block, near the walkway to the gas chamber. In his spare time he played music and looked for ways to get high.

In 1964, Pepper came up for parole. Shelly Manne wrote to the authorities, indicating that he had a job waiting for Pepper at the Manne Hole, Shelly's Los Angeles club. This made the difference, and soon Pepper was gigging at the Manne Hole, followed by an engagement at the Jazz Workshop in San Francisco. Pepper's style had undergone a major transformation since his last period on the outside, largely under the influence of John Coltrane and, to a slightly lesser extent, Ornette Coleman. Pepper's new sound was something of a surprise, if not a disappointment, to those familiar with his earlier work. For a while he seemed to have lost much of the individuality that had characterized his seminal work from the 1950s. But with time the altoist was able to blend these new influences into his own sound effectively.

During the comeback years of the 1970s, Pepper was a driven soloist with a slashing, pointillistic style that cut to the quick. Pepper's up-tempo numbers were cathartic in their fiery discharges, but his ballads were even more remarkable. On late ballads, such as "Everything Happens to Me," "Goodbye," and especially "Patricia," with its gripping coda, Pepper pulled together his whole range of musical and personal experiences into a riveting sound that mixed equal doses of the raw and the cooked. The lessons of jazz history suggest that it is music made best by young men, but Pepper seemed ready to turn the tables on this truism. Has any saxophonist played with such newfound energy so late in life? These late recordings stand as crowning achievements in Pepper's career. Unlike virtually every other musician examined in this book, Pepper created his greatest work at the end of his life, long after the glory days of West Coast jazz had passed.

When I interviewed Art Pepper, only a few weeks before his death, he showed the vitality of a player at the start of his career. He spoke of his plans and goals for the future—an album with Toshiko Akiyoshi's band, a recording of "down-home" bluesy music, another solo saxophone project, more performances in New York, and—his big goal—seeing his picture on the cover of Downbeat. None of these ambitions came to pass. Within a month, Art Pepper was dead, struck down by a cerebral hemorrhage. Toward the end he knew his days were numbered. He recorded prolifically in an attempt to set down as much music as he could while he could.

At that last stage in his career, Pepper's monomania would settle for nothing less than being acknowledged as the greatest alto saxophonist in jazz. Such arrogance may have been off-putting, but his playing was backing him up. His was heady music; seeing Art Pepper even on an off-night, at this time, was a memorable experience. There may be no one best player in today's pluralistic jazz environment, but if such an accolade existed, Pepper had to be in the running. Even back east, where he had rarely played, word of his music was going strong, and after his death a consensus slowly began to develop granting him the status of a jazz master. The praise he so wanted to hear, and so long eluded him, is now a matter of record.

CHAPTER FIFTEEN

LA Hard Bop

joy spring

Max Roach came to California in the fall of 1953 to replace Shelly Manne as drummer with Howard Rumsey's Lighthouse All-Stars. Despite his growing reputation as the outstanding exponent of modern jazz drumming, Roach had been working almost exclusively as a sideman. He had recorded as a leader for Debut—the label he had founded with Charles Mingus—but, by his own admission, had not yet "got seriously involved in bandleading."[1] In California, he was asked by jazz impresario Gene Norman to start a group of his own. Promised an extended booking at the California Club, Roach agreed to form a quintet. His next move was to send for a young trumpeter from back east named Clifford Brown. These two musicians, one already famous in the jazz world and the other soon to be so, were about to become the most prominent members in one of the finest—if not the best—jazz combos of the early 1950s.

Brown's work in jazz was as striking for its architectonic structure as for its emotional immediacy. And this quest for order was as much a part of Clifford's life as it was integral to his music. Studies of highly gifted youngsters have revealed that in three areas of human endeavor—music, mathematics, and chess—talent becomes apparent at an especially young age. Clifford Brown's biography (as well as those of many other jazz musicians) substantiates the view that these three highly structured ways of seeing the universe may be correlated. Brown showed early ability in all three disciplines. Born in Wilmington, Delaware, on October 30, 1930, he revealed, first and foremost, a prodigious musical talent. In addition to quickly mastering the trumpet, which he began in his early teens, he pursued studies in piano and arranging while still in high school. When he entered Delaware State College, he started as a mathematics major, only

switching to music after transferring to Maryland State. Brown's complementary skills as a chess player have been attested to by, among others,
his bandmate Max Roach. And Roach should know: He was a fine player
in his own right, who made the all-city chess team when still back in
Brooklyn. By his late teens, Brown's career as a promising musician had
come to overshadow these subsidiary interests. Even so, the ordered universe of mathematics and chess may have found its way into the trumpeter's music. At its best, his playing combined the raw passion of jazz with
the precision and logic of composed music.

In a macabre foreshadowing, Brown was injured in an automobile
accident in June 1950. For almost a year his promising musical career was
placed on hold. His comeback was slow at first, and his first record date,
with Chris Powell and His Blue Flames, did not take place until March
1952, almost two years after the accident. Only six weeks later, however,
Brown was back in the studio again, this time with a much finer band
consisting of Lou Donaldson, Elmo Hope, Percy Heath, and Philly Joe Jones.
From this point until his tragic early death in a second auto accident in
June 1956, Brown would record and perform regularly with the finest musicians in jazz. His few recordings are among the most important jazz
legacies from the 1950s.

By the time of his fateful journey to California, he had already impressed many with his precocious skills on the trumpet. Both Charlie Parker and Dizzy Gillespie were strong supporters of the young musician:
Parker's glowing recommendation had convinced Art Blakey to add Brownie
to his band for a brief period earlier in 1954, while Gillespie had been
among the first to tell Max Roach about the extraordinary talent of this
future colleague. In addition to these illustrious connections, Brown had
already gained valuable experience recording and playing with Tadd Dameron, Lionel Hampton, J. J. Johnson, and Gigi Gryce. These early sideman
sessions, as well as a few dates as a leader from this period, demonstrated
that Brown had already achieved a mature, poised style and a polished
virtuosity well before his twenty-third birthday.

Perhaps the most striking element of this provocative trumpet style
was Brown's distinctive sound. When many aspiring bop trumpeters were
willing to sacrifice tonal clarity in order to play fast, Brown proved that it
was possible to have it both ways: One could (or at least Brown could)
play complex, rapid-fire melodic lines while still maintaining a warm, well-
rounded tone. Building on the legacy of Fats Navarro, Brown could boast
of the purest, cleanest sound of any of the young bebop trumpeters. One
could well imagine Brown playing the classical trumpet repertoire—much
as Wynton Marsalis would do a generation later—without having to alter
his basic musical conception. (Nor is it a coincidence that Marsalis's earliest jazz work showed the strong influence of Clifford Brown. Brown was

the perfect role model for this latter-day master of both the classical and jazz idioms.) This keen sense of sound provided the foundation for Brown's other musical virtues: his melodic creativity, his speed of execution, his sense of phrasing and dynamics.

The Brown/Roach group was perhaps the strongest working jazz band of its day, the ensembles of Parker and Gillespie notwithstanding. At first, however, the personnel of the band underwent a number of changes. Roach's initial choice for the saxophone chair, Sonny Stitt, made the trip out west with Brown, only to leave the band after a few weeks. Stitt's replacement was Teddy Edwards, a powerful tenorist who had made a name for himself on recordings with Howard McGhee and Dexter Gordon a few years before. Edwards was playing in the San Francisco area during the summer of 1954 but returned to Southern California when Roach asked him to finish out the group's engagement at the California Club.

Although Edwards did not remain with the group when it went on the road a short while later—by then Harold Land had taken his place—he participated in the group's first recording for Gene Norman. This record proved to be Edwards's only jazz session until his 1958 date with Leroy Vinnegar—some four years later! Two other participants in this first recording, pianist Carl Perkins and bassist George Bledsoe, were also only briefly part of the quintent; they were eventually replaced by Richie Powell and George Morrow. Several technical problems mar these otherwise excellent performances: Awkward splices edit out much of Perkins's and Edwards's solos; the sound balance is poor, with Bledsoe and Perkins often disappearing behind Roach's drumming. Moreover, the resulting packaging on Gene Norman's GNP label (at least in the version in my collection) gives neither recording date nor place and provides incorrect personnel information. However, the recorded music overcomes the hatchet job done by GNP. Brown plays throughout with a complete, awe-inspiring command of the horn, while Roach takes several extended solos that find him at top form. Edwards's and Perkins's contributions are more difficult to evaluate because of the radical splicing of their improvisations. In light of their work elsewhere, as well as the tantalizing passages included on the released album, one suspects that they might have worked out as well as their eventual replacements with the quintet. In any event, by the time the Brown/Roach group returned to the studio in early August, the sidemen had changed to the very successful combination of Harold Land, Richie Powell, and George Morrow.

In the interim, Brown had participated in a very different session for Richard Bock's Pacific label. Tenor saxophonist Jack Montrose was called in as an arranger and proceeded to create a distinctive setting for Brownie's horn, one very different from the hard bop orientation of the Roach group. Montrose's tight, medium-groove arrangements were typical of the "West

Coast sound," but to counterbalance this tendency toward the cool, Montrose wisely drew on some of the more hard-swinging musicians in the area to complement Brown's energetic style. Zoot Sims and Bob Gordon both proved to be compatible front-line foils for the young trumpeter.

Sims would have been one of the most important musicians on the coast had he not left Los Angeles while still in his teens to initiate a career that kept him increasingly on the road or on the eastern seaboard. The son of a vaudeville husband-and-wife comedy team, Sims was born in Inglewood, California, on October 29, 1925, and grew up in the nearby community of Hawthorne. "My parents were pretty casual," Sims would later say. "I was the only one [of seven children] whose name was spelled right on the birth certificate."[2] Even so, his given name of John Haley Sims did not survive long into his career. By the time he went on the road, at age sixteen, with Kenny Baker's band, John Haley had already been christened by the bandleader as "Zoot." "He put these supposedly funny nicknames on the front of his music stands—Scoot, Voot, Zoot—and I ended up behind the Zoot stand, and it stuck." By 1949 Sims had settled permanently in New York, but Montrose managed to enlist the services of the tenorist during one of his occasional return visits to Southern California.

Bob Gordon, another sideman on the Brown sessions for Pacific Jazz, also might have made a major impact on West Coast jazz under different circumstances. A driving and creative baritone saxophonist, Gordon had created a distinctive style that stood out from the then predominant influence of Gerry Mulligan. Indeed, Gordon drew mostly on influences outside the baritone tradition. When he was asked by Leonard Feather, as part of the latter's research for his *Encyclopedia of Jazz*, to cite his favorite musicians on his instrument, he mentioned sessionmates Zoot Sims and Jack Montrose.

Born in St. Louis on June 11, 1928, Gordon came to Los Angeles in 1948 to study at the Westlake College of Music. In the early 1950s he participated in a series of successful recordings as a sideman for various West Coast jazz luminaries, including Chet Baker, Shelly Manne, Shorty Rogers, Red Norvo, Pete Rugolo, Bill Holman, and Maynard Ferguson.* In May 1954, only a few weeks before the sessions with Clifford Brown, Gordon recorded as a leader for Pacific Jazz. The resulting album, *Meet*

---

*Gordon discographer Gerard Hoogeveen suggests that Gordon's first recordings were made in 1949 with the Roy Porter Big Band for the Knockout label, while other sources suggest that Tony Ortega held the baritone chair. A check with the original copy of the form Gordon filled out for Leonard Feather's *Encyclopedia of Jazz*, now on file at the Rutgers archives, shows that Gordon himself cited his 1951 recording with Shelly Manne as his first date. This, combined with Gordon's absence from the other Porter recordings, as well as from Hunter Hancock's listing of the Porter personnel in a 1948 article on the band in the *Los Angeles Sentinel*, casts some doubt on Hoogeveen's assertion.

Mr. Gordon, showed that the young baritonist was on the brink of emerging as a major voice in the Southern California jazz scene. A short while later *Downbeat* awarded him its New Star Award on baritone sax. On August 28, 1955, Gordon was killed in a car accident while driving to San Diego to appear in a concert with Pete Rugolo's band.

In addition to Gordon and Sims, Montrose drew on a strong rhythm section consisting of Russ Freeman and Shelly Manne, with Joe Mondragon and Carson Smith alternating on bass. Stu Williamson, the brass-playing brother of pianist Claude Williamson, joined on valve trombone. For the first session, Montrose wrote arrangements for two Brown compositions, which eventually became widely known standards: "Joy Spring" and "Daahoud." Brown would record these songs again with the Max Roach group less than a month later, and it is interesting to compare the versions. The Pacific Jazz release features more elaborate arrangements, with Montrose relying on clever introductions and interludes to support his four-horn voicings of the Brown melodies. Brown, in response, counts off the two songs at slightly more relaxed tempos than on the later recording and settles into a comfortable groove during his solos. His playing is tastefully impeccable, with Sims and Gordon also contributing strong solos.

A month later Brown returned to the studio with the same front line and recorded four more Montrose arrangements. Two other Brown compositions, "Tiny Capers" and "Bones for Jones," were taped that day, along with two standards. "Tiny Capers" boasted an especially infectious melody with a baroque twist and an aspiring set of blowing changes. "Blueberry Hill" was also given a striking treatment, with Brown dancing over the shifting meters of Montrose's reconfiguration of the melody. A few more sessions along this line, and Clifford might have gained a reputation as a quintessential West Coast trumpeter.

There was little danger of that given the nature of his continuing work with Max Roach and company. Early August 1954 found the Roach/Brown unit camping out at the Capitol Studios in Los Angeles for a series of recording sessions. A date from the second week in August paired the two easterners with some of the more sympathetic locals for a loose jam session date. All but one of the numbers recorded that day last over fifteen minutes, as each soloist stretched out at length over the changes. Altoists Herb Geller and Joe Maini, Brown's front-line companions, were among the most bop-oriented of the white Los Angeles saxophonists of the day, and both fit in well with the musical proceedings.

Joe Maini was "probably one of the most talented [musicians]—raw talent—that ever lived," Terry Gibbs has commented. "He could play anything in any way. He was one of the greatest bebop alto and tenor players. He didn't own a clarinet, but he could play the hell out of a clarinet. He could sightread anything."[3] Born in Providence, Rhode Is-

land, on February 8, 1930, Maini began playing professionally at age fourteen. After a year and a half in a federal hospital in Kentucky on narcotics
charges, he came to California in the early 1950s. In the Golden State, he
developed a reputation—but often for things other than music. Maini was
perhaps better known as a sidekick of comedian Lenny Bruce and for his
wild demeanor both on and off the bandstand. Maini's taste for the extreme led to his death from a gunshot wound on May 8, 1964. Handling
a friend's gun—some say he was playing Russian roulette—Maini shot
himself. He was thirty-four years old.

Herb Geller, born in Los Angeles on November 2, 1928, was another
member of the Lenny Bruce clique—with a complementary taste for the
absurd and outrageous. Geller once devised a Rube Goldberg set-up for a
proposed Bruce bit in which a saxophone played "Groovin' High." The
twist: The horn was being blown not by a musician, but by a vacuum
cleaner. Starting on saxophone at age eight, Geller was initially inspired
by the playing of Benny Carter but later evolved into a high-energy altoist
in a Charlie Parker vein. Geller had apprenticed in New York with his
wife, pianist Lorraine Walsh Geller, for a short period after their marriage
in the early 1950s. Returned to Southern California in 1951, both the
Gellers became integral members of the Los Angeles jazz scene; Herb worked
with Howard Rumsey's Lighthouse All-Stars for some time, while Lorraine gigged with Shorty Rogers, Zoot Sims, and others. Both are featured
on strong recordings under Herb's leadership made for Emarcy—the same
label responsible for the date with Clifford Brown. Lorraine Geller died
from a heart attack in 1958, not long after recording her most successful
work as part of a quartet under the leadership of Red Mitchell. In more
recent years Herb Geller's career has found him most often based in Europe, where he continues to perform and record.

The week before the Maini/Geller session, the newly formed Brown/
Roach Quintet set down, during the course of four studio dates, what is
perhaps their most impressive body of work. As mentioned, both "Daahoud" and "Joy Spring" were recorded again, and Brown managed to give
both pieces fresh interpretations—indeed his treatment of "Joy Spring,"
with the comfortable virtuosity and easy eloquence of his solo, stands out
as the definitive performance of this now widely played jazz standard. In
general, the quintet succeeded remarkably in putting its own stamp on a
wide body of disparate compositions during these successive sessions. "De-
lilah," a movie theme that smacks of Hollywood superficiality in its original film version, is given a glistening jazz treatment. "Parisian Thorough-
fare" had been known, before the Brown/Roach recording, as an unusual
Bud Powell piano sketch—one whose lineage drew on French impressionism rather than bebop and Bird. Powell had recorded it as an ethereal
piano solo and as a fragmented, unsuccessful (and for a long time unre-

leased) trio number. Brown and Roach take this lovely, classically oriented melody and give it a powerful jazz foundation, complete with musical imitations of Paris street life à la Gershwin. A few oldtime standards—"Stompin' at the Savoy," "Ghost of a Chance," and "I Get a Kick out of You"—show up in new versions, the last in a clever Sonny Stitt arrangement with shifting time signatures that is reminiscent of Montrose's writing for the earlier Brown session.

This fastidious attention to material and arrangements is all the more striking given the hard-blowing orientation of the band. The Brown/Roach group boasted as fine a group of soloists as any working jazz combo of its day. The band could have easily gotten by, even have flourished, with unambitious head charts that simply gave the players room to stretch out. However, the band's new approach to jazz signaled the birth of hard bop. For years many, if not most, bebop performances had followed a strict formula of playing intricate melodies with straightforward unison horn lines. The main emphasis was on blowing solos over standard changes. Brown/Roach articulated a different sound, which expanded the tonal range of the combo with more elaborate polyphonic melodies, careful arrangements, and original chord progressions. These elements would later become staples of the Blue Note sound and in that form would be seen by many as the epitome of East Coast jazz.

Yet in the case of the Brown/Roach band, there likely was a West Coast influence on this group-oriented concept. Max Roach's work at the Lighthouse had found him working with similar musical values, making tight combo arrangements as important as the solos, and jazz composition on original chord changes the standard practice. Brown's music, as we have seen through the Pacific Jazz recordings, also fit in seamlessly with a West Coast approach (while his powerful influence on West Coast trumpeters such as Shorty Rogers and Jack Sheldon has seldom been noticed). Such considerations argue for the view, increasingly common among critics, that the gap between east and west was not as wide as the 1950s stereotypes might imply. Yet they also suggest that the West Coast players were not, as is often charged, merely "stealing" the musical ideas of their East Coast counterparts; the influences went in both directions. *Pace* Kipling, the twain could meet.

the land of jazz

At a round-table discussion on West Coast jazz held in 1988, Buddy Collette offered a few words about fellow saxophonist Harold Land:

Harold"'s been one of the finest tenor players I've heard and I have hardly
heard a write-up about what this man has been doing through the years. . . .
I've known him for 30 years, 35 years, and he's been playing jazz morning,
noon and night. . . . In New York he would have gotten more.[4]

It is all too telling that Harold Land is best remembered in the jazz
world for the brief time he was performing on the East Coast with the
Clifford Brown/Max Roach Quintet. Land's thirty-five years of exceptional work since that time are often treated as an elaborate footnote to
this early apprenticeship. The recordings, however, tell no lies. They document Land's major contributions to jazz both during and after his work
with Brown and Roach. They reveal that he was one of the most potent
voices on the West Coast scene throughout the period.

Those aware of Land's origins in Houston, Texas, where he was born
on February 18, 1928, often hear a lingering Texas tenor sound in his
playing. In fact, Land and his family spent only a few months in the Lone
Star State. Soon his family moved to Arizona, and just a few years later
they settled in San Diego. At an early age Land began taking piano lessons, at the instigation of his mother, but switched to tenor after hearing
Coleman Hawkins's influential 1939 recording of "Body and Soul." After
graduating from San Diego High School, Land began working at the Creole Palace and other local clubs.

"There was a strong jazz scene in San Diego," Land recalls.[5] San
Diego may not have been the place to build a national reputation, but it
offered regular work for Land and several other local musicians. Land continues:

> Froebel Brigham was playing at the Palace. He's still playing in San Diego. I
> was eighteen or nineteen, and he was in his late twenties or early thirties.
> They had dancers, shows, comedians at the club, but we could play whatever
> we wanted until the show started and after it was done. We were playing
> modern jazz. Sonny Criss, Hampton Hawes, Teddy Edwards, and others would
> come down from LA and play there.

In the 1950s, some twenty clubs flourished in the black side of town—
none of which has survived to the present day![6] Brigham, the king of the
local trumpeters, had turned down offers to play outside San Diego from
Duke Ellington, Billy Eckstine, Andy Kirk, and others, in order to stay at
home with his wife and three children. He maintained a twenty-year association with the Creole Palace, a large hotel and restaurant complex on
Market Street between 2nd and 3rd. The building, torn down in the 1960s
to make way for an apartment complex, housed a twenty-five-room hotel,
bar, restaurant, and dancehall with seating for five hundred patrons. Along

with the smaller Black and Tan Club, the Palace was the center of jazz in the black community. As a member of Brigham's group, Land played at both venues as well as at frequent private parties.

In April of 1949, Brigham's group made its way to Los Angeles to record for the Savoy label. For the occasion the leader gave the young tenor saxophonist virtually all of the solo space. Land was a prized pupil, and Brigham was determined to use the occasion to feature the younger musician's talent. Forty years later, Brigham explained to me: "Harold Land was a very brilliant saxophone player, and I felt he was going to go out in the world whereas I was going to stay with my wife and three children. I was trying to boost Harold so when he went out in the world he would have a letter."[7] The resulting record sides show the truth of Brigham's judgment. Land, a few months after his twenty-first birthday, comes across as a powerful tenor player, still very much under the influence of Coleman Hawkins, but with a strong sound and a rich flow of ideas. A touch of rhythm-and-blues figures in his playing, a trademark that would later become less noticeable, but never totally absent. The first hints of a bebop influence are also evident—by this time Land was listening to the modern jazz recordings of Charlie Parker, Bud Powell, Don Byas, and others.

Soon Land decided to expand his musical horizons by moving to Los Angeles, where he found performance opportunities few and far between: "Things were a little rough at first. But it wasn't just for me, it was for a lot of young musicians. So we spent a lot of time playing at each other's houses. Like Eric Dolphy—we'd go over to his house and play all day long."[8] Dolphy had a small music studio in the back of his parents' house, where many of the local and visiting musicians would congregate. It was at the Dolphy residence that Clifford Brown first heard Land. Impressed with the young tenor player, Brown returned the following day with Max Roach. On the strength of what they heard, they offered Land a job with their band. The tenorist readily accepted. "I thought it was a good opportunity."

Indeed it was! Land was fully ready for this apprenticeship with one of the most high-profile bands in jazz. His early Coleman Hawkins sound had by now broadened to include a fluent command of the bebop idiom, complete with a polished technique that could navigate the most challenging progressions and tempos. Throughout his career Land has shown a continued ability to assimilate new sounds and musical ideas. First grounded in the music of the big band era tempered with a dose of R&B, Land later assimilated the modern jazz vocabulary and made it his own, just as, in the 1960s, he would adopt many of the musical mannerisms developed by John Coltrane and his followers. A restless stylist, Land has been the jazz leopard who continually tries to change his spots. His stint with the Brown/

Roach Quintet was no exception: For two years Land further refined his craft within the confines of this world-class ensemble, slowly forging a quintessential hard bop sound that would reach its fullest expression in his later work as a leader and with the Curtis Counce group.

After the brief flurry of recording activity in August 1954, the Brown/ Roach ensemble changed seaboards, a move that was almost inevitable given the strong East Coast roots of Brown, Roach, and Powell. The next time Land entered the studio with the quintet, in February of the following year, the setting had changed to New York, and, perhaps in a conscious reaction to the new locale, the music had inched up a notch in intensity. Land's brilliant set of variations on "The Blues Walk," recorded on February 24, 1955, ranks among his finest moments with the band. This high-powered blues features inspired solo contributions from Land, Brown, Powell, and Roach and culminates in a series of breathtaking chase exchanges between the trumpeter and tenorist.

Land's association with the quintet ended abruptly late in 1955 when he learned that his grandmother was terminally ill back in San Diego. He left the band behind in Chicago and immediately returned to California. After his grandmother's death, he decided to remain on the Pacific Coast: "Once I got back, I decided to stay. I hadn't seen my wife in a while because I had been on the road so much." At this point in his career, Land was beginning to gain deserved recognition as one of the leading saxophonists in jazz—recognition that eventually faded into the background after he returned to Los Angeles. By a curious chance, it was Land's replacement in the Brown/Roach quintet, Sonny Rollins, who would come to hold center stage among the modern jazz saxophonists of the mid- to late-1950s. Land's two predecessors in the band—Teddy Edwards and Sonny Stitt—met complementary fates: The eastbound Stitt enjoyed a blossoming career, while the West Coast stay-at-home Edwards languished. For Land, the departure from the East Coast, and its attendant critical limelight, put the tenorist's reputation in an odd situation: His work with the Brown/Roach Quintet continued (and continues) to be lauded and appreciated by many listeners who only have the vaguest notion of his later work. "I think that's why Eric [Dolphy] moved back east," Land speculates. "There have been so many talented musicians out here that haven't received the attention they deserve. If you didn't get exposure back east you were sort of written off."

The group Land joined shortly after his return to Los Angeles proved the truth of this generalization all too well. This new band, nominally led by bassist Curtis Counce, was something of a West Coast counterpart to the Brown/Roach Quintet. The Counce Quintet used the same instrumentation and practiced the same brand of fiery, hard bop—and with almost equal fluency. Counce, born in Kansas City on January 23, 1926, had set-

tled in Los Angeles in the mid-1940s and made his name gigging with
Wardell Gray, Benny Carter, and Billy Eckstine as well as serving as an
early member of the Roach/Brown Quintet. A strong bassist in a Jimmy
Blanton mold, Counce boasted a warm, full tone and rock-solid time.

Counce formed his band shortly after returning from a disastrous experience with the Stan Kenton band on a European tour. Counce had been
fired by Kenton because of a heated conflict between the bassist and another member of the band. Returning to Los Angeles, Counce formed a
quintet for an engagement at the Haig. The bassist gathered around him
a strong rhythmic foundation for his band with drummer Frank Butler
and pianist Carl Perkins. Trumpeter Jack Sheldon, a polished soloist who
bridged the cool and hot schools on the West Coast scene, joined Land in
the front line.

The Counce Quintet is one of the great neglected jazz bands of the
1950s. The reasons for this neglect are difficult to pinpoint. Harold Land
suggests that the group's lack of opportunities to perform on the East Coast
was the major obstacle: "The group never really got to travel beyond the
immediate area. I thought that was very unfortunate because it was a very
good group, very talented musicians. Frank Butler was playing at his peak
during that period, and Carl Perkins was sounding beautiful, Jack Sheldon
was sounding very good."[9] Other factors may have contributed to the
group's limited success: Certainly the Counce Quintet was difficult for the
jazz establishment to pigeonhole, if only because the group offered all those
qualities supposedly lacking in West Coast jazz during the 1950s. The band
featured a strong-blowing front line backed by a forceful rhythm section,
solid arrangements, and plenty of room for soloists. This was an East Coast
band in spirit if not in geography.

Even with its initial inability to develop a national reputation, the
quintet might have experienced a revival if not for the individual tragedies
of some of the band's members. Counce's death in 1963, coupled with the
earlier passing of Carl Perkins in 1958 (as well as Frank Butler's disappearance from the scene during much of the same period), meant that any
recognition of the quintet's virtues would be, by necessity, posthumous.
The continued interest in the group with the passing years, along with the
renewed availability of the quintet's several recordings, suggests that just
such after-the-fact recognition is now coming Counce's way.

The quintet's first recording, *Landslide*, from two October 1956 sessions, already indicated the many virtues of this group. Land's extroverted
tenor is well complemented by Sheldon's cooler trumpet work, but the
contribution of the rhythm section is perhaps the most distinctive element
here—few West Coast bands pushed the soloists quite so hard. This recording marked Frank Butler's first session, according to Nat Hentoff, yet
he shows the poise of an established veteran, especially on medium- to up-

tempo cookers such as "Sonar," "Landslide," and "A Fifth for Frank."
Butler and Land would prove on several later occasions that they were
ideal group mates, and even on this initial pairing their give-and-take is
quite striking. The only weak point on the album is the ballad performance
of "Time After Time"; the band doesn't hit a groove until almost the end
of the number, while the poor sound mix obscures much of Land's work.
Sheldon's background musings often overwhelm the tenor melody statement.

Perkins's playing is florid and unconvincing on this number, but he
more than makes up for it with his persuasive contributions to "Mia" and
"Sonar." Here his crisp right-hand lines take flight in a manner reminiscent of Hampton Hawes, but his powerful left-hand accents are pure Perkins. Perhaps his unusual way of holding his left hand accounts for this
appealing addition to his rhythmic vocabulary. Red Callender once referred to it as a "crablike" technique—Perkins's forearm would lie almost
parallel to the keyboard, and his fingers would play the keys from a side-
ways angle. Sometimes his left elbow would not only rest on the keyboard, but even play bass notes.

Bassist Leroy Vinnegar, a childhood friend of Perkins from his days
in Indianapolis, recalls the pianist developing this unusual attack as a matter of necessity: "He developed his way of holding his left arm as a kid.
He couldn't really reach the keyboard and he had to play on tiptoe. So he
had to play like that. He told me that he just kept on doing it when he
started sitting on the piano stool. He got the bass notes with his elbow
because back in Indianapolis he wasn't playing much with bass players—
there weren't many bass players in town."[10] This unusual approach to the
instrument was the impetus for much speculation on the part of other
musicians. "There was a story going round," recalls pianist Dick Whittington, "that when Carl came out from Indianapolis with his brother Ed,
who played bass, they had just one suit between them, which they would
share for gigs. . . . Supposedly Carl had some gigs, but by the time Ed
got the suit back, the elbow was worn out on the suit."[11]

These techniques, despite their makeshift origin, gave Perkins a left-
hand piano sound unlike any other. As Vinnegar describes it, Carl "not
only played the chords, he played the beauty in the chords—his own way."[12]
Whittington picks up on the same point: "He had a real keen sense of
harmony. Carl was the first person I heard before Bill Evans using superimposed chords. Everybody does it now, but back then Carl was one of the
few who would, say, put a G flat triad over a C7—that would give him
the sharp eleventh and the flat nine." Harold Land explains: "His chord
constructions were beautiful; his solos always interesting; he knew how
to use space so that his phrasing was beautiful too. And there was no end
to the funk in his playing."

Perkins's funkiness was honed during his early work in the blossoming rhythm-and-blues idiom with Big Jay McNeely in 1948 and 1949. After his stint with McNeely, Perkins settled in California permanently. Born in Indianapolis on August 16, 1928, Perkins began piano at age nine and, like many of the local greats, was largely self-taught. After settling on the West Coast, he quickly established himself as a major presence on the Los Angeles scene. In 1950 he performed with Miles Davis, with whom he remained close for the remainder of his life. "Miles and Carl were good friends," Vinnegar explains. "When Miles came to town, he'd head straight for Carl. They'd be locked up for hours. I'd come by; and they would be playing. I think that's where Miles got some of his soft, pretty stuff."

This unique combination of the pretty and the funky, the percussive rhythmic feel and the harmonic depth, gave Carl a fresh and distinctive sound that stood out on the West Coast during the 1950s. Although Perkins was self-taught, his approach was not created in a musical vacuum. "I asked Carl once, this must have been around 1956, who the biggest influence had been on his piano playing," Whittington explains. "A lot of guys, you know, would be arrogant and wouldn't admit that anyone had influenced them. But Carl was really open. Who do you think he said? I would have thought maybe Oscar Peterson. But Carl said Nat Cole. And if you listen to Carl's attack on the piano and you compare it to the way Nat played eighth notes—that dancing feeling Nat got on his single-note lines—you can see what he meant."

In spite of his confident self-assertion at the keyboard, Perkins was described by those who knew him as a modest, unassuming man. "Carl was a shy kind of guy, very friendly, very nice," Whittington continues.

> I tried to get him to give me lessons, but he didn't think he could teach what he did. I said we could get together, he could play, and he'd stop and I'd cop. I'd figure out what he was doing. But he didn't think he could do it. A lot of those Indianapolis musicians did so much by ear rather than formal training—not so much Freddie [Hubbard] and that generation, but the earlier ones. They used to say that Carl couldn't even read chord charts—I don't know if that's true—but they'd say he could play classical pieces by ear.

In 1951, Perkins recorded with Illinois Jacquet, but then two years of service with the army took him off the scene until 1953. Vinnegar believes that the pianist's problems with alcohol, which eventually proved fatal when he developed cirrhosis of the liver, began around this time: "When he was in the service, he had to go up to the front line. This was in the Korean War. And he had to go up to the front line and he saw a lot of stuff which affected him, a lot. And then when he came back home, one thing led to another. . . . I moved to the coast and we started hooking up. And I noticed he was drinking a lot then."[13]

After his discharge in November 1952, Perkins picked up where he had left off two years before. The mid-1950s found him performing in the company of such jazz stalwarts as Miles Davis, Clifford Brown, Max Roach, Dexter Gordon, and Chet Baker. From the beginning of 1953 through November 1955, Perkins also pursued an intermittent association with Oscar Moore, who had risen to fame as guitarist with the Nat King Cole Trio. Starting the following year Perkins began his tenure with Curtis Counce, which continued until the pianist's death. It was Perkins's curse to be a perpetual sideman—his only date as a leader is a little-known trio project on the R&B–oriented Dootone label—but the Counce connection was an enviable one from almost every other perspective. It may not have been his group, yet Perkins could scarcely have found a more appropriate musical setting in California in the late 1950s. Along with his recordings with Art Pepper and his sole trio date, the Counce discography stands as Perkins's most lasting achievement.

A little over six months would pass after the sessions for the first record before the Counce group returned to the studio. In the interim, the band performed regularly. Around this time, the band also backed up Billie Holiday during her performances at the Peacock in Los Angeles. The results of the new sessions, released on the group's follow-up LP *You Get More Bounce with Curtis Counce*, show the progress the quintet had made. Counce had contributed no compositions to the earlier release, but now he was pursuing studies with Lyle "Spud" Murphy, a former arranger with the Benny Goodman Orchestra. Counce also participated in Murphy's recording *New Orbits in Sound*, as part of a strong line-up that included Frank Morgan, Buddy Collette, Bob Gordon, and Chico Hamilton. Murphy's "twelve-tone system of composition" was being promoted by his record label as "something entirely different . . . a fresh harmonic concept"—praise that is quite out of keeping with the music. The Murphy pieces, for all their virtues, hardly presaged a breakthrough in harmony. They certainly bore little resemblance to twelve-tone music as practiced in classical composition, and even from the standpoint of jazz his work is far from revolutionary, often sticking fairly close to conventional circle of fifths progressions.

The surprising result of Murphy's theorizing is the positive impact it had on Counce. For his follow-up album, the bassist penned two pieces, "Complete" and "Counceltation," which are among the album's highlights. The latter begins with Perkins playing some striking polytonal chords (which the liner notes suggest were influenced by the "Murphy twelve-tone system") behind a melancholy theme stated by Land and Sheldon. Counce adds a lustrous countermelody that anticipates the rhythmically freer bass sound Scott LaFaro would bring to the jazz world a few years later. The rhythm section—indeed the whole band—sounds very comfortable at the comparatively slow tempo on both this piece and "How Deep Is the Ocean?" This album, in contrast to the earlier project, showed that the Counce band could swing at any tempo. Except for the album's gaudy and inappropriate cover—a pouting brunette nurse in partial undress is shown applying a stethoscope to her chest, apparently gauging the increased heart rate induced by listening to the Counce Quintet—this was a first-rate project from start to finish.

The first three albums by the Counce band document the development of the group's trumpeter, Jack Sheldon. For most of his musical career Sheldon has been best known as an exceptional exponent of the cooler West Coast trumpet sound. His work on "I Had the Craziest Dream" from one of his first leader dates—from the summer of 1957—shows off his melodic instincts in the context of a polished Lennie Niehaus arrangement. The influence of Chet Baker and Shorty Rogers is apparent at such moments. The Counce band, in contrast, gradually brought out a different side of Sheldon's playing. A more forceful, Clifford Brown–inflected style, perhaps reinforced by the presence of former Brown bandmate Harold Land, emerged during his tenure with the group. While flashes of this new approach are apparent on the band"s earliest work, it is with Sheldon's composition "Pink Lady," released on the *Carl's Blues* album, that the trumpeter makes his strongest statement in the new idiom. His sinewy melody line and assertive solo are the work of a dedicated hard-bopper.

Sheldon was born in Jacksonville, Florida, on November 30, 1931. Much of his childhood was spent in Detroit, where he began playing trumpet at age twelve, as part of a local school program. He came to California in 1947, and at age sixteen he enrolled at USC. Disenchanted with the music program, he transferred to Los Angeles City College, where Jack Montrose and Lennie Niehaus were also students. After a stint in the air force, Sheldon began working and jamming in Southern California clubs. "I got started playing on Main Street in Los Angeles in real dives and playing in little trios—piano, bass, and trumpet. We played for two, three, five bucks a night."[14] Soon Sheldon was working with Wardell Gray and Earl Bostic and sitting in with older musicians like Shorty Rogers and Art Pepper. Sheldon talks with some reluctance about his early experiences in the Counce band: "That was a good band. I was a little intimidated, though. I was the only white guy and I was very young. I didn't think I played as good as them. I didn't have the self-esteem, but I sort of held my own. But now I think I could do much better with that band."

Sheldon's stay in the Counce band ended when he joined the Kenton orchestra. In this setting—as in his later leader dates—Sheldon's playing often returned to the cooler West Coast orientation of his earliest work. For example, an excellent March 6, 1959, date as a leader finds him contributing several thoughtful and tasty solos in the company of an impressive line-up of West Coasters—among others, Art Pepper, Chet Baker, Harold Land, Mel Lewis, and Paul Moer. In the 1960s Sheldon, like many of his contemporaries, reduced his involvement in jazz. But Sheldon's reasons for moving on were quite unusual: He pursued a modestly successful career in acting and even starred briefly in his own TV situation comedy. Like many of the musicians on the West Coast, Sheldon became more visible in the jazz world during the 1970s through his work with Benny Goodman, Bill Berry, and others, as well as more frequent performances as a group leader.

Sheldon's replacement with the Counce band was Gerald Wilson, a West Coast trumpeter who is far better known as a big band leader and composer. The quintet's January 6, 1958, record date also marks pianist Perkins's last session with the group. Frank Butler stands out on this session; his unaccompanied drum work on "The Butler Did It" showcases his extraordinary and often overlooked talent. Not long before the session, the great drummer Jo Jones had said in a *Downbeat* interview: "As of today, this very minute, Frank Butler is the greatest drummer in the world." Jones's insistence on the time period proved prescient, for a few years later Butler would almost disappear from the scene. Another victim of substance abuse, he never achieved the fame that, given his talent, could have been his due.

Of the surviving members of Counce's various bands, saxophonist Land was the one who kept truest to the hard bop legacy of the group. A week after the last session for the *Carl's Blues* release, Land returned to the studio as leader of his own date, eventually released as *Harold in the Land of Jazz*. Although the group was not a regular working band, the two carryovers from the Counce group—Carl Perkins and Frank Butler—mesh comfortably with Rolf Ericson on trumpet and Leroy Vinnegar on bass. Land's playing is forceful and assured, and still free of the marked Coltrane influence that would become increasingly evident over the next decade. A little more than two months before his death, Perkins proved to be in strong form, and his composition "Grooveyard" is one of the highlights of the album. Land and Ericson respond with passionate playing.

That same month Perkins participated in the Art Pepper Omegatape sessions, and these also show the pianist playing as well as at any point in his career. The previous spring, Pepper and Perkins had enjoyed a two-week stint at the Tiffany Club with Ben Tucker on bass and Chuck Flores on drums. The remarkably high quality of these sessions testifies to the wisdom of Pepper's decision to use the same group in the studio. *The Art of Pepper* recordings (as they came to be called) rank among the neglected masterpieces of the period—neglected, no doubt, because they were not initially released on LP but on 3 3/4 ips tape. Record collectors were unable to listen to these performances until the early 1970s, when Onyx finally made them available. One can scarcely believe, listening to these recordings, that Perkins would be dead within a matter of weeks. A year earlier Pepper had teamed up with Miles Davis's rhythm section to make a much-acclaimed record for Les Koenig's Contemporary label, but Perkins's rapport with the altoist is every bit the equal of Red Garland's work on that previous date. In the publicity surrounding the earlier record, even Contemporary was willing to further the myth that East Coast rhythm sections were a step ahead of their West Coast equivalents, but the Counce unit and the Pepper collaborations with Perkins (ably assisted by bassist Ben Tucker and drummer Chuck Flores, both playing at their best) of this period give the lie to such stereotypes.

On March 11, Perkins was admitted to the county hospital. Some months earlier he had been briefly hospitalized for an apparent heroin overdose. On this occasion he was believed to be suffering from the same cause. Subsequently, doctors discovered that his condition was acutely aggravated by the ravages of alcoholism. Even though Perkins was now under constant medical supervision, he died less than a week after being admitted, on the morning of March 17. Cause of death was given as cirrhosis of the liver. His body was shipped back to Indianapolis for burial.

Given the circumstances, Counce's ability to maintain his group at this time is something of a surprise. Perkins's death; Land's emerging work as a group leader; the loss of trumpeter Jack Sheldon and then the departure of Gerald Wilson; the termination of the group's affiliation with Contemporary; the paucity of serious recognition beyond the West Coast; lack of opportunities to tour—all of these suggest that the Curtis Counce band was at the end of its rope. Somehow the bassist managed to regroup for one more album. Dootsie Williams stepped in to record the band for his growing Dootone label. This move stands out as something of an enigma—a decade before, Williams had been a vocal critic of Charlie Parker and bebop music, and his successful record label had focused on the growing rhythm-and-blues market. In an odd reversal he began producing sessions with Dexter Gordon, Carl Perkins, and now Curtis Counce.

The Counce date for Dootone, released as *Exploring the Future*, comes across as hastily put together and somewhat contrived. Williams likely bears the blame for at least the latter complaint: The song titles and bizarre album cover—Counce is shown floating through outer space, clutching his bass and dressed in an astronaut's suit—obviously try to exploit a post-Sputnik interest in such things. Here questionable taste in design is matched by even more dubious ethics: The album label cites Dootsie Williams as composer of the title track as well as of the jazz standard "Move" (which was actually written by Denzil Best). It is little wonder that a few years later, Williams announced he was retiring from the record business: "I realized publishing was the best deal." [15]

Certainly the personnel for this Counce date was capable: Pianist Elmo Hope and trumpeter Rolf Ericson were now gracing the band. However, the new material failed to match the brilliance of the earlier Contemporary recordings. This would be the last recording for the Counce unit. In 1960, Counce traveled to Australia with Benny Carter's group. Upon his return he faced the same harsh economic climate for jazz that pushed so many of his contemporaries into the studios or into emigré careers in Europe. During his last few years Counce put together new groups, but they more often were small piano trios, which made little headway in what was becoming the age of rock-and-roll. On July 31, 1963, Counce was stricken unexpectedly by a heart attack and died in the ambulance on the way to Los Angeles Central Receiving Hospital. He was thirty-seven years old.

the fox

After the break-up of the Counce group, Land was one of the few musicians keeping the hard bop flame alive in Southern California. The West Coast scene, both cool and hot, seemed on the brink of disappearing as more and more jazz musicians were abandoning ship, going into studios, relocating back east or in Europe, serving time in prison or in a steady day job. Whether by choice or necessity, most jazz musicians were giving up on Southern California. For those who remained, everything indicated that it was, for better or worse, the end of an era. The great flowering of modern jazz on the West Coast, which had begun in the mid-1940s on the streets of Central Avenue, had reached a dead-end, financially if not creatively. Its place in Southern California musical culture was now taken over by innocuous studio pop records, the nascent sounds of surf music, and the steadily growing world of rock and roll. In retrospect, the music being playing by Harold Land, Sonny Criss, Teddy Edwards, and the few other straggling survivors of the modern jazz revolution stands out as the last futile effort to hold onto the ground painfully won over a decade and a half of jazz proselytizing in the Southland, of attempts to spread the gospel of a rich, complex, deep music, a music now on the brink of being drowned out by the amplified sounds of garage bands, three-chord wonders somehow made into media stars.

That Land survived at all in this setting is cause for celebration. That he managed to put together his greatest masterpiece, *The Fox*, is nothing short of astonishing. Given the opportunity to record a project for independent producer Dave Axelrod in the late summer of 1959, Land drew on a new group of musicians and a different approach to compositional structures. In the last dying days of hard bop on the coast, these musicians created one of the most powerful musical statements of the decade, which built on the foundations of Land's work with Brown, Roach, and Counce but moved ahead as well, extending a tradition even while it seemed on the verge of extinction.

Land not only asked pianist Elmo Hope to anchor the rhythm section for this date but also enlisted him to compose all but two songs on the album. Hope responded by providing some of the most powerful—and difficult—charts of his career. Hope, who had come to California with Chet Baker in 1957, long remained something of an outsider on both coasts. His complex compositions, dense harmonies, and aggressive piano attack have won increasing favor since his untimely death in 1967 but often generated only puzzled disdain during his lifetime. Bassist Herbie Lewis, only eighteen at the time, was making his first session with *The Fox* but had already won the praise of veteran bassists Red Callender and Red Mitchell for his outstanding promise. Drummer Frank Butler, the group member with the longest track record with Land, was the perfect choice to round out the rhythm section. The most hard-driving drummer to reside on the West Coast in the 1950s, Butler was the important catalyst on the session who pushed the soloists to peak performances.

The vital link and the greatest enigma in the band was trumpeter Dupree Bolton. Even before the release of the *The Fox*, the mystery surrounding Bolton was beginning to grow. On October 15, 1959, *Downbeat* published a page of photographs taken at the session. The captions read, in part:

> West Coast musicians who have heard the tapes from a recent recording session produced by Dave Axelrod are flipping over trumpeter Dupree Bolton. . . . In [the photo] Land looks as if he honestly didn't believe what is coming from Bolton's horn. Gifted with exceptional technique and fierce power, Bolton is being compared to the late Clifford Brown for the brilliance of his lines. But he's something of a mystery man: not even Land seems to know where he came from.[16]

Land had heard the extraordinary trumpeter at a local club and immediately knew he was the right man for the forthcoming session. Bolton boasted a flawless technique, an expressive tone, and—perhaps most striking of all—a fierce intensity, an electric quality that made his solos, especially at fast tempos, absolutely gripping. As if this were not enough, Bolton was a crack reader. Hope's complex charts for the date, which would give many hornplayers fits, were navigated by Bolton with ease. If any question remained about him, it was simply wonderment over where this full-fledged trumpet star had learned his craft. How could such a musician simply emerge, already at a mature level, with no known history or background, immediately capable of playing with the very best?

This mystery was apparently not to be solved. Bolton disliked talking about himself. When John Tynan tried to interview Bolton in 1960, the trumpeter would only tell him: "When I was fourteen I ran away from home." That was the extent of the interview, and it proved to be the only one Bolton gave before disappearing from the scene in the early 1960s. When *The Fox* was reissued a decade later, Leonard Feather—the ultimate expert on jazz biography—could only say of Bolton: "Nobody seems to know where he came from or where he is today."[17] Interviewed at the time, Land added: "If things had worked out for him, he could have been one of the most important trumpet players of our time."

If Bolton was taciturn in public, he spoke eloquently through his music. On the title song "The Fox," trumpet and tenor open by stating, at a lightning pace, one of the most complex bop melodies ever penned. Land immediately leaps into his solo with a blistering attack, with Butler behind him stoking the ultrafast tempo—certainly one of the tenorist's most impressive statements. Bolton follows, matching Land step-for-step with searing trumpet lines that crackle with energy. The song's closing four-bar exchanges with trumpet, tenor, and drums are textbook examples of hot playing, inevitably rekindling memories of the Brown/Roach Quintet.

The title song was composed by Land, but the Hope originals, which make up most of the remainder of the album, are much in the same vein. Intricate melody lines, ingenious chord progressions, complex compositional structures—these characteristics stand out in virtually every number. This is especially noteworthy given the climate of the jazz world in late 1959: The switch to less tightly structured music was very much evident in the various new schools of music, whether modal, free, or funk. *The Fox* definitely goes against the grain of the day, and perhaps for this very reason it seems almost a summation of the musical values then falling, whether rightly or wrongly, out of favor. Yet the most persuasive attribute of this recording is not so much its evident fascination with formal structure but the musicians' ability to make these arcane structures come to life. In its striking combination of fiery spontaneity and calculated formalism, *The Fox* stands out as one of the finest recordings of the closing years of the decade.

Perhaps under other circumstances these musicians might have made more outstanding recordings. But in that time and place, *The Fox* was destined to be a brief stopping place for a group of musicians heading in different directions. The individual stories of Hope, Butler, and Bolton, despite their superficial differences, are sadly similar in their depiction of great talents fallen upon hard times.

Hope would soon return to New York, where his career never brought him more than a small degree of recognition—indeed, along with the great

Herbie Nichols, Hope has almost become typecast as the quintessential "neglected" pianist of the 1950s, a neglect that has slowly given way to begrudging respect in the years following his death.

Frank Butler seemed on the brink of achieving widespread recognition when he joined Miles Davis's group in 1963. Had he stayed with the band for any length of time, his reputation as one of the leading masters of jazz drumming might have been assured. Butler, however, had the misfortune to join the band right before Davis discovered Tony Williams. Davis decided to go with Williams—an understandable decision, given the latter's brilliance—and Butler's big break disappeared as quickly as it had come. In 1965, Butler served another brief stint with a jazz master, this time John Coltrane, but once again his work was understandably overlooked, given Elvin Jones's memorable collaborations with Trane. Perhaps it is some consolation to realize that, although Butler's work in the 1960s was overshadowed, it took the two greatest drummers of the decade to do it. From the mid-sixties on, Butler was mostly absent from the jazz scene, surfacing briefly in the late 1970s to record a series of excellent albums as a sideman and leader. By then, however, he was viewed by most jazz fans as a figure from the past, one whose work was more often taken for granted than appreciated. A hot drummer on the cool coast, Butler died in 1984, never having fulfilled the promise of his earliest recordings.

Land's many varied and creative recordings of later decades showed little interest in repeating his achievements of the 1950s. In the early 1960s, he co-led a band with bassist Red Mitchell. This quintet's Atlantic release *Hear Ye!!!! Hear Ye!!!!* tried to recapture the spirit of *The Fox*, with trumpeter Carmell Jones sharing front-line duties. But by then the tenorist's playing was diverging sharply from the bop roots of his Brown/Roach and Counce work. The cause of this shift in perspective was the innovative work of John Coltrane, then causing waves in the jazz world. In the words of critic Francis Davis, writing in 1982, Coltrane meant for Land an "artistic mid-life crisis which gripped him (along with many other tenors his age) in the early 60's. The kind of pentatonic, modal, post-Coltrane thinking, which first rumbled through his work around the time of Elmo Hope's *The Fox* (when it promised to deliver great things) still colors his playing, writing, and choice of sidemen to some extent, and not always for the better."[18] Land acknowledges Trane's influence but believes that it has not clouded his own musical identity: "[Coltrane's] expression of so many emotions that we all feel touched everybody. I was no exception to that. Being inspired by his spirit, by the same token, I tried to maintain my own identify."[19]

Bolton completely disappeared from the jazz world in the early 1960s. In a final album with Curtis Amy, entitled *Katanga!* Bolton lived up to the high standards he set with *The Fox*, as he did in his few live performances. In a 1963 review of a club appearance Bolton gave with Amy, John Tynan wrote:

> This reviewer recently replayed a HiFi jazz album, *The Fox*, recorded about three years ago, which features Bolton in his first known recording. His playing was impressive then; today it is out of sight. . . . Since joining Amy, he's been turning heads around all over town. On trumpet he's a fireball equipped with fearsome chops and a seemingly bottomless barrel of ideas. His sound is big and honest and sometimes so raw it rips a listener's head off. . . . Bolton is shouting "Hear me!" every time he puts the horn to his lips. And one has no choice but to listen.[20]

The fans had to listen while they could. At almost the same time Tynan wrote these words, Bolton disappeared—as mysteriously as he had shown up—apparently never to return.

Over the quarter of a century that followed Bolton's last commercial recording, a number of details about the trumpeter came to light. In England resercher Bob Weir found that Bolton had recorded before *The Fox*, but in many ways Weir's findings only furthered the mystery: Bolton had recorded in the 1940s under an assumed name for the Buddy Johnson band. Even more intriguing, Bolton was said to be featured on a little-known recording made in 1980 by a group of Oklahoma convicts. Weir published these details in the 1987 edition of his *Dupree Bolton Discography*. Another story in circulation told of Bolton playing with Dexter Gordon in Oklahoma City as late as 1982. These tantalizing anecdotes suggested that Bolton had indeed long survived his last jazz recording with Amy in the early 1960s and had continued playing. Beyond that one could only speculate.

Late in 1988 saxophonist Mark Lewis told me about an elderly trumpeter he had heard playing on the streets of San Francisco. Lewis had been impressed by the older man's playing and made a point of finding out who he was. I paid only passing attention to his story until Lewis mentioned that the trumpeter's name was Bolden, like the great Buddy Bolden of jazz history (whose career rivals Dupree's for mysteriousness). With Lewis's help, I managed to track down this wandering street musician. He proved to be the long-missing Dupree Bolton.

In the back room of a ramshackle East Bay music store, I met Dupree and over the course of several days conducted the first extensive interview he had given in his career. It perhaps comes as little surprise that the ravages of drug abuse explain the many gaps in Bolton's career. Most of the quarter-century since his last recording had been spent in prisons and

government institutions. Born in Oklahoma City on March 3, 1929, Bolton ran away from home, as he had explained to Tynan years before, at
age fourteen to join the Jay McShann band. His early recordings under an
assumed name were designed to help him elude his parents, who were
actively searching for the runaway. Almost from the start, Bolton fell under the sway of drugs, and he already had a lengthy criminal record at the
time of his work with Land. His desire to keep quiet about his troubled
past motivated his legendary silence in the face of questions about his
private life. Much of the 1960s and 1970s was spent in San Quentin and
other prisons. Since the mid-1980s Bolton has been permanently on the
outside, residing in San Francisco. He participates in a methadone program, and the uncertain income from his street playing has recently become supplemented by a regular Social Security check. Except for a slight
limp, Bolton looks surprisingly fit as he enters his sixties, especially when
one considers the wear and tear of his lifestyle. However, his playing these
days shows only brief glimmers of the extraordinary fire that brought him
into the limelight in the late 1950s. His story is one of the most tragic
accounts of the devastating impact of drugs on the lives of jazz musicians.

CHAPTER SIXTEEN

Something Else!

Charles Mingus, Eric Dolphy, Ornette Coleman, Don Cherry, Charlie Haden, Paul Bley, Billy Higgins, Ed Blackwell, Scott LaFaro, Gary Peacock. This roster of names conjures up, in the minds of knowledgeable jazz fans, memories of the best in experimental jazz of the 1950s and 1960s, of daring attempts to push the music into uncharted waters, to develop nothing short of a new musical vocabulary for jazz. Often the brazen expressiveness of this music has been contrasted with the more conventional, sterile music being played on the West Coast during the same period.

Less known, or perhaps less easily acknowledged, is that each of these musicians developed his mature style, partly or mainly, while resident on the West Coast. But this should not be surprising. Despite the stereotyped view of West Coast jazz as an exercise in musical conventionality, the truth was that no other place in the jazz world was as open to experimentation, to challenges to the conventional wisdom in improvised music, as was California during the late 1940s and the 1950s. New sounds, new instruments, new compositional techniques—these were the salient, almost dominating characteristics of West Coast jazz from the time of the Kenton band in the late 1940s to the release of Ornette Coleman's first recordings on Contemporary a decade later. Stan Kenton, Bob Graettinger, Dave Brubeck, Pete Rugolo, Bill Smith, Shelly Manne, Chico Hamilton, Jimmy Giuffre, Shorty Rogers—these are not artists typically lauded by modern-day fans and practitioners of the avant-garde, but they remain integral parts of that music's ancestry. The unrelenting emphasis on experimentation by these forerunners paved the way for a later, more overt avant-garde.

Paul Horn describes this West Coast ethos in his autobiography:

When I moved from New York to Los Angeles in 1957, I quickly realized the East Coast was extremely conservative. California was wide open—an experimental, innovative and exceptionally creative environment. People felt free to try new ideas, anything at all. If it was new and interesting, they went for it.[1]

Bruce Ackley, a member of the ROVA saxophone quartet—one of the most important experimental ensembles of the 1980s—has commented in a similar vein:

> When I was first listening to jazz—it was in the 60s—and the emphasis was on the Black music, the new Black music, and the West Coast thing was in disfavor. I mean everyone said the white players just ripped the Black players off; that they just stole their ideas and the West Coast thing was bogus. Since then I found that Art Pepper and Jimmy Giuffre were just as important to me, if not more so, than Sonny Stitt. But you have to find these things out for yourself. I mean a lot of innovations come from people like Jimmy Giuffre in terms of orchestration and group sound. I think that influenced us.[2]

Anthony Braxton, the doyen of free jazz during the 1970s, has made similar comments on a number of occasions. Not only has he cited Paul Desmond as a major influence on his music, but Braxton went so far as to commit the ultimate heresy: He recorded an album with Brubeck!

Such comments, however isolated at present, suggest that a more broad-minded view of the contributions of West Coast jazz is developing. Thus the following accounts of the early careers of Mingus, Dolphy, Coleman, et al.—narratives that some might think tangential to any discussion of West Coast jazz—are in fact crucial chapters in the history of this music. Here more than anywhere else, we can give depth and breadth to the one-dimensional view of West Coast jazz that has too long passed for the real thing.

Baron Mingus and his symphonic airs

Charles Mingus often contended that his birthdate, April 22, 1922, was something of a numerological phenomenon, with its strange preponderance of twos. Some twenty-two years later, Mingus recorded his first two sides as a leader for the Excelsior label. Odd conjunctions of numbers followed him to his death at age fifty-six in Cuernavaca, Mexico. The day his body was cremated, his widow noticed an item in the paper: Fifty-six whales were found beached on the Mexican coast. The authorities had them burned.

In death Mingus had come almost full circle. Right across the Mexican border lay Nogales, Arizona, where he had been born, the son of Charles Mingus, Sr., a sergeant in the U.S. Army, and Harriett Sophia Mingus, a Texas native who would outlive the birth of her son by less than six months. Left in the care of his stern father—who, by all accounts, brought his notions of military discipline into the home—Mingus was raised, from the time of his mother's death, in the Watts neighborhood of Los Angeles. In an interview with Mike Dean from 1972, Mingus recalled his father:

> He was almost impossible to like, anyway, 'cause he was a soldier, you know, an ex-soldier. So the quick way to get you to do something was with his fist. Or a belt held tight by the fist, and you could feel the fist in the belt. . . . I know that he would fight anybody. You know, if that point came, he would fight even a white man.[3]

Not that black pride played an important part in the elder Mingus's orientation—his son continued: "I don't think he knew anything about it, about the fact that there was anything to be proud about. And I think he put his hopes in the strength of the fact that he passed for white." Photos of Sergeant Mingus show a light-skinned, serious-looking gentleman with strong, solid features. The resemblance to his son is quite striking. Charles Jr. could have pursued the same path of assimilation—he was of mixed African, Chinese, and European descent—but instead took a great degree of pride, sometimes a devilish pride, in this amorphous ethnicity. Janet Coleman relates that Mingus long toyed with the idea of naming his autobiography (later released as Beneath the Underdog) either Half Yaller Nigger or Half Yaller Schitt-Colored Nigger. "He hadn't decided which yet, though he was pretty sure no white man would let him use any of those words in print."[4] The final title retained, if in a less colorful version, Mingus's sense of himself as something of an outcast, a permanent outsider.

At around age six, Mingus began his musical education on a Sears Roebuck trombone. His early music lessons, first from the local choirmaster and then from an itinerant teacher named Mr. Arson, gave little direction to the youngster's intuitive musicality. Charles played mostly by ear. Fellow trombonist Britt Woodman, two years older than Mingus, convinced him to switch to the cello. Soon Charles was playing in the cello section of the Los Angeles Junior Philharmonic. Two different stories are told about his final switch to the bass. One has Buddy Collette pointing out to Mingus that the school band needed a bass player, not a cello player; the other version—not necessarily in contradiction—explains that a local violinist told Charles's father: "Why don't you get him a bass? Because at least a black man can get employment with a bass."[5]

Later Mingus approached bassist Red Callender, then resident in Los Angeles, for further instruction. Callender recalls:

One morning there's a knock on the door of my house on 20th Street. . . . It's Mingus, saying he wants to study with me. He was seventeen, still in high school. I told him I was no teacher, that I was still studying myself, but he persisted. That was typical of him; Mingus would go through walls to get what he wanted.[6]

The "veteran" Callender was only twenty years old. Even so, he was the best teacher Charles had yet encountered. For two dollars a lesson, Callender rehearsed Mingus on the fundamentals of the bass. ("Mingus knew little about the bass. . . . However, even then, he knew exactly what he aspired to be—the world's greatest bass player.") His student showed extraordinary dedication. Callender recalls his protégé practicing seventeen hours a day: "That's the secret of his greatness: the hours he put into it." Eventually Calender referred Mingus to his own teacher, Herman Rheinschagen, a German-born taskmaster formerly with the New York Philharmonic. Again the younger musician responded to the challenge with zeal, while Rheinschagen found in Mingus a pupil who would push himself even harden than the disciplinarian teacher required.

The other major influence in Mingus's musical development was Lloyd Reese, the pioneering LA jazz educator who served as mentor to a host of future jazz stars. Reese's rehearsal band, which met Sunday mornings at the segregated union branch (Local 767 of the AFM), provided a training ground for many of these up-and-coming players. Dexter Gordon, another of Reese's pupils, recalls: "He taught more than exercises in the books. He gave us a broader picture and an appreciation of music."[7] Buddy Collette, also a student of Reese's, adds: "He wanted all his students to play the piano, to learn the keyboard. He wanted you to learn all the chords to different songs in different keys, and he used the Roman numeral system so you could transpose easily."[8]

Two years before Parker and Gillespie made their way to California, Mingus began working high-profile gigs in the LA area, first with Lee Young, the drummer brother of Lester Young, then with the great Louis Armstrong. We know little about the latter association—Mingus may even have toured Louisiana and Texas with the celebrated trumpeter. The bassist hardly ever referred to this period in later years, and it is likely that he was less than enamored with the band's music. This was perhaps the low point in Armstrong's mature career. For years he had pursued a brand of watered-down swing music in settings that bore little resemblance to the extraordinary performanaces he had recorded in the 1920s. By the early 1940s, Armstrong's work was often a tepid approximation of his previous heights. James Lincoln Collier, the most controversial of modern jazz historians, has raised eyebrows by his assertion that Armstrong's work from 1938 to 1947 was "startlingly bad," but even a more generous assessment of these middle years of the master would confirm that Mingus's dismay with the music was not wholly unfounded. Dexter Gordon, the other Reese alum who served with Armstrong during these years, has made no bones about his unhappiness with the gig: "The band wasn't saying too much. . . . Everything was just blah."[9] Mingus had unabashed praise for drummer Sid Catlett, who also played with Armstrong's group: "His beat was so alive it made the other drummers I'd heard sound dead."[10] But his noncommittal remark on Armstrong is a classic example of damning with faint praise: "I like all kinds of music, so how am I not going to like Louis?" A short time later Mingus worked with Kid Ory, another New Orleans stalwart who was tapping the resurgent interest in early jazz on the West Coast. Mingus was much more positive in his assessment of this affiliation: "I was very happy with that band until other young musicians began kidding me; I liked their music."

Mingus's recordings as a leader during these early years bore tribute to the other great force in premodern jazz: Duke Ellington. Mingus, in his emulation of the "Duke," went so far as to adopt a similarly noble nickname for himself. Several of his early recordings list the bassist as Baron Mingus or announce even more resplendently that "Baron Mingus presents his Symphonic Airs." In addition to putting on such "Airs," Mingus pursued a brand of swing era music strongly indebted, in music even more than in choice of names, to Ellington and his collaborator Billy Strayhorn. A May 1946 recording by "Baron Mingus and His Octet" is in no way a forerunner of the later octet/nonet recordings that would dominate West Coast jazz a decade later, but rather a clear attempt to sound like the Ellington band with a scaled-down instrumentation. Despite the obvious mimickry, Mingus's skills as a composer and arranger are quite impressive: If he had been a student in a conservatory class on "Ellington's Compositional Methods," he would have earned an A[+] for this effort. "Honey Take a Chance on Me" (also known as "Baby Take a Chance on Me"), recorded at the same time, is an innocuous Ellington-inflected pop song—"I see your face in every flower/ My love for you grows more each hour"—with a vocal by Claude Trenier. Here again one hears a very talented composer hidden beneath the superfical mimickry. Years later Mingus would return to this approach with his sensitive tribute piece "Duke Ellington's Sound of Love," showing his admiration openly in the title. Mingus's bass playing on these mid-1940s recordings is also quite accomplished, although it reflects the preponderant influence of Jimmy Blanton, the masterful Ellington bassist who had died only a short time before.

It is important to note that these recordings took place some months after Parker and Gillespie's influential stint in Los Angeles. Although the presence of the two young lions of bop made a lasting impression on a whole generation of West Coast players, Mingus was not one of them—at least not at first. For some time Mingus insisted that his friend Buddy Collette could match anything Parker played note for note, and he only came around to the bop camp after a number of his fellow musicians had been converted to the new sounds. When he finally made the switch, however, Mingus made up for his status as a latecomer by the vehemence with which he embraced Parker's innovations. He had not been a regular attendee of Parker's performances at Billy Berg's, but Mingus had become a devoted Bird admirer by the time of the latter's engagement at the Finale.

Miles Davis recalls:

> Charles Mingus loved Bird, man, almost like I have never seen nobody love. Maybe Max Roach loved Bird that much. But Mingus, shit, he used to come to see and hear Bird almost every night. He couldn't get enough of Bird.[11]

Miles also notes that Mingus's mastery of the bass was already impressive: "Mingus could play the bass and everybody knew when they heard him that he would become as bad as he became. We also knew that he would have to come to New York, which he did."[12] As for Mingus's skills as a composer, Davis was both puzzled and impressed by what he heard:

> After Bird went off the scene, I would rehearse with Charlie Mingus a lot. . . . I used to argue with him about using all those abrupt changes in the chords in his tunes. . . . It was some strange-sounding shit back then. But Mingus was like Duke Ellington, ahead of his time. Mingus was playing really different shit. All of a sudden he started doing this strange-sounding music, almost overnight.[13]

We can hear this new stylistic development in a later Los Angeles period recording by "Baron" Mingus titled "Story of Love." One still notes the Ellington/Strayhorn influence, but the music has already adopted an "out" experimental flavor that is *sui generis*. This is Ellington as seen through a distorting mirror; the individual horn lines seem to be on uneasy terms with each other and the expected harmonic resolutions rarely appear.

This particular breed of experimentation anticipated many of the West Coast stylistic tendencies of the next decade. It was a reluctant modernism: It retained strong roots in the jazz tradition, especially the swing era tradition; composing and arranging were as important as improvising; tonality was rarely discarded but instead played with, modified, enhanced. In this regard, Mingus's approach to music was not far from what Giuffre, Rogers, Manne, and others would be doing over the next decade. Unlike the East Coast "new thing," which it would later learn to incorporate, this music reflected an unusual mixture of avant-garde and derriere-garde.

"In California it was different," Mingus wrote in a 1970s memoir, which recently came to light: [14]

> People I knew, their main thing wasn't solos, it was the ensemble, and maybe give one guy a solo. In New York if there's five men, all five men take a solo before you end the piece. We used to write the elaborate arrangements in California—Buddy Collette, Britt Woodman, John Anderson, Oscar Bradley, Spaulding Givens on piano. Spaulding wrote the most difficult compositions and good ones. This band stayed together quite a while; we called it the Stars of Swing, nobody was a leader. . . . That band today would be *avant garde*—it was then.

The Stars of Swing remains the most enigmatic ensemble from Central Avenue during the postwar years—and also, according to various accounts, one of the finest. No recordings of the group survive, although tapes were apparently made. Mingus and Collette, among others, have remarked that the band was one of the outstanding musical projects of their respective careers, and given their significant later achievements, this is no small claim. Mingus's brilliance is, of course, well documented, while Collette, despite disappearing for much of his career into the netherworld of studio music, has frequently shown that his skills as a jazz saxophonist and flutist are considerable. Lucky Thompson, on occasional member of the band, boasted a hybrid swing and bop style that made him an ideal candidate for a band that similarly represented a meeting ground for different styles. Britt Woodman, later an important contributor to the Ellington band, was an excellent trombonist schooled in the heart of one of Southern California's first jazz families. (His father, trombonist William Woodman, had taken part in some of the first West Coast jazz record sessions in the mid-1920s.) Spaulding Givens (known since the 1950s as Nadi Qamar), a fourth cousin and protégé of Art Tatum, was a first-class pianist. Trumpeter John Anderson and drummer Oscar Bradley rounded out the band. Mingus has mentioned that Miles Davis also served briefly as a member of the Stars, but Qamar is less certain: "I don't remember Miles being involved. That's not to say he wasn't. But I don't remember it. . . . He may have written something for the band." [15] Qamar recalls Miles coming to hear the band at the Downbeat, and it is quite likely that Davis sat in during one of these visits.

The Stars started as a rehearsal band that practiced for several weeks at Mingus's place. Qamar, who was living with Mingus at the time, recalls: "Buddy Collette was one of the main ones to suggest that we start rehearsing and writing. All the musicians wrote, and for about four or five weeks we rehearsed. We wrote songs and arranged standards." The music played by the Stars of Swing appears to have been fairly eclectic. The band's name might suggest a more traditional, swing era approach, while Mingus's comments cited above imply a more experimental, avant-garde approach. But then again, the stylistic proclivities of many of the members might suggest more of a bebop orientation. Qamar's comments underline this breadth of sound:

> We were just West Coast jazz musicians. We dealt with the blues, we dealt with standards. I liked songs like "Laura," "Somewhere over the Rainbow." My arrangements were as lush as I could make them with the group. I used counterpoint, different harmonies, endings. I was very influenced by some of the easy listening albums that were coming out of Hollywood at the time. Also, I had the knack of reversing voices—I would give high notes to instruments that normally wouldn't do that."

If these various accounts, when combined, suggest a strange, almost unclassifiable mixture, one need only recall that Mingus's whole career was spent in making music that defied easy categorization. Indeed, this early band seems to have foreshadowed Mingus's later musical activities to a striking degree. A proclivity for experimentation, an emphasis on compositional structures, a deep feeling for the blues and the jazz tradition, a stable of strong soloists—all these characterizations of the Stars of Swing could easily be applied to almost any Mingus band of later years. The only different twist comes from Mingus's and Qamar's description of the band as an indigenous West Coast group. Qamar's "lush" arrangements suggest that the Stars of Swing were playing a brand of cool West Coast jazz long before Mulligan or Baker (or even the Davis Nonet) hit the scene.

Certainly Mingus is not typically viewed as part of the "cool" school—a fact perhaps more due to his character, the antithesis of cool restraint, than to his music. As to the latter, Mingus, both early and late, ranks as one of the most sensitive composers of jazz ballads—"Goodbye Porkpie Hat," "What Love," etc.—even if other sides of his multifaceted musical personality may stand out more in listeners' minds. Over and above his work as a leader, Mingus's early associations point to this much different, more intimate side of the bassist/composer. His work in the early and mid-1950s, even after he left California, included sessions with Miles Davis,

Stan Getz, Lee Konitz, Teddy Charles, Ralph Sharon, John Mehagen, Hazel Scott, John Dennis, Wally Cirillo—"cool school" associations that tend to fade into the background behind the more celebrated work with Parker, Powell, and the later Jazz Workshop. In the early 1950s, Mingus told interviewer Nat Hentoff: "Individuals can swing alone like Bird, and groups can swing collectively like Tristano's."[16] Mingus's praise of Lennie Tristano—which his biographer Brian Priestley dismisses as a passing fancy attributable to the bassist's temporary "lack of understanding"—was no fluke. On Mingus pieces such as "Extrasensory Perception," the Tristano influence—amplified by Mingus's use of Tristano protégé Lee Konitz on saxophone—could be quite striking. And this "cool" influence, even when it became muted in later years, still played an important part in much of Mingus's music.

Yet if elements of the cool showed up in the mature Mingus, elements of virtually every other postwar style also somehow made their way into his music. Hard bop, avant-garde, neo-Dixieland, West Coast, rhythm-and-blues, Latin jazz—all these tonal colors found their place on Mingus's compositional palette. The impressive result of this approach is, however, not so much its eclecticism—other, lesser musicians have outdone Mingus in that regard—but more the bassist's ability to make each of these styles his own. This radical diversity never collapses into a shallow exposition of the history of jazz. It always remains, first and foremost, an exposition of Mingus.

In this regard, the Stars of Swing was an accurate reflection of the later directions Mingus would take. The various and diverse accounts of the band's music do not so much contradict each other as round out the picture of a true Mingus band. Not that the bassist was the leader of the ensemble: The group remained a collective affair, despite Lucky Thompson's brief attempt to assume leadership. Already a veteran of the Basie band, Thompson might have helped the group with his name recognition. As it was, the Stars of Swing disbanded after only six weeks at the Downbeat. During this engagement, agents and club owners reportedly expressed an interest in the band but hesitated because the group worked without singers, dancers, or any kind of floor show.

Even before the Stars of Swing, Mingus had shown an interest in expansive compositional forms, as well as his well-known knack for off-beat song titles. Mingus compositions "The Chill of Death," "Half-mast Inhibition," and "Weird Nightmare" all date from this early period. Shortly after the break-up of the Stars, Mingus did an octet date for a local label, then somehow convinced Columbia Records to record "The Chill of Death." The record was never issued, but given the bassist's low profile at the time, as well as the arcane nature of the piece, it is something of a miracle that it was recorded at all. Mingus tells that Charlie Parker came to the studio the day the piece was recorded and encouraged Mingus to continue writing in the same vein: "He never mentioned whether he thought my bass playing was good or bad, but he always thought I was a good writer. . . . He said ["The Chill of Death] was the sort of thing I should keep on doing, and that I shouldn't be discouraged."[17] It was not until 1971 that "The Chill of Death" was re-recorded and released—ironically by Columbia, the same company that neglected the original version!

By joining the Lionel Hampton band in 1947, Mingus got his first taste of national exposure. Hampton drew heavily from the West Coast in his band of that era—another of Hamp's Los Angeles discoveries was Dexter Gordon—and recognized in Mingus both a talented bassist and promising composer. A few months after the newcomer joined the band, Hampton recorded "Mingus Fingers," an up-tempo romp on rhythm changes, during a session for Decca. The strong bass work, the composition, and its title all contributed to Mingus's growing reputation.

"Local boy Charles "Baron" Mingus, who made good with Lionel Hampton's famous orchestra, has left that band to form one of his own," reported the *California Eagle* on its entertainment page for November 4, 1948.[18] The new band, it said, consisted of Buddy Collette, Chuck Thompson, Jimmy Bunn, and an unnamed singer. "Some smart local night spot should grab this band," it concluded. "They're definitely Big Time and their brand of entertainment would pack any club!" There were few takers for this promising offer. Work was sporadic for the Baron during this period, and, while several recording opportunities arose, they inevitably came from small, local labels with little national visibility. Mingus held down the bass chair at Billy Berg's Sunday jam sessions in late 1948, followed by a brief stint as a leader at the Last Word, and he even had a modest local hit with his recording of "These Foolish Things" for John Dolphin's label. The November 11, 1948, *Eagle* announced that the release was "soaring the heights."[19] Yet as with most of Dolphin's releases, distribution was terrible, and success was often equated simply with sales at Dolphin's local record store. Indeed, the release remained so hidden, despite its local notoriety, that H. L. Lindenmaier and Horst Salewski missed it in their massive 103-page Mingus discography of 1983.

The state of Mingus's performing career can perhaps best be gauged by the account of his next major employer, Red Norvo. Norvo had recently come out west with his innovative vibes/bass/guitar trio. The sudden departure of Red Kelly forced the leader to find a replacement bassist in short order. And not just any bassist: The Norvo Trio, without a drummer and with a repertoire of barn-burning fast numbers, required a virtuoso bassist with rock-steady time. Jimmy Rowles suggested to Norvo that Charles Mingus was the right man for the job. "We started looking for Charles Mingus," Norvo recalls. At first he had little success, but he finally found Mingus working in Watts as a mailman. Norvo elaborates:

> He wasn't playing. Hadn't played at all. When I called him, he said, "Oh, I can't. I haven't been playing. Haven't played for six months." So I said, "Don't worry about it. Come on, take a chance." Every night, every night for a month he'd cry, "Oh no, I can't do it. I can't play with you and Tal. It's too much."[20]

This crisis of confidence lasted for several months. At one point Mingus failed to show up for a television broadcast with the trio. When Norvo returned home that night he found a note from the bassist: "I'm just afraid—I can't do this." Norvo recalls that almost nine months passed before Mingus began to feel secure in his playing with the group.

The setting was a challenging one for any bassist. A few years later the Mulligan Quartet would cause a sensation by performing jazz without a piano player, but this earlier West Coast ensemble went a step further: It lacked both piano *and* drums. This put considerable pressure on the bassist—a pressure that was only aggravated by Norvo's preference for fast tempos. Mingus was not the only group member with misgivings. Guitarist Tal Farlow recalls, "I had all kinds of difficulties at first." In contrast he remembers Mingus as "a master when it came to playing fast."[21]

The recordings of the Red Norvo Trio tell a different story from these mutual laments about musical inadequacy. The ensemble work bristles with virtuosity; few trios of that period, perhaps only Art Tatum's or Bud Powell's, could boast as firm a command of fast tempos. Mingus emerges on these sides as a powerful young bassist with solid time and a strong, resounding tone. His solos are few, but his presence is constantly felt.

Farlow is perhaps best known as a consummate bebop guitarist: "In terms of guitar prowess," writes critic Stuart Nicholson about these sessions, "it was the equivalent of Roger Bannister breaking the four minute mile."[22] But on these recordings his speedy melodic inventiveness is matched by an extraordinary variety of rhythmic and harmonic variations. On "Cheek to Cheek" his elaborate chord substitutions hint at the polytonal work of the avant-garde. On "Night and Day" he pushes the group by playing the guitar body like a bongo. In essence, Farlow serves as soloist, accompanist, and rhythm guitarist—all with great skill. Freed by the absence of keyboard and drums, Farlow continually takes chances with the music.

Norvo himself is a more difficult musician to evaluate. He is one of those versatile players—too versatile, perhaps, for their own good—who do not fit easily into the accepted schemas of jazz history. Born in 1908 in Beardstown, Illinois, Norvo already had enjoyed a diverse and successful musical career before the bebop revolution. In the 1920s he was gigging with Paul Whiteman, in the 1930s with Charlie Barnet and (Norvo's wife) Mildred Bailey, and in the 1940s with the Benny Goodman Sextet. There was little in this background to prepare listeners for his path-breaking records of the mid-1940s with Charlie Parker and Dizzy Gillespie. These were among the first modern jazz records to gain widespread notoriety, and while much of the attention was focused on Norvo's up-and-coming sidemen, the leader's florid vibraphone style fit in surprisingly well with the new bop music. This leap into modernism proved to be no fluke: Like his contemporary Coleman Hawkins, Norvo was one of the few older musicians daring enough to attempt the new approaches of the younger generation. The Mingus/Farlow Trio proved not only that the vibraphonist could survive in the hothouse bop environment but that he could challenge the best of the new players. Even Charles Mingus and Tal Farlow had to summon up their best efforts to keep up with this old-timer. These sides are perhaps the best known of Norvo's later modern jazz efforts, but they are by no means the only ones. Norvo's 1957 record, the tautologically titled *Music to Listen to Red Norvo By*, is an outstanding project that finds the veteran vibist surrounded by a strong cast of West Coast musicians— Buddy Collette, Bill Smith, Barney Kessel, Red Mitchell, and Shelly Manne—and drawing on compositions by these artists as well as Jack Montrose, Lennie Niehaus, and Duane Tatro.

The Norvo Trio was Mingus's last major involvement before leaving the West Coast. In later years, Mingus often remarked that all of his important musical education had taken place before he moved east. The surviving recordings do not discredit this claim. Both in composing and improvising, Mingus established many of the trademarks that would remain part of his music until the end. But over and above their impact on his evolution as a player, Mingus's West Coast roots would also show in his continued musical and personal relationships with many other West Coast musicians. His ties with Buddy Collette were perhaps the strongest of his career: In later years, Collette was one of the few restraining influences on Mingus; the bassist would listen to Collette when no one else could get through to him. Years later, when Mingus's eccentric behavior threatened to turn his forthcoming Town Hall concert into a fiasco, the promoters flew Collette in from the West Coast to make a last-ditch effort to talk sense into the headstrong bassist.

Collette was not the only, or even the most celebrated, of Mingus's Los Angeles ties. A few years after Mingus's departure for the east, another young California musician came to play an important role in Mingus's life and music. His name was Eric Dolphy.

gongs east

Eric Dolphy was born in Los Angeles on June 20, 1928, toward the close of the boom ties of the 1920s and on the brink of the Great Depression. His father, Eric Dolphy, Sr., did better than most during the hard times, managing to keep his job with a Packard automobile distributor and providing a stable, comfortable home for his wife and only son. The family, of West Indian descent, was a close-knit, religious group, and music held a central place in the household: Eric's mother, Sadie, sang in a church choir—one whose repertoire tended more toward Handel's *Messiah* than gospel music—and often would bring her young son to rehearsals and performances. Only six years old—and having barely started grammar school—Eric began to study clarinet. In junior high he took up the oboe as well. Even at this early age, Eric was exhibiting the extraordinary dedication to practicing that distinguished him throughout his career. At age thirteen, in the spring of 1942, he won a certificate at a local school band competition; around the same time, he began playing with the Los Angeles City School Orchestra. While still in junior high he was awarded a two-year scholarship to study music at the University of Southern California.

The Dolphys attended Westminster Presbyterian Church in Los Angeles, presided over by Reverend Hawes—father of pianist Hampton Hawes—where Eric eventually taught Sunday School. Both the younger and elder Hawes had an impact on Dolphy's musical development, although in contrasting ways. The elder Hawes has been portrayed by his son as indifferent, if not outright hostile, to the music of the younger generation, but the pastor took a special interest in Eric's musical development and gave him a key to the church so he could practice at night on the church piano. This anecdote suggests that Dolphy was still primarily interested in classical music, a view substantiated by accounts of Dolphy's listening habits in his early teens; his favorite pieces were by Ravel, Webern, and Debussy. Apparently the youngster's musical ambitions at this point focused on becoming a concert oboe player.

His friendship with Hampton Hawes may have pushed Dolphy in another direction, fueling his growing interest in modern jazz. But Eric's studies with Lloyd Reese, which began during his high school years, probably had an even greater impact. Reese, however, only infuriated Dolphy's parents when he told them that a college degree was not necessary for pursuing a career in music. Reese himself had earned a college degree, but he realized that the reputation of his students in the jazz world (as well as Reese's own status as an outstanding musician) had little to do with diplomas. The Dolphys, however, still hoped to see their son pursue a symphonic career, and Mrs. Dolphy refused to pay for further lessons from

Reese. Eric was not so easily separated from his mentor; he responded by doing cleaning work for Reese in exchange for instruction. Buddy Collette, who met Dolphy around this time, recalls Reese's close supervision of the youngster's musical development: "Eric was at Lloyd's almost every day. He was there when eight or nine people would be taking lessons. He didn't get just one lesson a week. It was almost like he was in music school."[23]

The final break with the world of classical music came during Dolphy's brief period of study at USC. After some faculty members complained that his participation in the orchestra ruined the "color scheme," he dropped out of school. Dolphy continued formal music studies, but as a performer he gravitated more and more to the world of jazz. His studies with Reese and other teachers, as well as his disciplined practice regimen, had prepared him well for the new career upon which he was embarking. Although Dolphy was not a Central Avenue regular by any stretch of the imagination, he had occasional involvements with playing jazz from the time of his early teens. While still in junior high he had played in a band led by another youngster named Harry Allen, who had studied with Lester Young's father and apparently had more of a background in improvisation than Dolphy. Around this time, Eric experimented with several more popular forms of music, not just jazz but also blues (which he tried singing for a brief period) and rhythm-and-blues. Dolphy's first stint in an important jazz group did not come, however, until he joined, at the ripe age of twenty, Roy Porter's new big band. Soon he was put in charge of Porter's reed section, just as Art Farmer was assigned responsibility for the brass instruments.

Porter decided on Dolphy even though the drummer felt that his strongest alto soloist was Leroy "Sweetpea" Robinson. Despite some accounts to the contrary, Porter claims that Dolphy did not solo on any of the band's few available recordings. "Sweetpea had more of the feeling for solos, he was more relaxed," Porter notes, "but I put Eric over the reed section because he was a hell of a reader, a great musician." Indeed the very confusion some listeners experience between Robinson's sound and Dolphy's early style suggests that Sweetpea may have been a strong influence on his younger sectionmate. Porter's choice of Dolphy as section leader was, however, not only a response to the youngster's polished musical education but also a judgment on the altoist's strong and serious character. Porter elaborates:

> Let me tell you about Eric Dolphy. He was a clean-cut young man. He wasn't using, he wasn't interested in the women that hung out around the band. Cisco, the band's valet, asked him once, "What's the matter with you? Don't you like broads?" . . . But when Eric was done playing with us, he was ready to go home and practice. He had no time for girls.

This dedication and all-consuming concentration on music made Dolphy stand out in the context of the Porter band, which had a reputation for, to put it mildly, enjoying the many pleasures of life beyond music. Much like his future employer Charles Mingus, Dolphy exhibited an early devotion to mastering his instrument that bordered on the obsessive. This shared passion for the music would help bond together these two men who, in other aspects of their personalities, were strikingly different.

The Porter band broke up after an automobile accident cut short the group's national tour. Dolphy, who had continued classes at Los Angeles City College while with Porter, was drafted in 1950 and remained in the armed forces until 1953. His musical talent kept him out of Korea. While stationed in Fort Lewis in Washington, Dolphy performed with the Tacoma Symphony Orchestra; he later attended the U.S. Naval School of Music in Washington, D.C. After his discharge, he returned to Los Angeles.

Despite his varied and exceptional musical accomplishments, Dolphy remained virtually unknown for almost five years after his release from the navy. From 1953 until 1958, when he joined Chico Hamilton's group, Dolphy's musical activities were mostly restricted to occasional gigs in and around Los Angeles. There is speculation about recordings he may have made during this period (with Gerald Wilson, Eddie Beal, and/or Red Callender), but none of these has been documented with any certainty. Even if such records were made, they certainly did little to enhance Dolphy's reputation. In his late twenties, when most major jazz musicians have already begun to make their mark on the world, Dolphy continued to practice, study, and refine his craft.

Form the first Dolphy had established a practice regimen that bespoke uncommon self-discipline. "His parents built a little studio in the back," Buddy Collette recalls, "and I thought he was going to go crazy. He was practicing six hours, then later seven hours a day and eight hours."[24] Given this constant drive to expand his musical horizons, his interlude of anonymity in Southern California was not a complete loss. This lengthy stay in and around Los Angeles—with occasional road trips as far away as New Mexico—gave Dolphy the opportunity to be among the first to hear the new approach to improvisation being developed by fellow alto saxophonist Ornette Coleman. Dolphy was aware of Ornette's distinctive work almost from the start. He told interviewer Martin Williams: "Ornette was playing that way in 1954. I heard about him and when I heard him play, he asked me if I liked his pieces and I said I thought they sounded good. When he said that if someone played a chord, he heard another chord on that one, I knew what he was talking about, because I had been thinking the same things."[25] Most jazz fans would be unaware of Coleman's music for another five years. But by the early 1960s, both Dolphy and Coleman had transformed these new thoughts about music into action, most notably in a path-breaking series of recordings that pushed jazz music beyond the last vestiges of conventional harmony.

If the intellectual roots of Dolphy's later experimentation date back to his West Coast years, the music he was playing on gigs in the mid-1950s was more closely related to the bebop idiom. Lillian Polen, one of Eric's closest friends from this period, remarks that Dolphy "worshipped Bird" during these LA years: "I would fall by the Oasis and listen to him, and my opinions seemed important to him. The questions from him were almost intense. Did he sound like Bird to me? That seemed all-pervading."[26] Dolphy could hardly have found a better model than Parker: Bird, much more than Coleman, provided a striking example of a musician for whom technical mastery of the horn and musical expression went hand in hand. Both Parker and Dolphy, moreover, instigated a musical revolution in which transcending existing conventions necessitated first assimilating them. In short, they were both strange revolutionaries who appeared to negate the tradition but in fact were its truest heirs. Under the influence of Parker, the ultimate alto virtuoso, Dolphy used these years of semiobscurity to advance his technical command of the various reed instruments now in his arsenal. This fluency held Dolphy in good stead when he got his break with Chico Hamilton in 1958.

Buddy Collette had originally been approached by Hamilton about rejoining the band. Collette explains:

> He said, "You've got to come back with me." And I said, "Well, let's send you Eric. There's a guy that's playing all the keys off the horn." . . . And about a month after [Eric] got to New York, he called me up and said, "Hey, you've got to come to New York too." He said, "This is where it is." He said, "I met Coleman Hawkins and he likes what I do. They like my sound." And it was really joyful to hear that, you know, what he was doing *here* [in Los Angeles] was good enough but he didn't know it until he got to New York."

Collette adds, a moment later: "Without moving out it wouldn't have worked. You couldn't just do it here."

Dolphy's first released recording with the Hamilton Quintet, on the Warner Brothers release *The Chico Hamilton Quintet with Strings Attached*, suffers from the unfortunate addition of a string section to the already string-oriented instrumentation of the group. By this time cellist Fred Katz had left the Hamilton ensemble to concentrate on composing and scoring work in Hollywood, but he was called in to write the orchestrations for the Warner project. Katz brought with him all the slick studio aplomb of his new profession. The regular cello spot in the quintet was now taken by Nat Greshman, a graduate of Philadelphia's Curtis Institute and formerly a member of the Cleveland Symphony. Wyatt Ruther, an alumnus of the Brubeck band, held down the bass chair, while the other newcomer along with Dolphy was guitarist Dennis Budimir, a twenty-year-old Los Angeles native whose most notable previous gig had been with the Harry James Orchestra. Budimir would go on to record with Bud Shank in the early 1960s, and later he established himself as one of the leading studio guitarists in Southern California. This was one of Hamilton's strongest groups.

Easily the best of the Hamilton Quintet recordings from this period is *Gongs East*—which, its name notwithstanding, was recording in Los Angeles in the closing days of 1958. "Beyond the Blue Horizon" gave Dolphy a chance to show off his impressive flute technique; Budimir follows with his well-conceived guitar lines. The title song features Dolphy on bass clarinet, a seldom-heard reed instrument he had learned while studying with Merle Johnston, a Los Angeles music teacher whose other students include Frank Morgan and Buddy Collette. Merle had gone with Eric to the pawnshop where Dolphy had previously spotted the horn. Johnston examined the instrument, gave his stamp of approval to the purchase, and subsequently helped the young altoist develop his distinctive clarinet tone. On "Gongs East" Dolphy takes a warm blues-inflected solo, while the album closes with a delicate version of the Billy Strayhorn piece "Passion Flower," marred only by Greshman's somewhat saccharine cello work. The piece is redeemed, however, by Dolphy's strong playing. His contribution here shows more than a passing acquaintance with the work of that earlier alto master, Johnny Hodges—a surprising evocation coming from this would-be musical revolutionary.

In general, the recordings with Hamilton gave Dolphy little chance to stretch out. His solos are often just brief snippets. But the exposure given to Dolphy in the course of many performances with the band—at the Newport Jazz Festival, Birdland, and elsewhere—brought the young up-and-coming player to the attention of the New York critics. Little wonder that, upon leaving Hamilton, Dolphy decided to settle permanently in New York. A short time later, in the closing months of the decade, Dolphy reunited with Charles Mingus for the latter's new band, then debuting at the Showplace in Greenwich Village. Together the two exiled Los Angelenos came to gain a measure of success and recognition that none of the West Coasters who stayed in California could match. Dolphy's rising critical acclaim, however, was scarcely matched by a comparable increase in financial security and income. When he won *Downbeat*'s 1961 International Jazz Critics Poll as new star on the alto, Dolphy's reported response was: "Does that mean I'm going to get work?" Even at the height of his reputation in the mid-1960s, his opportunities to perform were often sporadic. But in the years since his death, on June 29, 1964, Dolphy's stature in the jazz world has come to loom larger and larger. His graceful combination of forward-looking modernism with a firm grasp of earlier jazz traditions has been a powerful model for many later musicians.

the shape of jazz to come

In 1960 when Eric Dolphy joined with Ornette Coleman to record the seminal album *Free Jazz*, it was a musical meeting of minds for the two most prominent saxophonists of avant-garde jazz. But only three years before, both players were unheralded musicians struggling to make their reputation in a declining Southern California jazz scene. Coming from radically different musical backgrounds—Dolphy building on years of formal study and work within the modern jazz idiom, Coleman developing in isolation in the face of continued rejection from the jazz establishment—these two pioneers grew from marginal figures in the jazz world to the doyens of the "new thing."

One could envision Dolphy, with his accomplished mastery of the horn, eventually succeeding in almost any musical environment, whether traditional or modern, classical or jazz. Coleman, in contrast, stands out as a more unusual and fragile talent, one largely unable or unwilling to adapt to other styles of music. The jazz world had to accept him on his own terms or not at all. For most of his early years, the latter held true.

Born in Fort Worth, Texas, on March 19, 1930, Coleman was raised far away from the fertile musical spawning grounds of the two coasts. The Texas tenor sound, perhaps the Southwest's greatest contribution to jazz, sets little store by either virtuosity or innovation but builds from a visceral feeling for the blues. That Coleman was able to retain this sense for the gut-bucket well into his mature sound is not surprising given his early musical surroundings. That he was able to grow from his early R&B/ swing jazz orientation into a major figure of musical modernism, without the benefit of formal training or even strong jazz credentials, is quite amazing. Propelled by his unique vision of music—a vision that has been derided and lauded by turns—Coleman developed into the key figure of avant-garde jazz.

Coleman has no recollection of his father, who died seven years after his son's birth. Another brother and sister had died in their youth, and Ornette grew up with his mother and sister in a household that was, he recalls, "poorer than poor." About the time he entered high school, Coleman became anxious to learn an instrument after many of his friends joined a church band. His mother managed to purchase an alto saxophone for her only son. "I must have had a pretty good ear," Coleman explains, "because about a year later I was making jobs. If some rhythm-and-blues tune would come out I would learn it on the horn and go right out and play it in a nightclub in a dance band."[27]

Soon Coleman had made the inevitable switch to tenor saxophone. Forced to support his mother and sister, Coleman realized that the tenor would afford him greater opportunities to work in an R&B setting. Although he later returned to the alto, these early experiences playing the tenor left a strong mark on Coleman's conception of music: "The tenor is a rhythm instrument, and the best statements Negroes have made, of what their soul is, have been on the tenor saxophone."[28] Ornette ultimately abandoned the instrument one night in Baton Rouge late in 1949. Coleman's unusual playing at a dance displeased the patrons. A group of them beat him up and ruined his horn. Over a decade would pass before he tried his hand again at the tenor. Coleman, in his strangely unassuming way, accepted much of the blame for the inexcusable actions of his attackers. The tenor, he realized, had "that thing . . . you can get to people with." It was a two-edged sword, he believed, which could provoke either love or violence.

Coleman's influences on the instrument were unusual by the standards of modern jazz but highly conventional given his surroundings. On one occasion Coleman heard Lester Young performing in Fort Worth but was markedly unimpressed with the elder tenorist's playing. Instead he was convinced that local saxophonist Red Connors, who sat in with Young that night, was the better player. At that time the saxophone styles of Gene Ammons and Arnett Cobb were more appealing to Coleman, as well as to many other aspiring Texas saxophonists. In later years Coleman tried to emphasize his early roots in bebop music, but it is clear that his exposure to modern jazz came slowly at best, as well as at a relatively late stage in his musical development. The first Parker tune he heard was "Now's the Time," perhaps the earthiest blues in Bird's repertoire, which was made into an R&B hit under the title "The Hucklebuck." Coleman was already familiar with "The Hucklebuck" and concluded that, since it was the same as the Parker tune, bebop must be almost the same as rhythm-and-blues.

After the incident in Baton Rouge, Coleman made his way to New Orleans, where a friend, clarinetist Melvin Lassiter, resided. Lassiter's brother had just quit playing the alto saxophone, and Ornette picked up the abandoned horn. Ornette cites this return to his first instrument as a turning point in his musical development. He looks back to these days in New Orleans for the first stirrings of the distinctive approach to improvisation that, ten years later, would bring him equal helpings of fame and controversy. "It was while I was staying at Melvin's that started playing like I'm trying to play now," Coleman explained to A. B. Spellman. "The things that me and Cherry were doing, Melvin and I could do that then, and that was 1949."[29] In New Orleans, Coleman also met Ed Blackwell, the innovative drummer he would encounter again in Los Angeles and eventually send for when Billy Higgins left Coleman's band during its New York debut. Blackwell, along with Alvin Batiste, was one of the few New Orleans musicians then sympathetic to Coleman's experimentations. He also proved to be one of the few drummers who could adapt to its unusual metric demands.

Coleman stayed in New Orleans for six months. From this period come the first accounts of musicians walking off the stand when Coleman tried to sit in—substantiating the altoist's claim that his musical "breakthrough" had already taken place. Coleman supported himself, as he would for some years to come, through a series of nonmusical jobs. When a former Fort Worth employer, Pee Wee Crayton, arrived in New Orleans late in 1949, Coleman took the open saxophone chair in Crayton's traveling band. Ornette came with the group to Southern California, although his relations with Crayton had long before deteriorated; Spellman reports that Crayton "was paying Ornette *not* to play by the time they reached Los Angeles."[30] Coleman decided to settle down in his new surroundings. For the next nine years (except for one brief interlude in his native Texas) Southern California would be his often inhospitable home.

Given the rapid rise to maturity of most of jazz's greatest talents, this nine-year period of virtual obscurity in Coleman's career, coming when he had already played professionally for years, is quite telling. Some may be tempted to assign this general neglect of Coleman's music to his lack of mastery over the traditional jazz idiom. Yet when one recalls that Eric Dolphy, a virtuoso who could play any type of jazz with mastery, languished in Los Angeles for most of this same period, one is forced to assume that these artists' lack of opportunity says more about the state of the LA jazz audience and critics during the 1950s than it does about these musicians' talent. The East Coast critics' unwillingness to look beyond their native borders for jazz talent was somewhat understandable: They were too far away from the California scene to assess local happenings. More pointed, however, was the almost complete lack of media coverage in Southern California for home-grown talents. The major Los Angeles papers were scandalous in their neglect of the local jazz scene during those days, while even the more perceptive black newspapers, like the *Sentinel* and the *Eagle*, seemed more impressed with what passed for jazz in New York than with what was happening under their own noses.

In Los Angeles, Coleman eventually reunited with Blackwell, who moved to California in 1951. They shared an apartment, and both continued to work on their music while supporting themselves with day jobs. For over two years Coleman worked as an elevator operator at a Bullock's department store in Southern California—finally being let go when the store introduced self-operating elevators—while Blackwell labored as a clerk in another department store. "We started playing together," Blackwell recalls, "because he couldn't find anybody else to play with. Nobody wanted to play with him. I thought that was amazing. Here's this cat playing all the music and nobody wants to play with him. . . . We'd play every day. The minute we'd get home, we'd get right in and start playing, man."[31]

Coleman continually tried to make his reputation by sitting in with various local bands—and indeed he soon made a reputation, although not the kind he sought. Howard Rumsey recalls that Coleman tried to sit in at the Lighthouse and adds that Ornette soon became an inside joke among Los Angeles musicians. "Everybody—the musicians, I mean—would panic when you'd mention Ornette. People would laugh when his name was brought up."[32] When Coleman tried to play with the Brown/Roach Quintet during their stint at the California Club, the band made him wait almost four hours, until right before closing. When they finally let him on the stand, they proceeded to pack up their instruments as soon as he started playing. One evening Coleman sat in with Dexter Gordon's rhythm section because the leader was late in arriving. When the statuesque tenorist showed up, he shouted Coleman off the stage: "Immediately, right now. Take the tune out, and get off the bandstand."

Even after Coleman gained some high-powered admirers, the incidents continued. Drummer Mel Lewis, who gigged in and around Los Angeles in the mid-1950s, recalls an engagement with Bill Holman, who was an early supporter of Coleman's music: "We were working over at the Jazz Cellar on Las Palmas, and one night Ornette Coleman came and sat in with us. You never saw a club empty out so fast. The woman who ran the club told us that if we let him sit in again, we were fired. The very next night, who comes in but John Lewis and Gunther Schuller. They want to hear Ornette with the band. Well, we let him sit in again, and the club emptied out again. This time she fires us."[33]

Despite the indifference, if not outright hostility, of most audiences and musicians, Coleman eventually gathered around himself a small group of fellow musicians who encouraged his experimentation. The fortuitous chain of events that led to his debut recording on the Contemporary label depended on just such outside support. Bassist Don Payne, one of Coleman's earliest sidemen, lived at the time in Hollywood near fellow bassist Red Mitchell. One day when Mitchell was visiting him, Payne introduced him to Coleman and played him one of Ornette's compositions. Intrigued by the different flavor of the music, Mitchell suggested that Coleman visit Contemporary president Les Koenig. Even at this point, however, Mitchell was noncommittal about Coleman's playing and intimated that the altoist should approach Koenig only in order to sell him some compositions.

On this note, Coleman came by Contemporary's offices. Koenig initially had no time to meet with him and suggested he come back a few days later. Coleman returned the following Friday, bringing Don Cherry along for moral support. He proceeded to sell Koenig on the virtues of his compositions. Koenig asked Coleman to sit down at the piano in the company's studio/warehouse and play some of his originals. After a half-hearted attempt to convey his music on the keyboard, Coleman gave up in frustration. Koenig continues the story: "I asked him, 'How did you hope to play your tunes for me if you can't play the piano?' So he took out his plastic alto and began to play."[34] Koenig was interested in what he heard—not only was he fascinated by Coleman's compositions, but he also found his alto playing quite compelling. On the strength of this impromptu performance, Koenig scheduled a full-scale audition with Coleman, Cherry, Payne, drummer Billy Higgins, and pianist Walter Norris. Payne recalls: "Red Mitchell sat with Les through the whole thing. The group played a few charts of Ornette's, and the next thing we knew we had an album date."[35]

Cherry served not only as a friend and musical colleague to Coleman at this time but also as one more, and a much-needed, stamp of legitimacy on the latter's experimental music. Cherry probably stood for everything that the altoist aspired to be at the time. One of the large contingent of Oklahoma musicians transplanted onto California soil—he was born in Oklahoma City on November 18, 1936—Cherry came from an established musical family. His father, a trumpeter who had run the Cherry Blossom jazz club while in Oklahoma, moved the family to Watts in 1940. His son's musical development took place during the heyday of Central Avenue, and Cherry assimilated the full range of musical sounds heard on the avenue, not just jazz but dance music and the R&B stylings of players like Johnny Otis. Cherry's later work with Lou Reed and Ian Drury, so surprising to many of his fans, was in many ways a harking back to these origins.

Of his first meeting with Coleman in a Watts music store, Cherry told Nat Hentoff: "He was trying a #4½ reed. That's the thickest reed you can get. He had long hair and a beard. It was about 90 degrees, and he had on an overcoat. I was scared of him."[36] On the bandstand, however, Cherry had little to fear. Although Cherry was anything but famous during his pre-Ornette days—his musical earnings had to be supplemented by a day gig delivering prescription drugs in Hollywood for Schwab's—he had nonetheless achieved respectability, if not stardom, in the Los Angeles jazz scene of the late 1950s. He was gigging in many of the same establishments where Coleman was *persona non grata*. Dick Whittington, who played with Cherry in an intermission band at the Lighthouse around 1956–57, recalls that the trumpeter was an accomplished player of standard tunes and changes before he developed his later reputation as a leader of the avant-garde. "He was playing sort of like Miles at times, but even then he was branching out into his own things," Whittington recalls. "He had his own sound." In tandem with Coleman's haunting plastic alto stylings, Cherry's distinctive brass approach became one of the most striking modern trumpet sounds of the last thirty years. It is no exaggeration to say that even Miles, especially around the time of the *Miles Smiles* album, learned quite a bit from Cherry and Coleman.

Over the course of three studio dates in February and March of 1958, the two players, supported by a more traditional rhythm section than would later be their wont, recorded *Something Else! The Music of Ornette Coleman* at Contemporary Studios in Los Angeles. Since Ornette had virtually no opportunities to perform during this period, the band had to prepare for the session at a series of private rehearsals. Walter Norris, pianist on the date, recalls:

> We rehearsed two or three times a week for about six months leading up to the recording. A number of times we rehearsed at my house. I would take a paper and pen and make notes about the compositions and about what we were supposed to be doing. But the funny thing was that at every rehearsal Ornette would change what we had done the last time. He would change the structure of the song, or change where the rubato was. And then when we finally showed up for the record date, he changed everything again. This whole process forced us to be intuitive, forced us to listen and be on our toes musically. Because of that the music we recorded is very much alive.[37]

Even before its release, word of the *Something Else!* date began to circulate not only in Southern California but throughout the jazz world at large. Only ten days after the first session, *Downbeat* announced that "Ornet [sic] Coleman may do an album (very, very avant garde) for Contemporary." *Something Else!* was appropriately named. Even before its release, listeners were preparing themselves for something out of the ordinary.

Nor did Coleman disappoint them: His music was innovative by the standards of the day. Even so, these early recordings by Coleman show much stronger roots in the jazz tradition than most of the early critics (or supporters) of the music realized. Ornette's knack for melody was the most innovative—and most compelling—feature of his new music on *Something Else!* In contrast, the harmonies used by the rhythm section are quite conventional: "Chippie" is based on "I've Got Rhythm" changes. "Jayne," written for Ornette's wife, falls into the "Out of Nowhere" progression after the opening melody statement. "When Will the Blues Leave?" is, as its name implies, built on a twelve-bar blues. But on top of these straightforward harmonic structures, Ornette's compositions reflected a different sense of melody and rhythmic placement than was the norm on either coast during the late 1950s. "Chippie," for example, starts off in a vein similar to the bop standard "Anthropology," but the jarring break in the melody in bar five creates a sense of disjunction unlike anything in the Parker/Gillespie idiom. Similarly the unexpected accent that closes bar two of the "When Will the Blues Leave?" melody or the turnaround of "Jayne" gives them a radical twist set against the conventionality of the underlying chord progressions.

Indeed, there is good reason to believe that Coleman wrote these pieces as melodies pure and simple without any specific chords in mind. The blowing changes often sound as if they were added after the fact—and often they hardly fit in with the structure of Coleman's melodies. The melody of "Jayne," with its tonic major in bars three and four, does not fit the "Nowhere" changes used in the solos. In the case of "Invisible," no standard progression could fit Coleman's AABA form, for the simple reason that his melody for the A theme is 8½ bars long! For the solos the rhythm section falls into a strict 32-bar form, but the melody stands out with its ungainly 33½-bar duration. "The Disguise" features a 13-bar melody but settles into a 12-bar blues for the solos. Time and time again, Coleman's distinctive compositions are squeezed into the standard jazz form that most closely approximates the melody. Sometimes the fit works reasonably well, sometimes not.

Norris is defensive about many of the critical reactions to this unusual combination of free jazz and traditional jazz harmony. He explains:

> I read this book that suggested that I was forcing Ornette to play changes on this session. But in fact this was what we had agreed on at the rehearsals. For example, we agreed on using "I've Got Rhythm" changes—Ornette was used to playing over those changes, and he was able to be very free in that setting. And when Ornette was playing, I was listening to what he was doing and opened up my comping in response.

Norris's point is substantiated by Coleman's comments to Nat Hentoff, reported in the liner notes to *Something Else!*

> I always write the melody line first, because several different chords can fit the same melody line. In fact, I would prefer it if musicians would play my tunes with different changes as they take a new chorus so there'd be all the more variety in the performance. On this recording, the changes finally decided on for the tunes are a combination of some I suggested and some the musicians suggested.[38]

This casual attitude toward harmony, unprecedented in jazz, is corroborated by Coleman's solos on his first Contemporary release. While Cherry and Payne typically play off the changes in their solos, Coleman's improvisations often disregard the harmonic underpinnings. For this reason, Coleman's "revolution" was likely to seem more radical to trained musicians, whose sophisticated ears detected the waywardness of his playing, while to the more tone-deaf listener the rhythmic freedom and internal consistency of Coleman's melodic line could be appealing, and the harmonic clashes passed by unnoticed.

Whether by choice or necessity, Coleman had created a fresh new sound that cut through the Gordian knot of modern jazz virtuosity and broke loose from the relentless jazz obsession with playing rapid-fire bebop patterns over changes. The dictates of modernism, which in classical music had been criticized for killing off melody, brought about a rebirth of melody with the music of Ornette Coleman. Sometimes the melodies were hummable ditties with a few eccentric twists; other times they danced over the bar lines with dazzling fluency, or they might bristle with an odd stop-and-start motion that coyly teased the listener. The melodic emphasis of Coleman's music was furthered by his distinctive saxophone sound, which broke with conventional notions of tone and pitch but still succeeded in its expressive emulation of the human voice.

Around the time of this first recording, Coleman landed one of the few paying jazz gigs from his Los Angeles years. The quintet, featured for a brief period at the Hillcrest Club in 1958, brought together a line-up that, only a few years later, would be heralded as an all-star collection of some of the most innovative musicians in jazz. The band was under the nominal leadership of Canadian pianist Paul Bley, who had moved to Los Angeles with his wife, Carla, the previous year. In addition to Bley and Coleman, the band included Don Cherry, bassist Charlie Haden, and drummer Billy Higgins. "The Hillcrest was a club on Washington Boulevard, which is the black section of Los Angeles," Bley explained in 1979. "That area had a tradition of live performance. Les McCann played our Monday night jam sessions. When I arrived in Los Angeles after a long college tour with a trio that I brought from New York, we added the vibraphone player, Dave Pike, and went into the Hillcrest and stayed roughly close to two years, six nights a week."[39] The original sidemen in Bley's band—bassist Hal Gaylor and drummer Lennie McBrowne—were soon replaced by locals Charlie Haden and Billy Higgins, two of the strongest of the up-and-coming Los Angeles jazz players. Bley at the time was already something of an established jazz artist—he had been profiled by *Downbeat* in 1954, when he was only twenty-one years old—and had recorded with Mingus, Art Blakey, and Percy Heath (as well as in a bootlegged live performance with Charlie Parker) before coming to California. In late 1957, shortly after making the move out west, he had recorded an impressive quartet album with Haden, McBrowne, and Pike for Gene Norman's GNP label. The liner notes to that project concluded with the prophetic statement: "As to future albums, Paul is again very specific. He intends to work with longer musical forms and less confined improvisational structures."[40]

The opportunity to do just that arrived one evening in early 1958 in the form of an ungainly alto saxophonist from Fort Worth. Higgins introduced Bley to Ornette Coleman, who had come to the club with Don Cherry, and although the pianist normally discouraged musicians from sitting in on the Hillcrest gig ("we sent them all to Monday night, and gave them to Les McCann") he made an exception for these particular newcomers because the request came through his drummer: "After playing one set with them, Charlie and I went out in the backyard and had a confrontation. We said, 'Look, we have been working in this club for a long time and most probably could stay here as long as we wanted. If we fire Dave Pike and hire Don and Ornette we won't last the week. We'll be lucky to last the night. What shall we do?' And we looked at each other and said, 'Fire Dave Pike!'"[41] The management of the Hillcrest was, as predicted, displeased by the new band. Although they allowed the group to continue for a few performances, Bley and company were fired within a month.

Eric Kriss has suggested that this early collaboration was to free jazz what the Minton's and Monroe's jam sessions of the early 1940s were to the formation of bebop. The Hillcrest gig represented, in his words, "the beginning of avant-garde jazz in America."[42] These high claims may be exaggerated—especially given the brief duration of the Hillcrest quintet— yet even so, the importance of this ensemble should not be minimized. Despite its brief lifespan, this was in every sense a landmark band. Some performances, captured in an amateur recording made at the Hillcrest, have been released commercially. Like the Contemporary date, these tantalizing bits and pieces of musical history in progress are an intriguing combination of the old and the new.

Despite the negative audience reaction to the band's experimentation ("Every set we'd go up and play and the club would totally empty out, they'd leave their drinks on the bar and everything.")[43] the music from the live recording is more overtly traditional than any of Coleman's studio dates. This is free jazz in the process of freeing itself. These recordings make clear—much more clear than was possible before their release—that the constraining tradition holding Coleman and company back was the bebop idiom of the 1940s. In their tempos, in their choice of material, in their sense of phrasing and tone, these musicians seem to be fighting their private battles with the ghosts of bebop past. It is enlightening to hear Coleman moving in and out of tonality—sometimes following the bop changes, sometimes ignoring them—with his uncertain allegiance to Parker's legacy. His playing here represents an attempt to push beyond Parker's music from the inside out. Coleman's long solo on Parker's piece "Klactoveesedstene" is, for this very reason, one of the most illuminating documents in his discography. It shows him in the process of trying to exorcise Parker's ghost, to purge his playing of the bebop idiom the composition represented.

Each of Coleman's colleagues on this recording was in a similarly ambiguous relationship with the jazz tradition. Charlie Haden had come to Los Angeles a few years before to study at the Westlake College of Music, one of the first academic music programs in the country that offered a jazz curriculum. Born into a family of performing musicians, Haden had begun singing at age two on the Haden family radio show. After learning bass lines by ear on an instrument borrowed from his older brother Jim, Haden soon decided to pursue formal training. Although he had won a scholarship to Oberlin—which he claims (with tongue in cheek?) attracted him because of the Dave Brubeck album recorded on the campus—he instead opted for Westlake, which he had learned about through reading *Downbeat*. After saving up money he made from selling shoes, Haden left Forsyth, Mississippi, where he then was living, to make the trip out west. Shortly after enrolling in the Westlake program, Haden found his education was furthered more by gigging in local clubs than by his classroom studies: "There were good teachers there—Dick Grove, for instance, who's got a whole school now. But I started playing gigs at night, so I couldn't make classes in the morning."[44] His early work with Art Pepper, Hampton Hawes, and other West Coast regulars found Haden mastering the postbop styles of the 1950s, but his work with Coleman required him to develop different skills. In time Haden created an extraordinarily flexible and brilliant bass style that allowed him to flow in and out of tonal music with ease, all the while maintaining a melodic logic rare in string bass players. Combined with his warm, solid tone and his impeccable time, this striking ability to fit into any type of musical surrounding has made Haden one of the bassists most in demand in the modern era.

Billy Higgins also used his experiences with Coleman to expand his musical horizons. A Los Angeles native, born on October 11, 1936, Higgins had grown up near Central Avenue during its final days as the western jazz mecca. By the time he was old enough to work in clubs, however, the jazz scene had shifted—into the suburbs, into the studios—and to a certain extent disappeared. Given this state of affairs, Higgins refined his skills while playing in rhythm-and-blues bands by night and working as a

stock clerk at UCLA Medical Center by day. He soon graduated from the
R&B bands to working with Teddy Edwards, James Clay, and other members of the Southern California jazz elite. These experiences, however, did
little to prepare him for what he was to encounter when Don Cherry, a
former high school classmate, introduced him to an alto saxophonist recently arrived from Texas. "He was as raw as you could possibly be,"
Higgins remembers. "His music was completely different from anything
I'd ever heard. It shocked me, but I was open enough to want to learn."[45]
Learn he did—so much so that, along with Ed Blackwell, he developed into
one of the few drummers able to mesh with Coleman's new musical dic-
tion.

Higgins's career seemed on the brink of taking off when he went back
east with Coleman for the New York debut that brought the latter to the
forefront of the jazz world. New York authorities, however, refused to
issue Higgins a cabaret card when they learned of his record of arrests—
several for narcotics, and one for assault—back in California. Losing one
of the few drummers who could adapt to his music, Coleman urged Ed
Blackwell, who was then living in New Orleans, to rejoin the band. Eventually Higgins would make his peace with the New York bureaucrats, returning to play with John Coltrane and eventually staying for six years,
during which time his playing graced many of the finest Blue Note recordings of the day. In 1977 he returned to Los Angeles to stay, although,
even as a local musician made good, he often finds more work these days
out of town than he does in his hometown.

Coleman and Cherry never needed to look back. The New York engagement generated fame and controversy in heaping doses, and their careers blossomed under the heated scrutiny the new music engendered. As
in the cases of Dolphy and Mingus, here again the West Coast proved that
it could develop an avant-garde but was capable neither of appreciating it
once it came to be, nor of establishing it as a legitimate form of jazz worthy of close attention, widespread dissemination, and emulation. Two decades later the same scenario was re-enacted when a new generation of
California-born modern jazz musicians—David Murray, Arthur Blythe, and
others—made their names as leading players after moving to New York,
in contrast to the virtual obscurity of their efforts on the West Coast.
Throughout the postwar years, California has been rich in modern jazz
music of many different stamps, but dirt poor when it came to the institutions needed to establish and boost that music. Outside of a few individuals such as Les Koenig and Richard Bock, the west largely lacked the
nonmusical resources—the behind-the-scenes support groups made up of
journalists, impresarios, and the like—that are often crucial in determining
what gets heard and what gets neglected. In the short run, such outside
figures often hold the key to a musician's commercial viability; in the long

run, they affect nothing less than how the history of the music is written. In many ways the hidden story of what distinguished West Coast jazz from East Coast jazz is the story of these institutions, social practices, and support groups. This history behind the history signifies nothing less than the secret code that dictated, and continues to influence, what West Coast jazz was, and is, all about.

CHAPTER SEVENTEEN

West Coast Jazz:
Final Considerations

If an east coast jazz musician is playing jazz on the west coast, is he an east coast jazz musician playing east coast jazz on the west coast or is he an east coast jazz musician playing west coast jazz on the west coast or is he a west coast jazz musician playing east coast jazz?

Question posed in Downbeat,
November 12, 1959

What is West Coast jazz? It's whatever the East Coast critics say it is?

Unidentified West Coast jazz musician

Too much of the debate surrounding West Coast jazz has focused on definitions. Was there a West Coast jazz? What constituted it? How was it different form East Coast jazz? Was it the last regional style in jazz history? Was it the final entry in a geographical tradition that includes Kansas City jazz, Chicago jazz, New Orleans jazz? Or was it merely an inventive fabrication of Hollywood record producers? Was it a true artistic movement, whatever that may signify, or was it only a publicity campaign or marketing hoax?

Such questions are not without their validity, but in many ways they miss the point. Jazz writers learned long ago, for example, that it is almost impossible to come up with a good, succinct, widely accepted definition of jazz itself. "If you have to ask, you better not mess with it," was Fats Waller's rejoinder to those who sought such definitions. And Fats's view, despite its joking intent, is worth taking seriously. No good definition is in sight, yet jazz continues to flourish. Jazz records continue to be released, listened to, reviewed. Concerts sell out. Jazz books continue to be written and read. The art form thrives. West Coast jazz is much the same:

The supposed crisis of definition has done little to hinder the music. Interest in the music is stronger than it has been at any time in the last thirty years.

The very health of jazz music is part of what makes formulating these definitions such a difficult and often futile practice. A healthy art form lives and grows and breathes on its own, with little care for critics' generalizations. In the past, one might have tried to define jazz on the basis of certain syncopated rhythms, but then a new generation of musicians showed that jazz could have a completely different rhythmic feel. At one time, one might have tried to define jazz on the basis of the blues tonality, but then a fresh crop of musicians showed that jazz did not need to rely on the blues tonality. One could go on and on. And this confusion of formal constraints is not restricted to jazz. Aristotle's definition of the dramatic unities was promulgated only to be ignored by later dramatists. The lesson learned should be that only dead art forms have rigid rules that allow no exceptions. Jazz does not fall into that category—thank God, at least not yet.

Nor do I have any interest in making West Coast jazz into something of that nature. It is most definitely not some kind of archaeological fossil that can be easily dated, classified, and then promptly thrust out of mind. The West Coast jazz music detailed in these pages still strikes listeners as tremendously alive and vital. The musicians followed no sacronsanct formulas; they did not go to some recipe book to concoct a standardized batch of West Coast jazz music. Often they broke whatever rules they found. They constantly tackled new things, sometimes with success and not infrequently with failure. Indeed, if one thing should stand out in this account of music in California during the postwar years, it is the enormous diversity of the music, the ceaseless, churning search for the different and new. It is this characteristic that unites a Stan Kenton and an Ornette Coleman, a Charles Mingus and a Jimmy Giuffre, a Shelly Manne and an Eric Dolphy. True, the more traditional mainstream sounds coexisted with this experimentation, but that was part of the pluralism and diversity as well. Even when a thousand flowers blossom, the garden roses are not uprooted.

If one is seeking geographical explanations, one can look to the sprawling suburban landscape of Southern California, the jigsaw of Los Angeles streets and neighborhoods in the years before the great freeway expansion. There was no uniform gathering place for West Coast jazz players after the decline of Central Avenue; there was no Jim and Andy's, the now legendary East Coast jazz bar. West Coast music reflected California's diverse spaces, its nooks and crannies and open fields. Years earlier, the movie industry had come to Southern California partly because one could find nearby the right landscape for almost any film setting: desert, beach, valley, mountains, city, countryside. The musical terrain of the 1940s and 1950s proved to be equally diverse. The musicians had the space to go their own way in a manner that may not have been quite so possible in Manhattan. In the San Fernando Valley, or half a county away at the Lighthouse, or in Watts or on Central Avenue, the musicians had a kind of artistic isolation that may have been frustrating at times—and one hears many complaints about the lack of community among West Coast players then and now—but was also liberating. Players had the space they needed to develop a separate identity.

The critics who claimed that a Brubeck or a Desmond or a Baker would never have "made it" in New York may, in their own way, have been stating a truth, but one that is less flattering to the east than they might think. Their assertion tells more about the opportunities for individualism in the 1950s New York jazz scene than it does about Brubeck or Desmond. These artists might well have never made it in Manhattan, but is that to New York's credit or disgrace? Herbie Nichols, now celebrated posthumously, never made it in the 1950s New York jazz scene either. But that wasn't his fault. His distinctive sound was simply not close enough to what passed as fashionable at the time. Perhaps he would have never made it out west either—certainly California was not the place to make a critical (as opposed to a popular) reputation in the 1950s, or even today for that matter. But his "eccentric" music would certainly have had a chance in the pluralistic West Coast scene that could land a recording contract for Ornette Coleman and a steady gig for Bob Graettinger.

This is not to say that there wasn't a West Coast sound. Critics who pretend that such a thing never existed are practicing an unusual kind of bad faith. Certainly such a sound never accounted for all of the music played at all times on the coast, and maybe not even most of the music played most of the time. But it was prominent enough, often enough to demand our acknowledgment. What was this West Coast sound? By and large it had a strong compositional emphasis; it delighted in counterpoint; it had a cooler demeanor than Bird and Dizzy's bebop; the drummers were not so dominating as Roach and Blakey; the horn players were not so heavily rooted in the bebop vocabulary as Stitt and Rollins. The West Coast sound was cleanly articulated, the execution fluid and polished. Desmond, Baker, Rogers, Mulligan, Giuffre, Niehaus, Manne, Sheldon, Hamilton, Montrose, Farmer, Guaraldi, Graas, Collette, the Stars of Swing— they were part, to a greater or lesser extent, of this breed of West Coast jazz player. This sound may not have figured in all their recordings or performances, nor might they be happy with being lumped together as part of a "regional school" (especially one that has been the frequent brunt of attacks), but these shared characteristics were common enough to make any attempts at denying them seem somewhat perverse and distinctly un-realistic.

But there was other music on the coast as well. And not only was it just as much a part of the story of West Coast jazz, but it is also in many ways the story that most needs to be stressed. Sonny Criss and Carl Per-kins and Harold Land had little to do with the stereotypical West Coast sound, yet their work included some of the finest jazz being played on either coast during the 1950s. Dupree Bolton and Hampton Hawes, Teddy Edwards and Curtis Counce, Dexter Gordon and Wardell Gray, Eric Dol-phy and Joe Gordon—they, too, warrant our attention. If my account of these careers says anything, it is that a whole range of exciting jazz styles could coexist on the coast. There was the West Coast sound, but there was much else besides.

But after this is acknowledged, one is forced to ask whether, given this diversity, there was really anything unifying to this music, anything that would justify concern with these musicians as "West Coast" jazz mu-sicians, instead of, say, individual players tied together only by a coinci-dental, but hardly crucial, shared geography. The answer to this question must be an unambiguous yes. Not because these musicians shared the same musical goals and precepts—they most obviously did not—but rather because they shared a group of institutions essential to West Coast jazz. The real story of West Coast jazz, as a somewhat unified phenomenon, may well be the story of these institutions—or, in some cases, their no-table absence—institutions that were crucial in establishing West Coast jazz in the postwar years.

It is no exaggeration to say that what made West Coast jazz possible, first and foremost, was a small group of local record companies dedicated to presenting the area's musicians to the nation at large. Without the Dial, Fantasy, Pacific, Contemporary, and Capitol labels, this music would not have happened and this book would never have been written. The existing jazz institutions can determine, to a great extent, the nature of a region's sound, and almost entirely dictate its level of visibility. As I described earlier, the whole West Coast sound might have been radically different had Dial Records and its bop-oriented sound stayed on the West Coast. Instead, the West Coast sound was left to others to shape and determine: Richard Bock at Pacific, Les Koenig at Contemporary, the Weiss brothers at Fantasy. The history of jazz has invariably been written as though mu-sicians are the only influencers, but any jazz musician who has been around the block will tell you a much different story. A single influential person behind the scenes—Jimmy Lyons in the case of Dave Brubeck, Dave Dex-ter in the case of Stan Kenton—can make a significant difference; and when several of them unite, as happened in the case of Ornette Coleman, a career can turn on a dime. In the case of West Coast jazz, these institutions played a crucial role in delineating, preserving and disseminating the music—and those three tasks have tremendous import even if they require no familiarity with harmony, melody, and rhythm.

The existence of opportunities to record represented by these labels not only presented the local musicians with a chance to make their names but helped attract legions of itinerant musicians to the area. The fact that so few West Coast musicians were born in California—another supposed disproof of the existence of West Coast jazz—simply reinforces the opposite conclusion. Musicians were attracted to the coast because there were a number of institutions in place—clubs and playing gigs in addition to record companies—to justify the move. If regional styles were simply a question of the birthplace of musical talent, one might, for example, talk with justification of Indiana jazz, with its development in the music of Wes Montgomery, Buddy Montgomery, Leroy Vinnegar, Benny Barth, Carl Perkins, Freddie Hubbard, and the like. And these musicians actually show more than a little stylistic similarity in their playing—one could persuasively argue that there was an "Indianapolis sound." But Indiana lacked the institutions at the time that would have been necessary to promote "Indiana jazz," and many of its finest musicians ended up on the two coasts. Those who stayed "back home in Indiana," as the song goes, did so at the cost of their reputations as major jazz players.

But although nonmusicians had a pronounced impact on many West Coast musicians' careers, they stopped far short of dictating how the musicians they recorded should play. In this regard, those who suggest that Dick Bock or Les Koenig "created" West Coast jazz are seriously off the mark. The many interviews with West Coast musicians that went into this book show that, if anything, the major West Coast jazz producers of the 1950s gave too little direction to the artists on their rosters. Jack Montrose's comments about Richard Bock are illuminating:

> His sessions were as free as they could possibly be. He hired people he trusted, and even if he didn't completely understand what they were doing, he would give them free rein. In fact, Richard ruined me—because in the 1960s, when that freedom and ambience ceased to exist, I found it very difficult to exist. . . . When the jazz thing ended, with its great creative parameters, I was too spoiled to write commercial music.*

The same sentiments were expressed, in interview after interview, by a host of other West Coast players. The major West Coast jazz record producers were distinguished, in almost every case, by their laissez-faire philosophy.

*Interview with author, March 5, 1990.

But the story of West Coast jazz is also the story of the failure of institutions. The development of a jazz scene on the coast grew in uneven spurts and bounds. Record companies and musicians, clubs and jazz educators sprang up in California very rapidly, but the jazz critics and major jazz periodicals maintained East Coast addresses. The lack of an influential, indigenous critical establishment was the one missing ingredient that plagued the whole development of the music. The colorful story of Kenton's manager, Carlos Gastel, literally driving *Downbeat*'s Dave Dexter across the country in a Cadillac to hear the Kenton band is a favorite Kentonian legend, but it could also stand as a symbolic tale of what it could take to get noticed east of the Rockies. With few exceptions, the musicians who went back east made the big reputations—Mingus, Dexter, Dolphy, Ornette, Mulligan—while the players who stayed out west, especially those with harder, bop-oriented styles, merely made music.

For the musicians resident in other parts of the West Coast—Portland, Seattle, Vancouver, San Diego—the situation was even more limiting. In these cities the paucity of institutions to record and promote the music proved all too decisive. The reason historians of West Coast jazz dwell on the Los Angeles and San Francisco scenes has nothing to do with California chauvinism but is due simply to the negligible preservation and dissemination of music from these other areas. Like the glib hold-up man who, when asked why he robbed banks, replied "because that's where the money is," so must the historian of the West Coast scene go where that history was preserved. It is all too indicative that when Froebel Brigham wanted to record his San Diego protégé Harold Land at the close of the 1940s, the band had to drive to Los Angeles to record the session. The situation in LA or San Francisco may have been far from ideal for jazz musicians in the 1940s and 1950s, but still it allowed some opportunity to make a modest name without leaving town—something that was virtually impossible in other spots on the coast.

This fame usually came in small doses and with only modest help from the Pacific Coast media. The task of going through the California newspapers from the early days of West Coast jazz is a stimulating exercise in seeing what was not covered. Charlie Parker, during his tenure on the coast, rarely warranted much more than a passing mention. Even in the black media he was less celebrated than his onetime sideman Jack McVea, or Nellie Lutcher, or Joe Liggins and the Honeydrippers. When a write-up in the media did make a difference for a West Coast player, as in the case of *Time* magazine's coverage of Mulligan/Baker or its later cover story on Brubeck, it was the national media that stepped in, not any local paper or periodical. This was a matter of necessity, for there simply were no periodicals out west, akin to a *New Yorker* or *Village Voice* today, where a review, if by some miracle it had appeared, could have made a difference.

This remains true to this day: A write-up in *Sunset* magazine does not generate much work for an up-and-coming jazz player. And finally, even when California did attract jazz critics from other, colder climes—Leonard Feather, Ralph Gleason, Stanley Dance—these writers rarely saw themselves as advocates for West Coast jazz. They were typically more interested in spreading the word of East Coast bands and players to their uninitiated West Coast readers. Even Gleason, who had a relation with Fantasy so close that he was on the company's payroll, was anything but a West Coast jazz advocate. The title of his major book is something of a giveaway as to his concerns in jazz: *Celebrating the Duke and Louis, Bessie, Billie, Bird, Carmen, Miles, Dizzy and Other Heroes.* Indeed these East Coast heroes richly deserved to be celebrated, but if Gleason was not going to celebrate Brubeck and Desmond, Hawes and Perkins, Baker and Rogers, Criss and Land, who would? There simply were too many good musicians and too few critics in California, and it was unfortunate that the best of the local San Francisco critics had little interest in what has happening in his own backyard.

The West Coast phenomenon made an impact, at almost every point, *despite* the critics. People liked the music. And this seemed, in fact, only to infuriate the critics all the more. This, too, is an essential part of the story of West Coast jazz. Brubeck, the one West Coaster to hit the pinnacle of the jazz world before moving back east, did it by relentless touring, developing his own audience night after night. Kenton did the same thing with his intense road schedules, which embraced clinics, concerts, dances, interviews, whatever his booking agent could drum up. West Coast jazz was a musical equivalent of a grass-roots campaign. Where it succeeded, it did so by bypassing the critics. And the response of jazz fans during the 1950s to what was happening out west was unabashedly positive. The *Downbeat* and *Metronome* readers' polls tell a story of jazz in those years strikingly at odds with what the jazz history books have to say.

The antagonistic critics at the time were often stymied by the public's response. They kept trying to write off Kenton or Brubeck or Baker or Hawes or Tjader. The general belief of those hostile to the music was that the success of the West Coast artists was simply a passing fad, like surf music in the 1960s or disco in the 1970s. But this proved to be anything but the case. In virtually every instance, these artists showed phenomenal staying power. Brubeck continues to sell out huge auditoriums and rack up big record sales over forty years after the octet. Chet Baker has more records in print now, after his death, than probably at any time in his life—this, again, some forty years after his first recordings. Art Pepper, Frank Morgan, Hampton Hawes, Cal Tjader—their names are not writ large in the histories of jazz, but dozens of their albums remain in print and continue selling at a brisk pace. And the few exceptions to this phenomenon only go against the critical consensus; for example, Jimmy Giuffre's work from the 1950s is mostly out of print and sadly neglected, yet he was one of the West Coasters with the strongest support among East Coast critics in the 1950s.

And when write-ups did appear in the 1950s on the phenomenon of West Coast jazz, they often distorted the music beyond recognition. The fact that only certain kinds of music were associated with the West Coast was in itself a gross misrepresentation, but even the artists who were touted as "West Coast players" suffered from the east versus west mentality that permeated discussions of the topic. In today's pluralistic jazz world, most listeners and critics are comfortable with different styles coexisting in peaceful harmony, but this multiplicity of musical methods was somewhat alien to the postwar listeners. It appeared that new styles had to supplant the old ones: Swing replaced traditional jazz, bop replaced swing, and so on. This either/or mentalitywas furthered by jazz publications such as *Downbeat*, which in its earlier days revealed a tabloid mentality (long since abandoned, one happily notes) in which such controversies were hyped rather than underplayed. Accounts of Charlie Parker and Dizzy Gillespie in that periodical went out of their way to fan the flames of contention between swing and bop—and, to be honest, probably sold more records and magazines by doing so. Little wonder that West Coast was made to do battle with East Coast, or that avant-garde was made to do battle with bop. The jazz world has taken a long time to shake off this mentality, and it still lingers in odd ways. One still encounters revealing comments from people who don't like West Coast jazz because, as they explain it, they prefer Art Blakey, Sonny Rollins, Cannonball Adderley and the like. The implication is that the two kinds of music are mutually exclusive. By this token, one would have to give up Louis Armstrong in order to appreciate Duke Ellington—a strange way of enjoying music! But with the passage of time, it is such crudely posed alternative accounts of jazz supremacy that begin to look a little ragged. The music itself holds up quite well.

These considerations are not raised simply to bash the establishment critics of days gone by, however satisfying that pastime may prove to be. One cannot and should not expect New York critics, then or now, to take the lead in sifting through the jazz scenes in each and every city on the globe, nor is it surprising that the New York critics have touted artists whose careers they have been able to follow closely and at firsthand. Rather such points are brought up with the aim of explaining the need for a historical reassessment of the music that was West Coast jazz. As we approach a half-century after the Kenton band's debut at the Rendezvous Ballroom, we perhaps are only now achieving the distance necessary to give a fair account of this often dismissed and discredited body of work.

One can no longer attribute the continuing appeal of the music to passing fad or fancy, a temporary aberration of the public taste, or the big promotional budgets of the major labels. Nor can we continue to dismiss much of the West Coast output because it "doesn't sound like bebop" or hard bop or what you will. The time has passed for continuing illusions about what jazz *should* sound like—especially given the here-to-stay diversity of jazz in the postmodern years. Models from social sciences, clumsily applied to jazz, imply that one paradigm replaces another, that the new replaces the old; but the growing realization among practitioners in the contemporary arts is that such models bear little resemblance to what is actually happening in modern music, painting, poetry, or jazz. We are blinded by our theories of paradigm shift.

If the history of jazz innovation—the heated battles waged by Parker, Gillespie, Coleman, Coltrane, and others—has one lesson, it is simply that jazz sounds the way it sounds. Any extension of any tradition can be dismissed out of hand if the old rules are applied without an appreciation for the new. In this regard, the Kenton band and the Brubeck Octet are no different from the bebop bands at Minton's. They must be evaluated on the basis of what they were trying to achieve, not some imposed standards that have nothing to do with what the players were aiming at.

No account of West Coast jazz can, however, shirk the subject of influence. The most ardent defender of the virtues of distinctive West Coast players such as Baker, Pepper, Guaraldi, Brubeck, Desmond, Rogers, and Manne—to name a few—cannot pretend that their contributions and fresh voices have had a major impact on the playing of later generations. Even in the pluralistic contemporary jazz environment, the models followed by the younger players are invariably drawn from the East Coast mainstream. In this regard, however, West Coast jazz does not stand alone. The revivalistic tendencies of the younger generation of jazz musicians seem to dwell recurringly on resuscitating a few specific sounds out of the past—a Blue Note sound, or a Miles Davis 1960s sound, or a Coltrane Quartet sound—but whole ranges of the jazz experience are neglected. Are these other sounds—Kansas City jazz, West Coast jazz, cool jazz, Third Stream jazz—simply museum pieces with no possible relevance to the future growth of the music?

One hopes not. Histories of this sort have full meaning only as part of an ongoing practice. The jazz musician of today or tomorrow may well go back to these once-explored sounds and find ways of making them new, of making them relevant to contemporary experience. The West Coast experiment that finally ran out of steam in the early sixties did not die for any lack of musical paths left to explore. Nor was it the hostile critics who killed the music. Economics and rock-and-roll, television sets and closing nightclubs, layoffs in the Los Angeles aerospace industry, the increase in attractive studio music jobs, the rising costs of providing live music, the growth of a Las Vegas entertainment establishment that lured audiences and artists away from California while bidding up the fees paid for major acts—these are what did in West Coast jazz. The music did not die of internal complications, as the later revived careers and musical growth of a Pepper or Morgan, a Shank or Hawes demonstrate. The musical trails the West Coast players laid down in the 1950s are far from aesthetic dead ends. They are still out there, waiting for someone new to clear the old path once more and find out where it might lead.

The West Coast jazz scene of the late 1940s and 1950s may seem nowadays like only a faint dream, a dim recollection of a time when California could confidently look at itself as a major center of musical activity. Today the musicians and other artists west of the Rockies apparently have lost that confidence in the centrality of their vision. They no longer feel that the West Coast experience is conducive to great art. Models from back east are invariably imitated by the California artists of the present day, and lauded in turn by the local critics. While Californians may be parochial in defending their weather or sports teams, they do little to hide their inferiority complex in the arts.

And yet a new flowering of West Coast jazz is not beyond the range of future possibilities. The long span of art history shows that great periods of culture go hand in hand with shifts of economic and political power. The rise of banking and merchant powers in Renaissance Italy was intimately connected with the great artistic developments of that age. The economic achievements of the Industrial Revolution coincided with the heyday of English Romanticism and the great Victorian novel. New York's role as the financial capital of the Western world has thrust it into a central position in the world of high culture. But economic forces are brewing out west. Silicon Valley, venture capital, high-tech start-ups, Pacific Rim trade—such topics may be anathema to practicing artists on the West Coast, but they bode well for such artists' futures. Who knows what interplay between West Coast economics and art, politics and culture, may develop? A new breeze may soon be on the rise—one blowing strong and hard out of the west. Perhaps it will show that this early golden age of California jazz, now seemingly so distant and outside the mainstream of current activity, was but a prelude of things to come.

Appendix
Fifty Representative West Coast Jazz Recordings 1945–1960

Although each of these releases ranks among the finest of the period, these selections do not pretend to include the fifty "best" albums from West Coast jazz. Instead, an attempt has been made to capture some of the breadth and scope of jazz on the coast. I have provided a single issue number for each release, although many of these recordings are available under several different names and in a variety of formats.

Chet Baker: *The Complete Pacific Jazz Studio Recordings of the Chet Baker Quartet with Russ Freeman* (Mosaic MR4 122). This Mosaic box set features the seminal Baker vocal and instrumental sides of the mid-1950s.

Chet Baker: *The Complete Pacific Jazz Live Recordings of the Chet Baker Quartet with Russ Freeman* (Mosaic MR4 113). A companion set to the above date, these performances include some of Baker and Freeman's strongest work of the decade.

Black California (Savoy SVL 2215). This Savoy compilation presents important work by Harold Land, Sonny Criss, Wardell Gray, Art Pepper, and the Roy Porter Big Band.

Clifford Brown/Max Roach Quintet: *Clifford Brown and Max Roach* (Emarcy 814 645-2). This LA date was the band's finest. It includes classic Brown performances of "Joy Spring," "Jordu," and "Daahoud."

Dave Brubeck: *Dave Brubeck Octet* (Fantasy 3-239). Brubeck's enormous success with his later quartet has tended to obscure the path-breaking music of this earlier ensemble. It was one of the most innovative bands of its day.

Dave Brubeck Quartet: *Jazz at Oberlin* (Fantasy 3-245). The Oberlin date ranks among the finest of Brubeck's live college concerts.

Dave Brubeck/Paul Desmond: *Jazz at Storyville* (Fantasy 3-240). This live date features many of the best early recordings of Brubeck and Desmond, including memorable performances of "You Go to My Head" and "Over the Rainbow."

Ornette Coleman: *Something Else!* (Contemporary 7551). Coleman's work for the Contemporary label was a turning point for modern jazz and a major statement of the free jazz aesthetic.

Buddy Collette: *Man of Many Parts* (Contemporary 3522). Collette's long studio exile kept him from the jazz scene during much of his career. This release showcases the versatility and depth of this often overlooked musician.

Bob Cooper: *Coop! The Music of Bob Cooper* (Contemporary 7544). Joined by an outstanding West Coast lineup—including the Candoli brothers, Victor Feldman, Frank Rosolino, and Lou Levy—Cooper presents five standards and his ambitious "Jazz Theme and Four Variations."

Curtis Counce: *You Get More Bounce with Curtis Counce* (Contemporary 7539). Counce's band was the hard bop successor on the coast to the Brown/ Roach Quintet and one of the finest LA bands of its day.

Sonny Criss: *Intermission Riff* (Pablo 2310-929). This live performance, released posthumously, captures the twenty-three-year-old altoist at his best.

Russ Freeman/Richard Twardzik: *Trio* (Pacific 7-46861-2). This reissue brings together two outstanding mid-1950s piano trio releases from the Pacific label.

Terry Gibbs: *Dream Band* (Contemporary 7647). For thirty years the tapes of this outstanding band stayed unreleased. They now establish Gibbs's unit as one of the top big bands of its day.

Jimmy Giuffre: *Jimmy Giuffre Clarinet* (Atlantic 1238). Giuffre's work from the 1950s covers a wide range of styles and approaches. The clarient album successfully tied a number of different strains together. It combined Giuffre's experimental tendencies with his lyricism and instinct for musical surprises.

Dexter Gordon: *The Chase* (Spotlite SPJ 130). These classic Dial sides feature Gordon, Wardell Gray, and Teddy Edwards. They include some of the finest bop performances, from either coast, of their day.

Dexter Gordon: *The Bethlehem Years* (Bethlehem 6008). This reissue includes outstanding Gordon performances from the mid-1950s.

Dexter Gordon/Wardell Gray: *The Hunt* (Savoy 2222). The sound quality is poor, and the songs stretch on for twenty minutes each—but few live jazz recordings of the postwar years can match the sheer excitement of this July 6, 1947, encounter between Gordon and Gray.

Wardell Gray: *Memorial Volume One* (Prestige 7008). This reissue captures first-rate Gray work from the close of the Central Avenue era.

Vince Guaraldi: *The Vince Guaraldi Trio* (Fantasy 3-225). In later years, this engaging pianist would have big successes with his "Cast Your Fate to the Wind" and his enduring soundtracks to the Charlie Brown TV specials. This 1956 date with guitarist Eddie Duran and bassist Dean Reilly showcases the lyricism and bluesiness that were Guaraldi trademarks.

Chico Hamilton: *Gongs East* (Discovery 831). With Eric Dolphy in the band, Hamilton put together his best leader date from the 1950s.

Hampton Hawes: *All Night Session* (Contemporary 7545, 7546, 7547). Starting late November 12, 1956, and going on until dawn the next day, Hawes laid down some two hours of his music. The three original recordings—now available together in reissue—present this exceptional pianist at peak form.

Bill Holman: *In a Jazz Orbit* (Andex 3004). Holman was the hardest swinging of the Kenton arrangers. *In a Jazz Orbit* was the best of Holman's 1950s leader dates.

Stan Kenton: *Cuban Fire* (Capitol 7-96260-2). One of the most satisfying Kenton dates and a landmark of Latin jazz.

Stan Kenton: *City of Glass and This Modern World* (Capitol W736). Kenton's taste for experimentation never took him any farther into the avant-garde than on this recording of Bob Graettinger's compositions.

Harold Land: *The Fox* (Contemporary 7619). A blistering hard bop from the close of the decade. The finest of the few existing recordings of trumpeter Dupree Bolton. Land has never played better.

Harold Land: *Harold in the Land of Jazz* (Contemporary 7550). Solid straight-ahead offering from tenorist Land.

Lighthouse All-Stars: *Music for Lighthousekeeping* (Contemporary 7528). The strongest release by the most hard-bop oriented of the Lighthouse bands. Features Frank Rosolino, Conte Candoli, Sonny Clark, Bob Cooper, Stan Levey, and Howard Rumsey.

Shelly Manne and His Men: *Volume One, The West Coast Sound* (Contemporary 3507). This music helped put the West Coast sound on the map.

Shelly Manne: *The Gambit* (Contemporary 3557). Manne's extended works of the mid- and late 1950s are among the forgotten masterpieces of the decade. Charles Mariano's "The Gambit" is perhaps the best of these.

Shelley Manne and His Men: *At the Blackhawk, Volume One* (Contemporary 7577). The four live albums recorded by Manne at the Blackhawk in 1959 show the influence of the hard bop currents from the East Coast.

The Mastersounds: *Introducing the Mastersounds* (World Pacific 403). The Mastersounds were a ballsier West Coast equivalent of the Modern Jazz Quartet. This release, their first recording, captures some of their strongest work.

Howard McGhee: *Trumpets at Tempo* (Spotlite SPJ 131). *Trumpets at Tempo* presents the McGhee band's best West Coast bop work—with Teddy Edwards and Dodo Marmarosa along for the ride—from the mid-1940s.

Charles Mingus: *The Young Rebel* (Contact ST-1010). This reissue features seldom-heard Mingus sides from his LA years.

Red Mitchell: *The Red Mitchell Quartet* (Contemporary 7538). This powerful mid-1950s hard bop band also included James Clay, Lorraine Geller, and Billy Higgins.

Brew Moore: *The Brew Moore Quartet and Quintet* (Fantasy 3-222). This Fantasy release highlights the skills of this hard-swinging tenorist from the Lester Young school. Moore's famous quip was: "Anyone who doesn't play like Prez is wrong."

Frank Morgan: *Bird Calls* (Savoy 1201). Morgan's career hit full stride in the 1980s, but this 1954 Hollywood date shows that the twenty-one-year-old altoist was a prepossessing musician from the start.

Gerry Mulligan: *The Complete Pacific Jazz and Capitol Recordings of the Original Gerry Mulligan Quartet and Tentette with Chet Baker* (Mosaic MR5-102). This box set includes the finest and most influential examples of Mulligan's West Coast work.

Lennie Niehaus: *Volume One, the Quintets* (Contemporary 3518). These outstanding selections reveal a virtuoso altoist seldom heard from in later years.

Red Norvo Trio: *The Savoy Sessions* (Savoy 2212). Joined by Charles Mingus and Tal Farlow, Norvo led this exceptional vibes/bass/guitar trio from the early 1950s.

Charlie Parker: *The Very Best of Bird* (Warner Bros. 3198). These are landmark recordings. Bird's LA dates for Dial Records witnessed some of the finest music of his career.

Art Pepper: *Meets the Rhythm Section* (Contemporary 7532). This powerful pairing of Pepper with Miles Davis's rhythm section led to one of the best Contemporary dates of the decade.

Art Pepper plus Eleven: *Modern Jazz Classics* (Contemporary 7568). Pepper's rendition of modern jazz clasasics—with charts courtesy of Marty Paich—has earned a place as a jazz classic in its own right.

Art Pepper: *The Art of Pepper* (Omegatape 2030). This was Pepper's strongest working band of the decade. Originally released only on Omega Tape, a 3¾ ips format, this dynamic session featuring Pepper with pianist Carl Perkins went unnoticed until its reissue in the 1970s. A real gem.

Bill Perkins: *2 Degrees East, 3 Degrees West* (Pausa 9019). The title comes from the felicitious combination of three West Coast musicians (Perkins, Chico Hamilton, Jim Hall) with two sympathetic players from the east (John Lewis, Percy Heath).

Shorty Rogers: *Courts the Count* (RCA LJM-1004). The influence of the Count Basie sound on West Coast jazz has seldom been noted, but it comes to the fore in this mid-1950s recording pairing Rogers with Basie trumpeter "Sweets" Edison in the context of an all-star LA band.

Shorty Rogers: *Short Stops* (RCA/Bluebird 5917). This RCA reissue includes classic Rogers sides from 1953 and 1954. These recordings were crucial in delineating a "West Coast" sound in jazz.

Frank Rosolino: *Free for All* (Specialty 2161). Released almost twenty years after being recorded, *Free for All* features Rosolino in a "Blue Note" setting with Harold Land, Leroy Vinnegar, Victor Feldman, and Stan Levey.

Bud Shank: *Live at the Haig* (Choice 6830). Shank's finest moments during the 1950s usually came when he didn't realize the tape was running. This amateur recording from the mid-1950s features outstanding stereo sound and captures the altoist (and pianist Claude Williamson) at a transition point between their early cool and later hot styles.

Cal Tjader: *Monterey Concerts* (Prestige 24026). Tjader's 1959 live date from Monterey captured one of his finest bands, which included Latin jazz masters Mongo Santamaria and Willie Bobo.

Notes

One: *Central Avenue Breakdown*

1. Interviews with author, March 29 and October 17, 1989.

2. Interview with author, July 19, 1989.

3. Pops Foster and Tom Stoddard, *Pops Foster: The Autobiography of a New Orleans Jazzman* (Berkeley: University of California Press, 1971), 130–31.

4. Interview with author, April 18, 1989.

5. Scott DeVeaux, "Conversation with Howard McGhee: Jazz in the Forties," *Black Perspective in Music*, Spring 1987, p. 71. This article contains extracts from several interviews DeVeaux—who later wrote a dissertation on McGhee and Hawkins at UC Berkeley—conducted with the trumpeter in New York in the early 1980s.

6. Letter to John Chilton, dated August 20, 1987, quoted in Chilton's *The Song of the Hawk: The Life and Recordings of Coleman Hawkins* (Michigan: University of Michigan Press, 1990), 227.

7. Interview with author, March 27, 1989. All further unattributed Roy Porter quotes are from this interview or interviews conducted on March 7 and 14, 1989.

8. Interview with the author, October 17, 1989. All further unattributed Nathaniel "Monk" McFay quotes are from this interview.

9. Interview with author, July 7, 1990.

10. Ross Russell, *Bird Lives: The High Life and Hard Times of Charlie Yardbird Parker* (New York: Charterhouse, 1973), 224.

11. Interviews with author, March 29 and October 17, 1989.

12. Valerie Wilmer, *Jazz People* (Indianapolis: Bobbs Merrill, 1970), 142.

13. Ira Gitler, *Swing to Bop: An Oral History of the Transition in Jazz in the 1940s* (New York: Oxford University Press, 1985), 166.

14. Ted Gioia, "Art Pepper: His Last Interview," *Jazz Times*, June 1984, p. 11.

Two: The Bird in the Basket

1. Correspondence with author. All further unattributed Harry "the Hipster" Gibson quotes are from correspondence and tapes sent to the author in fall 1989.

2. *California Eagle*, March 10, 1949, p. 1.

3. Interview with author, August 27, 1989.

4. "The California Cats: Sonny Criss Talks to Bob Porter and Mark Gardner," *Jazz Monthly*, April 1968, p. 8.

5. Ibid.

6. Ira Gitler, *Swing to Bop: An Oral History of the Transition in Jazz in the 1940s* (New York: Oxford University Press, 1985), 166.

7. Ross Russell, *Bird Lives: The High Life and Hard Times of Charlie Yardbird Parker* (New York: Charterhouse, 1973), 215.

8. Miles Davis with Quincey Troupe, *Miles: The Autobiography* (New York: Simon & Schuster, 1989), 93.

9. Scott DeVeaux, "Conversation with Howard McGhee: Jazz in the Forties," *Black Perspective in Music*, Spring 1987, p. 75.

10. Gitler, *Swing to Bop*, 182.

Three: The Chase

1. Hampton Hawes and Don Asher, *Raise Up off Me* (1974; rpt. New York: Da Capo, 179), 33.

2. Herbie Butterfield, "Wardell Gray," *Jazz Journal*, October 1961, p. 2.

3. Robert Reisner, ed., *Bird: The Legend of Charlie Parker* (New York: Citadel Press, 1962), 201.

4. Quoted in Thorbjørn Sjøgren, *Long Tall Dexter: The Discography of Dexter Gordon* (Copenhagen: Privately published, 1986), 7.

5. *Downbeat*, July 2, 1947, 10; see also Phil Schaap's liner notes to *Jazz Concert West* (SJC 407) on the Savoy label.

6. Shirley Klett, "Roy Porter Interview, Part 2," *Cadence*, October 1986, p. 6.

7. Art and Laurie Pepper, *Straight Life* (New York: Schirmer, 1979), 43.

8. Ira Gitler, *Jazz Masters of the Forties* (New York: Macmillan, 1966), 202.

9. Quoted in Sjøgren, *Long Tall Dexter*, 5.

10. Quoted in Gary Giddins, *Riding on a Blue Note* (New York: Oxford University Press, 1981), 248–49.

11. Quoted in Gitler, *Swing to Bop*, 38.

12. Quoted in Ross Russell's liner notes to *The Chase* (Spotlite SPJ 130).

13. Interview with author, April 18, 1989. All further unattributed Marshall Royal quotes are from this interview.

14. From Paul Bullock and David Hoxie's interview with Collette, reprinted in *Man of Many Parts: A Discography of Buddy Collette*, compiled by Coen Hofmann (Amsterdam: Micography, 1985), 9.

15. Gitler, *Jazz Masters of the Forties*, 203.

16. From Bullock and Hoxie's interview with Collette, in *Man of Many Parts*, 8.

17. This, and below, from Michael Ullman, *Jazz Lives: Portraits in Words and Pictures* (Washington, D.C.: New Republic Books, 1980), 93–94.

18. This, and below, quoted in Gitler, *Jazz Masters of the Forties*, 203–4.

19. Ibid., 206.

20. Quoted in Giddins, *Riding on a Blue Note*, 249–50.

21. Peter Keepnews, "The Lionization of Dexter Gordon," *Jazz*, vol. 1, issue 4, p. 30.

22. Quoted in Gitler, *Swing to Bop*, 145–46.

23. Bob Rusch, "Dexter Gordon: Interview," *Cadence*, November 1981, p. 7.

24. Klett, "Roy Porter Interview, Part 2," 6; Art and Laurie Pepper, *Straight Life*, 43.

25. Quoted in Gitler, *Jazz Masters of the Forties*, 209.

26. *Melody Maker*, July 31, 1954, p. 3.

27. Hawes and Asher, *Raise Up off Me*, 33.

28. Quoted in Gitler, *Swing to Bop*, 256.

29. This, and below, from Hawes and Asher, *Raise Up off Me*, 7–8.

30. Red Callender and Elaine Cohen, *Unfinished Dream* (London: Quartet Books, 1985), 79–80.

31. Interview with author, February 7, 1989. All further Vernon Alley quotes are from this interview.

32. This, and below, from Keepnews, "Lionization of Dexter Gordon," 31.

33. Hawes and Asher, *Raise Up off Me*, 76.

34. Quoted in Stanley Dance, *The World of Count Basie* (New York: Charles Scribner's Sons, 1980), 234.

35. Rusch, "Dexter Gordon: Interview," 7.

36. Callender and Cohen, *Unfinished Dream*, 79–80.

Four: Dave Brubeck and Modern Jazz in San Francisco

1. Quoted in Tom Stoddard, *Jazz on the Barbary Coast* (Essex, Eng.: Storyville Publications, 1982), 54.

2. Alan Lomax, *Mister Jelly Roll* (Berkeley: University of California Press), 170.

3. Interview with author, May 28, 1988. All further unattributed Max Weiss quotes are from this interview.

4. Quoted in A. B. Spellman, *Black Music: Four Lives* (New York: Schocken, 1970), 61.

5. Quoted in David Watts, "Take the Billy Joel Challenge," *Pulse*, November 1989, p. 79.

6. Interview with author, September 18, 1989. All further unattributed Dave Brubeck quotes are from this interview.

7. Ralph Gleason, "They Said I Was Too Far Out," *Downbeat*, August 8, 1957, p. 17.

8. This, and below, from Owen Goldsmith, "Dave Brubeck," *Contemporary Keyboard*, December 1977, p. 29.

9. Correspondence with author. All unattributed Dave Van Kriedt quotes are either from this correspondence or an interview on April 8, 1989.

10. Gleason, "They Said I Was Too Far Out," 18.

11. Ibid.

12. Quoted in Raymond Horricks, "Dave Brubeck," from *These Jazz-men of Our Time*, Raymond Horricks, ed. (London: Victor Gollancz, 1959), 163.

13. Ralph Gleason, "Perspectives," *Downbeat*, April 6, 1955, p. 18.

14. Gene Lees, *Meet Me at Jim and Andy's* (New York: Oxford University Press, 1988), 249.

15. Letter to Peter Bergmann, June 4, 1979. Emphasis in original. I am indebted to Mr. Bergmann for providing me with this letter and various other materials relating to Paul Desmond.

16. Quoted in Lees, *Meet Me at Jim and Andy's*, 244.

17. Marian McPartland, *All in Good Time* (New York: Oxford University Prress, 1987), 58.

18. Interview with author, February 9, 1989. All further unattributed Ron Crotty quotes are from this interview.

19. Lees, *Meet Me at Jim and Andy's*, 253.

20. Arnold Jay Smith, "The Dave Brubeck Quartet: A Quarter of a Century Young," *Downbeat*, March 25, 1976, p. 20.

21. Interview with author, January 18, 1989. All further unattributed Joe Dodge quotes are from this interview.

22. Dave Brubeck's liner notes to *The Dave Brubeck Octet* (Fantasy 3-239).

23. Interview with author, April 30, 1988.

Five: The San Francisco Scene in the 1950s

1. Owen Goldsmith, "Dave Brubeck," *Contemporary Keyboard*, December 1977, p. 27.

2. Marian McParland, *All in Good Time* (New York: Oxford University Press, 1987), 61.

3. Phil Elwood's liner notes to *Star Dust: The Dave Brubeck Quartet Featuring Paul Desmond* (Fantasy F-24728).

4. Nat Hentoff, "Jazz Fills Role of Classical Composition, Brubeck Learns," *Downbeat*, June 2, 1954, p. 2.

5. This, and below, from McPartland, *All in Good Time*, 34–35.

6. Quoted in Lee Hildebrand, "Drummer Sticks to Latin Jazz," *San Francisco Chronicle Datebook*, July 3, 1988, p. 36.

7. John Tynan, "Cal Tjader," *Downbeat*, September 5, 1957, p. 17.

8. Douglas Ramsey, "A Talk with Cal Tjader," *Jazz Monthly*, November 1962, pp. 9–10.

9. Quoted in Ralph Gleason, "Swing's the Thing, Says Cal Tjader," *Downbeat*, March 25, 1953.

10. This, and next quote, from Tynan, "Cal Tjader," 17.

11. John Tynan, "Caught in the Act: Cal Tjader," *Downbeat*, June 27, 1956, p. 8.

12. Ralph Gleason's liner notes to Vince Guaraldi, *A Flower Is a Lonesome Thing* (Fantasy 3257).

13. This and the following quote from Ralph Gleason are from Gleason's liner notes to *The Brew Moore Quartet and Quintet* (Fantasy 3222).

14. John S. Wilson, "Brew Brews Bop on Prez Kick," *Downbeat*, July 1, 1949, p. 7.

15. Ibid.

16. Cited in Stan Woolley, "Brew Moore," *Coda* 142 (1975): 25–26.

17. Ramsey, "Talk with Cal Tjader," 8.

18. Interview with author, September 15, 1989. All further unattributed Benny Barth quotes are from this interview.

19. Ralph Gleason's liner notes to the Mastersounds, *The King and I* (World Pacific WPM-405).

Six: Central Avenue Survivors

1. Interview with author, October 14, 1989. All further unattributed Jay McNeely quotes are from this interview.

2. Len Lyons, "Hampton Hawes: Challenging the Charts, on Wood," *Downbeat*, December 16, 1976, p. 23.

3. John Mehagen, "Jazz Pianists: 4," *Downbeat*, July 25, 1957, p. 17.

4. This, and below, from Michael Levin, Nat Hentoff, and Leonard Feather, "Dissonant Thirds," *Downbeat*, September 9, 1956, pp. 16–17.

5. Hampton Hawes and Don Asher, *Raise Up off Me*, (1974; rpt. New York: Da Capo, 1979), 95.

6. Ibid., 99.

7. Quoted in Gitler, *Swing to Bop; An Oral History of the Transition in Jazz in the 1940s* (New York: Oxford University Press, 1985), 170.

8. "The California Cats: Sonny Criss Talks to Bob Porter and Mark Gardner," 8. This two-part interview from the April and May 1968 issues of *Jazz Monthly* remains the most detailed interview Criss gave during his life. Further unattributed Sonny Criss quotes in this chapter are from the interview.

9. Interview with Lucy B. Criss, February 6, 1989. Further unattributed Lucy Criss quotes are from this interview.

10. Ross Russell, *Bird Lives*, (New York: Charterhouse, 1973), 125.

11. Quoted in Gitler, *Swing to Bop*, 167.

12. Ibid., 168.

13. Interview with author, September 5, 1989. All further unattributed Dick Whittington quotes are from this interview.

14. From an interview with John Detro. See "Sonny Criss Fund Set," *Jazz Times*, August 1988, p. 6.

15. Interview with author, March 29, 1989. All further unattributed Teddy Edwards quotes are from this interview.

16. Quoted in Peter Watrous, "Getting to New York at Last," *New York Times*, November 4, 1988.

17. Quoted in John Tynan, "Teddy Edwards: Long, Long Journey," *Downbeat*, May 24, 1962, p. 19.

18. John Tynan, "Hampton Hawes," *Downbeat*, December 28, 1955, p. 9.

19. Hawes and Asher, *Raise Up off Me*, 78.

20. Roger Hunter and Mike Davis, *Hampton Hawes: A Discography*, (Manchester, Eng.: Manyana Publications, 1986), 51.

21. Hawes and Asher, *Raise Up off Me*, 103.

22. Art Taylor, *Notes and Tones* (New York: Putnam, 1977), 181.

Seven: Big Bands Out West

1. Hunter Hancock, "Huntin' with Hunter," *Los Angeles Sentinel*, October 14, 1948, p. 19. See also an unsigned article in the *California Eagle*, "Roy Porter Has Exciting New Swing Orchestra," October 21, 1948, p. 16.

2. Interview with author, March 27, 1989. All further unattributed Roy Porter quotes are from this interview or interviews conducted on March 7 and 14, 1989.

3. Interview with auuthor, October 10, 1989. All further unattributed Gerald Wilson quotes are from this interview.

4. Quoted in Peter Watrous, "Dean of California Jazz in Fifty-Year Retrospective," *New York Times*, October 20, 1988, p. B6.

5. John Garelick, "In the Write Direction," *Boston Phoenix*, November 18, 1988, Sect. 3, p. 13.

6. Quoted in William Lee and Audree Coke, *Stan Kenton: Artistry in Rhythm* (Los Angeles: Creative Press, 1980), 119–20.

7. Quoted in Carol Easton, *Straight Ahead: The Story of Stan Kenton* (New York: William Morrow, 1973), 71.

8. Interview with author, October 16, 1989. All further unattributed Peter Rugolo quotes are from this interview.

9. Quoted in Lee and Coke, *Stan Kenton*, 80.

Eight: City of Glass

1. Carol Easton, *Straight Ahead: The Story of Stan Kenton* (New York: William Morrow, 1973), 138.

2. Quoted in William Lee and Audree Coke, *Stan Kenton, Artistry in Rhythm* (Los Angeles: Creative Press, 1980), 134.

3. Easton, *Straight Ahead*, 139.

4. Quotations that follow are from Carol Easton's excellent account of Bob Graettinger's work with the Kenton band from *Straight Ahead*, 135–40.

5. From Bob Graettinger's comments in the liner notes to *Stan Kenton Conducts Robert Graettinger's City of Glass and This Modern World* (Capitol W736).

6. Interview with author, October 20, 1989. All further unattributed Forrest Westbrook quotes are from this interview.

7. Quoted in Lee and Coke, *Stan Kenton*, 120.

8. Interview with author, September 22, 1989. All further unattributed Bill Holman quotes are from this interview.

9. Quoted in Les Tompkins, "Big Band Arranger Par Excellence Bill Holman," *Crescendo International*, February 1987, p. 6.

10. Interview with author, October 5, 1989. All further unattributed Lennie Niehaus quotes are from this interview.

11. Max Harrison, *A Jazz Retrospect* (New York: Crescendo, 1976), 168.

12. From the liner notes to *Terry Gibbs Dream Band* (Contemporary 7647).

13. From the liner notes to *Terry Gibbs Dream Band, Volume Three, Flying Home* (Contemporary 7654).

14. Quoted in Easton, *Straight Ahead*, 89.

Nine: Chet Baker and the Pianoless Quartet

1. Bob Rusch,"Chet Baker: Interview," *Cadence*, August 1978, p. 9.

2. From a transcript of a radio interview conducted in Holland in early 1988. I am indebted to Peter Pabst for providing me with tapes of this and other European radio interviews with Chet Baker. All further uncited Baker quotations are from this interview.

3. Quoted in Hans Henrik Lerfeldt and Thorbjørn Sjøgren, *Chet: The Discography of Chesney Henry Baker* (Copenhagen: privately published, 1985), vii.

4. Bob Rosenblum, "Chet Baker" (interview), *Coda*, Sept./Oct. 1977, p. 6.

5. Quoted in Lerfeldt and Sjøgren, *Chet*, vii.

6. Author's interview with Richard Bock, December 23, 1986. All further unattributed Bock quotes are from this interview.

7. Quoted in Bob Micklin, "Chet Baker Knows the Blues," *Milwaukee Journal*, September 23, 1973.

8. "Counterpoint in Jazz," *Time*, February 2, 1953, p. 36.

9. Bob Rusch, "Gerry Mulligan: Interview," *Cadence*, October 1977, p. 7.

10. Ibid., 6.

11. Quoted in Nat Hentoff, *Jazz Is* (New York: Random House, 1976), 117.

12. Quoted in Ira Gitler, *Swing to Bop: An Oral History of the Transition in Jazz in the 1940s* (New York: Oxford University Press, 1985), 252.

13. Ibid., 247–48.

14. Rusch, "Chet Baker: Interview," 9.

15. John Tynan, "Straight Talk from Russ Freeman," *Downbeat*, March 14, 1963, p. 20.

16. Quoted in Will Thornbury's essay accompanying *The Complete Pacific Jazz Studio Recordings of the Chet Baker Quartet with Russ Freeman* (Mosaic MR4-122).

17. Interview with author, September 2, 1989. All further unattributed Russ Freeman quotes are from this interview.

18. From the liner notes to Shelly Manne's *The Three and The Two* (Contemporary OJC-172).

19. Rusch, "Chet Baker: Interview," 33.

20. Quoted in Lerfeldt and Sjøgren, *Chet*, ix.

21. Fran Kelley, "Chico Making Time with Jazz Chamber Group," *Metronome*, August 1955, p. 20.

22. Interview with the author, August 9, 1989. All further unattributed Chico Hamilton quotes are from this interview.

23. This, and below, quoted in Didier Deutsch, "Chet Baker and the Demons That Haunted Him," *Jazziz*, May 1989, p. 13.

24. Quoted in Joe Goldberg's essay accompanying *The Complete Pacific Jazz Live Recordings of the Chet Baker Quartet with Russ Freeman* (Mosaic MR4 113).

25. Quoted in Micklin, "Chet Baker Knows the Blues."

26. Pauline Kael, "The Current Cinema: Fascination," *New Yorker*, May 1, 1989, p. 75.

27. Max Harrison, "Gerry Mulligan," in *These Jazzmen of Our Time*, ed. Raymond Horricks (London: Victor Gollancz, 1959), 74.

Ten: From the Lighthouse

1. I am indebted to Howard Rumsey for much of the background information included in this chapter. All unattributed Howard Rumsey quotes come from our correspondence.

2. Quoted in Leonard Feather, *The Passion for Jazz* (New York: Horizon Press, 1980), 168.

3. Quoted in Carol Easton, *Straight Ahead: The Story of Stan Kenton* (New York: Morrow, 1973), 57.

4. Author's interview with Teddy Edwards, March 29, 1989. I am also indebted to Edwards for providing me with a long biographical document from which some of this information is drawn.

5. Leonard Feather, "Howard Rumsey—Success by the Beach," *International Musician*, June 1966.

6. Interview with the author, July 31, 1987.

7. Quoted in Feather, *Passion for Jazz*, 169–70.

8. Quoted in Linda Dahl, *Stormy Weather: The Music and Lives of a Century of Jazz Women* (New York: Pantheon, 1984), 215.

9. Jack Chambers, *Milestones* (New York: William Morrow, 1983), vol. 1, p. 174.

10. I am indebted to John Miner for his help in tracking down the many permutations and combinations of the Lighthouse band.

11. Easton, *Straight Ahead*, 109.

12. Interview with author, July 31, 1987. All further unattributed Bob Cooper quotes are from this interview.

13. John S. Wilson, "Brew Brews Bop on Prez Kick," *Downbeat*, July 1, 1949, p. 7.

14. Interview with author, February 20, 1988. All further unattributed Bud Shank quotes are from this interview.

15. Gene Lees, *Jazzletter*, December 1988, p. 6.

16. Ibid., 4.

17. Interview with author, May 15, 1989. All further unattributed Claude Williamson quotes are from this interview.

18. Interview with author, September 5, 1989. All further unattributed Dick Whittington quotes come from this interview.

19. Quotations in this paragraph are from Fran Kelley, "Bud Shank Burning Brighter," *Metronome*, February 1956, p. 20, unless otherwise noted.

20. Quoted in Roger Cotterrell, "Bud Shank: A New Image," *Jazz Forum*, March 1987, p. 25.

21. Brian Priestley, "Requiem for Lennie," *Wire*, March 1989, p. 30.

22. Quoted in Gene Lees, *Meet Me at Jim and Andy's* (New York: Oxford University Press, 1988), 115.

23. Quoted in Arne Astrup, "Frank Rosolino," *Coda*, December 1, 1982, p. 9.

24. This, and below, from Leonard Feather's liner notes to Frank Rosolino's *Free For All* (Specialty Records SP 2161).

Eleven: A Ring-tail Monkey

1. Quoted in Ed Michel, "Jimmy Giuffre," in *These Jazzmen of Our Time*, Raymond Horricks, ed. (London: Gollancz, 1959), 146.

2. "Jimmy Giuffre: Four Brothers + Three Decades" *Downbeat*, December 1981, p. 29.

3. Graham Lock, "Coming In from the Cool," *Wire*, March 1989, p. 25.

4. Interview with author, July 31, 1990. All further unattributed Jimmy Giuffre quotes are from this interview.

5. George Avakian in the liner notes to *Orchestra USA: Sonorities* (Columbia CL 2395).

6. André Hodeir, *Jazz: Its Evolution and Esssence*, trans. David Noakes (New York: Grove, 1956), 275–76.

7. This, and below, quoted in Ed Michel, "Jimmy Giuffre," 149–51.

8. This, and below, from the liner notes to *Tangents in Jazz* (Capitol T634).

9. Quoted in "Jimmy Giuffre: Four Brothers + Three Decades," p. 29.

10. Lock, "Coming In from the Cool," 25–26.

11. Hodeir, *Jazz: Its Evolution and Essence*, 276.

12. Quoted in Martin Williams's liner notes to *Ad Lib: The Jimmy Giuffre 4* (Verve MGV-8361).

Twelve: Martians Go Home

1. Bud Shank: Fran Kelley, "Bud Shank Burning Brighter," *Metronome*, February 1956, p. 20. Dexter Gordon: Thorbjørn Sjøgren, *Long Tall Dexter: The Discography of Dexter Gordon* (Copenhagen: Privately published, 1986), 5. Shelly Manne: Dom Cerulli, "Manne!" *Downbeat*, July 25, 1956, p. 14. Art Pepper: Ira Gitler, *Swing to Bop: An Oral History of the Transition in Jazz in the 1940s* (New York: Oxford University Press, 1985), 39. Wardell Gray: Ted Hallock, "Return of the Thin Man," *Melody Maker*, July 31, 1954, p. 3. Shorty Rogers: Interview with author, July 31, 1987; all further unattributed Shorty Rogers quotes are from this interview.

2. Quoted in Steve Voce, *Woody Herman* (London: Apollo Press, 1986), 47–48.

3. Ibid., 55.

4. Robert Gordon, *Jazz West Coast* (London: Quartet, 1986), 58.

5. Quoted in Ralph Gleason's liner notes to *Shorty Rogers Courts the Count* (RCA LJM-1004).

6. Quoted in Todd Selbert's essay accompanying *The Complete Atlantic and EMI Jazz Recordings of Shorty Rogers* (Mosaic MR6-125).

7. This, and below, quoted in Robert Gordon, *Jazz West Coast*, 126–27.

8. Don Gold, "Shorty Rogers," *Downbeat*, July 10, 1958.

9. Quoted in Leonard Feather's liner notes to Bud Shank and Shorty Rogers, *California Concert* (Contemporary C-14012).

Thirteen: The Anti-drummer

1. Quoted in Leonard Feather, "Shelly Manne: All American Drummer," *International Musician*, September 1961, 20.

2. Interview with author, September 2, 1989. All further unattributed Russ Freeman quotes are from this interview.

3. Robert Gordon, *Jazz West Coast* (London: Quartet, 1986), 95.

4. Shelly Manne, "Shelly Manne Offers His Concept of Jazz Drums," *Downbeat*, December 14, 1955.

5. Ira Gitler, *Swing to Bop: An Oral History of the Transition in Jazz in the 1940s* (New York: Oxford University Press, 1985), 51.

6. Quoted in Dom Cerulli, "Manne!" *Downbeat*, July 25, 1956, 14.

7. From Bill Holman's program notes to "Quartet" included in the liner notes to *Shelly Manne and His Men, Volume 5* (Contemporary C3519).

8. From Nat Hentoff's review of *Shelly Manne and His Men, Volume 5*, *Downbeat Record Reviews*, vol. 22 (Chicago: Maher, 1958), 123.

9. Quoted in Nat Hentoff's liner notes to *The Gambit: Shelly Manne and His Men* (Contemporary C 3557).

10. Gitler, *Swing To Bop*, 43.

11. Quoted in Nat Hentoff's liner notes to *The Poll Winners* (Contemporary 7535).

12. Gitler, *Swing To Bop*, 157.

13. Miles Davis with Quincey Troupe, *Miles: The Autobiography of Miles Davis* (New York: Simon & Schuster, 1989), 262–63.

14. Quoted in Les Koenig's liner notes to *Shelly Manne and His Men at the Blackhawk, Volume One* (Contemporary 7577).

15. Interview with the author, September 5, 1989. All further unattributed Dick Whittington quotes come from this interview.

Fourteen: Straight Life

1. Art and Laurie Pepper, *Straight Life* (New York: Schirmer, 1979), 155.

2. Ibid., 90–91.

3. Ibid., 259, 335.

4. David Pepperell, "I Want to Play So Bad," *Wire*, June 1986, p. 26.

5. Art and Laurie Pepper, *Straight Life*, 44.

6. Quoted in the liner notes to *Art Pepper Discoveries* (Savoy 2217).

7. Bob Rusch, "Jack McVea: Interview," *Cadence*, April 1986, p. 18.

8. Brian Case, "Straight Life," *Melody Maker*, June 9, 1979.

9. Quoted in Art and Laurie Pepper, *Straight Life*, 174.

10. Interview with author, June 13, 1987.

11. Ira Gitler, *Swing to Bop: An Oral History of the Transition in Jazz in the 1940s* (New York: Oxford University Press, 1985), 153.

12. Ibid., 224.

13. Art and Laurie Pepper, *Straight Life*, 85–86.

14. Dick Bock, "Scanning," *Downbeat*, March 7, 1952, p. 2.

15. John Tynan, "Art Pepper . . . Tells the Tragic Role Narcotics Played in Blighting His Career and Life," *Downbeat*, September 19, 1956, p. 16.

16. Art and Laurie Pepper, *Straight Life*, 191.

17. John Tynan, "Art Pepper Quartet," *Downbeat*, May 16, 1957, p. 34.

18. Interview with author, April 30, 1988. All further unattributed Marty Paich quotes are from this interview.

19. *Downbeat*, May 15, 1942.

20. Art and Laurie Pepper, *Straight Life*, 216.

Fifteen: LA Hard Bop

1. Gene Santoro, "Max Roach," *Pulse*, December 1988, p. 88.

2. This, and below, quoted in Whitney Balliett, "Zoot and Louise," *New Yorker*, May 12, 1986, p. 113.

3. Bob Rusch, "Terry Gibbs," *Cadence*, October 1988, p. 22. See also part one of this interview in *Cadence*, September 1988, pp. 5–22.

4. Transcribed from a tape of a panel discussion on West Coast jazz held at the 1988 Jazz Times convention in Southern California.

5. Author's interview with Harold Land, December 21, 1988. All further unattributed Harold Land quotes are from this interview.

6. See Stanley Dance's informative "Jazz Musicians in San Diego," *Black Music Research Bulletin*, Spring 1988, pp. 10–11.

7. Interview with the author, March 8, 1989.

8. Marc Cobb, "Interview: Harold Land," *Bebop and Beyond*, Nov./Dec. 1984, p. 17.

9. Ibid., 18.

10. Interview with author, April 20, 1989. All further unattributed Leroy Vinnegar quotes are from this interview.

11. Interview with author, September 5, 1989. All further unattributed Dick Whittington quotes come from this interview.

12. This, and below, from Nat Hentoff's liner notes to *Harold in the Land of Jazz* (Contemporary C7550).

13. Bob Rusch, "Leroy Vinnegar Interview," *Cadence*, March 1989, p. 10.

14. Author's interview with Jack Sheldon, June 13, 1987. All further unattributed Jack Sheldon quotes are from this interview.

15. Quoted in Jim Dawson's notes to *The Dootone Story, Volume 1* (Ace CHD 242).

16. "West Coast Session," *Downbeat*, October 15, 1959, p. 15. Unattributed but likely written by *Downbeat*'s West Coast correspondent of the time, John Tynan.

17. From Leonard Feather's liner notes to *The Fox* (Contemporary 7619).

18. *Jazz Times*, December 1982, p. 14.

19. Cobb, "Interview: Harold Land," 18.

20. John Tynan, "Curtis Amy Sextet," *Downbeat*, March 14, 1963, p. 36.

Sixteen: Something Else!

1. Paul Horn and Lee Underwood, *Inside Paul Horn: The Spiritual Odyssey of a Universal Traveller* (San Francisco: Harper Collins, 1990), 116.

2. Quoted in Peter Szigeti, "Bruce Ackley: Interview," *Cadence*, June 1984, p. 20.

3. Quoted in Brian Priestley, *Mingus: A Critical Biography* (New York: Quartet Books, 1983).

4. Janet Coleman and Al Young, *Mingus/Mingus* (Berkeley: Creative Arts Company, 1989), 4.

5. Priestley, *Mingus*, 10.

6. Red Callender and Elaine Cohen, *Unfinished Dream: The Musical World of Red Callender* (London: Quartet, 1985), 38.

7. Quoted in Michael Ullman, *Jazz Lives: Portraits in Words and Pictures* (Washington, D.C.: New Republic Books, 1980), 94.

8. Quoted in Robert Gordon, *Jazz West Coast* (London: Quartet, 1986), 28.

9. Ira Gitler, *Jazz Masters of the Forties* (New York: Macmillan, 1966), 206.

10. This and the comments below on Louis Armstrong and Kid Ory are

quoted in Nat Hentoff, "Charles Mingus," in *These Jazzmen of Our Time*, ed. Raymond Horricks (London: Victor Gollancz, 1959), 180.

11. Miles Davis with Quincy Troupe, *Miles: The Autobiography of Miles Davis* (New York: Simon & Schuster, 1989), 86.

12. Ibid., 86.

13. Ibid., 93.

14. Mingus's complete autobiographical writings remain unpublished. In addition to the unissued portions of *Beneath the Underdog*, the existence of a second Mingus book, on music and musicians, became known in 1988. The section quoted above is from extracts of this latter work included in Tom Moon, "The Black Saint's Epitaph," *Musician*, June 1989, p. 65.

15. Interview with author, July 19, 1989. All further unattributed Nadi Qamar quotes are from this interview.

16. This, and below, from Priestly, *Mingus*, 48.

17. Quoted in Nat Hentoff, "Charles Mingus," 185.

18. "Charles Mingus Is Back in Town with New Combo," *California Eagle*, November 4, 1948, p. 17.

19. "The 'Baron' to Record When Ban Is Lifted," *California Eagle*, November 11, 1948, p. 16.

20. Quoted in Shirley Klett, "Red Norvo: Interview," *Cadence*, July 1979, p. 10.

21. Quoted in the liner notes to *The Red Norvo Trio* (Savoy SJL-2212).

22. Stuart Nicholson, "Axe of the Apostles," *Wire*, September 1990, p. 72.

23. David Keller, "Eric Dolphy: The Los Angeles Years," *Jazz Times*, November 1981, p. 14.

24. The comments here and below by Buddy Collette have been transcribed from a tape of a panel discussion on West Coast jazz held at the 1988 Jazz Times convention in Southern California.

25. Quoted in Vladimir Simosko and Barry Tepperman, *Eric Dolphy: A Musical Biography and Discography*, (Washington, D.C.: Smithsonian Institution Press, 1974), 36.

26. Ibid., 37.

27. A. B. Spellman, *Four Lives in the Bebop Business* (New York: Pantheon, 1966), 85.

28. Ibid., 102.

29. Ibid.

30. Ibid., 105.

31. Scott Fish, "Ed Blackwell: Singin' on the Set," *Modern Drummer*, November 1981, p. 17.

32. John Tynan, "Ornette: The First Beginning," *Downbeat*, July 21, 1960, p. 32.

33. Interview with the author, March 15, 1989.

34. John Tynan, "Ornette: The First Beginning," 33.

35. Ibid.

36. Quoted in Nat Hentoff's liner notes to *Tomorrow Is the Question: The New Music of Ornette Coleman* (Contemporary 7569).

37. Interview with author, April 5, 1990. All further unattributed Walter Norris quotes are from this interview.

38. From Nat Hentoff's liner notes to *Something Else* (Contemporary 7551).

39. Bill Smith, "Paul Bley," *Coda,* April 1, 1979, p. 4.

40. From Carla Bley's liner notes to *Solemn Meditation: The Paul Bley Quartet* (GNP 31).

41. Ibid.

42. From Eric Kriss's liner notes to *Live at the Hillcrest Club* (Inner City 1007).

43. Bill Smith, "Paul Bley," 4.

44. Howard Mandel, "Charlie Haden's Search for Freedom," *Downbeat,* September 1987, p. 21.

45. Lee Hildebrand, "Jazzman Billy Higgins: He's Had Time for Everyone but Himself," *San Francisco Chronicle Datebook,* October 5, 1986, p. 48.

Index

Hoogeveen, Gerard, 311n
"Hootie Blues," 123
Hope, Bob, 146
Hope, Elmo, 309, 325, 326, 327-28
Horn, Paul, 109, 189, 331-32
Horne, Arthur, 131
Horne, Lena, 187, 189
"House of Strings," 157
"How About You," 215
"How Deep is the Ocean," 322
"How High the Moon," 81, 93, 126
"How Long Has This Been Going On?" 212
Howard, Gene, 154
Howard, Joe, 139-41
Howard, Paul, 8
Hubbard, Freddie, 320, 364
"Hucklebuck, The" 349
Hula Hut (club), 47
"Hunt, The," 36-37, 125

"I Can't Escape from You," 44
"I Can't Get Started," 136
"I Fall in Love Too Easily," 181, 182
"I Get a Kick Out of You," 314
"I Had the Craziest Dream," 322
"I Hear a Rhapsody," 79, 82
"I Mean You," 178
"Igor," 249
"I'll Keep Loving You," 119
"I'll Remember April," 101, 178, 186
"I'm All Smiles," 137
"Impressionism," 151
In Concert, 113
In a Jazz Orbit, 160-61, 164
"Indiana," 87
"Infinity Promenade," 254
Intensity, 305
Interlude (club), 105
Intermission Riff, 126
"Intermission Riff," 142
"Introduction to a Latin Rhythm," 151
"Invisible," 354
"Ipca," 81
"Isn't It Romantic," 259
It Club, 279
"It Don't Mean a Thing," 303
"It Had to Be You," 243
"It's the Talk of the Town," 46
"I've Found a New Baby," 44
"I've Got News for You," 250
"I've Got Rhythm," 118, 353, 354

Jack's Basket (club), see Bird in the Basket
Jackson, Chubby, 222
Jackson, Daniel, 224
Jackson, Jack, 27

Jackson, Milt, 18, 103
Jacquet, Illinois, 41, 188, 320
"Jahbero," 50
Jamal, Ahmad, 118, 119
James, Henry, 170, 287, 347
Jarrett, Keith, 119
"Jayne," 353, 354
Jazz Cellar (club), 351
"Jazz City Blues," 190
Jazz Composition and Orchestration, 158
Jazz Goes to College, 95
Jazz Goes to Junior College, 98
Jazz Journal, 31
Jazz at Oberlin, 93, 357
Jazz at the Philharmonic, 127, 267, 277
Jazz Retrospect, A, 163
Jazz Rolls-Royce, 207-8
Jazz Showcase, 112
Jazz Showcase (club), 112
Jazz Story, The, 147
"Jazz Theme and Four Variations," 208
Jazz West Coast, 227, 251
Jazz Workshop (club), 306
Jazzin' Around, 222
"Jeepers Creepers, 229
Jefferson High School, 23, 40, 57, 124, 187
Jethro Tull, 68
Jimmy Giuffre Clarinet, The, 227, 237
Jimmy Giuffre 3, The, 238
"Jive at Five," 217
Joel, Billy, 68
Johnson, Buddy, 329
Johnson, Jack, 5
Johnson, J. J., 47, 289, 309
Johnson, James P., 227
Johnston, Dick, 224
Johnston, Foster, 21-22
Johnston, Merle, 347
Jolly, Pete, 119, 257-58, 260, 298, 300
"Jolly Rogers," 250
Jones, Carmell, 142, 218, 328
Jones, Elvin, 328
Jones, Hank, 118
Jones, Isham, 249
Jones, Jo, 12, 187, 323
Jones, Philly Jo, 142, 296, 309
Jones, Thad, 102
Jordan, Duke, 118
Jordan, Stanley, 111
"Joshua," 279
"Joy Spring," 312, 313
"Jubilation," 223
"June Christy," 157
Jungle Room (club), 117
Jupiter (club), 61
"Just One of Those Things," 117